SIXTH EDITION

Social Inequality

Forms, Causes, and Consequences

CHARLES E. HURST

The College of Wooster

PEARSON

Boston   New York   San Francisco
Mexico City   Montreal   Toronto   London   Madrid   Munich   Paris
Hong Kong   Singapore   Tokyo   Cape Town   Sydney

To Mary Ellen
with love always for who you are

Senior Series Editor/Series Editor: Jeff Lasser
Series Editorial Assistant: Heather McNally
Senior Marketing Manager: Kelly May
Production Editor: Susan McNally
Editorial Production Service: Integra
Composition Buyer: Linda Cox
Manufacturing Buyer: Jo Anne Sweeney
Electronic Composition: Integra
Cover Coordinator: Kristina Mose-Libon

For related titles and support materials, visit our online catalog at www.ablongman.com.

To obtain permission(s) to use material from this work, please submit a written request to Allyn and Bacon, Permissions Department, 75 Arlington Street, Boston, MA 02116 or fax your request to 617-848-7320.

Between the time website information is gathered and then published, it is not unusual for some sites to have closed. Also, the transcription of URLs can result in typographical errors. The publisher would appreciate notification where these errors occur so that they may be corrected in subsequent editions.

Library of Congress Cataloging-in-Publication Data

Hurst, Charles E.
  Social inequality: forms, causes, and consequences / Charles E. Hurst.—6th ed.
    p.   cm.
  Includes bibliographical references and index.
  ISBN 0-205-48436-0
  1. Equality—United States.   2. United States—Social conditions.   I. Title

HN90.S6H87 2006
305.0973—dc22

                                          2006001682

Printed in the United States of America

10   9   8   7   6   5   4   3   2   1   RRD-VA   10   09   08   07   06

CONTENTS

PREFACE

Social inequality is all around us, and its impact on our lives and the social structure of the United States is unmistakable. Changes brought about by technology and globalization have affected international inequality and the socioeconomic position of the United States in the world. It is unavoidable that the worldwide changes now occurring will affect all of us. Yet it is still an open question as to who will benefit most from these changes. Some things change, while others remain the same. Widening gaps in wealth and income, continued racial and sexual discrimination, threats to the democratic process, persistent child poverty, hunger, and homelessness continue to tear at our social fabric. The number of billionaires has increased at a record pace, but in 2003 almost 36 million were poor. International competition, corporate outsourcing, and the quest for corporate efficiency have left increasing numbers of both white-collar and blue-collar workers unemployed or in new temporary positions. Racial, ethnic, and gender-related tensions have resurfaced with an often brutal face as people try to assign blame for their threatened statuses and compete for a better life in a society in which the distant but constant glow of the American dream has dimmed. Women continue to push for greater equality in earnings and occupational opportunities. Gays and lesbians fight for social respect and equal treatment under the law.

This sixth edition of *Social Inequality: Forms, Causes, and Consequences* is intended as a user-friendly introduction to the study of social inequality. The assumptions upon which it is based are the same as in previous editions: (1) inequality is multidimensional; (2) explanations of the various forms of inequality are necessary for any resolution of inequality's

undesirable consequences; (3) couching a discussion of inequality in its broader, historical, cultural, and international context provides a deeper understanding of the nature and role of inequality in society; and (4) an evenhanded approach covering the full range of perspectives and information on inequality is most appropriate, especially for students being exposed to this material for the first time. My goal is to convey as simply, but as compellingly, as I can a sense of the pervasiveness and extensiveness of social inequality in the United States within a comparative context, to show how inequality can be explained, how it affects all of us, and what is being done about it.

The sixth edition benefits from the advice of students, colleagues, and reviewers who are familiar with past editions of *Social Inequality*. The result of this advice and changes in my own thinking have resulted in some major revisions in several chapters, reorganization of others, discussions of new issues and research studies, and thorough updating of statistics on all dimensions of inequality. I believe the sixth edition has been significantly strengthened by these changes. Following are among the more extensive changes in content:

1. Separate in-depth discussions of the relationships between globalization and the various forms of inequality in Chapters 2 through 7. Discussion of the global context and globalization processes is necessary to understand what is happening to economic, status, gender/sexual, racial/ethnic, and political inequality in the United States.
2. Extensive revision and reorganization of the chapter on racial and ethnic inequality, incorporating in-depth discussions on

the meaning of race and racial formation, colorism, and intra-class divisions within the Black community;

3. The addition of a section on multiracial feminist theory in Chapter 5;

4. More discussion on the importance of opportunity structure for understanding gender and racial/ethnic inequality as well as status attainment;

5. Discussion of the meaning of the concept of social class in the lives of individuals;

6. The addition of a section on power inequality in the workplace to complement the discussion of political inequality at the national level;

7. More material in the theory chapters on Marx's early work and on recent attempts to identify specific processes that produce inequality;

8. Discussion of the roles of threat and stereotypes in the high rates of incarceration rates of Blacks and the impact of incarceration on the political power of prisoners;

9. Addition of a longer section on the role of causal attributions in conclusions about justice and fairness in the system of inequality; and

10. A strengthening of the discussion of how wealth and power are built across generations through the incorporation of comments on inheritance and sedimentation in different chapters.

In addition to the above revisions, I have made the following changes:

1. Updated statistics and research information in all the chapters

2. Added several new Nutshells to provide concrete examples of issues being discussed

3. Added new questions and Internet sites at the ends of most chapters

4. Reorganized the chapters on economic inequality and personal consequences of inequality for purposes of clarification and

5. Rearranged the order of the chapters to reflect the need to separate outcomes for inequality (Chapters 2, 3, and 4) from bases of inequality (Chapters 5, 6, and 7), and to include social movements among the social consequences of inequality.

The sixth edition is divided into four major parts. *Part One* examines the extent of economic, status, and political inequality in a general sense, as well as the impact of gender, sexual orientation, and race/ethnicity on economic, status, and political inequality. Specific theories on gender and racial/ethnic inequality are also presented in detail. *Part Two* covers in-depth discussions of general explanations of inequality. The classical arguments included are those of Marx, Weber, Durkheim, and Spencer, while the contemporary theories discussed include functionalist, social constructionist, reproduction, labor-market, and process explanations. Rather than placing them at the beginning as other texts usually do, I have placed the theory chapters after discussions of the extent of inequality because I believe students will be more inclined to study theories once they realize how extensive inequality is in society. While scholars often think deductively, students are more likely to start with their own lives and what they see around them and then may be more inquisitive about the causes of what is happening in society. The chapters in *Part Three* demonstrate how inequality affects our physical health and most intimate mental selves as well as crime, social unrest, and social movements in the wider society. There is no question that inequality's effects are pervasive. Finally, *Part Four* addresses processes of change and stability in the structure of social inequality through discussions of social mobility and attainment, the justice and legitimacy of inequality, and the underpinnings and nature of political policies aimed at ameliorating inequality and poverty.

Although any shortcomings in the book are my own responsibility, any improvements in this edition are due in large part to the suggestions of students in my social inequality course at The College of Wooster and to colleagues, Pam Forman, Anne Nurse, and others, both anonymous and known. I am grateful to those who have used and reviewed the fifth edition and made suggestions for how to improve the text. These reviewers include Michael V. Miller, University of Texas at San Antonio, Myron Orleans, California State University at Fullerton, Richard A.K. Shankar, Stonehill College, and George Wilson, University of Miami. I kept their detailed reviews in front of me as I incorporated changes in the sixth edition that reflect their suggestions and, I believe, make this edition stronger. While no book can fully satisfy every reader, I have tried to make improvements that correspond to major and recurrent comments of the reviewers. I have also considered comments offered by colleagues who are using the text at other schools. I want to thank Karen Hanson, Jeff Lasser, Erikka Adams, and Susan McNally at Allyn & Bacon for making the process of writing smoother by being on hand to answer my numerous questions. Finally, I am grateful for the perceptive observations of my children—Katie, Brendan, and Sarah—who have shared experiences, articles, and photos that help make an academician see the reality of inequality in the everyday lives of people. Finally, and as always, I am deeply indebted to my wife, Mary Ellen, for her continued love, moral support, sense of perspective, and help in preparing the final manuscript for submission. She is one of the unsung, real heroes in my life. In an unequal world, she is without equal.

1 An Introduction to the Study of Social Inequality

Was there, or will there ever be a nation whose individuals were all equal, in natural and acquired qualities, in virtues, talents and riches? The answer in all mankind must be in the negative.

—John Adams

Several years ago, a student approached me to say how much she resented her wealthier acquaintances. What upset her was not merely the BMWs and Acuras some of the students drove, or the quality of their clothes, or their expensive computers, but the fact that they had not really earned these things; rather, they had been given to them by their parents. She herself had grown up with working-class parents who lived on a farm and who did not particularly value a seemingly nonpractical liberal arts education. She had been taught that one had to work for and earn the kinds of goodies other students had in abundance. This experience is not an isolated one. Over the years, knowing of my interest in social-class issues, numerous students have spoken to me about their discomfort of being at an elite liberal arts college where the fees are well above $25,000 per year. Some learn to accommodate themselves to their unusual and somewhat foreign situation, while others continue to wrestle with their marginality among students who are better off than they are, and some simply transfer to another school.

The same experience is felt by some faculty whose backgrounds are dissimilar from those of their colleagues and many of the students they

teach. Recently, I interviewed faculty at several highly selective liberal arts colleges. Some expressed their lack of ease, even though they had been at their institutions for years. One, for example, who came from a background where his father had not graduated from high school and had worked in a factory, told me, "I have always felt a little bit of an outsider to the general social class here, certainly the students." He went on to say that he "felt sort of intimidated." Keep in mind that these feelings were expressed by a full professor with a Ph.D. in a natural science—not a person one would expect to have a shaky sense of self-confidence. The theme of not fitting in or being unsure of oneself occurred often among the faculty I interviewed whose class origins were below the middle. Consider your own situation. Imagine that you had come from a family of noticeably different wealth or from a different region or nationality, or that you were of a different race or sex. How would your experiences, perceptions, and opportunities be different?

Inequality is present and affects us at all stages of our lives. Think of your own experiences. Even when young, we hear people speak of others as being from the "wrong side of the tracks," as being not "our kind," as being "above" or "below" us. We hear about racism and sexism. As youths, we notice that because of the way others dress, where they live, and who their parents are, some are treated differently and have greater opportunities than others. We are also smart enough to see that there are class differences associated with different neighborhood elementary schools.

Economically, the gap between the top and the bottom has increased and class mobility has stagnated in the last few decades. Recent analyses by newspapers as divergent as *The Wall Street Journal* and *The New York Times* have publicized the growing inequality. "As the gap between rich and poor has widened since 1970, the odds that a child born in poverty will climb to wealth—or a rich child will fall into the middle class—remain stuck," writes David Wessel in the *Journal* (May 13, 2005, p. A1). In the last 30 years, class "has come to play a greater, not lesser, role in important ways," agree Scott and Leonhardt in the *Times* (May 15, 2005, p. A1).

The statistics confirm the extensive inequality. For example, in 2003, almost 36 million or 12.5 percent of U.S. citizens were classified as poor by the Census Bureau. Almost 13 million of these were children under 18 years of age. For a single person under 65 years old, this meant having an income below $9,574, and for a family of two parents and two children, having an income of no more than $18,660 (U.S. Census Bureau, August 2004). In 2003, the median household income in the United States was $43,318. At the same time, however, the number of households with net worth in excess of $10,000,000 has increased dramatically to 430,000 (Frank 2005). Chief executive officers (CEOs) in the largest 365 U.S. corporations received an average of $8.1 million in compensation in 2003. Their pay was 301 times that of the average worker compared to only 42 to 1 in 1982 (Anderson et al. 2004). Moreover, CEO compensation has increased at a much higher rate than that of the ordinary worker. As we will see in the next chapter, wealth distribution in general is highly polar-

ized in the United States with a small percentage owning most of the wealth. Economic inequality is alive and well in the United States.

A wide variety of social, political, and economic forces are driving this inequality, not the least of them is economic globalization. While the outsourcing of jobs may leave many workers without immediate employment, for example, it also reduces labor costs and raises profits for corporations. The result is that in 2003 executives at companies with high rates of outsourcing received compensations much higher than that of the average CEO at a large corporation (Anderson et al. 2005). To further strengthen their economic positions, an increasing number of companies have also been able to successfully pass off their pension obligations on to the federal government, in which case, workers will likely receive only a small proportion of their originally promised pensions. "It's a hammer blow to thousands of retirees who will have to somehow make do with lower pension checks," complained Joseph Tiberi, a representative of the International Association of Machinists and Aerospace Workers, after United Airlines withdrew its pensions plans. "The promises United made to them are worthless" (Maynard 2005, p. C2). Similarly, James Roberts, who worked for Bethlehem Steel for 33 years but had to retire early because of serious health problems, lost a large percentage of his pension benefit and free health care when the company passed on its obligations to the federal government. The pension was money he counted on to "use for food or I could use for entertainment or I could use to help my kids who are in school. . . . [t]he promises were not kept. That makes me angry, because we gave up things in order to get those promises" (Dale 2005, p. D2).

The global marketplace affects not only the operations of companies, but the operations of individual workers at home. Like economic inequality, status, gender, racial, and political inequality have been impacted by globalization. At the end of the following chapters on these forms of inequality, I will address aspects of the relationship between globalization and inequality. Increasingly, not only internal factors, but external events and policies outside the United States are affecting the extent and nature of inequality within it. Certainly, individuals disagree on what causes people to wind up in the economic positions they are in. Erma Goulart, a 67-year-old retiree and widow with only a high school degree believes that she "worked hard for what I have" but feels that "[t]he rich get more benefits and tax breaks and the poor people don't." In contrast, Steve Schoneck, a 39-year-old college graduate and accounting official for a utility company, thinks that "[y]ou always have the opportunity to try and move forward financially. . . . Over all, I've achieved the American dream. I'm happy" (Scott and Leonhardt 2005, p. A16). These assessments suggest the different weights that people place on the relative roles of individual and extra-individual factors in explaining their class positions, and the fact that those who are less successful are less likely to be fully content with their positions.

The injurious impact of inequality is not confined to the working class and poor, however. In recent years, the effects of social and economic forces pushing people into different economic circumstances have been increasingly felt by those in the white-collar ranks as companies downsize to meet competition and maintain profits. Steven Holthausen, once a bank loan officer, is now a tourist guide because his job was eliminated in 1990. Since then, his wife has left him and his children avoid him, blaming him for his economic decline. He feels he has lost respect in the community. While part of his anger is directed at himself, he also blames the company and the government for his predicament. "The anger that I feel right now is that I lost both my family and my job. That is not where I wanted to be at this point in my life" (Uchitelle and Kleinfield 1996). Unfortunately, Steven's story is not unique. In 2001 alone, almost 2.5 million workers became unemployed because of mass layoffs in the private sector. About 42 percent of the layoffs were in manufacturing (U.S. Department of Labor January 29, 2002). Between January 1997 and January 2000, 3.3 million workers lost jobs they had held for at least three years because their positions were eliminated, or their plants closed or moved ("Worker Displacement during the Late 1990s").

The streamlining and downsizing of businesses have left millions of experienced, specialized workers with temporary part-time jobs or without jobs, and frequently the immediate response is like that of Edoardo Leoncavallo, a middle-aged recently unemployed architect who knows the family problems that result from downward mobility: "I think my wife initially felt resentment. I think she felt, Why can't you bring home the bacon?" (Labich 1993, p. 42).

At the same time, advances in computer and information technologies have created opportunities for others to become phenomenally rich. In the early 1990s, few people had heard of Michael Dell. Yet in 2004, this 39-year-old from Austin, Texas, who is the driving force behind Dell computers, was among the richest Americans, with wealth in excess of $14 billion (Forbes 400 Index, 2004).

SOME CONTROVERSIAL ISSUES OF SUBSTANCE

Inequality and its effects are all around us. Consider the breadth of inequality's impact one is likely to see during a lifetime involving differences in possessions, places, wealth, experiences, bodies, races, genders, and power. The extensiveness of it is almost overwhelming. And yet, there is a great deal of controversy about social inequalities. Are social inequalities inevitable, especially in a capitalist society that stresses competition and individual success? Why do some have more than others? Is this natural or unnatural? Do "you always have the opportunity to try" as Steve suggests above, and does "hard work" always pay off despite the odds against average people, as Erma believes exists? Is inequality really a *social* problem or an *individual* one? Is economic inequality increasing or decreasing in the United States? Is it desirable or not? Is inequality a source of divisiveness or a basis for integration in U.S. society? Are social classes the most important dimension of inequality in our society, and, if so, are classes really present in the United States? Can equality in political power exist even if economic resources are distributed unequally? Or does the Golden Rule operate— those with the gold rule? These are among the most intriguing and consequential of the questions that have been raised in the study of social inequality. We now examine some of these in more detail.

Is Inequality Inevitable?

Perhaps the most basic issue relates to the inevitability of inequality. It is important to clarify that reference is being made here to *institutionalized* rather than *individual* inequality (i.e., structured inequality between categories of individuals that are systematically created, reproduced, legitimated by sets of ideas, and relatively stable). We would not be studying this phenomenon if it was not a prominent feature of contemporary society with significant consequences. To ask whether it is inevitable is to address discussions of its origins (i.e., whether it is caused by natural or artificial factors). If social inequality is directly linked to conditions inherent in the nature of groups of individuals or society, then little might be expected to eliminate it. On the other hand, if such inequality arises because of the conscious, intentional, and freely willed actions of individuals or the structures they create in society, then perhaps it can be altered.

One side argues that inequality is always going to be present because of personal differences between individuals either in the form of basic differences in their own makeups or

differences in the amount of effort they expend. A large majority of Americans would appear to agree. A recent poll found that most people, regardless of their income, rank "hard work" more often than any other factor as being critical for economic success (Scott and Leonhardt 2005). In explaining his own success, Steve Schoneck believes he took advantage of the opportunities available to everyone and, as a result, was able to achieve the American Dream. In his view, he had what it took to get ahead. If there is an open society and if people vary in their talents and motivations, then this would suggest that inequality is inevitable, a simple fact of society. "Some inequalities come about as a result of unavoidable biological inequalities of physical skill, mental capacity, and traits of personality" argued Cauthen (1987, p. 8) in his treatise on equality. Some early philosophers also argued that there are "natural" differences between individuals, and some people, in fact, still maintain that there are differences of this type separating the sexes, resulting in the inevitability of inequality. Aristotle took the position that "the male is by nature superior, the female, inferior; and the one rules, and the other is ruled" (in Kriesberg 1979, p. 12). More recently, Goldberg (1973) argued that male dominance and higher achievement are probably inevitable because of the biological differences that he says exist between males and females. These and other explanations of inequality will be discussed in detail later.

Other theorists have argued that inequality is inevitable because as long as certain kinds of tasks are more necessary for the survival of the society than others, and as long as those able to perform those tasks are rare, social inequality of rewards between individuals is needed to motivate the best people to perform the most difficult tasks. Under these conditions, the argument goes, inequality cannot be eradicated without endangering the society.

On the other side of the fence are those who argue that economic inequality is not inevitable and is largely the by-product of a system's structure and not the result of major differences in individual or group talents, characteristics, and motivations. Rousseau, for example, linked the origins of inequality to the creation of private property (Dahrendorf 1970, p. 10). It is the characteristics of the political economy and the firms and labor markets within it that are primary determinants of differences in income and wealth. Where a person works and in what industry have a major effect on income. Certainly, the job changes resulting from downsizing would suggest this. Essentially, then, this argument states that it is not human nature and individual differences but rather structural conditions that determine where an individual winds up on the ladder of economic inequality. Discrimination is another of those conditions.

> *The theories that say . . . that women are "naturally" disadvantaged are of use to those who want to preserve and strengthen the dominant political and economic interests. . . . Contrary to the claims of biological determinists, studies of the contributions that biological factors make to human behavior can at most give only very limited information about the origins of present differences in human behavior and probably no information about the origins of present social structures. (Lowe and Hubbard 1983, pp. 55–56)*

Clearly, Erma Goulart suspects that her situation may be at least partially determined by forces (e.g., tax policies) beyond her control. If the conditions that generate social inequality are artificial creations of human actions, then they can be changed, and economic inequality is not inevitable, nor is it necessarily beneficial for the society and all its members. We will examine this controversy more thoroughly in later chapters.

Is Inequality Increasing or Lessening?

Another issue revolves around whether socioeconomic differences between classes, races, and the sexes are increasing or decreasing. One position is that the United States is largely a middle-class society and that government exerts pressure to limit the growth of the upper class's wealth, while at the same time it aids the lower classes through various social programs. The result is a *structural* tendency for most groups to move toward the middle—a class system with an ever-increasing bulge in the middle. This argument is related to the classlessness position in that if, ultimately, the pressure results in a largely middle-class society or middle mass, then in effect there is virtually only one large class. In *cultural* terms, this argument says that all classes are moving in the direction of the same values, and, specifically, that lower classes adopt the values of those above them. This has been particularly stressed in some discussions of the working class, which, it is said, takes on the values of the middle class as its economic fortunes improve.

Another version of this homogenizing scenario suggests that race may be becoming less important as a determinant of life chances and that the differences between the races are diminishing. In fact, it is suggested that class differences *within* racial groups may be more significant than those existing *between* such groups. Similarly, as women have moved increasingly into the labor market, their status has moved closer to that of men, and many argue that women have made great strides in reducing the socioeconomic differences between themselves and men.

In sharp contrast to these images of decreasing differences and merging groups, others have argued that polarization is occurring with respect to the social classes, with the gap between the top and the bottom increasing. They cite the number of poor, homeless, and an "underclass" as evidence for this trend, along with changes in governmental tax and poverty policies. In essence, they are saying that the rich are getting richer and the poor poorer. The same general kind of argument has been made regarding race and sex, stating that not only have race and sex continued to be important determinants of life chances but also there has been little reduction in the extent of differences that exist between the races and sexes in the United States. We will examine these issues closely in the next and succeeding chapters. If what is happening to James Roberts and the salaries of CEOs is fairly typical of what happens to many as the economy shifts, then perhaps the gap is increasing between the top and the bottom. On the other hand, if African Americans and women are breaking through the walls of discrimination and moving up, then perhaps some of the gaps are closing. We shall see.

Equality or Inequality: Desirable or Undesirable?

Some scholars think of inequality as a source of integration in society. The functionalist view, for example, which we will explore later, argues that inequality in rewards is a way of making sure that critical occupations become filled with the most qualified persons. That is, since rewards provide motivation to do certain tasks, the structure of inequality is really an incentive system helping the society to survive. Other analysts contend that economic and other kinds of inequality create divisiveness between the haves and the have-nots, men and women, minorities and majorities. This is in large part because these groups are not equally likely to believe that the system of inequality is fair. Because of this, inequality is more likely to instigate conflict than it is to strengthen cohesion between groups and in society in general.

A variety of studies have asked Americans how they feel about equality and inequality, and it is clear that they are ambivalent in their feelings. In some ways, they are attracted to equality; in other ways, they view inequality as justified.

Part of the problem here is that people think about different things when they think about inequality, and people feel differently about the various kinds of equality/inequality. Moreover, there are numerous inequalities/equalities; thus, the meaning of equality/inequality is not self-evident. "Trying to think clearly about equality," wrote Cauthen (1987), "is indeed like being tossed naked into a tangled thicket in the midst of a briar patch" (p. 2). For example, Bryan Turner (1986) cited four basic kinds of equality: (1) equality pertaining to all as basic human beings—that is, the notion that basically we are all the same and equally worthy as persons; (2) equality of opportunity—the idea that access to valued ends is open to all; (3) equality of condition—that is, that all start from the same position; and (4) equality of results or outcome, or equality of income. The latter is the most radical of the four and the one most likely to incite controversy.

Américans feel quite differently about equality of opportunity than they do about egalitarianism, and groups feel differently about the fairness of the system. A study of over 2,700 leaders in various areas, for example, showed that they feel any fair distribution of goods should be based on equality of *opportunity* rather than equality of *result*. At the same time, however, African American and feminist leaders are much less likely to consider the free enterprise system fair, and are more likely to consider poverty to be caused by problems in the system rather than by deficiencies in the individual (Verba and Orren 1985). We will examine the tangle of American beliefs about inequality and its fairness more fully in Chapter 14.

Are There Classes in the United States?

The economic differences that exist between families and between individuals can be easily recognized, but does that mean that social classes exist in the United States? There is much to discourage the belief in classes. The value system stresses individualism, liberty, and equality. The belief in individualism and liberty would work against the development of stably reproduced social classes in the United States. Following these values, it is inconsistent to have group inequalities in which a person's fate is largely determined by the group to which he or she belongs, nor is it legitimate to have individual liberty curtailed by the application of structural constraints (e.g., laws, admission requirements) to some groups and not others. Finally, the value of equality—that we are all one people, that, underneath, U.S. citizens are all "common folk" without formal titles (e.g., duke, lord)—helps to reinforce the basic notion that all Americans are equal.

In addition to some central U.S. values, other conditions moderate the belief in the existence of classes. First of all, as we will see later, there is a great deal of disagreement about the definition of *social class*. This lack of agreement in conceptualization makes it more difficult for there to be agreement on the existence of classes. Second, the lack of belief is further strengthened by the fact that in contrast to race and sex, there are far fewer reliable and clear-cut physical clues to class position. Walking down the street, it is much easier to tell accurately whether someone is Black or White and male or female than it is to tell what class he or she is in. Class is often invisible, and therefore we seem to be less often confronted by it. People do not always wear their class positions on their sleeves, so to speak. Think about it: Can you reliably and accurately tell the class positions of your classmates simply by their appearances?

Third, this very invisibility makes it much easier to create and manipulate ideas about the existence of classes in society. It is much easier to say that classes simply do not exist. Finally, the increasing concern for privacy and personal security in U.S. society, which isolates people from each other, enhances the belief in the absence of classes. It is hard to recognize classes and the predicaments of others if we live in shells. In this view, individual differences in wealth may exist, but basically Americans are all the same and equally worthy, and classes based on group or categorical differences do not exist. Any individual differences in wealth would be viewed as a continuum along which all individuals and families could be located. Here, the image of a system of inequality is one of a tall but narrow ladder. Discrete, wide, separate layers would not be a part of this perspective.

In fact, some social theorists have argued that the term *social class* has no relevance for the United States, at least in its Marxian definition. Social classes, as unified class-conscious groups with their own lifestyles and political beliefs, do not apply to the United States in this view, whereas they may still fully apply to European countries that have a tradition of class conflict. Frequently, part of this position is the conviction that there are differences in lifestyle and status between different occupational groups, but these differences are not class based. Much of the traditional research in the field of inequality, in fact, has focused on social lifestyle differences between groups rather than on economic-class differences. The focus of research is, of course, conditioned by the historical context in which it occurs, the cultural milieu, and the events of the times. As we shall see, this is clearly the case in U.S. research on social inequality.

One position, then, is that social classes as full-fledged groups antagonistically related to each other do not fit the U.S. condition today. Others suggest, however, that fairly distinct classes exist at the extremes of the inequality hierarchy but not in the middle, which is considered largely a mass of relatively indistinguishable categories of people. A third position is that distinct classes have always existed and continue to exist in the United States, and that *class* conflict has not been absent from its history and continues to this day. Distinct disparities in the incomes of those in different occupational categories would appear to reinforce the notion that classes exist in the United States.

But even if classes do exist, does this mean that they are the most important dimension of social inequality in the United States?

Certainly, there are other bases and forms of inequality that are important, such as those between the sexes and between races. Moreover, inequality can not only take an economic form, but also appear in a social or political form. We will be examining all these forms in the next several chapters, beginning with those forms of inequality that appear more as *outcomes* (i.e., economic, status, political) and then moving on to those forms that can be viewed more as *bases* for those outcomes (i.e., gender, sexual orientation, race/ethnicity). As we will see, Max Weber conceived of each of the three outcomes above as aspects of the distribution of power in society. Power can take each of these forms, and how much power one has in these areas appears to be at least partially *based* on one's gender, sexual orientation, and race/ethnicity. Oftentimes, the latter three bases intersect in their impact or have compounding effects. The combination of being not only a woman but also Black rather than White, for example, can have distinct effects on how far one can get economically, socially, and/or politically. In several of the following chapters, we will have occasion to look at the impact of this "intersectionality" on inequality outcomes.

Capitalism versus Democracy

Do economic and political inequality necessarily go together? The *economic* system of capitalism has been linked to the *political* system of democracy in both a positive and a negative manner (Almond 1991). It has been viewed as a determinant as well as an enemy of democracy. Can capitalism and democracy effectively coexist? Pure capitalism demands that markets be open and free and that individuals be able to freely pursue their economic goals, competing with others within the broad framework of the U.S. legal system. Capitalism's ideal conditions assume *equality of opportunity*, regardless of sex, race, or any other categorical characteristic. Presumably,

individual talents and motivations are the prime determinants of how far a person goes in the system. This is how many would explain the high executive salaries noted previously. "My view of executive compensation is like all compensation, it's market driven. The company pays what it has to pay to recruit and retain a person. . . . A person is worth what the market is willing to pay for him," said Charles Peck, an analyst for The Conference Board (Gladstone 1988, p. 4). A system like this presumably would result in the best people being in the highest positions, with the consequence being an efficiently run economy. But if this type of competitive capitalism operates in the United States, then economic inequality is unavoidable, since the talents and motivations of individuals and supply and demand for them vary. There is a potential for economic concentration under these circumstances, with a few having much while many may have little.

Alongside this capitalistic economic system exists a political democracy in which everyone is supposed to have a vote in the running of the government. "One person, one vote" is the rule. *Equality of result* is expected in the political arena in the sense that power should be equally distributed. The question is Can equality of political power and inequality in economic standing exist at the same time? Or does economic power lead to inordinate, unequal political power, thereby making a mockery of political equality? Can open economic capitalism and political democracy coexist? John Adams, one of the Founding Fathers of the United States, expressed concern that "the balance of power in a society accompanies the balance of property and land. . . . If the multitude is possessed of the balance of real estate, the multitude will have the balance of power and, in that case, the multitude will take care of the liberty, virtue and interest of the multitude in all acts of government" (Adams 1969, pp. 376–377). Bryan Turner wrote, "Modern capitalism is fractured by the contradictory processes of inequality in the marketplace and political inequality at the level of state politics. There is an inevitable contradiction between economic class and the politics of citizenship" (Turner, B. 1986, p. 24). How do individuals who lack economic resources react politically to this situation? Does the contradiction generate resistance? Is it possible to have a society that is both capitalistic and democratic?

Conservatives and radicals generally take different positions on each of the issues we have been discussing. Conservatives tend to praise the virtues of open capitalism and emphasize its benefits for the individual, rather than see the internal contradictions between capitalism and democracy. Radicals, on the other hand, view unbridled capitalism as destructive of human beings and stress the inter linkage between economic and political power. Conservatives also tend to consider social inequality to be inevitable, if not necessary and desirable, and perceive the United States as being largely classless, seeing the similarities among Americans as being more fundamental than the differences. In sharp contrast, radicals conclude that inequality is neither inevitable nor desirable, that the United States is a class society, and that basic social, economic, and political conditions create deep divisions within the population.

ISSUES OF METHODOLOGY

In addition to the preceding substantive controversies, there are also important methodological issues that must be considered in the study of inequality, most of which you will encounter as you read through the following chapters. How these questions are handled by scholars heavily affects the conclusions they draw about the nature and extent of social inequality. These issues frequently involve questions about definitions and measurement of concepts, levels of analysis, and the relative impacts of race, class, sex, and gender on individual lives.

Definitional Problems

One of the most fundamental questions involves the measurement of social class and poverty. As noted later, *social class* has been defined in different ways, using different indices. Some conceptualize given social classes as being characterized by particular levels of income, education, and occupational prestige, whereas others view class as having to do primarily with ownership and exploitation, or with class consciousness. Still others focus on lifestyle as the critical factor that distinguishes social classes. These different definitions result in different measures of social-class position. Hollingshead's Two-Factor Index of Social Position, for example, involves objectively rating a person from 1 to 7 on occupational and educational scales (Hollingshead and Redlich 1958). Wright's measure of social class, in sharp contrast, uses exploitation as its defining characteristic, and consequently separates different types of exploitation that individuals use or are exposed to while they work (cf., e.g., Wright and Cho 1992).

As in the case of social class, *poverty* has also been defined and measured in different ways, as you will see in Chapter 15. Some argue that being poor means more than not having money—it also means a lack of status and power. Even when money is used as the measure of poverty, there is disagreement about whether it should be gross or net income, whether it should include income from government programs, whether it should be current or long-term income, and so on. Other methodological issues arise when examining additional dimensions of social inequality. How to measure discrimination when discussing racial or gender inequality, how to measure the openness of a society using its mobility rates, how to measure political power, and how to gauge the comparability of situations when discussing how the degree of social inequality in the United States stacks up against that found

Social scientists often have called different aspects of inequality by different names.
There is always the danger that we may mistake one part of inequality for all of it.

in other countries—all are issues of significance and difficulty.

Why are these differences in measurement and definition so professionally and practically important? Professionally, varying definitions and measures make comparability of results difficult and raise problems of communication between scholars supposedly studying the same phenomenon. Practically, these different perspectives are significant and involve heated discussion among policymakers because such things as openness, discrimination, poverty, and class are measured affects how egalitarian or inegalitarian the United States is seen to be. The measure of poverty affects how much poverty exists, how big a problem it is, and how much, if anything, needs to be done about it. Simply recognizing poverty as a social problem, in fact, is the

result of some individuals or groups "making claims" about poverty's problematic nature and then using a particular style to convince others that it is a problem (Ibarra and Kitsuse 2003). Others may not see poverty as a social problem or may not be convinced by the styles used to demonstrate that poverty really is a social problem. The definition and measurement of poverty, therefore, is a political hot potato because so much rides on which approach is accepted at the time.

In addition to class and poverty, "race" is also a contested concept because while we have traditionally thought of it as designating innate and fixed biological differences between individuals, it has increasingly been shown to be a concept that has been *socially constructed* over time. Racial classifications and positions within them change as political, social, and other shifts occur in society. I will discuss the theory of racial formation more fully in Chapter 7.

With respect to the discussion of women, the trend in terminology has been to use the term *gender* rather than *sex* when discussing differences and inequalities between men and women. However, they mean different things. The former reflects the images, roles, and behaviors society assigns to men and women; the latter is a direct reference to biology. Thus, the terms *sex* and *gender* will both be used in the text. When the focus is on inequalities between males and females as sexes (e.g., income and poverty differences), the term *sex* will be used. When the focus is on social definitions or roles, often socially ranked and culturally assigned to males or females, *gender* will be used. For example, occupations are often "gendered" (i.e., associated with or considered most appropriate for either men or women). One would think that it is indisputable that there are only two sexes. But even that is open to question, as the discussions in Chapter 6 indicate. This suggests that definitions are always socially constructed.

The concept of *power* is also a fuzzy one. Power can exist in many forms and can be viewed on several levels. In the discussion of political inequality in Chapter 4, I will focus on power as impact in decision-making processes, as reflected in both the *political-institutional* realm (i.e., voting, office holding, etc.) and on the *personal* level. It is not unusual for us to think of power as a property of the political or governmental realm. But power inequality can also exist in the personal relationships between individuals, for example, between men and women, bosses and workers, Blacks and Whites. Both of these levels need to be addressed.

In addition to the definitional issues swirling around the latter sets of concepts, there is also a dilemma involving their interrelationship. Can one effectively separate the independent effects of race, class, sex, and gender on the individual? Although each is a distinct variable, all are inextricably intermixed in the lives of actual individuals. Persons simultaneously occupy positions on each of these, and, in real life, they are deeply interconnected. We must recognize both their separateness and their interconnectedness when considering their roles in people's lives.

Levels of Analysis

The study of social inequality is concerned with both individuals and groups, personal positions as well as structural arrangements. Thus, analysis proceeds on several levels. For example, we are interested in how an individual's class-related characteristics affect the probability of that person being arrested, but we are also interested in how the structure of inequality itself affects the crime rate for the society as a whole. We are interested in the process by which individuals attain higher or lower status positions, but we are also interested in how class structures shift in society. We will look not only at how an individual's race or sex affects his or her income but also at how institutionalized discrimination affects the overall structure of inequality between the races and sexes. Many of the chapters to follow contain discussion of these important methodological issues.

ORGANIZATION OF THE BOOK

The text is divided into four major parts. Part One addresses the extent of inequality in its various forms. Chapters 2, 3, and 4 focus on specific forms of inequality that concern resource *outcomes* (i.e., income/wealth, social status, and power) that are distributed unequally among individuals and groups in the United States. The following three chapters (5, 6, and 7), while viewed as specific forms of inequality in their own right, are also significant *bases* for inequalities in resource outcomes. Sex, sexual orientation, and race affect the distribution of wealth, status, and power in our society. To place the structure and dynamics of inequality within a global context, I will discuss the relationship between globalization and the particular form of inequality at the end of each of these chapters.

Several of the chapters in Part One include *specific* explanations of given forms of inequality. Part Two presents the major *general* explanations given for social inequality, with Chapter 8 including discussions of Marx's, Weber's, Durkheim's, and Spencer's classical perspectives on inequality. Chapter 9 analyzes more contemporary explanations, ranging from functionalist, to social reproduction and constructionist theories, to labor-market theories of inequality.

Having discussed the extent and explanations of inequality in earlier sections, Part Three demonstrates the pervasive consequences of inequality for individuals and society. Physical and mental health, hunger, and homelessness are all subject to the influences of individual positions in the hierarchy of social inequality. These personal effects are the focus of Chapter 10. The long arm of inequality reaches far into personal and private worlds, but its effects also extend into the wider society as well. In Chapter 11, the effects of inequality on family violence, crime, collective protest, and environmental equity are explored. Specifically, the effects of socioeconomic position, race, and sex and gender on criminal justice are examined, ranging from the chances of being arrested to the likelihood of being given a long sentence. Street crimes, white-collar crimes, and hate crimes are each discussed. Inequality also has played a role in generating high crime rates, fomenting unrest, and raising questions about environmental justice.

On a broader level, the labor, civil-rights, and women's movements can be viewed as reactions to economic and political inequalities based on class, race, and gender, inequalities that are perceived as unjust. Chapter 12 surveys the history of these movements and their relationship to inequality.

Part Four of the book examines what has been happening to the system of inequality and what is being done about it. Chapter 13 asks whether there is a great deal of mobility in U.S. society. Do rags-to-riches stories provide a typical picture of the careers of most Americans? How does the United States compare with other countries in its rate of mobility? Is it more open than others? Have African Americans and women become more upwardly mobile in recent years? What determines how far up people go in the occupational hierarchy? Chapter 14 discusses the thorny issue of the equity of inequality. What do Americans think about their system inequality? Is it fair? What is being done about it? This is the subject of Chapter 15. What kinds of policies exist to deal with inequality and poverty and how effective are they? Are there any better ways to address the problem of poverty? These comprise some of the central questions addressed in Part Four.

Each chapter ends with a short set of questions addressing some critical issues raised by the chapter. They are aimed at forcing you to come to grips with central problems in inequality, often by looking at inequality in your own life. *Web Connections* suggests various websites where you can get more information and use as bases for course exercises. These should broaden and deepen understanding of inequality. Many chapters also contain a brief *Nutshell* from the popular press. Each deals with an issue of inequality and can serve as a point of classroom discussion. Finally, a Glossary of Basic Terms follows the last chapter.

The lines separating the social sciences are often vague, the result being that discussions in the book often will draw on the work of economists, anthropologists, as well as sociologists, and others. In addition, there is material from other countries. These inclusions, hopefully, result in a more thorough and well-rounded perspective on the structure and process of social inequality.

CRITICAL THINKING

1. Try to think of a personal relationship you have with someone who is unequal to you in some way, and yet the inequality appears to have few negative effects on you or your relationship. What characteristics lessen the impact of the inequality in this relationship? Discuss some lessons from this relationship that might be used to diminish the negative effects of inequality in society as a whole.

2. Is social inequality a problem that demands the full attention of society or is it merely a personal trouble of those living below the middle class? Explain your answer.

3. If unequal rewards were not available in society, what would motivate individuals to do their best?

4. I have noted that race, sex, and sexual orientation can be bases for differential outcomes in income/wealth, prestige, and power. Can the reverse ever be true, that is, can one's income affect one's race or gender?

WEB CONNECTIONS

Several of the following chapters use information obtained from national polls, many of which are published on the Internet. The National Council on Public Polls suggests that among the questions you should consider before accepting poll results are the following: (1) Who sponsored and who conducted the poll? (2) Is the sample large enough and representative of the whole population? (3) Were any important groups excluded from the poll? (4) Was the technique used in the interview likely to affect the answers received? (5) Was the wording of the questions neutral or biased in some way? (6) Are the survey results still valid or are they out-of-date? (*Source*: Deborah Carr, 2005. "Political Polls," *Contexts* 4: 32.)

Economic Inequality

Everywhere we turn in our daily lives in this nation we are confronted with the widening gap between rich and poor.

—bell hooks

In the next several chapters, we will be considering several forms of inequality: economic, status, gender, racial, and political. In this chapter, we examine economic inequality in the form of social class and income/wealth differences. We begin with economic inequality because other aspects of inequality are often based on economic or class inequality in a society. As we will see in later chapters, economic position has a significant impact on the prestige, power, and life chances that individuals possess. Consequently, a discussion of social class and economic inequality is critical for a full understanding of other forms of inequality. Scholars vary in their perspectives on social class, as do average citizens who have particular views of U.S. class structure and their place in it.

THE EVERYDAY REALITY OF CLASS

In general, Americans do not like to talk about class. "Class is not discussed or debated in public because class identity has been stripped from popular culture. The institutions that shape mass culture and define the parameters of public debate have avoided class issues . . . [F]ormulating issues in terms of class is unacceptable, perhaps even un-American" (Mantsios 2004, p. 193). But their reluctance to discuss class does not mean that Americans do not have a mental picture of the class structure or their position in it. The meaning of class for the public is rooted in their everyday experiences and relationships. Awareness of class differences begins early; even preschool children categorize individuals as rich or poor. Early in elementary school, they already have a distinct image of how occupations vary in prestige (Ramsey 1991).

Class structure is also a subjective reality for adults. When asked about it, people in the United States are much more likely to agree on and have images of the top and bottom of the class structure than they are of the middle classes, which are seen as more amorphous and heterogeneous. The perceived distinctiveness of the top, for example, is based not only on their wealth, but by the social and cultural boundaries that are seen as separating them from those below. Because of their extraordinary wealth, those at the top of the economic hierarchy often take on notoreity or celebrity status (e.g., Bill Gates, the Walton family). Those who are "old wealth" are often very guarded about who is let into their group and who is not, which again identifies them as unique and different from those below them (cf., e.g., Kendall 2002; Frank 2005). The popular image of the bottom is similarly clear, with that perception being dominated by stereotypes of individuals regularly on welfare, being homeless, and often being of minority status. The economic middle, in contrast, is seen as mainly made up of white-collar professionals, semiprofessionals, and highly paid blue-collar "aristocrats," that is, a loose collection of widely varying individuals not nearly as homogeneous in the public's eye as those at the top and bottom. Below them, the working class is often described as being composed of those in less-skilled, routine white-collar and blue-collar positions.

Most Americans feel at least fairly strongly that they belong to a particular class (Jackman and Jackman 1983). When asked to place themselves in the class structure, usually 80–90 percent of adults say that they are either "middle" or "working" class. In 2003, a survey by the Gallup Organization indicated that 63 percent of the adults interviewed considered themselves as "middle" or "upper-middle" class, while 28 percent classified themselves as "working" class. Only 1 percent thought they were "upper class" and 7 percent labeled themselves "lower" class (Robison 2003). A 2005 *New York Times* poll found similar results—57 percent and 35 percent of respondents, respectively, considered themselves as belonging either in part to the middle class or to the working class (Scott and Leonhardt 2005).

But on other aspects of class structure, individuals vary in their perceptions. When asked in past surveys to describe the nature of

the class structure in the United States, individuals' images have differed depending on their own class positions. Historically, middle-class respondents have described the class structure more as a relatively smooth continuum with few major breaks between classes, while those in the working and lower classes have been more likely to see classes as discrete, distinct groups, and to perceive a smaller number of classes. However, a recent poll found that 61 percent of Blacks and 38 percent of Whites believe that the United States is divided into the "haves" and "have-nots." These percentages have grown over the last two decades corresponding to growth in the polarization of incomes and wealth (Ludwig 2003). Generally, those in the lower classes are more likely than those in higher classes to believe there is a greater distance between the top and the bottom (cf., e.g., Ossowski 1963; Wrong 1969; Giddens 1973; Vanneman and Pampel 1977).

Criteria used to place individuals in a given class also vary. Occupational positions that are seen as requiring mental ability or as having authority over others are generally classified as at least middle class rather than working class (Jackman and Jackman 1983). Class position itself affects what individuals think distinguishes persons in different class positions. For example, those in the working and lower classes are more likely to see the upper class as being distinguished by *money*, while those in the higher classes see their main distinction as lying in their *lifestyle*. Indeed, individuals in the higher professions are significantly more likely than persons in other occupational statuses to engage in "high-brow" cultural activities (Katz-Gerro 2002). With respect to other criteria, married men and women vary in how much they consider their separate incomes and educations when describing their class position. Married men and women, for example, agree that both the husband's and wife's incomes affects their class position equally, but they differ on whether their own as well as their spouse's educations help define their class position (Yamaguchi and Wang 2002). What all these studies suggest is that while Americans tend to agree on some broad ideas about U.S. class structure, there are also many ways in which their views vary, resulting in an overall uncrystallized, nonuniform image of the class structure as a whole.

TWO VIEWS OF U.S. CLASS STRUCTURE

In recent years, there has been a continuing debate among scholars about whether classes really exist in the United States. Their conclusions have depended heavily on how the concept of *class* has been defined. Some portrayals of class structure use sets of very diverse criteria, following closely a socioeconomic definition of class, whereas others try to be more faithful to Marxian criteria. Neither of these approaches is inherently better than the other, and each focuses on criteria that have been found to have separate effects on individuals' life conditions. Each approach attempts to identify meaningful breaks in the class system. In the following sections, we will examine both socioeconomic and Marxian images of the U.S. class system.

Socioeconomic Image of Class Structure

Traditionally, U.S. researchers have defined social class statistically in terms of occupational status, education, and/or income. Individuals or families that fall in the same category on these dimensions are then said to be in the same social class. Generally, persons receive a score based on their placement on these variables; in essence, social class is thus determined by statistical score. Since these scores are continuous, the class hierarchy is frequently viewed as a continuum where the boundaries between classes are not always clear and distinct. Classes may merge imperceptibly into one another and, as a result, boundary determination becomes an important problem.

Another characteristic of this approach is that the dimensions used to measure social class are not all purely economic in nature. Occupational status is essentially a measure of the prestige of an occupation—that is, it reflects the subjective judgment of individuals about an occupation. Education is also a noneconomic phenomenon. The result is that not only is this measure of social class multidimensional but it also mixes economic with social dimensions of inequality. Consequently, this measure is often referred to as *socioeconomic status*.

Finally, this measure does not assume any kind of necessary relationship between the classes. There is no assumption, for example, that the upper and working classes are in conflict with each other. Classes are merely the result of scores on a series of socioeconomic dimensions. In sum, the traditional, more conservative measure in the United States assumes that the structure of social class, or socioeconomic status, is (1) a continuum of inequality between classes, (2) partly the result of subjective judgments as well as objective conditions, (3) multidimensional, and (4) nonconflictual in nature.

As an example of this approach to *class*, Rossides defined a social class as being "made up of families and unrelated individuals who share similar benefits across the three dimensions of class, prestige, and power" (1976, p. 23). Similarly, Gilbert defined social class as "a large group of families . . . approximately equal in rank to each other and clearly differentiated from other families. . . . The various stratification variables tend to converge and jell; they form a pattern, and this pattern creates social classes" (2003, pp. 14–15).

Using the socioeconomic criteria of income, education, and occupation, Gilbert (2003) proposed that the United States contains six major classes. A condensed version of his model is presented here. Percentage of households in each class are enclosed in parentheses.

1. *Capitalist Class* (1%): Graduates of high-ranking universities who are in top-level executive positions or are heirs who have

an income average of $2 million mainly from assets.

2. ***Upper Middle Class*** (14%): Individuals with at least a college degree who are in higher professional or managerial positions or owners of medium-sized businesses who have incomes of about $120,000.

3. ***Middle Class*** (30%): Individuals who have high school degrees and maybe some college who are in lower managerial or white-collar, or high-skill, high-pay, blue-collar occupations who make about $55,000 a year.

4. ***Working Class*** (30%): Persons with high school degrees who are in lower-level white-collar (e.g., clerical, sales workers) or blue-collar positions (e.g., operatives) whose incomes are about $35,000 per year.

5. ***Working Poor*** (13%): Those with some high school who are service workers, or are in the lowest paid blue-collar and clerical positions who have average incomes of $22,000.

6. ***Underclass*** (12%): Individuals with at best some high school education who work part time, are unemployed, or are on welfare, and who have incomes under $12,000.

In surveying different models of U.S. class structure that use several kinds of socioeconomic criteria, there are some remarkable *similarities* as well as differences between them. These models usually see the structure as being composed of five to seven classes, rather than as a dichotomy or trichotomy. Also, the proportion of the population said to be in each class in each model is very similar. Generally, the working and middle classes, in which the majority of the population is placed, are considered to be about equal in size, and the upper class is generally said to be around 1 percent. Then, depending on whether employed as well as unemployed are included in the lower class, its percentage can range from 10 to 25 percent.

Some of the most significant *differences* in traditional models center on the criteria used to place individuals in various classes. One notable difference lies in the distinctions made about the lower class. Some researchers simply include all those who are poor, while others draw a line between those who are poor but work and those who are chronically unemployed and poor for long periods of time. The term *underclass* is frequently used to refer to the latter group. There is some debate about the actual size of the underclass; of course, the proposed size depends on the definition given to it. A conference of experts on the issue agreed on the definition of the *underclass* as "poor people who live in a neighborhood or census tract with higher rates of unemployment, crime, and welfare dependency" (McFate 1987, p. 11). By this definition, the underclass would include 5–10 percent of the population.

Another difference among the models of class structure concerns distinctions between particular kinds of white-collar and blue-collar occupations. Traditionally, blue-collar and white-collar categories were distinguished on the basis of whether the occupation involved manual or nonmanual work. (Manual work was generally viewed as requiring primarily physical and routine rather than mental and intricate skills/tasks.) Recently, however, the lines distinguishing the nature of blue-collar and white-collar jobs have become blurred. The routine nature of much low-level white-collar work has encouraged some analysts to place individuals who do this kind of work into the working class, and to place those who do complex, high-skill, well-paying blue-collar work into the middle class. As technological change occurs, and some physical labor by humans is replaced by machines, the character of the working class changes correspondingly.

The question of the relative importance of the manual/nonmanual and level-of-complexity criteria is the subject of some debate and has become focused in the debate about the *proletarianization* of some white-collar work and the *embourgeoisement* of some blue-collar work. Briefly, the proletarianization argument states that a significant and increasing number of white-collar jobs are routine and boring, demand little skill, and involve little worker control. Qualitatively, this makes them no different from many blue-collar jobs. Some have described those who occupy those positions as a "new working class," especially as the economy advances and becomes more automated. Generally, radicals tend to view the U.S. class structure in a manner consistent with the proletarianization thesis.

In contrast, the embourgeoisement thesis, embraced more often by those with a more conservative bent, proposes that complex, high-paying blue-collar jobs take on many of the sociocultural characteristics of the white-collar middle class. As society moves into a postindustrial phase and its labor force becomes more saturated with white-collar service positions, the size of the blue-collar work force shrinks. Most people become middle class in their standards of living and lifestyles. While blue-collar workers' job situations may be different from lower white-collar positions, many in the higher blue-collar ranks, argued Mayer and Buckley (1970), have a lifestyle that "resembles that of the lower-middle class much more closely than that of the poorer semi-skilled and unskilled manual laborers. . . . Away from the job, they cannot be distinguished from the lower-middle-class white-collar men" (p. 94).

Although several past studies have found that clerical positions have become deskilled (e.g., Crompton and Jones 1984), others have found a distinct trend toward *deproletarianization*. There has been an increase in the proportion of the labor force who are managers, experts, or supervisors, providing more support for the postindustrial theories than the Marxist thesis of proletarianization. Wright and Martin (1987) proposed that these results may mean merely that capitalism has internationalized itself and has shifted more proletarianized occupations into Third World countries. Thus, the proletarianization issue is still unsettled.

Marxian Images of Class Structure

In contrast to the socioeconomic approach, Marxian sociologists generally object to the mixing of economic, status, and other socioeconomic variables because they believe it dilutes what Marx considered to be the core economic meaning of social class. Marx believed class was basically an economic phenomenon and was defined by an individual's position in the social relations of production, by control over the physical means (property) and social means (labor power) of production. In other words, class is not defined by income or occupation but rather by ownership/control in the system of production. In this view, introducing other socioeconomic variables, such as prestige or occupational status, only distorts the meaning of social class. Thus, in the Marxian definition, class is much less multidimensional in nature. Moreover, the crucial differences between the social classes are qualitative in nature—that is, the class system is not a continuous hierarchy. The boundaries between the classes are discrete and clear. Finally, classes in this view are defined by the exploitation that exists between them and by the interconnection of the functions of each class. This means that a given class is defined by its relationship to another class. Workers are members of the working class, for example, *because* of the nature of their relationship to capital and capitalists. Different classes perform distinct but interrelated functions in capitalist society.

As we have seen, the basic Marxian definition of class is "first of all a place in the system" (Ollman 1987, p. 62). This "place" simply may refer to ownership or nonownership or it may refer to a variety of *structural* conditions that define an individual's place in the system of production.

While some Marxists define class strictly in terms of structural position, others incorporate a social-psychological dimension into their conception, arguing that class consciousness or a similar sense of belongingness and organized opposition must also be present for *social* classes to be present—that is, individuals must identify with each other and understand their real relationship to other classes and act on that knowledge. Ollman stated flatly that the concept of class has both subjective and objective dimensions, the subjective element being a sense of unity that develops as a class emerges. People "tend to acquire over time other common characteristics as regards . . . lifestyle, political consciousness and organization that become, in turn, further evidence for membership in their particular class and subsidiary criteria for determining when to use the class label. Here, class is a quality that is attached to people" (ibid., p. 64). In this approach, people become a real *social* class when they acquire a common culture and political awareness. In addition to occupying the same location or position in relation to the means of production, then, people in the same social class "share the distinctive traditions common to their social position" (Szymanski 1978, p. 26). This common identity, especially when it involves awareness of common exploitation and engagement in class struggle, Marx suggested, is what welds an aggregate of people into a social class, or a "class-for-itself" (Bottomore 1966).

It should be clear at this point that even among Marxists there is lack of agreement on the exact definition and measurement of social class. Marx never gave an explicit, clear-cut definition of class. Moreover, he suggested various definitions and different numbers and types of social classes at different points in his writing. Nevertheless, his approach and that of contemporary Marxian analysts are clearly different from those discussed earlier who define class in broader socioeconomic terms. In sum, Marxists generally view classes as (1) discrete rather than continuous, (2) real rather than statistical creations, (3) economic in nature, and (4) conflictual in their relations. In contrast,

traditional conservative approaches define classes as existing along a continuous hierarchy, largely statistically created, and being multidimensional and nonconflictual in their relationships.

Perhaps the most sophisticated recent attempt to analyze the class structure of the United States in Marxian terms comes from Erik Wright. At the heart of Marx's conception of class is a view that stresses the relational, antagonistic, and exploitative relationship between property owners and nonowners. Accordingly, Wright's most recent characterization of U.S. class structure uses exploitation as the defining element (Wright and Cho 1992; Western and Wright 1994). Classes and class locations are distinguished by an individual's ability to exploit or be exploited on the basis of (1) property, (2) organizational authority, or (3) expertise or skill.

Combining these three criteria, Wright identified several class "locations" within this structure of class relationships. The most elemental distinction involves those who have property from those who do not (owners vs. nonowners). Among *owners*, Wright has separated capitalists who employ others (employers) from those who do not (petty bourgeoisie). Application of the other two criteria of class location, authority and expertise, results in distinctions among *employees*, which create a number of class locations. Considering the criterion of bureaucratic authority, there are those who have it and those who do not (managers and nonmanagers). Individuals are considered managers if they are involved in policy decisions and are in a position to impose sanctions on others. Employees also differ in level of skill or expertise, which is the third criterion of class position. There are (1) managers and professionals who are experts, (2) workers and managers who are not experts, and (3) semiprofessionals (such as those in technical jobs) who are in between. In this scheme, the owners might be considered the capitalist class and the workers compose the working class. The remaining groups among employees (managers, professionals, semiprofessionals) might be viewed as the middle class because they have characteristics of both those above and below them. In a real sense, as Wright has put it, these employees occupy "contradictory" locations because not only are they exploited as employees but they also exploit other employees because of their authority and/or expertise assets. Frequently, this group of employees is referred to as a "new" middle class because of its relatively recent growth within capitalism. Figure 2.1 graphically depicts Wright's class structure.

The figure gives a rather static, broad view of the class structure and how persons might be located within it. But Wright has pointed out that class position also depends on the relationship a person has with others in his or her family—relationships that may link the individual to different classes. In other words, a person's own position is "mediated" by the position of others. For example, two individuals may both be professionals, but one lives in a family made up primarily of workers while the other lives in a family in which all the adults are professionals. These varying sets of relationships connect each of these professionals to the class structure in different ways. As suggested in Chapter 1,

the subjective meaning of social class and how they place themselves in the class structure may be different for college professors, whose parents are working class, for example, than it is for professors who come from a fully professional family.

In addition, two individuals may be in the same class at a given time, but one is located on a clear and recognized career path that will take that person to a higher position (e.g., being on the "fast track" to an executive position at a corporation) while the other person is in a dead-end job. This "temporal" aspect of class position means that to define class location fully, one must take into account the span of the broader career trajectory in which the current position is embedded. The addition of the concepts of mediated and temporal class position makes Wright's characterization of class structure more complex as well as realistic.

Common to this Marxian conceptualization of social class is the idea that classes are tied together by relationships of exploitation. In addition to Wright, Sorensen recently suggested a measure of class that uses exploitation as its central characteristic (2000). He defined *exploitation* in terms of the ownership or control of assets that produce returns or "rents"

OWNERS (approximately 15 percent)
(are self-employed in the system of production)

includes

(1) employers, (2) petty bourgeoisie

EMPLOYEES IN CONTRADICTORY (MIDDLE) LOCATIONS
(approximately 45 percent)
(have expertise and/or authority but are not owners)

includes

(3) manager/experts, (4) other managers, (5) professionals, (6) semiprofessionals

WORKERS (approximately 40 percent)

includes

(7) those who are in nonowner/nonexpert/nonmanagerial positions

---

FIGURE 2.1   Wright's Class Structure

for the individual. "Rents are returns on assets that are in fixed supply because single owners of the asset to the market control the supply of those assets . . . I propose to define *exploitation class* as structural locations that provide rights to rent-producing assets" (Sorensen 2000, p. 1525). Consequently, the class structure consists of classes who do or do not own such assets and who are fixed in an antagonistic relationship to each other. While Wright agreed with Sorensen on the importance of using exploitation to define class relationships and structure, recall that he believes the bases of exploitation and the nature of the relationships between exploiter and exploited are more complex than what is suggested by the concept of rent-producing assets.

However, several critics have raised questions about Wright's new measure of class position. Meiksins (1988) argued that it is not necessarily true that those with skills or credentials exploit those below them. This is an empirical issue and cannot simply be settled by conceptual fiat.

As a further reaction to Wright's model, Resnick and Wolff (2003) have suggested that the recent emphasis on basing a Marxian class model on the concept of exploitation has led to neglect in the use of another central concept in Marx's theory as a basis for class modeling, namely, "surplus value." Resnick and Wolff argue that classes of employees can be distinguished according to whether they (a) produce surplus, (b) appropriate (i.e., take) it, or (c) are given part of the distribution of the surplus that is produced. This would suggest that there are three main classes in a capitalist society like the United States. In a word, they view workers as *producing* the surplus, capitalists as *appropriating* it, and managers/supervisors as being given or *distributed* surplus because they provide the conditions under which workers produce surplus. Following Marx, Resnick and Wolff define workers as "productive" because they actually create the surplus, while capitalists, managers, and the like are classified as

"unproductive." Resnick and Wolff do not contend that their class model is better than Wright's, but only that there are potentially several models, each of which taps a different part of social and economic reality and, therefore, helps us to understand some parts of class reality while ignoring others.

Some Generalizations.   As you have seen, all analysts of U.S. class structure wrestle with recurrent issues of where to place given sets of individuals within the class structure. Most prominent among these issues are (1) whether to place lower white-collar positions (i.e., routine clerical, service, sales occupations) within the middle or working class; (2) whether to place high-level managers within the middle or upper class, or in a separate category such as the corporate class; (3) how and where to incorporate the rising number of "knowledge" workers or professionals within the class structure; and (4) whether to include the poor and/or unemployed among the working class or to consider them a separate lower class or underclass. As the nation's economy experiences downsizing and similar corporate moves, another increasingly relevant issue will be to figure out how temporary, floating, and new entrepreneurs fit into the U.S. class structure.

In reviewing both the multidimensional socioeconomic and Marxian models, a few generalizations may be made about U.S. class structure. First, there appears to be general agreement across all these models that the upper or capitalist class makes up only a very small percentage of the population, about 1 to 2 percent. Second, most of these schemes suggest that the working class comprises at least close to half of the population. Third, estimates of the lower class or underclass range from approximately 5 to 12 percent. Finally, most of these models place lower-level white-collar occupations in the working class rather than in the middle class. This is consistent with the perceptions of Americans in general surveys.

If you were to consider each of these conceptualizations of social class, how would your perception of U.S. class structure change as you went from one to another? Certainly, the definition a person has of something affects what he or she sees. This is no less true of class perceptions.

TECHNOLOGY AND THE SHAPING OF THE U.S. CLASS STRUCTURE

The class structure of any society is shaped by the political, cultural, economic, and technological context in which it is embedded. *Politically*, changes in rules and resources governing labor/management conflict, including unionization of workers, affect class conditions and relationships. Government trade and immigration policies, poverty programs, tax laws, and restrictions on business help determine the size and composition of classes, the extent of income and wealth differences, and the channels for moving up and down the class ladder. *Culturally*, broad-based values about democracy, equality, and justice can serve to temper the extent of social inequality, whereas the presence of prejudice, stereotypes, and derogatory ideologies about different groups can perpetuate such inequality. Finally, *economic* and *technological* developments have become increasingly significant for the changing composition of classes and for shifts in the distribution of individuals among classes. These developments need to be emphasized.

In recent years, technological developments have sped the integration of national economies into a global network. What happens to steelworkers in Ohio, textile employees in New York, and electronic-component workers across the country is directly tied to the international context within which the U.S. economy operates. The ties created between nations make each more vulnerable to economic and political shifts in other countries. Like a giant web, pressure on any part has reverberations throughout the system. Economic chaos in Russia, the economic union of European countries signaled by the new Euro-currency, and attempts by Latin American nations to better integrate their economies, all have economic repercussions for the United States.

The demand for goods produced by U.S. employees fluctuates with economic and political changes in other countries. For example, the disappearance of almost 170,000 U.S. manufacturing jobs in recent years is linked to economic problems experienced in Asian markets and the subsequent decline in prices for goods and reduction of U.S. exports to those countries. As economic crises occurred in Asian markets, their currencies were devalued, prices of their goods dropped, and importation of these goods into the United States became more attractive. Conversely, the higher cost of U.S. electronic and industrial equipment made them less attractive to economically strapped buyers in Asia, forcing a downturn in these exports to Asian countries. To compete successfully in world markets, many U.S. manufacturers had to reduce prices of their goods. Increases in cheaper imports, declines in U.S. exports, and reductions in prices have led to increases in unemployment in manufacturing (Slater and Strawser 1998; Goodman and Consedine 1999).

Downsizing, lean production, and the exportation of jobs to cheaper foreign labor markets have been primary ways used by U.S. manufacturers to reduce costs and respond to foreign competition. *Successful* penetration of U.S. firms into foreign countries may mean higher profits for some, but it also spells lower incomes for many workers, white-collar and blue-collar alike. Higher unemployment means lower incomes for those affected, in part because it means lower pressures for increased wages. Not surprisingly, job loss and fear of job loss dampen appeals for wage increases, as does the weakness of U.S. labor's power (Volgy, Schwarz, and Imwalle 1996; Aaronson and Sullivan 1998). *Unsuccessful* foreign penetration, on the other hand, means fewer exports for U.S. firms, lower profits, and very likely, lower stock prices. The latter means declines in the wealth of those who own these stocks. Thus, individuals throughout the entire class system are affected by international economic events, but not in the same ways.

The interconnectedness of the world economy has been intensified by progress in the technology of communication networks and information systems, which has brought together larger networks of individuals and organizations around the globe. This technology also has repercussions for the occupational structure. Increased computer usage in all kinds of organizations has provided the impetus for increases in jobs for systems analysts, software programmers, and computer technicians. Between 1996 and 2006, for example, employment of computer scientists, computer engineers, and systems analysts is expected to more than double to almost 2,000,000 workers. The number of temporary workers who are hired out to provide expertise in these fields to client companies is also expected to increase by 123 percent during this period (U.S. Department of Labor 1998; Melchionno 1999).

In addition to their effects on occupational distribution, advances in computer technology and the rapid growth of the Internet have also created greater possibilities for flexible work patterns and new forms of economic organizations. Because the technology allows dispersion of workers across space, even across countries, work groups are being formed in cyberspace, resulting in the creation of "virtual organizations" (Crandell and Wallace 1998). The Internet technology has opened up scores of opportunities for individuals who are adept in it. New companies made possible by the powerful computer technologies have arisen overnight and their stocks have rocketed so suddenly that their youthful creators have become millionaires in a very short time. Amazon.com, eBay, eTrade, and similar companies have made their management very wealthy

on paper. More individuals have become billionaires since 1985 in the United States than in its entire previous history, and technical knowledge and opportunity have provided the bases for their wealth (Thurow 1999).

Employment and unemployment patterns are being dramatically affected by computer technology and the Internet. The freedom from restrictions of space and time that the Internet provides means that the line between home and work can easily become blurred. Employees can stay at home and still be employed in computer tasks. Even though the success rates of such businesses is low and self-employment accounted for less than 1 percent of all job growth in the United States in the 1990s, enterprising employees can start their own businesses and become entrepreneurs. Workers who are interested in moving but wish to remain employees are not limited in their job searches by local newspaper advertisements. Rather, they can search the Web for employment in a wide variety of geographic areas. Conversely, because of new communication technologies, employers can hire qualified individuals who live in very diverse locations. Knowledge and skills in new computer technologies have become a critical avenue for success. These possibilities hold the potential to complicate the processes of status attainment and diversify the compositions of given classes.

Moreover, new technology has made corporations and their workers less loyal to each other. It has created employment for some, unemployment for others; higher profits for some, and lower incomes for others. All this means that some will benefit from the ongoing technological revolution while others will remain onlookers, lacking access to and/or participation in it. A recent national survey found that households with incomes of at least $75,000 are 20 times more likely than those with lower incomes to have Internet access, and the gap has grown over the last few years. Similar discrepancies exist for individuals at different levels of education, and between individuals who live in rural and urban areas (National Telecommunications and Information Administration 1999).

Race is also involved. Historically, for example, Blacks have frequently been left behind in times of technological progress. Not surprisingly then, "blacks have traditionally been poorly educated . . . and deprived of the sorts of opportunities that create the vision necessary for technological ambition. . . . Not channeled to follow the largely technological possibilities for success in this society, black folkways have instead embraced the sort of magical thinking that is encouraged by the media and corporations whose sole interest in blacks is as consumers" (Walton 1999, pp. 17–18). Instead of encouraging education and the development of technical knowledge, these folkways have identified uniqueness of individual talent, as in sports or popular music, as avenues of attainment. But these folkways are reactions to real living conditions. Recent research suggests that less than one-third of Blacks own a personal computer, compared to just under one-half of Whites. Racial differences in ownership and usage are especially great in lower-income groups with differences declining or disappearing with increasing income and education (Hoffman and Novak 1998). Since computer skills and related access are important bases for attainment in the knowledge professions, to be left out is to be relegated to a "cyberghetto" separating the technological haves from the have-nots (McKissack 1998).

INCOME INEQUALITY

Because "class" has been first and foremost thought of as an economic phenomenon, it should not be surprising that "income" has frequently been used as a measure of class position. As such, its distribution can provide clues about character of U.S. class structure and trends within it. *Money income*, as defined by the Bureau of the Census, includes money from virtually all sources, including wages or salaries, social security, welfare, pensions, and others. There are some advantages to using *total money income* when assessing the extent of economic inequality. In the first place, it is certainly more immediately quantifiable than many other measures, such as real estate. Second, income is highly valued in U.S. society and serves as a base on which people are evaluated by others. Third, income inequalities saturate and are reflected in a number of other economically related areas. Unemployment, inflation, farm and food prices, rent control, women's liberation, racism, and welfare are all areas that involve income-differential issues. In your own case, think about the number of ways that income is implicated in different areas of your life. Income, then, at least at first glance, would appear to be a more than adequate measure of economic inequality.

However, when interpreting the following statistics, several factors should be kept in mind. First, income is only a partial measure of a family's or individual's economic well-being. It does not include the value of stocks, real estate, or other noncash economic assets, and if it is *current* income, it does not take into account the income trajectory an individual may be on if, for example, he or she is just beginning in a lucrative career. Second, some of the estimates of income are based on pooled findings from several government studies that are not always identical in methodology or measures of income. Finally, and most significantly, the Bureau of the Census contends that there is an underreporting of income, with some sources of income being more likely to be reported than others. Tax filers tend to underreport their incomes on their income tax forms, and not all persons are required to file income tax returns. Independent estimates suggest that incomes from government benefit programs and property income are among those most likely to be underestimated (U.S. Bureau of the Census, August 1992b).

In recent decades, manufacturing has fallen on hard times. Traditionally associated with many well-paying, unionized jobs, manufacturing accounted for 42 percent of all mass layoffs and almost half of all initial claims for unemployment insurance in 2001. Transportation equipment, electronic, electrical, and industrial equipment were sectors that were hit especially hard.
Photo by Brendan R. Hurst.

Table 2.1 presents information on how U.S. households are distributed among different income categories. The top and bottom lines indicate that although the percentage of families with incomes below $15,000 has declined over time (from 19.8% in 1970 to 15.9% in 2003), the percentage of those with incomes of at least $100,000 went up much more during that same time (from 4.2% to 15.1%). However, the percentages of those in the $25,000–$49,999 categories have generally declined. While shifts in the top and bottom

TABLE 2.1   Percentage Distribution of Households by Income Level: 1970–2003

INCOME	1970	1980	1990	2003
Under $15,000	19.8	18.8	16.9	15.9
$15,000–24,999	14.3	14.3	13.6	13.1
$25,000–34,999	14.9	14.0	12.9	11.9
$35,000–49,999	21.1	17.9	17.0	15.0
$50,000–74,999	19.1	20.0	19.2	18.0
$75,000–99,999	6.5	8.6	10.0	11.0
$100,000 and over	4.2	6.3	10.3	15.1
Median income	$35,832	$37,447	$40,865	$43,318

Source: U.S. Census Bureau, *Income, Poverty, and Health Insurance Coverage in the United States: 2003.* Current Population Reports, Series P-60, No. 226, Table A-1, p. 27.

categories in this table may suggest that economic conditions have improved since 1970,
we need to reserve that judgment until we
explore the matter further.

One way in which income inequality
shows up clearly is when comparisons are
made between racial and ethnic groups. Over
27 percent of Black and almost 19 percent
of Hispanic households had incomes below
$15,000 in 2003, compared to under 14 percent
of non-Hispanic White households. On the
other end of the income scale, over 17 percent
of non-Hispanic White households had
incomes of at least $100,000 in 2003, yet only
about 7 percent of Black and Hispanic households had such incomes (U.S. Census Bureau,
August 2004). Not surprisingly then, as they
have in the past, the median incomes of households varied as well in 2003, ranging from
$29,645 for Black to $32,997 for Hispanic to
$47,777 for White households.

Incomes also vary between family types. As
might be expected, households with married-
couple families are generally better off than
those headed by only males or females. This is
the case among Whites, Blacks, and Hispanics,
but as Figure 2.2 demonstrates, Blacks and
Hispanics are worse off than Whites in each
type of family. Female-headed families have

the lowest incomes within each racial and
ethnic group. Overall, such families have less
than half of the income of married-couple
families.

IS THE MIDDLE CLASS SHRINKING?

The decline in the percentage of families in the
$25,000–$49,999 categories is one indication
that the middle class has been shrinking. Of
course, one's conclusion about such shrinking
depends heavily on the income measures used
and the definition given to the *middle class*.
These variations in measurement constitute
the primary reason for the controversy surrounding economic fortunes of the middle
class.

Most of the analyses on the middle-class
issue do indicate a shrinking in the size of
the middle-income categories. Horrigan and
Haugen (1988) reexamined this issue, using
family income and two ways of comparing
changes in family income distributions overtime.
They were interested in examining any changes
that may have occurred between 1969 and
1986. Regardless of the method used, they
found that the middle was being reduced, but
whether only the top or both the top and bottom
were increasing in size depended on the method

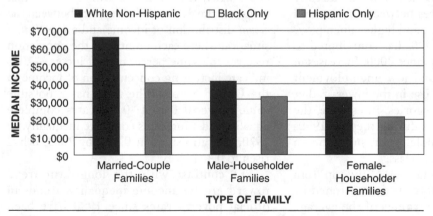

FIGURE 2.2   Median Incomes for Family Types by Race: 2003
Source: U.S. Census Bureau, Table FINC-01 at pubdb3.census.gov/macro/032004/
faminc/new01_000.htm.

used in making comparisons over time. Part of the increase of families in higher earnings categories is due to the increase in two-earner families, especially with the increase of women into the labor force on a full-time basis. The shriveling of the middle class continued into the 1990s, in part due to declines in upward mobility from the bottom (Gottschalk in Bernstein 1996, p. 90).

The conclusion that the middle is shrinking is also based on current trends in earnings, the major source of middle-class income. Median wages and salaries have declined over the last two decades. Between the late 1970s and the mid-1990s, median wages fell for the bottom two-thirds of the work force, and especially among those in the lowest categories (Mishel, Bernstein, and Schmitt 2001). In contrast, earnings for those in the upper third of the labor force rose during this period. The result of these trends was a distancing of the top from the middle and the middle from the bottom. In the mid-to-late 1990s, wages increased across the board, but wage inequality continued in a different form. Those in the top 5 percent of the labor force experienced the greatest increases, and consequently, moved further away from those in the middle, while those at the bottom of the wage scale also went up and moved closer to the middle. In the early 2000s, wage differences between the top and the middle have grown, and higher unemployment since the late 1990s has contributed to higher wage inequality since 2000. Increases in the minimum wage and low unemployment especially benefited those in the lower- rather than middle-wage categories. In essence, the top made greater gains during the late 1990s than those in the middle, again suggesting a weakening of the middle class.

The continued distancing of the top from the rest of the labor force is demonstrated by the fact that median earnings of the average CEO went up 79 percent during the 1989–2000 period, with the result that the average CEO received pay that was 185 times

the wages of the average worker (Mishel, Bernstein, and Allegretto 2005). In mid-2004, the average weekly pay for blue-collar employees was about $526, which is the lowest since 2001 (Strobe 2004).

Large numbers of mass layoffs involving 50 or more employees have also contributed to the growing gap between the top and the rest of the labor force. In 2004, there were almost 16,000 layoff events involving about 1.6 million employees. Thirty-five percent of these events were in manufacturing. Large numbers of jobs also disappeared for professionals in information technology following the burst of the high-tech bubble in 2000 and an increase in white-collar outsourcing to countries like India.

In addition to the decline of well-paying manufacturing jobs and white-collar outsourcing, there are other clues that suggest the decline of the middle class. One of these lies in the changes that have occurred in the distribution of income among sections of the population. Figure 2.3 confirms the decline in income shares going to those below the top 20 percent. As the figure indicates, the percentage of all income going to the bottom 80 percent of the population has declined since 1980, whereas that going to the top 20 percent increased from 43.7 percent in 1980 to 49.8 percent in 2003.

Finally, trends in the Gini ratio—which measures the extent of discrepancy between the *actual* distribution of income and a *hypothetical* situation where each quintile of the population receives the same percentage of income—also indicate increasing concentration of income in the United States. The ratio has a possible value range of 0 to 1; 0 indicates complete equality and 1 indicates complete inequality. In 1970, the ratio stood at 0.394; by 2003, it had risen to 0.464.

In contrast with the long-term trend toward greater income inequality, trends in official poverty rates since 1980 have been more erratic, going up in the early 1980s before declining and then rising again in 1989. They began to decline again in 1993 and did so

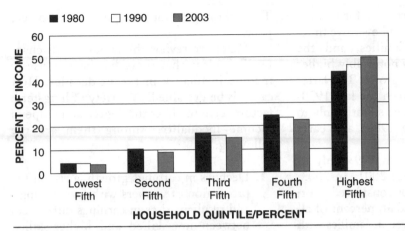

FIGURE 2.3 Percentage Share of Aggregate Income Received by Each Fifth of Households: 1980, 1990, 2003

Source: U.S. Census Bureau, *Income, Poverty, and Health Insurance Coverage in the United States: 2003*. Current Population Reports, Series P-60, No. 226, Table A-3, pp. 36–37.

for the remainder of the decade before increasing again in 2001. In 2003, the poverty rate stood at 12.5 percent (35.9 million), up from 11.3 percent (31.6 million) in 2000 (U.S. Census Bureau, August 2004).

Whether a person or family is defined as "poor" by the Bureau of the Census depends on whether their income falls below a given threshold. These thresholds vary by one's age,

and family size and composition. For example, in 2003, individuals under 65 years old were defined as poor if their total income fell below $9,573. On the other hand, a family of four with two parents and two children under 18 years of age had to have a gross income of under $18,660 to be classified as poor.

Table 2.2 shows that Hispanics and Blacks have poverty rates that are almost three times

TABLE 2.2 Poverty Rates by Race, Age, and Family Status: 1980, 1990, 2003

POVERTY RATE (% IN POVERTY)			
	1980	*1990*	*2003*
All persons	13.0	13.5	12.5
Under 18 years old	18.3	20.6	17.6
18 to 64 years old	10.1	10.7	10.8
65 and older	15.7	12.2	10.2
Whites, non-Hispanics	9.1	8.8	8.2
Blacks	32.5	31.9	24.4
Hispanics	25.7	28.1	22.5
Married-couple families	6.2	5.7	5.4
Female-headed families	32.7	33.4	28.0
Male-headed families	11.0	12.0	13.5

Source: U.S. Census Bureau, *Income, Poverty, and Health Insurance Coverage in the United States: 2003*. Current Population Reports, Series P-60, No. 226, August 2004, pp. 9–13.

those of Whites. The poverty rate for families with female householders is still over five times that of married-couple families, and the poverty rate for children is noticeably higher than that for any other age group. The latter had risen significantly between the late 1970s and early 1980s, then declined slightly only to rise again during the late 1980s and early 1990s.

The rate began falling in 1993 only to begin increasing again since 2001. In 2003, about one in six children was considered poor; together, children composed 36 percent of all the poor in that year. Children in families with a female householder are five times more likely to be poor than children living in families with a married couple. Their poverty rate is almost 40 percent (U.S. Bureau of the Census, September 2001).

Within the poor population, some people are poorer than others. Some have incomes that are very near the poverty threshold, whereas the incomes of others fall well below that poverty line. Two measures are used to indicate how far an individual's or family's income falls below their poverty threshold (ibid.). One of these is a *ratio* that compares their actual income with their poverty threshold. A ratio of 1.00 would indicate that their income is exactly the same as the threshold. A ratio below 1.00 is a measure of how far *below* poverty the person's or family's income falls; conversely, a ratio above 1.00 indicates how far their income is *above* the poverty threshold.

About 42 percent of poor families, involving over 10 million individuals, had incomes that were *less than half* of the amount that the government uses to classify them as poor.

The second measure used to show the depth of one's poverty is the *income deficit*, which is the difference between a family's income and its poverty threshold. In 2003, the average poor family's income deficit was $7,627, which means that their income was actually $7,627 below their poverty threshold.

Thus, they were not only poor, but also very poor.

When we review the tables in this chapter, it is clear that there has been a rise in income inequality in recent decades. How can this be explained? A variety of long-term factors seem to affect the degree and shape of income inequality. Among them are the following:

1. Declines in earnings growth, a rise in the proportion of workers with low earnings, and resultant rises in earnings differences between low-skilled and higher-skilled workers

2. Shifts in the economy from production of goods to services, which contain wider variations in salaries and wages

3. Recessionary and expansionary forces in the economy

4. Shifts in the demands for high- and less-skilled workers, in part creating more temporary positions with few benefits

5. Changes in employment rates with a tighter labor market in the late 1990s

6. Changes in the age structure of the population and labor force (e.g., influx of the baby-boom generation into the labor market) and in the composition of households (e.g., rise in single-parent families)

7. An influx of poorly educated immigrants into the work force and the rising use of less-expensive foreign labor

8. Declining unionization and power of unions

9. Industrial streamlining, reengineering, and downsizing

10. Governmental policies such as minimum wage changes, tax reform, and cuts in programs for the needy (Grubb and Wilson 1992; Levy and Murnane 1992; U.S. Bureau of the Census, March 1992; Hershey 1993; Mishel, Bernstein, and Schmitt 2001)

11. Effects related to globalization.

It is common to associate poverty with the inner city, and indeed central cities have the highest poverty rates of any residential area. But rural poverty is also higher than the national average. Although it has declined in the last decade, the poverty rate in 2003 for those living outside metropolitan areas was 14.2 percent. Almost two-thirds of the poor live in the South and West. Rural states such as Alabama, Arkansas, Louisiana, and New Mexico have high poverty rates compared to other states. The photo above of a now largely abandoned home was taken in Knox County, Kentucky.

Photo by Sarah Brownlee.

WEALTH INEQUALITY IN THE UNITED STATES

Although extensive income inequality exists in the United States, there is even greater wealth inequality, and it has grown since the 1980s. Since 1983, it is those at the top whose wealth has grown most rapidly. In contrast, the bottom 40 percent lost 76 percent in wealth. While the average wealth of the top 1 percent rose to over $10 million, that of the bottom 40 percent fell to $1,100. In 1998, the richest 1 percent held 38 percent of all household wealth. On the other end, the percentage of those with zero or negative wealth rose since 1983 from 15.5 to 18 percent (Wolff, April 2000). Among industrial countries in the 1990s, the United States has the greatest degree of wealth inequality between families (Keister and Moller 2000).

As significant as the increase in income inequality has been, the increase in wealth inequality is even more significant because wealth is a more complete measure of a family's economic power, since it consists of the value of all the family's assets minus its debts. Wealth includes the value of homes, automobiles, businesses, savings, and investments.

But although the amount of personal wealth gives a fuller picture of an individual's or family's economic position, even it does not fully suggest the fact that the wealthy also have at their disposal a greater number of economic tools that serve to enhance their economic opportunities and market situation. For example, ownership of a great deal of stock in a corporation that is interlocked or directly connected with other corporations may give an individual indirect influence over the economic behavior of the latter organizations. Like poverty, wealth has economic implications beyond the actual size of the holdings. Economic opportunities are at least in part a function of the economic tools a person has at his or her disposal.

The methodology used to uncover the distribution of wealth is not as agreed upon as one would desire. Some of the difficulties associated with present methods are clear. Information about wealth is difficult to obtain. Virtually all data about it come from various field surveys and administrative records. Often, individuals are hesitant to be interviewed, and this is especially true of the wealthy who, for several reasons, may be sensitive about their wealth. "As a rule," stated Allen (1987), who has conducted an extensive analysis of the country's richest families, "the members of wealthy capitalist families refuse to divulge even the most rudimentary details of their wealth. . . . In order to maintain their anonymity, the members of corporate rich families typically refuse to disclose even basic biographical information about themselves" (pp. 26–27). What is requested of individuals in surveys and what is given are frequently not the same (J.D. Smith 1987).

Social scientists, in general, have produced hundreds of studies of the poor and poverty, even the middle class, but good broad-based information about the wealthy and wealth concentration has always been and remains difficult to find. Why this has been the case remains an interesting political question (Pessen 1973; Turner and Starnes 1976). Another problem with wealth data is that cash

and personal items such as jewelry and art are often undervalued. To complicate these matters, researchers use different units of analysis in discussing the distribution of wealth. Sometimes the unit used is the individual, while in others the family or consumer unit is the basis of analysis. I will discuss the sources of data on wealth distribution in greater detail later. But first, let us examine wealth differences in their historical context.

Wealth Concentration before the Civil War

If ever there was a time when equality was present, it surely must have been when the United States was first being established. When this nation was being politically formed, many left their European homelands because of oppression of one kind or another to escape to the "land of the free," where the streets were thought to be paved with gold. The Founding Fathers, using "the voice of justice," forged a document that not only enumerated the offenses committed against the then new American people but also demanded freedom and equality for all. While some, such as Alexander Hamilton and Thomas Jefferson, argued about whether the government should or should not take a strictly egalitarian form, many believed the period was an "era of the common man" (Pessen 1973). The Founders recognized the belief that "all men are created equal" and later devised a constitution that had among its objectives to "establish justice." In his famous visit to the United States, Alexis de Tocqueville (1969) was surprised by the "equality of conditions" that seemed to prevail in the youthful country. And although he believed wealth was certainly present, no one group held a monopoly on it. Indeed, de Tocqueville believed that wealth moved about quite a bit in the country.

Recent studies have simply not borne out these beliefs. Social historians, poring over probate records, tax forms, and old census documents, have found a decidedly different America than one might have expected. The studies of wealth distribution in the early United States consistently point to the fact that wealth inequality was a clear and constant condition during this period. This was especially true for the period between the Revolution and the Civil War, a time in which inequality was on the rise.

Before the Revolution, however, the increases in inequality do not appear to have been as great or as consistent, but differences in wealth were quite noticeable. Studies in Philadelphia and Chester County, Pennsylvania; Boston and Salem, Massachusetts; and Hartford and rural Connecticut point not only to evident variations in wealth among people, but in some cases to increasing differences as time passed (Pessen 1973). However, uniform evidence about a trend toward increasing inequality before 1776 does not exist. But after 1776, the trend toward increasing inequality is present everywhere.

In his studies of cities in New England, the Middle Atlantic, the South, and the Midwest, Sturm (1977) found some sobering results for believers in the "romantic hypothesis." Using probate data, he found distinct and increasing inequality in estate wealth for the period from 1800 to 1850. During this time, per capita holdings of the very wealthy had gone up about 60 percent (Sturm 1977). An examination by Pessen for this period in Brooklyn and Boston likewise confirms the general trend toward inequality. In Brooklyn in 1810, 1 percent of the population held 22 percent of the private wealth, and in 1840, 1 percent owned 42 percent (Pessen 1973, p. 36). Figures for Boston and New York duplicate these findings.

Concentration of wealth in the nineteenth century appears to have peaked during the period from 1850 to 1870. Soltow found that while wealth inequality remained fairly constant during this period, it was also very high. Using census data on real and personal estate holdings among free adult males, he found that

in 1860, the top 1 percent owned almost 30 percent and the top 10 percent owned about 73 percent of estate wealth, again demonstrating a strong degree of wealth concentration. During the period from 1850 to 1870, "there very definitely was an elite upper group in America in terms of control of economic resources" (Soltow 1975, p. 180). A small percentage had great wealth, but large numbers had little, if any. In 1850, over half of free adult males owned no land even though it was quite cheap. Nor did the situation change much in the years following 1850 (p. 175).

Given the period, as one might expect, a person was more likely to be an owner of real estate if that person was native born, older, and a farmer (Soltow 1975). In 1860, there were an estimated 41 millionaires, 545 in 1870, and 5,904 in 1922. But if one uses constant 1922 dollars, the real estimate for 1870 would be between 1,800 and 2,600.

The main conclusion from all these data is that at least from the mid-eighteenth to the mid-nineteenth centuries, wealth concentration was high and tended to increase during that period. Little is known about the extent of concentration during 1870 to 1922 "except that it was lower after the Civil War than before and lower in 1922 than it was to become by 1929" (Lindert and Williamson 1976, p. 31).

Wealth Concentration in the Contemporary United States

Estimates are that the richest 1 percent held about 30 percent of all wealth during the 1920s, although their wealth decreased to under 30 percent in the 1930–1950 period. By the late 1950s, however, their assets increased to almost 35 percent of all wealth (Keister and Moller 2000). During the first half of the 1970s, the proportion of wealth going to the top 1 percent declined, but then began to rise significantly during the late 1970s and continued through the 1990s although at a slower rate (Nasar 1992; Wolff 1992). Currently, the richest 1 percent hold about one-third of all privately held wealth in the United States (Mishel et al. 2005).

The median household wealth in 2001 was about $74,000. But as Figure 2.4 shows, in 2001 the *wealthiest 20 percent owned over 84 percent of all wealth, while the bottom 40 percent held well under 1 percent.* In fact, while the richest 20 percent owned an average of $1.6 million in wealth, the bottom 20 percent actually had negative net worth or wealth, averaging a minus $8,200. That is, on average, each household owed $8,200 more than they owned. *Financial wealth, that is, wealth involving only stocks, mutual funds, and other investments, was even

more concentrated than overall net worth in 2001, with the top 10 percent possessing 80 percent of all financial assets and the *bottom 90 percent holding only 20 percent* of all financial wealth. In sum, all the evidence indicates a highly unequal distribution of wealth in the United States (ibid.).

The reasons for the increasing concentration of wealth in recent years are related to the differences in the types of wealth held by various income groups. That is, their assets are distributed differently. Those on the top are more likely to have much of their wealth in stocks, bonds, and related kinds of investments, whereas those with much less wealth are likely to have

---

NUTSHELL 2.1

Sources of Wealth Measurement

The observations drawn below about the extent of wealth inequality rely heavily on the work of economist Edward Wolff who uses data from the Survey of Consumer Finances (SCF) conducted by the Federal Reserve Board since 1983. This data source yields a more accurate picture of wealth distribution because it uses a broader and more inclusive definition of net worth and a sample that includes a better representation of the wealthiest households. The SCF is the source used most often in investigations on wealth distribution (Keister and Moller 2000). Other surveys, such as the U.S. Bureau of the Census's Survey on Income and Program Participation (SIPP) and the Panel Survey of Income Dynamics (PSID), underrepresent the richest families and, therefore, significantly understate the wealth of the richest segments of society and the extent of wealth inequality in the United States. Consequently, Wolff contends that these two surveys "are probably useful for studying the wealth accumulation behavior of the middle class, but are not reliable for analyzing the behavior of the very rich" (Wolff 1998, p. 134). Moreover, since the sample used in the SCF is different from those of the two other surveys, so is the composition of the wealth found in its top 20 percent and bottom 80 percent.

Two of the important terms used by Wolff in his analyses are *net worth* and *financial wealth*. *Net worth* refers to "the current value of all marketable or" cash-convertible "assets less the current value of debts" (Wolff 1998, p. 133). It includes the value of housing, real estate, cash, savings, certificates of deposit, money market accounts, bonds, stocks, and equity in businesses and trust funds owned by the household. It also includes the cash value of retirement, life insurance, and pension plans. Wolff believes that this measure is important because it "reflects wealth as a store of value and therefore a source of potential consumption" (Wolff 1998, p. 133). Spilerman also views wealth for its potential "as a capitalized income stream" (2000, p. 500). Wolff goes on to say that "I believe that this is the concept that best reflects the level of well-being associated with a family's holdings" (Wolff, April 2000, p. 3). In contrast to net worth, *financial wealth* is a narrower concept and is defined as one's net worth less the net equity in one's house. Financial wealth includes only those forms of wealth that are easily convertible to cash. Therefore, home equity is excluded because "it is somewhat difficult to liquidate one's housing wealth in the short term" (Wolff 1998, p. 133).

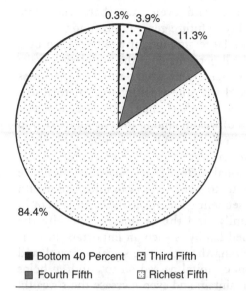

■ Bottom 40 Percent   ⊡ Third Fifth
■ Fourth Fifth   ⊡ Richest Fifth

FIGURE 2.4   Distribution of Net Worth by Quintile and Bottom 40 Percent: 2001

Source: Mishel, Bernstein, and Allegretto 2005, *The State of Working America 2004/2005.* Ithaca, New York: Cornell University, Table 4.3, p. 282.

their wealth in savings accounts and home ownership (see Figure 2.5). Stocks did very well during the late 1980s and the 1990s, and those who had invested profited handsomely.

Between 1983 and 1998, the richest 20 percent gained 91 percent of the growth in overall wealth and 89 percent of the growth in financial wealth. In each case, the top 1 percent accrued over half of the increase (Wolff, April 2000). One million dollars invested in stocks in 1983 would have increased 14-fold by the end of 1998 (Collins, Leondar-Wright, and Sklar 1999). Few Americans have such an amount to invest; those who do can reap large rewards as a result. Such investments paid off in the 1990s. Between 1989 and 1998, the number of millionaires increased 54 percent, and the number of those worth at least $10 million almost quadrupled (Wolff, April 2000). As Figure 2.5 shows, the richest 1 percent had almost 80 percent of their wealth in stock, financial securities, real estate, and businesses. Less than

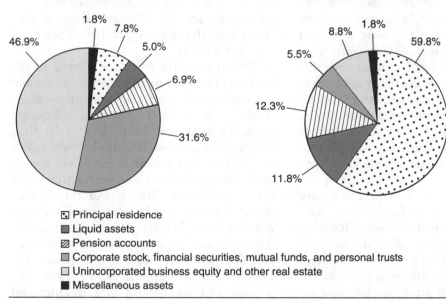

⊡ Principal residence
■ Liquid assets
▨ Pension accounts
■ Corporate stock, financial securities, mutual funds, and personal trusts
□ Unincorporated business equity and other real estate
■ Miscellaneous assets

FIGURE 2.5   Distribution of Asset Types in Top 1 Percent and Middle 60 Percent of Wealth: 1998

Source: Edward N. Wolff, "Recent Trends in Wealth Ownership, 1983–1998." April 2000. Working Paper No. 300, Table 5.

8 percent was invested in their homes, and only 5 percent was in liquid assets, such as bank deposits or money market funds. The pattern of distribution of assets for the middle 60 percent of the population contrasted markedly. Almost 60 percent of their wealth was invested in their principal residences. About 24 percent was in pension funds or liquid assets. Finally, and most significantly, only about 14 percent was in the form of business investments, stocks, real estate, or securities. Yet, it is the latter kinds of investments that experienced the greatest growth in the 1980s and 1990s.

In 1998, the wealthiest 10 percent owned over 85 percent of all *assets* in stocks and mutual funds, 84 percent of financial securities, 91 percent of trusts, and 92 percent of all equity in private businesses (ibid.). In contrast, the bottom 90 percent held 73 percent of all *debt*. Investment in stocks and mutual funds is difficult if income has to go toward debt payments, and a higher percentage of the incomes of households with incomes below $10,000 go toward debt payment than is the case among households with incomes of at least $100,000. Almost a third of households with incomes below $10,000 compared to only 2 percent among $100,000+ households were experiencing "economic hardship," that is, spending more than 40 percent of their incomes on debt payment (Mishel, Bernstein, and Schmitt 2001). After their debt payments, poor families are constrained to spend the remaining income on items (e.g., automobile) that will not produce wealth and will depreciate over time (Spilerman 2000).

The constraints placed on them also mean that poorer families are less able to leave inheritances to their children, leaving the latter with little or no wealth on which to build (Oliver and Shapiro 1995). This is another reason why wealth inequality is so important— its accumulation has direct implications for economic inequality among the children of today's families. As a basis for future economic status, wealth (or its absence) helps to stabilize, reproduce, and even exacerbate economic inequality in future generations (ibid.).

The large amounts of wealth owned by a very small percentage of the population make one curious about where the wealth comes from and who the wealthy are. Historically, family and inheritance have been major sources of wealth among the corporate rich in the United States. Only a minority obtained their initial wealth through entrepreneurship or personal saving. Gift and estate laws have done little to stem the flow of inherited wealth to subsequent generations. Wealth is kept in the family, and this is one reason why the extended family is such an important institution among the rich. The social, cultural, and economic capital passed on to children helps them maintain and even increase their wealth. The odds of the children of wealthy parents keeping their wealth is probably about 3 to 1 (Currie and Skolnick 1988, p. 106). In addition to inheritance, however, technology innovation is becoming a much more prevalent source of wealth. Less than 10 percent of those on the 2004 list of Forbes richest 400 Americans actually inherited their wealth, down from 50 percent in the 1980s (Scott and Leonhardt 2005).

What characteristics are related to the amount of wealth one has? Certainly race and ethnicity are factors that are involved. As Table 2.3 demonstrates, Blacks and Hispanics generally have significantly less wealth than Whites, and are more likely to have no wealth at all. In 1998, the median net worth among non-Hispanic Whites was over 8 times that for non-Hispanic Blacks, and the median financial wealth was 31 times greater among non-Hispanic Whites (Wolff, April 2000). The medians of net worth and financial wealth, however, were even lower for Hispanics than for Blacks. In 1998, the median financial wealth of Hispanics and Blacks as a group was close to zero, and at least twice as many as non-Hispanic Whites have negative wealth (ibid.).

TABLE 2.3 Mean (Median) Net Worth and Financial Wealth by Race and Hispanic Origin, and Household Type: 1998 (in thousands)

	MEAN NET WORTH	(MEDIAN)	MEAN FINANCIAL WEALTH	(MEDIAN)
Non-Hispanic Whites	320.9	(81.7)	254.8	(37.6)
Non-Hispanic Blacks	58.3	(10.0)	37.6	(1.2)
Hispanics	79.2	(3.0)	50.4	(0.0)
	MEAN NET WORTH		**MEAN FINANCIAL WEALTH**	
Married couples, under 65				
with children	253.7		200.8	
without children	415.1		338.6	
Female head, under 65				
with children	63.0		51.0	
without children	109.1		77.6	

Source: Edward N. Wolff, "Recent Trends in Wealth Ownership, 1983–1998." April 2000. Working Paper No. 300, Tables 7, 8, 11.

Since 1998 and the recession of 2000–2001, Hispanics and especially Blacks appear to have lost ground in wealth to Whites, with the wealth gap becoming larger in 2001 than it had been in 1998 (Kochhar 2004; Mishel, Bernstein, and Allegretto 2005). With its implications for inheritance, this change would only exacerbate the economic distinctions in the next generation. Indeed, estimates are that racial differences in inheritance will be even more important in widening the wealth gap between the races among baby-boomers than inheritances in previous generations (Avery and Rendall 2002).

In sum, wealth is distributed much more unequally between Whites and others than is income. The reader should notice the differences in the mean and median figures. The means tend to be much higher because, as a simple average, they are skewed upward by the inordinately high wealth held by those on the top. In contrast, the median shows the wealth of the individual who is in the position where 50 percent of the individuals are above and 50 percent are below. That is, he or she is the case in the exact middle of the wealth hierarchy. Medians are less affected by extreme cases,

and consequently, they tend to be significantly lower here.

Wealth also varies by family type, with married-couple households with children possessing about four times the wealth of female-headed households with children. Families without children are significantly wealthier than those with children. Among age groups, those in the 55–64 bracket have the greatest net worth, those under 35 the lowest (Wolff, April 2000).

Studies of the richest people in the United States further clarify the characteristics of the wealthy. Table 2.4 lists the top 20 richest individuals in the United States in 2004. Several characteristics jump out immediately. Most are men. Most have derived their wealth from extensive activities in crucial areas of the economy (e.g., stocks, technology, communications). The list suggests the importance of new technologies and their development as a source of wealth. In addition to being men and under 60 years of age, the majority of millionaires work and are self-employed. Only about 20 percent are retired. Most have college degrees and just over one-third have advanced degrees (Stanley and Danko 1996).

TABLE 2.4   Richest 20 Individuals in the United States and Principal Sources of Wealth: 2004

NAME	AMOUNT OF WEALTH (IN BILLION DOLLARS)	PRINCIPAL SOURCE OF WEALTH
William Henry Gates III	48.0	Computer software
Warren Edward Buffett	41.0	Investments
Paul Gardner Allen	20.0	Software, investments
S. Robson Walton	18.0	Retail merchandise
John T. Walton	18.0	Retail merchandise
Jim C. Walton	18.0	Retail merchandise
Helen R. Walton	18.0	Retail merchandise
Alice L. Walton	18.0	Retail merchandise
Michael Dell	14.2	Computers
Lawrence Joseph Ellison	13.7	Computer software
Steven Anthony Ballmer	12.6	Computer software
Abigail Johnson	12.0	Investments
Anne Cox Chambers	11.3	Communications
Barbara Cox Anthony	11.3	Communications
John Werner Kluge	11.0	Entertainment media
Pierre M. Omidyar	10.4	Internet sales
John Franklyn Mars	10.0	Candy
Jacqueline Mars	10.0	Candy
Forrest Edward Mars, Jr.	10.0	Candy
Sumner M. Redstone	8.1	Entertainment media

Source: Forbes, Inc., www.forbes.com/lists.

THE GLOBAL CONTEXT AND THE IMPACT OF GLOBALIZATION

It is clear from the discussion so far that Americans believe not only that classes exist in the United States but that there are several ways to describe that class structure. The existence of significant economic inequality in the United States is further demonstrated by Census and other data that reveal extensive income and even greater wealth inequality in the population. Poverty also is a condition of life for almost 36 million in the United States. To better evaluate the significance of these economic inequalities, we need to consider them in a comparative perspective, even though this can be difficult. Cross-national comparisons of economic-inequality systems have always been hazardous because of variations in definitions, measures of economic status, units of analysis, and data-collection

times. Nevertheless, some gross comparisons can be made.

When we look across the world, we find that some populations not only have much higher rates of poverty, but levels of poverty that are significantly more abject than those found in the United States. In some sub-Saharan African countries such as Zaire, Sudan, Malawi, and Rwanda, at least 80 percent of the rural population is poor. In 1995, the per capita income in the United States was 89 times higher than that found in the least developed countries of the world (United Nations 1998). The World Bank estimates that 1.1 billion people were living in "extreme poverty" in 2001, meaning that they were trying to exist on less than $1.00 a day. Extreme poverty has been aptly described as "the poverty that kills" (Sachs 2005: 47). The greatest numbers living in these conditions are in South Asia, Africa, and East

Asia, respectively. India alone is estimated to have 350 million living in extreme poverty (Waldman 2005).

Like poverty, income inequality also varies across nations. In 1960, the top 20 percent richest countries had an income that was 30 times that of the poorest 20 percent, but by 1995 that gap had increased to 82 times. In 1997, it was estimated that the total wealth of the richest 225 people in the world was over $1 trillion, which equaled the combined income of the poorest 47 percent (2.5 billion people) (United Nations 1998). Overall, in most cases, the poorer a country, the greater is the income discrepancy between the richest and poorest 20 percent of the population. In about half of the developing countries, the income of the top 20 percent is at least 15 times that of the bottom 20 percent. For example, in Kenya in 1992, a "low income" country, the poorest 10 percent owned 1.2 percent of all income compared to 47.7 percent being owned by the richest 10 percent. In contrast, in Denmark, a "high income" country, the poorest 10 percent possessed 3.6 percent of income while the top 10 percent held 20.5 percent (United Nations 1998; The World Bank 1999).

A traditional argument has linked greater income inequality to lower economic development. Briefly, the argument goes that early in development, inequality is low, then it increases along with development, but eventually it declines while the country continues to develop. Basically, the trend in inequality takes an inverted U-pattern (Alderson and Nielsen 2002). Past historical trends in the United States have sometimes been depicted this way, with economic inequality reaching a peak in the latter part of the nineteenth century and early part of the twentieth century, and then declining with greater industrialization, increases in population size, and enhanced modernization of institutions, including higher education (Nielsen and Alderson 1995). As logical as this argument seems, however, it does not appear to be universally applicable. In their study of 43 countries, Stack and Zimmerman (1982), for example, found that development led to greater economic equality for only the top 80 percent of the population. The bottom 20 percent did not share in any income redistribution. "Development does not result in the redistribution of income to low income groups" (1982: 355). Indeed, in their analysis of the severely unequal distribution of resources in Latin America, Hoffman and Centeno found that much of the inequality is due to extreme concentration of wealth at the very top, leading them to refer to that region as "the lopsided continent" (2003).

Income distributions also differ among industrial nations, with the United States having among the highest concentrations of income. Table 2.5 presents the shares of income going to each income quintile in various industrial countries. Keep in mind that data were collected in different years from these countries. But among them, the United States has the highest degree of income inequality (Gini index = 40.1). In 1994, the poorest 20 percent owned only 4.8 percent of income compared to over 45 percent for the top 20 percent. In contrast, in Norway, for example, the corresponding figures were 10 and 35.3 percent, respectively. The differences in income inequality among industrial countries, however, while significant, pale in comparison to the differences noted earlier between groups of nations whose economic development is great and those whose development is much less.

Given the widespread inequality between nations, coupled with the breakdown of national boundaries in the world economy, it is not surprising that the relationship between global economic inequality and globalization has become a hot topic of research. Does more extensive involvement of all nations in the world economy reduce the economic inequality between them? Is globalization a

TABLE 2.5   Percentage Share of Income or Consumption among Population Quintiles in Selected Industrial Market Countries

COUNTRY	BOTTOM 20%	SECOND 20%	THIRD 20%	FOURTH 20%	TOP 20%	GINI INDEX[a]
Australia (1989)	7.0	12.2	16.6	23.3	40.9	33.7
Belgium (1992)	9.5	14.6	18.4	23.0	34.5	25.0
Canada (1994)	7.5	12.9	17.2	23.0	39.3	31.5
Denmark (1992)	9.6	14.9	18.3	22.7	34.5	24.7
Finland (1991)	10.0	14.2	17.6	22.3	35.8	25.6
France (1989)	7.2	12.7	17.1	22.8	40.1	32.7
Germany (1989)	9.0	13.5	17.5	22.9	37.1	28.1
Ireland (1987)	6.7	11.6	16.4	22.4	42.9	35.9
Italy (1991)	7.6	12.9	17.3	23.2	38.9	31.2
Netherlands (1991)	8.0	13.0	16.7	22.5	39.9	31.5
Norway (1991)	10.0	14.3	17.9	22.4	35.3	25.2
Spain (1990)	7.5	12.6	17.0	22.6	40.3	32.5
Sweden (1992)	9.6	14.5	18.1	23.2	34.5	25.0
Switzerland (1982)	7.4	11.6	15.6	21.9	43.5	36.1
United Kingdom (1986)	7.1	12.8	17.2	23.1	39.8	32.6
United States (1994)	4.8	10.5	16.0	23.5	45.2	40.1

Source: Adapted from The World Bank 1999, pp. 198–199.

Note: The dates in parentheses are the years in which data were collected. [a] The Gini index measures the dispersion of income across the whole income distribution. The index ranges in score from 0 to 1.0, with 0 representing perfect *equality*, where each person or group gets an equal share, and with 1.0 representing perfect *inequality*, where one person or group owns all the income. In other words, the higher the index score, the higher the inequality. Gini scores were multiplied by 100.

way out of world poverty? Has globalization reduced or exacerbated economic inequality within the United States? We need to address these questions.

Globalization itself has been defined in two basic ways, one which is narrowly economic and another which incorporates a variety of dimensions and is sometimes referred to as the "grand" theory of globalization (Goldthorpe 2002). In the latter view, globalization is seen as an economic, political, and social force that has enveloped most of the world. In its *economic* aspect, globalization involves a marked acceleration in international trade and the flow of financial capital and technology between nations. *Politically*, globalization involves the opening of national borders to products and services from other countries, creating more free trade and rendering borders much more

porous than in the past. *Socially*, it includes the flow and exchange of cultural ideas and structural arrangements among nations. The broad central impact of globalization is to create greater interdependence between parts of the world and to compress the world into a smaller place (Harvey 1989; Guillen 2001). A narrower conceptualization of globalization views it as a strictly economic phenomenon, involving the increase in direct investment, flow of workers, and free trade between countries. It is this definition that we will use in our assessment of globalization's impact on inequality between nations and within the United States.

There is no agreement over whether globalization has been primarily a positive or negative force in the world at large. The positive or "neoliberal" view envisions globalization as raising the average economic fortunes of all nations as members of a world community through the opening up of opportunities and sharing of skills and technologies (Taylor 2002). Globalization encourages internationalism and opens up all countries to the same set of market forces. Since the global marketplace is an open competition, it creates pressures on countries to use their resources efficiently and to find their niche or specialty that puts them at a comparative advantage in the market. The supposed result is a reduction in poverty, a decline in inequality between nations, and, consequently, a wholesale breakdown in the dichotomies that have characterized the world (e.g., rich/poor, core/periphery, North/South) (Wade 2004). Globalization would also reduce economic inequality *within* countries because it is a win–win situation for everyone involved.

The critical view, in contrast, interprets globalization as a force that strengthens the opportunity of powerful nations to take advantage of more vulnerable and less powerful ones through the dismantling of traditional protections for the less wealthy and the consequent exploitation of their labor. Transnational corporations have weakened the power of labor and unions, intensifying competition between home-based and foreign labor. The deindustrialization accompanying globalization reduces the number of high-paying manufacturing jobs and pushes more workers into lower-paying service work (Alderson and Nielsen 2002). One result is a widening of economic inequality between skilled/educated and less-skilled/uneducated workers within countries and between developed and underdeveloped nations (Scholte 2000; Makoba 2002). Poorer countries are more likely to subscribe to this critical view, because they believe that their countries enter the world economy with many disadvantages. Free trade is supposed to operate in the global marketplace, for example, but they know that wealthy nations often subsidize their farmers, putting farmers from poorer countries at a disadvantage.

A more mixed view of globalization states that while globalization harmed less-developed countries in the 1970s, it has more recently hurt employees in developed countries through the exportation of work to lower-wage countries. It has been argued that the effect of globalization on world inequality may vary with its stage at the time. As globalization becomes initially established, inequality between nations grows, but in later stages the advantages of rich nations are slowed and inequality between nations declines (Krugman and Venables 1995).

So what is the answer; has globalization had a positive, negative, or mixed impact on economic inequality? "On this very important question, responsible opinion tends towards diametrically opposing views" (Seshanna and Decornez 2003: 354). Goldthorpe says flatly that globalization theorists have not made their case one way or the other (2002).

Since the early 1800s and up to the recent past, most world inequality has been due to economic inequality *between* nations (Goesling 2001). Economic inequality between nations grew significantly during the Industrial Revolution and twentieth century at the same time that globalization was occurring. And some argue that globalization has continued to create more inequality and has either increased or had no effect in poverty in the world (Prabhakar 2003; Seshanna and Decornez 2003; Kiely 2004; Wade 2004). They find that direct investment in the world market is concentrated in the developed countries rather than evenly spread among all countries, resulting in a concentration rather than dispersion of capital.

Others disagree, contending that in the last few decades of the twentieth century inequality between nations, though extensive, appears to have stabilized (Schultz 1998; Firebaugh 1999; Goesling 2001) or that globalization fosters a reduction in economic inequality (Minnich 2003; Dollar and Kraay 2004; Firebaugh and Goesling 2004). Countries that are most globalized are more likely to thrive economically.

In their study of countries across the economic spectrum, for example, Firebaugh and Goesling found that, while still large, economic inequality between nations declined in the last part of the twentieth century "primarily because of [globalization's] role in the spread of industrial technology in Asia" (2004: 285). Moreover, they anticipate that it will continue to decline because of industrialization and the fact that most of the growth in the working-age population will be in these poor nations. But even though its contribution has declined, economic inequality between countries still accounts for roughly two-thirds of world inequality (Firebaugh 2000; Goesling 2001).

In sum, there are conflicting findings on whether globalization has a positive or negative effect on economic inequality between countries. It has been suggested that among the main reasons for these disagreements are differences in methodology. Earlier I alluded to the difficulties of finding comparable data and definitions in assessing inequality between nations. Those who argue that globalization has reduced inequality criticize the methodology, conceptualizations, and logic of those on the other side. For example, proponents say that critics of globalization define "technology" as meaning information/communications rather than industrial technology. While the former may indeed worsen between-nation inequality, the latter does not (Firebaugh and Goesling 2004). What dimensions of globalization are included in studies also makes a difference because some dimensions may be related to economic inequality in some countries while others are not. In their study of 69 developed and less-developed nations, Reuveny and Li found that open trade reduced inequality within less-developed countries but not developed ones. Foreign direct investment by multinational corporations increases inequality in both types of countries. On the other hand, the free flow of financial capital does not seem to affect income inequality (2003).

Despite these variations, on the whole there seems to be much more agreement that globalization raises economic inequality within countries including the United States (Alderson and Nielsen 2002; Firebaugh and Goesling 2004; Wade 2004; Moore and Ranjan 2005). Despite any possible slowing in international inequality, inequality *within* nations has increased and has become a greater contributor to worth inequality as a whole (Goesling 2001; Guillen 2001). Declining inequality in many industrialized nations has been replaced with increasing inequality. The "great U-turn" in income inequality within advanced nations is partially explained by globalization. In the global marketplace, countries that exercise fewer controls on the movement of capital experience greater earnings inequality as a result (Mahler 2004). Examining data from 16 industrial countries, Alderson and Nielsen found that while direct investment abroad has led to more capital for employers, it has also spurred a decline in high-paying jobs, reduction in demand for low-skill compared to high-skill labor, and an increase in the number of immigrants who have varying levels of skills. These developments have widened the economic gaps within advanced countries (2002). Mishel and others add that globalization has also reduced employment in traditionally high-paying manufacturing jobs, lessened investment in the U.S. manufacturing base, and reduced the price of many goods thereby indirectly causing a decline in the average wages of U.S. workers. They also note that competition from foreign workers can cause U.S. employees to reluctantly accept wage reductions. Finally, the "offshoring" of many high-tech white-collar service jobs appears to be having a depressing effect on the salaries of U.S. white-collar professionals (Mishel, Bernstein, and Allegretto 2005). "Whatever the causes," writes Robert Wade perhaps with some exaggeration, "the fact is that the United States is now back to the same level of inequality of income as in the decades before 1929, the era of the 'robber barons' and the Great Gatsby" (Wade 2004: 578).

SUMMARY

This chapter has analyzed economic inequality as a fundamental form of social inequality. Economic inequality was defined as including social-class, income, and wealth differences in the United States. Americans have complex views of the class structure itself and on what determines their places within it. Scholars as well vary in their depictions of it, usually seeing the class structure either as a socioeconomic continuum or as a set of more discrete classes. Despite these variations in class models, there are some general agreements on the proportions found in different classes. Disagreements about U.S. class structure include the question of the placement of lower-level white-collar workers, the issue of the shrinking middle class, and the question of proletarianization or embourgeoisement of the working class.

Discussing class structure is only one way to depict economic inequality. Describing the extent of income inequality is another. Such inequality has increased in recent years with the top 20 percent receiving a greater and the bottom 80 percent a smaller proportion of total income. These differences are in part manifested in the growth in wage inequality between CEOs and other workers. In recent years, this gap has been propelled by technological and globalization processes that affect unemployment and the bargaining position of labor on the worker side, and lower costs, better tax positions, and higher profit on the CEO/corporate side. The U.S. poverty rate has also increased since 2001 after having fallen between 1993 and 2000.

The increases in income inequality are overshadowed by even greater wealth inequality. Latest estimates show that the richest 20 percent own over 84 percent of all wealth, while the bottom 40 percent possess well under 1 percent of all wealth. As a broad measure of an individual's or family's economic position, wealth is a better indicator than income because it incorporates a broader range of assets that can be used to perpetuate economic inequality across generations. In sum, whether measured by social-class indicators, income, wage, or wealth distributions, economic inequality is extensive and appears to have grown since the early 1980s in the United States. The extent and shape of such inequality has been influenced by national and international forces.

While economic inequality is often fundamental for understanding other forms of inequality because it often serves as a basis for inequality on other dimensions, other kinds of inequality can also be seen in their own right because they are not always strictly based on economic differences. Thus, different kinds of inequality are often, but not always, interlinked. Status inequality, for example, is often based on wealth or class position, but it has also been based on differences in education, lifestyle, values, physical characteristics, and place of residence. In the United States, certainly, status inequality along these lines has gained prominence. It is to this status dimension of inequality that we now turn our attention.

CRITICAL THINKING

1. Why is income an inadequate measure of a family's economic position?

2. Consider the jobs you have held. What factors do you think led to your being employed and affected the earnings you received?

3. Are social classes in the United States cohesive, self-conscious groups in any sense? Or are they merely categories of people who just happen to be in the same economic positions?

4. What do you think economic and technological conditions will be like 10 years from now? How will this affect your chances of moving up or down in wealth?

WEB CONNECTIONS

The U.S. Census regularly collects data on income and poverty in the United States. Go to their website at www.census.gov and click on "income" and "poverty." United for a Fair Economy is an independent, nonprofit organization interested in greater equality that also gathers information on wealth, earnings, and income distribution and their relationship to race and democracy. They also write reports on this information. Visit www.FairEconomy.org. Do you think inequality undermines democracy?

3 Status Inequality

Wealth or political power may be a prerequisite, but they are not sufficient. . . .
The key boundary assumption of the theory of status relations is that status is not
reducible to economic or political power.

—Murray Milner, Jr.

As the quote above suggests, social status is largely about "*being* things" rather than "*having* things." It is about having a particular lifestyle and set of social characteristics. It is about being viewed as a certain kind of person, as a member of a specific subgroup that has attached to it a definite degree of high or low prestige. The previous chapter discussed the various types of *economic* inequality present in U.S. society—namely, class, income, and wealth inequality. But the ranking system is more complicated than that, and experiences in everyday life tell us that invidious distinctions are made between individuals on grounds other than economics. It is not just the *amount* of wealth, but the *kind* and *source* of wealth as well as how it is *used* that are ranked. It is not just the amount of education, but the kind and place of education. It is not just the earnings of the occupation, but the kind of occupation it is. If economic inequality is primarily about *quantities*, status inequality is about *qualities*.

People often are evaluated and ranked on the basis of their education, religion, possession of "culture," type of occupation, and even their speech patterns and clothing styles. Think about how students are evaluated by their peers. In addition to gender and race/ethnicity,

fraternity/sorority membership, academic major, athletic status, the regions of the country they are from, and even the dormitories in which they live serve as criteria for status rankings. In each case, these serve as systematic bases for high or low prestige.

Evidence presented in the last chapter supports the existence of *economic* classes, and there is no doubt that inequality includes *social* dimensions as well. More often than not, we notice these social distinctions in our contacts with others; that is, they become most salient when we interact with individuals whose characteristics and lifestyles differ from our own. Research suggests that we often rank people differently depending on those characteristics and lifestyles. Indeed, the term *social stratification* suggests that alongside economic inequality we have a system of status inequality, and often these two forms are intertwined with each other, as we shall see. Quite often, for example, an individual's economic position will affect his or her social position. But an individual's or group's social status need not be tied to either economic or political power. This requires that we examine social status as a separate form of ranking system. In this chapter, we will examine the nature of this status dimension of inequality.

THE THEORY OF SOCIAL STATUS

Social status refers to an individual's ranking with respect to some socially important characteristic; thus, some people are thought to be low in social status, while others are high on this scale. Max Weber, the great German sociologist, stressed the importance of distinguishing between (economic) class and (social) status inequality, while he pointed out that they could be empirically related to each other, as when social *status* is dependent on *class* position. Weber viewed a person's *status situation* as "every typical component of the life fate of men that is determined by a specific, positive or negative social estimation of *honor*. This honor may be connected with any quality shared by a plurality" (Gerth and Mills 1962, p. 187). This means that individuals are or are not given homage and respect because they possess or lack some characteristic the community considers honorable or dishonorable. That quality is social rather than economic in nature; for example, one's family name, the street where one lives, the kind and degree of education one possesses, or one's race or gender all may elicit such honor or dishonor. Weber argued that this "claim to positive or negative privilege with respect to social prestige" may be based on (1) a "mode of living," (2) "a formal process of education which may consist in empirical or rational training and the acquisition of the corresponding modes of life," and/or (3) "the prestige of birth, or of an occupation" (Weber 1964, p. 428).

Status groups that are ranked in a certain place on a community's social hierarchy are characterized by (1) a set of conventions and traditions, or lifestyle; (2) a tendency to marry within their own ranks; (3) an emphasis on interacting intimately—for example, eating only with others in the same group; (4) frequent monopolization of economic opportunities; and (5) emphasis on ownership of certain types of possessions rather than others (Weber 1964). All of these features reflect the tendency in status groups to establish and maintain the integrity of the boundaries that separate them from other groups. Wearing team jackets or particular types of clothes, associating with only particular kinds of people, and participating in an initiation process when becoming a member of a group are all signals that social status is operating.

Murray Milner, Jr. explains that an individual's status within a group is dependent upon conformity to the group's norms. These norms may involve expectations with respect to behavior (e.g., involvement in rituals), social relationships (e.g., friends and enemies), certain physical characteristics (beauty, race, gender), and use of appropriate symbols (e.g., dress, language). Since high status is coveted and in short supply, those at the top may change the norms or make them more complicated to maintain their position, making it more difficult for those below them to move up and displace them. One's own status is always at the expense of someone else's social position (Milner, Jr. 2004).

To be an accepted member of a status group, a person is expected to follow the normative lifestyle of the group and to have "restrictions on 'social' intercourse" (Weber 1964, p. 187). This means that the person is expected to associate intimately with only similar kinds of people. Consider what might happen if a person in a distinct status group steps out of line by violating the expected customs of the group. A good example is provided by *Frasier*, the well-known TV comedy. The principal players are two snooty psychologists who are brothers and their father, who is a retired police officer and has a set of tastes and values entirely different from that of his sons. Their lifestyles, manners of speaking, and friendships differ markedly from each other. Beer, homespun and earthy language, and flannel shirts characterize the father, whereas fine wines, expensive European suits, and an arrogant professional demeanor characterize the sons' lifestyles. Not surprisingly, their eating habits are quite different, as well. In one hilarious episode, the sons condescend to go to dinner with their father at one of his favorite haunts, a rustic steak house. The sons, of course, do not fit in and violate the customs associated with those who frequent such places. Although the effects are funny, they are also sobering as they show what happens when status groups clash and expected norms are violated.

A group tries to set itself apart from other status groups, especially those that might contaminate the purity of the group. An extreme instance of this process exists when individuals of a particular status group agree to marry only among themselves (i.e., to practice endogamy) and to chastise or shun anyone who marries outside the group. Lewis Lapham recalled his own experiences in this regard: "At college I knew several boys whose mothers discouraged their sons' acquaintance with anybody who lived in towns not adequately represented in the Social Register. If a boy didn't come from Grosse Pointe or Burlingame or Fairfield County, then his place of origin was listed under the heading *terra incognita*" (1988, p. 160). After all, status honor rests on "distance and exclusiveness." In her study of upper-class women's involvement in voluntary associations, for example, Diana Kendall (2002) notes how carefully new applicants are screened and the elaborate application process that is involved before a new person is accepted as a member. To maintain the integrity and value of membership, applicants need to negotiate a complex application process. The extent and intensity of the application process is a direct indicator of the strength of the social boundary of a status group. The maintenance of a status group's cultural and social integrity requires continual vigilance of its boundaries with the outside. Not just anyone is accepted.

It should not be surprising that to be accepted as a member of a particular status group requires possessing certain credentials. Credentialism is a major tool in the practice of exclusion (Parkin 1979). Having the proper credentials might mean, for example, having a given license or educational degree, to be accepted into the "club." Because they help to control the labor supply, for example, requiring particular education credentials and/or licensing even enhances the earnings associated with an occupation (Weeden 2002).

Moreover, "exclusion" is a primary mechanism by which those in powerful status groups keep others from gaining power (Parkin 1979). Voluntary residential segregation in a secure gated community on the part of a high-status group might also be seen as an attempt at separation from people of lower status. Or men may attempt to keep their corporate positions exclusive by preventing women from moving to the top of the ladder.

The various conventions, rules, traditions, and rituals of a particular status group help to sustain it over time. Thus, it is not surprising that there are attempts to enforce them within the group. Status groups are the "bearers of all 'conventions' . . . all 'stylization' of life either originates in status groups or is at least conserved by them" (Gerth and Mills 1962, p. 191).

So far, we have seen that status groups (1) are associated with different estimations of social honor, (2) are based on a variety of socially relevant characteristics such as occupation or ethnicity, and (3) tend toward closure—that is, toward restrictions on contact with those outside the group. In addition, Weber contended that status groups tend to monopolize particular types of economic opportunities and acquisitions, while they discourage the possession of other kinds. For example, a status group whose honor or prestige is based on its class position may allow its members to acquire fancy homes in particular neighborhoods, but it may be considered bad form to spend money acquiring a new bowling ball or a gaudy automobile. In societies where there is extreme *social* stratification, this monopolization may be legalized. The *social* privileges of a group are based on their economic and political power. It follows from this view that status groups are "phenomena of the distribution of power within a community" (ibid., p. 181).

What kinds of institutions people can or cannot get into depend heavily on whether they meet the requirements of entrance, which in many cases include the magnitude of their economic resources. In both of these cases, membership exclusivity is stressed, even though in each case it appeals to a different level of clientele.
Photos by author.

When social and economic conditions in a community are stable, Weber argued, stratification by status becomes dominant, and after status has been "lived in" for a while, status privileges can become legal privileges. In the United States, these conditions are frequently found in small towns where the same kin groups have lived for generations, where relationships are based on family name, and where social connections are important. Ironically, status also becomes salient when change threatens or tradition is in danger of being upset as when politically or economically powerful newcomers come to town (Milner, Jr. 2004). The "old guard" may try to maintain their high position by stressing their social status in the community, for example the fact that they have lived there all their lives and are leaders in the culture of the community.

When legalization of status privileges occurs, a society may be on the road toward a full-fledged caste system. According to Weber, the extreme of a caste system developing out of a status system happens only when the "underlying differences . . . are held to be 'ethnic' " in nature (Gerth and Mills 1962, p. 189). There is a clear hint that supposedly inherent and even biological distinctions are being considered here. Race is a basis for deference/honor, or its opposite, because "it is thought to represent the possession of some quality inherent in the ethnic aggregate and shared by all its members." This "essential quality" is "manifested in . . . external features such as colour, hair form, physiognomy and physique" (Shils 1970, p. 428). Indeed, there is evidence that ranking does take place on the basis of such external features (Lasswell 1965). The existence of varying degrees of social distance between various ethnic groups in the United States provides ample evidence of such a ranking system. In this instance, various ethnic status groups that may have been horizontally related are converted into a set of hierarchically arranged groups, those on the top being the most pure and those on the bottom being impure, contaminating, or even untouchable. The later "pariah" groups may be tolerated only because of economic necessity; that is, the lower castes may perform necessary but dishonorable, dirty, and onerous work. For example, lower castes may be the only groups ritualistically permitted to collect garbage or dead carcasses from the street.

Groups that are dishonored or low in status may attempt to usurp prestige by creating their own ranking system. This enhances their own social status often to the denigration of other groups. The Black Power Movement of the 1960s is an example of this kind of attempt (Milner, Jr. 2004). Another example is provided by Lamont (2000) who found in her interviews that working-class men use their own criteria to distinguish themselves as an honorable and distinct status group from those above and below them. Rather than wealth or political power, which would relegate them to a lower status, these men use moral criteria (being hardworking, responsible, having integrity, etc.) to separate themselves from others. These are the kinds of criteria that define the social and cultural boundaries that distinguish their own group from others, and they are the criteria that render them a higher social status in their own eyes.

When ranking does occur among status groups, *deference* is expected to be shown toward those in more prestigious or honored groups. The act of showing deference to persons in higher status positions manifests itself in various presentational rituals that essentially indicate to them how they are being regarded. The ways by which individuals greet and compliment others, as well as similar behaviors of homage, are examples of deferential behavior (Goffman 1959, 1967). For example, students are often concerned with how they should address me: Should it be "Professor," "Doctor," "Mister," or simply "Chuck"? Some clearly feel uneasy using the latter form of address because they think it suggests a lack of respect or deference.

While those in lower statuses may show deference for those at the top, the latter can use their resources to present themselves in ways that elicit and justify such respect. They typically have the resources and motivation to appear impressive, and so manage situations to obtain the responses they desire. Through their *demeanor*, individuals of higher status can suggest that they are worthy of such deference. Demeanor is "that element of the individual's ceremonial behavior typically conveyed through deportment, dress, and bearing, which serves to express to those in his immediate presence that he is a person of certain desirable or undesirable qualities" (Goffman 1967, p. 77).

Deference behavior between individuals in differently ranked status groups can be based on a variety of criteria. An individual may be considered entitled to such behavior from others because of occupation and race or ethnicity, as we have already suggested, but also on the bases of level and type of education, gender, lifestyle, political or corporate power or one's nearness to it, family name or kinship network, income, and amount and type of wealth. Service work on behalf of a community or society and formal titles also can serve as grounds for status honor in some locations. All these factors are deference relevant because they are linked with basic values and/or issues in the society. A region or area can also be the basis of deference because it is thought to be associated with a particular occupational role (e.g., Appalachia with coal mining, Manhattan with the stock market, etc.), with the exercise of power in a society, or with some other valued criterion (e.g., New England with quality education).

SPHERES OF STATUS IN THE UNITED STATES

As suggested earlier, the esteem in which a person is held in the United States can be related to a number of areas of life, for example occupation, education, lifestyle, and wealth. Less noticed, but also arenas of status, physical appearance and place also are analyzed. A brief comment is also made on race and gender as factors that call forth status ranking.

Occupation

Occupational role, of course, is frequently associated with both social class and social status, but the most commonly used measures of occupational ranking tap the prestige/esteem dimension rather than the economic one. Occupation is a basis for deference and honor not only because of its association with valued goals (income, power, etc.) but also because there are often lifestyles associated with particular roles—lifestyles that receive different degrees of honor. Plumbers and professors clearly are accorded different levels of honor because of what people associate with each of these occupations. Individuals in higher-ranking occupations, for example, have been found to have broader tastes in music—that is, to enjoy and appreciate a wider range of music types (Peterson and Simkus 1992).

A good analysis of a particular occupation as being the basis of status is given in Bensman's (1972) discussion of professional musicians. He argued that musicians form a "status community" in that they adhere to a particular and somewhat unique set of values that shapes their lifestyles. The institutions, behaviors, and practices that organize and constitute their lives, in turn, are based on those core values. Insiders are clearly separated from outsiders. There are regularized interactions and rituals that help keep the community cohesive. When the musicians get together informally, they perform, discuss music, or attend concerts, all of which increase their allegiance to the community's values. In addition to having its own subcultural values, the music community is internally stratified according to a number of musically relevant criteria such as the instrument one plays and the skill with which it is played.

We can, of course, conceive of other occupational groups forming status communities. In fact, each of us is a member of several such communities and organizations in which our particular status may vary. Social rankings are at least implicit within and between many churches, civic associations (e.g., Rotary Club, Lion's Club), and social organizations (e.g., country clubs, square-dance groups). The existence of a large number of such status communities made up of individuals who have positions in several of them creates an image of a societal prestige/status system that is extremely complex. However, some of these status communities may be more central and important than others and, therefore, may have more of an impact on one's status position in the society.

Generally, status communities based on occupation are socially relevant and prominent. Over the years, there have been several attempts to rank occupations according to prestige or status. Early efforts to measure occupational status suffered from the fact that they generally were based on inadequate samples of respondents, were of a subjective nature, and contained prestige differences within the general occupational categories that were often almost as great as those between such categories (see Counts 1925; Edwards 1943; Smith 1943). It is also difficult to arrange these occupations along a single dimension using one criterion. Although it may seem obvious that skilled blue-collar work would rank above semiskilled in prestige, it is not at all clear why professionals should rank above proprietors using the same dimension of skill.

Several attempts were later made to perfect an occupational status ranking, the most influential being the North-Hatt scale developed in the mid-1940s. It differed from the earlier scales in that a much wider range of occupation types was considered, and it relied less on the creator's judgment of rankings. The prestige rankings obtained were based on a 1947 survey of 2,920 individuals who were asked to classify the *general standing* of each of 90 occupations. No mention was made of prestige. The five-point evaluations ranged from "excellent," "good," and "average" to "somewhat below average," and "poor." The most frequently cited reasons for awarding a given occupation an excellent standing, in order of decreasing frequency, were that it paid well (18%), served humanity (16%), required a lot of previous training and investment (14%), and had a high level of prestige associated with it (14%).

The reliability and accuracy of the North-Hatt scale, which was heavily used in the past, have been called into question because of the unrepresentative sample upon which it was based, its neglect of "female" occupations, and other reasons (Reiss 1961). However, a replication of the study in 1963 yielded very similar rankings for the 88 distinct occupation types (Hodge, Siegel, and Rossi 1964). The rankings appear to be stable over time. There appear to be fairly consistent feelings among Americans in general about the prestige ranking of occupations, a ranking that has not changed significantly since World War II.

Later, using the knowledge that occupational prestige was highly correlated with income and education, Duncan (1961) was able to develop an equation to estimate the prestige scores of all occupations. From these, a socioeconomic index (SEI) was developed for all occupations.

Education

Like occupation, education is also considered an important and valuable aspect of one's life in the United States. Consequently, it has also been an area in which processes of prestige ranking have been played out. Level of education is supposed to be related to the level of knowledge and skill one has in a particular field. In addition to that, however, education also prepares one for a particular status group and ensures the continuation of status groups. The type of education as well as the place where it is received are bases for prestige. A degree from an Ivy League school such as Yale or Harvard, or a small private school such as Amherst or Smith is quite prestigious compared to a degree from a local community college. The elitism and degree of selectivity associated with a school is linked to the level of prestige accorded to it. Think about the differences in the students you might know who graduate from each type of school. Schools like to pride themselves on the kinds of students they produce. Different types of schools instill different sets of values and outlooks in their students, thereby encouraging the development of different cultural groups.

The cultural/status effects of education have been analyzed in depth. Bourdieu suggested that higher education helps to reproduce the class structure by functioning to reinforce the value and status differences between the classes (1977a). It does this by honoring the *cultural capital* held by those in the higher classes. This capital—which consists of a group's cultural values, experience, knowledge, and skills—is passed on from one generation to the next. In organizing itself around the linguistic and cultural competence of the upper classes, higher education ensures that members of the upper classes are successful in school. This legitimates the class inequality that results because, on the surface, it appears that the inequality is largely the result of individual performance in a meritocratic, open educational system. That is, the language used, the cultural knowledge expected for success in school, and the values and behaviors honored are those of the upper class. In short, in the words of one interpreter, "The school serves as the trading post where socially valued cultural capital is parleyed into superior academic performance. Academic performance is then turned back into economic capital by the acquisition of superior jobs" (MacLeod 1987, p. 12). The experiences in school and in the workplace of those in the working and lower classes, coupled with the general outlook and specific attitudes they have acquired because of their class milieu, lead them to believe that they cannot succeed in school, thus lowering their aspirations to do so (ibid.). The result is stratification within the educational system, which then reinforces the class stratification in the wider society.

From early childhood, middle- and upper-class parents engage in what Annette Lareau has termed "concerted cultivation," the conscious preparation of their children in the skills and values they will need to be successful and to maintain their higher position in the social hierarchy (Lareau 2003). Or as Kendall describes it in her study of how upper-class women go about perpetuating their social-class positions, "Most elite parents strongly believe that, early on in their children's lives, the parents should start putting together all the right 'building blocks' that their children will need in order to take their own places in elite circles in which the parents live, and that the parents need to continue this process of social reproduction as the children grow into adulthood" (Kendall 2002, p. 81). As several of the studies indicate, schools play a central role in the social reproduction of the class structure from top to bottom.

One of the principal functions of education is to prepare students for the cultural status groups they will be entering after graduation (Collins 1971). In his biting satire at the beginning of the twentieth century, Thorstein Veblen observed that elite schools of higher learning had as their primary purpose "the preparation of the youth of the priestly and the leisure classes . . . for the consumption of goods, material and immaterial, according to a conventionally accepted, reputable scope and method" (Veblen 1953, p. 239). Similarly, authors of a more recent empirical study of elite prep schools observed that "curriculum is the nursery of culture and the classical curriculum is the cradle of high culture" (Cookson and Persell 1985, p. 74). But they also observed, in sharp contrast to Veblen's emphasis on the nonfunctional learning of the "leisure" class, that the education is deadly serious.

Analysis of the history of U.S. boarding schools supports the conclusion that they were developed to help the established upper class isolate and reaffirm its cultural characteristics. Initially, the founders hoped that these schools would help separate their cultural group from the new wealth developing in industry and from the increasing amounts of lower-class immigration. This suggests again the strong impetus toward social closure among the old rich. But the need for financial support of these schools necessitated taking in some of the sons of individuals who had become recently wealthy from industrial, manufacturing, or other enterprises in the latter part of the nineteenth century (Levine 1980). These *nouveaux riches*, consequently, infiltrated the boarding schools even though the established patrician families winced because the former were often seen as lacking in manners and polish. One of these new-wealth parents, Phillip Armour, once described his occupation as converting "bristles, blood, and the inside and outside of pigs and bullocks into revenue" (ibid., p. 83). This kind of comment is hardly the type that would have won over persons from the established old-wealth families.

While stressing the rigor and difficulty of attainment within them, studies of elite prep schools confirm the importance of cultural capital and the role of these schools in perpetuating the class system. A large part of the education for students in these status seminaries involves learning how to hide or mask their wealth, to acquire "taste," and to prepare themselves to be "soldiers for their class"— that is, to occupy and carry out the responsibilities of their class (Cookson and Persell 1985). As Shils (1970) observed, some schools are thought of as more important than others, and "those educated in them acquire more of a charismatically infused culture" (p. 426). The rules of eating, sleeping, and playing together along with peer expectations and formal discipline help forge cohesiveness at the same time that the classical curriculum, the emphasis on dialogue and discussion, and extracurricular activities such as sports encourage the development of specific values. The hothouse, intense, closed setting of the prep school helps to foster a "brick wall syndrome," a belief that exclusivity should be the norm and that there is nothing wrong with the separation of this

Even the classical architecture and spacious, finely manicured grounds of prestigious prep schools conspire to create a feeling of tradition and specialness among their students.
Photo by author.

group of students from those in the outside society (Kendall 2002).

The formal and informal curricula of these schools are designed to make sure that these results occur. Even the architecture of the school and demeanor of the headmaster or headmistress conspire to create an atmosphere in which such learning and value development can take place. "The cultural capital that prep school students accumulate in boarding schools is a treasure trove of skills and status symbols that can be used in later life" (Cookson and Persell 1985, p. 30).

For their students, elite prep schools also serve as a major linchpin between parental class position and obtaining positions of power in the wider society. These students tend to get into the better colleges and universities and, ultimately, to obtain positions of influence in the leading political, cultural, legal, and corporate institutions of society.

Earlier studies of prep school graduates reinforce the conclusion that these students need to go on to the "right" Harvard, Yale, or Princeton; that is, they have to get into the appropriate clubs and societies at these universities, and to do this a student has to come from the "right" boarding school.

Getting into the right sorority or fraternity, especially one in which your parent was a member, is an important step in the process of class cultivation. Among the values and skills learned in these organizations are the importance of screening potential members, allegiance to your own kind of people, and the development of social networks that will be helpful in later years (Kendall 2002; Robbins 2004). As Nutshell 3.1 shows, within these groups there is generally strict enforcement of approved values and behaviors that they will carry with them once they graduate.

NUTSHELL 3.1

Sororities as Tightly Knit Status Groups

Alexandra Robbins, a *New York Times* reporter, spent a year "undercover" observing sorority life and talking with several hundred sorority sisters. Brooke was one of those interviewed in depth. The excerpt below describes the control that "the ten" had over their sisters, the exclusive nature of members' behavior, and the continuing hold sorority membership has on its members long after they have left college. These qualities show the sorority as a social-status community.

> The Ten, as the sisters eventually called these materialistic members, were a clique within a clique. They were girls who were so blindly into the sorority that all other activities and aspects of college life paled by comparison. They had the attitude, Brooke explained, that "If you're an EtaGam, you're an EtaGam through and through. You bleed blue and cream." These were the girls who unoffi-

cially controlled the Eta Gammas by deciding the homogeneous characteristics to impose on the group. The Ten had the power to "make your life hell," Brooke told me. "If you weren't hanging out with the Delts, they made fun of you. They planned parties and wouldn't include you. They made you feel unimportant, like something was wrong with you. They had a 'You're not cool enough' attitude and would blow you off." . . .

> In a sense, sorority girls are in a clique for life. A sorority is more than an affiliation; it's a label that a girl can't simply unstick after school ends. A few years after graduation, Brooke attended the wedding of a Texas friend who was a member of another sorority. A thousand people circulated in the ballroom, starting their conversations with guests like Brooke not by asking what they did for a living but by inquiring which sorority they were in.

Source: Alexandra Robbins, *Pledged: The Secret Life of Sororities* (New York: Hyperion, 2004), pp. 115–116, 118.

Upon graduating from the university, these students can take up their memberships in the most exclusive city clubs and become established in a high-status Wall Street law or brokerage firm. This process, covering the youths from their teen years through their attainment of an occupation, helps ensure the exclusivity of this high-status group. A not insignificant reason for this attainment relates to the networks of relationships and values developed during the prep school years. The Cookson-Persell study confirms that going to the so-called right schools helps instill those values and aids movement into those positions most highly honored in U.S. society. In this manner, prep schools help to reproduce the values and positions necessary for the legitimation and maintenance of the class structure. In prep schools, class and status intersect.

School and Lifestyle

Status inequalities between groups can be found in a variety of school levels. Unambiguous categorization of individuals according to appearance, behaviors, values, and attitudes develops early in childhood. Social cliques and categories have been found even among elementary-school children, as well as in junior and senior high schools. Initial analyses of school killings in the 1990s by students suggest the significance of popularity, social isolation, and social labeling for self-esteem, identity, and conflict between groups of students. While certainly not the only factor in these incidents, attachment of a student to a social category or clique has real consequences in the school setting. Self-esteem and identity appear to be linked to the status of one's "crowd" in school (Brown and Lohr 1987; Adler and Adler 1998).

The students responsible for the deaths at Columbine High School in Colorado were linked to a category of students called the Trenchcoat Mafia. But social clusters at different schools go by many names: jocks, burnouts, preppies, trendies, leading crowd, nerds, brainiacs, goths, wannabees, earth queens, stickup boys, geeks, freaks, grits, punks. People with similar interests, backgrounds, or accomplishments join together to separate themselves from others and to solidify their identities and sense of membership at school. Belonging to a clique or category is a way of avoiding social isolation. It is also a means of ranking different kinds of individuals. From his own study of high schools, Milner, Jr. suggests that the status ranking of cliques or groups in schools depends upon their adherence to expectations regarding areas such as "beauty, athletic ability, clothes and style, athletic uniforms and letter jackets, speech, body language, collective memories, humor, ritual, popular music, dancing and singing, and space and territory" (Milner, Jr. 2004, p. 44). None of these is necessarily linked to income or class position, again confirming the frequent noneconomic nature of social status.

Although membership can be unstable and rankings within each of them can shift, these social clusters have many of the properties of status groups (cf. Eckert 1989; Kinney 1993; Cairns and Cairns 1994; Eder 1995; Adler and Adler 1998). As such, they represent a type of status inequality. Among these qualities is *group ranking* in terms of popularity and prestige at school. A second feature following from this are explicit attempts to attract certain youths while keeping others out (i.e., *attempts at maintaining boundaries* between insiders and outsiders). Being mean, picking on outsiders, and "putting them down" are techniques to keep outsiders at arm's length. Careful recruitment and monitoring of behavior and attitudes are common ways of ensuring insider loyalty once in a group. "Cliques' boundary maintenance makes them exclusive. . . . The dynamics of inclusion lures members into cliques, while the dynamic of exclusion keeps them there" (Adler and Adler 1998, p. 72). People outside the cliques are thought of as different. "You don't even date outside of your clique. It's like a kind of racism," a senior high school girl observes (Brett 1999, p. A6).

A third status feature of these groups is a *lifestyle* that is perceived to be distinctive. A large part of the unique lifestyles among student groupings is suggested by the clothing and adornments they wear. Students labeled as "goths" tend to wear black clothes, whereas more mainstream "jocks" wear Polo or J. Crew. Tattoos, jewelry, and hairstyle also symbolize given social categories at school. As part of the distinctive lifestyles, involvement in school activities, musical tastes, and language also systematically vary. Fourth, *exclusive places or locations* tend to be associated with different social clusters. Given lunch tables are "owned" by clusters, as are places where students socially hang out. Finally, *stigmatization and avoidance of social contamination* is also found within these school groups. Because of recurrent jockeying for status within groups, individuals pick on each other and single out some for intense ostracism. Avoidance with outsiders antagonistic to the group is also enforced. Paradoxically, meanness to others is a way of maintaining popularity because it avoids the problems of being thought of as "stuck-up" or "supernice." Being stuck-up reduces popularity while being super-nice to everyone reduces one's rank and distinctiveness (Merten 1997).

The cool relationships between members of different social clusters at school broadly reflect their different lifestyles. Lifestyle itself can be a principal source of status honor for adults as well, because the manner in which one lives is a concrete demonstration of one's social and cultural values. In essence, it is a symbol representing what one stands for. Such lifestyles are generally internally consistent (i.e., they contain behavior or style arrangements that go together by common agreement in the community or that are found frequently enough to be considered normative). Just as rap music is not likely to be found in a yuppie's CD collection, one does not mix general stylistic elements.

Stylistic unity, then, becomes the basis of lifestyle (Sobel 1983a).

Wealth

Having a particular amount and type of *wealth* and/or *income* also can be a basis for status. Since each class may form its own status group, it should not be surprising that sociologists have found that certain lifestyles and values are found in each class.

For example, a number of scholars have focused on the status honor of the upper class. The use of inherited wealth, family lineage, club membership, quality of education, and general lifestyle as criteria for membership into the established upper class helps maintain the exclusivity of that class. We have already seen how early boarding schools functioned in this regard. Practicing endogamy within the class helps determine who can get into "Society." Maintaining a closed circle in the face of an ostensibly open democratic society demands that there be mechanisms present to keep just anyone from getting into the circle.

E. Digby Baltzell, a member of the upper class himself, insisted that "there exists one metropolitan upper class with a common cultural tradition, consciousness of kind and 'we' feeling of solidarity which tends to be national in scope." This upper class has been buttressed historically by institutions that serve its members, such as boarding schools, select eastern universities and colleges, and the Episcopal Church (Baltzell 1958; see also Domhoff 1971; Ostrander 1984). The upper class as a status group practices a particular kind of lifestyle with particular kinds of rules associated with it. Specifically, children are expected to be well bred, with manners and a sense of their importance in society. Boarding schools are a principal source of this training, but family ties are also central. Keeping the family line intact and marrying the right kind of person are important. Marriages are not made as facilely as might be the case in other social classes. But some restricted social activities, such as debutante balls and fox hunts, which once were prominent elements in the lifestyle of the upper class, have declined in recent years. Acceptable occupations include financier, lawyer, business executive, physician, art collector, museum director, and even architect. Membership in exclusive metropolitan social clubs, often composed only of males, is also important if an individual is to be part of the upper-class status community. Living in an exclusive residence separate from middle class and other neighborhoods and maintaining a second summer home are also means by which separation from outsiders is preserved.

Upper-class families tend to be patriarchal, but even the female spouse may be a member of a private social club. Frequently, she is expected to be involved in charitable activities and other social events. There is a division of labor between the sexes in these families. Evidence suggests that members of this upper-status group are concerned with maintaining their separation from others, even in death. Their burial customs and sites tend to be different from those of lesser mortals (Kephart 1950). A historical analysis of cemeteries in the United States noted the long-term attempts by the middle and upper classes to segregate themselves physically in burial sites from those of a more lowly status, and to freely use monuments and mausoleums to proclaim their status. In recent years, mausoleums and monuments have again increased in popularity. Advertisements for these tout these structures as symbols of prestige that will remind viewers of how much success was attained during one's lifetime (Sloane 1991). As these characteristics indicate, "members of the upper class not only have *more*, they have *different*" (Domhoff 1971, p. 91).

Weber thought that status groups are ranked according to their patterns of consumption as manifested in their lifestyles (cited in Gerth and Mills 1962, p. 193). Many possessions have a level of prestige that differs drastically with their actual monetary value. For example, consider the relative prestige of a new Chevy pickup and an older Jaguar coupe, both of which may cost the same amount. It is not so much the economic value per se of the consumed goods that is important, but rather the fact that these goods, especially if owned by a higher-ranking status group, serve as symbols of worth and ability. It becomes a matter of self-respect and honor to conspicuously display such goods, not merely to "keep up with the Joneses" but to surpass them if possible (Veblen 1953).

Veblen's Theory of the Leisure Class.   The linkage of class position to status is most clearly seen in the arguments of Thorstein Veblen, an early American sociologist and economist who grew up in rural Wisconsin and Minnesota. His discussion of status applies most directly to the periods up to the early part of the twentieth century. Writing his most important work around the turn of the twentieth century, Veblen contended that manual labor had become defined as dishonorable and undignified, not becoming to one who wished to be considered of high social status. On the other hand, he argued that nonproductive labor, such as that of being a business executive, increased the probability of owning great amounts of property, which in turn, increased one's status honor. Owning property had become, in Veblen's view, the equivalent of possessing honor. In order to show this honor and property to others, one then had to engage in ostentatious displays of wealth and status—namely, various forms of what he called "conspicuous consumption." This display served as a symbol of one's worth and ability.

Women were really the first type of private property owned by men. During an early historical period of "predatory barbarism," according to Veblen, the major class distinction was between men and women. While women did all the essential, productive labor, men engaged most often in honorific hunting and various types of exploits and plunder, eager to produce trophies for themselves. This is the period in which industrious, productive labor came to be defined as dishonorable and dirty, whereas the kind of activities in which men engaged were considered to be honorable and praiseworthy. In a manner of speaking, men's work allowed them to avoid getting their hands dirty. In order to show their worth, men led a life of conspicuous leisure. It was an indication that one is not doing ignoble labor (i.e., working). Time was consumed nonproductively. It became a sign of the decency of one's life. Men competed with each other in demonstrating their worth by the accumulation of various possessions and trophies, so that they could make an invidious comparison of themselves with others. By *invidious*, Veblen meant "a comparison of persons with a view to rating and grading them in respect of relative worth or value—in an aesthetic or moral sense. . . . An invidious comparison is a process of valuation of persons in respect of worth" (ibid., p. 40).

In the civilized state of industrial society— a quasi-peaceable barbarian stage according to Veblen—the cultivation of manners and decorum is a central part of this leisure-class lifestyle. In modern times, the distinction between industry and business parallels the earlier difference between female and male labor. Modern-day businesspeople are industrial society's predatory class, whereas those directly involved in industrial work are those who are doing the productive labor.

Veblen argued that the modern leisure class of the industrial era engaged not only in conspicuous consumption and leisure but also in conspicuous waste. Women, for example, had become, in Veblen's view, not only the "property" of men but also an ornament with which men could display their wealth and power. Women took on a ceremonial function with the rise of the Industrial Revolution and were expected not to engage in industrious, productive work. Rather, in their behavior and appearance, women were to symbolize the status of their husbands. Men, even those in busi-

ness, could satisfy their "instinct of workmanship" (i.e., the feeling needed by everyone that one is doing something useful), but women were essentially servants of the household head and were expected to be well bred and to use their time cultivating their beauty. Women were in charge of the household—the so-called woman's sphere—and were expected to engage in conspicuous leisure and consumption, since their behavior reflected the status of the men who owned them. In their dress, they were expected to be especially wasteful; that is, their dresses were to be nonfunctional waste material. "Special pains should be taken in the construction of women's dress, to impress upon the beholder the fact (often indeed a fiction) that the wearer does not and cannot habitually engage in useful work. . . . [It is] the woman's function in an especial degree to put in evidence her household's ability to pay" (ibid., p. 126).

We can summarize Veblen's ideas by indicating that he felt that people's worth and honor, in modern times, were linked to their ability to pay—that is, their wealth and possessions. The more a person can display such resources, the greater the respect attributed to him or her. This leads to an ostentatious show for others in a desire to impress and to a competition to outdo others in such display. Such display covers a wide range of possessions, even such things as better-groomed lawns, ownership of prize horses, and conspicuous dress. Everyone tries to battle in this competition, according to Veblen, but the leisure/business class is most successful.

Since Veblen, there have been other analyses of the lifestyle of the upper class. As noted earlier, status often rests on class position, and high-class position makes it possible for individuals to pursue desired lifestyles. Brooks (1979) argued that Veblen's ideas must be updated because the lower classes do not revere the upper class as in Veblen's day, nor is leisure strictly the province of the upper class today. More often, people engage in "parody display" of honored status symbols. Just as in a literary parody, people poke fun at possessions that, in the past, have commanded great respect. He views this parody as the result of a mixture of admiration and ridicule by the lower classes. But still he finds that competitive display and conspicuous consumption are alive and well in U.S. society. Speech, clothing, and membership in exclusive clubs, for example, continue to be used in making invidious comparisons. Using beautiful women as ornamentation or as trophies also continues today. " 'Beauty' is a currency system like the gold standard. Like any economy, it is determined by politics, and in the modern age in the West it is the last, best belief system that keeps male dominance intact" (Wolf 1991, p. 12). By encouraging women to spend a lot of time on how they look and act as they attempt to meet culturally enforced standards, the "beauty myth" weakens their ability to fully develop their mental, political, and economic potential (Wolf 1991).

Physical Appearance and Status

Clearly, physical appearance can provide clues to and is often a basis for social status. Here I will focus on physical attractiveness and dress as areas that manifest status distinctions; in Chapters 5 and 7 the emphases will be on gender and race as bases of inequality.

Beauty, of course, is in the eyes of the beholder, but what the beholder sees and how it is interpreted are shaped by culture's values. Beauty is a social construction, and in U.S. society it has significance. "In twentieth-century American society, physical beauty emerged as a resource, like wealth or talent" (Rubenstein 2001, p. 212). Apparently, the power of beauty as a resource is evident very early in life. A recent study found that parents give more attention and care to beautiful than to less attractive children (cited in Dowd 2005). While beauty is a resource, it may also be used to reinforce gender inequality.

Popular folktales that have been most often reproduced (e.g., Cinderella, Snow White) are those that stress the value of female rather than male beauty. This consistent encouragement to be beautiful may discourage women from pursuing roles, activities, or positions that will make them appear less attractive. For men, women's entrapment in the beauty myth serves as a means of social control over women because it removes a source of potential competition (Baker-Sperry and Grauerholz 2003).

To further realize the importance of beauty, one need only look at the media to see how it is used to sell everything from automobile transmissions to cologne. It implies that those who possess it have other qualities as well. Research has suggested that individuals who are considered physically attractive also are considered to have happier marriages, have better mental health, and be more confident and likeable than those who are considered unattractive. They also are thought to be more attentive when being interviewed, to be better performers in the classroom, and to deserve more room on the street (Webster and Driskell 1983). In criminal cases, defendants who are more physically attractive tend to be treated more leniently, especially in cases where beauty is not relevant to the type of crime. When beauty is used as a weapon in a crime, however, more attractive individuals receive more severe punishments. "It is as if beauty is a gift, and its malevolent manipulation is condemned" (Rubenstein 2001, p. 215).

A study by Webster and Driskell, conducted among college students who examined photographs of males and females, indicated that people who are labeled as beautiful are considered to be "better at situations in general, things that count in this world, most tasks, and abstract ability" (1983, p. 158). It is also considered more desirable to be beautiful than to be unattractive. Many, especially younger White women, are deeply conscious of their body shape and weight and have negative feelings about them (Cash and Henry 1995). The widespread use by women of elective plastic surgery, liposuction, and cosmetics that promise to make them look younger suggests the importance of appearance in their lives. Eating disorders, such as bulimia and anorexia, are also attempts to make one look thinner and more attractive in present-day society.

Of course, the definitions of beauty and other status symbols vary with societies and over time within the same society. The beauty of the human figure portrayed in a Rubens painting is not the same ideal of beauty seen today in the clothing ads of Calvin Klein or Ralph Lauren. Especially in open and democratic societies, the salience and ranking of status symbols waxes and wanes. In one year, having a particular characteristic or possession may result in great status honor or prestige, but a few years later, that same possession may be of little social importance, while another has ascended to a position of high prestige.

In large and impersonal urban settings where individuals do not know each other personally, displays of status symbols are more common indicators informing strangers *who* their owners really are (Form and Stone 1957). It does not take long to pick up on the social meaning of what we put on our bodies. Even the smallest, seemingly insignificant adornment can suggest status. Pharoah, one of two Chicago elementary-school African Americans studied intensively in *There Are No Children Here*, was eager to have a pair of glasses, even if he did not need them, because "he suggested, if he wore glasses, his teachers would choose him more often to run errands or to answer questions. They would, at the very least . . . make him look smarter" (Kotlowitz 1991, p. 62). There is no question that what we wear sends signals about our status.

It has been well established that one of the most often-used status symbols in urban settings concerns fashions in clothing. Veblen (1953) observed that at the turn of the twentieth century, clothing was particularly well suited to being a status symbol since "our apparel is always in evidence and affords an indication of our pecuniary standing to all observers at the first glance" (p. 119).

A study at Michigan State University considered "the degree to which clothing is used as a guide in identifying the role and status of unknown persons" and "the various shades of meaning attached to clothing in particular social situations" (Rosencranz 1962, p. 18). When asked to evaluate individuals in pictures shown to them, characters in the pictures who were dressed more formally than others were accorded a higher status, whereas other inappropriately attired individuals were viewed as being of a lower status. Dressing in a manner that was foreign to U.S. culture or considered inappropriate for the gender of the person resulted in a kind of negative sanction. A man dressed in a skirt in one of the pictures, for example, was described as being "dressed like a foreigner" or, in particular, "a Chinaman." When it comes to what kind of dress is most honored, it is the upper class that defines which tastes are valued and which are devalued (Holt 1997).

Undoubtedly, how we dress affects the attitudes and behavior of others with respect to us (Kaiser 1985). "Clothing itself is the beginning and end of human display, touching on one side the skin of the person and reaching out on the other to announce to all what the person inside the skin is or wishes to be" (Brooks 1979, p. 201). Clothing takes on a moral character in that people assume that your dress indicates something about the kind of person you are. "A cheap coat makes a cheap man," observed Veblen. The appearance of secondhand clothing stores in Washington, DC, which cater to the not-quite affluent, for example, testifies to the importance people place on trying to make an impression. Originally expensive suits can be purchased for a low price. Noted one customer: "It pays to shop in a place like this in a town like Washington where clothes are a big part of how you are perceived" (Barringer 1990, p. 10).

Such concerns start early, with parents tramping off to buy Baby Gap, Baby Dior, and Baby Ralph Lauren designer clothing.

Some research suggests that clothing frequently brings out status-related reactions. Alison Lurie suggested a number of ways in which clothing can be used to give an impression of high status. She labeled these as "conspicuous" addition, division, multiplication, and labeling. Conspicuous addition refers to the technique of layering clothes—that is, wearing several kinds of clothing over each other, even though it is not functionally necessary. Scarves and vests, for example, when worn ornamentally, would be a demonstration of conspicuous addition and an example of what Veblen called conspicuous waste. Conspicuous division and multiplication are different forms of the technique of wearing a wide variety of different types of clothing, especially for separate occasions. The point here is that, to indicate high status, a person does not want to wear the same piece of clothing twice consecutively and does want to wear different kinds of clothes for evening, dinner, casual, and other sorts of situations.

"Life itself has been turned into a series of fashionable games, each of which . . . demands a different costume—or, in this case, a different set of costumes. . . . The more different looks a woman can assume, the more fascinating she is supposed to be: personality itself has become an adjunct of Conspicuous Waste" (Lurie 1987, p. 129). "The constant wearing of new and different garments is most effective when those you wish to impress see you constantly—ideally every day. It is also more effective if these people are relative strangers" (p. 127). The latter comment reinforces the notion mentioned earlier that it is in large cities that these symbols become most significant as emblems of status.

A good example of conspicuous multiplication is found in the inner city of Harlem where status among youths is related to the number and kinds of sneakers worn ("The Well Heeled"

1988). One's status is indicated by the use of different sneakers for different occasions and activities. "A man's got to have style, or he's half a man," explained one youth named Mr. Washington. "The fact is, in the inner city you are what you wear—on your feet" (ibid., p. A1). One has to be careful not to wear the wrong brand or style of sneakers in the wrong place or on the wrong occasion. There are regions, sections of cities, even streets, that are closely identified with particular brands of shoes. "In Boston, there are Nike streets . . . and Adidas streets . . . and woe to anyone caught wearing the wrong brand on the wrong street" (ibid., p. A6). Shoes are used to identify not only one's status but also one's turf. Some youths are willing to sell drugs to keep themselves in shoes, some of which cost over $100 a pair. The youth quoted earlier, Mr. Washington, owns 150 pairs of sneakers. "Black adolescents are more likely than white adolescents to define their masculine identities through fashion" and to choose clothing that is associated with their race (Crane 2000, p. 191).

Finally, a fourth form of clothing technique mentioned by Lurie, conspicuous labeling, is a way of ensuring that the knowledgeable would be able to distinguish the high-status piece of clothing from an imitation. Otherwise, a status crisis could occur for those who wish to use clothing as a status symbol, since several brand names of clothing may look virtually identical. Labeling on the outside, rather than the inside, of a garment is an obvious way of advertising your status to those around you.

Place and Status

Think for a moment of the United States as a large geographical grid on which different groups travel and reside in particular places. If you could see this grid from above, what would it look like? Social patterns of enclaves, segregation, inclusion, and exclusion would become evident.

Historically, sociologists have not paid much attention to the role that the physical environment plays in our understanding of society's social structure. Indeed, the arrangement of space and the role of place have been neglected in the study of inequality. But in the past few years, space and place have been increasingly recognized as being related to social status. Recently, Daphne Spain has even argued that space is used to acknowledge and reinforce inequalities between men and women. Earlier in U.S. history, the lower status of women was used to keep them out of college, and later to relegate them to separate women's colleges. At work, women's workplaces are most often open spaces characterized by a lack of doors and walls (e.g., as in a secretarial pool), in sharp contrast to the privacy found in the closed-door higher-status jobs of men. Finally, at home, different spaces and entrances are often assigned to men and women, especially in nonindustrial societies and in nineteenth-century United States (Spain 1992).

Where people live is also associated with their status. Regionally, for example, high concentrations of the upper class reside in New England, Florida, and California, whereas few upper class live in heartland states such as North and South Dakota, Iowa, Kansas, Oklahoma, West Virginia, Indiana, and Arkansas (Higley 1995). The United States has neighborhood clusters, many of which are clearly and intentionally connected with specific groups occupying different status levels. The elegant mansions of the so-called blue blood estates neighborhoods of places such as Beverly Hills and Scarsdale hold those at the top of the status ladder, while the public assistance neighborhoods of West Philadelphia and Watts are disproportionately dwelling places of African American and single-parent families. Public housing has also become increasingly occupied by female-headed families, and contains disproportionate numbers of elderly and children (Spain 1993). Throughout the status ladder are found neighborhoods known as "young

suburbia," "middle America," "shotguns and pickups," and "sharecroppers." Each of these has its own core values and lifestyle. That these distinct cultural pockets exist should not be surprising: "People seek compatible neighbors who share their family status, income, employment patterns and values" (Weiss 1988).

We must not forget, however, that living in a particular community or neighborhood is not always the result of free choice. Resources and status help dictate where one lives. Constraint also enters the picture when people try to keep undesirables out of their neighborhoods through mortgage-loan practices, building restrictions, and zoning procedures. Increasingly, one can find new housing developments for the affluent and cultured that are surrounded by walls and maintained by armed guards at secured entrances. Often, these communities are planned and monitored by electronic surveillance devices, and constitute another, perhaps more blatant, form of segregated neighborhood. Mike Davis offered Los Angeles as a good example of "where the defense of luxury lifestyles is translated into a proliferation of new repressions in space and movement, undergirded by the ubiquitous 'armed response.'" He saw this approach to living as "a master narrative in the emerging built environment of the 1990s" (Davis 1992c, p. 223). As noted earlier in this chapter, Weber made a point of identifying exclusionary tactics as devices used by higher status groups to keep their position intact. Privacy and security, and, most importantly, seclusion from undesirables, mark these "walled communities" (Schneider 1992). Turf wars are perpetrated not only by those at the bottom of the status system but also by those at its pinnacle. The control of physical space is one reflection of status inequalities in our society.

INEQUALITY IN APPALACHIA

On a broader scale, not only do neighborhoods and communities conjure up different perceptions and evaluations but so do regions. There are stereotypes and lifestyles, for example, that have been attributed to Californians, New Englanders, the Old South, the New South, Midwesterners, and Appalachians. Regions can be and have been the basis for status grouping and ranking, even though the cultural, social, and sometimes even topographical homogeneity attributed to these set-apart places is usually mythical rather than factual. Nevertheless, some of these regions, perhaps most notably Appalachia, have been identified as constituting not only a separate subculture but also a status group that has been consciously ranked as being low in prestige. Let us explore Appalachia as an example of status based on region.

A discussion of Appalachia helps us in at least two ways. First, it allows us to examine economic inequality within a region sometimes described as a colony for more powerful economic interests. Second, it allows us to examine the cultural mystique and folklore associated with a section of the country that has often been thought to be out of touch with the mainstream of U.S. society and its culture. Associated in the public mind with mountain men, the region has been portrayed as being inaccessible and isolated. As such, it has been viewed in the popular press and mind as constituting a separate and often homogenous culture. It is principally the latter that we wish to investigate in this section. Does Appalachia constitute a separate subculture and, if so, how is it viewed in terms of social status? What is the origin of this subculture, and how is it linked with the economic inequality that prevails in the region?

As a strip in the eastern part of the United States, Appalachia covers an area involving parts of 13 states, bordered on the north by southern New York state; on the south by parts of Mississippi, Alabama, and Georgia; on the west by the eastern sections of Kentucky and Tennessee; and on the east by the western portions of Pennsylvania, Virginia, and the Carolinas. It includes all of West Virginia.

Most of the discussion of Appalachia as a subculture, however, is based on material from southern Appalachia (northern Georgia, Alabama, North and South Carolina, and parts of Tennessee and Virginia), whereas discussions of the coal industry focus on central Appalachia (Kentucky, West Virginia, southwestern Virginia, and eastern Tennessee). Northern Appalachia is composed of parts of New York, Pennsylvania, Maryland, Ohio, and West Virginia.

Poverty and Economic Development in Appalachia

Poverty and uneven economic development in Appalachia are often associated with the introduction of large-scale coal mining, timber, and other outside corporate intrusions into the region. However, recent historical studies of Appalachia demonstrate that social, political, and economic conditions that had helped to perpetuate poverty in Appalachia had already been present in many places (Duncan 1999; Billings and Blee 2000). The notion that Appalachia was completely isolated from the outside world is erroneous. Even before the Civil War, for example, Appalachia was tied to the wider U.S. economy through its salt-making and iron industries. The importation of slaves into the region also fostered outside ties and allowed some to gain control of their local communities (Billings and Blee 2000). As a consequence of elites taking control of local settings, the kind of politics that was generally exercised was aimed at satisfying and maintaining their personal and narrow interests, rather than helping communities as a whole. Little investment was made in the infrastructure that would have laid a foundation for the future and spurred development and raised all citizens economically. The result was communities with strong systems of inequality on the one hand, and weak civic cultures and polities on the other. Political corruption was not uncommon and served to maintain social and economic inequality. Thus, conditions were not fertile for the elimination of poverty or inequality, but only for their perpetuation (Duncan 1999; Billings and Blee 2000).

Racial segregation and educational and employment discrimination between families further divided many communities. Rich and poor, Black and White often did not even share religious institutions. Powerful White farmers kept out new industries so that they could maintain a captive and dependent labor force who would work for low wages (Duncan 1999). Racial inequality deepened throughout the nineteenth century as White landowners strengthened their economic position while landless Blacks sunk deeper into poverty (Billings and Blee 2000). Because of their poor educational facilities and lack of social and political connections, Blacks were ill-equipped to take advantage of the few new economic opportunities that did arise.

Finally, the subsistence agriculture that was practiced and the growing population provided a formula for continued poverty for many and outmigration for others. Local economies were not developed that would have allowed more independence from outside economic interests. Underemployment at low wages created a labor force that was ripe for exploitation by incoming coal, timber, and other industries (ibid.). In sum, the uneven development and entrenched poverty found in much of Appalachia are rooted in a history replete with economic, political, and racial inequities. That history provided a hospitable environment for further profit-taking by industry.

Outside timber, mining, and manufacturing interests were gaining increasing access to and ownership of much of the land and other natural resources in the region. Coal was becoming a major industry, and without understanding all the implications, many residents "sold their land and/or mineral rights for pennies an acre to 'outsiders.' . . . Appalachians became not the entrepreneurs but the labour-

ers" (Appalachian Regional Commission 1985, p. 8). The "patterns of corporate exploitation were established that continue to dominate the resource utilization today" (Beaver 1984, p. 82). John Tiller, a former miner from Trammel, Virginia, described Appalachia as a colony: "It has all the earmarks—the absentee landlords; nothing built of permanence. You can look at the whole area—the poor roads, the poor schools, the lack of facilities—and realize that there's no solutions" (Carawan and Carawan 1975, p. 26). Hundreds of thousands of acres have been stripped for their lumber and coal resources by absentee owners, individuals who live outside the region but take its resources.

Thus, the region is wealthy in resources, but the native people have been relatively poor. During the late 1950s and early 1960s, about one-third of the families in the area lived below the official poverty level, unemployment was about 40 percent higher than in the rest of the nation, and net migration from the region was over 2,000,000 (Appalachian Regional Commission 1985, p. 13). In the 1990s, rural Appalachia continued to have higher poverty rates and a higher percentage of working poor than the national average (Duncan 1992; U.S. Bureau of the Census, April 1996). In many parts of Appalachia, the percentage of persons who had graduated from high school was much lower than the national average, and one in four rural dwellings were considered to have fundamental structural weaknesses. The 1960 presidential election brought many of these problems into the public eye for the first time. In the early 1980s, in many Appalachian counties, less than one-third of the people had a high school education. Almost as many (30%) adults in the *entire* region and almost half of the unemployed were functionally illiterate (Darling 1984).

Resource ownership in Appalachia has been very concentrated. Around 1980, over half of the land was owned by 1 percent of local residents working together with absentee owners, government, and corporations. This means that 99 percent of the local people controlled less than half of the land. Some of the largest owners were and still are multinational corporations. While the 1970s brought some economic growth to the region, the early 1980s brought renewed economic decline fueled by worldwide recession and foreign competition. Coal, oil, electricity, and steel industries all suffered setbacks. Between 1980 and 1983, Appalachia lost more than 500,000 jobs (Appalachian Regional Commission 1985, p. 77). Gaventa (1980) argued that the 1980s brought an intensified attempt to recolonize Appalachia because of the belief in some circles that if the United States drew energy resources from within the nation, the country would be less dependent on foreign sources for coal and other minerals. As we will see in a later chapter, the whole process of economic dependence and exploitation of Appalachia fits a general Marxian explanation of the dynamics of economic inequality.

The events and conditions just noted brought attention to the region, and media presentations helped form the images and conclusions outsiders developed about Appalachia. They even helped shape the perceptions of Appalachians about their region. Since the turn of the twentieth century, when major changes in the economy and ownership had already begun, the image portrayed of Appalachian culture has been one of stagnation and backwardness attributed in large part to the supposed physical isolation of the region.

But in his study of a central Appalachian valley, Gaventa (1980, 1984) argued that the proliferation of the cultural model of Appalachia as being backward, uncivilized, and so on was a creation that helped justify the exploitation (development) of that region by

Strip mining, which leaves noticeable scars on the landscape, has been common in Appalachia. This photo was taken in Whitley County, southeastern Kentucky.
Photo by Sarah Brownlee.

outside interests. The presence of excess investment capital and an ideology that encouraged development of undeveloped rural areas led to the purchase and control of Appalachian property by outside investors. Part of the justification of this easy appropriation of resources was couched in the specious argument that the inhabitants were quiescent and backward simpletons. Gaventa pointed out that the image of Appalachians was molded to fit and justify the exploitation that occurred. While those in his study were not ostensibly aggressive in defending themselves against the domination of outside financial interests, Gaventa demonstrated that this reaction suggesting passiveness and apathy was really a rational response to their condition of powerlessness. Repeated defeats, the greater resource power of outside forces, the construction of various barriers, and the perpetuation of myths and stereotypes about the Appalachian people all have conspired to create less rebellion, even though extensive grievances and discontent on a variety of issues lie just below the surface.

The Subculture of Appalachia. Following the Civil War, Appalachia was "discovered" by journalists and others who viewed it as an offbeat place with unfamiliar vegetation inhabited by a people with odd customs. ("A Strange Land and Peculiar People" cited in Beaver 1984, p. 86). A variety of values have been associated with Appalachians, many of them negative in nature. "The Appalachian is fatalistic," wrote Lewis (1974), "while mainstream Americans believe they can control their environment and their lives. The Appalachian is impulsive, personalistic and individualistic while mainstream Americans are rational, organized, can handle impersonal role relationships and have a social consciousness" (p. 222). Individualism, a love of and dependence on family and an attachment to home, a belief in personal liberty and independence, fatalism and resignation, a belief in the essential equality of all individuals, a disdain for and suspicion of formal education, and

the centrality of personal religion all have been characteristics frequently associated with Appalachians (cf., e.g., Vogeler 1975; Erikson 1976; Batteau 1984; W.H. Turner 1986).

As was indicated earlier in this chapter, the social status given to another person or group is a subjective process, one in which the group is portrayed as having a specific lifestyle and set of beliefs that distinguish it from surrounding groups. In most groups, there is more heterogeneity than is suspected by outsiders, but it is the latter's perceptions, whether based on fact or not, that govern their reaction to the group. The fact is that despite the stereotypical view often taken of it, Appalachia is a region with varied resources, differentiated geography, and people with varied ethnic backgrounds.

Alongside the negative image of Appalachia as a stagnant and backward region, another more patronizing image exists. This interpretation fosters the view of Appalachia as an area of great natural beauty being despoiled by greedy economic interests. Unsullied nature and the rugged individualism of mountain men are integral components of this perspective of Appalachia as an innocent victim (Batteau 1984). In this view, the mountains take on a mystical, romantic quality.

A problem with such subcultural descriptions—especially of an area that has been said to be socially, culturally, and physically shut off from the rest of the country—is that they tend to become caricatures over time, ignoring internal differences within the region and changes that have occurred in its relationship with other parts of the world. These subcultural characteristics also have been interpreted as the principal causes for the unusually high rates of poverty found in Appalachia. This constitutes a form of blaming the victim, however, because evidence suggests that it has not been primarily subcultural values or isolation but rather the nature of a region's ties to the outside that have exacerbated and perpetuated the high poverty rate. Numerous scholars, many from the region, have labeled Appalachia as a rich land with poor people, poor because their resources have been exploited by outsiders (cf., e.g., Caudill 1962; Gaventa 1980; Eller 1982).

Even though Appalachia is a heterogeneous area, where many lead urban and middle-class lives, few have questioned the traditional stereotype associated with the Appalachian. Too often, images of an Appalachian character (1) are derived primarily from descriptions of adult *males*, (2) ignore the fact that many of the characteristics are shared by other Americans, and (3) minimize or deny the inconsistencies and differences found within Appalachian culture (Erikson 1976, pp. 75–78). With respect to the latter, for example, the African American ethnographer William Turner (1986) suggested that many Blacks in Appalachia do not share the values and beliefs of their White neighbors. Rather than being fatalistic, traditional, and so forth, they are attracted to materialism and individual achievement and do not identify psychologically as strongly with the land and the region as White Appalachians do.

Despite the fact that changes have occurred in the region, many traditional values have become weakened, and many Appalachians are becoming integrated culturally and socially into the wider society, stereotypes still abound. Old images die hard deaths. Berger cautioned that "myths are potent enough to survive evidence; they are not disarmed by understanding. Once myths gain currency . . . they become real and fiction as self-fulfilling prophecies" (cited in Billings 1974, p. 322).

The image of Appalachia as being composed of backward, fundamentalistic, individualistic mountaineers has lowered the status prestige of this region for most Americans. In the late 1960s, "in some popular and scholarly circles Appalachia was second only to Black America as a repository for social pathos" (W.H. Turner 1986, p. 279). Appalachia occupies "the lowest rung in [our] socio-economic ladder" (Coreil and Marshall 1982). Data collected in interviews with long-term rural Kentuckians suggested that a large majority of them feel that

Appalachians are given "much less respect than other Americans." Many also believed that Appalachians experience greater occupational, educational, legal, and income inequality than other Americans. They also were inclined to view the inequality involving Appalachians as being separate from racial and class inequality, suggesting that they identify themselves as a separate group when it comes to the problems of inequality (Smith and Bylund 1983).

How do the elements of this discussion of Appalachia relate to our earlier conclusion that status can be based on region? Let us review the core factors that determine status and status-group ranking. We noted that status honor/prestige is subjectively given by a community to another person or group. This perception, in turn, depends on the characteristics attributed to the person or group and on how valued these characteristics are in mainstream culture. Status honor can be based on (1) lifestyle, (2) extent of empirical/rational formal education, (3) family genealogy, and/or (4) occupation, according to Weber (1964). We also said that a distinct lifestyle and isolation from outsiders characterize status groups. Weber further argued that individuals in similar status situations tend to form cohesive communities. This cohesiveness is reaffirmed and maintained through intimate associations among themselves and by their wariness of and distance from outsiders. Status groups also are characterized by some uniqueness in their acquisitions; that is, their possessions may be exclusively associated with members of the group. Finally, higher status groups try to avoid contaminating contact with lower status groups, since they represent "impure" qualities and, in the extreme case, may be considered pariah groups.

The evidence we have reviewed strongly suggests that most Americans have a fairly coherent conception of Appalachians as a group and that they perceive them as having distinctive values and behaviors. Moreover, this subculture is more often than not portrayed in negative terms; that is, it is attributed with low-status honor. As Bensman stated, all status communities make claims for prestige, but "the validation of that claim, however, is based less on the claim itself than on the ability and willingness of others to experience and evaluate favorably the activities, characteristics, and institutions buttressing the claim" (Bensman 1972, p. 126). As we pointed out earlier, status honor/prestige is subjectively and willingly given.

This subculture of Appalachians is thought to have a unique lifestyle, according to the traditional conception, that includes a denigration of formal education, a genealogy composed of so-called common folk, and traditional occupations that are usually blue collar or agricultural in nature. None of these characteristics enhances the status honor accorded Appalachians. The mountain people frequently have been portrayed as being physically, socially, and culturally isolated from the outside world, and conversely, as having close relationships among themselves, especially within families. The qualities assessed as different by the standards of the dominant culture help justify the ridicule and romanticism rained upon mountaineers and "hillbillies" by outside urbanites. In correspondence with the romantic view of mountain culture, some of the artifacts associated with this culture, such as musical styles and instruments, have been viewed as being unique and worthy of preservation, especially by intellectual outsiders. In sum, what exists in Appalachia is an interesting confluence of economic, colonial, and status factors that must be understood within their historical context. Most importantly, our traditional image of Appalachians, while not consistent with much empirical evidence, has encouraged us to label Appalachians as a separate status group having low prestige.

Gender, Sexual Orientation, and Race as Bases for Status

There is no question that individuals of different races and genders are ranked unequally in U.S. society. Both Blacks and women have been thought of as separate status groups and, in some cases, even separate castes. Do Blacks and women constitute status groups that are distinct from those of Whites and males? Does it make sense to view them as being members of a caste? Does the concern for contact with homosexuals suggest that they, too, occupy a castelike position? Does this model help us understand and explain the situation of these groups better than other models? A fuller discussion of this matter will take place in later chapters, but we should briefly address this general issue since we are dealing with the various bases of status in this chapter.

Weber (1964) argued that, ultimately, the caste system is based on ethnicity, and that it is also legally sanctioned. Movement between castes is restricted, endogamy is expected, and traditional occupations are associated with each caste. On the surface, at least, there would appear to be a parallel between this description and a system in which ranking is based on either sex or race, both ascriptive characteristics. Some U.S. laws, in the past especially, have restricted areas or behaviors on the basis of sex and race, and race mixing and homosexuality have been frowned upon. One's attitudes toward Blacks and homosexuals can be partially attributed to the purity/impurity dimension associated with caste systems. The concerns for social distance, racial purity as typified by White supremacist and other extremist groups, and various forms of segregation suggest that purity/impurity is a fundamental dimension of races and homosexuals as status groups.

Although these comments on purity do not apply directly to an understanding of women and homosexuals in U.S. society, it is clear that assumptions about the basic characteristics of these groups, and associating these with specific types of skills, are relevant to explaining the socioeconomic predicament of women and homosexuals today. Clearly, the histories of women, homosexuals, and Blacks in the United States have been different, and thus it would be a mistake to assume that the same model can be used in the same manner to understand all of them. Blacks, for example, have never been expected to refrain from manual work or even participation in the labor market, whereas the nineteenth-century cult of true womanhood expected this of middle class, respectable women.

GLOBALIZATION AND AXES OF SOCIAL STATUS

In Chapter 2, I discussed the relationship between globalization and economic inequality in part because, not surprisingly, the major emphasis in globalization studies has been on its economic implications. There has been much research on how different economic dimensions of globalization affect economic conditions both within and between countries. There have also been studies of the political ramifications of globalization, which will be discussed in Chapter 4. However, there has been virtually no research on the potential impact of globalization on status inequality or status communities. In some ways, this is rather curious because globalization generally involves the movement and intermixing of people with different cultural, religious, political, and educational backgrounds. What I will do here is briefly suggest some possible relationships between globalization, on the one hand, and the development of new bases of status resulting in the rise and fall of status communities within and between nations. So consider the following few paragraphs as food for thought.

It seems to me that increased immigration from Latin America and Asia, public discussions about various religious groups, and concerns about the global educational and digital divide are all seedbeds for the development of new status communities and the strengthening of nascent ones. Historically, adaptation by immigrants to the United States sometimes took the form of economic, social, and cultural enclaves. Within them, immigrants could maintain their distinct cultural ways of life, creating a sometimes voluntary and sometimes involuntary boundary between themselves and the outside

society. Given the continuing controversy about the economic, educational, environmental, and other effects of immigration on U.S. society, and the conviction on the part of some that we ought to severely limit immigration and be more rigorous in our monitoring of recent immigrants, it may be that the boundaries between recent immigrant enclaves and the rest of society will become more solidified, reinforcing any tendencies toward exclusion and exclusivity now present. The result could be more stratification by status based on immigrant position, where immigrants are labeled and stigmatized. Might this not encourage them to turn inward to develop more fully their own communities to the neglect of ties with others? The immigrant/native divide may have political and economic implications as well.

A second axis of status ranking that may become more prominent involves religion. Recent "terrorist" activities have sensitized more Americans to the religious division of Islam, Judaism, and Christianity, and have led to retributions of members of one religion against those who follow a different creed. At least in the short term, these actions and reactions solidify the boundaries that separate these religious communities both within and between countries as some individuals "look down on" members of different religions. The religious differences are often viewed with ethnic overtones, suggesting that Muslims, Christians, and other religious groups are basically viewed as being made up of different *kinds* of people, and confirming Weber's belief that status communities are perceived as groups of people who are *inherently* different. This situation can lead to the reinvigoration of religion as an important basis of status honor or dishonor.

Finally, there has also been discussion by international leaders about the "global digital divide" that separates developed from less developed nations. In 2000, members of the major economic powers in the world—the "G-8" as they are called—met to assess the extent of the digital gap and propose policies that might help to close it. The gap is large: In North America, for example, there are 61 computers for every 100 individuals whereas in South Asia there is only 0.5 computers and in Sub-Saharan Africa only 1 computer for every 100 people. The Internet is rarely if ever used in these regions, whereas in North America over 50 percent of the citizens use the Internet (Chinn and Fairlie 2005). While this may change, the current situation conjures up an image of a world community in which some parts are left "out of the loop" about what is happening in the world and others are not. This again strengthens a boundary between different kinds of people. Do you think new status communities may develop as a result of globalization? Will the continuing infiltration of new values, styles, and technologies into countries create new social disparities where none had existed?

SUMMARY

This chapter has addressed the topic of social status, a form of inequality that is analytically separate from economic inequality, even though it is frequently based on an individual's economic resources. Status also can be based on occupation, education, lifestyle, physical appearance, region, race, gender, and sexual orientation. The prestige of our occupation, the kind of education we receive, the lifestyles we pursue, and the way we appear in public are each badges of status. They affect how others perceive us and how they treat us. In their extreme, status groups can be legally sanctioned and exclusive. Veblen was acutely aware of the invidious comparisons that groups made with each other in the early 1900s, and these continue today. Even the labels attached to various places and regions of the country suggest that they have implications for social status. We examined Appalachia in depth because differences in economic and political power and social status all converge in this region. By analyzing it, one can see several forms of inequality at work all at once. In Chapters 5, 6, and 7, attention is turned to gender, sexual orientation, and race/ethnicity as additional bases of status. But first we return to a final political dimension of inequality.

CRITICAL THINKING

1. Discuss the new forms or bases of status developing in the United States. What are they and how important are they? Will they replace status based on older grounds? Explain your answer.

2. How can individuals present themselves to others to indicate their membership in particular status groups?

3. The discussion in this chapter suggests that social status is often based on economic differences between groups. What kinds of social rankings are not rooted in economic inequality?

4. What does the case of Appalachia teach us about the sources of poverty and economic inequality?

WEB CONNECTIONS

Appalachia has often been described in contradictory ways—as beautiful but ravaged, and as rich in resources but impoverished. The Appalachian Regional Commission's website will give you a better idea of trends in its population, employment, education, and poverty. Visit www.arc.gov/appalachia. To help dispel stereotypical images you may have of the region, visit http://cass.etsu.edu/ARCHIVES/index.htm.

CHAPTER 4

Political Inequality

Every social act is an exercise of power, every social relationship is a power equation.
—Amos Hawley

The exercise of power and the experience of powerlessness are implicit in all the forms of inequality. The relationships between wealthy and nonwealthy, men and women, gays and straights, and Blacks and Whites are frequently mediated by the relative power of these groups. Power also has a narrowly political meaning as well, relating to the varied involvement and impact of individuals and groups in the national government. Thus, inequality in political power exists on the national level as well as in the everyday relationships between individuals. We will examine each of these in turn, beginning with a discussion of images of political power structure in the United States then moving to a review of evidence that bears on those images.

PORTRAITS OF NATIONAL POWER STRUCTURE

The founding architects of the U.S. national government did not agree on how large or how strong it should be, nor did they consistently agree on whether everyone should have an equal influence on government. Washington and Adams, for example, believed in the need for a strong, centralized government, while Jefferson and Madison worried that such a government would move the country toward a European-style monarchy rather than a democracy.

Arguments on how widespread such power is have continued to this day. Some argue that the majority is dependent on a minority, and that a power elite or ruling class exists. Others believe the evidence supports a more pluralistic interpretation of the national power structure. Basically, the argument boils down to one over the extent of inequality in political power.

Most of these theories can be listed under one of the following types: (1) pluralist, (2) power elite, or (3) ruling class. A brief description and critique of each of these approaches follows. The principal issue on which these approaches differ is the degree to which they see power as being concentrated in the United States. After the summaries of these perspectives, a survey of the empirical evidence that bears on them will be presented.

The Pluralist View

Basically, this widely accepted position argues that there are a number of competing groups and organizations that hold much of the power in the country, but no one of these groups holds power all of the time. There is no central or inner circle that dominates or coordinates the connections between these groups, because each is relatively autonomous and self-interested. Each group pursues issues that are of narrow interest to its organization; in those areas it can have influence,

71

but in others it has little or no power. Generally, social inequality is "noncumulative, i.e., most people have some power resources, and no single asset (such as money) confers excessive power" (Manley 1983, p. 369). Although there is some contact between organized groups, it tends to be inconsistent and deals with specific issues rather than broad orientations (Higley and Moore 1981). For example, conservative and liberal religious organizations may join together and have some power in their support of proposed policies revolving around rights of the fetus or unborn, but on other issues, they may differ or have no influence or interest. The shifting of power from group to group as issues fluctuate keeps power in a rough balance throughout the society. Individuals can exercise power in part by becoming members of these groups.

In sum, although the pluralist approach has spawned a number of specific theories, most share these core ideas:

1. Power is shared rather than concentrated among a variety of groups and individuals.
2. These groups are relatively autonomous of each other and become politically active primarily when political policies are at issue that directly affect their narrow interests.
3. The average citizen can be politically influential through membership in these groups and through voices of responsible journalists and intellectuals.
4. The consequence of items 1 through 3 is that there really is no single, permanent structure of power. Power is mercurial and its distribution is somewhat balanced by the existence of varied competing groups (Riesman, Denney, and Glazer 1950; Galbraith 1952; Berle 1959; Rose 1968).

In these theories, one is given the impression of a society that, although made up of a variety of different groups and categories of people, is fundamentally based on *a system of values on which there is a widespread consensus*. In this society, each individual is rational and free, and interests are taken into account in one way or another by those organizations such as government or corporations that might be seen as having greater power. Power and powerlessness do not appear to be problems. The sharing of power actually helps the society to function.

A variant of the pluralist model was proposed by Keller (1969), who contended that the increasing complexity and differentiation in modern societies makes the existence of "coordinating elements" essential. To prevent this society from disintegrating because of all of its different parts, some groups must play a central role in keeping the parts together. These "strategic elites," as Keller calls them, perform this function and serve as the "guardians and creators of common purpose and . . . managers of collective aims and ambitions." (Keller 1969, p. 521). These elites have knowledge that is both expert and critical for the functioning of the entire society. Obviously, not all organized groups in the society qualify for this elite status. Included among the strategic elites are leaders in the political, economic, military, cultural, and recreational fields.

Because strategic elites are specialized, none of them dominates according to Keller, nor do these elites constitute a ruling class. Unfortunately, this theory is not very informative about the *degrees* of importance of each of the strategic elites; nor does it explain what happens when strategic elites, such as those in economic, political, and military domains, collide with each other.

Finally, what makes these groups strategic elites is their expert knowledge in critical areas. But a theory that stresses specialized knowledge as the important basis for power neglects the fact that ideology and outlooks frequently are the bases for advancement in power (Prewitt and Stone 1973, pp. 126–127).

For over 40 years, pluralism has been roundly criticized (Mills 1956; Bachrach and Baratz 1962; Connolly 1969; Prewitt and Stone 1973; Cunningham 1975–1976). Social and historical events during the 1960s and 1970s helped develop a critical stance in all the social sciences, especially economics, political science, and sociology. The central criticisms of pluralism frequently reflect skepticism about the reality of democracy in society today and are based on an analysis of current events on the political scene. First, the issues of concern to many people frequently are not dealt with by the government. In large part, this occurs either because these individuals are not in positions to make their interests known or because their interests are of less concern than those of people who hold positions of economic and social power and whose values are represented and reflected in the government (Connolly 1969; Prewitt and Stone 1973).

Second, voluntary associations are no longer effective representatives of the average citizen as they have themselves become oligarchical in nature. In addition, individuals in positions of organizational power do not represent the average membership. These members do not have access to power (Presthus 1962; Kariel in Connolly 1969, p. 16). Finally, nondecisions and problems that never become publicly defined as issues must be examined. Pluralism examines issues but ignores "the values and biases that are built into the political system and that, for the student of power, give real meaning to those issues which do enter the political arena" (Bachrach and Baratz 1962, p. 950).

The Power-Elite View

The idea of a power elite differs drastically from pluralist conceptions and Keller's concept of strategic elites, but it is not the same as the ruling-class concept, which we will discuss shortly. Perhaps the most famous U.S. power-elite theory was developed by Wright Mills (1956). Because Mills's portrayal of the power elite has drawn an inordinate amount of attention in the years since it was written, and because it represents a prime example of a theory in opposition to the pluralist position, it is presented here in detail. Mills's essential argument is that power is centralized in a power elite. According to Mills, certain historical changes

have brought about the development of a power elite. As the society has grown, institutions have become more complex, and national functions have become centralized in specific institutions— namely, the economic, military, and political institutions. Mills contended that with historical changes, the tasks in top positions in each of these institutions have become so similar that it is now possible for those at the top to interchange positions. Consequently, in addition to centralization in institutions, there has been an increasing coalescence, so much so that *three* separate political, military, and corporate elites are now *one* power elite made up of individuals in the highest positions in an interconnected set of institutions. "By the power elite, we refer to those political, economic, and military circles which as an intricate set of overlapping cliques share decisions having at least national consequences" (Mills 1956, p. 18). The nucleus of the power elite consists of those who hold high positions in more than one of the three major institutions, as well as those, such as prestigious lawyers and financiers, who serve to knit the three institutions together (ibid., pp. 288–289).

The persons within this structure have their power because of their positions. They do tend to come from the same kinds of economic, social, and educational backgrounds and do informally intermingle. Ultimately, however, it is their position that makes them powerful in national decision-making.

Mills described the top part of the power structure as possessing a "higher immorality." What he was talking about is not personal immorality (i.e., one caused by a corrupt personality) but a structural immorality, in that because of the way society is organized and because of the way its institutions are structured, certain individuals can take advantage of others and their positions. It is similar to what has recently been called "structural corruption," a situation in which structural avenues are open in society that allow outside money to influence the political and intellectual stance of those in positions of power (Judis 1990).

In Mills's view, part of the higher immorality is reflected in the fact that such characteristics as cynicism, personality selling, conformity, and mediocrity have replaced values based on knowledge, skill, and independent thinking.

Some may feel that Congress is part of the power elite, but Mills did not agree. Rather, he referred to the Congress as a "semi-organized stalemate" made up of people who, since they have their eyes on reelection, are concerned largely with the fluctuating local issues of their constituencies back home. In other words, such groups as the farm bloc, labor unions, white-collar workers, and Congress really have little to do with decisions of national consequence. These groups, specifically Congress, make up a middle level of power in the United States. If the competition of groups in pluralism operates at all, it is at this level, as Congressional members exchange favors, make compromises, and balance each other out. Mills further believed that the wealthy and political officers who are entrenched in local interests will not become nationally important. As he stated, "to remain merely local is to fail" (1956, p. 39). Local society has, by and large, been swallowed up by the national system of power and prestige. This is in part due to increasing urbanization, increasing satellite status of smaller towns, improved transportation networks, and now the World Wide Web. Again, it has been changes in the structure of the society that have resulted in the appearance of a particular kind of power structure.

On the bottom of this pyramidal power structure are the large majority of people who are quickly developing into a mass society. Masses are characterized by the fact that they are always on the receiving end of opinions, cannot or do not effectively respond to opinions expressed in the mass media, and really have no outlet for effective action in society. Mass media, largely controlled by those on the top of the power structure, have only served to weaken communications between the top and the bottom of the structure. The media tell people what their experiences are or should be and stereotype them. Education only serves to help people to "adjust" to a society that is very hierarchical in terms of power. Voluntary associations, although theoretically may be viewed as a link between the individual and the people at the top, do not perform this function because as they have grown, the individuals in them feel less powerful. Power is distant and inaccessible to average members.

Gusfield's (1962) neat summary of the central characteristics of mass society fits in nicely with Mills's description. In a mass society, there is a:

1. Weakening of primary and local associations
2. Strengthening of impersonal bureaucratized relationships in large-scale organizations that have replaced smaller and more informal systems of loyalty and affiliations
3. Homogenization of the population and a leveling of conditions and ideologies that have reduced traditional authority systems characteristic of stratified communities
4. Lengthening of the chain of organizational authority, which makes local groups less viable and more amenable to control from above
5. Personality disintegration in the individual characterized by alienation, lack of commitment, and malaise (in addition to the structural disintegration indicated).

It should be pointed out that Mills was not saying that there is a conspiracy on the part of a small group of individuals to control political power in the United States. Rather, it has been a sequence of historical and structural events and changes, such as the growth in major institutions, that has led to the development of such a power structure. For example, the military is not powerful because it is conspiring against civilian populations, but it is in a position of power because the United States as a nation is now within an international military neighborhood, surrounded by allies and enemies. This means that what in the past may have been simply and purely political issues have now become largely military issues. Foreign aid is no longer just an economic or political issue but a military issue as well.

The *current* power elite is a relatively recent phenomenon that, in Mills's view, came into existence only after the New Deal in the 1940s and 1950s. Before that time, the power structure passed through several other epochs in which either no single institution or one of the three major institutions was dominant. Today, the hierarchy among these institutions is much less clear, and they are much more equal and intertwined.

Mills's power-elite theory has been criticized on several grounds, including the arguments that his terminology is vague and his selection of issues to test his theory is biased. He has also been faulted for choosing data that support his theory and ignoring contrary evidence. Third, some critics have attacked his conception of power, questioning his decision to use "position" as a measure of power and to see power as flowing only from the top down. Finally, some have branded his a conspiracy theory because of its emphasis on the interrelationships among institutional sectors and the similar backgrounds of those occupying high positions in them.

Despite these criticisms and others, however, Mills's analysis is not without its strengths. Among other points, Prewitt and Stone (1973, p. 90) mentioned that "whatever else it accomplished, *The Power Elite* raised the level of debate to a higher plane" since the author was the "first major analyst of American society" to anchor his analysis in concrete and major institutions.

The Ruling-Class View

As we have seen, Mills's description of the power structure is one in which a group of individuals in high positions in core institutions dominate, while those at the bottom

comprise an unorganized, ineffectual mass. They have little power and offer little active resistance. Rather, they are manipulated and educated in a manner that makes them almost willing subordinates in the society. The ruling-class view similarly proposes that a small group has inordinate political power in the society and that there are important interconnections between economic and political institutions. However, aside from these similarities, the ruling-class model differs from the power-elite model in several ways:

1. Rather than stressing several types of institutions as being involved in the elite, the ruling-class view emphasizes the dominance of the economic institution and position within it.
2. The ruling-class model often views the bottom of the power structure as being more active and effectual as a working class. It can organize and bring about change in the society. In the case of the power-elite model, the mass is largely passive in response to its position, whereas in the ruling-class model the working class can be class conscious and organized. Thus, the relationship between those on the top and those on the bottom is characterized more fully by conflict (Bottomore 1964).
3. The relationship between the upper class or bourgeoisie and political power is portrayed as being much tighter than is the case in Mill's power-elite theory where the upper class and celebrities are more tangential to the political process. In Mills's view, it is strictly *institutional position*, not *personal wealth*, that leads to political power.

G. William Domhoff's argument that the corporate rich and owners constitute a "dominant class" that largely controls the political process is perhaps the best representation of a ruling-class theory of U.S. politics. Briefly, Domhoff contends that a cohesive power elite dominates federal governmental affairs, and it is composed of those members of the upper class whose wealth is heavily concentrated in corporate holdings and who actively become involved in corporate affairs and political policymaking (Domhoff 1998). Consequently, their power is based in both class position and corporate attachment. In addition, these individuals have similar backgrounds, often know each other, and have general political and economic interests in common. Because of the cohesiveness founded on these similarities, the upper class "is a *capitalist* class as well as a *social* class" (ibid., p. 116, emphasis added). Although there may be internal disagreements over specific policies, there is broad agreement over the general direction that policy should take. The corporate-based elite dominates the political arena through its heavy influence on public opinion, participation in lobbying through its powerful interest groups, and involvement in policy formation through foundations, board room discussions, and various research groups.

In contrast to Mills's view of the power elite, Domhoff does not present a picture of power structure in which there is a mass society without voice and in which no group but the elite can have any power of consequence. Rather, he notes that unions and different liberal groups frequently conflict with the corporate rich, but that, generally, it is the latter group that sets the parameters within which conflict occurs. Domhoff is quick to point out that, given the size, internal disagreements, and bases of the dominant class, his is not a conspiracy theory. Rather his argument focuses on providing evidence that there is "an upper class that is tightly interconnected with the corporate community . . . [and] that the social cohesion that develops among members of the upper class is another basis for the creation of policy agreements" (ibid., p. 71).

DISTRIBUTION OF POLITICAL POWER

Each of the positions just discussed suggests a different distribution of power and political influence. But the data that bear on them must be examined before conclusions can be drawn about the concentration and dispersion of political power. The degree of political power and political participation can be measured in a variety of ways, and each of these measures provides clues concerning the actual distribution of power.

Though some people feel they have little influence, perhaps they are wrong. To what extent are all individuals really politically influential in the United States? Does being a citizen mean by definition that a person is a participant? One means by which to assess the potential political impact of a group is through its history of participation in the political process. "Participation is a potent force; leaders respond to it. But they respond more to the participants than to those who do not participate" (Verba and Nie 1972, p. 336). A group obviously has to make its desires known if it is to have the possibility of gaining political power under the present system. "Party politicians are inclined to respond positively not to group *needs* but to group *demands*, and in political life as in economic life, *needs* do not become *marketable demands* until they are backed by 'buying power' or 'exchange power' because only then is it in the 'producer's' interest to respond" (Parenti 1970, p. 528; emphasis in original). Individuals and groups can make their demands known by participating in the political process through (a) voting, (b) holding political office, and/or (c) putting pressure in the form of lobbying and monetary support.

Voting

Voting is a frequently used measure of political participation. Voting turnouts for national elections in this country are well below the 80 percent turnouts found in other industrial democratic nations. This lower voting rate is somewhat surprising, given the fact that evidence suggests that Americans tend to be more politically aware than adults in other similar countries. The party system's lack of close connection with many other social groups, along with voluntary registration, has weakened participation in the U.S. political process (Powell 1986).

Generally, there are clear relationships between selected social characteristics and voting behavior. Historically, Whites have been much more likely than African Americans or Hispanics to register and to vote in congressional and presidential elections. The data show that during the 1960s—the period of the Civil Rights movement, racial disorders, and War on Poverty—a greater percentage of African Americans voted in presidential elections than did in 2000. That percentage declined during the 1970s only to rise again to almost 56 percent in 1984. Since 1984, the percentage of Blacks voting has remained in the low-to-mid 50s; in 2004, about 56 percent of the Black voting-age population went to the polls in the presidential election. An even lower percentage of Hispanics vote. Generally, under one-third of voting-age Hispanics vote in national elections (Casper and Bass 1998). Only 28 percent of voting-age

Hispanics participated in the 2004 election. The difference between the sexes has not been as great; in the 2004 presidential election, a slightly higher percentage of women than men voted. Figure 4.1 shows the voting percentages for the voting-age *populations* of various groups in the presidential elections between 1968 and 2004.

One of the reasons for the lower percentage of voters in the Hispanic *population* is that a significant percentage of them are not citizens, and thus, cannot vote. In 2000, 39 percent of Hispanics in the population were not citizens. The pattern and extent of immigration in recent years accounts for this situation. If only *citizens* in the Hispanic population are considered, the percentage who voted jumps to over 47 percent. A similar shift exists for Asians in the population. So it is important to separate the percentage of a *total population* that votes from the percentage of the *citizen population* that participates. It is not possible to do this in Figure 4.1 since the U.S. Census Bureau has regularly separated these out only since 1994.

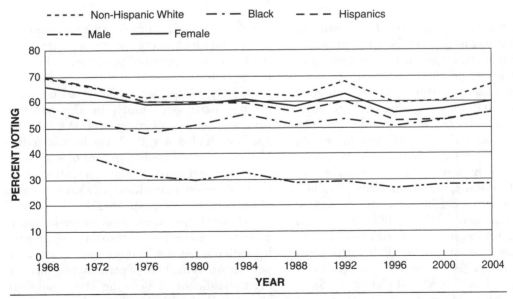

FIGURE 4.1   Percent of Voting-Age Population Who Reported Voting in Presidential Elections, by Race, Hispanic Origin, and Sex: 1968–2004

Sources: Jamieson, Shin, and Day, *Voting and Registration in the Election of November 2000*, U.S. Census Bureau, Current Population Reports, Series P-20, No. 542, February 2002; U.S. Census Bureau. *U.S. Voter Turnout Up in 2004, Census Bureau Reports*, at www.census.gov/Press-Release/www/releases/archives/voting.

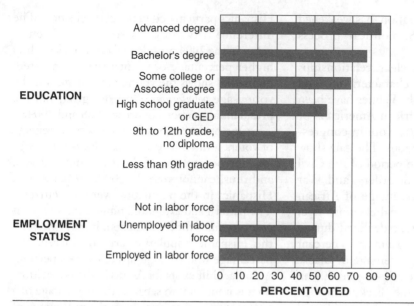

FIGURE 4.2   Percent of Citizen Population Voting in 2004 U.S. Presidential Election, by Education and Employment Status

Source: U.S. Census Bureau, *U.S. Voter Turnout Up in 2004*, Census Bureau Reports, at www.census.gov/Press-Release/www/releases/archives/voting.

But Figure 4.2 does provide the patterns for 2004 voting by those in the *citizen population* by education and employment status, giving us a general idea on the relationship between one's social class and voting. Those with more education and who are employed are more likely than others to have voted. For example, more than twice the proportion of those with advanced degrees compared with those who have had no high school experience voted in 2004. Historically, those with higher incomes have also been more likely to vote than those with low incomes. In the 2000 presidential election, for example, 75 percent of citizens with incomes of at least $75,000 voted, compared to only 34 percent of citizens with incomes of less than $5,000 (Jamieson, Shin, and Day 2002). Homeowners and those who have lived in their homes at least 5 years are also much more likely to vote than nonowners and those who have lived in their residences

less than a month. In sum, it is those who are most integrated in the society who are most likely to participate politically in it through voting (ibid.).

Cleary, a large percentage of some groups do not participate much in the political process, even at this basic level. What Verba and Nie concluded in 1972 remains true today. Voting patterns reveal "a picture of low levels of citizen participation and concentration of political activity in the hands of a small portion of the citizens" (1972, pp. 26–27).

If people did vote, would they be more politically powerful? Unfortunately, if past legislation is any guide, it does not appear that popular will is the kind of participation that has been significant in bringing about political changes. Rather, it has been the organized efforts of groups with resources that have been effective in the past (Prewitt and Stone 1973). Platitudes about popular control and the average citizen's importance simply have not held up (Parenti 1970; Prewitt and Stone 1973). Modes of participation other than voting have been more effective.

Some groups are, at best, only minimally involved in the political process. Those who are totally inactive have disproportionate numbers from low-income and low-education backgrounds, whereas "complete activists" have an overrepresentation of high-status individuals in their ranks (Verba and Nie 1972, pp. 97–99). The complete activists are individuals who participate in a variety of ways (voting, attending meetings, campaign contributions, contacting officials, etc.). Regardless of how it is measured, political inequality is present and present to a large degree. Simply put, those who are better off vote more and are more involved.

Changing Bases of Political Involvement. The data just presented indicate that socioeconomic factors are related to the probability of voting. There is also evidence to suggest that this inequality in political participation is perpetuated over generations through educational differences. Parents who are highly educated tend to be politically involved, provide a variety of politically relevant experiences to their children, and perhaps most significantly, maximize the chances of their children becoming highly educated themselves. "In turn, well-educated offspring are likely to . . . have challenging and financially rewarding jobs, to develop civic skills and to receive requests for participation in non-political institutions, to be politically informed and interested, and so on. . . . Most of the proximate causes of political participation have their roots, at least in part, in social class background" (Verba, Burns, and Schlozman 2003, p. 58). Those who are better off not only participate more, but are also better organized than those who are not so well off. This difference in participation means that "ordinary Americans speak in a whisper while the most advantaged roar" (quoted in Dionne 2004, p. B2).

While class position affects political participation, some have argued that, as a basis for political advocacy, class has been supplanted by "cultural" factors. Prominent issues like gay marriage, abortion, medical malpractice, stem cell research, marijuana usage, and immigration incite groups that are not organized around *class* but around religious and other *cultural* dimensions. *Status*-based politics has moved into the foreground while *class*-based politics has receded. Michael Hechter observes, "[t]hat status politics may be gaining in recent times is suggested by the increasing political salience of ethnicity, religion, nationalism, gender, and sexual orientation" (2004, p. 404). As noted in Chapter 3, status is a significant basis for inequality in the United States, and is one that is rooted in the prestige or "honor" of given lifestyles or consumption habits. Certainly, the issues mentioned above resonate with status lifestyles and, consequently, instigate participation by individuals on that basis.

In addition to status, ethnicity may also be becoming a more significant factor in voting and holding office. The Hispanic vote has become increasingly courted by national candidates, in part because this segment of the population is expected to compose one-quarter of the total population by 2050. Moreover, 80 percent of the Hispanic population is concentrated in just 10 states, states which contain 80 percent of the electoral votes needed to win the presidency (Campo-Flores and Fineman 2005). Finally, religious-related and moral issues of the kind that have become prominent (e.g., abortion, gay marriage, etc.) are central to the lifestyles of many Hispanics. In combination, these facts make them an increasingly important political constituency.

Holding Political Office

Holding political office is another and more substantial means by which to wield political power. White males dominate political positions at the federal level. In terms of absolute figures, the number of Black elected officials has gone up dramatically since 1970. In 2001, there were 9,101 Black elected officials, compared to 1,469 in 1970. But Blacks still compose only about 2 percent of all elected officials, even though Blacks make up over 11 percent of the voting-age population. Under 1 percent of these positions are at the federal level. As a result of the 2004 elections, there were 42 Black members of the House of Representatives, but only one in the Senate. This compares to 24 Hispanic and 5 Asian American/Pacific Islander members of the 109th House of Representatives. The 2004 elections resulted in two Hispanic and two Asian Americans being members of the Senate. American Indians had one person in the House and no one in the Senate. In total, minority persons made up about 16 percent of the House in 2004 ("Minorities in the 109th Congress" 2004).

Among Blacks historically, while men have outnumbered female elected officials significantly, that trend has shifted with many more women than men being elected. Currently, about 35 percent of all Black elected officials are women. Women in general are underrepresented in elected political positions. Sixty-eight of the 435 members of the 2004 House of Representatives were women; 14 of the members of the Senate were women.

In addition to sex and race, socioeconomic status has also been tied to holding political office historically. Matthews's (1954) study of the 81st Congress in 1954 suggests that upper-class origin is linked to being a member of Congress. While 63 percent of the employed in 1890 were low-salaried workers, wage earners, servants, and farm laborers, only 4 percent of the senators in the 81st Congress had fathers in any of those categories. As the cliché might put it, the Senate was largely made up of White Protestants, most of whom were born into middle- and upper-class families, and a majority of whom were lawyers. Matthews concluded that his and other findings suggest a class ranking of political office, with those from the

Although working-class families have been among the most openly patriotic and have generally contributed their members disproportionately to serving their country militarily, they are less likely to vote or occupy political positions than are those in higher classes.
Photo by Brendan R. Hurst.

higher classes occupying the highest political offices. The Congress of 2000 was similarly composed. Seventy-four percent were businessmen, bankers, or lawyers (Hirschfeld 2001). The overrepresentation of individuals from higher-status backgrounds has clearly continued in the Congress.

The executive branch has also contained disproportionate numbers of higher-status individuals. Mintz (1975) and Freitag (1975) researched the class backgrounds of *all* cabinet officers during the period from 1897 to 1973 and found that there were strong ties to the upper class. A full 66 percent of these officers were from upper-class backgrounds and 90 percent had occupied a top corporate position before or after being appointed or had upper-class origins. The particular political party that happened to be in power at the time did not make much difference (Mintz 1975). Freitag's analysis supports Mills's conclusion that there is a clear connection between corporate and political elites and does not support Keller's and other pluralists' arguments about autonomous elites. His study, based on biographical information for all cabinet secretaries from McKinley to Nixon's first term, involving 358 cabinet positions, shows that *at least* 76 percent of cabinet members were tied to the corporate sector by being either corporate executives, officers, or corporate lawyers. Since President Truman's administration, this percent is even higher (86% under Eisenhower, 77% under Kennedy, 86% under Johnson, and 96% under Nixon) (Freitag 1975). Freitag concluded that the data do not prove that the corporate and governmental elite sectors are unified in terms of policies, but they do suggest that it is a "serious possibility" that the Cabinet may be accountable to large corporations.

Top federal officials are not likely to come from working-class or lower-class families. Presidents also tend to come from higher educational and occupational backgrounds, and certain ethnic backgrounds are overrepresented in these positions. For example, 32 of the first 42 presidents (Washington through Clinton) had college degrees, and the vast majority of them received their educations at elite schools in the Northeast. Twenty-seven of them were lawyers by occupation. Finally, all but a few of these White men had had previous political experience prior to becoming president (Ragsdale 1998).

For over two decades, Dye has documented the characteristics, backgrounds, and interconnections of the institutional elite in the United States. He included in his definition of elites all those who occupy positions of high authority in the governmental, media, educational, civic/cultural, military, financial, industrial, and legal institutions in the United States. Based on this definition, Dye concluded that there are 7,314 such positions. Taking all of the corporate, public-interest, and governmental elite together as a group, Dye estimated that about 30 percent come from upper-class origins, measured in terms of education and occupation of parent. However, while that class is disproportionately represented, the remaining 70 percent come from middle-class backgrounds. Ten percent of these institutional leaders are women and a much smaller percentage are African Americans (Dye 2002). Considering only the governmental elite—that is, those who occupy the top positions in the executive, legislative, and judicial branches—almost 75 percent have law or other advanced degrees. Over 40 percent are graduates of highly prestigious, private universities or colleges. Women and African Americans, as might be expected, are grossly underrepresented.

What is the meaning of these studies in terms of the perspectives on power presented earlier? If the essence of pluralism is the presence of a rough balance of power between constituencies with different interests, then these data clearly do not support the pluralist position. Some groups—most notably women, racial minorities, and working- or lower-class members—are seldom found in offices of political power. To the extent that these offices are a principal means by which to gain and exercise political power, and that incumbents reflect and work for their own interests, then some groups have much less power than others.

INTERLINKAGE OF ECONOMIC AND POLITICAL POWER

As noted in Chapter 1, there has been a long-standing concern for keeping economic power from contaminating the political arena and thereby keeping those who are wealthy from controlling the political process. The studies discussed earlier show that office incumbents are most likely to come from high social classes. This class connection raises several questions about the relationship between economic and political power. First, does this connection necessarily mean that, as officeholders, incumbents will press only for policies that benefit their own classes? Second, are political action committees (PACs) and lobbying groups so influential in the political process that it suggests dominance by one social class? Does money buy elections and votes? Third, and perhaps most important, is the upper class in general and its ruling "power elite" as united as Domhoff suggests? Each of these issues will be addressed next.

With respect to the first question, there are clear dangers in assuming that once in office, a person will automatically represent the interests of his or her class. Consider the following:

1. Although most of the elite are from wealthy backgrounds, not all wealthy individuals become members of the elite.
2. Not all of the wealthy who become members of the elite were born into or inherited their wealth. Some are more obviously self-made individuals, although they are wealthy. Those of poor backgrounds may certainly act differently from those who inherited their wealth.
3. The values of the elite can change even though recruitment continues to be from the wealthy (Prewitt and Stone 1973, pp. 146–147).
4. Finally, internal conflicts and competition within the elite among those with different capital interests hinder unity on specific policy content (Poulantzas 1973).

Despite these factors and the possible wide range of specific policies the elite may introduce, these differences are outweighed by the cohesiveness of broader agreements on how policies should be made and by concern for the preservation and protection of U.S. values and institutions (Prewitt and Stone 1973, pp. 148–157).

Candidate Selection and Campaign Funding

Short of actual occupancy in a political office, another substantial manner in which an individual or organization can attempt to have political impact is through direct influence of officeholders. In the recent past, direct lobbying has been carried out by various groups with financial power. Since the 1960s, there has been a significant increase in the number and activity of interest groups, an increased centralization of their headquarters in Washington, DC, a rise in the number of public-interest and single-issue interest groups, and more "formal penetration" on their part into governmental activities (Cigler and Loomis 1995). The number of PACs has spiraled upward in recent years, going from 1,653 in 1977–78 to 4,594 in 2001–02 (Zuckerman 2005). Basically, PACs are interest groups that collect money from individuals sympathetic to their cause(s), and present it to desirable candidates. Many are worried about their influence because candidates rely heavily on money to run successful campaigns.

Political action committees represent many different interest groups. Corporations, labor, assorted trade, and nonconnected specific-issues groups are among the organizations with PACs, and each follows different strategies. For example, the National Rifle Association is frequently cited as a formidable interest group, having great influence on governmental policies involving gun control. PACs come in handy because running for office is very expensive. As a group, candidates for positions in the House of Representatives, for example, spent almost $645,000,000, while those for the Senate spent a total of about $490,000,000 in the 2004 election. From PACs alone, the top recipient of House candidates received just under $2,000,000. Running for the presidency is also expensive. The 2004 presidential candidates spent $828,000,000 (opensecrets 2004).

Contributions by PACs are part of the "soft money" candidates receive during their

Many citizens believe that money has become a ticket to political power because it provides access to influential officeholders that is not as easily available to those who are not major donors to political campaigns.

Source: Non Sequitur © 2005 Wiley Miller. Dist. by Universal Press Syndicate. Reprinted with permission. All rights reserved.

campaigns. Such funds also include money from individuals, unions, and corporations. Loopholes in federal legislation have fostered growth in the amount of soft money in political campaigns. Among individual contributors in the 2004 election, the most generous contribution totaled almost $460,000. One hundred individuals gave at least $210,000 each.

The concern over the influence of PACs is based on the assumption that, *as a monolithic group*, contributors have disproportionate influence over federal policies. But it should be kept in mind that these groups vary widely in their specific interests and are not monolithic in this sense. In fact, the proliferation of these varying interest groups might be viewed as an indication of pluralism at work (Alexander 1992). At the same time, however, there is some question about whether the attention paid to *specific* interest groups will hinder the ability of governing officials to effectively address problems that affect the *general* interest of U.S. society (Cigler and Loomis 1995).

Regarding the issue of PACs and their impact, studies suggest that although PACs may increase an individual's access to given members of Congress, they do not systematically affect how these members vote. However, Senator

Russell B. Long once said that "the distinction between a large campaign contribution and a bribe is almost a hairline's difference" (quoted in Stern 1988, p. 146). But in a research study on 20 labor-related issues in the U.S. House of Representatives, Jones and Keiser (1987) found that the amount of contributions from union-approved PACs was related to voting only on issues that had little media attention. In other words, the less visible the issue, the greater the effect of contributions on voting behavior.

A second analysis of 120 PACs connected to 10 different organizations examined the effect of PACs on the voting behavior of members of the House of Representatives and no significant influence on voting was found. However, these PACs and the organizations they represent can influence voting to the extent that they can influence the election process in the districts from which these congressional members originate (Grenzke 1989). It is not through the amount of the PAC contribution itself, but through other mechanisms that economically powerful groups can influence voting patterns.

Concern for their potentially heavy influence has led to legislation to curb the economic involvement of special interests and individuals in the election process. In 1971, Congress passed the Federal Election Campaign Act (FECA) as a means by which to limit and clarify sources of monetary contributions. Although amendments were added to it throughout the 1970s and later, the Act's effectiveness in changing the system of contributions has been questionable. Congress has been reluctant to make sweeping changes in part because incumbents benefit from the present rules. "It's much easier for incumbents to raise campaign money than it is for challengers. Persons currently in office can provide access and influence legislation in ways impossible for those who aren't" (West 2000, p. 167).

The Enron scandal fueled demands for greater scrutiny and regulation of the connection between those with economic power and those with political power. With allegations of misrepresentation of company assets, faulty auditing, direct involvement in the massive loss of employee pension monies, and numerous meetings between top company officials and members of the executive branch of the government over energy policy, the scandal gave new impetus to campaign reform initiatives. Enron had been a heavy contributor to White House and congressional candidates (Foerstel 2002a; Oppel, Jr. 2002).

A U.S. House sponsor of campaign reform, Martin Meehan, stated Enron's alleged influence bluntly: "Enron is a textbook study on money's influence in Washington. At a minimum, the taint of big money contributions undermines confidence in government decisions" (in Foerstel 2002a, p. 168). In March 2002, both the House and Senate passed campaign-reform legislation which aims to curb soft money's impact on the political process by "barring unrestricted donations to political parties, increasing limits on contributions to candidates and regulating broadcast advertising by non-candidates" (Foerstel 2002b, p. 803). The heavy presence of money in the political process creates fervent political adversaries because what is at stake is the prize of political power.

RULING-CLASS UNITY

Concerns about soft money and the power of PACs are related to suspicions that those with plentiful resources are unified and will exercise disproportionate control of the political process. Mills's and Domhoff's descriptions of the social backgrounds of the elite and the historical circumstances in which they rule suggest that they are unified. Domhoff described their common membership in and interaction at exclusive clubs, attendance at elite schools, and frequent listing on the Social Register, while Mills described not only their social-psychological similarities but also the concentration and coalescence that occurred among the major institutions involved in the power elite. Domhoff detailed some evidence of intermarriages, unique schooling, and leisure activities that point, he argued, to the existence of a cohesive upper class of which the public is conscious:

> The corporate rich are drawn together by bonds of social cohesion as well as their common economic interests. This social cohesion is based in . . . common membership in specific social institutions and friendships based on social interactions within those institutions. . . . Social cohesion is important from a class-dominance perspective because the most socially cohesive groups are the ones that do best in arriving at consensus when dealing with a problem. (Domhoff 1998, p. 72)

Ostrander's (1984) and Kendall's (2002) studies of upper-class women suggest that they are highly conscious of their class and their responsibilities in maintaining their social-class position. In supporting their husbands' economic activities, and as members of voluntary associations and social clubs, upper-class women work to perpetuate their social class.

> A central aim of upper-class women's community volunteer work, as they describe it, is to keep private control over community organizations. Private control comes to be identified as the control of their own class. . . . Their social life is the social life of a class, and their relations weave the fabric of upper-class

life. As community volunteers, upper-class women work almost entirely as members of their class. They have little in common, here, with other women. (Ostrander 1984, pp. 148–149)

Although there are tensions and individual disagreements within this group, as a whole they are united in defense of their class. This not only helps to maintain their class, but because it is male dominated, the subordinate position of these women within it (ibid.).

The studies cited focus on the unity of the upper class as a whole. Other studies reviewed earlier on political activity, however, also imply unification of the elite as a group, many of whom are not of upper-class background. In his study of elites, involving individuals from a variety of institutional areas, Dye (2002) also concluded that there is general unity of opinion among the elite, even though there is some evidence of rising factionalism within it.

Verba and Orren's study of 2,762 leaders from various institutional areas in the late 1970s also suggests unity on *basic values.* They found that all types of leaders tend to agree, for example, that a fair distribution of economic resources is one in which everyone has equal opportunity to pursue legitimate goals. They do not feel that everyone should have an equal amount, however. This solidarity of opinion included African American, feminist, and labor leaders. However, when it comes to opinions on *specific* matters rather than *general* values, or to descriptions of actual rather than ideal situations, there is disagreement among these leaders. For example, only 9 percent of business leaders view poverty as the result of the workings of the economic system, whereas 86 percent of African American leaders and 76 percent of feminist leaders see it this way (Verba and Orren 1985, p. 74). Seider's (1974) content analysis of the speeches of big business executives also indicated that although there are differences among them on specifics, there is fundamental unity on beliefs supporting the capitalist economic system that are never challenged.

Even though he has concluded that the elite are generally united on basic values, Dye (2002) argued that a split has developed within the elite between those he labels the "sunbelt cowboys" and the "established yankees." As the labels suggest, the "cowboys" as a group are individualistic, conservative, and often from non-upper-class backgrounds. Their wealth has been recently acquired. In contrast, the "yankees" tend to be more liberal and have established family wealth. They have attended the best Ivy League schools and are also likely to have occupied high positions in prestigious corporate, financial, or legal institutions. Thus, as to the issue of how unified the elite or upper class is, it is important to indicate whether one is speaking of the *general* or *specific* level, in *ideal* or *real-situational* terms, and of *social background* or *behavioral* unity. In some ways, these groups appear unified and in others they do not; the results from attitudinal and positional studies on unity are clearly mixed and one can find statistics to support both positions.

Like Domhoff, Dye, and others, Useem has dissected the capitalist class and its unity in detail. His studies concern the structural texture of that class (cf. 1978, 1979, 1984). Useem defined the capitalist class as "those who own or manage major business firms and their immediate kin" (1980, p. 200). In one analysis, he studied 2,843 officers from 200 corporations that varied in size and sector. The officers also differed in the number of corporations to which they were tied through directorships. Generally, Useem found that members of the capitalist class are not equally powerful. Those from larger firms who were also directors at other corporations were significantly more likely to have served on advisory committees for government at the local, state, and federal levels. They were also more likely to participate in national business groups such as the Business Roundtable, Business Council, Council on Foreign Relations, National Association of Manufacturers, and U.S. Chamber of Commerce and to be involved in significant cultural organizations (elite university boards, and art and research organizations) (1980). Useem, however, did not find significant participation differences between major industrialists and financiers.

In other research, Useem directly addressed the issue of the political unity of what he calls the "inner circle" of business, looking at whether members of this group act on behalf of their own separate corporations or on behalf of the capitalist class as a whole. Useem drew his information and conclusions from a wide variety of data sources, including personal interviews and documentary and survey data. The inner circle he described is a network of leaders from large corporations who serve as top officers at more than one firm, who are politically active, and who serve the interests of the capitalist class as a whole rather than the narrow immediate interests of their individual companies. To be a member of the inner circle, it helps to (1) have been successful in a major corporation, (2) have multiple directorships, (3) have occupied a senior position, (4) be a member of business associations, and (5) have been a consultant or advisor to government. Members of the inner circle are more often members of the upper class than are other business leaders—that is, they are richer, have attended elite prep schools, and are in the Social Register (Useem 1984, pp. 65–69). The circle's political style is to adopt a "posture of compromise" and accommodation rather than to be directly confrontational on every specific issue. Its interests are in the general protection of capitalism as a whole, not in the interests of specific companies.

Useem viewed capitalism in the United States as having moved from (1) "family capitalism" in which individual upper-class families dominated corporate ownership, through (2) "managerial capitalism" in which managers began to replace the dominance of upper-class owners around the turn of the twentieth century, to (3) "institutional capitalism" in which networks of intercorporate ties characterize the core of capitalism. The increasing control of corporations by their managers rather than owners and the increased concentration and interlocking in the corporate sector during this century have helped lay the basis for the development of this powerful circle (Useem 1984).

Indeed, Dye's study of individuals in top institutional positions revealed that 6,000 individuals have formal control over 50 percent of the country's industrial, banking, communications, insurance, educational, legal, and cultural assets. The top 500 out of 5 million corporations control about 60 percent of all corporate assets. Twenty-five banks out of 12,000 possess over 50 percent of all banking assets in the United States, and 30 of the 2,000 insurance companies control over half of all insurance assets (Dye 2002). Some 15 percent of the 7,314 institutional leaders studied by Dye occupied more than one top position (i.e., were interlockers) and a smaller percent held as many as six or more such positions. He viewed this "inner group" as cohesive for a number of reasons, and, like Useem, found that multiple corporate interlockers were more likely than single directors to participate in governmental and other major organizations.

There are a number of ways in which this elite group of business leaders gets politically involved. One principal mechanism is through governmental ties. As Useem's and others' research indicated, for example, they are more likely to serve as cabinet officers. During Ronald Reagan's first term, Weinberger (Defense), Regan (Treasury), Baldridge (Commerce), Haig (State), and Pierce (Housing and Urban Development), as well as Smith (Attorney General) had all been multiple corporate directors. This is not unusual. As noted earlier, historically most Cabinets have had deep connections to powerful economic interests. Several top members of President Bush's 2004 administration (e.g., Cheney, Rumsfeld) have strong ties to corporate and financial institutions. Like Dye and others, Useem also found that the inner-circle members play crucial political roles by directing nonprofit organizations, serving as political fund-raisers, endorsing candidates, giving larger campaign contributions, and influencing media content (Useem 1984, pp. 76–94).

This inner circle is much more politically active than business in general because its members occupy several important positions at once, which (1) creates cohesiveness among its members, (2) helps mobilize economic and other resources, and (3) provides a powerful platform from which to express political positions. Moreover, its members are also closely tied to the upper class, which increases the circle's influence (Useem 1984). In contrast to other research, Useem found that if members of the upper class are in the business elite, they are more likely than persons from other classes to get into the inner circle. In sum, characteristics of the U.S. political economy create opportunities for the interconnection of political and economic power.

A significant part of the reason for the tie between economic and political power lies in the interlocking between private and corporate wealth and political opportunity. It takes wealth, or at least access to wealth, to run a viable campaign for a major national political office. The connection between economic and political power may be deeper than this suggests, however, and may be based not on the characteristics of particular *individuals* but on the *structure and functioning* of the society.

The *structuralist* position suggests that given the structure of a capitalist society such as the United States, the government *must* act in a manner that supports the capitalist class and capitalism in general. This occurs regardless of who is in office. The political and economic institutions are so intertwined that the government, although it may be "relatively autonomous," is constrained to support and pass policies that maintain the capitalist economy. The state needs to provide a hospitable environment for investment and create a stable

and smooth running economy because it relies upon the returns from the economy for its revenue. A stable economy also encourages political support for the government. In addition, the state provides programs (e.g., welfare, unemployment compensation) to deal with the fallout that comes from the operation of a capitalist system in which a relatively small number of corporations exercise inordinate influence. Inevitably, the state becomes involved in economic matters (O'Connor 1973; Offe 1975; Block 1977).

The preceding studies on campaign financing, holding office, and the capitalist economy indicate that both individuals and structural arrangements foster a relationship between economic and political power. Structural ties among institutions make it possible for some individuals to have access to positions of great power. According to some, however, one of the major problems with both these analyses is that they assume that all major policies are made within the government and, therefore, the focus of both approaches is on the state. In fact, it has been suggested, many major policies are created outside the government, principally by the actions of corporations. Industrial change, for example, to the extent that it can be considered a "policy," has largely been the result of actions by the private sector, not the government (Schwartz 1987).

POWER INEQUALITY IN THE WORK EXPERIENCE

The discussion so far should leave little doubt that, by a variety of measures, there is extensive inequality in power at the national level. An analysis of political inequality, however, also requires examination of the power differences that exist in the everyday lives of individuals. The focus in this section will be on power differentials that are experienced at work and at home, and the behavioral dynamics associated with these differentials. These differences are often related to issues of race, gender, and class.

As we will see in Chapter 12, there have been social movements going on for decades based on class, race, and gender that are generally organized attempts to gain greater power in society. The historical conflict between labor and management, for example, was generally one over the relative power and control of each side. Within a society, organizations, and those in control of them, exercise power over their members in a variety of ways. Total institutions such as the military and strict religious orders with their clear, fixed, and legitimate hierarchies and complete control over members perhaps provide the best expression of the use of power in organizations. Developments in technology have allowed contemporary corporations to expand their monitoring power and control over their employees. With cell phones, blackberries, and e-mail, is it ever possible for a manager to escape from work? Technology has broken down the traditional divide between work and home, public and private spheres.

Power itself can be situational or trans-situational, that is, it may be operative only in particular contexts (e.g., at work but not elsewhere), or it may be trans-situational, that is, apply regardless of the situation (e.g., as against a minority person). Power can also be derived from a number of sources. Sometimes power is based on one's formal position in an organization (*legitimate* power). In the situations, power is based on one's knowledge (*expert* power), attractiveness (*referent* power), ability to reward (*reward* power), or ability to punish (*coercive* power) (French, Jr. and Raven 1959). *Information* can also be a base of power (Raven 1965) as can connections or associations one has with others (*referred* power). In each of these cases, but for different reasons, one person is *dependent* on the other, and can be constrained to act in a particular way despite their resistance.

Dependency is the opposite of power in that a lack of independence or autonomy in making decisions would signal a lack of power. In their classic study of working-class employees, for example, Sennett and Cobb found that workers desired college educations for their children so that they could become professionals rather than manual workers like themselves, that is, they wanted them to have autonomy in their jobs and be able to exercise greater control over their own lives (1973).

The different bases of power conjure up some interesting scenarios about the relationship between power, on the one hand, and race, class, and gender on the other. Men, for example, are thought to possess more expert and legitimate power than women, while women are believed to have more referent power, that is, their greater likeability gives them some leverage in relationships (Carli 1999). Individuals in lower-authority positions can exercise power through their control or possession of information, for example, secretaries. Professionals who have a specialized expertise can exercise power over higher-ranking individuals who are dependent on their expertise. Persons who appear threatening to others, for example, Black males, can exercise control over others with higher status based on their perceived power to coerce. These are just a few of the ways in which power and its bases are linked to race, class, and gender in everyday life.

Most adults spend a large part of their lives working in some organization. There has been a great deal of research on power inequality in the work setting, much of it focusing on the forms of power noted above, especially legitimate power. But oftentimes the power to reward, punish, and the like has broader and deeper roots. Gender ideology, racism, and class distinctions are three of these roots. In fact, race, class, and gender can each engender power plays even against individuals in positions of higher authority, as when, for example, a male subordinate harasses a female supervisor (Rospenda, Richman, and Nawyn 1998). Thus, power at work and at home are also derived from the dominant society-wide ideologies and policies about gender, sexuality, race, and class.

Bullying is a good example of how cultural ideologies about women and minorities affect power in the workplace. *Bullying* refers to "*repeated* and *persistent negative* acts towards one or more *individual(s)*, which involve a *perceived power imbalance* and create a *hostile work environment*" (Salin 2003, pp. 1214–1215; italics in original). While supervisors, who have power because of their formal position, can and sometimes do bully subordinates, bullying can also occur between individuals who are formally equal in their work positions, but who differ in race, class, or gender. In other words, power imbalances between groups in the wider society can infiltrate the work setting. "Thus, for example, power differences associated with traditional gender roles and minority status may also affect bullying behaviour, as it can be assumed that women and minorities are perceived to have less power and status" (ibid., p. 1219). Power and bullying are especially likely to operate when serious competition exists and significant rewards are at stake. When a company is bought out or merges with another, it becomes apparent how dependent and how powerless employees are. It is often when the economic environment is changing or uncertain, resources are limited or strained, or when the decision-making process is not fixed that many of the nonlegitimate forms of power cited above become most important in an organization because battles over turf, position, and rewards become more prominent under these conditions. Battles for power in the workplace often bring racial, gender, and class ideologies and related discourses to the foreground.

Women and minorities, for example, generally tend to occupy positions of lower authority and greater dependence than White males. As we will see in the next chapter, women dominate in positions of lower status, such as clerical and service work. Individuals in these positions often complain about the lack of respect they receive (cf., e.g., Johnson 2002). Moreover, positions in which women dominate tend to be lower in authority, especially in those occupations that recruit nationally (Huffman and Cohen 2004b). Men, on the other hand, are more likely to dominate positions of high authority, and to work to screen potential colleagues so that individuals who are similar to them are admitted into those positions while those who are dissimilar are screened out. Because the duties of executive positions tend to be central to organizations, yet broad in scope, it is important to those already at the top that reliable (i.e., similar) persons be brought in when vacancies occur. The result is "homosocial reproduction" in which White men in high-level positions recruit other men similar to themselves (Kanter 1977a). Minorities and women have less power than White men at work, in part, because of less education and/or experience. But even if these deficiencies did not exist, women and minorities would still have difficulty gaining power because of racism and gender bias that could be used by White men to keep these groups out of power (Elliott and Smith 2004).

To move up the authority ladder, one will need a "cognitive map" of the social network at the organization and may have to be a "team player" (i.e., similar) as well. To be such a player, one has to appear to be similar to colleagues, subscribe to the dominant approach or ideology of the organization, and spend a lot of time at the office. All these qualities make other managers or executives feel comfortable with you (Jackall 1988). It is when people step out of line, violate traditional cultural expectations, or are believed to have a distinct outlook or lifestyle that difficulties arise for them. In their study of sexual harassment, for example, Uggen and Blackstone found that "women in supervisory positions and men who do more housework are likely to experience the behavioral harassment syndrome" (2004, p. 83).

If a "token" or dissimilar person such as a woman, working-class, or minority person does reach a high level in an organization, she or he will be under intense pressure to perform and conform to racial, class, or gender expectations. Research indicates that women, for example, face greater pressure and discrimination as they gain experience and move up the corporate ladder (Kanter 1977b; Carli 1999; Elliott and Smith 2004; Uggen and Blackstone 2004). In part, this is because they are viewed as outsiders to the males who dominate the positions, and because they are expected to conform to mainstream gender expectations about women at the same time that they are also expected to excel at their jobs. This often produces such a high degree of pressure that some women resign their positions. "A woman who behaves in a competent and assertive manner is often less influential, particularly with men, because she lacks legitimacy. At the same time, when a women does not exhibit exceptional ability, her competence is doubted by both genders and she is less able to influence women. These findings underscore the dilemma that women face in the workplace" (Carli 1999, p. 95).

Such pressure and the power used with it can be justified by gender, class, or racial ideologies, or by one's perception of the "target" of the pressure. Bruins theorizes that "the stronger the means of influence used by the agent [of power], the more the agent [e.g., White male] will tend toward making an internal attribution for the target's [e.g., minority, woman] compliance, in turn leading to a more negative evaluation of the target and a tendency to increase the social distance toward the target" (1999). In other words, claims about the basic inferiority or inadequacy of the target will be used as justifications as more force or power is exercised over the subordinate.

Jennifer Pierce's findings on women lawyers from her research on legal firms demonstrate these pressures, and reveal how "masculine" traits (e.g., aggressiveness, direct-ness, competitiveness) of "Rambo litigators" are thought to be more valuable and effective in the courtroom than "feminine" qualities (e.g., empathy, emotionality, sociability), even though this does not always prove to be the case (1995). Female paralegals in these firms were as well dominated by being expected to defer to and "take care of" their male bosses. In sum, these women were expected to be therapists, mothers, listeners, and supporters for male lawyers. Male paralegals did not have the same expectations placed on them. The result is that women needed to engage in more emotional labor to appear successful to colleagues.

The success or power one has at work affects power relationships at home. Traditionally, husbands' power at home has been tied to their ability to support their families through their occupations. Their work in the public sphere has generally meant, especially in past generations, that their wives' efforts were restricted to the private sphere of family. The balance of power and dependence has shifted as more women have entered the labor force and have earned their own salaries. However, this does not always mean that their increased independence is always accepted at home, because it violates traditional beliefs about appropriate gender roles. A recent study of U.S. born–Mexican Americans found that the more women earned outside the family and participated in decision-making at home, the more abuse they reported by their spouses (Harris, Firestone, and Vega 2005).

POWER INEQUALITY IN A GLOBAL AND GLOBALIZING CONTEXT

I have noted above that power plays and differences are most likely to become salient when economic conditions are in a state of flux, when one's employment and income are at stake. An unpredictable economy nurtures a sense of competition among its workers, workers who will use the tools at their disposal to maintain or attain scarce positions. Among these tools are cultural ideologies and policies that privilege some groups over others. Increasingly, the operation of national economies has become less predictable because of their involvement in the worldwide network of economies and states.

Over the last few decades, there has been extensive discussion about the structure of the world economic system, the shifting relationships among nations, and the effects of globalization on the relative power of nations in the international order. In broad terms, the world system is often described as consisting of interdependent core, semi-peripheral, and peripheral countries. Each of these types tends to perform particular functions in the world system. Core nations are those that are wealthy, industrialized, and technologically advanced. They hold a privileged position in the world economic system because they possess an inordinate amount of the world's capital and also have strong, stable political systems. Peripheral nations, on the other hand, are described as poor, technologically deficient, generally "underdeveloped," and lacking in political stability. Semi-peripheral countries occupy an intermediate position in the system. Because many of the poor and working class in peripheral nations are composed of racial minorities and women, economic, political, and immigration relationships with core nations take on racial and gender overtones.

For all of the twentieth century, the West, particularly the United States, held a dominant economic and political position internationally. In recent years, however, some parts of Asia, especially China, have strengthened their international economic position. In the next decade or two, China's productivity is expected to increase threefold. It is now a manufacturing giant, producing most of the world's toys, microwave ovens, shoes, and DVD players. In 2004, Wal-Mart alone imported $18 billion in products from China (Zakaria 2005). Its surging economic power and large population have also meant greater political leverage in the world system. With increasing openness in

trade and foreign investment across the globe, China's progress suggests that a significant realignment in international power arrangements may be taking place.

Also part of the world's "new geography of power" are (a) transnational corporations that are beyond the full control of any given nation, (b) transnational legal institutions that regulate international economic relationships, and (c) the growth of electronic technology, which makes economic transactions possible independent of space. While these three developments may appear to reduce the regulatory power of sovereign states somewhat, they also mean that the state's role in the world political economy is also changing (Sassen 2000). Evidence indicates that between 1960 and 2000, core nations have strengthened their global power position by increasing their ties to international nongovernmental organizations and creating new ones (Beckfield 2003).

Historically, the economic power and political power of a nation have been intertwined. International economic expansion generally leads to more political power, power which is then used to maintain economic dominance. But today, capital and national governments are bases of international political power that are more autonomous than in the past. As Hanagan puts it, "[i]n an age when capital can electronically flee continents in nanoseconds, can national states resist national markets? Despite the claims of distinguished scholars, most nations simply cannot" (Hanagan 2000, p. 83). The developments mentioned above also have implications for the sources, nature, and extent of immigration to be discussed in subsequent chapters, and the structure of economic inequality within nations.

The political structure of a country affects the degree of inequality within it. Numerous studies have found that political democracy is related to less economic inequality. In his study of 50 countries, for example, Muller (1988) found that the more stable and longer the democratic tradition in a country, the less income inequality there is. Conversely, when income inequality continues for a number of years, political democracy is undermined. These relationships persist even when a country's level of development is considered. Reuveny and Li's research using data from 69 developed and less-developed nations also revealed that democratic characteristics reduced income inequality in both types of nations (2003).

Wider political input within a society also promotes less economic inequality. The greater the percentage of individuals who vote and the more wages are determined on a national basis, the lower is the earnings inequality. A larger proportion of workers who are union members also means less income inequality (Mahler 2004). Finally, increased governmental spending on social programs (e.g., education, health, social security) also has a depressing effect on income inequality (Rudra 2004). Clearly, the greater power of citizens as measured by democratic policies and structures can reduce economic inequality.

SUMMARY

We began this chapter with a brief discussion on the importance and difficulty of conceptualizing power. We then moved to an analysis of pluralist, elite, and ruling-class views of the national power structure, and the data that bear on the validity of each.

There are clear relationships between socioeconomic position and voting, holding political office, and other forms of political participation. Those closer to the bottom of the class hierarchy are less likely than those in the middle and upper classes to vote, be elected to office, and be represented in powerful lobbying groups. Research indicates that those from higher socioeconomic levels, especially the upper class, are disproportionately represented in elite positions in a variety of institutional spheres. The tie between economic and political power, however, is more than just individual in nature; it is also structural. The fates of government and economy are linked, each needs the other. Consequently, a government in a society with a capitalist economy, for example, must support capitalism because its revenue and stability heavily depend on the smooth operation of that economy.

In addition to power differences at the national level, power inequality also exists at lower levels, for example in the workplace. Power has a variety of immediate sources within organizations but can also be rooted in broader cultural ideologies surrounding race, class, and/or gender. The global nature of our economy creates uncertainties that may intensify power battles over rewards and jobs. The structure of the global economy and polity is changing, putting more power into the hands of nongovernmental, transnational organizations. The structure and policies of government within a country also affect economic inequality within countries, with democratic structures being more consistent with less inequality.

CRITICAL THINKING

1. Are information technology and the World Wide Web creating new bases for power and domination? Is it the corporate rich who will claim these bases or are new, powerful groups being created by these technological developments? Discuss your answer.

2. Discuss the connections that exist between international economic and political developments on the one hand, and inequalities within the United States and within economic organizations on the other.

3. If the working and lower classes are underrepresented among those who vote, hold

office, donate large sums of money to elections, and have effective lobbying power, how can representative or democratic government be ensured in the United States?

4. How can economic and political power be separated to ensure the influence of all in government, regardless of wealth?

WEB CONNECTIONS

The Center for Responsive Politics lists the amount of money spent on federal elections, along with the amounts given by major individual and organizational donors. The Center also gives information on the political leaning of these donors. Visit www.opensecrets.org. Another source, the Joint Center for Political and Economic Studies, presents summary information on Black elected officials at every level of office. Its information also allows you to compare rates for Black men and women as well as differences in rates between states. Where does your state stand on electing Blacks to office? Visit www.jointcenter.org.

CHAPTER
5

Sex and Gender Inequality

*It is their [women's] differential role in the reproduction of labor power that lies
at the root of their oppression in class society.*

—Lise Vogel

*I believe that not only must the hierarchical nature of the division of labor
between the sexes be eliminated, but the very division of labor between the
sexes itself must be eliminated if women are to attain equal social status
with men and if women and men are to attain the full development of their
human potential.*

—Heidi Hartmann

Race and sex are ascribed statuses in the sense that people have no control over whether they are Black or White, male or female. However, race and sex also are given particular meaning within the context of a culture's values and beliefs, which in turn may be based on dominant economic and political arrangements. What is immediately significant about race and sex, therefore, is not the differences in themselves, but the fact that these characteristics are socially defined and have meanings attached to them. These interpretations often result in races and sexes being hierarchically arranged in society.

In Chapter 7, we will pursue an analysis of racial inequality and demonstrate how race, gender, sex, and economic inequality are intertwined. In this chapter, we will be surveying the forms and extent of gender inequality, as well as explanations for it. We begin with a brief overview of the historical condition of women in U.S. society.

THE STATUS OF WOMEN IN THE EARLY UNITED STATES

What has it meant to be a woman in the United States? When I was growing up in the 1940s, my parents had a traditional arrangement—my mother was a homemaker and my father "brought home the bacon." Earlier, however, my mother had worked in a hosiery factory. Throughout our nation's history, women have consistently contributed to the economy while still maintaining a family.

In our own agricultural preindustrial colonial society, women were directly involved in a variety of ways in production. On the one hand, their work contributed significantly to the prosperity of the society, but on the other hand, the nature of the labor was more often than not based on gender (Chafe 1977; Blau 1978; Marshall and Paulin 1987). The cultural norms of that time, as well as for following periods, dictated that first and foremost, women should be good wives and mothers; but, in fact, women were involved in the economy and often had difficult lives. They were involved in raising stock, weaving, gardening, and even running businesses. While some women took over for their deceased or disabled husbands, most of the unmarried and widowed women went on the market as hired domestic workers (Marshall and Paulin 1987).

Although there is some debate about the actual diversity of employment undertaken by women during this period, they made valuable contributions to the local economies, but were deprived of many of the political-legal, economic, and personal rights accorded men. They were attached to their families in a literal way, dependent on and subservient to their husbands (Matthaei 1982). A woman's identity was defined by her relationship to her husband and children. Moreover, wife beating was fairly common at this time. "The husband had the right to chastise his wife physically, and he had exclusive rights to any property she might have owned as a single woman, to her dower, and to any wages and property that might come to her while she was his wife. In short, like slave or servant women, married women whether rich or poor were legal non-entities" (Foner 1979, p. 11). Thus, the idealized life of the female as someone removed from the harsh realities of economic life was strongly inconsistent with the actual circumstances of her life.

Through their economic activities, women helped to contribute to the development of the first significant *industrial* organizations in the United States. The first textile factories, built around 1800 in Rhode Island and Massachusetts, recruited unmarried women from the farms of New England.

Despite the promises of a proper place to work, conditions at these early factories left much to be desired. Even though Lowell, Massachusetts, among the most famous early textile mills, was considered an advanced factory for its time, women worked an average of 13 hours a day, 73 hours a week, including 8 hours on Saturday (Dublin 1979). Working conditions were stifling. Windows in the plant were nailed shut and the air was periodically sprayed with water to keep it humid enough so that the cotton threads would not break. The vapors from whale-oil lamps and floating lint made the air in the shop quite oppressive (Eisler 1977). The Lowell Corporation paid women mill workers $1.85 to $3.00 per week, depending on abilities, from which $1.25 was deducted for board. Female workers were paid only half of what men were paid, even though they made up approximately 75 percent of the workers at Lowell (ibid.). Neighboring states exhibited similar sex differences in wages (Marshall and Paulin 1987).

Jobs in these early plants were also sex segregated. Men held all supervisory positions as well as jobs in the mill yard, watch force, and repair shop; women were restricted to particular jobs operating equipment such as the looms and dressing machines. The immediate reasons given for this segregation concerned differences in the skills developed and monopolized by men and women over the years, perceived physical strength and dangers associated with various jobs, and the general cultural values prescribing particular roles for men and women (Dublin 1979). Men also were concerned about the entrance of women into the labor market because they felt that it would have a depressing effect on their wages. They fought to keep women out of the craft unions that later developed. Women held strikes in the 1830s and 1840s to protest reductions in wages, speed-ups in work pace, and increases in working hours (ibid.).

In 1900, just over 20 percent (5,000,000) of all U.S. women 15 years of age or older were employed as breadwinners, but only 15 percent of native White females were, compared to 43 percent of Black females and 25 percent of White females with at least one foreign-born parent (U.S. Department of Commerce and Labor 1911, p. 262). Many young women

10–15 years of age also worked outside the home. In 1900, almost 6 percent of White, native-born females did so, compared to over 30 percent of non-White females 10–15 years old (ibid., pp. 256–259). From the end of the Civil War, the percentage of females in the work force had increased (U.S. Department of Labor 1947, p. 34).

At the turn of the twentieth century, women made up a disproportionate number of workers in several occupations. For example, in 1900, they constituted 80–90 percent of all boarding and lodging housekeepers, servants, waiters, and paper box makers and over 90 percent of all housekeepers and stewards, nurses and midwives, dress makers, milliners, and seamstresses. Men, on the other hand, dominated agricultural, common labor, bookkeeping, clerk/copyist, watch and shoemaker, printer, dye works, and photography positions (U.S. Census Office 1903, Plate 90). Perhaps surprisingly, women composed over 70 percent of the teachers and professors in colleges and over 50 percent of teachers of music, and men made up the majority of artists and teachers of art (ibid.). Black females, however, were more likely to be wage earners than either native or foreign-born White females.

Those who were "native White of native parents" dominated the higher status professions, with over 50 percent of college teachers and clergy and about 75 percent of lawyers and physicians coming from this group. In contrast, they made up less than 30 percent of those in servant, tailoring, laundering, and textile mill working positions (ibid., Plate 88).

PRESENT OCCUPATIONAL AND ECONOMIC CONDITIONS FOR WOMEN

The influx of women into the labor force has continued in recent years. Over the last several decades, the percentage of women in the civilian labor force has increased dramatically, while the percentage of men 16 years of age and older in the labor force has consistently declined. In 1970, for example, just over 43 percent of women were in the labor force, compared to 60 percent in 2001. In contrast, the involvement of men slid from 80 percent in 1990 to 74 percent in 2001 (U.S. Department of Labor, January 2002). The labor-force participation of women is expected to increase well into the twenty-first century. Women made up 42 percent of the full-time labor force in 2001, compared to only 29 percent in 1967.

Among the most important factors behind the increased participation of women in the labor force are the shift toward a service and information-based economy, increased possibilities for flexibility in work scheduling, lower marital stability, and a greater need for dual-earner families (Gerson 1998; Presser 1998). In most cases, the income brought into households by women is a necessity, and makes a major difference in the incomes of families.

Since 2000, wives, on average, have been responsible for over one-third of their families' incomes. In 2003, the median weekly earnings of wives were $588, significantly higher than those of women who were either single, divorced, separated, or widowed. Both the proportion that wives contribute and the proportion of wives who earn more than their working husbands have increased in the last few decades. In 2001, for example, almost one-quarter of all wives earned more than their husbands (U.S. Department of Labor, February 2004; U.S. Department of Labor, September 2004).

But the impact of wives' incomes on family economic status is not equally distributed across the income hierarchy. Rather, the contributions of wives are especially noticeable among lower-income families. Without their incomes, family incomes in the bottom 40 percent would suffer significantly. Wives' incomes make much less of an impact in families with the highest incomes. This suggests that were it not for wives' earnings in lower-income families, the degree of income inequality between families would be much higher than it is (Mishel, Bernstein, and Allegretto 2005).

The greater commitment of women to employment has resulted in a continuing struggle to balance home and work responsibilities. The related stresses are greater for women because of traditional gender-role expectations regarding women's responsibilities to families. Most employed married men and women agree that it is the woman who ends up being most responsible for cooking, cleaning, shopping, and child care. If a child is ill, it is the employed mother rather than the father who is most likely to miss work because of it (Galinsky and Bond 1996). Women's contribution to housework does decrease as they earn more relative to their spouses, and the housework done by husbands increases. But ironically, at the point where wives begin to earn more than their husbands, the latter also reduce their housework, suggesting an attempt by husbands to counter their income dependency on their wives by reinforcing traditional gender roles at home (Bittman et al. 2003; Evertsson and Nermo 2004).

Due to their traditional role as caregivers, "women in the middle" are often expected to take care of not only their children but also an elderly parent as well. And as the U.S. population ages, the need and responsibility for elder care is likely to intensify (Singleton 1998). Opting for contingency or part-time employment, having fewer children, and choosing a nonstandard work schedule are some of the ways women juggle home and work responsibilities (Gerson 1998; Presser 1998; Raabe 1998). More often than not, it is the mother who makes the compromise at work and who feels that she is not doing as well as she could in either family or work. Under these conditions, neither family life nor work is fully satisfying (Galinsky and Bond 1996). Until a better integration of home and work conditions is reached, stress will remain high for the majority of employed mothers.

Occupation and Sex and Gender

The gender inequities involved in balancing home and employment is just one area of the inequalities between employed men and women. Inequalities also extend to the nature of employment. To identify occupational inequalities between men and women in their work experiences, however, it is important to examine how they are distributed (1) across broad occupational categories, (2) among specific occupations, and (3) among specific occupations within specific organizational contexts. The resulting inequality varies in each of these cases.

Despite this rise in labor-force participation by women, occupational distinctions between the sexes remain within *broad occupational* groupings. The analysis of broad occupational categories suggests some recent decline in overall sex segregation, but most of it has been in middle-level white-collar rather than in blue-collar positions, and the major declines have been restricted to a few occupations (Beller 1984). Much of this trend has been due to the decline of some traditionally male occupations in the labor force, such as agricultural, unskilled, and self-employment occupations (Blau and Ferber 1986). Figure 5.1 presents current information on the distribution of men and women over broad occupational categories. In general, women tend to be concentrated in white-collar and service occupations, while men are more spread out among white-collar and blue-collar positions. But among women, there are also significant variations. While White women are more likely than Black women to be managers or professionals, Black and Hispanic women are much more likely to be found in service positions.

Although Table 5.1 indicates some gender differences in occupation, as we examine more *detailed occupational* categories, the nature and extent of occupational segregation become clearer. A decline in occupational segregation has occurred in broad occupational categories,

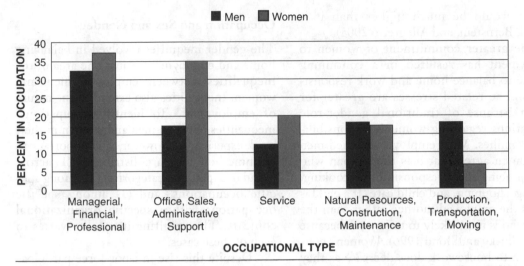

FIGURE 5.1   Occupational Distribution of Employed Civilians Aged 16 and Older, by Sex: 2004

Source: U.S. Department of Labor, *Employment & Earnings*, January 2005, Table 10, p. 208.

largely because of shifts in technology and organizational structures. But despite these general improvements, women still are found disproportionately in particular kinds of occupations. For example, women have increasingly moved into the ranks of managerial and professional occupations, but they tend to be concentrated among sex-typed occupations, such as teaching and nursing, and hold only a small percentage of positions as computer specialists, scientists, and engineers. Similarly, a man and a woman may both be in sales, but the woman is much more likely to be in clothing sales, while the man is involved in the selling of stocks and bonds. Craft occupations (carpentry, electrical contractors) are another group of occupations

TABLE 5.1   Sample of Occupations in Which Women Represented over 90 Percent or under 5 Percent of Employed Labor Force: 2004

OVER 90%	UNDER 5%
Kindergarten teachers	Logging workers
Teacher assistants	Brickmasons
Registered nurses	Carpenters
Occupational therapists	Construction equip. operators
Speech-language pathologists	Plumbers
Dental hygienists	Structural iron and steel workers
Licensed practical nurses	Highway maintenance workers
Restaurant hosts/hostesses	Heavy vehicle mechanics
Hairdressers/cosmetologists	Heating/air conditioning installers
Child care workers	Power-line installers/repairers
Bookkeeping/auditing clerks	Tool and die makers
Receptionists	Boiler operators
Secretaries	Truck drivers
Word processors/typists	Excavating machine operators
Maids and housekeepers	Roofers

Source: U.S. Department of Labor, *Employment & Earnings*, January 2005, Table 11, pp. 210–215.

in which women continue to be severely underrepresented (Herz and Wootten 1996).

An increasing number of women have moved into professions that promise high levels of rewards, such as the legal profession, but in those positions they still do not fare as well as men. A recent study of almost 800 lawyers found that even when background training, experience, seniority, preferences, and personal values are taken into account, female lawyers are less likely than men to become partners or practice in lucrative firms. If women choose to work fewer hours or leave a high-powered legal firm and, consequently, lower their chances of becoming highly-paid partners, it is at least in part due to the fact that difficulties in balancing work and family demands have a negative effect for women (but not for men) on the probability that they will become partners (Hull and Nelson 2000).

Becoming fully integrated into the military institution has been another struggle for women. Women have served in the military in typical feminine roles (e.g., cooks, nurses, laundresses) since the American Revolution, but it was not until 1901, when the Army Nurse Corps was developed, that they were given an established role. Currently, women compose about 14 percent of military personnel, but they are disproportionately found in health, administrative, and other support positions. Since 1993, women have gained access to naval and air combat positions (Youngman 2001). Within the military, the U.S. Coast Guard and Air Force are the most open to women, followed by the Navy. Central ground-combat positions in the Army and Marine Corps that are ladders for promotions are still closed to women. Part of the reason for women's continuing exclusion is the "warrior culture" nurtured within this quintessentially male institution. This culture reinforces traditional perceptions of male–female relationships with its view of men as more aggressive, protective, and stronger, and women as weaker, more fearful, and destructive of male bonding (ibid.).

Recently, however, there may have been a slight move away from the almost total domination of males in combat-related roles. The government has ordered that women be allowed to be combat pilots in the military. Although there have been some older veterans who have objected to this development, first responses suggest that the majority of current pilots appear to be supportive.

Despite small movement toward sex desegregation, many aspects of the occupational profiles are quite similar to those that existed in earlier years. In 1940, almost all of the servants, stenographers/secretaries, housekeepers, and nurses were women, and they comprised over half of the teachers (not elsewhere classified), apparel and accessories operators, waitresses, and bookkeepers. As far back as 1870, women dominated in servant, clothing, certain kinds of teaching, and nursing occupations (cf. U.S. Department of Labor 1947, p. 52).

Table 5.1 suggests that this sex-typing has continued. As one glances over the lists, it is easy to see that the positions in which women dominate tend to be those that demand "feminine" or "motherly" characteristics. Being able to work directly with people and to take care of others are qualities that are required in these occupations. In contrast, the list of positions that contains virtually all men are characterized by a different set of qualities; they are manual or require certain physical attributes, often contain an element of danger, involve work with a product rather than a person, and demand technical or scientific skill. In essence, these occupations are distinguished by their "feminine" or "masculine" character.

Many of the occupations dominated by women also do not have the protections afforded other positions. For example, nannies and maids often suffer long hours, low pay, few legal protections, and physical harassment. "Nannies are among the most exploited workers in the country. There are almost no legal protections for this relatively new, mostly female class of workers that is more than 350,000 strong. Nor are there even social pressures to keep employers from subjecting nannies to abuses—from low wages and long work weeks to sexual harassment and physical violence." They are a "dirty little secret in middle- and upper-middle-class America" (Lipman 1993, p. A1). Said one nanny of the family for which she worked, "Their cats were treated better than I was." Another confessed, "I was like a slave" (ibid.). Often these nannies are recent immigrants and are left dependent on their employers for fair treatment. Maids often find themselves in a similar position of exploitation and dependence. Mary Romero, a sociologist who has served as a maid, suggests reforms involving higher wages, Social Security benefits, unionization, and, above all, the elimination of the idea that household work should be done primarily by women (Romero 1992).

When we move on to examine specific occupations *within specific organizational contexts* in the private economy, occupational segregation again becomes magnified. Not only are women spread among fewer occupations than men, but within the same occupation, they are employed in different kinds of organizations and economic sectors, tend to have less authority in the same occupation and have different job titles, and make less money in their jobs than men do. Just breaking into the authority hierarchy, especially at the lower ranks of management, appears to be very difficult for women regardless of their personal qualifications, resulting in significant gender differences in authority among employees (Baxter and Wright 2000).

Occupations that draw applicants from across the country and are dominated by women tend to have less work authority than other occupations. The gender of the person most often doing the work negatively affects how much authority is associated with the position (Huffman and Cohen 2004b). The incumbents of most of the female-dominated positions in Table 5.1, for example, are accountable to someone else.

Moreover, not only is it difficult for women to obtain positions of authority, which are usually dominated by men, but if they do get such a position, a variety of gender-related pressures make it hard for them to retain or want to stay in the position. The result is that women then often move on to other less-prestigious, less-authoritative, and consequently, lower-earning positions in smaller firms. A result is continued sex segregation in occupations. Roth's recent study of women in securities positions on Wall Street bears out the problems that they face in a male-dominated profession. These women were much more likely than men to leave their positions because of family pressures or outright discrimination:

> Around here, at least, if you're liked, you don't have to be star performer to get ahead as a guy, whereas women, I think that category doesn't exist. It doesn't matter whether they like you or not, they base it more on your performance. But for guys, it can be a very mediocre white male, but because he's liked and he's congenial, then he gets through the ranks. (Roth 2004a, p. 220)

Another comments:

> They were downright hostile, to the point where I would do a lot of the recruiting and interviewing for our group, and I was told things like, 'Don't bring a woman, I wouldn't hire a woman into this group.' (ibid., p. 219)

In relation to the last quote, Roth also found that the belief that securities clients (who are primarily male) prefer male employees to work with further strengthened sex segregation in these occupations (Roth 2004b).

When women leave positions, they often end up in smaller firms. In general, women are more likely to be found in the *peripheral* than in the *core* sector of the economy. The peripheral sector is largely made up of small, less stable, local, nonunionized organizations lacking a clear career ladder, while the core consists of the larger, stable, multimarket, unionized organizations with career systems. These differences between men and women exist even when experience, education, and other factors are taken into account (Coverdill 1988). Factors that are characteristic of each of these sectors, moreover, appear to contribute to differences in unemployment rates and earnings levels between the sexes (Bibb and Form 1977; Beck, Horan, and Tolbert 1980; Coverdill 1988). Given the organizations in which they tend to find jobs, it should not be surprising that women are more likely than men to be in occupations with short career ladders and, therefore, have comparatively flat career trajectories.

Women have been underrepresented in higher posts even in those institutions that

Historically, women have had a difficult time entering into traditionally male occupations that are unionized and pay good wages. In 2002, only 2–3 percent of workers in the construction trades were women.
Photo © Corbis.

have publicly indicated a concern for equality and fairness. In higher education, for example, women are more likely than men to be employed at less-prestigious institutions and at nonresearch universities. They are less likely to be found at the full-professor level or to be among the tenured faculty. Even when men and women are equally productive, they are likely to be in different ranks (Long and Fox 1995). Women are also much less likely to be found in leadership positions of unions. Even in occupational areas where they dominate (e.g., elementary education and social work), they are often not in the decision-making positions of principals or department heads. And, as Kanter's research in corporations demonstrates, when women are put in unusual positions of authority, they are watched closely and under great pressure to perform because they are seen as "tokens" (1977b).

Despite all the difficulties discussed above, or perhaps in part because of them, the number of businesses owned by women has increased significantly since the 1970s and so have their revenues. In 2003, Omega World Travel, which was the top-ranked woman-owned business, had revenues of $1 billion, while each of the remaining 499 of the top 500 had sales of at least $5 million (DiversityBusiness 2005).

Accounting for Occupational Sex Segregation. What are the reasons behind the sex segregation in the occupations just discussed? Some have suggested that differences in education and skills, experience, and career aspirations may account for women moving into particular kinds of jobs, but recent evidence suggests that individual factors such as these do not fully account for differences in occupations and earnings between the sexes (e.g., Blau 1984; England et al. 1988). Gender-role socialization appears to have affected choice of occupation, but differences based on such socialization have declined in recent years. Younger women now plan for more continuous lifetime employment (England and Farkas 1986). Those who argue that gender-role socialization is an important source of sex segregation also overestimate the incompatibility of home and employment responsibilities.

One should keep in mind that the free choice of an occupation takes place within a gendered structure with particular characteristics. In a broad sense, employment is limited by shifts in the types of jobs on the market and by the supply of and demand for qualified workers. This context also includes cultural values into which both employers and employees have been socialized and a historical record, both of which encourage the employment of men and women into certain kinds of occupations. As Risman argues, "[g]ender itself must be considered a structural property of society. It is not manifested just in our personalities, our cultural rules, or other institutions. Gender is deeply embedded as a basis for stratification, differentiating opportunities, and constraints" (Risman 2005, pp. 296–297). Consequently, the choices women make about jobs and their work at home are conditioned by broader labor-market discrimination in the first place. This means that labor-market opportunities affect the role and amount of time spent in home labor by men and women. If women spend more time in the home than men because of fewer opportunities open to them in the market, it seems questionable, at best, to argue that it is their free choice alone that determines the amount of time spent in accumulating experience and education which in turn affects their occupational positions (Blau 1984, pp. 124–125).

The following are among the more prominent barriers that have prevented women from obtaining more well-paying occupations:

1. Less access to training and apprenticeship programs
2. Appointment to perceived gender-related tasks ("light" work)
3. Nonbureaucratized, patrimonial relationships with males in authority positions
4. Less access to information about job openings
5. Less fully developed job and contact network
6. Seniority systems that limit women
7. Protective laws inhibiting women from pursuing certain positions and restricting the number of hours and time of day they could work
8. Pressure on women to take on the bulk of family obligations
9. Tendency for co-workers or clients to prefer employees of matching sex
10. Stereotyping, discrimination, and the consequent crowding of women into certain kinds of positions
11. Lack of internal mobility ladder for many so-called female occupations within organizations (i.e., dead-end or flat-career jobs) (cf. Roos and Reskin 1984)
12. Prevalence of informal recruitment practices (Reskin and McBrier 2000).

Some factors do appear, however, to contribute to a decline in occupational sex segregation. Among these are the development of new forms of work resulting from broad economic changes and white-collar service employment of an unspecialized nature. On the other hand, it has been suggested that the large size and increased specialization in the core sector, along with the presence of a union and manual work, appear to have fostered greater sex segregation (Baron and Bielby 1984). Greater formalization—that is, increased presence of written rules, tasks, procedures, and so on—has been linked to sex segregation, but also to the greater hiring of women. Research indicates that when organizations use formal, standardized procedures when recruiting rather than an informal network and word-of-mouth, they hire a greater proportion of women, including more for managerial positions (Szafran 1982; Reskin and McBrier 2000).

NUTSHELL 5.1 _____

Suggestions for Hiring Women during World War II

The list below appeared in *Transportation Magazine* in 1943. The magazine no longer exists, but some of these ideas are still around. The suggestions for hiring reflect many of the attitudes, personality traits, and imagined behaviors present in popular stereotypes about women in 1943. The list demonstrates some of the biases exercised against women at the time. The guide recommended the following when hiring women:

1. Pick young married women. They usually have more of a sense of responsibilities than their unmarried sisters, they're less likely to be flirtatious, they need the work or they wouldn't be doing it, they still have the pep and interest to work hard and to deal with the public efficiently.

2. When you have to use older women, try to get ones who have worked outside the home at some time in their lives. Older women who have never contacted the public have a hard time adapting themselves and are inclined to be cantankerous and fussy. It's always well to impress upon older women the importance of friendliness and courtesy.

3. General experience indicates that 'husky' girls—those who are just a little on the heavy side—are more even tempered and efficient than their underweight sisters.

4. Retain a physician to give each woman you hire a special physical examination—one covering female conditions. This step not only protects the property against the possibilities of lawsuit, but reveals whether the employee-to-be has any female weaknesses, which would make her mentally or physically unfit for the job.

5. Stress at the outset the importance of time, the fact that a minute or two lost here and

there makes serious inroads on schedules. Until this point is gotten across, service is likely to be slowed up.

6. Give the female employee a definite day-long schedule of duties so that they'll keep busy without bothering the management for instructions every few minutes. Numerous properties say that women make excellent workers when they have their jobs cut out for them, but that they lack initiative in finding work themselves.

7. Whenever possible, let the inside employee change from one job to another at some time during the day. Women are inclined to be less nervous and happier with change.

8. Give every girl an adequate number of rest periods during the day. You have to make some allowances for feminine psychology. A girl has more confidence and is more efficient if she can keep her hair tidied, apply fresh lipstick, and wash her hands several times a day.

9. Be tactful when issuing instructions or in making criticism. Women are often sensitive; they can't shrug off harsh words the way men do. Never ridicule a woman—it breaks her spirit and cuts off her efficiency.

10. Be reasonably considerate about using strong language among women. Even though a girl's husband or father may swear vociferously, she'll grow to dislike a place of business where she hears too much of this.

11. Get enough size variety in operator's uniforms so that each girl can have a proper fit. This point can't be stressed too much in keeping women happy.

What do these guidelines say about the image of women. Which aspects are still operative today?

Source: *Transportation Magazine*, July 1943. List located on the Internet at: www.tiac.net/~cri/2000/women1943.html.

Earnings and Sex

As in occupational distribution, there are also significant earnings differences between men and women. Overall, between 1979 and 2003, it was the earnings of those in the top 5 percent among both men and women that grew at the fastest rate, leaving those below further behind them (Mishel, Bernstein, and Allegretto 2005). *Weekly* earnings, however, continue to differ between men and women, with median earnings for full-time working women in 2004 being about 80 percent those of men ($573 vs. $713). The differences exist across all major occupational groups (see Table 5.2). In 1979, women earned only 63 percent as much as men. Since 2000, wages among women have grown faster than those among men. The trends suggest a decline in the gender wage gap in recent years, a gap reduction fueled by a combination of declines in men's wages and slight rises in women's median wages (ibid.).

The gender differences in wages vary by race. Increases in earnings among White women have been much higher in the last 20 years than those for minority women. Still the differences between men and women are greater among Whites than among either Blacks or Hispanics. In the latter groups, women earn about 88 percent of what men earn, compared to 79 percent among Whites (U.S. Department of Labor, September 2004).

The information given above is for *weekly* earnings. But we must keep in mind that weekly earnings are the result of *both* the number of hours worked and hourly wage rate. *Hourly* wage rate is often considered a more accurate gauge of earnings because it discounts the role played by hours worked, which is not the case when using weekly earnings as a measure. Just as in weekly earnings, however, women make lower hourly wages than men at every earnings and educational level. In 2003, median hourly wages for women were $10.08 versus $11.89 for men. Even among those in the top 5 percent, women's hourly wages were still only 77 percent those of men in 2003. Moreover, in 2003, a significantly larger percentage of women than men earned hourly wages that did not put their families above the poverty level (29% vs. 20%) (U.S. Department of Labor, September 2004; Mishel, Bernstein, and Allegretto 2005).

How are differences in wages between men and women to be explained? Differences in human capital (experience, skills) may continue to account partly for the earnings gap. But differences in work effort or work interruptions,

TABLE 5.2   Median Weekly Earnings of Full-Time Workers Age 16 and Older, by Occupational Category and Sex, Annual Averages: 2004

OCCUPATIONAL CATEGORY	MEDIAN EARNINGS		RATIO OF WOMEN'S TO MEN'S EARNINGS
	Men	Women	
Managerial and prof.	$1,098	$780	0.71
Office, sales, adm. support	669	512	0.77
Service occupations	476	374	0.79
Natural resources, construction and maintenance	626	453	0.72
Production, transportation, moving	578	406	0.70
Median earnings for all workers	713	573	0.80

Source: U.S. Department of Labor, *Employment and Earnings*, January 2005, Table 39, pp. 250–254.

or attachment to labor force, which can take one away from the job, are not major variables in explaining sex earnings differences (Bielby and Bielby 1988). Even census data indicate clearly that differences in earnings persist even when work interruptions are taken into account. Women earn less than men even when their tenure on the current job is the same (U.S. Bureau of the Census, August 1987, Tables D and F). In sum, differences in work interruptions and work effort do not appear to be major factors in accounting for the earnings differential between men and women. However, "interruptions" can be of many kinds. A study conducted recently in Indiana suggests that domestic work, especially childcare, negatively affects women's earnings significantly more so than men's. This is especially the case for women who are in non-working-class jobs. The earnings of non-working-class men, however, benefit when their wives work only part-time as opposed to full-time (Shirley and Wallace 2004). Women appear to experience domestic and work pressures that men do not, and their earnings suffer as a result.

One structural factor that is clearly important is the distribution among and concentration of men and women in occupational categories. Occupations that are culturally defined as appropriate for women and in which there is a high proportion of women tend to have lower earnings attached to them regardless of who occupies them. Jobs of comparable worth do not have equivalent earnings because of the sex compositions (Treiman, Hartmann, and Roos 1984; England and Farkas 1986). Earnings tend to be lower in those jobs in which sexes are most segregated (Cohen and Huffman 2003; Cotter, Hermsen, and Vanneman 2003). For example, faculty in nursing, library science, and social work positions, all of which contain a high percentage of women, have significantly lower salaries than faculty in male-dominated departments such as engineering, physics, and dentistry (Bellas 1994).

Within occupational categories, women are less likely to be in positions of authority and to be given distinct kinds of tasks—factors that also influence earnings (Wright and Perrone 1977; Parcel and Mueller 1983; Blau 1984). A recent study of U.S. companies suggested that most of the differences in compensation that existed between male and female executives were due to women not only being in smaller firms, but also to the fact that they were less likely than high-ranking male executives to be heads of their companies (Bertrand and Hallock 2001). In their study of variations in power at work, Elliott and Smith (2004) conclude that "there are strong findings to indicate that most superiors, regardless of their race and sex, tend to fill power positions they oversee with ascriptively similar others, . . . [and] because there are more white men at higher levels of workplace power than members of other groups, white men have greater opportunities to exercise this self-similar preference and, in the process reproduce their advantage over successive generations of employees" (2004, p. 384).

Another factor in accounting for the earnings gap, the crowding of women into specific kinds of jobs, of course, increases the supply of women and thereby reduces the wages associated with those occupations and jobs (Bergmann 1974). Evidence also suggests that female-dominant jobs yield lower earnings, even when men are in those jobs. "Net of human capital, skill demands, and working conditions, those who work in occupations with more females earn less" (U.S. Bureau of the Census, August 1987; England et al. 1988). These jobs frequently have shorter career ladders, which may further affect long-range earnings. Consequently, in addition to differences in characteristics between individuals, occupational, job, and organizational factors play significant roles in explaining earnings discrepancies.

Related to the occupational clustering of women and relegation to positions of lower authority are more subtle stereotypical beliefs about women that also lower their earnings.

These include the perception that a woman's earnings are not as important to a family as those of a man, and that she is more committed to her family than to her job. Also involved is "that women sell themselves cheap—and companies know it. . . . Women tend to be more reluctant than men to talk money" (Krotz 1999, p. 47). This behavior, in turn, may be related to their socialization into the traditional feminine gender role.

Finally, a smaller percentage of employed women than employed men belong to unions, and union members consistently have had higher median earnings than nonunion workers. In 2003, the average hourly earnings of union workers was almost 32 percent higher than those of nonunion workers (Mishel, Bernstein, and Allegretto 2005). Part of the reason for women's lower union membership rates relates to their lower percentage in occupations such as protective service and precision craft, where a significant proportion of employees are union members.

While the gender gap in pay remains, there has been a decline in its size in recent years. Two of the immediate factors that have increased annual earnings among women in working-class occupations have been an increase in the number of wives who work and an increase in the number of hours worked by women. In contrast to women, however, the slower wage growth for men in working-class occupations since 2000 has been instigated in part by declines in the economic power of unions along with declines in and movement abroad of manufacturing and other jobs. Among women in higher positions, it has been a rise in their real hourly wages relative to men that explains most of their increases since 1979 (ibid.).

MICROINEQUITIES IN THE TREATMENT OF WOMEN

Beyond the occupational and earnings differentials just discussed, there are other forms of inequalities experienced by women. Sexual harassment on the job is one of the areas that demonstrates this inequitable treatment. While forms of inequity relating to occupation and earnings have been in the public eye for years, microinequities between the genders permeate the everyday world that we take for granted. "*Microinequities* refer collectively to ways in which individuals are either *singled out*, or *overlooked, ignored,* or *otherwise discounted* on the basis of unchangeable characteristics such as sex, race, or age" (Sandler 1986, p. 3). These microinequities generally take the form of different kinds of language, treatment, or behavior exhibited toward women on a regular basis. This brief section merely points to some inequities that appear in everyday language, communication, the media, and education.

As suggested, these inequities are often deeply rooted and seemingly unconscious. Growing up, we seldom sift through the reasons why we think the way we do. For example, young boys rarely think about the everyday difficulties of being a woman:

> It was not my fate to become a woman, so it was easier for me to see the graces. I didn't see, then, what a prison a house could be, since houses seemed to me brighter, handsomer places than any factory. I did not realize—because such things were never spoken of—how often women suffered from men's bullying. Even then I could see how exhausting it was for a mother to cater all day to the needs of young children. But if I had been asked, as a boy, to choose between tending a baby and tending a machine, I think I would have chosen the baby. . . . So I was baffled when the women at college accused me and my sex of having cornered the world's pleasures. (ibid., p. 68)

Even educated adults often find it difficult to identify with the deep unseen inequities. Reflecting on her work in Women's Studies, Peggy McIntosh observed that she had "met very few men who are truly distressed about systemic, unearned male advantage and conferred dominance. . . . Many men likewise think that Women's Studies do not bear on their own existences because they are not female; they do not see themselves as having gendered identities" (McIntosh 1988, p. 15). All these experiences and events give evidence to our lack of conscious recognition of many everyday inequities.

Microinequities of a subtle sort permeate our culture. In language, the generic term *man*, for example, has historically been meant to include both men and women. Yet when most people think visually of that term, they think of men rather than women. In other words, this term does not suggest all of humanity to most individuals, but rather men in particular (Martyna 1978; Richardson 1987). Similarly, the pronoun *he* when used in a generic sense is supposed to represent both males and females; yet it is often attached to various kinds of occupations in a way that perpetuates gender-typed career ambitions and expectations (Richardson 1987). For example, the pronoun *she* is often used when speaking of occupations in which a majority of persons are women. Nurses, elementary school teachers, and the like are almost always referred to as *she*, whereas mechanics, doctors, and mathematicians are usually spoken of in terms of *he*. Our own names, which are part of our identity, reflect gender inequities. Traditionally, women who marry have been expected to give up their surnames and take on that of their new husbands. Women who are named after their fathers frequently have names that are diminutive versions of their father's first names—for example, Georgina (after George), Paulette (after Paul), and so on. These names "are copies, not originals, and like so many other words applied to women, they can be diminishing" (Miller and Swift 1993, p. 79).

Even the styles of speaking and communication are often different between the genders, reflecting their social positions in society. For example, women's language tends to involve a greater use of qualifiers and to be less direct and forceful than men's language (Parlee 1979). Men also talk more than women, interrupt

women more often than they do other men, and are more likely to initiate conversation on a topic that is then carried on by others (Bernard 1972; Zimmerman and West 1975; Eakins and Eakins 1978; Parlee 1979). People in an audience are also more likely to respond in depth to comments made by a man than by a woman, and to be more attentive to a speech by a male (Sandler 1986). It has been suggested that many of these differences are due to inequities in power rather than to the sex of the communicators. Research among undergraduates indicates that when individuals with different levels of formal authority communicate, subordinates are more supportive, cooperative, and speak less than leaders, regardless of the sex involved (Johnson 1994).

The images of women in the popular media similarly mirror the stereotypes we have of them (Andersen 1993). In music videos and commercials, women are most often displayed as sexual objects expected to be pleasing to the eye and satisfying to the opposite sex. Almost every year, someone does a survey on which colleges have the most beautiful women. The differences among various countries in the physical beauty of their women have also been commented upon, with the sex appeal of women in democratic, wealthy nations being greater than that of women in totalitarian, poorer countries ("Girl Watching" 1992).

In addition to how they are expected to appear physically, stereotypes of women's psyches are further perpetuated in the media. Muriel Cantor's survey of popular fiction indicated that despite women's increased movement into the economy and other changes, the dominant view of women remains. These images include the beliefs that (1) women's sexual relationships are the most important element of their lives, (2) women are subordinate to men whose work and choices are more important than theirs, and (3) women need romantic relationships to be happy and fulfilled (Cantor 1987). In their study of the top 100 U.S. films in 2002, Lauzen and Dozier also found gender stereotypes to be alive and well. Not only were men much more likely to be the leading characters in the films, they were also more likely to be depicted in positions of leadership and power (2005).

A recent Gallup poll revealed that both men and women in the United States continue to associate particular characteristics with women rather than men. Consistent with media images, women are much more likely than men to be viewed as emotional, affectionate, talkative, patient, and creative (Newport 2001). As in our earlier history, stereotypes and images have not kept pace with the reality of changes in women's social and economic lives. What is important about these media images of women's appropriate physical and psychological traits is that they help to lock women into traditional roles and reinforce their subservient position in society.

Within schools, sex and gender biases remain significant. In primary and secondary schools, females are more likely than males to be ignored by their teachers and get less attention and encouragement in math and science. Textbooks used are rarely authored by women. "Students sit in classrooms that, day in, day out, deliver the message that women's lives count for less than men's" (cited in Chira 1992, p. A8). The contents of elementary-school textbooks continue to portray men as competitive and aggressive while portraying women as characteristically warm, emotional, and nonconfrontational (Evans and Davies 2000). All of these treatments are part of the unofficial hidden curriculum of what schools teach their students.

Reports of sexual harassment in schools have also increased (Chira 1992, p. A8). An incident of the so-called Spur Posse in a California school illustrates the extent to which systematic harassment can go. A group of male high school athletes formed the group, in which status was measured by how many girls they could get into bed. Some "scored" into the 60s, and involved girls ranging from 10 to 16 years of age. Some of the parents of the boys were not particularly concerned; one father even bragged about the virility of his sons ("Mixed Messages" 1993).

Inequity problems can even be found in colleges and universities, and the comparatively small numbers of women in top positions increase the chances of their being treated differently from men. A review survey by the Project on the Status and Education of Women reported that women are provided with fewer resources and less desirable offices, are not taken as seriously as male colleagues by students or male faculty, are considered less for their scholarly accomplishments than for their feminine characteristics, and are subject to a variety of forms of sexual harassment (Sandler 1986).

Sociologist Theda Skocpol also reflected on the significance of gender for her career. She noted that in 1984 she "was offered the Harvard tenured professorship that I am convinced would have been mine in 1981 if I had been 'Theodore' rather than 'Theda'" (Skocpol 1988, p. 155). She went on to comment that, in general, "ambitious women are still not accepted at the top and, no matter what their achievements, they still have to endure the worst personal insults and struggle without end against virtually insuperable obstacles to their having real power" (p. 156).

Traditionally appropriate gender roles are further reinforced by many college textbooks. A recent study of texts from several decades in the areas of human sexuality and marriage and the family concluded that traditional photographs of women's roles are dominant in them. Although the proportion of such images was higher in the 1970s, a large majority of images were still traditional in texts of the 1990s. This is especially disturbing because there was an increase in the number of photographs with women at their center (Low and Sherrard 1999).

These examples suggest the variety of problems that groups of lower status face in U.S. society. Benokraitis and Feagin (1986) summarized the kinds of subtle sex discrimination that exist. Some are intentional and others are not, but generally they occur on an informal basis. Following are among the types they cited:

- Chivalry, which treats women in an overly protective manner and thereby encourages the image of them as nonadults
- Encouraging women to be ambitious and active but then creating blockages that make it difficult for them to perform effectively
- Forms of humor and suggestion, which on the surface may appear innocuous but are demeaning and embarrassing
- Treating women as objects—that is, as sex symbols or as status objects
- Devaluating the talents and abilities of women and focusing on stereotypical or superficial characteristics to honor them
- Overloading or overburdening women in their tasks or jobs under the guise of allowing them full participation or equality with men
- "Benevolent exploitation" in which women are exploited in an often unnoticed manner—that is, showcasing token women, using their talents and then not giving them appropriate credit
- Portraying dominant males as considerate and concerned with the welfare of women
- Socially and physically isolating women in professional settings.

This list should serve as a reminder that sex discrimination can occur in several forms, not only in the formal institutional areas of occupation and earnings. The list also parallels the kinds of subtle discrimination that African Americans have experienced historically under paternalistic treatment of them as simple-minded children and tokens of their group.

GENERAL THEORIES OF SEX AND GENDER INEQUALITY

In addition to specific sources of gender inequality mentioned earlier, several types of general theories of sex inequality (i.e., inequality between males and females) have also been suggested. Because of the broad range of theories available, our discussion will be limited to theories that are more sociological or anthropological in nature. That is, the focus will be on explanations that emphasize the importance of social structure, ecology, or cultural contexts rather than biological or psychological elements. Biological explanations of sex inequality that suggest that basic genetic, hormonal, or physical differences determine sex inequality are inadequate for several reasons. Although there are some hormonal and physical differences between the sexes, they do not mandate that men will dominate women. These differences and any behaviors associated with them still have to be culturally and socially interpreted (i.e., gendered). For example, aggressiveness is related to domination only if it is interpreted in a particular way. In some societies, such behavior may be not only tolerated but also admired; in others, it may be considered deviant and those who engage in it may be assigned low status (Coontz and Henderson 1986).

Even in limiting this discussion to cultural and social explanations of sex inequality, only samples of each type of theory can be presented. Moreover, in some cases, such as in theories involving patriarchy and capitalism in their explanations, you should be aware that there are differences among specific theorists about details. The goal here is to present a general picture of the kinds of explanations that exist to account for sex inequality.

Largely for the sake of convenience, the theories on sex inequality are divided into four general categories: (1) cultural, (2) social-structural, (3) ecological, and (4) capitalist/patriarchal. This set of categories does not, of course, exhaust all the types of theories of sex inequality that have been developed, nor are they mutually exclusive. The categories in the list overlap to some degree, but they also serve to separate theories whose foci and thrusts differ from each other. One other point should be made. The theories discussed are principally concerned with addressing the *origins* rather than the *maintenance* of sex and race inequality. Theories involving socialization and the role of education in inequality, on the other hand, shed light on the maintenance of such inequality across generations.

Cultural Values, Sex, and Gender Inequality

When we speak of a person's *sex*, we ordinarily are referring to the biological status of being female or male. However, cultures assign different meanings to the definitions of *male* and *female*. To differentiate it from the term *sex*, the term *gender* frequently is used to denote the definitions and assignments that different groups and cultures associate with the sexes. In other words, *gender* is a "cultural construct" (Caplan 1987; see also Ortner and Whitehead 1981).

Cultures expect different attitudes and behaviors from members of each sex, but those expectations vary among cultures. In some cultures, what we consider so-called masculine behavior is expected of women, and in some cultures, men engage in what we would consider to be so-called feminine (i.e., effeminate in the U.S. value system) behavior. All this is to say that *sex* is a term used to describe a biological constant and *gender* is a term used to describe socially and culturally approved expectations, and these vary between societies. For example, we might argue that being a bouncer at a night club is quintessentially a male role; however, among the Dahomeyan of Africa, rulers used women as bodyguards because they considered women to be excellent fighters (Light, Keller, and Calhoun 1989). Among the Tchambuli of New Guinea, women were the dominant figures, the principal breadwinners, wore no jewelry, and kept their heads shaved. Margaret Mead's research uncovered some societies where both sexes were expected to be nurturant and gentle, and others where

men and women were expected to be aggressive and arrogant (Mead 1963).

Thus, although women are members of the same sex and are therefore biologically the same across cultures, their gender roles may be markedly different and differentially ranked among those same cultures. One of the pitfalls of equating sex with gender has been to define the gender roles given to each sex as being natural, that by their nature men and women perform particular roles and have particular characteristics. The old phrase "men are men and women are women" captures this belief. In this view, there is a consistency between sex and gender that cannot or should not be changed. For example, in U.S. culture, "male homosexuality threatens male solidarity and superordination because some men take on what are thought of as female characteristics. Lesbianism is likewise seen as threatening to male superiority because the women who engage in it appear not to need men." We assume that there needs to be a "correct fit between sex, gender, and sexuality" (Caplan 1987, p. 2).

In eighteenth- and nineteenth-century Europe, it was common to associate women with nature. Women's nature was thought to reflect natural laws and their behavior to reflect a basic emotionalism and passion. Ortner (1974) has argued that because of women's reproductive role, they have been and still are viewed as being closer to nature than men, who, "lacking natural creative functions, must . . . assert [their] creativity externally, 'artificially,' through the medium of technology and symbols. In doing so [the man creates] relatively lasting, eternal, transcending objects, while the woman creates only perishables—human beings" (p. 75). Women are also seen as mediating between nature and culture, and men are seen as divorced from nature. Since nature is generally interpreted as being lower than culture and subject to the constraints of culture, Ortner argued, men are accorded more prestige and women less.

While realizing that not all cultures neatly divide the sexes in terms of nature versus culture, Ortner said that most of the differences between the sexes are seen in dichotomous terms, nature/culture being one of them. Others of a similar kind involve the notion that women's activities and values are circumscribed by the domestic sphere or self-interests, whereas men's roles are in the public domain or for the social good. Since the public or social sphere of life encompasses the narrowly focused domestic sphere, higher value is attached to it (Ortner and Whitehead 1981, pp. 7–8).

The proposals that these dichotomies are central to the explanation of sex inequality have been severely criticized in recent years. Why are women necessarily seen as more natural than men when the procreative role of men and many of their other activities (eating, sleeping, etc.) are just as natural as those of women? Moreover, many of the forms taken by natural behaviors surrounding reproduction are limited by cultural constraints and are not, therefore, purely natural (MacCormack 1980).

While incorporating the element of cultural beliefs into her theory, Ortner appeared to ignore the structural constraints placed on behavior by the social and natural context of the society (Schlegel 1977). Not all cultures devalue what is natural, and the meaning of "natural" changes historically rather than remaining timeless and static as it appeared in Ortner's view (Coontz and Henderson 1986; Yanagisako and Collier 1987). Perhaps the most serious deficiency of the nature/culture dichotomy is that it simplifies the complex reality of diverse cultures. Research indicates that even where such a dichotomy can be derived, nature and culture may be defined in a manner different from Western society, or males may be viewed as being closer to nature than females, or the dichotomy may not be associated with the sexes at all (Gillison 1980; Harris 1980; Strathern 1980).

The importance of Ortner's work is that it called attention to the significance of symbols and cultural constructs in understanding how individuals interpret the sexes and the relations between them. What distinguishes most of the theories discussed next from Ortner's view is that they emphasize the centrality of social structure in the process of inequality development between the sexes. Sex inequality is viewed as an outcome of particular kinds of social or economic structures, and not, therefore, historically universal.

Social-Structural Explanations

Several of the most significant social-structural theories highlight the importance of women's work activities and kinship structure in generating inequality between the sexes (e.g., Blumberg 1978, 1984; Chafetz 1988). They are usually cross-cultural in nature in that they propose to explain the degree of sex inequality in societies that are radically different in technology, size, culture, and so forth. Janet Saltzman Chafetz's explanation is a good example of a social-structural theory.

Chafetz's Theory of Sex Stratification. Chafetz argued that there has never been a situation in which women dominated men on a systematic and long-term basis, so that societies vary "from near equality to radical inequality favoring males" (Chafetz 1988, p. 51). She has tried to explain the "degree of sex stratification" in a given society—that is, "the extent to which societal members are unequal in their access to the scarce values of their society" (Chafetz 1984, p. 4). These values include material goods and services, prestigious roles, political power, interpersonal decision-making, freedom from unwanted constraints, and educational opportunities. In other words, Chafetz views stratification as multidimensional in nature. Moreover, some of these dimensions may vary independently of each other, causing women's positions to be high on some and lower on others.

Three of the factors most directly related to sex stratification, according to Chafetz, are (1) the nature of the work organization, (2) the type of kinship structure, and (3) the degrees of ideological and stereotyping support for sex inequality in the society. Of these, the most important is the work organization, which includes a number of specific elements (see Figure 5.2). Sex inequality will be high in a society when the following circumstances exist: (1) women do not contribute significantly to highly valued tasks, (2) women are easily replaced, (3) occupational tasks are sex-typed, (4) attention span is an important variable in a valued task, and (5) women do not have ownership and control over the means and products of their production.

The work organization itself is affected by several other independent variables, most of which are directly related to the level and type of technology in the society. Specifically, the more the time women have to spend on child-rearing activities, the greater the distance between workplace and home, the more the need for physical strength and/or mobility, and the less the emphasis that is placed on subsistence rather than surplus production for exchange, the less women can be meaningfully involved in valued work tasks and, conse-quently, the higher the degree of sex stratification will be.

In addition to work organization factors, kinship structure also has an impact. When (1) married women live with or in the same places as their husbands' families (patrilocal), (2) a society traces lineage through the male line (patrilineal), and (3) there is a domestic division of labor based on sex, then inequality between the sexes will be high.

Finally, Chafetz included both the *degree of ideological/religious support* for sex stratification and the degree of *gender stereotyping* as factors that affect the acceptance of inequality between the sexes. For example, some societies may support the notion that "women's place is in the home" or that a wife must be submissive to her husband, while other societies may emphasize above all the belief in the worth and equality of all individuals as human beings. In addition, cultures usually contain stereotypes of male and female characteristics and appropriate behavior for each sex. According to Chafetz, these factors are more important for sustaining and justifying inequality than they are for generating it.

There have been conflicting reactions to Chafetz's argument. In a discussion of his view of how sociological theory should be struc-tured, Gerhard Lenski praised Chafetz's model for being presented in a diagrammatic and essentially propositional form. Lenski believed that this makes the theory clearer and more amenable to empirical testing. In sharp con-trast to the praise of Lenski, Pierre van den Berghe was quite critical of Chafetz's formalis-tic approach to theory, which appears to be becoming more dominant in the field. In assessing her theory, he bluntly stated that "an exercise in loosely linking a grab bag of 'vari-ables' does not constitute anything that a real scientist would recognize as a theory" (1985, p. 1350). However, this is an extreme reaction to what is a useful predictive model. It brings together variables that have been cited as important by others into a somewhat coherent

(1)   Nature of Work Organization
(sex division of labor; nature of work contribution; labor substitu-tion; ownership/control of means of production)

(2)   Kinship Structure
(descent; residence rules; sex division of labor in family)

(3)   Degree of Ideological Support for and Degree of Gender Stereotyping

SEX STRATIFICATION

FIGURE 5.2   Factors Most Immediately Related to Sex Stratification
Source: Based on Chaftez 1984, pp. 10–22.

and testable package. One variable minimized by Chafetz, considered central for Sanday's theory, which is to be discussed next, is the role of cultural factors in explaining and maintaining sex stratification.

Ecological Explanations

The structural theories of Chafetz and others often rely on the cross-cultural evidence and ideas of anthropologists who have developed theories of sex inequality. The latters' theories usually focus on societies that are simpler in technology, whereas sociological theories usually emphasize complex industrial societies when trying to explain inequality (Chafetz 1988).

Sanday's Theory of Male Dominance. Peggy Sanday's theory is based on her analysis of information from over 150 societies, most of them not known to the average reader and many of them extinct. But they provide clues to the origins of male dominance. Sanday defined male dominance in terms of the "exclusion of women from political and economic decision-making" and "male aggression against women" (1981, p. 164). Her principal question addressed the origins of male dominance. Where does it come from? *The basic generating cause for male dominance relates to the nature of the environment in which a society operates.* If that environment is one in which risk is great, danger is present, or resources are uncertain or in scarce supply, then the society is more vulnerable to male dominance. For example, when a society's ability to feed itself is dependent on hunting large migrating animals, its continuity is not as certain. This means that people's tie to the environment is more negative than positive under these circumstances. Survival is at risk. This contrasts with situations in which the immediate environment supplies abundant food without risk or uncertainty, as, for example, among the Mbuti, an African forest people.

These two different environments generate different stresses for the people exposed to them, their relationships to the environment are defined differently, and the general cultural orientations and consequent sex-role plans they develop also differ as a result (Sanday 1981). In other words, a group develops its sense of peoplehood and cultural orientations as responses to its environmental circumstances. When those circumstances involve risk, uncertainty, and so forth, as in the case of societies that rely heavily on the hunting of large animals, then there is a greater reliance on the aggression of men. These societies, in which animals must be killed, in which death and destruction predominate, develop what Sanday calls an "outer orientation" in their worldview. "Men hunt animals, seek to kill other human beings, make weapons for these activities, and pursue power that is *out there*" (1981, p. 5). On the other side are societies whose environments produce abundantly and with certainty, cultures that rely on the surrounding plants for sustenance. Nature is viewed in a friendly manner, as freely satisfying human needs. In many cases where this situation is present, a basic affinity is seen between women and nature. As women produce, so does nature. Women are seen as being more in tune with nature and men are largely extraneous to this relationship. In these cultures, an inner orientation is dominant.

The cultural system that develops in a society contains scripts for the relationships not only between humans and the natural environment but also between the sexes. In societies in which the environment is potentially hostile, men spend much of their time in activities in the outer environment, outside the family, wrestling with forces beyond the family. In these kinds of societies, the ultimate source of power is believed to reside either in animals or in a supreme being of some kind who lives in a place beyond human beings. In these societies, because of their hunting activity, men are distant from their children and do not engage much in nurturing activity. The myths surrounding origins of the culture or world are imbued with masculine characteristics. The opposite is the case when a society, especially a technologically simple one, relies on plants in plentiful supply. Here, the earth supplies the food and men are close to their families and children. Growth and life are an inherent part of the culture. Like women, the earth provides and creates life. Tales of life origins have a feminine quality to them. Under both these circumstances, "the phrases 'man the animal' and 'mother earth' make a great deal of sense" (ibid., p. 73). There is a close connection between the economy of a society and the role of the sexes in myths and childrearing.

A strict sex-based division of labor is more likely when the society depends heavily on hunting as its means of subsistence, whereas a society that depends equally on hunting and gathering or inordinately on the latter for food is more likely to produce a division of labor that is sexually integrated. Cooperation rather than competition is likely to be emphasized. Females *achieve* power when a society has to depend on their economic activity for survival. This makes men more dependent on them. Women are *given* power when they are associated closely with nature and the society's continuity, as in the origin myths just mentioned (ibid., pp. 89, 114).

With Western colonialism, women lost much of the higher status they held in tradi-

tional societies. The infusion of new weapons, new technologies, and the increased importance of aggression helped to redefine the roles of the sexes, with male activity becoming more highly valued. In many cases, the increased complexity of economic technology also led to the decline of women's status. In her survey of societies, Sanday concluded that "male dominance is associated with increasing technological complexity, an animal economy, sexual segregation in work, a symbolic orientation to the male creative principle, and stress" (1981, p. 171). Sex inequality is much more likely when the environment is unfavorable and unstable than when the opposite is the case.

To summarize Sanday's explanation, the nature of the surrounding environment gives shape to the economy and the stress in society and determines the relative worth of men's and women's behavior. Cultural orientations, myths, and sex-role plans develop that are consistent with these conditions. When environmental conditions create stress because they involve risk, danger, or uncertainty, greater reliance is placed on the economic efforts of men. An outer cultural orientation develops along with origin myths in which men dominate and create, sex-segregation of roles follows, ultimately leading to male dominance. Sanday's basic model is suggested in Figure 5.3.

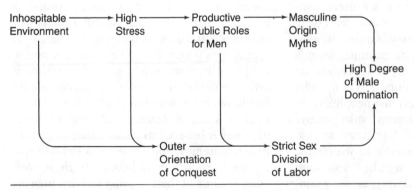

FIGURE 5.3   Sanday's Basic Model of the Genesis of Male Dominance
Source: Based on Sanday 1981, pp. 11–12, 64–75, 163–172ff.

Sanday's theory has been criticized for overemphasizing the role of the environment in determining cultural beliefs and for ignoring the internal sources of stress in society. It also does not take into account the fact that different cultures may react differently to similar environmental circumstances (Coontz and Henderson 1986). Additionally, her theory neglects the possibility that the difficulties men encounter in dealing with a harsh environment may strengthen them enough to dominate women directly.

Randall Collins has suggested, for example, that the form of the economic system and the habitability of the surrounding natural and political environments influence the extent to which warfare is an important element in the society. When the economic system is advanced enough and involves the protection of private property or settled territories, warfare is often part of a society's existence as it tries to defend itself against outside encroachment. Men are generally larger and stronger than women and are therefore more likely to control the fighting that occurs. In this kind of a potentially hostile environment, political alliances become important, and males use the exchange of females through marriage with surrounding groups as a means of establishing political, economic, and social ties. This control of females by males results in separate cultures and roles developing for each of the sexes (Collins 1971, 1986, 1988). In other words, the

need for the mediation of the environment's impact on male domination through the intervening factors of cultural scripts and orientations may either not be necessary or involve the operation of other variables like warfare.

The causal nature of the relationships outlined by Sanday also needs to be more fully examined (England and Dunn 1985). One would suspect, for example, that cultural orientation and beliefs would have an impact on the degree to which the environment is interpreted as being hostile or friendly. In other words, not only can the environment affect the culture, but the culture may affect the definition of the environment as well.

Capitalism, Patriarchy, and Sex Inequality

Generally, structural theorists, as well as many anthropologists, recognize the significance of broadly defined economic factors for sex inequality. Many point to the significance of labor, work organization, and family structure in shaping inequality. In a general way, then, their perspectives have been affected by Marxian thought as well as by perspectives that focus on the family structure and the sex/gender divisions within it. Some explanations, however, explicitly focus on the effects of capitalism and patriarchy on sex inequality. Figure 5.4 gives a basic model showing some of the alleged major impacts of capitalism/class on sex inequality.

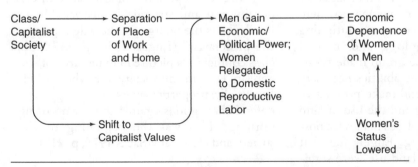

FIGURE 5.4   The Relationship of Class/Capitalism to Sex Inequality

Again, there are a large number of individuals who present such explanations (e.g., Sacks 1975; Vogel 1983; Leacock 1986). Some of them address the adequacy and insights of Engels's theory of the origins of sex inequality, so we will begin with an overview of his position.

Engels's Theory of Sex Inequality.   Frederick Engels contended that early in human history, people lived together communally and engaged in tasks together to produce goods principally for their own use. Since all resources were communally owned, individuals worked for the group as a whole. Separate nuclear families as we know them, as distinct productive units, did not exist. Rather than being wives within separate families, women were members of society and contributed fully and equally to society (Sacks 1975). Being a mother was a central role in those societies, according to Engels. Since all members of both sexes were involved in producing goods of direct value and use to their own communities, the work of both sexes was considered equally valuable. Women were full participants in the society. Although there was a division of labor based on sex, each sex was a master in its own sphere of work.

This situation changed, according to Engels, when certain material conditions changed. Specifically, the development of privately owned productive resources in the form of domesticated animals and land laid the groundwork for the differentiation of the sexes and the subordination of women to men. These resources appeared on a continuing basis when the technology and natural resources accessible to the group made possible the development of the abilities necessary to domesticate animals and make productive use of the land. Herding and the use of land made possible greater surpluses than were possible under mere hunting. Engels felt that once domestication and land use were stabilized and part of the society, then private ownership would also be stabilized. He also believed that men were the earliest owners of property (ibid.).

Once private property was entrenched in society, economic and other divisions developed between individuals and families; that is, the *preclass* days were over. The extensive domestication of animals and land use made possible greater surpluses, allowing individuals to produce not only for themselves and their families but for others as well. Production for *exchange* began to become more dominant than production for *use* by the households themselves. With private property owned by men and the increase in production for exchange, the kind of work that dominated the lives of women changed, and with it their status in society (Sacks 1975; Leacock 1986). Because men now had property they could pass on to their children, men became more concerned about making sure they had children. This encouraged them to usurp more control in the nuclear monogamous family and the procreation process.

Consequently, women changed from being contributing adults equal to men to wards, wives, and daughters in a subordinate and increasingly domestic position. Their reproduction of children was now for producing heirs and workers for their own families rather than for producing another child for the societal group. Individual families and their economic statuses could then be preserved generation after generation. This domination of men over women in the nuclear family setting was, for Engels, the first instance of class domination and struggle in history. "In the family, he is the bourgeois; the wife represents the proletariat" (Engels 1973, p. 247). This class conflict is "a picture in miniature" of what appears later in the society as a whole (ibid.). Eventually, property owners joined together to defend their goods against those who owned nothing. This was the beginning of class society and class state (Sacks 1975, p. 217).

Vogel's Reproduction Theory.   Lise Vogel reviewed and assessed Engels's analysis of women's oppression, but came to the conclusion that his theory was seriously flawed. For example, she said Engels does not clearly trace and explain the development of a separate domestic arena out of class or capitalist society. Also, he does not elaborate on the subordination of women in precapitalist class societies (Vogel 1983, p. 86). These problems led Vogel to attempt development of her own theory based on Marxian concepts.

Vogel began the development of her theoretical framework by reviewing several Marxian concepts: production, reproduction, and labor power. *Labor power* refers to the capacities, mental and physical, an individual exercises whenever he or she produces something of use. *Production* is a result of labor power. But every act of production is also an act of *reproduction*, because whatever is produced lays the basis for its being reproduced later.

Specifically, a society needs a labor force to continue to produce products, and this labor force, in turn, needs food to maintain itself. In other words, part of the reproduction process involves reproducing the laborers who are involved in the labor process. These workers must be maintained and, when necessary, replaced. Sex becomes a significant factor in the generational replacement of bearers of labor power, because it is only women who can perform this function. But regeneration or replenishment of the labor force does not have to occur within the family. Other sources— such as migration, enslavement, and the enlistment of nonworkers within the family—also may serve as potential sources of labor power.

In order for the capitalist system of production to continue, labor power must produce the conditions necessary for the constant renewal of the labor process. The labor needed to reproduce the workers and their replacement is *necessary* labor. For example, a certain minimum amount of labor is needed to provide basic subsistence to the workers and to produce new workers. Part of this necessary

labor is done at the workplace and is paid for by wages, with which the worker can buy those necessities needed to reproduce himself or herself and other nonworkers in the working class. As it takes place in the social or public sphere it is the *social* aspect of necessary labor. But as mentioned, biological reproduction and the rearing of children are also needed, and as such constitute a second *domestic* component of necessary labor. In addition to necessary labor, there is *surplus* labor. This is the labor time that is left over after socially necessary labor has been subtracted from the total labor time spent on the job. It provides the profit to the employer.

It is the unavoidable performance of the domestic component of necessary labor by women that creates a basic sex division of labor. But their involvement in reproduction creates a dilemma for capitalists and constitutes an internal contradiction in the capitalist system. On the one hand, this domestic labor reduces any time women could spend in the labor force producing profit for employers. So in the short run, capitalists suffer because of the smaller direct contribution of women to profit. On the other hand, if capitalism is going to continue over the long run, replacement and reproduction are necessary. So in these terms, capitalism benefits.

In order to benefit both ways, capitalists try to minimize the amount of necessary domestic time needed for reproduction in order to maximize the surplus value of labor, thereby increasing their profit. Thus, employers may allow maternity leaves for their female workers, but the leaves are kept short so as to maximize the work time of new mothers. At the same time, however, male workers try to get the best conditions and wages they can for themselves, their families, and their wives. This may mean more and better-quality domestic time for their wives. So while employers may be trying to enlist wives in the marketplace, husbands are trying to create conditions that will make it more possible for them to stay comfortably at home. In trying to resolve this contradiction, according to Vogel, what almost invariably occurs is the involvement of men in the labor force and the production of surplus labor and profit on the one hand, and the involvement of women in the reproduction of the labor force at home on the other. Accompanying this resolution is a male supremacy based on males as the laborers who produce the means of subsistence and receive a wage.

It is in capitalism that a distinct and strong division is accentuated between the arena in which surplus labor is carried out and that in which domestic labor is performed. In order to increase profit, separate factories in which workers are concentrated are needed that are socially and culturally isolated from the home. "Capitalism's drive to increase surplus . . . forces a severe spatial, temporal, and institutional separation between domestic labor and the capitalist production process. . . . Wage labor comes to have a character that is wholly distinct from the laborer's life away from the job" (Vogel 1983, p. 153). Men are clearly associated with the social, working sphere, whereas women are associated with the domestic sphere. This is a carryover from earlier class societies.

Of course, exceptions exist. Depending on the specific historical circumstances of a given society, either the importance of women's power of reproduction or their involvement in the labor force may be stressed. Migration and natural or other disasters may tip the scales in such a way that the participation of females in the work force is more important than their domestic labor. But the usual division of labor consists of men and women being associated with distinct spheres of labor. This clear division of labor, when accentuated in a situation of male supremacy, is the source for ideologies that serve to explain and maintain the sexual basis of the division of labor. Since this division of labor is so prominent and obvious, it comes to be viewed as natural even though it is

rooted in the capitalist mode of production (ibid., p. 154).

As noted previously, according to Vogel, women's involvement in and relegation to domestic labor is the basic source of their subordination. In fact, she suggested that in advanced capitalist societies, sex sometimes is more important than class in determining differences between individuals. Men support women by working and receiving wages, and this gives them economic power over women.

> It is the provision by men of means of subsistence to women during the childbearing period, and not the sex division of labor in itself, that forms the material basis for women's subordination in class society. (ibid., p. 147, emphasis added)

Since many of the immediate conflicts take place within the context of the family, it is easy to conclude that it is the sex division of labor within it that is at the source of the problems experienced by women. But Vogel reminds us again that it is the nature of the relationship of men and women to the capitalist system of production and women's role in reproducing it that is the basic cause. As long as capitalism remains unchanged, inequality between the sexes will continue. Figure 5.5 presents the core of Vogel's argument.

One of the problems with Vogel's theory is that she dated the beginning of women's oppression with the advent of class societies. Many would argue that male domination predated class society (Nicholson 1984). Vogel's theory also heavily stressed economic factors to the exclusion of cultural, psychological, and other possible contributors to male domination.

The Role of Patriarchy. Vogel acknowledged the division of labor and the inequality that exists between the sexes in capitalist society, but Sacks (1975) noted that in many nonclass societies the sexes were also unequal. This suggests strongly that sex inequality preceded

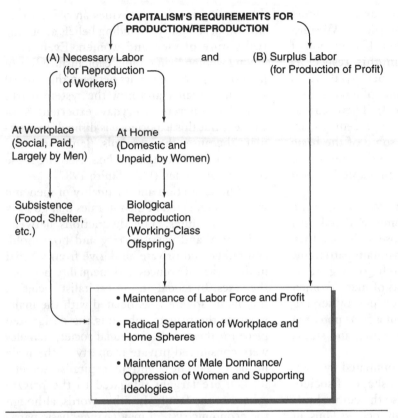

FIGURE 5.5 A Simplified Version of Vogel's Theory of Women's Oppression

capitalism and indeed is a form of domination distinct from class inequality.

In brief, many feminists argue that patriarchy not only preceded capitalism but also existed even in the earliest societies. The term *patriarchy* has been defined in a variety of ways, but basically it refers to a whole complex of structured interrelationships in which men dominate over women. It is a "system of sexual hierarchical relations" (Eisenstein 1981, p. 19). Just as capitalism is based on the relationship between capitalists and workers, so patriarchy is a system based on the unequal relationship of men and women (Phelps 1981). Because of its early appearance, patriarchy is considered by

most radical feminists to be the most fundamental of all forms of social inequality, as one in which "men learn how to hold other human beings in contempt, to see them as nonhuman and to control them" (Lengermann and Niebrugge-Brantley 1988, p. 306).

In other words, in this view, sexism and the domination of women did not appear with class societies as some Marxists would have it; rather, it existed long before capitalism came on the historical scene. The roots of patriarchy have been tied to the reproductive function of women in society (Firestone 1970; Eisenstein 1981; Phelps 1981; Chafetz 1988). "On the basis of this capacity she has been excluded from other human activities and contained within a sphere defined as female" in Western society (Eisenstein 1981, p. 14). The division of labor between the sexes in this respect is ancient: "Where there is society, there is gender, and the gender division of labor is pervasive" (D.E. Smith 1987, p. 4). There was no primordial matriarchal society preceding class society. Table 5.3 suggests some of the basic elements tied to patriarchy and some of the forms it has taken under precapitalist and capitalist societies.

Once men dominate in areas outside the family and gain the economic and political resources attendant with those activities, they can use these resources to maintain patriarchy. The maintenance of patriarchy over generations is clearly in the interests of men. Women serve the material interests of men by serving not only as sexual partners but also as potential laborers, childbearers, ornaments, and status enhancers.

The social institutions dominated by men, then, influence not only the shape of society and relations within it but also the cultural values and ideas that dominate in society. Thus, in present-day society, education and socialization agents instill those values consistent with patriarchal structure. Under capitalism, the culture consists largely of the ideas and values sanctioned by those in power—that is, men.

This ruling ideology provides an official version of social reality, including beliefs about the real nature of men and women. Eventually, among women living under capitalism, a line of fault or disjuncture occurs between this official version of reality and how the system works and the concrete everyday experiences of women. But this experience is difficult to articulate because the symbols, language, and organization of thought in the society are those of men not women (D.E. Smith 1987).

The separation and inequality of men and women is reflected in dichotomies that go back to ancient times. The distinctions between rationality and passion, city and household, and public and private all derive from a belief in the basic differences and inequality between the sexes. In feudal and in capitalist societies, the public sphere is associated with the male, whereas the private sphere is the designated place for the female. In feudal society, females were considered private property of the male heads of families, and in capitalist society, women are largely relegated to the private sphere of the family. In other words, although the economic system may change, basic patriarchal relationships remain intact and only change form.

One of the difficulties with patriarchal theories is that the original source of patriarchy is not always clearly spelled out. Sometimes it

TABLE 5.3 Patriarchy and Sex Inequality

GENERAL FEATURES OF PATRIARCHY	UNDER PRECAPITALIST SOCIETIES	UNDER CAPITALISM
1. Power, force of men 2. Control of outer resources by men 3. Separate work spheres 4. Division of labor based on sex 5. Reproductive capacity of women critical	Men engage in status-enhancing hunting; men control domesticated animals; women used as exchange, women were purchased (bridewealth); men control military	Radical separation of home and work; women cheap labor for market, women largely confined to home, women economically dependent on men

is associated with the differences in the reproductive function between the sexes, sometimes with the physical force of men over women, and other times its source is left undescribed. Collins (1988) argued that the basic problem with theories that propose patriarchy as the fundamental, original cause of sex inequality is that they are merely restating the question using a different label. That is, if "patriarchy" *refers* to male domination of one sort or another, then how can it be used to *explain* male domination? This seems to be too severe a criticism, given that many of those proposing such theories do attempt to locate the sources of patriarchy itself. Since that source is often viewed as being tied to the elemental function of reproduction, the task remains to identify the exact conditions under which such distinctions in the division of labor do *not* lead to patriarchy. For example, can socializing or spreading a large part of the childrearing function free women to a degree from the destiny of remaining in the domestic sphere, thereby potentially raising their status in society?

Socialist-Feminist Theories of Sex Inequality.
In contrast to those who would opt for viewing either capitalism *or* patriarchy as the principal cause of women's subordination, there are those who see the two as complementary causes. Women's oppression by men cannot be reduced to a matter of class exploitation, according to these scholars. *Exploitation* of women, Eisenstein (1977) argued, exists when men and women are wage laborers. But women are also in a lower sexual hierarchy in their roles as mothers and housewives. "The study of women's oppression, then, must deal with both sexual and economic material conditions if one is to understand oppression rather than merely understand economic exploitation" (Eisentein 1990, p. 124). As we will see, those who use an internal-colonialism model in explaining Black/White inequality in the United States make a similar argument about understanding racial oppression.

Eisenstein and Hartmann both emphasized the mutual reinforcement between capitalism and patriarchy. On the one hand, patriarchy supplies capitalism with generations of laborers it needs at minimal costs and with the techniques of control needed to keep oppressed women in their place. All the tasks carried out and raw materials worked on by housewives (e.g., children, husbands) are "future worker-commodities" (Secombe 1973, p. 19). In turn, capitalism reinforces patriarchy by only hiring women for certain low-paying positions, thereby encouraging job segregation, women's relegation to the domestic sphere, and their continued economic dependence on males.

> *Job segregation by sex, in my view, is the primary mechanism in capitalist society that maintains the superiority of men over women, because it enforces lower wages for women in the labor market. Low wages keep women dependent on men because they encourage women to marry. Married women must perform domestic chores for their husbands. Men benefit, then, from both higher wages and the domestic division of labor. (Hartmann 1990, pp. 147–148; see also Eisenstein 1990)*

The domestic division of labor is the linchpin that connects capitalism and patriarchy (Philipson and Hansen 1990). Patriarchy defines the role of women as being in the home, whereas capitalism defines men's role as being in the wider economy and women's role as reproducer of workers in the economy. The division of labor, as it were, brings the private/domestic and public/economic spheres into contact. This has raised a number of questions about the nature of the relationship between the marketplace and the home.

One issue pits the obvious contributions of domestic work to the continuance of capitalism against the fact that domestic labor is basically unpaid low-status work outside the economy. If such work contributes to the economy by providing functioning laborers, why is it not paid labor? Because it is not paid, it has lower status in a society in which the amount of money labor brings in is a measure of its status (Benston 1969).

A second issue concerns the basic character of domestic labor. In contrast to work in the marketplace, which is seen by some as being alienating and rationalistic, work in the home is sometimes seen as much less alienating and more leisurely (Sontag 1973; Vogel 1983). The home and family life are viewed as the areas in which love, warmth, spontaneity, cooperation, and fun have a central place. In sharp contrast, the public sphere of paid labor is interpreted as one where work is forced, competitive, and rational. It is, of course, questionable whether those who feel trapped in the home would describe it in the glowing terms just used. But part of our socialization is aimed at fostering the belief that these terms accurately describe family life in modern society.

A third issue among scholars relates to the effects of involvement in the marketplace on women. Engels viewed industrialization as providing women with a means of escape from the drudgery of housework and the oppression of domestic life. Work outside the home was interpreted as a liberating experience. However, if capitalism creates work that is fundamentally alienating, a legitimate question can be raised about how liberating and beneficial such an escape would be for women. Are they not just escaping into work that is also alienating and compounding their alienation by doing not only paid labor but unpaid domestic labor as well?

A final area concerns the family's role in socializing new members of society into a dominant set of values and ideas that perpetuate patriarchy and capitalism (Hartmann 1981). The traits attributed to the ideal male—competitiveness, rationality, coolness—are those valued in the marketplace, whereas those attributed to the ideal female under capitalism—emotionality, sentimentality, and so on—are those valued in the family. These are values that keep patriarchy and capitalism intact.

The last point demonstrates that the concerns with profit in capitalism and with social control in patriarchy are "inextricably connected" and "cannot be reduced to each other." Capitalism and patriarchy, being mutually reinforcing, become an "integral process" (Eisenstein 1977/1990, p. 134). The conditions in the marketplace affect what goes on in the family in terms of production, reproduction, and consumption; conversely, production, reproduction, and consumption in the family affect the production of commodities in the marketplace.

The centrality of the sexual division of labor in maintaining both patriarchy and capitalism has caused both Eisenstein and Hartmann to call for its elimination. Eisenstein argued forcefully that it is this division of labor that must be changed because it is the principal means by which men maintain control. It suggests that the roles and activities that divide men and women are rooted in nature (ibid., p. 140). Eisenstein stated that for conditions to change, women must organize and they can do so by becoming conscious of what they have in common with each other. They may differ in their ties to the marketplace, but their "commonality derives from the particular roles women share in patriarchy. From this commonality begins the feminist struggle" (ibid.). Similarly and even more pointedly, Hartmann believes that both men and women will be better off and more equal only when "we eradicate the socially imposed gender differences between us and, therefore, the very sexual division of labor itself" (1977/1990, p. 170).

One of the great values of seeing capitalism and patriarchy as dual systems is that it encourages us to examine the interlinkage between class and sex in trying to understand the relative roles of men and women in society. Clearly, an individual's position in the general system of inequality is an outcome of the confluence of economic, sexual, and racial/ethnic factors. Understanding the nature of this intersection and its origins will provide us with a more comprehensive and exact explanation of sex inequality. There is no question that women as a group are in a unique position in contemporary society.

Multiracial Feminist Theories

All of the theories discussed above focus on the position of women in general. In recent years, however, numerous feminist theorists have stressed that we need to take women's experiences as they have lived them along with their accumulated wisdom into account when developing an explanation of women's situation. In doing that, it is necessary to realize that all women do not have the same experiences or live the same kinds of lives. While they may have some experiences in common because they are women, they vary along other dimensions, for example, in their races and social classes. These dimensions intersect in different ways for different women and affect each other, the particular combination characterizing a given woman having a unique effect on her life chances. As Browne and Misra put it in speaking about the relationship of gender and race, "[r]ace is 'gendered' and gender is 'racialized' so that race and gender fuse to create unique experiences and opportunities for all groups— not just women of color" (2003, p. 488). We could add that race and gender are also "classed," and class has been "gendered" and "racialized" as well in our history. That is, the particular pattern *itself* has an impact independent of the separate effects that might flow from one's gender, race, or class. This is what is meant by the importance of "intersectionality" and what Patricia Hill Collins calls "the matrix of domination" (Collins 1990). Each of these patterns has particular cultural images or stereotypes associated with it. For example, Black, lower-class men are often seen as dangerous, Black women as unusually sexually active, White women as dependent and feminine, and so on (Browne and Misra 2003).

A woman's race, class, and her gender may all affect her position in society. As we have seen in several instances, for example, the occupational and earnings positions of women vary with their race. The situation of women also depends upon their class. In their study of power at work, Elliott and Smith found that "men and women of various races and ethnicities experience increasing inequality in workplace power, relative to white men, but they experience it to different degrees and via different mechanisms. . . . Evidence here suggests that a one-size-fits-all explanation hides more than it reveals" (2004, pp. 384–385). Since each group faces problems that are in part unique, the solutions to their domination need to vary as well.

In addition to the intersection of race, class, and gender, recent issues on employment, welfare, and wages revolving around immigration have added *nationality* to the mix. Globalization and the continual movement of people, jobs, and capital across national boundaries associated with it have also had an impact on women's position in our own society and in others. Having examined a variety of general explanations of gender inequality, let us now examine the position of U.S. women in a global context and assess the specific roles played by globalization in determining women's statuses.

THE GLOBAL CONTEXT AND THE IMPACT OF GLOBALIZATION

The examination of gender inequality in the United States showed that women are generally below men in their earnings, income, and occupational statuses, and the families that they head are more likely to be poor. However, gender inequality and oppression encompasses a broader range of life chances than just narrow economic opportunities. The life conditions for women often entail subjection to extreme forms of discrimination.

Genital mutilation, euphemistically referred to as female circumcision, has been a common practice in many African countries. The operation, which involves surgical removal of segments of a female's sexual anatomy, has been maintained by the myth that such an operation will dampen the female's sexual drive and thereby guarantee chastity. In other words, it is used as a means of gender control. The painful procedure, often performed with unsterile knives, has been done on an estimated 140 million girls and women, mostly in African countries. Girls as young as age 6 have been subjected to the operation (Scott 2000; Smucker 2001).

So-called *honor killings* constitute another form of extreme discrimination against women aimed at controlling their behavior. These killings take place because of alleged disobedience or sexual indiscretions on the part of women. Muslim countries in the Middle East have been among the most cited for this discrimination. Between 1998 and mid-1999, for example, 36 women were killed in Jordan for family honor. Islam is used as justification. The Koran has been interpreted as supporting wife-beating and the assignment of much lighter sentences for the murders of women than of men. In the 5,000 cases of honor violence against women recorded in 4 Pakistani hospitals in the 1990s, 97 percent of the women died but guilty verdicts were reached in only 3 percent of the cases (Ligner 2001). Customs and laws often entrap girls in relationships and make it difficult for them to escape. Marriage to girls under the age of 12 is not uncommon in some Middle Eastern countries, and it is much more difficult for a woman than a man to divorce ("The Women of Islam" 2001).

Finally, in some countries, conditions for women prove so unbearable that many commit *suicide*. China, for example, has one of the highest suicide rates in the world, and more than half of these are rural women. This contrasts with most other countries where the male suicide rate is higher. Each year, approximately 157,000 Chinese women commit suicide. Part of the reason for the higher female suicide rate in China is that women who attempt suicide there are more successful at doing it. More

significant, however, is the fact that rural Chinese women are generally not considered as valuable or worthy as their male counterparts and are thought of as the property of males (Fackler 2002). Gender mutilation, honor killings, and suicide are all indicators of the extreme gender oppression that women, but not men, face in some cultures. In the small village of Umoja in northern Kenya, a group of women have tried to escape the widespread oppression they have faced from their husbands and men in general by creating a village composed almost entirely of women (Lacey 2004). The leader of the village complained that their only reason for being had been to give men children and to be treated like property. In this new setting, the women seem to be prospering economically and psychologically.

As these examples suggest, there are great variations between countries in the quality of life experienced by women. In its analysis of gender inequality in 163 countries, a recent United Nations study took into account women's (1) life expectancies, (2) educational attainment, and (3) incomes in its measure of gender-related development. Results showed that, *compared to men*, women are worst off in Oman, Saudi Arabia, Iran, Syrian Arab Republic, Algeria, Libya, and the United Arab Emirates. But in no society are women as well off as men. The country with the least gender inequality is Armenia, followed by Latvia, Slovakia, Sri Lanka, Kazakhstan, Czech Republic, Bulgaria, and Poland. This list of countries shows that less gender inequality is not directly related to a country's income.

Keep in mind that the "gender-related development index" used by the United Nations merely measures the *relative disparity* between men and women on the above three variables; it does not directly tap the level of quality of life in an *absolute* sense. In *absolute* terms in the United Nations study, women are best off in Canada, Norway, Sweden, Iceland, Finland, United States, France, New Zealand,

Australia, and Denmark, respectively. In terms of women's opportunities to participate fully in the economic and political life of a country, Sweden, Norway, and Denmark rank highest. The United States is 11th among 102 countries. Most of the top-20 on this measure are industrial countries (United Nations 1998).

"Save the Children" is an independent, nonprofit organization that, for the last several years, has conducted an evaluation of conditions for women across the world. Its 2004 survey of conditions for mothers and children in 119 countries revealed results similar to those of the United Nations. Sweden, Denmark, Finland, Austria, Netherlands, Norway, Australia, Canada, and the United Kingdom ranked highest, respectively, in measures of mother's well-being. The United States was ranked 10th best. The 10 countries with the lowest rankings, starting with the worst, were Niger, Burkina Faso, Mali,

Ethiopia, Guinea-Bissau, Yemen, Sierra Leone, Chad, Mauritania, and the Central African Republic. In general, Scandinavian countries, and industrial nations in general, rank highest, while sub-Saharan African countries dominate the lowest rankings on this measure. The measure includes rates of maternal mortality, anemia, use of contraceptions, births by qualified professionals, female literacy, and participation of women in national government (Save the Children 2004).

Considering the importance of intersectionality discussed earlier, however, one should keep in mind that women who belong to some ethnic, religious, geographical, political, or racial groups may be worse off than those in other groups. One of the problems of national-level data is that it obscures inequalities between subnational groups in a country. Ethnic cleansing, violence, and oppression in general have targeted some groups of women more than others.

NUTSHELL 5.2

Africa Worst Continent for Mothers

Study ranks conditions for children globally

ADDIS ABABA, ETHIOPIA: Africa is the worst continent on which to be a mother or child, and Mali is one of the worst countries, where one in eight children will die before seeing a first birthday, according to a study published Tuesday.

The State of the World's Mothers 2005, a report by Save The Children USA, studied 110 countries and details health and educational opportunities for mothers and their children.

"Conditions for children and mothers in the bottom-ranked countries are devastating," said Charles MacCormack, president of Save the Children. "Many children are fortunate just to survive the first five years of life and have a chance to go to school."

In Burkina Faso, fewer than one in 10 women can read and write.

In Ethiopia just 25 percent of the population has access to clean water.

Scandinavian countries sweep the top rankings for the best places to be a mother, while countries in sub-Saharan Africa dominate the bottom tier, the report said. Out of the 10 worst countries to be a mother or child, seven are in Africa.

In Sweden, which tops the list, nearly all women are literate. In Ethiopia, only 34 percent of women are literate. A mother in Ethiopia is 37 times more likely to see her child die in the first year of life than a mother in Sweden.

The United States ranked 11th.

Source: Akron Beacon Journal, May 5, 2005, p. A13. Used with permission of the Associated Press, copyright 2005, all rights reserved.

In addition to their involvement in the formal economy, women throughout the world also spend significantly more time than men on unpaid housework. In industrial countries, women spend at least 30 hours per week on housework, compared to 10 to 15 hours for men. In developing countries, the figures are 31 to 42 hours and 5 to 15 hours, respectively. How equally housework is distributed between men and women is affected by *individual-level* variables such as belief in gender inequality and the time that women have for housework, and these factors in turn are affected by *national-level* factors that provide the context in which individual elements operate. Among the national-level variables that are important in this regard are level of economic development, gender ideology, and welfare policies (Fuwa 2004). This research supports several of the general theoretical arguments discussed earlier.

As in the United States, the world's employed women are unevenly distributed across occupational categories. About half of them are in various services (e.g., retail, restaurants, communications, insurance, personal services, etc.) and over one-third are involved in agricultural work. The rest are in manufacturing (Neft and Levine 1997). Overall, women are heavily represented in professional, technical, clerical, and service positions. By and large, these patterns follow those found in the United States. In Europe, Latin America, and the Caribbean, women occupy about half of all professional and technical positions and about two-thirds of clerical and service jobs (United Nations 1995).

Although women are concentrated in some positions, they are underrepresented in others. Women are most underrepresented in administration, managerial, production, and transport occupations. Underrepresentation applies to positions of political importance, as well. In 1997, only about 9 percent of parliamentary seats in developing nations were occupied by women. About 15 percent of such positions were held by women in industrial countries (United Nations 1998).

Among industrial countries, the gender gap in authority in the private economy appears to be lower in the United States than in many other countries. A recent study of employed individuals in Canada, the United Kingdom, Australia, Sweden, Norway, Japan, and the United States revealed that the gap was smallest in the United States and Australia, whereas Japan showed the widest difference in male and female authority. These differences persisted even after differences in characteristics in workplaces, jobs, and individual characteristics were taken into account (Wright, Baxter, and Birkelund 1995).

As in the United States, the expected attitudes and behavior of women in their occupations reflect cultural values. Kanter (1977a) found that U.S. women in corporations were often expected to perform the social duties of a wife or servant, even though their job descriptions did not specify these as part of their work. But these expectations are consistent with beliefs about women's general roles and place in society. The same is the case in other societies.

Jeannie Lo's fascinating study of "office ladies" (OLs) and factory women in a Japanese company reveals similar expectations. Office ladies are expected to "carry out their 'domestic' responsibilities: they serve tea to their superiors (the men in the office), keep themselves presentable and feminine, and do the cleaning" (Lo 1990, p. 100). These ladies are careful to maintain the delicate network of relationships (*shigarami*) underlying the work system, and expect to leave their jobs and marry before the age of 30. Female factory workers find their work more physically exhausting, but do not put up with as much harassment on the job as OLs do. Women's pay is low, even for those in senior worker positions. They work to save money for their dowries and quit to marry. "Marriage is the ticket out of suffering and hard work" (ibid., p. 101).

Earnings is another area in which gender inequality is prominent. In none of the

50 countries in which men's and women's earnings have been analyzed are women's earnings equal to those of men. Unfortunately, these studies focus on earnings from manufacturing or nonagricultural occupations. Since many women work in agricultural jobs, especially in developing nations, the picture given of wage discrepancies between the genders in these studies is, at best, incomplete. Those countries in which women receive earnings that are at least 85 percent of what men receive include Norway, Sweden, and Australia among industrial nations, and Tanzania, Vietnam, Sri Lanka, Colombia, Kenya, and Turkey, among developing countries. In 2004, U.S. women earned about 80 percent of what men did, which puts the United States near the middle in earnings differences between men and women. Among industrial countries, the United States has lagged behind Australia, Norway, Sweden, France, New Zealand, Denmark, Finland, Netherlands, Germany, Belgium, Italy, Portugal, Greece, Austria, and Poland in gender earnings equality. Among the nations with the greatest earnings inequality are Russia, Bangladesh, Japan, and Guam, where women's earnings equal no more than half those of men (United Nations 1995; Neft and Levine 1997). In sum, women's involvement in the economy, occupation segregation by sex, and lower authority for women are common around the world, but when compared to many other industrial countries, earnings differences between men and women have been higher in the United States.

International differences in gender inequality as well as disparities within the United States are affected by globalization. Rather than being gender-neutral or impartial, globalization has profound and unique gender effects, effects that are generally more costly for women than for men (Chow 2003; Mills 2003; Gottfried 2004). This should not be surprising because globalization is simultaneously an economic, cultural, social, and political process; and in each of these spheres there are gender differences. Among the economic costs for women are "feminization of labor in segregated and low-paying work, wage dependency, labor exploitation, economic marginalization, poverty, sex tourism, and international human trafficking of women and young girls" (Chow 2003, p. 454). Economically, global capitalism can enlist sexist ideology to justify and perpetuate lower wages for women in a variety of cultural contexts. Women migrating from poorer to richer countries in search of better lives serve as domestic workers and nannies for two-career families in wealthy countries. As low as their wages may be by Western standards, the conditions and opportunities that immigrants experience in their new countries are often better than those they had in their countries of origin. We need to understand that a group's cultural and social experience will affect its views of the costs and benefits of globalization. Whether globalization is seen as a largely positive or negative force depends in part on the vantage point from which it is viewed (Kabeer 2004).

The prevalence of women working in the United States along with continued gender inequities in housework and lack of childcare support, for example, creates a need and opportunity for domestic workers, many of whom are immigrants who expect better economic conditions than in their home countries. In other words, gender inequalities *within* a nation help spur the immigration of women *between* countries. The migration of women as workers is a widespread phenomenon. "In the United States, African-American women, who accounted for 60 percent of domestics in the 1940s, have been largely replaced by Latinas, many of them recent migrants from Mexico and Central America. In England, Asian migrant women have displaced the Irish and Portuguese domestics of the past. In French cities, North African women have replaced rural French girls. In western Germany, Turks and women from the former East Germany have replaced rural native-born women"

(Ehrenreich and Hochschild 2005, p. 52). Lacking political, union, and economic power, these workers are open to exploitation by their employers.

The trafficking of women for sexual labor is a major illustration of gender exploitation. In 2000, the United Nations estimated that sex trafficking yielded $5–7 billion in profit and involved at least 700,000 women (Shifman 2003). Rather than finding more prosperous lives, these women often end up as virtual slaves to traffickers (Ehrenreich and Hochschild 2005). The technology of the Internet has made the buying and selling of women more accessible and prevalent (Shifman 2003). In the demand for sex laborers, gender often intersects with racial, class, and age characteristics in that men may have desires for particular kinds of women. Gendered values in a society may privilege certain qualities: "perhaps some of this demand grows out of the erotic lure of the 'exotic.' Immigrant women may seem desirable sexual partners for the same reason that First World employers believe them to be especially gifted as caregivers: they are thought to embody the traditional feminine qualities of nurturance, docility, and eagerness to please . . . some men seek in the 'exotic Orient' or 'hot-blooded' tropics a woman from the imagined past" (Ehrenreich and Hochschild 2005, pp. 53–54). In this way, globalization activates the use of gendered values in the perpetuation of gender inequality.

While domestic work and sexual labor offer two specific areas in which globalization has an impact, globalization has also had a broader effect on labor-force segregation. It has reinforced and reproduced traditional gender differences in the workplace, relegating women to positions of lower pay and authority than those of men. At the same time, globalization has created some economic independence for some women and encouraged labor activism among them (Mills 2003). Some have even found that greater foreign investment by transnational corporations reduces occupational segregation (Meyer 2003).

How much globalization reproduces sex segregation in occupations within a nation depends in part on the relative position of the country in the world economic system as a whole. Globalization may exacerbate gender occupational inequality in some countries while lessening it in others. For example, Meyer (2003) found that high levels of trade and increased foreign investment have more of a weakening effect on segregation and inequality in the occupational structure in less-developed than in more-developed countries. This results in part from the resulting movement of women into traditional male occupations, such as manufacturing. But she cautions that this lessening of segregation does not reveal many of the qualitative properties of the jobs that women get nor does it take into account the prevalence of women in the underground economy. She also observes that the segregation reductions may be temporary.

Occupational segregation and inequality in industrial countries appear to be much less affected by these globalization processes. From her study of 56 nations, Lisa Meyer contends that "[t]his is likely due to the fact that the economic structures in advanced industrialized nations counteract global forces and societal features . . . thereby promoting nominal segregation through the incorporation of women's traditional tasks into the formal economy" (ibid., pp. 270, 272).

While occupational segregation may not be as affected by globalization in industrial countries like the United States as it is in less industrialized nations, globalization does have other implications for gender inequality in the United States. For example, globalization has created more competition for major stockbroking firms on the international market and, consequently, greater pressure for increased effort and longer work hours for employees, most of whom are men. The result is the perpetuation and even intensification of gender inequity in housework. More time at work means less time for family, and higher pay means less need for the spouse to work, thereby solidifying the traditional division of labor between husbands and wives (Blair-Loy and Jacobs 2003). More generally, globalization in the form of increased trade appears to be more likely to reduce gender wage inequality in concentrated than in competitive industries in the United States because it opens up these traditionally sheltered industries to international competition (Black and Brainerd 2004). Thus, as in other areas of inequality, conclusions about the effects of globalization need to take into account the economic and cultural contours of the units being examined.

SUMMARY

This chapter has documented the historical socioeconomic position of women in the United States. Despite having been consistently involved in the economy, women have generally held lower positions in it. Even in colonial times, women who worked received lower pay even though they made valuable economic contributions, and factory jobs were segregated on the basis of sex. By the beginning of this century, women already dominated certain occupations, although those of higher ethnic and class positions controlled most of the prestigious occupations. Gender roles culturally associated with women (e.g., homemaking, clerical work, etc.) generally are given lower status in our society, resulting in gender inequality. Occupational conditions today still reveal distinct inequalities between men and women. Women (1) are spread over a smaller range of occupations, (2) are less likely to be in positions of authority, (3) are more likely to work in smaller organizations in the peripheral sector of the economy, (4) are more likely to occupy positions with short career ladders, and (5) make less money than men even when they work full time, year round, and have

comparable educational levels. A variety of microinequities involving language, popular media and stereotypes, and education also pervade relationships between men and women.

Attempts to account for the inequalities between the sexes suggest that differences in human capital, commitment to the labor force, work effort, and interruptions due to childbearing and rearing do not account substantially for the differences in earnings and occupational placement. The differential arrangement of women and men along the occupational hierarchy is, however, directly related to the discrepancy in earnings between the sexes, especially when we consider the differences in the characteristics of the jobs most often held by men and women.

Broader theories of sex inequality have also been advanced, and we focused on those that are more sociological or anthropological in nature. Among the factors that have been linked with sex inequality are (1) the cultural association of women with nature and men with culture or society, (2) the position of women in the work organization of society, (3) the hostile or friendly character of the natural environment, (4) capitalism's requirements and women's role in necessary labor, and (5) early patriarchal structures. Women's roles in the domestic and economic public spheres appear to have direct consequences for their overall position in society. It seems reasonable to conclude that in our own society, the demands and expectations of capitalism and traditional or patriarchal views of what is appropriate for men and for women have affected the kinds of occupations and levels of earnings that each of these groups is likely to attain. At the same time, we must keep in mind that not all women are in the same position because each one's position is affected by the intersection of their race, class, and gender. Multiracial feminist theories warn us against the dangers of generalizing too broadly.

Oppression against women varies widely across the world. The extent of extreme forms such as genital mutilation, honor killings, suicide, and sex trafficking differs among societies. Women also spend significantly more time on housework than men. There is also sex segregation in the occupational structure. Globalization has had an impact on the constraints and opportunities afforded women across the world. Its effects vary among nations depending on the position of the country in the world economic system. For example, the movement of women into careers in the industrial world has fostered a demand for more domestic workers, many of whom are immigrants from technologically less-advanced countries. This creates opportunities for some women but also the possibility for continued oppression.

CRITICAL THINKING

1. Think about a specific occupation and its likely occupant (e.g., police officer, elementary school teacher, home builder). Does a specific sex come to mind? Why?

2. In your own life, how have sex and gender limited you or allowed you to act a certain way or get involved in particular kinds of activities? What was it about your sex or gender that created this effect?

3. In terms of conditions in the United States, how do you think foreign investment, immigration, and outsourcing of jobs have affected gender inequality?

4. What needs to be done to reduce gender inequality in occupations and earnings?

WEB CONNECTIONS

The Global Policy Forum is a nonprofit, tax-exempt organization that consults with the United Nations on issues of international law and equity among nations. It recommends articles on gender inequality and compares countries on the gender gap. Visit www.globalpolicy.org/socecon/inequal/indexgen.htm.

CHAPTER 6

Sexual Orientation and Inequality

The greatest debates and ethical dilemmas of our time are about drawing boundaries. This is because placing lines here or there has definite implications for how we treat each other and the world around us.

—Christena E. Nippert-Eng

In the previous chapter, we focused concern on sex and gender and discussed a variety of inequalities that exist between males and females as the two traditionally recognized sexes. In this chapter, we will examine status inequality that results from sexual orientation, principally the inequities associated with being gay or lesbian. Unfortunately, sexual orientation has generally been ignored as a basis for inequality. "With some noticeable exceptions . . . sociologists of race, class, and gender nonetheless tended to treat sexuality as a weakly integrated addendum to the list of intersecting oppressions" (Gamson and Moon 2004, p. 52).

Historically, Western society has viewed sex, gender, and sexuality as dichotomous and interrelated. The conceptual sets of male/female, masculine/feminine, and hetero-sexuality/homosexuality have been thought to accurately and completely characterize sexual possibilities. Moreover, men are supposed to behave in a masculine manner while women are supposed to perform femininity, and heterosexuality is a part of their masculine and feminine performances.

Rather than being a fixed attribute of the individual or as something that we *are*, gender

and heterosexuality are something that we *do* (West and Zimmerman 1987). Further dichotomies in social science, such as public/private, instrumental/expressive, and rational/emotional, have built on these typologies and helped reinforce their perceived legitimacy. The continued emphasis on these dichotomies as "natural" lends them a seemingly timeless and universal quality. Consequently, individuals who do not fit into these neat categories or do not behave in the culturally prescribed manner for their category have been thought of as deviant. Judeo-Christian dogma views normal, moral, and legitimate sex as having a reproductive function and as belonging in monogamous marriages between men and women, and views same-sex relations as sinful and abnormal (Herdt 1997). Heterosexuality is generally conceived of as being normal, while homosexuality is defined popularly as outside the mainstream. But traditional binary categories of sex and related genders are neither timeless, universal, or natural. They are social constructions found only in some societies during specific periods of time. Katz observes that " 'homosexual' and 'heterosexual,' the terms we moderns take for granted, are fairly recent creations. Although presented to us as words marking an eternal fact of nature, the terms 'heterosexual' and 'homosexual' constitute a normative sexual ethic, a sexual-political ideology, and one historically specific way of categorizing the relationships of the sexes" (Katz 2004, p. 45). How one defines oneself sexually is also not permanent but rather varies according to historical, situational, and cultural circumstances, and can be affected by one's race and class. The meaning of sexuality intersects with cultural images of gender, race, and class, and this intersection helps to reinforce stereotypes and justify oppression and inequality (Gamson and Moon 2004). The meanings of masculinity, femininity, and sexuality in general vary with one's race and class.

THE COMPLEXITY OF SEXUALITY AND GENDER

The simplistic, traditional, either/or categories of male/female, masculine/feminine, and heterosexuality/homosexuality miss much of the variety of actual human experiences (Lorber 1996). While most Westerners think of man and woman as mutually exclusive categories, a number of countries around the world recognize more than two sexes, sexualities, and genders. For example, in India, the *hijras*, while male at birth, define themselves as neither men nor women but as a third gender. They wear women's clothing and may marry men. Yet they are not stigmatized, but are thought to exemplify the time-honored Hindu belief that each person possesses both male and female elements. *Hijras* personify this dualism and the valued "ambiguity of in-between sexual categories" (Andersen 1997, pp. 21–22). Another illustration of the complexity of sexuality concerns individuals born biologically as hermaphrodites. At birth, members of this intersexed group lack an enzyme that would allow them to develop male genitals and so they are initially defined as female, even though male features begin to develop later

during puberty. These "manlike" women are placed in a third sex category (Herdt 1997).

The oversimplified dichotomy of male and female is further demonstrated in studies of *transgendered* individuals—that is, individuals who deviate from the traditional gender binaries of Western society and who sometimes define themselves as belonging to a third gender category (Gagne and Tewksbury 1998). These include individuals who wish to be women or men and who may or may not undergo surgery for sex reassignment. But whether or not one can afford sex-change surgery depends upon one's class since the surgery involves significant costs. In this way, as well as others, sex, sexuality, and gender intersect with class position.

Men who are transsexuals may describe themselves as being heterosexual, bisexual, or lesbian. Ironically, a majority of these individuals do not challenge the idea that men should be masculine and women should be feminine. That is, they accept the traditional gender categories. However, they define themselves as women rather than men, and therefore adopt many of those roles and attitudes traditionally associated with women. Some argue that sexual identity involves a variety of elements and thus their combinations can result in multiple possible sexual identities. Among others, these elements include one's biological sex at birth, self-identity of gender, biological sex of partner, and the distribution of masculine and feminine traits in one's personality (Sedgwick 1998). The wide variety of self-identities, gender practices, and even biological differences found in contemporary society have led a growing number of scholars to urge replacement of the traditional dichotomies of male/female and masculine/feminine with more complex classification systems of sexuality and gender (e.g., Lorber 1996; Andersen 1997; Herdt 1997).

Because of their mixing of gender, sex, and sexuality, the position of transsexuals and bisexuals remains ambiguous within the gay and lesbian community. In other words, they violate the norms within the homosexual community of what it means to be a "normal" or "good" homosexual. They are not fully accepted and are stigmatized by "ordinary" homosexuals. The final result is that transsexuals and bisexuals are often relegated to a position of low status within a community that is itself stigmatized by the larger heterosexual society (Phelan 2001, pp. 115–117).

In the discussion that follows, I will concentrate on *homosexual* groups. It appears that while knowledge of same-sex relations goes far back in history, the technical dichotomy of heterosexuality and homosexuality as we know it today is of nineteenth-century origin, that it "is a product of the transition to modernity. . . . This sexual transformation involved such factors as the institutionalization of bourgeois middle-class values, the secularization of social medicine and state discourse on sexuality, the individualized concept of desire and identity, and the premium placed on reproduction within the nuclear family" (Herdt 1997, p. 39). At that time, homosexuality was considered abnormal and a disease, a kind of degeneracy from the healthy condition of heterosexuality. In fact, up until the early 1970s, homosexuality was listed as a mental illness by the American Psychiatric Association (APA). Recent studies indicate that homosexuality *itself* is not a good predictor of mental illness. Child gender identity disorder and transsexualism are still formally listed as mental disorders by the APA (Bailey 1996).

Despite evidence to the contrary, and even after its removal from its list as an illness by the APA, some psychoanalysts and Christian counselors continue to view homosexuality as a pathological condition (Gonsiorek 1996). In large part, this is because the standard heterosexual view of the strict, accepted relationships among sex, gender, and sexuality is broken by homosexuals. Instead of a female desiring a male, there is sexual inversion in which a female, for example, desires another female. In heterosexual society, this defines homosexuality as an aberration (Phelan 2001). In each of the traditional dichotomies of male/female, masculine/feminine, and heterosexual/homosexual, one category has been given higher social status in the United States over the other. In the case of the last, heterosexuality is valued and honored over homosexuality. This belief was manifested in the recent political controversy surrounding gay marriages, which most opponents viewed as being antithetical to traditional moral values.

PUBLIC OPINIONS ON HOMOSEXUALITY

The preceding comments suggest that there continues to be a deeply held view that homosexuality is unnatural and unhealthy, if not immoral. When one adds to this the strong negative reaction to homosexuality by staunchly religious groups, it is not surprising that, up until the early decades of the twentieth century in the United States, gay networks tried to avoid harassment by keeping out of the public eye. In the mid-twentieth century, the anti-alien crusades of Senator Joseph McCarthy and FBI director J. Edgar Hoover as well as city police across the country continued to single out gays and lesbians as legitimate targets who were thought to undermine the heterosexual family as a cultural foundation. These attacks were viewed as legitimate because of the legal status of homosexuality. "Homosexual acts were illegal in most states under existing anti-sodomy statutes. . . . Furthermore, gays and lesbians were specifically excluded from laws and policies regulating fair employment practices, housing discrimination, rights of child custody, immigration, inheritance, security clearances, public accommodations, and police protection" (Button, Rienzo, and Wald 1997, p. 24).

The public's attitudes about the morality of homosexuality became more positive during the 1990s. Analyses of data from the General Social Survey collected over the 1973–2002 period revealed that in 2002, 53 percent felt that homosexuality was "always wrong." This contrasts with the approximately two-thirds who considered it wrong during the 1973–1993 period. The historical dislike of homosexuality is reflected in the fact that, up until very recently, a number of states still had laws against sodomy. Sodomy laws in 18 states were only repealed after 2000, several of these in 2003. However, a small majority continue to believe that homosexuality is always wrong. A slight majority (55%) think that homosexual behavior is sinful; this is especially the case among individuals who are very religious. Almost nine out of ten of these persons believe such behavior is sinful, contrasted with only 18 percent of individuals who are not religious (Pew Research Center 2003). Close to half the population considers homosexuality to be an acceptable lifestyle. A 2003 Gallup poll in mid-2003 found that 49 percent considered it acceptable (University of California-Davis 2005).

When it comes to gay marriage, several polls indicate that a majority of Americans disapprove of it. Almost two-thirds were against any law that would permit homosexuals to get married in a traditional sense. A large percentage, but still not a majority, are in favor of allowing some kind of civil union between same-sex partners. A plurality are against legal recognition of same-sex unions of any kind (Pew Research Center 2003; Polling Report 2005).

Many adults may not like homosexuality, but that does not mean they advocate discrimination against homosexuals as a group. With respect to *specific* economic areas of civil rights, there does appear to be an increase in the percentage of those who would not exclude homosexuals from teaching, sales, medical, clerical, and political professions. In most cases, this includes a majority of those sampled. By and large, the belief that civil liberties ought to be curtailed among homosexuals has steadily declined since the early 1970s (Loftus 2001; Pew Research Center 2003).

The public appears to be split on allowing gays and lesbians to serve in the military, but most recent polls suggest that close to a majority

may be in favor of their participation. In general, over 75 percent of adults feel that homosexuals should have equal job and housing opportunities. At the same time, however, a majority contend that homosexuals, as opposed to women and racial minorities, should not be explicitly covered under *broad* civil rights laws (Gallup 1997; Yang 1997).

The sharp contrast in Americans' reactions to homosexuals' *morality*, on the one hand, and their rights to *civil liberties*, on the other, may in part be explained by how each of these is interpreted. While *morality* relates to *individual behavior* and activates traditional heterosexual and religious beliefs of Americans, *civil rights* relates to homosexuals as a *group*, does not refer to a specific behavior, and is not as easily linked to religious beliefs. Rather, the civil-rights issue is more easily tied to traditional American values of equality and fairness (Loftus 2001). The difference in respondents' attitudes in these two areas exposes contradictions within the value systems of most Americans.

Not all subcategories of adults are equally likely to hold positive or negative attitudes about homosexuals, however. One should be cautious in drawing conclusions on this matter because most studies have involved either small, student, or nonrandom samples. There are also fewer studies of lesbians than gay men, perhaps suggesting a gender bias. Nevertheless, several research patterns emerge that suggest systematic variations in prejudice against homosexuality. Those who believe that it is something one is born with or cannot be changed are more sympathetic toward homosexuals than are those who view it as a chosen lifestyle (Button, Rienzo, and Wald 1997; Pew Research Center 2003). Men appear to be more heterosexist than women on a variety of dimensions. They are more hostile (1) toward homosexuals as *individuals*, especially when this involves gays rather than lesbians; (2) toward homosexual *behavior*; and (3) toward *civil rights* for gays in traditionally masculine roles such as service in the military (Kite and Whitley 1998). In addition to gender, education is also related to homophobia, with more education being associated with lower degrees of prejudice. Within educational institutions, students in the arts and social sciences are more positive in their attitudes than are those majoring in business or science (Schellenberg, Hirt, and Sears 1999). Among age groups, a greater proportion of those aged 65 or older are prejudiced, compared to those under 30 years of age. This may be partially accounted for by the generally lower education and greater religious traditionalism among older adults. Table 6.1 lists the population categories found by Loftus to be most negative about the morality of homosexuality and most willing to restrict the civil liberties of homosexuals (2001). Results from a 2003 Pew survey reveal similar results, with men, older, rural, lesser educated, southern, conservative, and evangelical Protestants having more negative views of homosexuals. With regard to race, a review of 31 national surveys conducted between 1973 and 2000 indicates that while Blacks are more likely to be against homosexuality on moral grounds, they are more supportive than Whites of protecting the civil rights of homosexuals (Lewis 2003).

Not unexpectedly, political conservativism and right-wing authoritarianism have also been found to be linked to hostility toward homosexuality. "Right-wing authoritarians" are individuals who adhere to "the traditional family structure and feel threatened by liberalization and individuals who threaten their conventional values" (Haddock and Zanna 1998, p. 85). Relatedly, conservative religious groups have demonstrated their opposition to homosexuality by being in the forefront of battles against gay-rights policies around the country.

A recent survey of gay-rights ordinances in 126 communities identified evangelical, charismatic churches as most likely to oppose gay-rights legislation (Button, Rienzo, and Wald 1997). This includes Black evangelical groups as well. Within the Black community, the heritage of seeking justice and supporting the underdog coexists with more conservative social attitudes that, in turn, are tied to fundamentalist religious beliefs. The result has been a wide variation in the attitudes of Blacks to homosexual issues. The survey also identified communities with gay-rights ordinances as being (1) larger and growing, with (2) higher average incomes and educational levels, (3) lower median age, and (4) greater proportions of Blacks and nonfamily households in the populations, than communities that do not have such legislation. The South is less likely to be supportive of homosexual rights than other regions. These results are consistent with those

TABLE 6.1   Demographic Categories Most Negative on Morality and Civil Liberties of Homosexuals

Most likely to view homosexuality as immoral or to believe in restricting civil liberties of homosexuals are those who are

- older
- less educated
- male
- from South Central part of the United States
- other than White or Black
- persons who lived on farm or in country at age 16
- fundamentalist Protestant in religious affiliation.

Source: Loftus 2001.

found in other surveys. Individuals with lower incomes and education, who are older and from the South and rural areas are more likely to feel that homosexuality is morally evil (Newport 1998).

In most cases, these variables interact with others in individuals to either intensify or weaken antagonism toward homosexuals. Sherrod and Nardi's 1998 three-year study of 3,542 mock jurors in 15 states sought to identify characteristics of individuals who are most likely to be biased against persons who were either gay or lesbian. Using an established homophobia scale that tapped the extent of personal prejudice and beliefs about homosexual rights in a variety of areas, the researchers developed profiles of those most likely to be antihomosexual as jurors. They found that White and Latino males were the most homophobic, and Latina and White females the least. Black males and females were in the middle. Generally, the most important predictors of homophobia were found to be political conservatism and the absence of close homosexual friends. As Table 6.2 shows, within each racial and gender group certain types of individuals were most likely to harbor such hostility.

The attitudes adults hold about homosexuals are at least moderately related to stereotypes held about them. These stereotypes include beliefs about gays' personality traits, behavior, and physical characteristics. Popular stereotypes of gays and lesbians suggest that negative reactions to them are due in part to the fact that they are seen as violating traditional gender rules about behavior and interests. The hostility toward men who violate masculine roles appears to be stronger than that toward women who violate feminine prescriptions (Kite and Whitley 1998). When questions about homosexuals make distinctions between gay men and lesbians, results show that heterosexual men and women view gay men more negatively than lesbians. This emphasizes the need to disaggregate the homosexual population when designing attitudinal surveys about them. Herek found that, in general, greater hostility is felt toward gay men than lesbians. This was the case even among the heterosexual men in the sample. Gay men are also more likely than lesbians to be seen by respondents as being mentally ill, as potential child predators, and as less likely to make good parents. These feelings are more prevalent among heterosexual men than women. Although this was found to be true for both, heterosexual men are also more likely than women to feel uncomfortable around a homosexual of the same sex. Finally, the homosexuality of lesbians is more likely than that of gay

TABLE 6.2   Characteristics of Potential Jurors within Selected Groups Who Are Most Homophobic

White men	No homosexual friends, traditional in values, actively religious, politically conservative, Protestant, from the South
Latino men	No homosexual friends, conservative, guided by religious values, military veterans
Black women	Actively religious, politically conservative, no close homosexual friends, do not read newspaper regularly
Black men	No close homosexual friends, conservative, traditional in values, do not read magazines regularly
Latina women	No close homosexual friends, guided by religious beliefs in daily life, married, conservative, traditional in values
White women	Politically conservative, religious in daily life, no close homosexual friends, live in South, traditional in values, attends religious services regularly, do not read newspaper regularly, have high school or less education, believe in fate

Source: Based on Sherrod and Nardi 1998, pp. 32–35.

men to be viewed by both men and women as being the result of an intentional choice (Herek 2002). Herek's results reinforce those of earlier work that also found stronger reactions against violations by men of traditional masculine roles (e.g., Kite and Whitley 1996) and are consistent with research that finds victimization to be higher among older gay men than lesbians (D'Augelli and Grossman 2001).

Stereotypes about gay men suggest that they are viewed as being feminine, emotional, security-seeking, neat, interested in fine arts, creative, with high-pitched voices (see Simon 1998 for a summary). In her multimethod study among Rutgers University students, Stephanie Madon found that there are also subtypes within stereotypes of gay men. On the one hand, they are generally viewed as possessing some positive feminine personality traits (e.g., compassionate, gentle), while on the other hand, they are seen as violating masculine roles (e.g., "walk like girls," "transvestites"). Of these two components, it is their violation of traditional masculine roles that is more strongly held in popular stereotypes, and it is this dimension of the stereotype that may be most clearly linked to prejudice against gay men (Madon 1997). Stereotypes about lesbians, like those of gay men, contain violations of traditional feminine roles in featuring many masculine traits. Lesbians are characterized as being independent and independently minded, open and loud, stubborn, and not being good for children.

Labeling an individual as having the traits of either of these stereotypes, and therefore as being automatically lesbian or gay, can have significant consequences. Consider the case of Sara Harb Quiroz, a permanent and employed U.S. resident who, on her way back into Texas from Juarez, Mexico, was stopped by an immigration agent (Luibheid 1998). Evidence indicated that she was stopped because her appearance revealed several masculine characteristics. She wore pants and a shirt instead of a dress and her hair was cut "abnormally" short for a female. Ms. Quiroz may or may not have been a lesbian.

Since as late as 1990, lesbian immigrants could be refused entry into the United States, and conscious attempts were made by border agents to identify lesbians. They looked for visible cues to the individual's sexual preference. Lesbian immigrants were often aware of this kind of screening, so they dressed and prepared themselves physically so that they would not appear to violate traditional images of what a woman *should* look like. This is known as "straightening up," which "includes practices like growing one's hair and nails, buying a dress, accessorizing, and donning makeup. . . . [The fact that one has to do this only] confirmed the 'bug'-like status of lesbians within the immigration system" (ibid., pp. 485–486).

HOMOSEXUALS AS A STATUS GROUP

As the surveys just discussed indicate, homosexuals, like women and Blacks, form a status category with low prestige or social honor in the United States. As such, they possess all the core attributes of status groups. Most notably, they are subjectively viewed by others as sharing certain lifestyle characteristics while being qualitatively different from outsiders. Being gay or lesbian is associated with having certain kinds of occupations (e.g., hairdresser) and dress (high fashion, artsy) (Madon 1997). However, their differences are defined as even deeper. Recall that in his depiction of status groups, Max Weber argued that extreme status separation between groups is most likely if the differences that separate them are thought of as being "ethnic" in nature. Consistent with this conception, gay scholar Stephen Murray has referred to the homosexual community as a "quasi-ethnic group" (1996, p. 4). This suggests that the differences must be viewed as fundamental, almost biological in nature, for castelike arrangements to develop between groups. Indeed, depending on the survey used, somewhere between one-third and one-half of U.S. adults currently believe that homosexuality is either biologically based or something with which one is born that cannot be changed (cf., e.g., Yang 1997; Newport 1998). In their fight for political legitimacy and equal rights, the earliest gay-rights organizations in the United States (e.g., the Mattachine Society) characterized "homosexuals as a sexual minority, similar to other ethnic and cultural minorities" (Button, Rienzo, and Wald 1997, p. 25). Those currently at the forefront of the gay-rights movement also "argue that homosexual orientation is a genetic condition like skin color or gender" (Newport 1998, p. 14).

The latter comment is quite revealing because in the case of each of the three principally involved groups implied in the statement (i.e., homosexuals, Blacks, women), fundamental values are at stake. Specifically, sexual orientation, race, and gender are each controversial and sensitive areas of conflict. They are touchstones for battles in the United States over basic values involving sexual behavior, racial superiority, and appropriate gender roles. Since these are important matters in U.S. society, it should be expected that status boundaries should separate those who fall on different sides of these values. In the case of sexual orientation, homosexuals are clearly defined as being on the wrong side regarding moral values. One consequence is their exclusion from full citizenship in U.S. society (Phelan 2001).

In addition to being viewed as qualitatively different in lifestyle, being seen as a different "kind" of people, separated from the rest of society, and occupying a distinctive place on a hierarchy of social honor or prestige, a status group is also perceived as having an internal social cohesion that unites them. That is, they are seen as sticking together and being mutually supportive of each other. As with most status groups, outsiders lump them all together, even though there are sources of internal division, such as race, within the homosexual community. On the other hand, given that the crucial factor of sexual orientation is what divides them from and is the prime basis for conflict with outsiders, it is defense involving this factor that helps to unite them. This has resulted not only in the creation of informal friendship networks among gays and lesbians, but also in the development of neighborhoods with high concentrations of homosexuals, separate institutions catering to a homosexual clientele, and political-rights organizations.

Finally, what further marks homosexuals as a negatively defined status group are fears of contamination and contact on the part of outsiders. Concerns about purity on the part of traditionalists and heterosexuals are indicative of concerted attempts to keep boundaries between heterosexuals and homosexuals intact. Publically known association by a heterosexual with homosexuals, especially of a personal kind, creates the risk that some of the ostracism held for homosexuals may "rub off" on the individual. The recent murder involving guests on Jenny Jones's television show is a good example of the stigmatization felt by a man who had been connected to a gay acquaintance. In front of live and national audiences, the gay guest professed his love for the man. The man later killed his gay friend because he felt "humiliated" by this profession of love (Turner, May 17, 1999).

Fear of association is also suggested by polls that indicate that less than 10 percent of U.S. adults feel warmhearted about gays and lesbians and less than one-third feel homosexual couples should be allowed to adopt children (Yang 1997). This is despite the fact that concerns that homosexuals are more likely than heterosexuals to be sexual predators on unsuspecting children or that children who are raised by gays or lesbians will be damaged or turn out to be homosexuals themselves are simply not supported by evidence (Andersen 1997). Still, these beliefs persist in part because they are consistent with prevailing stereotypes and help justify hostile treatment of homosexuals. In their campaigns, opponents of gay rights often use "lurid stereotypes of gays as child molesters, sources of disease, and an abomination in the eyes of God" (Button, Rienzo, and Wald 1997, p. 195). It is feared that unless gays and lesbians are held in check, traditional morality and family structure as foundations of our society will become contaminated and seriously weakened. In the eyes of these opponents, social, cultural, and moral purity must be maintained, and contamination avoided at all costs.

DISCRIMINATION, LEGAL CONFUSION, AND SEXUAL ORIENTATION

No federal laws explicitly prohibit discrimination based on sexual orientation. For example, Title VII of the 1964 Civil Rights Act prohibits employment discrimination because of an individual's race, color, religion, national origin, or sex, but it offers no such prohibition based on sexual orientation. Arguments in favor of protection for homosexuals under Title VII generally involved reference to the inclusion of "sex" in the law.

The meaning of the phrase "because-of-sex" has been a subject of debate, and its interpretation has varied between courts and levels of courts. Some judges have argued, for example, that just because a man harasses a woman on the job, this does not mean he does so because of her sex. Others have suggested that simply showing interest in the other sex constituted discrimination. Many recent courts have argued that harassment is often based on hostility that has nothing to do with the recipient's sex, and, therefore, is not protected under Title VII (Hebert 2001). The confusion over this issue is explored more fully below.

The battle to gain protection based on sexual orientation has not been fully successful. As of 2000, twenty states continue to prohibit sexual activity between individuals of the same sex. The lack of specific mention of sexual orientation as a basis for punishment in many state hate-crime laws similarly suggests the absence of attention paid to the interests of lesbians and gay men by some state public officials (Wald 2000). However, state hate-crime laws are more prevalent than any other kind of pro-homosexual law and, in general during the 1990s, both pro-

and anti-homosexual legislation increased at the state level (Haider-Markel 2000).

The fate of proposed legislation on sexual orientation is strongly tied to (1) the extent to which it is seen as supporting or undermining traditional values and social order, and (2) how effectively and in what manner the issue is framed by proponents and opponents to the legislation. The 1996 Defense of Marriage Act (DOMA) provides a good example of this process. The subject of DOMA related directly to the moral dimension of public opinions on homosexuality. As we saw earlier, polls often uncover a clear schism in the public's view of the morality of homosexuality on the one hand, and the affording of civil rights to homosexuals on the other. While a majority of the public views homosexuality as immoral, a large majority also feel that the economic rights of homosexuals should be protected. On a broad level, the conflict experienced by the majority is one that pits religious values against those of a secular democracy, and highlights the issue of separation of church and state.

Traditional U.S. values assign privilege to heterosexual over homosexual relationships, and assume a narrow and clear relationship between one's sex and gender role. Congressional sponsors proposed the DOMA bill "to define and protect the institution of marriage" and "to make explicit what has been understood under federal law for over 200 years; that a marriage is the legal union of a man and a woman as husband and wife, and a spouse is a husband or wife of the opposite sex" (Barr et al. 1996, p. 2). In arguing for its passage, the proponents of DOMA focused on the need to preserve traditional values of family and morality and on alleged attempts by the gay community to undermine "civilized" society. Traditional marriage was praised "as a 'corner-stone,' 'foundation,' 'bedrock,' and 'fundamental pillar' of any civilized society" (Lewis and Edelson 2000, p. 202). In these ways, proponents of DOMA sought to frame the legislation in *moral* rather

The controversy over gay and lesbian marriage hinges on the conflict between civil rights and moral values.
Photo by Brendan R. Hurst.

than *civil-rights* terms, knowing the public's perception of homosexuality as immoral.

In contrast, opponents to DOMA—for example, those who wished to extend marriage rights to gays and lesbians—emphasized the need to enforce the *rights* of homosexuals as citizens. In this case, the moral framing of the issue won. Because of the public's continued negative reaction to homosexuality as a behavior, interest

groups that wish to succeed in getting legislation passed that ensures homosexuals' full citizenship, "will be most successful in the states if they can frame the issues in terms of *rights*, effectively mobilize group resources and sympathetic heterosexuals, and demobilize conservative religious groups" (Haider-Markel 2000, p. 314, emphasis added). Historically, success has been more likely in areas such as labor discrimination than on morally tinged issues such as sodomy and same-sex marriages (Lewis and Edelson 2000).

It is estimated that over 3 million people are in same-sex relationships, and that several million children are being raised by them (Human Rights Campaign 2005a). Currently, Massachusetts is the only state that allows same-sex marriage, while 40 states had laws banning such marriages in 2004. The DOMA does not recognize same-sex marriages at the federal level, the result being that persons in long-term, same-sex relationships are not protected in the same ways that individuals in traditional marriages are. Proponents of gay marriage argue that same-sex couples are now denied many of the rights afforded persons in traditional marriages. Among others, the rights which are fully or partially denied to homosexuals include hospital visitation, social security survivor benefits, health insurance to partners, estate taxes, family leaves, pensions to survivors, and living together in nursing homes. As a whole, the federal government offers 1,138 benefits based on marital status, benefits that are not offered to same-sex couples (Human Rights Campaign 2005b; National Gay and Lesbian Task Force 2005).

More inclusive laws on hate crimes, marriage, employment discrimination, adoption, and military service remain issues in the homosexual community. In viewing the United States as "a heterosexual regime" with its denial of many protections to homosexuals, Shane Phelan argued that gay men and lesbians are not full citizens because "citizenship does not concern only what rights, offices, and duties are to accrue to citizens, but also how the polity decides who is eligible for them; that is, it concerns the structures of acknowledgement that define the class of persons eligible for those rights, offices, and duties" (Phelan 2001, p. 14). Acknowledgement means recognition and respect for a group's lifestyle and for *being* who one is. As noted in Chapter 3, social status is about *being* something, and in this

case, being homosexual does not afford the same recognition as being heterosexual.

Fierce opposition is one of the reasons for the paucity of specific laws to protect homosexuals. In addition, effective and uniform legislation to protect homosexuals has been hampered by the legal profession's lack of clear understanding of basic terms relating to sexuality. Confusion and inconsistency in conceptualizing and defining "sex," "gender," and "sexual orientation" abound in legal venues. The manner in which these have been linked in legal cases reveals the biases in favor of traditional definitions and connections among these terms. Underlying these interpretations is the acceptance of heterosexuality as opposed to any other form. In this view, one's sex (defined biologically in terms of genitalia) is thought to automatically determine one's gender demeanor and role (social) as well as one's sexual orientation (sexual attractions and behavior). For example, males are expected to act in a masculine manner and to be attracted to females. They are not meant to be homosexual in their sexual orientation.

One consequence of these assumed associations is that courts often confuse sex, gender, and sexual orientation, and confuse them in a way that results in denying the rights not only of gays and lesbians, but also of those who do not present themselves or act in a manner traditionally expected of their sex. A man, for example, who acts "effeminately" and who may or may not be homosexual might not be protected by a court because judges directly link such behavior with being homosexual. As a consequence, while individuals who bring their complaints to court may argue that they are being discriminated against because they do not act in a "masculine" manner, courts often make decisions in these cases on the basis of sexual orientation, assuming that such behavior *means* that the persons are gay. In this way, gender role and sexual orientation are conflated and incorrectly tied together (Valdes 1995; Nathans 2001). This results in plaintiffs losing because, as noted earlier, Title VII does not cover discrimination based on sexual orientation. An example of the narrow manner in which courts have often interpreted Title VII is revealed explicitly in a 1979 case involving a female employee who was having a sex-transformation operation. The Ninth Circuit Court judge argued that in including sex as a basis for discrimination in Title VII, "Congress had only the traditional notions of '*sex*' in mind," and that it "applies only to discrimination on the basis of *gender* and should not be judicially extended to include sexual preference such as homosexuality" (quoted in Zimmer et al. 2000, pp. 624–625, italics added).

Ironically, the word *sex* was added to Title VII at the last minute by a powerful anti-civil-rights representative who thought that, by adding it, Title VII would be voted down (Eskridge Jr. and Frickey 1995). It passed anyway. It is still difficult to know exactly what Congress had in mind, however, since *sex* was added to Title VII only a day after it was presented. Consequently, there was little time for discussion of the meaning of this inclusion (Nathans 2001). Attempts to use other bases, such as the right to privacy, free speech, and equal protection to protect gays and lesbians, have not been very successful (Zimmer et al. 2000). The ruling discussed above shows how the court used the terms *sex* and *gender* interchangeably (see also Case 1995). The easy substitution of the terms *sex* and *gender* in legal arguments adds to the confusion concerning the terms' meanings. The case also reveals the narrow manner in which sexuality is framed by the court. Finally, the legal situation is further complicated by the fact that some courts define *sex* according to the biology of the person at birth, while others consider later operations that change an individual's biological makeup (Valdes 1995).

Although Title VII of the 1964 Civil Rights Act prohibits discrimination on the basis of sex, it is not clear what this means. As we have seen, the result has been confusion. Another example will illustrate the confusion of gender and sexual orientation. In the case of *Smith* v. *Liberty Mutual Insurance Co.*, Smith was not hired as a mail clerk because he was seen as "effeminate" and, consequently, "not too suited for the job" (quoted in ibid., p. 138). The representative for the Equal Employment Opportunity Commission, which examined the case, reported that Smith liked "playing musical instruments, singing, dancing and sewing." These were viewed as "interests . . . not normally associated with males" (ibid.). Smith argued that he had been denied employment because he had hobbies that were not consistent with the masculine role and, therefore, was a victim of gender stereotyping. That is, his argument had to do with the traditional connection made between sex and gender behavior. In contrast, the employer argued that he had not been hired because Smith was "suspected" of being a homosexual. In other words, the employer drew a conclusion about Smith's sexual orientation based simply on his gender behavior. The court ended up drawing the same connection, noting that Title VII did not cover an individual's sexual orientation. Thus, it ignored the argument of Smith and the fact that the evidence demonstrated that the discrimination had been based, as Smith proposed, upon his *gender behavior* (effeminacy) and not his *sexual orientation*. This shows how the court used the plaintiff's behavior as a measure of his sexual orientation, and how stereotypical misinterpretations can result in legal defeats for homosexuals and others.

Men who exhibit gender behaviors traditionally associated with females are more likely to face defeat in court than women who act in masculine ways. For example, in the famous 1989 case of *Price Waterhouse* v. *Hopkins*, the U.S. Supreme Court found that Ann Hopkins had been discriminated against because partners refused to propose her as a partner in the firm on the basis of her gender behavior. To them, Ann displayed many of the characteristics traditionally associated with masculinity. She was described by some partners as "macho," as having "overcompensated for being a woman," and in need of "a course at charm school" (*Price Waterhouse* v. *Hopkins* 1989). In spite of her evidenced abilities and experience, Hopkins was passed over for partnership. In ruling against Price Waterhouse because of sex stereotyping, Justice Brennan stated that:

> [W]e are beyond the day when an employer could evaluate employees by assuming or insisting that they matched the stereotype associated with their group. . . . An employer who objects to aggressiveness in women but whose positions require this trait places women in an intolerable and impermissible catch 22: out of a job if they behave aggressively and out of a job if they do not. Title VII lifts women out of this bind. (490 U.S., p. 251)

The disposition in the Ann Hopkins case was the opposite found in the Smith case discussed earlier. It appears there is less tolerance for "sissies" than for "tomboys" (Valdes 1995, p. 179). "The man who exhibits feminine qualities is doubly despised" (Case 1995, p. 3). This is consistent with public opinion surveys, which find a greater contempt for men who violate their traditional roles than for women who act similarly. Consequently, gay men who act effeminately are likely to bear a disproportionate amount of the discrimination leveled against homosexuals.

While legal protection for those with nontraditional sexual orientations has been weak at best at the federal level, a number of local and state governments have passed laws granting protection. Before 1985, only two states and 30 local governments provided protection for private and public employees, but by 1994, 9 states and 81 local governments had done so (Klawitter and Flatt 1998). In these statutes, sexual orientation typically includes bisexuality, homosexuality, and heterosexuality (Zimmer et al. 2000). Even in many of these statutes, however, there are limitations to the protection of homosexuals. Some statutes exempt religious organizations, and if it can be proven that one's sexual preference is actually a "bona fide occupational qualification" for a position, then homosexuals may be excluded from that job (ibid., p. 634). Full legal protection for homosexuals has a long way to go.

A SOCIOECONOMIC PROFILE OF HOMOSEXUALS

Like data on the wealthy, we do not know very much about the actual socioeconomic position, or even the number of homosexuals, because many still fear "coming out" and can remain hidden because of the generally lower visibility of sexual orientation compared to one's race and sex. This alone tells us a great deal about the stigma attached to being homosexual. Moreover, the measurements of homosexuality have varied wildly. Persons who have sex with others of the same gender do not necessarily define themselves as homosexuals, nor are individuals who have had a homosexual experience at one time or another necessarily thought of as homosexuals. The *invisibility* of homosexuals in society is a key feature differentiating this group from those based on gender and race. On one hand, it provides a group that the majority may attack without concern regarding damage to family and friends who are unknown members of the group. On the other hand, the invisibility of homosexuals prevents young gays and lesbians from finding local positive role models and supporters. The unique invisibility aspect of homosexuals as a group is revealed by reference to the military's "don't ask, don't tell" policy which, if applied to Blacks, would basically say it is acceptable to be Black and in the military as long as one does not identify oneself as such.

Measurement issues have revolved around how to define homosexuality and how to procure a representative sample so as to estimate the size of this population. Some estimates have put the figure as high as 10 percent, but that is considered by some to be too high. A national survey of sexual practices suggested that about 2.4 percent of men and 1.3 percent of women (1) consider themselves homosexual or bisexual, (2) have same-sex partners, and (3) are attracted

A variety of groups have banded together to support the rights of non-mainstream sexualities. Such organization has also taken place across national boundaries.
Photo by Brendan R. Hurst.

to homosexuality (Laumann et al. 1994). This may help account for the regional differences in prejudice against homosexuals discussed earlier.

Most recently, three national data sets have been used to determine the gay/lesbian population in the United States. The General Social Survey (GSS), the National Health and Social Life Survey (NHSLS), and the U.S. Census provide the most accurate estimates. Each also provides several measures of sexual orientation. Historically, and cross-culturally, determining a person's sexual identity on the basis of sexual behavior has been problematic (Badgett 2001).

Not surprisingly, the estimates of this population vary with the measure used. Pooling GSS and NHSLS data from the early and mid-1990s, Black and others estimated that while 4.7 percent of men have had at least one homosexual experience since age 18, only 2.5 percent had only same-sex partners in the year before the survey, and only 1.8 percent of men defined

themselves as gay. The figures for women also vary with the measure. For the same definitions, the percentages for women are 3.6, 1.4, and 0.6, respectively. The authors estimated that about 28 percent of men and 44 percent of women who had only same-sex relationships in the prior year had partners—that is, were living with a person of the same sex with whom they were having sexual relations (Black et al. 2000).

According to U.S. Census data, the gay and lesbian population tends to be concentrated in larger urban areas. For example, almost 60 percent of gay men are in 20 cities. While also concentrated, the lesbian population is somewhat more widely dispersed. In smaller cities, those with universities or colleges are more likely than others to have a significant number of homosexuals in their populations. But unfortunately, data from these cities are not very reliable (ibid.). This may reflect regional differences in prejudice against homosexuals discussed earlier.

Education is also related to the incidence of homosexuality, with those in the college ranks being more likely than those with less education to have had homosexual experiences. This relationship is stronger for women than for men, however (Laumann et al. 1994).

Educationally, data from the three national surveys show that a greater percentage of lesbians and gay men than other individuals have higher degrees. For example, data from the U.S. Census indicated that over 31 percent of lesbian-partnered women have college degrees compared to under 18 percent of married women. About 30 percent of gay-partnered men in the 25–34 age bracket have college degrees compared to under 7 percent of married men.

One might think that the apparently higher education of homosexuals would mean that their earnings would be higher than those of others as well. Indeed, small samples from earlier surveys conducted by magazines often suggested that gay men had higher incomes. "Readers of mainstream media are bombarded with this message of affluence from columnists and political figures, and the message seems to get through" (Badgett 2001, pp. 23–24). Explanations for these high incomes often reflect stereotypes about homosexuals. One explanation is that gay men, for example, may put in extra effort at work to show their manliness; another is that homosexuality is the pastime of an idle, rich, and decadent group (ibid.). The fact is, however, that the conclusion that lesbians and gay men have inordinately high incomes is based on surveys whose samples are biased toward the more affluent. The samples usually come from readers of magazines or participants in social events or marches, which most often draw those with higher incomes. In addition, the samples tend to be very small. Consequently, conclusions about the high income of homosexuals are misguided.

In contrast, national data of the early 1990s from GSS and NHSLS surveys suggest that the earnings of gay men who work full-time are significantly lower than those of comparable heterosexual men, while those of lesbians are somewhat higher than the earnings of heterosexual women who work full-time. These differences hold even when age, education, and area of residence are taken into account (Badgett 2001). Similar findings have been uncovered using U.S. Census data on same-sex and married couples, although much of the difference among women appears due to variations in weeks and hours worked (Klawitter and Flatt 1998; Black et al. 2000).

Ironically, the presence of state or local laws prohibiting discrimination against homosexuals does not appear to have a significant impact on their earnings. Rather, the earnings of both heterosexuals and homosexuals tend to be higher in places with such laws. Laws of this kind are more likely to be found in more urban areas where populations have higher levels of education (Klawitter and Flatt 1998). These are likely of be areas where gays and lesbians experience lower levels of discrimination and, consequently, prosper more easily.

Occupationally, evidence cited by Hewitt indicates that gay men are more likely to be self-employed than other men and to be in the labor force, probably because of the greater likelihood that they are younger and single. With respect to the distribution among occupations of gay men, information from different sources reveals the same kinds of patterns. First, gay men are not as broadly distributed along the full range of occupations as are heterosexual men. Like minorities and women, they tend to be concentrated in a smaller number of occupations. Second, the concentration is especially great within white-collar occupations. A much greater proportion of gay men than heterosexual men are in white-collar, higher status jobs. Well over half of gay men are in managerial, administrative, "artistic-creative," or "nurturant" occupations, the latter category referring to traditionally female jobs in which a customer or client receives a face-to-face service of some kind. Under 10 percent are in blue-collar occupations. Third, within broad white-collar categories, there are concentrations of gay men in specific occupations. Although frequently based on small samples, it has been estimated that a disproportionate number of male artists, hairdressers, librarians, architects, entertainers, and fashion designers are gay. Although gay men are heavily overrepresented in these fields, they appear to be very underrepresented in quintessentially "male" occupations such as the military, business, law, and sports (Hewitt 1995). Again, this information must be treated with caution because of the problems of data collection noted earlier.

It has been suggested that concentrations of gay men in particular kinds of occupations are linked to several factors, including discrimination. Despite the military's intent to keep homosexuals out, historically gay men have served in proportions that are similar to those of other men. During World War II, for example, almost 73 percent of partnered gay men had

military service compared to 75 percent of other men. There was also little difference during the Korean War. In recent years, however, gay men have been less likely than other men to be in the military. Overall, among men aged 18–67, about 16 percent of partnered gay men are veterans compared to just over 31 percent of other men. Among women, lesbians have been more likely than heterosexual women to have had military experience (Black et al. 2000).

The hostility expressed by the military establishment to former President Clinton's proposal that gays freely be allowed to enter the military suggests the homophobia involved in discrimination. In fact, despite this attempt by Clinton to lessen discrimination, there have been more gays coerced into leaving the military since the "don't ask, don't tell" policy was installed in 1994. In 2001, 1,250 individuals were dismissed from the armed forces

---

NUTSHELL 6.1

Amid recruiting woes, 'don't ask' under fire

Critics of ban on openly gay soldiers are gaining allies for repeal of policy

BY DAVID CRARY, Associated Press

NEW YORK: Critics of the military's "don't ask, don't tell" policy are gaining new allies, including a few conservative congressmen and a West Point professor, as they press on multiple fronts to overturn the ban on out-of-the-closet gays and lesbians in the armed forces.

As part of their strategy, opponents of the policy are now highlighting the ongoing struggles of Army and Marine recruiters. The Servicemembers Legal Defense Network says in a new report that many highly trained specialists – including combat engineers and linguists – are being discharged involuntarily while the Pentagon "is facing extreme challenges in recruiting and retaining troops."

On other fronts:

- A federal court hearing is scheduled in Boston next month on a lawsuit by 12 former service members challenging the 12-year-old policy.

- In Congress, four Republicans – including stalwart conservatives Wayne Gilchrest of Maryland and Ileana Ros-Lehtinen of Florida – have joined 81 Democrats co-sponsoring a bill to repeal the policy. Gilchrest, a former supporter of the ban, said he changed his view partly out of respect for gay Marines he served with in Vietnam and for his brother, who is gay.

- A U.S. Military Academy professor, Lt. Col. Allen Bishop, wrote a column this spring in Army Times urging Congress to repeal the ban. "I thought I'd get lots of hate mail, and my colleagues would walk on the other side of the hall – but there's been none of that," he said Tuesday.

Still, neither the White House nor the Pentagon has given any signal that they would drop their support for the policy, implemented in 1993 under the Clinton administration. It prohibits the military from asking about the sex lives of service members but requires discharge of those who acknowledge being gay.

On July 6, the Bush administration plans to ask a federal court in Boston to dismiss the lawsuit challenging the policy. The suit cites a 2003 Supreme Court ruling that state laws criminalizing homosexual sex were unconstitutional; the government says that landmark decision has no bearing on "don't ask, don't tell."

More than 9,400 troops have been discharged since the policy was implemented. Discharges peaked at 1,273 in 2001, and declined to 653 last year, a drop that critics attribute to reluctance by war-zone commanders to deprive their units of experienced gay and lesbian personnel during difficult missions.

"The services are far less likely to discharge gays and lesbians serving on the front lines," Servicemembers Legal Defense Network said in its report, released Monday.

"The military continues to sacrifice national security and military readiness in favor of simple prejudice," said SLDN Executive Director C. Dixon

Osburn. "Americans do not care if the helicopter pilot rescuing a wounded soldier or the medic treating that soldier is gay."

A Pentagon spokeswoman, Lt. Col. Ellen Krenke, noted that dismissals under the policy are only a small fraction of overall military discharges. She also noted that the Defense Department could change the policy only if Congress acted first.

Among recently discharged soldiers is Robert Stout of Utica, Ohio, who was wounded while serving in Iraq and wanted to remain in the Army as an openly gay soldier. He is scheduled to visit Washington this week to lobby for repeal of the ban.

Gilchrest said he was unsure how many of his fellow majority Republicans were ready to join in seeking repeal but suggested the momentum was shifting in that direction.

"When this issue comes up, members who believe that gays shouldn't be in the military are now more hesitant to voice their opinion," Gilchrest said Tuesday. "Many of us who feel the other way have come out of the closet, so to speak. A year ago, I would have been uncomfortable expressing my feelings."

Discharges under policy

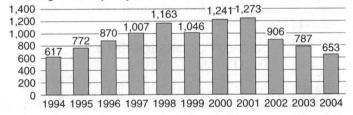

Discharges under 'don't ask, don't tell' policy

A gay rights group notes in a new report that hundreds of service members were discharged under the "don't ask, don't tell" policy last year as the Army struggles with recruiting.

Note: Numbers include United States Coast Guard for all years except 2004

Source: Servicemembers Legal Defense Network

because of their homosexuality, compared to only 617 in 1994 ("Bigotry in the Military" 1999). Harassment in the military has also increased (see Nutshell 6.1). Legal attempts to protect homosexuals in the military on the grounds of privacy or free-speech rights have not been very successful (Zimmer et al. 2000, p. 630).

Prejudice against homosexuality has also been used as a weapon against women in the military who report harassment by men. In doing so, they have been labeled as lesbians, and could then be dismissed because of their alleged sexual orientation (Damiano 1998/1999). In fact, women have been more negatively affected than men by the "don't ask, don't tell" policy. While in 1996 women composed only 13 percent of the military, they were 29 percent of those discharged because of alleged homosexuality (Ransom 2001). These instances demonstrate how homophobia has been used to perpetuate inequality between men and women. Sex, expected gender roles, and heterosexual culture are intertwined in a way that allows continued discrimination by dominant groups.

In addition to discrimination, networking and connections also provide part of the explanation for the concentration of homosexuals in some occupations and their exclusion from others. As noted by Murray (1996):

> *In most places the prototypically masculine occupation of construction worker requires knowing someone to get him into the union or hired by a patron (foreman or employer) at a nonunionized site. Obtaining a position in what hairdressers consider a good salon similarly depends upon personal sponsorship from inside. In any field, there is routine insider trading of information about job vacancies and even secrecy about them. Therefore, any concentration . . . is likely to be replicated and reinforced over time. (p. 159)*

Surveys reveal some broad similarities among gay men, but this does not mean that there are no significant internal differences in this population. One of the problems of being viewed as a separate status group is that outsiders tend to see everyone within that group as being essentially the same. This is the case for women, professors, Blacks, the Amish, and other status groups—including homosexuals. Yet, as in any large group, there are significant differences and conflicts among homosexuals. In addition to differences in attitudes toward and identification with homosexuality within the gay and lesbian communities, alienation often exists between those who consider themselves working class and those in higher status occupations. Race has also been a divisive factor. Ethnic lesbian groups have formed as a reaction against the whiteness of established lesbian organizations and as a desire to celebrate distinct ethnic backgrounds. Generational differences in attitudes and lifestyle also appear to exist (ibid.). The fact that older lesbians and gay men grew up in and had to develop mechanisms to survive the significant difficulties of living in a society that has been broadly and actively hostile toward homosexuality may help account for the high degree of self-acceptance and satisfaction among them (Jacobson and Grossman 1996).

NEGATIVE CONSEQUENCES OF STIGMATIZATION

As an ostracized status group, homosexuals have historically experienced a wide variety of systematic stresses and obstacles in the United States, ranging from psychological difficulties, to personal physical attacks, to institutional and legal discrimination. While the eighteenth-century extreme reaction of legally putting persons to death because of their homosexuality no longer exists, physical victimization has been experienced at one time or another by almost all gay men and lesbians (Button, Rienzo, and Wald 1997). In this section, I will touch on the significant consequences of being homosexual for suicide rates and stress at school and in the work place. A brief discussion of hate crimes is included in Chapter 11.

Suicide

Heterosexism, social isolation, self-blame, and other stresses can have dire outcomes for the individuals who are victims of these conditions. Reviews of research suggest that gay and lesbian youths are two to three times more likely to attempt suicide than their heterosexual counterparts. It has been fairly typical for studies of homosexual youths to cite suicide attempt rates of 20–40 percent (Savin-Williams and Cohen 1996; D'Augelli 1998). Adolescence has its own set of stressful events, and when adding homosexuality to these, its problems are intensified.

However, suicide attempt rates are not spread evenly over this minority population. Gays and lesbians most likely to attempt or seriously think about suicide tend to (1) be younger, (2) be victims of physical assault, (3) feel more confused about sexual identity, (4) have lower self-esteem, (5) have more family problems, and (6) recently have "come out" or have been exposed as homosexual (ibid.). It has also been suggested that gays and lesbians who are members of a racial or ethnic minority may be more vulnerable to these problems because of the singular problems they face as both racial/ethnic and sexual minorities (Savin-Williams and Rodriguez 1993).

Despite the obvious need for various kinds of social support for these individuals, however, the seeking out and offering of such support is problematic because of the demeaned social status of gays and lesbians in U.S. society. Homosexual youths find themselves between a rock and a hard place. On the one hand, they may be willing to seek out individuals who might be able to help, but at the same time, they may be unwilling to risk rejection or reveal their problems because of the stigma attached to the homosexual label. Finally, the invisibility of the homosexual group presents a further barrier for youths who are seeking a support network or role model to guide them through a difficult period.

Minority Stress

The stigma placed on homosexuality exposes gay men and lesbians to a wide array of stresses ranging from everyday microinequities, such as slurs and constant sensitivity to not to be too obvious in one's identity, to problems in their families, religious practice, and the labor market. The stresses themselves, in turn, affect health and feelings of well-being, having been related, for instance, to recurrent headaches, depressive moods, and more serious psychological conditions. In the case of women and minorities who are homosexual, these stresses can be intensified because of their added status as gender and ethnic/racial minorities (DiPlacido 1998). The negative labeling of same-sex intimacy and the consequent uneasiness among some homosexuals about their own behavior and feelings can also lead to problems in developing and maintaining intimate relationships, and greater stress and adjustment problems in general (Meyer and Dean 1998).

Growing up as a homosexual in a social context in which there are strong expectations of heterosexuality can create deep stresses for an individual. Interviews with gay men from a small working-class town in England bear out the agony felt by many gays in a culturally hostile setting as they realize that they do not fit in: "I knew there was something wrong, something different in my life," commented one of the gay men (Flowers and Buston 2001, p. 54). Another remarked, "I remember going home at night and crying myself to sleep because I knew that I was different, and I was terrified of being different" (ibid.). Many of the men in this study kept their feelings to themselves, resulting in a sense of alienation from others: "I never really talked to anyone about my sexual feelings. I used to lay in bed and hide them away thinking about these things and 'I'm not normal'" (ibid., p. 56).

During school years, when boys are dating, and are culturally expected to date girls, homosexual youths find themselves at a psychological and social disadvantage. These same expectations apply to everyone. A lesbian recalls from her youth: "Love of women was never a possibility that I even realized could be. You loved your mother and your aunts, and you had girlfriends for a while. Someday, though, you would always meet a man" (quoted in Savin-Williams 1996, p. 170). A gay youth remembers experiencing a similar plight: "Throughout high school and college I had no way to meet people of the same sex and sexual orientation. These were more years of isolation and secrecy. I saw what other guys my age did, listened to what they said and how they felt. I was expected to be part of a world with which I had nothing in common" (ibid.). Gay youths may experience the stress of their family's bigotry because of their invisibility, unlike Black children whose status is obvious and generally the same as that of their parents and siblings. All of these consequences exist on the personal and interactional level, but stresses that result from the homosexual label exist on the institutional level as well.

Despite the stigmatization and often intense pressures faced by them, a number of homosexuals have "come out" and have prospered. These include Ellen DeGeneres who came out publicly on her own TV series and now has a highly popular talk show. Amelie Mauresmo and Rosie Jones, both professional athletes, also went public with their sexual orientation. Mauresmo is ranked among the top female players in the world and has become much more accepted since her outing in 1999. Jones came out publicly in 2004, and has won over a dozen professional golf tournaments. Finally, in addition to being the author of several books, Roberta Achtenberg has held several political offices, including assistant secretary of the U.S. Department of Housing and Urban Development.

In employment, up until the late 1960s, some occupations—such as those in law, education, medicine, and the military—were not open to homosexuals in most of the United States. Evidence suggests that one-third of gays have experienced discrimination in employment (Button, Rienzo, and Wald 1997). Even now, despite the then President Clinton's attempts to make the military more open for gay men, harassment and footdragging in making the institution more hospitable for gays continue. I have already discussed the hostility of some Christian religious groups toward homosexuality. It is viewed by them as a sin and abomination in the eyes of God. These beliefs serve to justify, and even encourage, hostility toward homosexuals. Interestingly, religious beliefs, such as the "curse of Ham," that were used to justify and encourage racism against Blacks in the past have diminished, leaving gays and lesbians as a religious target.

GLOBALIZATION AND SEXUALITY

At the beginning of this chapter, I commented on the subjectivity and variety of sexual classifications across time and cultures. I also mentioned that members of different racial and class groups define and highlight masculinity and femininity in varying ways. In other words, there is no one way to classify sexualities nor is there only one meaning for how one *does* sexuality. "Different cultures and different periods of history construct gender differently. Striking differences exist, for instance, in the relationship of homosexual practice to dominant forms of masculinity" (Connell 2005, p. 37). The complexity of classifications and sexual identities can only be expected to grow in the United States with globalization and the continued immigration of peoples of varying ethnicities and cultural backgrounds (Gamson and Moon 2004). The open borders that come with these events will have an impact on our views of sexuality and the meanings that we give it. Individuals whose sexual identity is not honored in their own society can immigrate to another more hospitable society and thereby affect and be affected by that society's cultural views.

Given that societies often differ in their sexual mores, meanings, and classifications, when different cultures meet, it should not be surprising that clashes would occur over these matters, as a host society seeks to impose its own hegemonic culture upon those who immigrate into it. Movements by some rights groups to push for a more positive attitude toward homosexuality can inadvertently lead to backlashes by host governments, which establish policies that reinforce traditional meanings and definitions of sexuality (Massad 2002). Western religious missionary work has also reinforced the idea of heterosexual marriage as ideal and served to denigrate and weaken homosexual and other nontraditional sexual behaviors. Technological innovations have also allowed the mass media to promulgate alternative images of sexuality (Connell 2005).

The effects of globalization on definitions of sexuality and gendered behavior and their acceptance depend in part on the relative positions of countries in the world political-economic system. "The conditions of globalization, which involve the interaction of many local gender orders, certainly multiply the forms of masculinity in the global gender order. At the same time, the specific shape of globalization, concentrating economic and cultural power on an unprecedented scale, provides new resources for the dominance of particular groups of men" (ibid., pp. 41–42). Thus, as groups and individuals flow between countries, there are likely to be changes in and reactions to varying definitions of gender and sexuality, including homosexuality. Which definitions and practices become dominant and accepted depends upon relative power in the world order.

Altman contends that homosexual communities in other industrialized nations model themselves after such communities in the United States. The language used and histories evoked are those that originate not in their own coun-

tries, but in the United States. For example, the Stonewall riots that occurred in the United States as a result of police harassment are cited by European gays as giving birth to gay activism even though such activism occurred earlier in their own countries (Altman 2005). This suggests the hegemonic position held by the United States in the world community.

While globalization may help ignite international cultural clashes over the meaning of sexuality, it has also fostered the development of a transnational network of gays and lesbians. Similar movements have been underway to unite transgendered individuals as a means of protecting them against the harassment they regularly experience (ibid.).

SUMMARY

This chapter has presented a brief overview of the inequities involved in being homosexual rather than heterosexual in sexual orientation. The concept of homosexuality has served to single out and stigmatize a group that does not fit dominant cultural ideas about appropriate sexual behavior and lifestyles. Although sympathy and opinions in specific areas of civil rights appear to have improved in recent years, significant proportions and subgroups within the United States continue to be hostile to homosexuality. Stereotypes for both gay men and lesbians continue, and they continue to be a minority with distinct status-group attributes, yet without the legal protections afforded other minority groups.

Because of the difficulties involved for homosexuals and the disregard in which they have been held, reliable and thorough statistics on this group are nonexistent. Estimates about the size of the homosexual population and its characteristics vary from study to study. Lack of knowledge about this community can only help to reinforce existing stereotypes about them. The consequences for individuals in this group are momentous. Few areas of their lives are left untouched; psychological, economic, social, legal, and health problems arise from their position as a stigmatized status group. At the same time, however, some homosexuals have prospered despite the difficulties they have faced, excelling in areas as diverse as sports, entertainment, literature, and politics.

Globalization has had an impact on the sex categories used as well as the meanings ascribed to sexuality and masculinity and femininity. In the case of disagreements, which of these categories and meanings is privileged depends in part upon the position of a society in the global context. Finally, globalization has helped to unify gay and lesbian groups across national boundaries.

CRITICAL THINKING

1. What would be the social consequences if everyone accepted the belief that sexual variation is a continuum rather than a dichotomy (i.e., if we believed that there are many more than two sexes)?

2. How does the invisibility of being homosexual affect the homosexual individual and the status image of homosexuals as a group?

3. How necessary is it that homosexuals be singled out as a group to be legally protected? What are the likely consequences of such legal protection?

4. What do you think should be done about gay marriage? Do bans against it discriminate and perpetuate inequality or do they justifiably protect a viable tradition of marriage? How can we reconcile a desire for fairness with a desire for morality on this issue?

WEB CONNECTIONS

For brief discussions of issues of concern to gay, lesbian, bisexual, and transgender groups, see the websites of the Human Rights Campaign (www.hrc.org) and the Washington Blade (www.washblade.com). Visit also www.thetaskforce.org/reslibrary for reports on issues related to same-sex marriage, civil unions, race and same-sex, and related matters.

7 Racial and Ethnic Inequality

What is a black person?
7-year-old Bridget

The positions of women and minorities are often thought to have a lot in common. Moreover, as mentioned in Chapter 5, race and sex have both been associated with biological differences that have been given social and cultural meanings. While their specific histories and socioeconomic conditions are different, both women and members of minority groups tend to occupy lower positions than White males in our system of inequality. Both groups have even been referred to as being in a lower caste when compared to White males. Finally, the terms "sex," "gender," and "race" each have specific meanings that vary with the cultural, historical, and social context in which they are used. Consequently, none of these terms has a fixed, unvarying definition.

THE MEANING AND CREATION OF RACE

"Race" is a slippery term. The question posed above by 7-year-old Bridget seems pretty straightforward: *"What is a black person?"* Bridget is a U.S. citizen who has been living abroad for the last several years; she has spent most of her life in England, not in the United States. Her mother responded to her question by saying that a Black person is a person

who is "dark-skinned." Bridget responded: "You mean like Tarush" [who is Indian]? Her mother then went on to further explain the traditional racial distinctions, but it was clear that Bridget thought her mother meant that a Black person is distinguished solely by the color of her/his skin. "Color" is an important social and cultural trait, and we know that within "races," individuals can vary in the color of their skin. In our society, individuals with lighter skin generally are accorded higher status than those with darker skin. I will discuss the issue of "colorism" more fully later in this chapter.

The exchange between Bridget and her mother hints at the complexity involved in defining race. There have been past attempts to define it "scientifically" and to develop clear classifications of race, but these have always been found to be faulty for one reason or another, and virtually all have fallen by the wayside. Some of the earliest attempts classified individuals by their ancestry rather than physical features. These tended to conflate ethnicity, nationality, and physical characteristics (e.g., Jewish or Irish "race"). Other classifications tended to identify and rank groups in an ethnocentric fashion, separating the socially dominant group from others and ranking it highest. The features chosen to distinguish the "races" were those that appeared to separate the dominant from lower-ranking groups, groups which could then be exploited for their alleged inferiority. The attempted annihilation of the "Jewish race" by the "Aryans" is an example of how racial categorizations can be based on and used for political rather than scientific reasons. As the social, economic, and cultural positions of groups changed, so did their race. While we usually think of a person's race as affecting their class position, in this case, their *class* position helped to determine their "*race.*" For example, with assimilation, Jewish, Irish, and Italian immigrants, once defined as "non-White" became defined as "White."

The continual changing of racial categories in society and by governmental offices indicates that "race" is something that is created and anchored in the social, economic, and cultural conditions of the time. In the words of Omi and Winant, it involves "racial formation," which is a "sociohistorical process by which racial categories are created, inhabited, transformed, and destroyed" (2005, p. 195). As historical conditions and contexts change, so do racial classifications. In a real sense, racial classifications reflect the structure of inequality in a society.

We need only to review changes that the U.S. Bureau of the Census has made since its first census in 1790. Native Americans and Blacks were separated out from others because of their political status, but it was not until 1820 that "race" or color was used in the Census (Snipp 2003). Throughout the rest of the nineteenth century, the racial classifications used by the Census were rooted in cultural, social, and intellectual developments going on in the wider society. The addition of "Chinese" and "Japanese" to the 1890 Census racial classification reflected growing concern on the part of the dominant group about the increasing numbers and potential competition of

these groups with native citizens on the West coast. The added inclusion of "Octoroon" (1/8 Black) and "Quadroon" (1/4 Black) to the classification symbolized the growing interest in and concern for racial purity at the end of the nineteenth century in the United States (Snipp 2003; Schaefer 2006). States often defined a person as Black if they had only one drop of Black blood and used this definition as a means of fighting and outlawing racial intermarriage (Brunsma and Rockquemore 2002). Racial categories continued to fluctuate in the twentieth century, and reflected changes in social and cultural conditions. The term "Hispanic" is still used even though Hispanics can be of any race. It is considered more as a description of ethnicity and is separated out because Latinos often do not agree on their race or view themselves as belonging to another race, and because they are considered a minority group by the government (Lee and Bean 2004).

In part because of problems encountered by Census workers in accurately classifying a person's race, in 1960 the Census began to allow individuals to identify their own race (Snipp 2003). In 2000, because of increased recognition of the mixed backgrounds of individuals, the Census Bureau made it possible for a person to identify themselves as belonging to more than one race. Tiger Woods helped to call attention to this issue by calling himself a "Cabalinasian" (i.e., part Caucasian, Black, American Indian, Thai, and Chinese) (White 1997). Currently, about 2.5 percent of individuals in the United States identify themselves as multiracial.

When we examine historical fluctuations in the definition and meaning of race, it becomes apparent that racial definitions and classifications have served as indicators of which groups have political, economic, and social power and which ones do not. "Throughout the history of racialization, material (economic, social, and political resources) and ideological elements of race have been inextricably linked" (Lewis

2004, p. 625). Moreover, as we will see, high rates of immigration from Hispanic, Asian, and other groups will continue to accelerate the multiracial character of the United States and further complicate the racial/ethnic picture. Finally, the move toward self-identification has further revealed the fluidity and complexity of race as a concept.

Interestingly, most Whites do not think of "White" as a race. Rather, when speaking of race, the tendency is to think of racial "minorities" as belonging to a race. Whiteness is invisible in this sense. "From an early age," observes Rothenberg, "race, for white people, is about everyone else" (Rothenberg 2002, p. 2). Whiteness is not racialized. "Most White people, in my experience, tend not to think of themselves in racial terms. They know that they are White, of course, but mostly that translates into being not Black, not Asian-American, and not Native American. Whiteness, in and of itself, has little meaning" (Dalton 2002, p. 15). The fact that most Whites do not recognize "White" as a racial category poses a problem for those researching "whiteness" (Lewis 2004).

It is clear that the term "white" has various meanings for different people. For some it has a distinct racial connotation while for others it does not. The same is found for the term "black." It has even been suggested that research in this area should focus not on "who is black" but "what does 'black' mean?" (Brunsma and Rockquemore 2002, p. 109). This is essentially what Bridget was asking earlier. The meaning of a given racial category to individuals has been explored by asking individuals to identify their race. In their study of 177 college students with mixed parentage, Brunsma and Rockquemore, for example, found that students varied in their racial self-identifications. Almost two-thirds identified themselves as neither Black nor White, but as biracial, adopting a "border identity," while the remaining one-third saw themselves as (a) either Black or White,

(b) varying in their race depending on the situation, or (c) not thinking of race as part of their identity at all (2002). How one defines oneself or others racially appears to depend on the geographical context, education, age, race of the identifier, and nativity (Farough 2004; Roth 2005). On nativity, for example, Pyke and Dang found that the adult children of Korean and Vietnamese immigrants thought of themselves as bicultural, but described others in their group as being either "fresh off the boat" or "whitewashed." In using these terms, these children were able to minimize or eliminate the stigma they faced by distancing themselves from their coethnic *others*. Doing this is a response to the racial hierarchy in U.S. society and the desire to maintain a respected position within it (2003).

The discussion above reveals how reflective the concept of race, racial classifications, and racial identification are of the structure of inequality in U.S. society. While researchers continue to use standard racial categories in a manner that suggests that they are fixed and stable, we must keep in mind that they are historical, social, political, and economic creations of society. This is especially important when examining the relationship between race and socioeconomic position. With this in mind, we turn now to a brief historical overview of race and ethnic relations in the United States.

U.S. RACIAL AND ETHNIC RELATIONS: AN HISTORICAL SKETCH

The unequal treatment of racial minorities in the United States goes back to the early years of colonization. Anglo-Saxon colonists' earliest contact with a visibly different group were with American Indians. Ideas and stereotypes of the "savage" had developed in the sixteenth and seventeenth centuries and provided colonists with a framework within which to interpret American Indians. Rather than color or racial distinction, religious and ethnocentric criteria were used initially to separate groups into superior and inferior categories. Specifically, distinctions were made between "Christians" and "heathens" and between "civilized" and "savage" (Fredrickson 1981). Clearly, the American Indians were placed in the heathen and savage categories. Thus, distinct attitudes about this group were entrenched by the time the American Revolution occurred.

Despite these beliefs, early relations between colonists and American Indians were frequently cooperative since both groups were interested in trade and barter. In fact, American Indians frequently had quite a bit of power when it came to bargaining because of their prowess in the fur trade (Lurie 1982). But this cooperation was short-lived. Relationships with the British became increasingly belligerent, since the British were farmers and interested in obtaining American Indian land, whereas the French were primarily traders (Garbarino 1976). The American Indians whose economy emphasized agriculture and who were located near the coast were the first to be overwhelmed by the colonists (Lurie 1982).

In order for the colonists to spread their civilization, land held by American Indians had to be obtained. Many of the latter resided in villages and cultivated crops in a manner not very different from the traditional European way. But arguments about the savage and heathen way of life of American Indians were used as devices to justify taking over this land. Many of the arguments were similar to those used to justify slavery (Farley 1988). The belief was that such action would rescue the earth from these savages and speed progress and Christianity (Fredrickson 1981). This is an early instance of a group using an ideology to justify the taking of economic resources from another.

In the period roughly between 1880 and 1930, over 65 percent of the 138 million acres that had been held by American Indians moved to White ownership (Carlson and Colburn

1972). By the last decade of the nineteenth century, most American Indians were on reservations where they were forbidden to practice their religions and their children were forced to go to boarding schools run by Whites where they had to speak English (Farley 1988). Much of the policy of this period was aimed at forcing American Indians to assimilate into the dominant White culture (Marden and Meyer 1973). Nevertheless, they were not allowed to vote since they were not considered citizens. The Constitution had never actively incorporated concerns for the rights of these groups, and it was not until the 1920s that American Indians were granted citizenship. Even as late as the 1920s and 1930s, there was a feeling among some influential individuals that American Indians were biologically inferior to White Anglo-Saxons (Carlson and Colburn 1972). The consequences of this poor treatment bore bitter fruit.

In the 2000 Census, 2.5 million, or 0.9 percent, identified themselves as only American Indian or Alaska Native. An additional 2.6 million reported a mixed race identity that included American Indian or Alaska Native (U.S. Census Bureau, February 2002). The West has the largest number of American Indians (43%), followed by the South, Midwest, and Northeast, respectively. New York and Los Angeles were the cities with the highest American Indian populations. About one out of eight American Indians live on reservations.

Currently, American Indians have unemployment and poverty rates that are well above those of Whites, and have household incomes that are well below the U.S. median. In 2002–2003, the median household income for American Indians and Alaska Natives (which are grouped together by the Census Bureau) was $32,866 compared to $47,876 for non-Hispanic White households. Their poverty rates for 2001–2003 averaged just over 23 percent, compared to 8 percent for non-Hispanic Whites. During the same period, almost 28 percent were without any health insurance, compared to about 11 percent of non-Hispanic Whites. Their unemployment rates tend to be roughly twice those of the general population. Two areas in which some progress has occurred are education and business. About 73 percent of American Indians aged 25 years or older are at least high school graduates, compared to over 80 percent of Americans in general in that age group. But in the last 20 years, there has been a dramatic increase in enrollment in postsecondary education. In business there has also been a significant rise; 40 percent of tribes have some kind of gambling business operating, bringing in about $15 billion each year (Bruchac 2004; U.S. Census Bureau, August 2004).

Black–White Relations

Land in early America was plentiful but greater labor power was needed to take full advantage of its resources. The absence of large numbers of willing free laborers led to attempts to obtain forced labor that could be justified on ideological or philosophical grounds. American Indians were difficult to subdue and were a potential major threat since they were familiar with the countryside and could put up fierce resistance. On the other hand, large-scale, prolonged use of indentured White servants was unrealistic because they were freed after a period of servitude. This made the importation of non-White slave labor attractive. It created a large labor

The education of Native Americans remains a serious issue. Underenrollment is higher than that found among Hispanics and Blacks, a major reason being differences between the values and cultural expectations of Native Americans and education officials. One positive development has been the appearance of tribal community colleges, which help students maintain their cultural identity while at the same time preparing them for positions in outside society. Still, however, federal financial support for these colleges has been meager. The above photo is of the Keweenaw Bay Ojibwa Community College in Baraga, Michigan.
Photo by author.

pool of workers who did not know the land, and it helped to elevate all Whites to a higher status (Fredrickson 1981). A major difference in the initial contacts, of course, was that whereas colonists conquered American Indians and annexed their land, in initial Black–White contact, it was a case of involuntary immigration (O'Sullivan and Wilson 1988).

Given English views of Blacks as evil, animalistic, uncivilized, and un-Christian, it is not surprising that the early colonies passed laws banning sexual mixing and intermarriage. Children of mixed parentage were considered Black (Fredrickson 1981). Enslavement was a thorny issue that troubled some of the Founding Fathers (e.g., Washington, Hamilton) more so than others (e.g., Jefferson). The result was that the problem of what to do with slavery after the Revolution was put off again and again. Several thousand African Americans had fought in the Continental Army, but nevertheless at the Constitutional Convention it was decided that a Black man was only three-fifths of a man. Although Thomas Jefferson is associated with the belief that "all men are created equal," he owned 180 slaves when he died and thought of Blacks as inferior to Whites: "I advance it therefore as a suspicion only, that the Blacks, whether originally a distinct race, or made distinct by time and circumstances, are inferior to the Whites, in the endowments both of body and mind" (quoted in Feldstein 1972, pp. 52–53). Beliefs in the different endowments helped to justify slavery. After all, inhuman treatment could be tolerated if the members of a race were not considered fully human.

At the time of the first official census in 1790, the Black population was approximately 757,000 of whom almost 700,000 were slaves. The Black population grew to almost 4.5 million in 1860, of whom 89 percent were slaves. Between 1790 and 1860, about 90 percent of all Blacks in each Census were slaves. Even though the slave trade was officially outlawed in 1808, it still flourished along the long east coast of the country (U.S. Bureau of the Census 1979; Schaefer 1988). In 1790, 23 percent of all families had slaves, while in 1850, 10 percent of families owned them. Most of these owned only a small number, the average being seven to nine slaves per family (U.S. Bureau of the Census 1979).

The system of inequality that developed between the races during the heyday of slavery up to the Civil War was essentially a caste system. Laws forbade Blacks to (1) intermarry with Whites, (2) vote, (3) testify against Whites in legal cases, (4) own firearms, (5) use abusive language against Whites, (6) own property unless permitted by a master, (7) leave the plantation without permission or disobey a curfew, (8) make a will or inherit property, and (9) have anyone teach them to read, write, or give them books (Elkins 1959; Franklin 1980; Fredrickson 1981; Blackwell 1985).

The end of the Civil War, Emancipation, and Reconstruction did not end the misery for Blacks, and, in fact, appear to have done little to change their caste relationship with Whites (Turner, Singleton, and Musick 1984). Legal, intellectual, economic, and population changes were occurring that provided support for continued discrimination against Blacks. The Jim Crow laws in the South and beliefs about the inferior nature of Blacks, along with increased labor competition from a continuously rising number of White immigrants from all parts of Europe conspired to keep Blacks in a lower socioeconomic position. Lynchings increased in the latter part of the nineteenth century. IQ tests, developed as early as the 1890s, were erroneously used to test native intelligence, and then used to demonstrate the intellectual inferiority of Blacks. This occurred even though some of the early inventors of such measures cautioned against using them for this purpose (Gossett 1963). Social Darwinism, an intellectual application of the notions of the "survival of the fittest" and "natural selection" to whole groups and societies, provided another basis to explain the differences in the accomplishments of the races (Turner, Singleton, and Musick 1984).

Racist feelings were fueled by several events during this period. The rising number of immigrants from Europe, especially eastern Europe, in the latter decades of the nineteenth century and the early twentieth century helped to create a fear on the part of some that the White race was in danger of being extinguished. The Eugenics Movement of the early twentieth century also argued that Blacks could not serve as builders of the country, but could only serve to threaten its progress (Carlson and Colburn 1972). World War I and the Russian Revolution of 1917 with its attendant "Red Scare" only helped to bolster a hatred for individuals of different nationalities and races. During and immediately after World War I, membership in the Ku Klux Klan grew dramatically (Johnson 1976). Black southern migration to the industrializing North during and after World War I resulted in severe clashes between Black and White workers, and in the years from 1917 to 1919, riots broke out in several cities (Brody 1980). Protectionist nativist feelings ran high, and in the 1920s, legislation was passed that restricted immigration.

In the 1920s, anthropologist Franz Boas spoke out forcefully against the racially based theories being propagated at the time, and by the 1930s and 1940s, other important scientists joined him in attacking the idea that Blacks were inferior to Whites (Gossett 1963). Nazi racism also contributed to a reexamination of race domination in this country (Turner, Singleton, and Musick 1984). But discrimination continued, with Blacks still having problems within unions and industry. Blacks also were segregated within the military. Riots occurred during World War II, which further demonstrated that the United States still had a long way to go to bring about equity between the races. Increasing organization and political power of African Americans

during the late 1940s and 1950s helped to bring about some legislative changes and, eventually, the Civil Rights movement.

Other Minority Groups in History

The preceding historical sketch reveals how extensive racial inequality has been in U.S. society. American Indians and African Americans were not, of course, the only minority groups to be treated unequally. Mexican Americans have been exploited for their land and labor. In the last half of the nineteenth century, Mexican Americans frequently had their land taken away by Anglos. Historically, the use of Mexican workers waxed and waned, depending on the demand for labor. They were used and then dispensed with when no longer needed. For example, early in the twentieth century, many Mexican immigrants came to the United States as agricultural laborers, only to be deported or repatriated after demand for their services declined. During World War II, Mexican workers were again imported, only to be sent back during the 1950s under "Operation Wetback" as expendable and undesirable. Illegal raids, threats, and expulsions have not been uncommon in our treatment of Mexicans (Farley 1988).

Asian Americans have also suffered the effects of stereotyping and unfair treatment. Near the end of the nineteenth century, Japanese immigrants took laboring jobs but were disliked by unions and other employees. They were lumped in with the Chinese as part of the "yellow peril," the fear that yellow races would overtake the White race. The events at Pearl Harbor, initiating the entry of the United States into World War II, exacerbated negative feelings toward Japanese Americans. Under Executive Order 9066, people on the West Coast with virtually any Japanese ancestry at all were rounded up and taken to way stations for removal to concentration camps. This was not done to either German or Italian Americans, even though the United States went to war against Germany and Italy as well as Japan.

This strongly suggests a heavy influence of racism. The 113,000 Japanese sent to these camps without the benefit of trial could take only personal items, leaving behind and often losing most of their property. After the war, terrorism and bigotry against Japanese Americans continued, although no instances of espionage by them had ever been proved. Even while in the camps, they remained loyal to their adopted country. Today, when we examine the low rates of social problems among Japanese Americans, they appear to be model citizens. They also have achieved levels of earnings and education that are higher than those of Whites. But continued friction and trade difficulties between the United States and Japan are likely to keep ethnic prejudice simmering between these two nations.

Immigration of Latinos and Asians to the United States has been especially heavy in recent years. By 2050, it is estimated that the Hispanic segment will compose 26 percent and Asians 8 percent of the population in the United States. By 2100, those percentages are expected to increase to 33 and 14 percent, respectively (Smith and Edmonston 1997; Schaefer 2006). These influxes will undoubtedly help to complicate the issue of developing a more adequate and acceptable racial classification or to make the idea of developing such a classification unlikely. We will explore the implications of immigration and globalization for socioeconomic inequality near the end of this chapter.

RACIAL AND ETHNIC INEQUALITY TODAY

We now turn to an analysis of present-day racial and ethnic inequality. Despite some advances, Blacks, Hispanics, and Whites continue to have significantly different incomes, occupations, and earnings.

The tables to follow include data on Whites, Hispanics, and Blacks only because these groups constitute roughly 95 percent of the U.S. population, and thus provide a broad idea of the extent of inequality involving racial and ethnic groups.

Wealth and Income

As we saw in Chapter 2, there are significant differences in the wealth of Whites, Blacks, and Hispanics, and these differences appear to have widened since 2000. The median net worth of non-Hispanic Whites was 8 and 27 times, respectively, that of Blacks and Hispanics. The median financial wealth of the latter groups hovered around zero, with many more than non-Hispanic Whites having negative wealth (more debt than assets) (Wolff, April 2000). Over one-quarter of Blacks, for example, have zero or negative net worth, almost twice the rate found among non-Hispanic Whites. To a large extent, the wide differences between means and medians with respect to wealth noted in Chapter 2 reflect the extreme variations in wealth within these groups. As mentioned earlier, wealth is much more unequally divided than income.

Historically, inheritance of family wealth, or lack of it, has been a significant factor in the "sedimentation of racial inequality. . . . Between 1987 and 2011 the baby-boom generation stands to inherit approximately $7 trillion. . . . One-third of the worth of all estates will be divided by the richest 1 percent, each legatee receiving an average inheritance of $6 million" (Oliver and Shapiro 1995, p. 6).

Wolff's analysis of national data from the Survey of Consumer Finances (SCF) indicates that 24 percent of White households, but only 11 percent of Black households, received an inheritance sometime during their lives. Moreover, the average amount received by Whites was $115,000 compared to only $32,000 for Black inheritors (Wolff, April 2000). The future does not look any brighter for greater equality in wealth. Estimates are that we can also expect racial inheritance differences to increase when the baby-boom generation nears retirement. "The mean white baby boomer's lifetime inheritance will be worth $125,000 in current

(2000) dollars at age 55, as compared to only $16,000 for the black baby boomers and around $70,000 for the preceding generations of whites" (Avery and Rendall 2002). The differences in these amounts indicate the differences in the size of the bases upon which more wealth can be built.

The building of Black wealth for the next generation has been further hindered by discrimination in the mortgage industry. Regardless of credit history and income, Blacks tend to be given less information about loans, be denied loans more often, and be charged higher rates (Turner and Skidmore 1999). Loan denials appear to be especially likely when Blacks seek housing in higher-income, predominately White neighborhoods (Holloway and Wyly 2001). These denials help to perpetuate wealth differentials and "sediment" Blacks into lower levels of wealth.

Wealth inequality between Blacks and Whites has been perpetuated since early in U.S. history, beginning with slavery, by governmental policies that prohibited Blacks from beginning certain kinds of businesses or entering particular markets, agencies such as the Federal Housing Authority which made loans and mortgages for Blacks more difficult to obtain, and the lack of opportunity to take advantage of the wealth-accumulation benefits of lower capital gains taxes, home mortgage deductions, and social security benefits. White mob violence has also weakened attempts to build up wealth that could be passed on to future generations. Consequently, 75 percent of Black children grow up in families with no wealth assets (Oliver and Shapiro 1995).

Income differences between groups are not as extensive as those in wealth. Between 1980 and 2003, the income gap between Black and non-Hispanic White households closed slightly. In those years, the median incomes of Black households went from 57 percent to 62 percent that of non-Hispanic White households. In 2003, the median income for Black households was $29,645, compared to $47,777 for non-Hispanic White households. In that same period, the gap between the median incomes for Hispanic and

non-Hispanic White households increased. In 1980, Hispanic household income was 72 percent that of White households, but dropped to 68 percent in 2003 ($32,997 vs. $47,777) (U.S. Census Bureau, August 2004).

A significant factor in the increase in family incomes among lower-income Blacks has been the increase in their number of hours worked. By the late 1990s, lower- and middle-income Black families were working roughly between 100 and 500 more hours per year than either comparable Hispanics or Whites. Among the highest income quintile, Black families put in about 500 more hours than high-income White families (Mishel, Bernstein, and Schmitt 2001). This suggests that Blacks have to work longer to remain in the middle- and upper-income groups. Among families, the contributions of wives' earnings to total family income has increased among all these groups. In addition to being behind Whites on median income, as we saw in Chapter 2, Hispanics and Blacks also have poverty levels about three times that of Whites, and they are poorer.

The later part of the 1990s witnessed the most equal income growth in two decades (ibid.). This is reflected in the closing of the income gap between Whites and others just mentioned. Since 2000, however, things have changed. Incomes for all households and families dropped between 2000 and 2003; minority groups were hit especially hard because of a softer labor market and industrial shifts, including those out of manufacturing. The result is that the household income gap between groups that had been closing has grown since 2000.

Table 7.1 shows the trends in household incomes between 1980 and 2003 for different groups. While the percentage in households with incomes below $25,000 went down for all groups over the period, and that for households with incomes of at least $75,000 went up, the proportion of White households with incomes of $75,000 or more is still significantly higher than those for Blacks and Hispanics.

TABLE 7.1   Percentage of Households with Incomes under $25,000, $25,000–$74,999, and $75,000 or Higher, by Race and Hispanic Origin: 1980–2003

	HOUSEHOLD INCOMES BELOW $25,000		
	1980	1990	2003
Non-Hispanic Whites	30.0%	27.1%	25.6%
Black	53.8%	49.5%	43.4%
Hispanic	43.5%	42.3%	36.5%
	HOUSEHOLD INCOMES BETWEEN $25,000 AND $74,999		
	1980	1990	2003
Non-Hispanic Whites	53.5%	50.3%	44.9%
Black	40.5%	41.3%	42.9%
Hispanic	49.0%	47.1%	48.4%
	HOUSEHOLD INCOMES $75,000 OR HIGHER		
	1980	1990	2003
Non-Hispanic Whites	16.4%	22.5%	29.4%
Black	5.8%	9.2%	13.7%
Hispanic	7.6%	10.6%	15.2%

Source: U.S. Census Bureau, *Income, Poverty, and Health Insurance Coverage in the United States: 2003*. Current Population Reports, Series P-60, No. 226, Table A-1, pp. 28–32.

Note: All incomes are in 2003 adjusted dollars.

Conversely, the percentage of households with incomes below $25,000 remains noticeably higher for Blacks and Hispanics.

Concentrations in income distribution increased within all major subpopulations during the 1979–1999 period. Increases in the total proportion of income went to the top 20 percent, and decreases in the percentages went to the middle 60 percent and bottom 20 percent (see Figure 7.1). Income concentration is highest

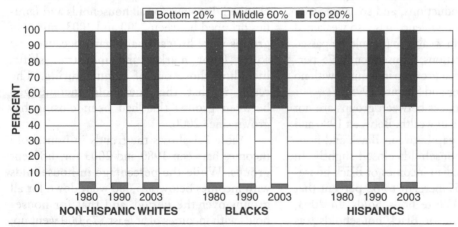

FIGURE 7.1   Share of Aggregate Income Received by Bottom 20 Percent, Middle 60 Percent, and Top 20 Percent within White, Black, and Hispanic Populations: 1980, 1990, and 2003

Source: U.S. Census Bureau at www.census.gov/hhes/www/income/histinc/h02n.html, Table H-2.

among Black and lowest among Hispanic households. The increased polarization of income suggests a growth in class distinctions within these groups. Among Blacks especially, it complicates relative allegiances to class and race. The special vulnerability of Blacks to weak labor markets, reductions in manufacturing employment, the decline of union power, and the fact that the richest 25 percent of Blacks possess more than 90 percent of all Black wealth suggest that economic discrepancies will continue to grow within this group.

Earnings and Occupations

Given the differences in household incomes, it should not be surprising that there are also inequalities in the earnings of these groups. The median *weekly* earnings of Blacks and Hispanics working full-time are lower than those of Whites, among both men and women (see Table 7.2). Differences are also found in *hourly* wages. Blacks and Hispanics, especially those who are women, are much more likely than Whites to earn poverty-level wages or below. In 2003, 30 percent of Black and almost 40 percent of Hispanic employees had wages at this level. In the same year, the hourly wages for White men ($16.82) were about $6.00 higher than those for Hispanic men ($10.67) and over $4.00 higher than those of Black men ($12.23). Wage discrepancies also exist among women, but to a much smaller extent (Mishel, Bernstein, and Allegretto 2005).

TABLE 7.2   Median Weekly Earnings of Full-Time Wage and Salary Workers 16 Years and over, by Race, Hispanic Origin, and Sex: 2004

	MALE	FEMALE
White	$732	$584
Black	$569	$505
Hispanics	$480	$419

Source: U.S. Department of Labor, *Employment & Earnings*, January 2005, Table 37, p. 248.

The earnings gap increased dramatically during the 1980s, and while it has slowed since then, significant disparities remain. Interestingly, Black/White wage differentials appear to be greater in high-earnings occupations. Consequently, while occupational mobility may increase Black earnings, it appears to accelerate the inequality between Black and White private-sector employees (Grodsky and Pager 2001). The availability of manufacturing jobs and union membership appear to be especially important for reducing Black/White wage inequality. The movement of industry out of the city and declines in manufacturing jobs have reduced the employment rates and earnings of Blacks, while immigration has had a dampening effect on the earnings of Hispanic workers (Mouw 2000; McCall 2001).

Part of the reason for the differences in earnings between racial and ethnic groups relates to differences in their occupational distributions. There seems to be at least a three-step process involved in producing the earnings discrepancy. First, Blacks are segregated into jobs that are dominated by other Blacks (Huffman and Cohen 2004a). Then, secondly, jobs in which there is a high concentration of minority employees have lower wages attached to them regardless of the qualifications of the workers or the characteristics of the place of employment. Evidence indicates a causal relationship between racial composition of jobs and their wages (Catanzarite 2003; Kmec 2003). Finally, minority workers tend to lose ground in wages to White workers as they get older and move through their careers (Willson 2003; Maume, Jr. 2004). The initial lower levels of wages for these workers coupled with their cumulative disadvantage is another factor that makes it difficult to accumulate wealth or develop an inheritance for their children.

Examining broad occupational categories, we find that Blacks, Whites, and Hispanics are variously concentrated among them. There has been some occupational upgrading for Blacks in recent decades, however. A greater percentage of Blacks have moved into white-collar and blue-collar/manufacturing positions since World War II, and a smaller percentage are service and farm workers.

These changes are largely a result of broader changes in the U.S. economy and polity. Principal among the changes that have reshaped the distribution of occupations among Blacks have been

- The shift away from agriculture since 1900
- A decline in the centrality of unskilled work
- The movement toward a service-oriented economy
- The movement of industry out of central cities into suburbs, different regions of the country, or even different countries
- Attacks on unions, and the general weakening of the power of labor relative to corporate management
- "Retrenchment of civil rights enforcement" (see also Blau and Ferber 1986; Glasgow 1987; Wacquant and Wilson 1989).

Not only are these macrolevel shifts important for understanding the distribution of occupations among African Americans and Whites but they are also directly tied to unemployment and poverty levels, the *hyperghettoization* of the inner city, and the size of the underclass discussed in Chapter 2. The decline in basic blue-collar jobs, especially those requiring little formal education, and the mismatch between the location of jobs and Blacks have intensified the unemployment problems of inner-city Blacks (Lichter 1988; Kasarda 1989). These shifts in the economy, however, do not mean that race itself has become unimportant as a factor in accounting for occupational differences between Blacks and Whites. The relative significance of economic class and race will be discussed shortly.

Table 7.3 presents the current broad occupational distribution for Blacks, Hispanics, and Whites of each sex. The greatest concentration of White males is in the managerial/professional category, while Black males are most often in production/transportation occupations, and the highest percentage of Hispanic men are found in the natural resources/construction group. Among women, the greatest concentration of White women is in managerial/professional occupations, while a plurality of Black and Hispanic women are in office/sales/support positions. Black and Hispanic women are also much more likely than White women to be in service positions.

But these general categories mask greater discrepancies among more detailed classifications of occupations. As is evident in Table 7.4, Blacks are most underrepresented in certain high-level professional and upper-level skilled

TABLE 7.3   Occupational Distribution of Employed Civilians Age 16 and over, by Race, Hispanic Origin, and Sex: 2004 Annual Average

OCCUPATION	WHITE MALE	WHITE FEMALE	BLACK MALE	BLACK FEMALE	HISPANIC MALE	HISPANIC FEMALE
Managerial/professional	33.1%	38.6%	21.7%	30.6%	14.0%	22.4%
Office/sales/adm. support	17.1	35.6	18.2	33.3	13.5	33.2
Service occupations	12.3	18.8	20.0	27.0	20.2	30.3
Natural resources/ construction/maintenance	19.7	1.0	13.6	0.9	28.5	2.0
Production/transportation/ moving	17.9	6.0	26.5	8.2	23.8	12.2

Source: U.S. Department of Labor, *Employment & Earnings*, January 2005, pp. 208–209.

TABLE 7.4   Sample of Specific Occupations in Which Blacks and Hispanics Are Significantly Over- and Underrepresented: 2004

BLACKS			
Underrepresented	%	*Overrepresented*	%
farm/ranch managers	0.1	telephone operators	39.8
chiropractors	0.3	barbers	34.9
small engine mechanics	0.9	nursing/home health aides	34.6
surveying and mapping	1.0	postal service clerks	30.4
cabinetmakers	1.5	refuse collectors	29.5
jewelers	1.6	taxi drivers/chauffeurs	28.7
engineering managers	1.7	security guards	28.4
aircraft pilots/flight engineers	1.7	bus drivers	24.4
artists	2.2	machine feeder	22.6
real estate appraisers	2.4	eligibility interview., gov.	22.4
HISPANICS			
Underrepresented	%	*Overrepresented*	%
farmers/ranchers	1.8	drywall installers	49.6
chiropractors	1.9	garment pressers	47.1
directors, religious activities	2.0	graders/sorters (agri.)	44.7
speech pathologists	2.1	butchers/meatcutters	44.3
biological scientists	2.2	hand packers/packagers	44.1
environmental scientists	2.3	concrete/terrazzo workers	44.0
writers/authors	2.6	packing machine operators	42.4
millwrights	2.6	grounds maintenance work	40.2
engineering managers	2.9	roofers	39.4
personal financial advisors	2.9	maids/housekeepers	38.2

Source: U.S. Department of Labor, *Employment & Earnings*, January 2005, Table 11, pp. 210–215.

white-collar positions involving authority or decision-making and they are overrepresented in various private and governmental service and aide occupations. Those positions in which they are typically underrepresented require specialized training or high levels of education. Their overrepresentation lies in certain mid-to-lower level service jobs, such as telephone operators, refuse collectors, and bus drivers. Some of these positions have direct or indirect ties to government (e.g., postal clerks, government interviewers), suggesting to many that the government is a significant route to the middle class for Blacks. However, the economic benefits for Blacks of working for the government seem to have eroded in the 1980s and 1990s (Zipp 1994). Moreover, even when

Blacks do gain high-level positions in the public economy, their positions are tenuous because of the volatility of political conditions (Collins 1993). Similar to Blacks, Hispanics are underrepresented in many professional, high-authority occupations and overrepresented in manual labor, agricultural, and personal-service positions.

Blacks, Hispanics, and Whites differ, like males and females generally, (1) on the authority they possess in their jobs, (2) on the specific kinds of organizations in which they are employed, and (3) in the economic sector in which they work. Similar to the situation for females, human-capital variables do not fully account for these discrepancies. Rather, structural factors, such as place of employment, along with discrimination, appear to be implicated in inequalities in the occupational structure.

MICROINEQUITIES IN THE TREATMENT OF RACIAL AND ETHNIC MINORITIES

Like women, racial and ethnic minorities have been subjected to a host of everyday indignities. These indignities are independent of class position. Language, which reflects cultural values, helps to undergird the system of social inequality as it pertains to minorities, and yet because it is so much a part of our everyday lives, we seldom step back and look at it in any depth. The derogatory terms used to describe different ethnic and racial groups suggest the value placed on these groups, and reinforce this negative imagery when terms referring to these groups are used to describe some disliked or despised behavior (e.g., "an Indian giver," to "Jew down," to "gyp," to "nigger lip," etc.). Language is a powerful tool for shaping the attitudes toward and general beliefs about groups, and what makes it exceptionally influential is the fact that these terms are part of the matrix of everyday life and often used without intentional thought being given to their implications.

Embedded in this language are stereotypes of different racial and ethnic groups. Stereotypes, in turn, often have subtle yet negative effects on those affected. For example, a recent study of Atlanta employers found that many employers carry a negative stereotype of Black women as single mothers who are more concerned about their children than work, and are therefore generally late to work, lack education, and are not good role models for their children. These stereotypes, based on a lack of specific knowledge, affect the attitudes employers have toward prospective and current employees, and put Black women at a disadvantage (Kennelly 1999).

One reason for stereotypes is the lack of personal, concrete familiarity that individuals have with persons in other racial or ethnic groups. Lack of familiarity encourages the lumping together of unknown individuals. This happens even among social scientists. White interviewers have been found to view Black respondents as much darker than do Black interviewers, and conversely, Black interviewers perceive White respondents as being much lighter than do White interviewers. In addition, each type of interviewer sees members of the opposite race as having little variation in color, while seeing much more color variation among members of their own race. Familiarity encourages images of variation and individuality, while unfamiliarity fosters images of sameness (Hill 2002).

The media, especially movies and television, also have perpetuated stereotypes of African Americans learned in other contexts. Traditionally, African Americans and other non-White individuals have either been absent from the media or have been portrayed in negative terms—for example, the African American as lazy, slow thinking, and subservient, and the American Indian as savage and hostile (Marger 1997). The stereotype of the "drunken Indian" is also found among Whites. American Indians are viewed in the minds of many Whites as lacking a sense of control and responsibility. Such psychological factors are often used by Whites to explain alcoholism rates among American Indians, although the latter more often trace the problem to White invasions into Indian territory and culture. Allegations of psychological and cultural deficiencies are then used by Whites to explain the continued poverty and related problems among American Indians and to justify the paucity of attempts to alleviate these problems. In other words, such explanations continue to be used as part of an ideology to legitimate the inequalities that exist between Whites and American Indians (Holmes and Antell 2001). Even the image of Asian Americans as a "model minority" (i.e., as educated, family oriented, and successful) glosses over educational and economic distinctions within the Asian American community, and recently has taken on a negative cast as others look for scapegoats for our economic difficulties. Instead of being viewed positively and as consistent with American values, the competitiveness displayed by some of these groups has been seen as a reason for the nation's problems. Just as competitive women are often seen as being unfeminine and aggressive, Blacks who are competitive are often considered pushy and uppity.

There are many additional, subtle, taken-for-granted advantages that are attached to the status of being White. In a thoughtful, reflective essay, Peggy McIntosh listed 46 conditions that she feels are connected primarily to the privilege of being White in our society, and that non-White individuals cannot take for granted. Among these, she included her being able to:

- Freely choose a place that she wants and can afford to live in
- Go shopping, feeling secure that she will not be harassed or followed
- See others of her race prevalently displayed in the media
- Be fairly sure that her voice will be heard even in a non-White group
- Rely on her skin color to protect her from being seen as financially unreliable
- Feel that her children will receive an education that acknowledges the contributions of her race and in which teachers treat her children fairly
- Talk with her mouth full and not have people put this down to her color
- Not worry about acknowledging the views of non-White people
- Consider a wide variety of options in her life without worrying about whether her race would be a factor in limiting them
- Select a service or public accommodation without considering whether she will be treated poorly because of her race
- Not worry about her "shape, bearing, or body odor" being seen as a reflection of her race
- Use a flesh-colored bandage and have it blend with her skin (McIntosh 1988).

In Nutshell 7.1, Gregory Williams shares the personal experience of being White and being Black.

THE INTERSECTION OF CLASS, RACE, SEX, AND GENDER

In the preceding few chapters, we have been examining the economic, racial, and gender dimensions of social inequality, and although they have been, to a large extent, treated separately, in the context of a *society* and in the lives of real *individuals*, these dimensions are interconnected. If we wish to understand how the dynamics and effects of each of these dimensions play out in actuality, we need to probe the nature of these interconnections at both the social/societal and individual levels. The significant meaning of these relationships can be uncovered by examining them at both levels.

When we speak of analyzing the interaction of class, race, and gender at the *social/societal level*, we are essentially considering each of these as separate variables that affect each other at the group or aggregate level. For example, consider the discussion of the relationship between the class measures of occupation and earnings on the one hand, and race on the other. The search for a statistical relationship among these variables can be carried out without ever addressing the psychological effects or experiences of individuals. We are concerned with effects at the level of the group or society.

The intersection of race and class can also be understood at the *level of individual experience*. Here, we are concerned with how race and class interact in the lives of individuals. How do people *experience* race and class in their lives? In their everyday lives, individuals accumulate *simultaneous* experiences as members of particular races, classes, *and* gender groups. A person is all of these things at the same time. This is the meaning of "*intersectionality*." The dimensions are not as readily separable. How

One Boy's Experiences of Being White and Being Black

Gregory Howard Williams had always thought that he was White, but he learned midway through his childhood in Muncie, Indiana, that his paternal grandmother was Black. The experience of a boy who had always received the privileges of being White changed when he experienced the feelings of being Black in a racist society. He lived as a White boy in White society, and then as a Black boy in White society. In his autobiography, Williams relates his experiences and feelings of going from being thought of as White to being Black. Even now as a respected lawyer and law professor, remembrance of those experiences of living in a racist society come back to haunt him:

> I often think about life in Muncie and even some-times in the middle of the night, halfway between sleep and consciousness, I go to the place where that bewildered boy of long ago still dwells in me, and my eyes fill with tears. We share the disbelief that all the things that happened to him in those early years of his life could have occurred. We cry together, and I tell him that he is now in a safe place and that a wiser and stronger friend is here to pro-tect him. But the wounds are deep, the scars on his soul ache, and he is able to draw little solace from my presence. He wishes me well, but in his little manly way asks why it had to happen to him. . . .

I do believe that there was some reason I was called upon to live the life that I was given. Maybe to share it with others in the hope that no child will have to experience what I did. In spite of all the pain and grief of my early years, I am grateful to have been able to view the world from a place few men or women have stood. I realize now that I am bound to live out my life in the mid-dle of our society and hope that I can be a bridge between races, shouldering the heavy burden that almost destroyed my youth.

I was fortunate to be able to achieve my goal of becoming a lawyer, and later my dream of being a law professor. I have held positions that even in my wildest fantasies during the nights at 601 Railroad Street I could not envision for myself. Yet when I stand in front of students, my mind often wanders back to the pain and rejection of the Muncie years. Almost as if it were yesterday, I vividly recall watching Dad being beaten by the police, and the day we were chased from the "white" waiting room in Louisville. I never felt more impotent and powerless to control my life than I did in those days. When I think of those times, I remem-ber what Dad used to say: "Son, one day this will all pale into insignificance." He was wrong. Muncie has never paled into insignificance. It has lived inside me forever.

Source: Gregory Howard Williams, *Life on the Color Line* (New York: Dutton, 1995).

---

do these elements interact *within* the individ-ual? Consider a person who is Black, upper class, and male—a Black surgeon, for example. What is it like to be him? How do the effects of class and race and gender interact in his life? And, at the same time, what is it like to be poor, White, and female? To address these questions is to examine the intersection of race, class, and gender at the individual level.

One of the most publicized relationships among these variables involves the relative importance of race and class in the lives of indi-viduals. Another area concerns the reciprocal interaction between class and race, with class affecting one's race and one's *color* affecting

class position. A third topic of interest focuses on the increased class divisions within the Black community and their effect on that commu-nity's solidarity. A final area to be discussed addresses the interaction among sex, gender, race, and class as a group. We now turn to a discussion of each of these areas of study.

The Relative Significance of Race and Class

One of the most controversial and prominent discussions on the intersection of race and class involves arguments about the relative effects of race and class on the life chances of individuals.

Scholars differ on which they think is most important. Around the turn of the twentieth century, W.E.B. DuBois suggested in his study of *The Philadelphia Negro* (1973) that not only racial discrimination but economic factors as well affected the everyday living conditions of Blacks. E. Franklin Frazier (1937) also suggested that both race and class play a role in determining what happens to Blacks, but finally felt that economics may be more important than race, an opinion later shared by Oliver Cox. Cox viewed race relations in the United States as stemming from and continuously being conditioned by economic-class relations. Racism exists as one of several devices used by capitalists to control, exploit, and keep workers down. As a result, it is rooted in economic conflict.

William Julius Wilson has argued that class has become more important than race in determining the life chances of Blacks today. This is because even though political and economic changes in society have opened up more potential opportunities for Blacks, these changes have also helped create urban joblessness. Blacks have been particularly affected, for example, by the shift from a manufacturing to a service economy, by the broadening split between low-wage and high-wage labor markets, and by the movement of industries out of the central cities (Bonacich 1985; Wilson 1987). "The net effect is a growing class division among Blacks, a situation, in other words, in which economic class has been elevated to a position of greater importance than race in determining individual Black opportunities for living conditions and personal life experiences" (Wilson 1982, pp. 399–400). Wilson has not argued that race is irrelevant today but he has said that historically racism has had a major effect on the lives of Blacks that continues today. However, this *historical* discrimination has a more significant impact on Blacks' lives today than does *contemporary* discrimination. Still, it is broader economic and political forces that are most immediately important for

understanding events and behaviors within the Black community.

In sharp contrast to those like Wilson and assorted exploitation theorists, who stress the primacy of economic-class factors in explaining the socioeconomic condition of Blacks, others emphasize the greater and, in some cases, increasing significance of race in understanding the economic predicament of Blacks. They suggest that the gains that Blacks have made relative to Whites have been blown out of proportion (Willie 1979).

Analyses of national surveys done from 1972 to 1996 revealed the continuing influence of race on one's quality of life. Over this period, Blacks continued to score lower on measures of happiness, life satisfaction, and health, and were more mistrusting and anomic than Whites.

Class differences have been a source of division within racial and ethnic groups, just as racial and ethnic differences have hindered unification of those in the same classes. The above is a poster for a rally in Columbus, Ohio.
Photo by Brendan R. Hurst.

"What is clear is that being black in U.S. society results in a lower quality of life than does being white. Also clear is the substantial degree of racial inequality in U.S. society . . . and the continuing experience of racism in the lives of African Americans. . . . The coexistence of these facts suggests that racial differences in quality of life are produced by racial inequality and the experiences it produces" (Hughes and Thomas 1998, p. 792).

The interaction of race and class factors is certainly complex. We saw that, historically, economic and racial factors interacted in the treatment of American Indians and African Americans. Economic motives played a role in driving American Indians from their land and developing African American slavery into an extensive labor force. At the same time, we found that class distinctions existed among African Americans and women that were important for understanding the differences in life conditions. We also found that racism as a fully developed ideology was used to legitimate and sustain the economic systems that were being constructed. In the same way, ideologies about the sexes and their proper roles have helped to keep occupational sex segregation intact. Economic as well as other conditions helped bring about the migration of Blacks to the North and the consequent form of the class structure within the Black population.

In contemporary times, Wright (1978) has shown in his studies that race as well as class, measured in largely Marxian terms, has an influence on income. Race plays a different role at different class levels. Among managers, Blacks receive less income return for their education than Whites, but Black supervisors and workers receive returns that are similar to those of Whites. Ethnicity, race, and class background all play a role in determining earnings (cf. Hirschman and Kraly 1988). Blacks and women both earn less than White males, even when they have the same qualifications, but Black women are the worst off of these groups. Another study by Tienda and Lii (1987)

indicated that the earnings of non-Whites, including African Americans, suffer when they are derived from participation in a labor market with a concentration of minorities, whereas the earnings of college-educated Whites benefit from association with such a labor market.

Class, Color, and Race

Usually we think of race as a biologically fixed category that cannot therefore be affected by class. But as we saw earlier, races are socially constructed, and how one identifies with a given race and is placed in a racial category can depend on one's class position. As discussed earlier, some ethnic and "racial" groups became "White" as they became more assimilated, successful, and accepted in U.S. society. The Irish, Jews, and Italians were all at one time considered separate races but have since been "Whitened," that is, included in the "White" category. Their race is historically constructed as a result of social, political, and economic changes. In this sense, their success or class position has affected their race membership. Recently, Bonilla-Silva has argued that increased multiethnicity, immigration, and globalization are among the forces leading the U.S. into a three-tiered racial system. Within the first two of "White" and "Honorary Whites" categories are varieties of ethnic groups that, traditionally, have been thought of as separate from "Whites" (e.g., Japanese Americans, Arab Americans, Asian Indians). The third category, labeled "Collective Black," includes not only African Americans, but newer, generally poorer East Asian immigrants, "dark-skinned and poor Latinos," and "reservation-bound Native Americans" (Bonilla-Silva 2004, pp. 225–227). This suggested classification clearly shows the interaction of economic and racial/ethnic forces.

Within races, skin tone can affect the treatment a person receives. " 'Colorism' is the discriminatory treatment of individuals falling within the same 'racial' group on the basis of skin color. It operates both intraracially and interracially" (Herring 2004, p. 3). In her study of women involved in high-society organizations, Diana Kendall found that colorism operated not only within White organizations, and between White and Black organizations, but within Black "high society" as well. The "brown-bag test" was used to screen potential members of these organizations, meaning that one's skin should not be darker than a brown grocery bag (Kendall 2002, p. 129). This is significant if only because it is within such organizations that social capital can be developed that may enhance one's socioeconomic position. More directly, skin color has been found in several studies to have an effect on occupational status and income. Tracing the occupational attainments that several hundred Black men reached over their lifetimes, for example, Hill found that lighter-skinned Blacks attained higher positions than darker-skinned Blacks, regardless of their social origins (2000). The extent to which the effects of skin color continue to operate is still an open question, especially in light of the class polarization that has been developing within the Black community (Bowman, Muhammad, and Ifatunji 2004).

Class Divisions among Blacks

Economic dislocations and restructuring along with globalization forces have helped foster class polarization among Blacks. During the past three decades, at least three major classes appear to have developed as a result of broader economic changes. These include (1) an underclass living below poverty, (2) an above-poverty class just getting by, and (3) a relatively well-to-do class with high education levels and professional occupations (ibid.). However, the class structure among Blacks is more compressed than that among Whites and each class is different from its White counterpart. The position of the Black middle class, for example, is more precarious than that of the White middle class because of the generally lower stability of their jobs and the smaller "nest eggs" available for future expenses.

"Wealthy" Blacks are not as rich as wealthy Whites, the white-collar positions held by members of the Black middle class tend to be of lower status than those occupied by middle-class Whites, and poor Blacks are generally poorer than poor Whites. Also, in contrast to the *invisibility* of whiteness as a color and of Whites as a race, consciousness of race is more prominent among Blacks, in part because of the continued segregation and other problems they face regardless of class. On a day-to-day basis for adults, race often overrides class in its importance for getting along with life (West 1993).

There are other areas in which unity exists among Blacks in general. Regardless of class position, Blacks have a strong positive identity with their race and do not subscribe to negative images held of them by others (Bowman, Muhammad, and Ifatunji 2004; see also Carter 2003). There is also some evidence to suggest that Blacks identify more strongly with their race than with their class, and agree in their opinions on social policies and programs (Jackman and Jackman 1983; Cannon 1984; Welch and Combs 1985; Gilliam 1986). Black English is also a unifier because of the necessity to communicate with others within their community of varying statuses. Finally, Blacks in general also have views of the class system and alleged equality of opportunity that are different from those of White males (Kluegel and Smith 1986).

Despite these similarities among Blacks, class-related pressures still create fissures and disagreements within the Black community. Many of the issues between classes revolve around differences in lifestyles, attitudes, and childrearing. In her study of a Black middle-class neighborhood on the south side of Chicago, Mary Pattillo-McCoy found that residents often distinguish area individuals on the basis of whether or not they are "bourgie" (i.e., have a *bourgeois* lifestyle) or are "uppity" (i.e., thinking they are better than everyone else). The economic middle class consisted of both law-abiding and criminal elements. Perhaps most significantly, residents had to negotiate their daily lives using both "street" and "decent" lifestyles (see also Anderson 1999). While the decent lifestyle professes adherence to traditional, more mainstream middle-class values and behaviors, the street lifestyle requires values and behaviors that reflect the street-smarts necessary for survival and respect in the neighborhood. The battle to balance these two lifestyles is constant, but especially intense during adolescence (Pattillo-McCoy 1999).

The conflict between traditional dominant lifestyle values and subgroup values also is found in school settings. In the hothouse environment of the elite prep school, all students, regardless of background, are expected to adhere to a given set of principles. But these principles often come into conflict with the values and attitudes that Black, working-class, and poor children have been taught at home. These children are marginalized in the school setting that is structured to prize and honor children from elite backgrounds. Kuriloff and Reichert (2003) found that Black students can effectively combine the methods and findings taught at home with those taught at school to successfully navigate their way through the elite school. In other school settings, poor and middle-class Black students are often divided in their lifestyle codes, with poor Blacks adopting what they consider an "authentic," "black" code, and middle-class Blacks subscribing to a "minority culture of mobility" that distinguishes them from middle-class Whites and other Blacks (Carter 2003, p. 150).

Annette Lareau (2003) also discovered lifestyle differences among Blacks of different classes. Her interviews and participant observation of Black and White families in different communites revealed that middle-class parents, regardless of race, used a method of childrearing that Lareau dubbed "concerted cultivation." These parents worked hard to provide crucial tools, and intentionally prepared their children for successful adulthoods. This meant greater monitoring and control of the everyday schedule of their children. It also meant that they enrolled their children in numerous activities, nurtured debate abilities and language development, and taught them how to negotiate and compete with adults to accomplish their goals. In children, not only did this cultivation provide them with advantages that will serve them later, but it also fostered a "sense of entitlement" within the middle-class children (Lareau 2003, p. 6).

In sharp contrast, working-class and poor parents, both Black and White, engaged in a "natural growth" form of childrearing. This is a less directive and controlling, in a sense more easy-going, form of childrearing in which children are more likely to be on their own for much of the day. The worlds of adults and children are kept separate. Children were not treated as equals. Parents did not intentionally develop argumentation skills among their children or encourage them to debate with authority figures. Working-class children engaged in fewer formal, scheduled activities. Clearly, the differences uncovered in Lareau's research indicate significant lifestyle and class differences among Blacks. Not only do class and race intersect in interesting ways; gender further complicates the picture.

Gender, Race, and Class

Sex and gender discrimination appears to be an important element in the continuance of occupational segregation, thereby affecting class position. At the same time, class and race divisions among women historically helped to determine the nature of their involvement in the labor market. Almquist (1984) found, for example, that some female minority groups have different occupational patterns than others. The patterns of Asian women approximate those of Anglo women, whereas those of American Indians are closer to the patterns found among African American and Hispanic women. Educational patterns also vary among these groups. "People's class position at birth, even for those of the dominant ethnic group, is an overarching factor in determining their eventual wealth, power, and prestige. . . . But for minorities, the chances of winding up at the bottom are much greater" (Marger 1997, p. 63). In essence, we can say that race, sex, and class are each important and often interact in their influence on the individual.

The Census data on incomes of full-time workers make it evident that race *and* gender have an influence on income, earnings, and the distribution of occupations. Blacks and Whites differ on each of the latter, but within each race males and females are differently situated with respect to income, earnings, and occupation. Census data clearly show that although Blacks and women, in general, have increased their representativeness in professional occupations, they continue to be severely underrepresented in professions dominated by males. Even though the proportion of male professionals declined, males continue to dominate certain high-ranking professions. In fact, their over-representation in these professions has increased. Black men are the next group most represented in these professions, followed by White women and Black women, respectively. These findings again suggest the complex interplay of race and gender that affects class position.

Attitude toward the feminist movement is another area that demonstrates the detailed interworking of race, gender, and class. Many African American women do not identify with the movement because they associate it with White, middle-class women, a group whose interests and needs differ in many ways from their own (hooks 1981; cf. Davis 1981; Reid 1984; King 1988). Historically, African American women have been suspicious of White women (Chafe 1977). Many view their class and race interests as separating them from the feminist movement that has developed in the United States. hooks (1981) wrote:

We were disappointed and disillusioned when we discovered that White women in the movement had little knowledge of or concern for the problems of lower class and poor women or the particular problems of non-White women from all classes. . . . Black feminists found that sisterhood for most White women did not mean surrendering allegiance to race, class, and sexual preference. . . . It did not serve the interest of upper and middle class White feminists to discuss race and class. (pp. 188, 190)

Some argue that the race-versus-gender stance suggested here is unfortunate because it hinders Black women from working against *both* racism and sexism (Reid 1984). The development of Black feminism was one response to these issues raised about traditional feminism.

The influences of race, class, and sex on the life chances of an individual are multiplicative because they interact in complex and different ways depending on the specific sociohistorical and cultural context and the area of life chances in question (King 1988). In this sense, African American women are often in a situation of "multiple jeopardy" because of their racial, sexual, and class positions. It is inappropriate to lump Blacks and women into the same category because their current life experiences and past histories are unique, even though, in general terms, the two groups share some characteristics. For example, both (1) are readily physically distinguishable from White men, (2) have endured similar kinds of social control to keep them "in their place," and (3) are assigned characteristics of excessive emotionality and childlike qualities (Hacker 1951; Chafe 1977). But these somewhat superficial and broad similarities disguise what are more specific and deeper differences between the groups in terms of their concrete historical experiences, as our earlier historical summary of these groups indicates.

Moreover, whereas the races have been expected to restrict intimacy with each other, men and women have been expected to do the opposite. In this manner, Blacks have occupied a caste-like position while women have not (Keller 1987). Even more specifically, Black women are often left to fall between the cracks when discussions of Blacks (usually meaning Black men) and women (usually meaning White women) are carried out. The lesson here is that even though the histories of the sexes and races have been unique in many ways, the influences of race, sex, and class interweave when affecting individual lives.

THEORIES OF RACIAL AND ETHNIC INEQUALITY

As is the case for sex and gender inequality, there have been a variety of attempts to explain race inequality, ranging from biological to cultural and structural. Attempts to anchor an adequate explanation in biology have been widely criticized. The work of Herrnstein and Murray (1994) has elicited an avalanche of commentary, most of it negative. Basically, these scholars have argued first that an elite of highly intelligent people has developed that is increasingly separated from the rest of society, socially and economically. The high demands for intelligence and education in our sophisticated economy have funneled these elite into the high-paying, high-prestige occupations and left the rest of the population behind. The result is greater social inequality. The second part of their argument is that intelligence has been shown to be significantly linked to a wide array of social effects, including wages, poverty, school dropouts, crime, and having an illegitimate child. A highly controversial position follows this discussion in which Herrnstein and Murray suggested that racial groups vary on intelligence, that a large portion of intelligence is very likely genetically based, and that most of those at the bottom of the socioeconomic ladder are also those who score low on intelligence. The society stands to suffer since this group is also more likely than the more intelligent to have high fertility rates. In essence, their argument appears to be that intelligence has become more significant for the class placement of individuals, that intelligence has a strong genetic component, and that the

United States is moving toward a more volatile class-stratified society based on intelligence in which classes are isolated from each other.

Briefly, Herrnstein and Murray's work has been criticized for, among other things, (1) its reliance on intelligence tests given later in life and whose results might thus reflect both genetic and environmental influences, (2) the omission of other significant factors that can affect socioeconomic outcomes (e.g., labor-market experience), and (3) the belief in the fixity and rigidity of genetic mechanisms and related social problems (Haynes 1995; Massey 1995; Nielsen 1995). Earlier research by the psychologist Arthur Jensen, who argued that there are significant differences between Blacks and Whites in native intelligence, also had been heavily criticized. But even if such differences could be demonstrated, their relevance for social and economic inequality between the races would still be problematic given the fact that numerous studies demonstrate that individual characteristics do not fully explain such inequality. Finally, the whole idea of racial differences in biology is based on the assumption that different races can be accurately, indisputably, and objectively identified. As we have seen, this is not the case.

In the sections that follow, various interpretations of race relations and explanations for racial inequality will be presented. Most will focus on the United States even though they are frequently based on analyses developed for the characterization of intergroup relations in other countries such as India and Third World countries in general. The caste model is one of these.

The Caste Analysis of Race Relations

The application of the caste concept to race relations in the United States has not served to explain those relations as much as to describe them. It will be recalled from Chapter 3 that caste relations fall under the category of status relations; that is, caste structure is an extreme form of status inequality in that relationships between the groups involved are said to be fixed and supported by ideology and/or law. Membership in a particular caste is hereditary, mobility is virtually impossible, marriage within one's caste is mandated, and occupation is strongly related to caste position. These are the fundamental characteristics of a caste structure.

In *An American Dilemma*, Gunnar Myrdal described Black–White relations in the United States as constituting a caste system. Caste characteristics are largely a remnant from the slavery system and are to be distinguished from the class distinctions found within each racial caste (1944, pp. 221, 667–668). One can move *within* one's caste but not *between* castes. "The boundary between Negro and White is not simply a class line which can be successfully crossed by education, integration into the national culture, and individual economic advancement. The boundary is fixed. . . . It is a bar erected with the intention of permanency . . . against the whole group" (p. 58). Like most caste theorists who followed him, Myrdal argued that a caste system was incompatible with the characteristics of democracy. The ultimate result of both existing alongside each other is not only a conflict in values but a "split in American personality," creating the "American dilemma."

The caste model has continued to be used in recent times (Berreman 1960, 1972; van den Berghe 1967; Willie 1979). Van den Berghe (1967) viewed race stratification as "an extreme case of status ascription making for rigid group membership," one that is comparable to the Hindu caste system and stratification by sex (p. 24). He also argued that before the Civil War, race relations were *paternalistic* in nature, and afterward *competitive*. Under a paternalistic system of master and servant, the socially dominant group treats subordinate group members as if they were children with an "ideology of benevolent despotism." Members of both castes are expected to abide by a code of race relations in which appropriate behavior and position are expected by each group.

In virtually all areas of life, there is a wide gap between the races and government is tyrannical. While conflict is present, the uneasy stability is maintained partly by the constant undercurrent of force, but also by the enforced complementarity and acquiescence of the subordinate group (van den Berghe 1967). This type of system, according to van den Berghe, is most likely to be found in complex agricultural systems, especially those that produce cash crops on a large scale, such as slave plantations. A paternalistic ideology also heavily informed our treatment of American Indians on nineteenth-century reservations (Farley 1988).

In contrast, a *competitive* system of race relations is more characteristic of industrial societies and developed abruptly in the United States after the Civil War, according to van den Berghe. Briefly, under this system, although caste relations remain, class positions within each caste become more elaborated and more important. In industrial societies, human-capital factors take precedence over race in determining position, and competition characterizes the relationship between African Americans and working-class Whites. Mobility is more likely, with the result that relationships between the races are more aggressive than accommodative. The stereotypes of African Americans change from being perceived as easy-going, immature children to that of an aggressive, "uppity," and dangerous people (van den Berghe 1967).

One of the implications of van den Berghe's description of the conditions under which caste or class predominates is that the former is more likely in a static agricultural society while the latter becomes more important with the advance of industrialization and industrialism. Caste is viewed as being associated with rural areas (e.g., the early twentieth-century South) and class with industrialization (e.g., the North). Frazier (1957) took a similar position when he said that the conflicts surrounding African Americans' status in the United States are symptomatic of the attempt to "force into the mold of a static agricultural society the dynamic economic and social relations which characterize an industrial urban society" (p. 268). The general image of the structure of race relations in a society in which a dominant agricultural economy is in the process of being supplanted by an ever-growing industrialism is one in which caste and class are both components, as described by Warner, Dollard, and others (e.g., Willie 1979).

The caste model of U.S. race relations has come under severe attack from both conservative and more radical scholars. On the conservative side, there is the belief that race either is or is becoming largely irrelevant in modern industrial society. Position in the system of inequality is allegedly based on achieved rather than ascribed characteristics, and movement is based on results of an open contest between individuals rather than on the sponsorship of influential others. Critics have commented on the inappropriateness of comparing U.S. race relations with the Indian caste system, arguing that in contrast to the Indian situation, Black/White relations are (1) not stable, but changing; (2) characterized by mobility for Blacks; (3) conflictive and pathological; and (4) characterized by upward aspirations on the part of Blacks. Other significant differences between India and the United States, it is argued, are that whereas each caste in India is tied to a particular occupation, in the United States, Blacks are not relegated to a single type of occupation. Furthermore, the Indian caste system is legitimized through religion, but in the United States, racial inequality has been justified on the basis of biological or subcultural differences (Cox 1942, 1948; Simpson and Yinger 1965; Barrera 1979). Finally, as mentioned earlier, the caste model has been used more as a descriptive device than as an historical explanation of racial inequality.

Not all of the preceding criticisms are valid, however. There is evidence that as in the United States, the caste system in India has been challenged by those in the lower groups. There is no consensus on the part of all to see it as a legitimate system (Berreman

1960, 1972). Despite the Constitution in India guaranteeing certain rights and outlawing castes, caste relations still operate and contrast sharply with Constitutional provisions, creating an inconsistency between what is on paper and what really exists in society (Sivaramayya 1983). Similarly, in the United States, a distinction has been made between de jure and de facto segregation. In other words, this condition is not unlike the internal contradiction between the tenets of American democracy and the reality of racial inequality—what Myrdal called the "American dilemma." Moreover, as in the U.S. case where classes are divided by race, in India, the primordial loyalties of caste have weakened the unity of classes and prevented poorer classes from organizing (Chakravarti 1983, p. 170). What several of these comments suggest is that it is not acceptable to compare an *idealized* model of the Indian caste system with a *realistic* view of the U.S. race structure (Berreman 1960; Das and Acuff 1970).

Domination Theories of Race Relations

A variety of specific theories are included under this general category, but all of them incorporate the historically crucial role of power and/or domination in shaping racial inequality. Thus, they tend to be more dynamic and historically rooted than caste approaches. They do not anticipate the eventual automatic assimilation of minorities, nor do they emphasize the stability of the system of inequality or the active complicity of the minority group as is often suggested in caste analyses. Three of these approaches are (1) Noel's theory of ethnic stratification, (2) imperialist/colonial explanations, and (3) class-based explanations of racial inequality. Because of the focal role of power in each of these explanations, these theories are not incompatible and attempts have been made to synthesize them (Barrera 1979; Bonacich 1985).

Noel's Theory of Ethnic Stratification.   Noel (1968) generated a broad theory of the origins of ethnic stratification which he then tested by applying it to the development of slavery in the United States. By ethnic stratification, he means "a system of stratification wherein some relatively fixed group membership (e.g., race, religion, or nationality) is utilized as a major criterion for assigning social positions with their attendant differential rewards" (p. 157). He begins with the assumption that before the possibility of such stratification even exists, there must be a period of prolonged contact between the groups involved. Whether or not contact results in stratification depends on the existence of (1) ethnocentrism, (2) competition, and (3) differential power. All three of these factors must be present for ethnic stratification to emerge.

Ethnocentrism, of course, refers to the belief that one's culture is the best, the center of the universe so to speak. All others are judged according to it. Cultures that are similar to one's own are ranked highly, and those that are radically different are looked down upon. Consequently, ethnocentrism fosters an in-group/out-group or us/them orientation toward others. Since people are so classified, double standards may be applied to the groups involved. What one expects of oneself may not be what is expected of others. It is important to note that each group is ethnocentric, thinking of the other in terms of mild or severe disdain. Each group measures the other in terms of its own values and beliefs, and of course, the other group is always found to be wanting to some degree. Each group also remains separate and autonomous from the other.

However, mere ethnocentrism is not enough to create ethnic stratification according to Noel. Groups can remain independent and relatively equal with a mutual and healthy respect for each other even though both are ethnocentric. Thus, it is also crucial that competition exists between the two or more groups in question. *Competition,* as defined by Noel,

refers to the interaction between groups who are trying to attain "the same scarce goal." What is important about this interaction is that the goal is the same and that it is scarce. This could be competition over a prime neighborhood area or desirable jobs, for example. If the groups were after different goals, there would be no sense of competition and perhaps even lack of concern over the goals of the other group. If the goal is easily attainable and in abundant supply, there is no reason for one group to try to exploit or stratify the other. There is plenty for all.

If, on the other hand, the desired object or goal is actually or believed to be in scarce supply, then stratification may be seen as functional by each group. The intensity and terms of the competition along with the relative adaptive capacity of each group will affect the probability and form of ethnic stratification. Competition is more likely to be highly intense if there are many valuable, scarce goals that are shared by both groups, and will be less intense if those shared goals are few in number and relatively unimportant. The more intense the competition, the greater the likelihood of ethnic stratification, other factors being equal. The terms of the competition concern the values, rules, and structural opportunities present in the setting. If competition is regulated by agreed-upon rules and some basic humane values are shared by the two groups, then ethnic stratification is far less likely to occur than if the competition is essentially a free-for-all and the groups had no values in common. Moreover, if there are few structural outlets in the form of opportunities, then competition is more likely to lead to stratification.

Finally, the adaptive capacity of a group relative to its competitor also has an impact on ethnic stratification. Basically, the group that has more cultural and other internal resources to call on when problems of adaptation and adjustment arise will be more likely to be able to dominate the other group. The chances of stratification occurring are lower when both groups are equal in their adaptive capabilities.

According to Noel, in addition to ethnocentrism and competition, a third variable, *differential power*, is also necessary for the emergence of ethnic stratification. "Highly ethnocentric groups involved in competition for vital objects will not generate ethnic stratification unless they are of such unequal power that one is able to impose its will upon the other" (Noel 1968, p. 112). Ethnic stratification simply will not appear in the absence of differential power. Once the greater power of one group is established, the more powerful group develops measures to subordinate and regulate the other group and to stabilize the current distribution of differential rewards.

In sum, Noel argued for an interactive model in that all three variables—ethnocentrism, competition with particular characteristics, and differential power—are needed to produce ethnic stratification. In applying this theory to the development of slavery in the early English colonies of the United States, Noel concluded that it adequately explains ethnic stratification. "Given ethnocentrism, the Negroes' lack of power, and the dynamic arena of competition in which they were located, their ultimate enslavement was inevitable" (ibid., p. 117). Earlier, we saw how these factors also were implicated in the subjugation of American Indians.

In our early contacts with Mexican Americans throughout the Southwest, competition for land, accompanying racial/ethnic stereotyping, and imbalances in numbers and power contributed significantly to the inequality that developed between Whites and Chicanos (Farley 1988). Although Noel's theory does not identify all the specific historical and societal factors that might affect stratification in specific settings, his theory does identify in broad brush strokes three core factors that make it likely.

The next two theories, which also focus on differential power, have a great deal in common. The colonial model of race relations owes a significant amount to the Marxian class framework, and early architects of that model generally acknowledge their debt to Marx (e.g., Fanon 1963; Memmi 1965). In recent years, there has been a lot of cross-fertilization of both the colonial and class perspectives, with each using concepts from the other. But since the primary impetus that gave rise to each was not the same, they will be presented as if they are distinct approaches. However, their overlap in general orientation will become clear as each is discussed.

Internal Colonialism and Race Inequality. This approach to understanding the domination of Whites over Blacks in the United States is based on discussions and analyses of relationships between colonizing countries in the First World and those who have been colonized in the Third World. In this way, it bears a striking resemblance to world-system and dependency theories. The popularization of the internal-colonial perspective arose during the tumultuous 1960s when the War on Poverty, Civil Rights movement, and major urban racial confrontations were at their height. Militancy and discussions of "Black power" and "Black Nationalism" made the parallel between the Black predicament and that of other oppressed racial groups seem viable. In other words, the times were ripe for a colonial theory of U.S. race relations. Fanon and Memmi, who wrote about colonial relationships in the Third World, had their writings adapted to the U.S. racial setting. Following them, a large number of scholars suggested and elaborated on what they felt was a basic parallelism between the dynamics in those relationships and those that occur in Black/White relations (cf. Carmichael and Hamilton 1967; Allen 1969; Blauner 1972).

One of the noted differences between classic colonial relationships and the internal-colonial relationship said to exist between Blacks and Whites in the United States is that the former generally involves groups from one territory invading and dominating the territory of another group, whereas in the latter case, both groups are from and occupy the same country. What can be said in response to this difference is that it is the character of the relationship rather than the factor of geography that defines a relationship as colonial (Barrera 1979; Bonacich 1980).

While acknowledging that the analogy is not perfect, Carmichael and Hamilton argued that Blacks in the United States "stand as colonial subjects in relation to the White society. . . . That colonial status operates in three areas—political, economic, social" (Carmichael and Hamilton 1967, pp. 5–6). *Politically*, while Blacks are technically just as free as Whites, Whites dominate the power structure of society, holding the most influential positions. Moreover, they exercise "indirect rule" by coopting and controlling selected influential Blacks to help maintain the Black community in a subordinate position. *Economically*, Blacks are more likely to be poor and unemployed and to pay exorbitant prices for shoddy goods. In this manner, the Black ghetto is sapped of its resources, which are transferred to the dominant part of society. *Socially*, Blacks are looked down on and demeaned in everyday contacts with Whites. Racial ideologies arguing their basic inferiority and presenting negative stereotypes help justify and maintain control over Blacks. This interpretation presents all Whites as benefiting from the colonial structure.

Perhaps the most often-cited architect of the colonial model of race relations in the United States is the sociologist Robert Blauner. Blauner argued that *assimilationist* theories, which view minority groups as being on a one-way road to blending into the rest of society, do not accurately characterize the historical conditions of African Americans because they draw a false analogy between the present situation of African Americans and that faced by White ethnic immigrants about a century ago. He pointed out that this analogy cannot hold up because the histories and circumstances of their arrival in the United States were qualitatively and highly different. Not only the slavery experience, but the non-

voluntary nature of their entrance into the country and the more permanent control of their lives by those outside their communities distinguishes African Americans from earlier White-ethnic immigrant groups. African Americans are not merely the latest batch of immigrants who are waiting to be assimilated and upwardly mobile.

Although there are some differences between classic colonialism and internal colonialism, Blauner felt that they share several basic characteristics. First, the political domination and advanced technological level of the West was the basis for both slavery of African Americans and the colonization of many countries by Europe. Second, the economic and political superiority of the dominant group encourages a feeling of racial superiority used to justify the exploitation of the other group. In other words, since both types of colonialism have similar roots, Blauner said that they share "a common process of social oppression" (Blauner 1972, p. 84).

Blauner (1972) suggested that there are five basic characteristics in the colonization complex:

1. The dominant–subordinate relationship begins with forced, involuntary entry; that is, African Americans were brought here as slaves and ghettos are controlled from the outside by the dominant group. White settlers also, of course, forceably took over American Indian lands.

2. The indigenous culture and social organization of the dominated group is altered, manipulated, or destroyed; that is, African American culture and institutions are undermined. Native American culture also has been subjugated.

3. Representatives of the dominant group control the subordinate group through their legal and government institutions; that is, White institutions control much of the lives of African Americans. The placement of American Indians on reservations

also serves as an example of control by the dominant group.

4. Racism as an ideology is used to justify the oppression of the subordinated group; that is, Blacks and other racially or ethnically distinguishable groups are seen as biologically or otherwise inferior to Whites.

5. The colonizers and colonized occupy different positions in the labor structure and perform different roles; that is, by and large, African Americans are relegated to menial, nonprestigious jobs while Whites dominate in higher-ranking positions. The dual-labor market characterizes the occupational positions of dominant and subordinate groups.

The listed characteristics suggest that the Black ghetto, instead of being isolated from the rest of society in some kind of autonomous culture of poverty, is in fact tied to White society by bonds of exploitation and dependency. The educational, political, economic, and legal institutions of the dominant society infiltrate and permeate the dominated colony. Then racism is used to maintain and justify the lower status of Blacks.

In addition to these structural characteristics, there are also cultural and psychological ramifications to the colonial relationship. In the colony, individuals cannot break through the racial-ethnic barrier. Colonized individuals can move up in class but cannot change their position of being colonized except through successful revolutionary movements that transform the structure of society. They may try to gain entrance into the larger society but "everything is mobilized so that the colonized cannot cross the doorstep, so that [they understand and admit] that this path is dead and assimilation is impossible" (Memmi 1965, p. 125).

In attempting to assimilate, colonized persons may initially admire and even adopt aspects of their oppressors, but when it is realized that full structural assimilation is not possible, they begin to reassert themselves in part through resurrecting old traditions and through the advocacy of violence. "Those who understand their fate become impatient and no longer tolerate colonization" (ibid., p. 120).

Most of these stages appear to apply to African Americans and their movements in the United States, although some of the protest behaviors of African Americans could be interpreted in ways other than through the colonial model (Omi and Winant 1986). Among the strengths of this model are its historical and comparative dimensions and the fact that it can account for a relatively large number of factors within a fairly straightforward theoretical framework (Barrera 1979). Among the weaknesses of the internal colonial model is one that Blauner recognized himself:

> When the colonial model is transferred from the overseas situation to the United States without substantial alteration, it tends to miss the total structure, the context of advanced industrial capitalism in which our racial arrangements are embedded—a context that produces group politics and social movements that differ markedly from the traditional colonial society. . . . It lacks a conception of American society as a total structure beyond the central significance that I attribute to racism. (ibid., p. 13)

To effectively deal with this shortcoming, Blauner suggested that an adequate theory must incorporate elements dealing with characteristics of both colonialism and capitalism. Indeed, several of the attempts to develop a class-based theory of race inequality include references to both of these (e.g., Bonacich 1980; Hunter and Abraham 1987). Omi and Winant (1986) also pointed out that the internal-colonial model does not take into account class differences within the colonized (African American) group or relationships between minority groups. Despite these difficulties, the colonial model probably provides a more accurate analysis of Black/White relations in the United States than either the assimilationist or caste perspective (Wilson 1970; Barrera 1979).

Class-Based Explanations of Race Inequality.
Wilson (1970) has argued that economic and class dynamics are becoming more important for determining the life chances of Blacks. But well before Wilson developed his theory, others also argued that economic factors lie behind the inequality between Blacks and Whites in the United States. One of the most sophisticated class-based theories of race relations in the United States was developed by Oliver C. Cox in the late 1940s. Cox was very critical of the caste model presented earlier, arguing that the structural, cultural, and historical conditions in India were radically different from those characterizing U.S. Black/White relations. For example, he contended that a caste structure is ancient, nonconflictive, static, nonpathological, status oriented, and contains caste-fixed occupations. In contrast, he said, race relations and racism are relatively recent, conflictive, and pathological, do not usually involve narrow occupational restrictions, and are rooted in political-class conflict and capitalism (1942, 1945, 1948).

Cox viewed race relations and inequality in the United States as a product of economic exploitation. Forcibly bringing slaves to the United States was essentially a way of getting labor to exploit the natural resources of the country. Racial exploitation is only one form of the proletarianization of labor according to Cox. Racism as an ideology was not the root of exploitation; rather, it followed from it and was used to justify economic exploitation of Blacks. Racism, therefore, is a relatively recent phenomenon. Given its character and economic basis, "racial antagonism is essentially political-class conflict." Racial antagonism is used by employers to divide Black and White workers, and racial ghettos are maintained because they facilitate control over Blacks and perpetuate a self-defeating lifestyle. Blacks may want to assimilate but it is not in the interests of dominant Whites for them to do so (1948, 1976).

What is attractive about Cox's arguments is that he intermingled elements of racism, colonialism, class inequality, and capitalism in a comparative framework. Racial inequality is bound up with the development and expansion of European empires and the rise of capitalism and its labor needs.

Trade is the lifeblood of international capitalism. The need to control potential markets and sources of raw materials strengthens the tendency of capitalism to colonize and exercise political control in the world economic system. Loans, raw materials, markets for manufactured goods, and imperialism each play a part in creating and fastening ties (chains) between dominant and subordinate nations in the worldwide capitalist system (Cox 1959, 1964). Race prejudice is then used to justify imperialism. Much of Cox's later writing anticipated many of the ideas associated with world-system and dependency theory.

One of the thorny areas of disagreement among class-based theorists of race relations concerns who benefits from racism and the nature of the relationship between Blacks and the White working class. From one point of view, racism is used by employers to drive a wedge between Whites and Blacks in the working class, and nationalism is used to divide members of the working class from different ethnic/racial groups in different countries. White workers come to view foreign workers who labor for low wages as unfair competitors, and their racism, which is ultimately rooted in the worldwide development of capitalism, is an attempt to protect their own jobs (Bonacich 1980). Although White or dominant workers may benefit from this racism in the short run, in the long run, the inequality within the working class creates divisions that weaken its collective power against employers. Employers exploit members of the minority for greater profits and money with which to pay the dominant working class. Accordingly, the principal beneficiaries of racism are employers rather than all Whites (Reich 1977).

In general, having an ethnic/racial working class provides capitalism with a surplus army from which to draw poorly paid workers to perform jobs that are necessary but that no one in the dominant group wants to perform. But as the capitalist economy advances and the revolutionary potential of minority groups grows, many large employers begin to feel that the long-run costs of race inequality may be too high and that it should be eliminated (Baran and Sweezy 1966). One obvious cost of racism to employers is the loss of bright minority members to employers who could use them to increase productivity.

Edna Bonacich (1980) attempted to integrate and synthesize many of the arguments in class-based theories of race inequality. She began by commenting on the motivations for imperialism abroad. One important source for this movement is the desire to find more malleable and cheaper labor since the cost of labor rises as capitalism develops within a country. Wages rise because (1) the absorption of the entire labor supply into the expanding economy creates increased demand for it, (2) workers have a need for higher wages to purchase the increasing number of commodities produced in the economy, (3) large factories create social conditions conducive to the political organization and greater union power among workers, and (4) increased state support of workers cushions them and enables them to hold out for higher wages (see also Piven and Cloward 1982).

Because of these pressures for higher wages by domestic workers, then, employers look outside national boundaries for new sources of cheap labor. Pick up a piece of clothing from a well-known and expensive brand (e.g., Gant, Polo, etc.) and notice where the item has been sewn. The labels frequently cite places such as Honduras and the Dominican Republic. The public scandals dealing with the making of celebrity-endorsed clothing in Third World sweatshops is another example of attempts to profit through the use of low-wage workers. Wages are lower in less-developed countries because of the existence of additional sources of

subsistence (production for use) and a traditionally lower standard of living. Members of the domestic working class then see themselves as competing with cheap laborers in Third World countries, and may (1) react with nationalist and racist fervor against such groups or (2) see both themselves and other working-class groups from around the world as victims of capitalist development. Which of the two reactions is pursued by the domestic working class depends in part on the extent to which capitalists can control the colonized working class and manipulate the domestic working class, on how imminent the experience of competition with outside cheap labor is in the domestic working class, and on how proletarianized this class is itself (Bonacich 1980).

In terms of their relationship with upper-class elements in the host country, outside capitalists can try to use the native elite classes in the colonized countries for their own benefit as a sort of intermediary between themselves and the local labor force. This causes some of these elite to benefit in the short run from this arrangement while others lose by foreign capital's intervention into their country. Those who receive short-run gains will encourage native workers to work for outsiders for nationalist reasons, whereas those who are themselves immediately exploited will attempt to eliminate foreign intrusion into the home economy and press for the development of their own national industries.

The essential theme of Bonacich's argument is placing class and race dynamics in an international context and tracing racism and race inequality to the expansion of capitalism. It should be obvious by now that there are several similarities between the class and colony theories of race inequality. First, both have as central themes the notion of the exploitation (especially economic) of a lower group—African Americans and/or the working class. Both perspectives view top and bottom positions in relational terms—that is, the position of one group is considered to be inextricably linked to that of the other group. Second, in both models, justifications (ideologies) are crucial for legitimating the power relationships that exist. But in both, the relationship is both "destructive and creative" (Memmi 1965). Third, both perspectives emphasize the polarization of society and the importance of rising consciousness among the exploited. In general theoretical terms, these basic congruences between internal colonial and class theories outweigh their differences (Tabb 1970; Wilson 1970; Blauner 1972; Barrera 1979).

THE GLOBAL CONTEXT, IMMIGRATION, AND GLOBALIZATION

Racial and ethnic inequality, a form of what Charles Tilly (1998) calls "categorical inequality," is found throughout the world. Historically, among the most well-known of these systems of inequality were those found in South Africa, India, and Japan. In each of these societies, a significant axis of the system of inequality was centered around racial/ethnic differences.

Beginning in the late 1940s and lasting until the early 1990s, South Africa had in place a system of apartheid that enforced social, economic, and legal separation between Whites and Blacks. Even though Whites were heavily outnumbered by non-Whites, they dominated the country politically, socially, and economically. Blacks were required to live in certain areas, lacked political rights, had to use separate facilities, were limited in their job prospects, and were closely monitored by authorities. Under apartheid, the poorest 40 percent of the population, who were mostly Black, lived in conditions that were far worse than those of the richest 20 percent, who were mostly White. For example, in 1993, near the end of the apartheid era, among the crowded households of the poorest in South Africa only about one-fifth had electricity, one-quarter had inside water, and less than one-fifth had toilets in their houses (United Nations 1998). A combination of growing Black organization and political power, economic requirements, and

international sanctions and developments led to the decline of apartheid. In 1994, Nelson Mandela was chosen as president in the country's first general election.

Since the formal breakdown of apartheid, significant racial differences exist about national priorities in South Africa. Blacks see unemployment and the need for widespread access to basic services like housing and water as critical issues, while Whites are more likely to be concerned with crime and political corruption. Despite these differences and more positively, however, there is a multiracial government and general agreement that democracy is the government of choice (Schaefer 2006).

Parallels have been drawn between apartheid and the Jim Crow system that flourished in the southern United States after the Civil War. As in South Africa, more powerful colonists and settlers pushed native peoples off the land and captured important resources. Also similarly, racist ideologies were used to justify the growing inequality between dominant and dominated groups. The elements of Noel's theory of racial inequality—competition for resources, ethnocentrism, and unequal power—all operated in the U.S. and South African situations.

As noted earlier, similarities have also been suggested between India's traditional, now outlawed, caste system and Black–White relations in the United States. The caste system that was dominant in India provides an example of an extreme case of status stratification in Weber's sense. It had been both a system of inequality and a means of integration for India, with each layer assigned specific and unique functions (Lannoy 1975). The four major castes or varnas, beginning with the top, were the Brahmans, Kshatriyas, Vaishyas, and Sudras. Those at the top were assigned to perform the most honorific functions and were considered purer than those below. Legitimation for the caste system was rooted in early Hindu texts in which the four varnas are described and portrayed as metaphorically representing different part of the Indian social body. A fifth stratum, the Untouchables (Harijans) were not part of the formal caste system itself; they were outside it. The real, everyday structure and operation of the caste system at the village level was much more complex than the four-varna system would suggest. Although loosely associated by residents with the national caste system, castes or "jati" at the local level vary in number and character (Kolenda 1978).

There is increasing evidence that the Indian caste system is not the monolithic system as it is sometimes portrayed to be. While still influential in more rural areas, educated, Westernized Indians are less likely to believe in the purity/pollution theory, and industrialization, trade, and globalization have helped to weaken the hold of the caste system and spurred a growing class system (Lannoy 1975; Sivaramayya 1983; Beteille 1996). There is some evidence of avenues of social mobility, and some lower-caste persons have started their own religious movements, others have married upward, and the relatively new Indian democracy and constitution have formally outlawed the caste system. At the same time, however, as in the United States, old traditions die hard. As Milner observed, "while the caste system has undergone great changes over the long period of its existence, it has been relatively stable compared to most human institutions" (Milner 1994, p. 56).

Japan provides an interesting variation on the caste system. One of the minority groups discriminated against in Japan is the *burakumin* or "hamlet people," but in contrast to most minority groups elsewhere, the roughly 3 million burakumin are physically indistinguishable from other Japanese. Thus, they are sometimes called an "invisible race" (DeVos and Wagatsuma 1966). The only way to really know that a person is a burakumin is to know where he or she lives (DeVos and Wetherall 1983).

Historically, individuals in this group were considered unclean and were forced to live in certain areas. Their invisibility was reinforced by the absence of their village location on maps

(Rowley 1990). While some attempts have been made to ban them, prejudice and discrimination against burakumin remain, for example, in the areas of marriage, job application, occupation, and earnings.

As is the case in the United States, South Africa, and India, traditional cultural values and practices retain a grip in Japan even in the face of technological advances and globalizing forces. In many countries, immigrants bring in new ideas, cultural values, and practices that often clash with and foment change in the native culture. Since changes took place in U.S. immigration laws in 1965 that weakened the old quota system and opened the nation more fully to immigration from relatives, the proportion of immigrants coming from Asia and Latin America has grown significantly. Twenty years after passage of the 1965 Immigration and Nationality Act, almost 85 percent of immigrants were from Asia, Latin America, and the Caribbean (Lee and Bean 2004). In 2002, an estimated total of 1,064,000 individuals immigrated to the United States, including 342,100 from Asia, 219,400 from Mexico, 96,500 from the Caribbean, 74,500 from South America, and 69,000 from Central American countries (U.S. Census Bureau 2005). If immigration trends continue, about 45 million new immigrants will have come to the United States between 1995 and 2050, expanding the Asian and Hispanic numbers to 8 and 25 percent of the U.S. population, respectively (Smith and Edmonston 1997).

The manner and extent of adaptation of these U.S. immigrants have varied, and most of the recent Latino immigrants have not found assimilation to be a smooth or easy process. Nor has assimilation followed the same paths or resulted in the same experiences for different groups. The variation between immigrant groups has resulted in "segmented assimilation," where the quality of adaptation varies depending on the human capital of the immigrant group, the strength of its family structure, and the reception it receives in the host country (Portes and Rumbaut 2005). Some groups, such

Immigrants often come to the United States in search of better lives for themselves and their families. Eloisa appears pleased by the variety of choices at a discount superstore grocery chain called H.E.B. in the southwest region of the United States.
Photo © Janet Jarman/Corbis.

as Jewish immigrants, form economic enclaves that develop into a source of support and income for new immigrants. Other groups, like Koreans, become prominent as "middlemen," providing services for a variety of clients.

Generally, greater social and economic inequality in a country encourages emigration of poorer residents out of them and into less unequal countries. Thus, the movement is often from less to more developed countries like the United States (Hao 2003). These new immigrants have less education and fewer high-level skills than native citizens. In 1990, for example, the average educational attainment of "recent immigrant" men to the United States was 11.8 years, compared to 13.2 years among native U.S. citizens. Well over one-third of

male immigrants had dropped out of high school. Their lower educational levels were reflected in the lower earnings they received. In 1990, recent male immigrants from Mexico, for example, had average annual earnings of $14,251, compared to $37,551 for native men. Women who immigrated from Mexico had annual earnings of $8,738 compared to $20,196 for women born in the United States. Immigrants in general tend to fall near the bottom of the wage hierarchy. Their concentration in certain kinds of jobs like textiles, cooking, tailoring, and other service positions helps account for their lower earnings (Smith and Edmonston 1997).

In the United States, immigration has been an issue of concern again recently not only because of the shift that has taken place in most immigrants' countries of origin, but because of the potential effects of immigrants on the employment and earnings of native citizens. The influx of lesser educated and lower-skilled Hispanic immigrants, for example, has led many to believe that they have damaged the economic positions of native residents by either taking away jobs from them or lowering their wages because of the competition they provide. While immigration helps to account for an increase in wealth inequality in the United States because of the diversity of newcomers, evidence indicates that immigration has little effect on the wages of native-born employees (Smith and Edmonston 1997; Hao 2003).

Despite their minimal impact on natives' wages, the increase in Hispanic and Asian immigrants affects the character of the American racial hierarchy. "At this time, America's shift in color lines points to the emergence of a new split that replaces the old black/white divide and one that separates blacks from nonblacks. . . . In the black/nonblack divide, Latinos and Asians fall into the nonblack category. . . . The birth of a black/nonblack divide could be a disastrous outcome for many African Americans" (Lee and Bean 2004, p. 237). Another possibility is the incorporation of darker-skinned, poorer Hispanics and Asians into a "collective black" category in a new racial hierarchy (Bonilla-Silva 2004).

The concerns about new immigrants as a social and economic threat have raised questions about the need to control immigration. Yet attempts to screen and limit immigrants' entrance into a country fly in the face of the image of globalization as a process that opens the doors to technology, products, influences, and people from abroad. Concerns like this have led Ronen Shamir to argue that while theorists advocating globalization may see it as a liberalizing, open process, it is also a conservative, limiting, exclusionary process (Shamir 2005). This paradox arises from the desire for

nations to control their borders and maintain their national identity even in the midst of globalization. Globalization produces "closure, entrapment, and containment" through the "prevention of movement and the blocking of access" since some immigrants are seen as potential threats, even terrorists. This produces a "paradigm of suspicion" in which profiling, quarantining, imprisonment, and other forms of containment are put in place to control the mobility of suspect immigrants (ibid., pp. 199, 206–206, 210). Most of these "suspects" are from poorer countries. These modes of control are "a structural response to the problem of maintaining high levels of inequality in a relatively normatively homogenized world" in which there is a "tension between universal rights and universal fears" (ibid., p. 214). In this manner, globalization helps to maintain racial hierarchies and status exclusion.

SUMMARY

Historical and contemporary evidence documents the inequality that has existed between Whites and various minority groups, including African Americans, American Indians, Asian Americans, and Hispanic Americans. The exploitation of African Americans for their labor and American Indians and Mexican Americans for their land was justified by racist ideologies, stereotypes, and the force of law. Like women, many minority groups have incomes, earnings, and occupational statuses that are lower than those of Whites, while their poverty rates are higher. Differences in family compositions, educational levels, and labor-force participation do not fully account for these economic discrepancies. African Americans and other minorities also experience day-to-day microinequities, frequently of a type similar to those experienced by women. Biases in language, education, and the media constitute many of these, but there are many, such as those noted by McIntosh, that occur in a variety of settings.

A variety of theories have been developed to explain racial and ethnic inequality, ranging from the caste model to more radical internal-colonial and class explanations. In general, the latter are more sophisticated and focus on the centrality of differential power and economic domination in accounting for race inequality. As is the case with some gender inequality theories, several of these theories are couched in a comparative framework and intertwine class and economic processes in their explanation, which lends them some depth.

These theories and research evidence show how the variables discussed in the last several chapters—class, sex, and race—have been intertwined and influence each other. Debates in recent years have centered on the relative importance of race, sex, and class in producing these inequalities between groups. Some have argued for the primacy of one of these over others, but it seems clear that all affect the life chances through complex routes. Early racial and ethnic antagonisms helped to justify the economic exploitation of American Indians, Mexican Americans, and African Americans, and sexual stereotypes had the equivalent effect on women. At the same time, class differences within these groups created divisions that are sometimes hard to bridge. Sex and race also interact. For example, women of different races have different occupational and educational patterns. Race has been a source of division within the feminist movement, as well.

Across the globe, most societies struggle with ethnic and racial divisions. Among the most notable of these have been South Africa, India, and Japan. Increased Latino and Asian immigration to the United States has reignited concerns about open immigration and its effects on economic inequality. Little support has been found for the argument that such immigration has a depressing effect on the earnings of native workers. Globalization encourages the free flow of material and human resources between countries, which suggests that every country might benefit from the process. But globalization has also renewed attempts by nations to monitor and maintain the security of their boundaries, the integrity of their cultures, and their position in the world economic order. Consequently, globalization also encourages tendencies toward closure and exclusivity at the same time that neoliberals publicize its open and fluid qualities.

In the last six chapters, we have surveyed the extent of inequality along several axes: economic, status, power, gender, sexual orientation, and race/ethnicity. It is now time to examine in greater detail the most prominent explanations that have been given for social inequality in general. We begin in Chapter 8 with a discussion of classical explanations, and then move on to an analysis of contemporary theories in Chapter 9.

CRITICAL THINKING

1. How do historical events continue to play a role in racial and ethnic inequality today? Can the effects of these events ever be erased? How?

2. Does degree of darkness or shade of color play a role in the inequality between individuals that is independent of race? Explain and give examples.

3. Will changes in the *class* positions of racial and ethnic minorities affect their position as *status* groups in the eyes of the majority? Why or why not?

4. What explains the content of stereotypes? How and why do stereotypes of groups change over time?

WEB CONNECTIONS

Segregation is still widespread in many major cities in the United States. A website for the Bureau of the Census allows one to see how racial and ethnic minorities are distributed in cities. Choose a major city, perhaps your hometown, and request the percentage of Black residents by census tract at the site (see "theme" and "level") to visually see the distribution of races in the city. A map is produced that shows the location and degree of concentration of racial and/or ethnic minorities. Are your results surprising? Find out at: www.census.gov/cgi-bin/gazetteer.

Classical Explanations of Inequality

Society as a whole is more and more splitting up into two great hostile camps, into two great classes directly facing each other.

—Karl Marx

Under the natural course of things each citizen tends towards his fittest function.

—Herbert Spencer

The discussions throughout Part One make it clear that multidimensional inequality is extensive in the United States, and, in a number of ways, is becoming even more pronounced and disconcerting for many. The widespread nature of social inequality makes explaining it all the more important. Several previous chapters have offered specific explanations tailored for understanding particular forms of inequality. This chapter examines the broad classical explanations of Marx, Weber, Durkheim, and Spencer, from which many modern thinkers have drawn. Karl Marx is discussed first because virtually all of his central ideas were formulated before any of the others and because subsequent theories are often viewed as reactions to Marx's own work.

KARL MARX (1818–1883)

Few social scientists have had as great a political and economic impact as Karl Marx. His perspectives on society have been used by social scientists and ideologues, and his influence on modern sociology, and even society, has been pervasive. The ideas of all scholars are

in large part shaped by the historical events and life situations they experience. This appears clearly in the case of Marx, as well as Weber. Karl Marx was born on May 5, 1818, in the city of Trier, Prussia (now part of Germany). His family was of Jewish background and provided a bourgeois setting for Marx in his youth. His father and a neighbor, Ludwig von Westphalen, introduced him to the thinkers of the Enlightenment. Ludwig von Westphalen in particular became an intellectual companion with whom Marx discussed philosophy and literature. Marx later married von Westphalen's daughter, Jenny.

While studying at the universities of Bonn and Berlin, Marx became a friend of a group known as the Young Hegelians. Although Hegel was dead, his ideas survived as an intellectual force at Berlin. The Young Hegelians helped to convert Marx from the study of law to the study of philosophy. The increasing radicalism of his ideas encouraged his departure for Paris in late 1843. It was in Paris, a center of invigorating intellectual activity, that Marx began his close association and collaboration with Frederick Engels, the son of a manufacturer who acquainted Marx more fully with the real conditions of the working class. Marx's writing again caused his expulsion, and he moved from Paris to Brussels in 1845. By then, Marx already considered himself a socialist and revolutionary. He had aligned himself with several workers' organizations, and in 1848 he and Engels produced the *Manifesto of the Communist Party*.

After some moving around, Marx left in 1849 for London, where he stayed for most of the remainder of his life. It was there that he produced most of his major writing. During his stay, his life and that of his family were marked with poverty, which was relieved only by his occasional employment as a European correspondent for the *New York Daily Tribune* and periodic help from his friend, Engels. He became a leader of the International, a radical movement made up of individuals from several European countries, and in 1867 published the first volume of his monumental *Capital*. In the last decade of his life, Marx was already an honored figure among socialists and was able to live somewhat more comfortably than in his earlier years in London. He died on March 14, 1883, only one year after the death of his elder daughter and two years after the death of his wife, Jenny (Coser 1971).

Despite the familiarity of Karl Marx's name to most, many of his ideas are still not properly understood by numerous students. Two of these are especially relevant to his statements concerning class relations. First, Marx did not believe that everything is determined by the economic structure, that all other institutions are merely reflections of the economic system and are without causal influence. Although Marx considered the economic aspect the "ultimately determining element in history" and the "main principle," he did not think it was the only determining one. In a personal letter, while admitting that he and Marx had probably contributed to the confusion on this point, Engels put the matter succinctly: "The economic situation is the basis, but the various

elements of the superstructure . . . also exercise their influence upon the course of the historical struggles and in many cases preponderate in determining their *form*. There is an interaction of all these elements in which, amid all the endless host of accidents . . . the economic movement finally asserts itself as necessary" (Marx and Engels 1970, vol. 2, p. 487, emphasis in original). Thus, political, religious, and cultural factors play a role, though the "ultimately decisive" one is economic.

A second misconception is that Marx argued that only two classes exist in any society. On the contrary, Marx was aware of the diversity of classes that can exist at any one time, as well as the factions that can be present within a given class. His discussions in *The Class Struggles in France* and in the third volume of *Capital* make this abundantly clear. We will explore further comments on Marx's ideas after a discussion of the core elements of his theory.

The Theoretical Context of Marx's Class Analysis

Marx subscribed to a materialist conception of social life. That is, he argued that activities are what characterize and propel human history. History consists of human beings going about producing and reproducing themselves in interaction with nature. Humans are a part of nature, and both nature and humans change as they interact, making both of them a part of human history. History is really a process of "active self-making" (Simon 1994, p. 98). It is *activity*, especially labor, that defines who we are. Consequently, a concentration on economic activity is fundamental for understanding history's process.

Labor is an expression of our nature. When freely engaged in, it allows us to realize our true human nature and satisfy our real basic needs (not manufactured ones). When freely done, labor is also an enjoyment because it is spontaneous. However, when forced or artificial, that is, alienated, it becomes more of a misery than an enjoyment. It twists our human nature. Alienated labor exists when private property and its owners hire or control others and define their labor for them. Instead of being for oneself, labor becomes a task that primarily benefits owners of property. One works to get food, shelter, and so on, that is labor becomes a *means* to an end rather than an *end* in itself. Under capitalism, as in other class societies, the laborer and her or his labor belong to the capitalist. As a commodity, laborers have been hired at a price to work for the capitalist; for this period, the capitalist owns the workers and exploits them. It is out of the exploitation of the laborer by the capitalist that new value or profit is created because what is needed to reproduce the laborer (i.e., wage) is less than the value of what the laborer produces. It is this difference in value that defines exploitation and generates surplus value or profit for the employer. It is also private property and its control that defines classes and their relationship.

Historically, there have been several types of societies with class systems. According to Marx, the earliest societies were classless, being based on a "common ownership of land" (Marx and Engels 1969, vol. 1, pp. 108–109). But all known subsequent societies have been class societies, and the engine of change in history has been class struggle. Private property spurs the development of classes. Although societies change and the specific names given to the various classes may change, the presence of dominant and subordinate classes remains. The particular form that relations take between the classes depends on the historical epoch and the existing economic mode of production. The mode of production refers to the particular type of economic system in operation, such as feudalism, capitalism, and so on. Within every mode of production are (1) means of production and (2) social relations of production. The *means of production* refers to the tools, machines, and other resources used in production, whereas the *social relations of production* refers to

the property and power relationships among individuals in the economic system. Marx contended that up to his time there had been four major "epochs in the economic transformation of society" (ibid., p. 504). These were the Asiatic, ancient, feudal, and capitalist modes of production. Our primary focus is on the last of these.

Generally, classes are defined by their relationship to the means of production. Hence, in the capitalist mode of production, "by bourgeoisie is meant the class of modern capitalists, owners of the means of social production and employers of wage-labour. By proletariat, the class of modern wage-labourers who, having no means of production of their own, are reduced to selling labour-power in order to live" (ibid., p. 108). But when specific treatment is given, Marx's definition of class appears loose, and a variety of criteria are used differentially in different places. A full-fledged class that satisfied the criteria suggested by Marx would be one that possessed the following:

1. A distinct relationship to and role in the mode of production (in terms of ownership of means of production, employment of wage labor, and economic interests)
2. A clear consciousness of its existence as a unified class with objective interests that are hostile to those of other classes
3. An organization of the class into a political party aimed at representing and fighting for its interests
4. A distinct set of cultural values and a separate style of life (Ollman 1968).

"The owners of mere labour-power, the owners of capital, and the landowners, whose respective sources of income are wages, profit, and rent of land . . . form the three great classes of modern society based on the capitalist mode of production" (Bottomore and Rubel 1956, p. 178). Other transition classes exist, such as the petty bourgeoisie and small land-owning peasants, but these would disappear as capitalism inexorably reached its peak as a mode of production. Marx believed that in his day of the "two great hostile camps," the "two great classes" that were being polarized were the bourgeoisie and the proletariat (Marx and Engels 1969, vol. 1, p. 109). However, his use of such terms as "strata," "gradation," "middle classes," and "dominated classes" makes it clear that Marx was aware of the complexity that can characterize a concrete system of inequality. What is also apparent is that mere occupation or source of income is not the criterion used by Marx to define a class. Each class has within it a hierarchy of strata. Thus, within the proletariat, for example, individuals vary by specific occupation and income.

Because of the classes' different relationships to private property (i.e., owners vs. nonowners), conflict is inherent in class society. Class antagonism is built into the very structure of society. Marx's theory is one of class struggle. The existence of a given class always assumes the existence of another hostile class. " 'Who is the enemy?' is a question that can be asked whenever Marx uses 'class' " (Ollman 1968, p. 578). When the economic bases for classes are eliminated, they will disappear since the proletariat will be without the enemy, the capitalist.

In the process of class struggle, however, the proletariat develops from an incoherent mass (a class in itself) into a more organized and unified political force (a class for itself). The conditions that bring about this change are discussed in detail later.

Maintenance of Class Structure

The system of inequality—class positions, the given relations of production, and the profits of capitalists—is maintained and protected by a variety of mechanisms. The state, of course, is the ultimate arbitrator and represents "the form in which the individuals of a ruling class assert their common interests" (Bottomore and Rubel 1956, p. 223). "The executive of the modern State is but a committee for managing the common affairs of the whole bourgeoisie" (Marx and Engels 1969, vol. 1, pp. 110–111). The state has used its force and legislation to maintain capitalist-class relations (Marx 1967, pp. 734–741). Struggles that do occur within the state are always class struggles.

A second mechanism used to maintain class relations is ideology, and the dominant ideology supports and legitimizes the position of the capitalist. "The ideas of the ruling class are in every epoch the ruling ideas: i.e., the class which is the ruling *material* force of society is at the same time its ruling *intellectual* force." Just as the ruling class has control over "material production," so too does it control "mental production," and the form these ideas take is clear: "The ruling ideas are nothing more than the ideal expression of the dominant material relationships" (Marx and Engels 1969, vol. 1, p. 47). Of course, the ideas generated have been mentally separated in their association with the dominant class and hence can appear as eternal laws (such as the "free market") or rules generated by all of the society. Members of the ruling class have themselves believed that. The ideas that support class relations are frequently promoted by bourgeois intellectuals who are often nothing more than "hired prize-fighters" for capitalism (Marx 1967, p. 15). Religion as an ideological institution similarly helps maintain the class system by preventing labor from seeing its real situation.

A third factor serving to bolster the set of economic relations is much less obvious than the two just mentioned. The capitalist structure itself strengthens its seeming inevitability by creating a working class that because of custom and training comes to view "the conditions of that mode of production as self-evident laws of Nature" (ibid., p. 737). The condition of workers freely hiring themselves out to capitalists who freely employ them to work in factories run for maximum efficiency makes capitalism appear as an entirely natural process and creates a dependency of workers on it that makes it difficult for them to resist or rebel. As Miliband wrote, "The capitalist mode of production . . . veils and mystifies the exploitative nature of its 'relations of production' by making them appear as a matter of free, unfettered, and equal exchange" (1977, p. 45).

Development of Capitalism

The meaning and utility of Marx's central concepts bearing on inequality are embedded in his analysis of historical changes in the mode of production. To fully understand Marx's concept of class, one cannot legitimately remove it from his theory of capitalism but must view it in the context of capitalist development.

Several factors aid in bringing about early forms of capitalism. One of these is the accumulation of capital by some individuals. Increased trade and the opening up of the New World fueled the accumulation of capital. When feudal serf groups were broken up in the fifteenth and sixteenth centuries, "great masses of men [were] suddenly and forcibly torn from their means of subsistence, and hurled as free and 'unattached' proletarians on the labour market" (Marx 1967, p. 716). The direct motivations behind these expropriations of land were most often economic and political in nature. Larger tracts of land then became owned by fewer individuals. By the end of the sixteenth century, England had a group of rich capitalist farmers (ibid., p. 744). The forcible expropriation of all this land through various means "made the soil part and parcel of capital, and created for the town industries the necessary supply of a 'free' and outlawed proletariat" (ibid., p. 733).

The newly developing capitalism required a stable labor force, but it could not possibly absorb all those thrown off the land. Many became "beggars, robbers, vagabonds." Laws were then passed against such individuals and against laborers who tried to organize. Capitalists found it necessary to use legislation to mold these workers into a compliant but disciplined labor force (ibid., pp. 737–742).

Moreover, the means of production they brought with them, which had been scattered in individual homes (spindles, looms, etc.), could then be brought together under one capitalist's roof. And the raw materials freed up by the expropriation of this population provided a fuller basis for the production of goods by capitalists. The need of these individuals to work as employees who manufactured goods owned by capitalists rather than by themselves meant that, as a group, they became a mass market to which such goods could be sold. The products that the worker would have developed at home as a means of subsistence became commodities of the capitalist. In sum, freed labor power, raw materials, means of production, and a new market became available to capitalism as a result of the removal of part of the agricultural population from the land.

Capitalists then did all they could, including resorting to force, to speed up the fuller development of capitalism in "hothouse fashion." "Force is the midwife of every old society pregnant with a new one" (ibid., p. 751). The increasing prominence of the colonial system in the seventeenth and eighteenth centuries aided capitalist development by providing slave labor power, raw materials, and markets. Systems of trade protection and taxes further strengthened capitalism, as did the increasing use of children and women in the factories. Capital and its accumulation, then, were not attained by owners through careful saving and hard work, according to Marx, but rather came into the world "dripping from head to foot, from every pore, with blood and dirt" (ibid., p. 760).

As capitalism develops, in Marx's view, larger capitalists swallow up the smaller ones; centralization occurs and with it the increasing inclusion of a broader and broader circle of peoples in the world market. Capitalism takes on an international character. The problem of creating a secure, collective labor force in the new colonies, where land is available and where potential laborers might otherwise labor for themselves through their acquisition of such land, is dealt with by placing artificially high prices on the land, which then means that the laborer has to work longer to earn the wages needed to buy the land. The money saved from the sale of land can then be used to bring more laborers to the colonies to keep the labor supply full (ibid., pp. 771–772).

As centralization of capitalism grows, so does the misery and manipulation of the working class. But this misery is not without consequence, because the capitalist system of production serves as a crucible that perfects the discipline and unification of the expanding working class. Eventually, the control of capital by the few hinders the production system and speeds the dissolution of capitalism. "Centralization of the means of production and socialization of labour at last reach a point where they become incompatible with their capitalist integument. This integument is burst asunder. The expropriators are expropriated" (ibid., p. 763). Individual private property had been taken by the capitalists; now capitalistic property is expropriated by the masses. It becomes socialized property.

Stages of Capitalism.   According to Marx, capitalism as a mode of production has gone through three principal stages: (1) cooperation, (2) manufacture, and (3) modern (machine) industry.

Cooperation.   Capitalism begins when a large number of laborers are employed in one place working together to produce a given product. "A greater number of laborers, working together, at the same time, in one place . . . in order to produce the same sort of commodity under the mastership of one capitalist, constitutes, both historically and logically, the starting point of capitalist production" (ibid., p. 322). It is when workers are thus brought together that "the collective power of the masses" for the individual capitalist can be realized. Workers become more productive

and efficient under these conditions, resulting in greater profit for the capitalist. This and each successive change in the mode of production are motivated by the desire to increase the surplus value of labor power and, therefore, the level of profit.

Manufacture.   "While simple cooperation leaves the mode of working by the individual for the most part unchanged, manufacture . . . converts the laborer into a crippled monstrosity, by forcing his detail dexterity at the expense of a world of productive capabilities and instincts" (ibid., p. 360). The period of manufacture begins in the sixteenth century and extends to the last part of the eighteenth century. Its characteristic is a strict and detailed division of labor among workers who have been brought together to cooperate in the production of the capitalists' products. Everyone has a specific function to perform; no one carries out all the tasks. Thus, with this change there no longer exists a group of independent artisans cooperating, but rather a group of individuals performing minute tasks dependent on each other. "Its final form is invariably the same—a productive mechanism whose parts are human beings" (ibid., p. 338).

Weber's later description of work under rationalized capitalism is strikingly similar, as we shall see. In manufacture, each person performs the same task over and over again until the job becomes routine and the laborer becomes a mere mechanism, but efficiency and perfection in production become reality. Skills that had been learned in apprenticeship become less necessary, and manufacture creates a set of unskilled laborers. The collective laborer, when organized in this fashion, increases production, and as a result, increases the surplus value of his labor power to the capitalist. The profit for the capitalist goes up, and conditions for him could not be better. Larger manufacturing factories develop different departments that produce different products, with each having its own division of labor. To further speed production and the growth of profits, some workshops produce the new tools of labor—machines.

For the laborers, however, conditions worsen. Under the capitalist mode, their labor is no longer their own, because to increase capital, each worker must be "made poor in productive powers" (ibid., p. 361). They become unfit to produce independently, and their labor power becomes productive only within the factory. They need the factory. Working on minute operations rather than whole products, they become "a never failing instrument," "a mere fragment of his own body . . . a mere appendage" (ibid., pp. 349, 360). And the constant regularity and monotony of the task "disturbs the intensity and flow of a man's animal spirits, which find recreation and delight in mere change of activity" (ibid., p. 341).

In essence, the workers become alienated from their own labor. The work being done (1) is not an end in itself but a *means* to an end, (2) is not voluntary but *forced*, (3) is not part of human nature (i.e., it is *external*), (4) is not work for the workers but for *someone else*, and (5) is *not spontaneous*. The object of their labor does not belong to the workers even though they have put a part of themselves into it. Rather, the product "becomes an object, takes on its own existence . . . exists outside him, independently, and alien to him, and . . . stands opposed to him as an autonomous power" (Bottomore and Rubel 1956, p. 170). As appendages, workers become alienated from themselves, each other, and nature.

Under manufacturing, therefore, capitalists prosper as workers' conditions deteriorate, and the real nature of capitalism as a mode of production becomes clear. Capitalists prosper because laborers suffer. The two classes are not merely different levels but are inextricably interlinked in the capitalist mode. People and their labor power become commodities, things of use value to the capitalist, who owns and controls the instruments of production, the raw materials—everything. The laborers, in turn, have nothing but their own labor power to sell, and even that becomes twisted into a form suitable for maximum production.

Modern (Machine) Industry.   Like other forms of capitalist production, the development and use of machines are aimed at reducing the cost of commodity production for the capitalist by reducing the part of the day when the worker is working for himself or herself, and increasing that part when he or she is working for the capitalist. That is, it is a way of increasing surplus value for labor. "The machine . . . supersedes the workman" (Marx 1967, p. 376). In modern industry, machines are organized into a division of labor similar to that which existed among laborers during the manufacture period. Since machines replace labor power, physical strength becomes less important, and capitalists seek to hire children and women. The result is a decrease in the value of the man's labor power, and a concomitant increase in the general exploitation of the family overall. When the value of the workman's labor power vanishes, laborers flood the market and reduce the price of labor power. Supply then outweighs demand for labor. In effect, machines are a means of controlling the collective laborer. "It is the most powerful weapon for repressing strikes, those periodic revolts of the working class against the autocracy of capital" (ibid., pp. 435–436).

With the advance of machines, production becomes more and more centralized, forcing many small bourgeoisie who cannot compete or find little use for their skills into the proletariat (Bottomore and Rubel 1956, p. 188).

Crises in Capitalism and Class Struggle. The increased competition for profit among capitalists generates crises at both the top and the bottom of the class structure, ultimately leading to the polarization of large capitalists and the massive class of the proletariat. The initial result of the introduction of machinery is to increase profit, but problems arise.

Employees are thrown out of work, or work for low wages because they are not in demand. The proletariat increases in number and becomes more concentrated, and life conditions among members become equalized at a level of bare subsistence.

Competition among capitalists produces commercial crises, an "epidemic of overproduction" which in turn leads to increased concentration of capital, since many go bankrupt (Marx and Engels 1969, vol. 1, p. 114). Overproduction serves as an indication that the forces of production have become too strong for the property relations by which they are controlled ("fettered"). The capitalist responds by destroying productive forces and by trying to find new markets, but these solutions are, at best, stopgap measures and crises recur, each more serious than the previous. "Modern bourgeois society . . . is like the sorcerer, who is no longer able to control the powers of the nether world whom he has called up by his spells" (ibid., p. 113). The means of production that the bourgeoisie originally brought into existence to benefit their own position and that permitted them to supplant feudalism now become the means that destroy them.

Bourgeois society becomes the stage for the impending class struggle between the capitalist and the collective laborer, between the bourgeoisie and the proletariat. As capitalism improved from simple cooperation through modern industry, the bourgeoisie became more powerful and entrenched, their ideology and ideas became dominant, and the organization of the state more evidently reflected their power. But so, too, did the proletariat develop as a class with the progress of capitalism. Initially, struggle against the bourgeoisie takes the form of individual protests, then protests by larger groups—not against the relations of production, but against the forces of production: workers smash tools, machines, and so forth in order to maintain their status as workers. At this point, they are still just a mass rather than an organized whole. But as conditions for them worsen—that is, as they become increasingly massed together on an equal basis in a minute division of labor under conditions of extreme alienation and emiseration—and as their livelihood becomes more uncertain, their actions become more those of a united class and less those characteristic of individuals competing among themselves. The conditions under which the proletariat labor forge it into a class.

During the struggle that has its roots in the domination of the means of production and appropriation of its products (i.e., in a peculiar set of property relations), the proletariat becomes honed as a class, and the struggle takes on a greater political character. Ironically, the bourgeoisie has created the conditions that develop the class that revolts against it. As the decisive hour approaches, and the class and crisis nature of the society becomes increasingly evident, those in the bourgeoisie who see what is happening on the historical level also join the working class (Bottomore and Rubel 1956, pp. 184–188).

Marx argued that a given social order is not replaced until all the forces of production that can be produced under it have been developed, and new relations of production (i.e., new social orders) do not appear until the material basis for their existence has been formed in the old society. This is essentially what happens, according to Marx, when revolution occurs. Revolutions do not take place until the material conditions for their appearance are present. The mode of production shapes all other aspects of social life, and "at a certain stage of their development, the material productive forces of society come in conflict with existing relations of production. . . . From forms of development of the productive forces these relations turn into their fetters" (Marx and Engels 1969, vol. 1, pp. 503–504).

With proletarian revolution, the bases for the class system are removed and the proletariat is emancipated. In the interim, between the capitalist and classless society, a "dictatorship of the proletariat" exists, paving the way for a communistic society and the beginning of truly human rather than class history. Figure 8.1 summarizes some of the key elements of Marx's model that we have been discussing on the last several pages.

Some Comments on Marx

There are few areas in social science that have not had to confront the work of Marx. The sheer number of analyses and critiques of

Marx's theory of class struggle and capitalism is voluminous (e.g., Dahrendorf 1959; Mills 1962; Bottomore 1966; Giddens 1973; Miliband 1977). Consequently, only a few of the recurrent comments and criticisms about that theory are presented here.

Marx's theory has had a significant impact not only on the contemporary analysis of class structures but on the orientation taken in the study of society in general. Marx's approach allows us to see at once the simultaneous

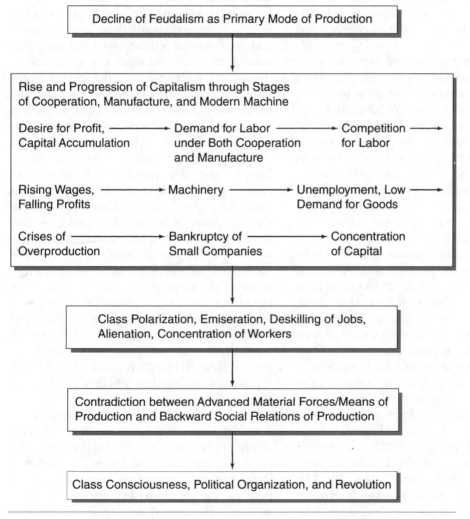

FIGURE 8.1   Core Elements in Marx's Theory of Class Struggle within Capitalism

existence of organization and conflict and their historical roots. In this sense, Marx's theory is a comprehensive one, in many ways unparalleled in social science. Individual actions and emotions, such as alienation, organizations, and class structure, are analyzed against the backdrop of societal settings and historical change. Marx was aware of their mutual interaction, and should not be considered as a simple economic determinist. His impact radiated beyond social science to philosophy and the study of morals and to the political arena. That his work continues to generate not only discussions but explanations and analyses built on his own is a tribute to the continued cogency and relevance of his theory.

Still, his conception of class is often vague and inconsistent, though the main thrust of his criteria—relationship to means of production, employment of labor, and class consciousness—is clear. His description of the classless society and the problems associated with the dictatorship of the proletariat as an interim period are not clear and precise. The state and bureaucracy in what are called communist societies have certainly not withered away. On the other hand, it is doubtful that Marx, who believed in uniting theory, practice, and human needs to help bring about a more humane society, would have considered these societies to be the kind he had in mind. Nevertheless, that these societies have turned out as they have suggested a basic flaw in Marx's view of how and why societies become structured as they do. Some have traced this fault to Marx's perspective on human nature which, they argue, is overly optimistic and does not consider the selfishness of people. "The most monumental error in Marx's thought" wrote Lopreato and Hazelrigg (1972), "is his failure to accept the fact . . . that man is by nature a fallible and 'sinful' animal" (pp. 40–41). Moreover, Marx appears to have "seriously underrated" the ability of individuals to adjust to inequality (Duke 1976, p. 34).

It certainly seems true that Marx also underestimated the strength of nationalism as a force inhibiting the international union of classes, and the "right to self determination" is something on which many early Marxists could not disagree. Miliband observed that "'nationalism' has proved a much more enduring and therefore a much more difficult problem to confront than early Marxists thought likely" (1977, p. 105).

Another criticism that has some validity is that the extent of pauperization and polarization of classes that Marx expected has not, as yet, come about. How much one makes of this comment depends heavily on the time frame one selects, because certainly there are indications that the extent of relative economic inequality has not declined and that corporate concentration has increased over the last 75 years. Capitalism has proved exceptionally resourceful in maintaining itself and forestalling widespread revolution. Being able to internationalize has provided capitalism with a mechanism for obtaining wider and wider markets and, therefore, has put off a crisis caused by its internal contradictions. The capitalist state, in being reformist and offering welfare programs, has alleviated some of its immediate problems. But, according to Marxists, reformism serves only to disguise the real class character of the state, and concrete reforms support the long-run maintenance of the existing economic order and are meant to solve only immediate problems rather than fundamental underlying ones (cf. Piven and Cloward 1971). Moreover, Miliband contended, "capitalism, however many and varied the reforms it can assimilate, is unable to do without exploitation, oppression, and dehumanization" (1977, p. 39).

Marx thought that the members of the working class would be the "gravediggers of capitalism," but, to use Giddens's colorful phrasing, "the grave remains undug, a century later; and its prospective incumbent, if no longer in the first flush of youth, does not seem seriously threatened by imminent demise" (Giddens 1982, p. 63). But the fact that the working class has not revolted is not conclusive proof of the inadequacy of Marx's theory or that capitalism is not a class society. This is because an effective class society, as Marx argued, can have a number of economic, political, and ideological characteristics that encourage false consciousness and minimize the chances for revolt by workers. Sooner or later (and he believed sooner), however, Marx thought, workers would become aware of their situation and act accordingly.

Although Marx's main predictions have not turned out exactly as he thought, many of the phenomena that he foresaw do exist to a degree. As we have seen in an earlier chapter, there has been a consistent trend toward more concentration of corporate power. There is also quite a bit of wealth inequality and there are business fluctuations, ups and downs, that capitalism follows. Moreover, every capitalist society has "class-based, working-class politics" to a certain degree (Collins 1988).

A final criticism is that Marx defined the concept of property too narrowly and misread its role (Dahrendorf 1959). To Dahrendorf, authority is a broader concept than property, and it is really authority that is the basis of class position. "Dahrendorf would have us believe that Marx, *of all people*, did not understand that property relations refer most fundamentally to power and domination with respect to the production of resources" (Hazelrigg 1972, p. 480). Dahrendorf's criticism on this count is weak; it is hard and erroneous to imagine that Marx was not aware of the importance of control of property as well as sheer ownership or of their separation. In *Capital*, discussing the organization of capitalism, he wrote: "The joint-stock companies in general . . . have a tendency to separate the function of management more and more from the ownership of capital, whether it be self owned or borrowed" (Bottomore and Rubel 1956, p. 153).

Despite the criticisms that have been leveled against Marx's theory of class and class struggle, some of which are ill-founded, the theory has much to offer as an approach to the analysis of class structure. Moreover, to use Marx's propositions in his general theory of capitalism as predictions about concrete capitalist societies without reference to a specific historical society is a mistake. The exact operation of a society depends on a variety of factors other than the abstract characteristics of capitalism (Giddens 1973, p. 37). Reissman's advice still holds: "Marx should be read today with understanding rather than with misplaced pedantic precision" (Reissman 1959, p. 44).

MAX WEBER (1864–1920)

Many of those who immediately followed Marx in time, and especially the major social theorists of the period, were engaged in a "debate with Marx's ghost" (Zeitlin 1968). Among those most evidently aware of Marx's work and some of its shortcomings was Max Weber.

Weber is often considered to be the greatest sociologist whoever lived. His "shadow falls long over the intellectual life of our era," wrote Mitzman (1971, p. 3). Much of what he contributed to social science still remains intact and even those of his ideas that have proven weak or been discarded still provide a foundation from which further analysis can begin. Indeed, it is difficult to imagine what sociology would have been like without his influence. Like Marx and other great theorists, whose specific theories fit into a coherent whole, Weber's formulations regarding inequality must be considered in the context of his broader theory of the rationalization of the modern world. We will examine what Weber had to say about inequality, how U.S. sociologists have interpreted his work in this area, and if and how he added to Marx's own analysis of class structure.

Max Weber's life was quite different from Marx's, but like Marx's, his life experiences were clearly related to propositions about society that he developed. Weber was born in Erfurt,

Germany, in 1864, 16 years after the publication of *Communist Manifesto* and three years before the publication of the first volume of *Capital.* His family was upper middle class. His father was a fun-loving conformist who disliked and feared upsetting existing political arrangements. In sharp contrast, Weber's mother was an extremely religious person of Calvinist persuasion, who often suffered the abuses of her much less moralistic husband, a fact that later became central in Max's repudiation of his father.

Despite its drawbacks for Weber, his parents' home was the site of frequent and diverse intellectual discussions featuring many of the well-known academicians of the day. So from the beginning, Max was exposed to a potpourri of ideas. Though he was a sickly child, he was very bright, becoming familiar with the writings of a variety of philosophers before setting off at the age of 18 for the University of Heidelberg, where he studied law, medieval history, economics, and philosophy. At age 19, Weber left for Strasbourg to put in his military service. It was there that he developed a lifelong and deep friendship with his uncle Hermann Baumgarten, a historian, and his wife, who was a devout Protestant and was effective in putting her religious fervor into action. Consequently, Weber developed a greater respect for those religious virtues found in his mother and less of a regard for the worldly and cowardly qualities of his father.

A year later, he returned to live with his parents and to study at the University of Berlin, where he wrote his dissertation on medieval business. Carrying on a very disciplined and rigid life, he served as a barrister in the Berlin court system and as an instructor at the university and wrote several works on agrarian history and agricultural laborers. These investigations included discussions of the social and cultural effects of commercialization and the role of ideas in economic behavior.

After getting married and serving at the age of only 30 as a full professor of economics at the University of Freiburg, Weber along with his wife, Marianne, left for Heidelberg, where he took a professorship, became more politically involved, and quickly developed a close circle of intellectual friends. During this period, Weber suffered a severe emotional breakdown and was able to do little of anything, even reading. He was only 33 years old at the time, and it was a number of years before his energy was restored. The breakdown may have been precipitated by a harsh confrontation with his father, very shortly after which the father died.

In the early 1900s, Weber's health was restored, and it was between this time and his death that Weber produced most of the works for which he is best known. He became enmeshed in German politics, volunteered for service during World War I, but later became disillusioned by it and the German government's incompetence. Weber, unlike Marx, was accepted in polite society and was not a political radical, but he was generally a liberal and participated in the writing of the Weimar Constitution. There were many occasions when he fought bigotry and close-mindedness. Weber died of pneumonia on June 14, 1920, his broad knowledge leaving an unmistakable mark on social theory (Coser 1971; Mitzman 1971).

Rationalization of the World

Much of what Weber wrote had an undeniable unified theme. His discussions of bureaucracy, the Protestant Ethic, authority, and even class, status, and party fit into his overall concern for social change and the direction in which he thought the Western world was moving. Thus, as is the case with Marx and many of the other nineteenth-century theorists, Weber's work on stratification must be understood in the context of his general perspective.

In contrast to Marx, who believed that capitalism and its accompanying denigration of the human spirit were necessary conditions that would eventually lead to a communistic, more humane society, Weber contended that alienation, impersonality, bureaucracy, and, in general, rationalization would be permanent societal features. Weber agreed with Marx that modern modes of technology have dehumanizing effects, but he contended that bureaucracy and alienation are not temporary or peculiar to a passing period, but rather are at the core of the disenchanted world. What the future promised in Weber's view was not a wonderful free society where people are reunited to themselves and nature, but rather an "iron cage," what we have to look forward to is not "summer's bloom," but rather a "polar night of icy darkness and hardness." Bureaucratization and technical rationality are not likely to decrease but to increase under socialism.

A bureaucracy is characterized by its impersonality, hierarchy of rational-legal authority, written system of rules, clear division of labor, and career system. According to Weber, it is technically more perfect than other methods of organization and is the most efficient. "Precision, speed, unambiguity, knowledge of the files, continuity, discretion, unity, strict subordination, reduction of friction and of material and personal costs—these are raised to the optimum point in the strictly bureaucratic administration" (Gerth and Mills 1962, p. 214). Bureaucracy is the perfectly rational system. Business is carried out "without regard for persons," under "calculable rules." The lack of regard for persons is a central characteristic of all purely economic transactions. Since status honor and prestige are based on who the person is, the domination of the bureaucratic organization and a free market mean "the leveling of status 'honor'" and "the universal domination of the 'class situation'" (ibid., p. 215). The leveling of status strengthens the rule of bureaucracy by weakening status as a basis for position and encouraging the equal treatment of all regardless of background.

Capitalism and bureaucracy support each other; bureaucracy hastened the destruction of feudal, patrimonial organizations and local privileges. Whereas feudalism was characterized by ties of personal loyalty and was grounded in small local communities, bureaucracy denies or destroys personal loyalty and demands loyalty to position and thereby equalizing individuals. Capitalist production requires it. Conversely, capitalism can supply the money needed to develop bureaucracy in its most rational form (Roth and Wittich 1968, p. 224). Bureaucracy and capitalism are characteristics of the contemporary modern society.

Bureaucracy and capitalism increase the prevalence of authority based on rational-legal, as opposed to charismatic or traditional, grounds. In the rational-legal form, authority is based on the acceptance of rules regarding the right to issue commands as they apply to formal position in the organization. Authority is attached to the office, not the person; it is impersonal.

Putting all of this together, we see that capitalism and the secularized Protestant Ethic, class, bureaucracy, and rational-legal authority are mutually supportive and are integral parts of the increasingly rationalized modern society that Weber saw emerging. They stand in stark contrast to feudalism, the personalism of status honor, tradition and charisma, and premodern forms of organization. An adequate understanding of Weber's perspective on class and status, their relationship, and their distinction can be obtained only if his broader theory of historical development and its associated concepts are incorporated in the analysis. Wrenching them out of this context distorts the meaning of what he had to say about inequality. Keeping Weber's broader theory in mind, we turn to discussion of his more specific ideas on inequality.

Tripartite Nature of Inequality

Weber argued that power can take a variety of forms. "Power," in general, refers to "the chance of a man or of a number of men to realize their own will in a communal action even against the resistance of others who are participating in the action" (Gerth and Mills 1962, p. 180). A person's power can be shown in the *social order* through his or her status, in the *economic order* through his or her class, and in the *political order* through his or her party. Thus, class, status, and party are each aspects of the distribution of power within a community. For example, if we think about an individual's chances of realizing his or her own will against someone else, it is reasonable to believe that the person's social prestige, class position, and membership in a political group will have an effect on these chances.

Social order refers to the arrangement of social honor (prestige) within a society. Different status groups (e.g., professors, construction workers) occupy different places along the prestige continuum. *Economic order,* in turn, refers to the general distribution of economic goods and services (e.g., owners and nonowners)—that is, to the arrangement of classes within a society. Finally, *political order* relates to the distribution of power among groups (parties) to influence communal decisions. Weber's general scheme for inequality is presented graphically in Figure 8.2.

Although these are presented as three distinct and separate orders, it is a mistake to see them strictly as such. All of them are manifestations of the distribution of power and can

and usually do influence each other, often in a quite predictable manner. The inclusion of the social and political dimensions is ordinarily seen as a "rounding out" of the economic determinism of Marx (ibid., p. 47). But, as already pointed out, Marx was not a simple economic determinist; he viewed causal relationships in a more complex fashion. Moreover, Weber's own writing suggested that he did not view the three dimensions as being equal in salience in capitalist society. Parkin (1971) persuasively argued that neo-Weberians have stressed the independence of these dimensions of stratification and thereby ignored, where Weber did not, the systematic relationship between the dimensions of inequality. Weber did not fully develop his political dimension, and the economic factor, as we shall see, outweighs the status element in the capitalist system of inequality. But at this point, it is necessary to examine each of Weber's three dimensions in greater detail.

Class.   More so than Marx, Weber deliberately set out a number of formal definitions for his concepts (Roth and Wittich 1968). But Weber acknowledged his debt to Marx: "Whoever does not admit that he could not perform the most important parts of his own work without the work that those two [Marx and Nietzsche] have done swindles himself and others" (Mitzman 1971, p. 182). Weber's own conception of class parallels Marx's in

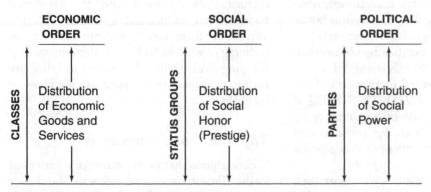

FIGURE 8.2   Weber's View of the General Distribution of Power

several ways. Class, at its core, is an economic concept; it is the position of individuals in the market that determines their class position. And it is how one is situated in the marketplace that directly affects one's life chances, "a common condition for the individual's fate" (Miller 1963, pp. 44–45). Just as Marx indicated that capital begins when capitalist and laborer meet freely in the market, when the laborer is free to sell his or her labor and form a relationship with the capitalist, Weber pointed out that persons are members of a class only if they have "the chance of using goods or services *for themselves* on the market" (ibid., p. 45, emphasis added). Consequently, slaves are not members of classes.

Weber distinguished three types of classes: property classes, commercial (acquisition) classes, and social classes. Individuals belong to the same class if they are in the same "class situation," which refers to the probability of individuals obtaining goods, position, and satisfactions in life, "a probability which derives from the relative control over goods and skills and from their income-producing uses within a given economic order" (Roth and Wittich 1968, p. 302).

Property classes are "primarily determined by property differences." There are those who monopolize costly foods and status privileges, such as education, and those who control the bulk of wealth, capital, and sales in the society. Such classes usually are composed of "rentiers," who get income from a number of sources, including people, land, factories, and bank securities. Those who are not privileged are those who are unfree or are paupers. Weber stressed the distinction between the top and the bottom classes but did mention that in each set of classes there are "middle classes" (ibid., pp. 302–303).

Weber is not clear, but he does not appear to make a complete separation between property and commercial classes. Rather, he has a broad conception of property in terms of ownership, and it is " 'property' and 'lack of property' " that

are "the basic categories of *all* class situations" (Miller 1963, p. 44, emphasis added). These general categories in turn can be broken down "according to the kind of property that is *usable for returns*; and, on the other hand, according to the kind of *services* that can be offered in the market" (ibid., p. 44, emphasis added). In a manner of speaking, one can own and dispose of property as well as skills and services.

Commercial-class position is determined by "the marketability of goods and services," in other words, by the opportunity to exploit the market (Roth and Wittich 1968, p. 302). Commercial classes, then, are determined by the skills and occupational characteristics members bring into the market. Hence, those who are privileged in this regard may monopolize management and exercise influence over government political policies that affect their interests. Merchants, industrial and agricultural employers, bankers, ship owners, professionals, and workers who have cornered certain skills are examples of the entrepreneurs who are members of privileged commercial classes. In contrast, those who are unprivileged are usually laborers (skilled, semiskilled, and unskilled) (ibid., p. 304). Again, there are middle classes, but these are treated more as residual categories when compared with the other classes.

Social classes make up all class situations "within which individual and generational mobility is easy and typical" (ibid., p. 302). That is, a social-class structure is one in which there is fluidity and movement of individuals between class situations. Upward mobility is most likely, however, between adjacent classes. Examples of such social classes are the "working class as a whole," "the petty bourgeoisie," "the propertyless intelligentsia and specialists," and "the class privileged through property and education" (ibid., p. 305).

Class Consciousness and Class Struggle.   According to Weber, classes of whatever kind need not be class conscious as Marx conceived them; they are not necessarily unified "communities."

Class organization can occur in any one of these three types of classes, but class consciousness and class (communal) action are likely only under certain conditions. Weber argued that just because there are different property classes, for example, it does not mean that they will necessarily engage in class struggle, although they may when circumstances are right. And when struggles do occur, they may not be over a basic change in the entire economy but may be more superficially over the distribution of wealth.

Class-conscious action is most likely if, first, "the connections between the causes and consequences of the 'class situation'" are transparent, or clear. If individuals can plainly see that there is a connection between the structure of the economic system and what happens to them in terms of life chances, class action is more likely. Weber believed this had happened among the proletariat. A second condition for class unification exists if there is an immediate opponent on whom the class can focus. Hence, workers will react against their immediate employers rather than those who are most distantly and perhaps even more profitably involved (such as stockholders). Third, class organization is also more likely if large numbers of individuals are in the same class position. The increasing growth of the proletariat would increase the chances of class action by them. Fourth, if all of the individuals are in one place and therefore are easier to organize, class unity is more probable. Finally, if the goals they have are directed and interpreted by a group of intelligentsia who are actually outside their class, class organization is more likely (Henderson and Parsons 1947, pp. 427–428; Miller 1963, p. 46; Roth and Wittich 1968, p. 304). These are not inconsistent with the conditions that Marx thought would forge a mass of individuals in the same class situation into a "class for itself." However, Weber cautions us about the belief that fully developed classes are never wrong—that is, "falsely conscious"—about their own interests. They can be.

Class struggles have changed in content throughout history, according to Weber. The focus of conflict has altered from struggles over debt and credit in antiquity, to struggles over the availability of consumer goods and their prices in the market during the Middle Ages, to struggles over the price of labor in the modern world. Historically, class struggles begin when a credit market exists in which debtors pay high and often increasing rates of interest to the wealthy, who monopolize the credits (Miller 1963, pp. 45, 48). But in each case, by definition, the struggle is of an economic character.

Status.   Standing in theoretical opposition to the market principle of class, which "knows no personal distinctions" and "knows nothing of 'honor,'" is the principle of status. Traditionally, status groups are ranked in terms of the "*consumption* of goods as represented by special 'styles of life,'" whereas classes are determined by their relations to the production system and acquisition of goods (ibid., p. 56, emphasis in original).

In addition, then, to being ranked in terms of market situation, individuals can be ranked on the basis of honor or prestige. A person's "status situation" consists of all aspects of his or her "life fate" determined by a "social estimation of honor" (ibid., pp. 49, 54). Status groups are based on a particular style of life, formal education, and/or inherited or occupational prestige. Certain groups may lay claim to (or, in other words, may usurp) a certain level of honor because of their hereditary background or family tree (such as "First Families of Virginia"), because of their peculiar lifestyle (such as liberal arts professors, perhaps), or because of their power. The existence of status groups most often shows itself in the form of (1) endogamy or a restricted pattern of social intercourse, (2) sharing of food and other benefits within groups, (3) status conventions or traditions, and (4) monopolistic acquisition of certain economic opportunities or the avoidance of certain kinds of acquisitions. Thus, because of their formal education and occupational prestige, liberal arts professors might tend to socialize only among themselves and might have certain unwritten rules about how a member of the group should act or what kinds of goods and services are suitable for use in the status group and what kinds are not. The conventions associated with the status group control the kind of lifestyle allowable (Roth and Wittich 1968, pp. 305–306). It is clear that some of the bases of class and status may concern the same factor, such as occupation. However, their characteristics mean that status groups are usually cohesive communities. They tend toward closure—that is, restriction of their memberships (Grabb 1984; Collins 1988).

The stability of status groups is linked to political and economic conditions in a society and is one way in which the latter two aspects of inequality are related to the social dimension. The likelihood of a conventionally recognized status group developing into a *"legal privilege*, positive or negative, is easily traveled as soon as a certain stratification of the *social order* has in fact been 'lived in' and has achieved stability *by virtue* of a stable distribution of *economic power"* (Miller 1963, p. 51, emphasis added). Weber is saying that status groups can be legalized and, therefore, become bases for political power differences when they have been around for some time and are buttressed by parallel differences in the distribution of economic resources. A belief in the long-run consistency between economic and social power is clear in his writing.

Where such stability exists, *caste groups* develop. Castes become supported by ritual (e.g., of purity), convention, and law. Separate castes may even develop their own religious beliefs. Usually, the status structure approaches this extreme form only when the fundamental differences between the groups are considered ethnic in nature (e.g., Jews). Caste is more than just simple ethnic segregation. The latter still permits each group in question to consider its own values (honor) to be high, but a caste

system arranges these groups hierarchically, allotting one more honor than the rest. Any sense of dignity a lower-caste group might have would derive from its belief in a *future* beyond present conditions in which it would have an elevated status. In contrast, the privileged caste groups can and do derive their own sense of dignity from their *present and/or past* situation (ibid., pp. 51–52, emphasis added).

Weber stressed that class, status, and political power can be reciprocally related, with each affecting the others. Status can influence and even determine class (Roth and Wittich 1968, p. 306). However, his writing emphasized the effect of class on status in capitalist society. "Property as such is not always recognized as a status qualification, but in the long run it is, and with extraordinary regularity" (Miller 1963, p. 49). Frequently, the richest person has the greatest prestige, and those in similar economic situations normally socialize with each other rather than with persons from different classes. Equality of status among individuals in unequal classes can "in the long run become quite precarious" (ibid.). Weber observed that although race, political power, and class have all been bases for status in the past, "today the class situation is by far the predominant factor, for of course the possibility of a style of life expected for members of a status group is usually conditioned economically" (ibid., p. 53).

Despite the controlling importance of the class factor, Weber emphasized that status and class are not necessarily connected. Individuals who are low in class position can be high in prestige and vice versa. Analytically, status is opposed "to a distinction of power which is regulated exclusively through the market" (ibid., p. 54). If individuals who were high in class automatically received high status, "the status order would be threatened at its very root" (ibid., p. 55). Groups who base their high status on their lifestyle rather than crass property are likely to feel threatened when the basis for honor shifts to the economic order.

Weber said very little about the conditions under which stratification by class or status predominate. In fact, his whole definitional classification of class and status is too brief. Parkin (1971, Chapter 1) argued that there was greater justification for seeing class and status as distinct and separate orders in the Middle Ages than is the case today, when status seems increasingly to be based on occupational and economic considerations. Weber maintained that "when the bases of the acquisition and distribution of goods are relatively stable, stratification by status is favored" (Miller 1963, p. 56). If a status order is entrenched by virtue of a monopolization of certain goods by particular groups, then the free-market principle is hindered; it cannot operate. Under these conditions, "the power of naked property per se, which gives its stamp to 'class formation,' is pushed into the background." But "every technological repercussion and economic transformation threatens stratification by status and pushes class situation into the foreground" (ibid., pp. 55–56). In contrast to commercial-class societies, which ordinarily operate in market-oriented economies, status societies are economically organized around religious, feudal, and patrimonial factors (Roth and Wittich 1968, p. 306). In capitalist societies, classes play a more important role than status (Giddens 1973).

Parties.   Political power generally is considered to be a third dimension of inequality included by Weber, though some interpret Weber to be saying that class, status, and party are each different forces around which the distribution of power can be organized (ibid.). Although Weber's entire specific treatment of class and status is brief, vague, and sometimes even ambiguous and confusing, his treatment of parties is even briefer.

Parties are associations that aim at securing "power within an organization [or the state] for its leaders in order to attain ideal or material advantages for its active members" (Roth and Wittich 1968, p. 284). Thus, Weber is not referring narrowly to what we think of as political parties (such as the Democrats) but to political groups more broadly conceived. Instead of parties being an outgrowth of class struggle, they can represent status groups, classes, or merely their own members and may use a variety of means to attain power. Since parties aim at such goals as getting their programs developed or accepted and getting positions of influence within organizations, it is clear that they operate only within a rational order within which these goals are possible to attain and only when there is a struggle for power. Parties themselves, however, can be organized around a charismatic or traditional leader as well as being structured in a rational way with formal positions to which members are elected. Formally recognized political parties are not the only kind that exist; parties also can be organized around religious issues or those that concern the traditional rights of a leader in an organization (ibid., pp. 285–286).

Marx and Weber

Weber's theory of stratification has traditionally been hailed in U.S. sociology as a major improvement over the supposed narrowness of Marxian theory. Why is this so? To some extent, it reflects the nature of U.S. sociology and the interpretation of Weber by U.S. sociologists. The vagueness in parts of Weber's treatment has encouraged multiple interpretations of what he said on the subject of inequality and the unintentional shaping of what he said to fit the peculiar characteristics of one version of sociology. The U.S. sociology has tended to focus on the individual and has, until very recently, tended to ignore the role of the market in generating and perpetuating inequality. Weber's incorporation of noneconomic (status, party) and more general economic elements (such as market situation) is more appealing to a sociology rooted in a society that has been anti-radical and staunch in the belief that individuals can distinguish themselves in a variety of ways other than economic.

Despite superficial measures such as income and occupational status, until recently U.S. sociologists have generally neglected the development of measures of Marx's concept of class and an adequate measure of Weber's market situation. Part of the reason for this appears to lie in the fact that many sociologists have an ideological dislike of purely economic and especially Marxian theory, and that Weber's multidimensional theory offers a more complete portrait of social inequality than does Marx's.

It is very easy to exaggerate the differences between these two men. Lopreato and Hazelrigg (1972, p. 90), in fact, argued that Weber added little to what was at least already implicit in Marx's theory. For example, certainly the assignment of prestige (honor) to given positions can be viewed as one way in which the dominant ideology maintains the class system.

There are two basic similarities between Marx and Weber. First, both argued that capitalist society is a class society. Capitalism is characterized by laborers and capitalists meeting freely in the market; it creates a large pool of dehumanized workers of all types and it broadens the market. Second, even though Weber talked about status and party as well as class, he argued that in a rationalized market society, such as capitalism, class becomes predominant, and there is a "leveling of status honor." This distinct separation of status honor from the market principle and property is most characteristic of traditional or premodern societies (Parkin 1971, p. 38). Thus, on the importance of class in capitalist society, Marx and Weber appear to agree.

In light of these core similarities, a good argument can be made that many U.S. sociologists have accepted Weber because they have trivialized his ideas by latching onto the multidimensional aspect of his theory and minimizing the systematic nature of the relationship between those dimensions. Their interpretation of Weber is that class, status, and party are separate and independent dimensions along which each individual can be ranked. By abstracting these concepts while ignoring their systematic interrelationship and the historical context in which they are embedded, Weber's theory becomes seriously distorted.

Of course, there are some basic differences between Marx and Weber. As mentioned earlier, Marx had a more optimistic view of the long-term future than Weber, who believed society would become increasingly rationalized and bureaucratized even under socialism, because bureaucracy once established was virtually "escape proof" (Grabb 1984). Socialism would only intensify the bureaucratic characteristics of the state. Thus, future society would not see the removal of alienation and impersonality but rather their enhancement. A second major difference between the theorists is that because Weber was concerned with status and party and defined class generally in terms of market situation, the system of inequality contained within it many more groups than are suggested by a class society in which only a few groups dominate. Market situation, for example, if defined broadly enough and in detail, could ultimately mean that each individual is in a distinct class position, meaning that there are as many classes as there are persons. Perhaps the greatest weakness in Weber's discussion is the brevity and ambiguity in his treatment of class, status, and party.

EMILE DURKHEIM (1858–1917)

In contrast to the theorists we have discussed, Emile Durkheim was not principally concerned with social equality. Rather, his emphases were establishing sociology as a scientific discipline, uncovering the sources and forms of integration and moral authority, and tracking and understanding the place of individualism in modern industrial society (Giddens 1978). Most of his works revolve around issues of integration and cohesiveness—that is, the question of order in society. Although liberal and reformist in outlook, Durkheim was a central founder of the functionalist school of thought in sociology, which views society as a social system tending toward equilibrium. The organic analogy of society is clear in his writing. Despite his preoccupations with questions of order and the evolutionary growth of societies, however, Durkheim had something to say about social inequality, and it is for that reason that this brief discussion is included here.

Emile Durkheim was born in 1858 in Alsace-Lorraine into a Jewish family, which expected him to become a rabbi. Later, as a young man, he turned away from religion and became an agnostic, even though his study of the "elementary forms of religious life" is one of his major works. Durkheim was a terrific student in his early youth, but was not entirely happy with the lack of scientific and moral emphases at the normal school he attended (Coser 1971). Later, he was to become a highly successful teacher at the high school and university levels.

Durkheim wanted to study a subject that would directly address issues of moral and practical guidance for society, and he wanted to use a scientific approach in the analysis of issues. He turned to sociology as the discipline of choice and, to the disdain of many colleagues, became an imperialistic advocate of sociology rather than the other social sciences (Giddens 1978). It is not surprising that topics related to order, development, and the relationship between the individual and the society would run as a common thread through Durkheim's body of work because of conditions in French society at the time. The early years of the Third Republic in France, when Durkheim was a young man, were filled with instability and conflicts between the political right and left. While events calmed down briefly in the late 1800s, conditions were shaken again by the Dreyfus affair in which a Jewish officer was wrongly accused and convicted of selling sensitive information to Germans. The affair pitted right against left again. At the same time these political events were occurring, France was moving toward more industrialism and a socialist movement was developing. In sum, French society was not experiencing complete stability; it was a time of change.

Durkheim was a defender of Dreyfus and became actively involved in public affairs, including aiding in the restructuring of the university system and helping early in the World War I effort by completing articles attacking Nationalist German writing (Coser 1971). Durkheim's major sociological works did not begin to appear until the end of the nineteenth century. *The Division of Labor,* the source we will be concerned with here, was completed in 1893, followed by *The Rules of Sociological Method* in 1895 and *Suicide* in 1897. Later, in 1912, he finished *The Elementary Forms of Religious Life.* Durkheim died in 1917 at the age of 59.

Durkheim and Inequality

In *The Division of Labor,* Durkheim developed his theory of the movement of society from "mechanical" to "organic" solidarity. A society based on mechanical solidarity is homogeneous, with a simple division of labor, and based on the similarity of the individuals in it. There is a strong collective conscience that serves as a principal source of moral cohesion. The individual ego is not prominent in this kind of society. In sharp contrast, societies organized around the organic form of solidarity are characterized by differences and interdependence in their division of labor. This specialization, along with the increased individualism, can threaten the cohesiveness and stability of society. Corporate groups, according to Durkheim, are to serve as means for integrating individuals in this kind of society. They stand midway, as it were, between the state and individual.

In a fully developed organic society, characterized by individualism, equal opportunity, specialization, and interdependence, inequality is to be expected because at this point in evolution it should be based on differences in the internal abilities of individuals. A "normal" division of labor is based on these internal differences between individuals, including differences between men and women. Differences in the division of labor between men and women should persist, but other differences, including classes, based on external qualities (e.g., race, inheritance) should decline and eventually disappear. As society evolves, differential rewards should, because of equal opportunity, directly reflect *individual* differences in abilities and differences in the social value of occupations. In short, Durkheim believed that as time moved on, modern society would be characterized by social inequalities between individuals based on their inner abilities rather than external characteristics. He believed that such internal differences existed between the sexes, and thus justified social inequalities between men and women, but he also argued that class and racial inequalities would diminish. Although there is some ambiguity in his treatment, this is Durkheim's primary position (Lehmann 1995).

Until this point in evolution is reached, however, the division of labor can take on "abnormal" forms that prevent its appropriate and efficient functioning. Durkheim argued that this occurs when individuals' positions in it are forced or determined without moral regulation. Individuals must recognize the rights of others in the division of labor and their duties to society as well as to themselves. Each person must have the opportunity to occupy the position that fits his or her abilities (Grabb 1984). When these conditions are not present, abnormal forms of the division of labor develop. Two of these are the *anomic* and *forced* forms of the division of labor.

In the first type, relations between people in the workplace are not governed by a generally agreed upon set of values and beliefs. Two of the developments that divided people were the split between "masters and workers" in which the organization is privately owned by the masters and the arrival of large-scale industry in which workers were each given very narrow and different functions to perform. Both of these factors served to drive a wedge between employers and workers. With large industries, "the worker is more completely separated from the employer." And "at the same time that specialization becomes greater, revolts become more frequent" (Durkheim 1933, p. 355). In smaller industries, in contrast, there is "a relative harmony between worker and employer. It is only in large-scale industry that these relations are in a sickly state" (p. 356). Large industry develops as markets grow and encompass groups not in immediate contact with each other. Producers and consumers become increasingly separated from each other. "The producer can no longer embrace the market in a glance, nor even in thought. He can no longer see its limits, since it is, so to speak, limitless. Accordingly, production becomes unbridled and unregulated" (p. 370). That is, a condition of anomic or normlessness exists. Economic crises develop but industry grows as markets grow.

With the growth of industry and an increasingly minute division of labor, the individual worker becomes more "alienated," to use a Marxian term. Like Marx, Durkheim concluded that the worker becomes a "machine," performing mind-numbing, routine, repetitive labor without any sense of the significance of his or her role in the labor process.

Every day he repeats the same movements with monotonous regularity, but without being interested in them, and without understanding them. He is no longer anything but a living cell of a living organism which unceasingly vibrates with neighboring cells, . . . He is no longer anything but an inert piece of machinery, only an external force set going which always moves in the same direction and in the same way. . . . One cannot remain indifferent to such debasement of human nature. (ibid., p. 371)

Although this description may sound intriguingly Marxist, Durkheim's view of the division of labor in modern society was quite different from that of Marx. Because of its nature, Durkheim viewed the division of labor as a central basis for integration in modern industrial society. It is only in certain abnormal forms that it becomes a problem. But basically, a complex division of labor is a necessity in *industrial* society. It is expected that as societies develop they become increasingly complex. In contrast, Marx viewed the division of labor as a source of basic problems in *capitalist* society. Class conflict was over fundamental issues in the property and social relationships involved in the division of labor. For Durkheim, class conflict was a surface symptom of an anomic state in which the employers and workers conflicted because of the absence of a common, agreed-on set of moral rules. The problems of the modern society are not due to contradictions within capitalism, "but derive from the strains inherent in the transition from mechanical to organic solidarity" (Giddens 1978, p. 36). Marx sees regulation in capitalist society as stifling human initiative, whereas Durkheim sees moral regulation as necessary for individual liberty and happiness.

However, the mere presence of rules is not enough to prevent problems in the division of labor because "sometimes the rules themselves are the cause of evil. This is what occurs in class-wars" (Durkheim 1933, p. 374). The problem here is that the rules governing the division of labor do not create a correspondence between individual talents or interests and work functions. The result is that the division of labor creates dissatisfaction and pain instead of integration and cohesiveness. "This is because the distribution of social functions on which [the class structure] rests does not respond, or rather no longer responds, to the distribution of natural talents" (p. 375). When the rules regulating the division of labor no longer correspond to the distribution of true

talents among individuals, then the organization of labor becomes *forced*. (This is the forced division of labor referred to earlier.) Durkheim felt that inequalities that were not based on "internal" differences between individuals were unjust. "External" inequality, which is based on inheritance or membership in some biological group, must be eliminated, according to Durkheim, because it threatens the solidarity of society. Superiority that results from differences in the resources of individuals is unjust. "In other words, there cannot be rich and poor at birth without there being unjust contracts" (p. 384). The sense of injustice associated with the significance of external inequalities becomes greater as labor becomes more separated from employers and the collective conscience becomes weaker.

Despite his realization of the injustices suffered by workers in the division of labor, Durkheim was not an advocate of class revolution. As mentioned, he did not feel that there is anything inherently wrong with a complex division of labor and, consequently, only reformist change was needed to eliminate the problems associated with it. Durkheim felt that complete revolution would destroy the delicate and complex membrane that made up society. "I am quite aware when people speak of destroying existing societies, they intend to reconstruct them. But these are the fantasies of children. One cannot in this way rebuild collective life: once our social organization is destroyed, centuries of history will be required to build another" (quoted in Fenton 1984, p. 31). Durkheim felt that deep, lasting change would take place gradually and through ameliorative reform rather than through drastic conflict. In this way also, he differed from Marx. Nor did he feel that the state was an instrument of oppression, but rather felt it could serve as an instrument of reform for a better society (Giddens 1978). However, like Marx and in contrast to Weber, he had an optimistic view of future society. Fundamental class conflicts would be minimized once problems in the division of labor could be ironed out with appropriate policies and moral regulations over time.

HERBERT SPENCER (1820–1903)

Spencer's star in social science fell as quickly as it had risen. At the turn of the twentieth century, Spencer was highly regarded and popular in academic and public circles. But by the early 1930s, his fame and reputation had suffered greatly. Near the end of the 1930s, Talcott Parsons, who was to become the leading social theorist in the United States, indicated his belief in the irrelevance of Spencer by asking directly: "Who now reads Spencer?" By and large, attitudes have not changed. Spencer does not have the high standing in social theory today that is accorded to Marx, Weber, and Durkheim.

Despite this generally negative reaction, I include a brief discussion of Spencer for three reasons: First, there are some today who argue that Spencer has been inappropriately neglected or ignored despite the value of some of his ideas (e.g., Turner 1985; Adams and Sydie 2002). Second, as we will see in Chapter 15, Spencer's arguments about inequality and its sources, as well as his beliefs about the proper role of the state in addressing poverty and related issues, are reflected in U.S. beliefs about poverty and welfare policies. Third, Spencer's individualistic orientation contrasts significantly and especially with the more collectivistic views of Marx and Durkheim and, consequently, provides an alternative perspective on inequality. As in other instances, I will focus only on those ideas of greatest relevance to social inequality.

Herbert Spencer was born in 1820 in England to parents who were religious dissenters and who believed in religious freedom and social egalitarianism. Consequently, he grew to dislike the blind subjugation to authority demanded by traditional religion. His father was an independent, self-employed teacher who encouraged skepticism and free thinking. As a young boy, Spencer loathed formal education, and at 16 quit formal education for good. His greatest intellectual interests were in pragmatic and hard-scientific areas, such as mathematics and physics. Spencer's interest in concrete practical matters was evident in his inventions of a velocimeter, a fishing-rod joint, and other mechanical devices. He was not a romantic. He cared little for the softer fields of literature and poetry, and consequently, he was rather narrow in his reading. Because of his upbringing and the influence of the Enlightenment, he subscribed to belief in combining individual reason and the judicious use of scientific method as the means for uncovering social laws.

As a young man, Spencer took a job as an engineer with a British railway firm, all the while continuing with his scientific reading. In 1848, the publication year of Marx's *Manifesto of the Communist Party*, Spencer moved to London. His first book, *Social Statics: Or, the Conditions Essential to Human Happiness Specified, and the First of Them Developed*, appeared in 1850. Later works of relevance to the area of social inequality include *The Study of Sociology*, *The Principles of Sociology*, *The Man versus the State*, and *The Principles of Ethics*.

Spencer was not fully healthy for much of his life, and in later years suffered from what may have been nervous breakdowns. His last years were marked by a bitterness resulting from the lesser publicity given to his later over his earlier works and his distaste for what he saw as England's aggressive militarism against other nations (Ashley and Orenstein 1990; Adams and Sydie 2002). Spencer died in 1903 and is buried in Highgate Cemetery, about 30 feet away and directly across from the tomb of Karl Marx. The worn-away state of his tombstone may be symbolic of the lack of attention and recognition his theories have received in recent years. In contrast, Marx's gravesite is quite grand and impressive.

Spencer's experiences as an engineer and his expertise in biological and physical/mechanical sciences informed his own interpretations of social evolution and equilibrium, and his work was quite influential in the latter half of the nineteenth century. Indeed, his texts on biology, sociology, and psychology were used at prestigious universities in England and the United States. This is despite the fact that Spencer held no higher degrees and never held an academic position. Part of the reason for his popularity was that his views on societal evolution, the state, and the sanctity of the free individual resonated with the ethos of the emerging U.S. capitalist industrial order of that time.

In Spencer's view, industrial societies are to be differentiated from militant ones. Clearly, he viewed militant societies with their heavy regulation of individuals as more primitive and unequal in their social structure. Inequality originates in militancy, first involving men as a ruling class and women as a subject class. War then creates a slave class of the conquered. The slave class increases when slaves are bought or individuals are brought into slavery because of debt or crime. Serfdom also arises with military conquest and the annexing of land. Male descent rules and kinship with those in power increases men's wealth, as does the possession of slaves. Rank and wealth are tied together. Increases in inequality build on themselves, as more wealth allows greater accumulation and defense of it. Militancy and regulation in the larger society are reflected in the social structure of the family. Men are dominant in the domicile over women just as they are in the wider society.

The class structure created is perpetuated by the abilities and habits developed over time by each respective class. Those on top become adept at control and domination, "an inherited fitness for command," while those below develop "an inherited fitness for obedience." These differences result in "strengthening the general contrast of nature." Eventually, these class relations are seen by all as "natural" (Spencer 1909, pp. 302, 309).

As a society becomes industrial, original class divisions based on rank, kinship, land, and/or locality are broken down. Classes and the distribution of rewards become based more "on differences of aptitude for the various functions which an industrial society needs," that is, on ability and performance in a competitive market (ibid., p. 310). Mental habits change as the increased economic exchange required in industrial society cultivates a "growing spirit of equality," that is, individuals become more "habituated to maintain their own claims while respecting the claims of others" (ibid., p. 307). Because human attitudes change, class and gender relations become more egalitarian. Industrial societies mean more freedom and greater reverence for the individual.

As suggested, Spencer's theory of evolution included the Lamarckian beliefs that some acquired personality traits could be inherited and that the process of evolution was basically proceeding in a progressive direction. Drawing on both biological and physical analogies, he viewed society as naturally becoming larger, more complex, integrated, and adaptive. In its free and natural course, societies evolve in a manner that increases their adaptability. Spencer argued that, left to its own devices and like any natural species, a society's best components survive, while its weakest die away. Evolution performs a cleansing function that makes society more adaptive to its environment. In the long run, this makes society stronger.

In the competitive battle of life, winners survive while losers die away. In this sense, inequality is to be expected in society. Spencer coined the phrase "survival of the fittest," which captures the spirit of this social competition. This is a natural process with which there should be no interference from any quarter. "Under the natural course of things each citizen tends towards his fittest function. Those who are competent to the kind of work they undertake succeed, and, in the average of cases, are

Karl Marx and Herbert Spencer are buried right across from each other at Highgate Cemetery in Highgate, England. As the photo shows, Marx's tomb is much grander and more well-kept than is Spencer's.

Photos by author.

advanced in proportion to their efficiency; while the incompetent, society soon finds out, ceases to employ, forces to try something easier, and eventually turns to use" (Spencer 1892/1946, p. 138). As humanity evolves, Spencer believed, it develops traits that promote its survival. Unnecessary governmental legislation and other attempts to modify this process damage the natural evolutionary process. "Let the average vitality be diminished by more effectually guarding the weak against adverse conditions, and inevitably there come fresh diseases" (Spencer 1961, p. 310).

Freedom allows each individual the opportunity to develop their own adaptive traits. If individuals develop positive traits, they can be strengthened and passed on to future generations, making society as a whole much stronger and more adaptive. Even well-intentioned interference in this natural process only weakens the possibility of individuals developing these traits. Overall, it also weakens society's ability to survive since it encourages, or props up, its weakest members at the expense of everyone else. Because weak individuals do not have the properties necessary for survival, their dependence on state aid is "evil" because "all evil results from the non-adaptation of constitution to conditions," and it is in its advance to build its strength that society rids itself of "evil" (Spencer 1897, pp. 28–29).

In modern industrial nations, such as the United States, Spencer envisioned a free-market capitalist economy and a government that performed only basic defensive and protective functions for the nation's citizens. He argued that, by and large, the state should minimize its role in the individual's life. The free individual is a hallmark of an advanced society, and Spencer fiercely believed in the protection of individual rights. As members of society, and at least before marriage, this applies to women as well as to men: "[N]o restraints can equitably be placed upon women in respect of the occupations, professions, or other careers which they may wish to adopt. They must have like freedom to prepare themselves, and like freedom to profit by such information and skill as they acquire" (ibid., p. 160). The pursuit of happiness by an individual should not impinge on the freedom or happiness of others (ibid.). "The root of all well-ordered social action is a sentiment of justice, which at once insists on personal freedom and is solicitous for the like freedom of others" (Spencer 1892/1946, pp. 77–78).

In contrast to Durkheim, Spencer believed that the State would become smaller and less intrusive and the individual freer as society evolved: "[T]he liberty which a citizen enjoys is to be measured . . . by the relative paucity of the restraints [governmental machinery] imposes on him . . . [especially] such restraints beyond those which are needful for preventing him from directly or indirectly aggressing on his fellows" (ibid., p. 19).

State size has implications for both the powerful and the powerless in society. What this means for the powerless and poor is that, in Spencer's view, governmental welfare programs should be eliminated for the good of society as a whole. Such programs actually weaken the poor and create bitterness among those who must be taxed to support them. In contrast to help given by volunteers to the needy, this aid is not freely given. No one benefits in the long run. It also weakens society because such suffering on the part of the weak must be endured if only to perfect society:

> *Blind to the fact that under the natural order of things society is constantly excreting its unhealthy, imbecile, slow, vacillating, faithless members, these unthinking, though well-meaning, men advocate an interference which not only stops the purifying process, but even . . . encourages the multiplication of the reckless and incompetent by offering them an unfailing provision, and discourages the multiplication of the competent and provident by heightening the difficulty of maintaining a family. . . . The process [of natural adaptation] must be undergone and the sufferings must be endured. (Spencer 1897, p. 151)*

What smaller government means for the powerful is the creation of fewer opportunities for the rich and powerful to use it for selfish purposes: "It is a tolerably well-ascertained fact that men are still selfish . . . and will employ the power placed in their hands for their own advantage . . . directly or indirectly, either by hook or by crook, if not open then in secret, their private ends will be served" (ibid., p. 95). One need only think of recent governmental and corporate scandals to realize the applicability of this observation. In the long run, smaller government benefits all.

Increased governmental regulation also promotes class distinctions and foments class hostility. If Spencer saw governmental organizations as distorting and slowing the progressive evolution of individuals and society, so too did he consider class-based organizations to be a hindrance to the free individual. Strong class organizations require an obedience on the part of their individual members and, because of the class bias built into these organizations, prevent an accurate understanding of the real causes of worker problems. This is true for working-class unions as well as for upper-class organizations. Unions control workers' lives as much as employers do. When you look at a union worker's situation, "it becomes clear that he and the rest have made for themselves a tyranny worse than the tyrannies complained of" (Spencer 1961, p. 225). Moreover, the class bias that workers hold "prevents them from seeing that each of their unions is selfishly aiming to benefit at the expense of the industrial population at large" (ibid.). It also prevents them from seeing that the problems they are facing are largely a product of the evolutionary stage of industrial organization and, at bottom, of human nature's evolution. "The relation of master and workman has to be tolerated, because, for the time being, no other will answer as well" (ibid., p. 229).

Upper-class organizations also encourage a class bias that bolsters the upper class and defines the working class as existing only for their benefit. Upper-class members do not see that their present class distinction harms them by encouraging class hostility and promoting their "idle lives" (ibid., p. 235). Nor does it help them see "that there is anything mean in being a useless consumer of things which others produce" (ibid., p. 236).

Spencer acknowledged the difficulties that the less fortunate face and the indignities and discrimination they suffer at the hands of the higher classes; he admitted that the distribution system gives too much to those on the top. But he contended that the problems that individuals face reflect the limitations of human nature at any given time. Unfortunately, governmental legislation and class organizations hinder this understanding. "[T]he welfare of a society and the justice of its arrangements are at bottom dependent on the character of its members. . . . The defective natures of citizens will show themselves in the bad acting of *whatever* social structure they are arranged into. There is no political alchemy by which you can get golden conduct out of leaden instincts" (Spencer 1892/1946, pp. 52–53; emphasis added).

In criticism, Spencer put too much faith in the natural process of evolution as the proper avenue through which inequality and its ills had to be solved. He appears to have been largely unaware of the negative consequences for many workers of the social-structural arrangements that evolve as a free-market economy "progresses." To wait for human nature to become less selfish seems a long time. Outside of voluntary charity and negative regulation that protected the rights of individuals, he left little room for using human activities of any kind as a means of alleviating poverty or inequality. This is because he viewed some inequality as a product of the survival of the fittest. On the positive side, Spencer's arguments call renewed attention to the selfish interests and biases of the powerful that are often present in governmental and other large organizations. As a champion of individual freedom, he also reminds us to be wary of constraints on both the rich and the poor, which may hinder their development as individuals. He reminds us that big government, regardless of its form, is no solution to the problem of social inequality.

SUMMARY

It was mentioned at the outset of the chapter that a thorough understanding of what Marx, Weber, Durkheim, and Spencer had to say about inequality depends on seeing and analyzing that work in the context of their broader theories and perspectives on society and human beings. Too often, as a reflection of our specialization and departmentalization, we wrench out only those segments of an individual's theory in which we have an immediate interest. This is not the way in which these theories were developed, and so taking them out of context can lead to distortions and, at best, only superficial understanding. Consequently, the specific observations made by these individuals on inequality should be couched in the broader frameworks of their overall perspectives and life experiences. Hopefully, this leads to a fuller comprehension of what each of the given theorists was trying to convey.

It is clear from the discussion in this chapter that theorists differed significantly in their views on human nature, the forms that inequality could take, and the bases and future of inequality. Weber saw human beings as self-seeking, whereas Marx viewed them in more selfless terms. Durkheim felt that individuals required regulation and guidance. Spencer believed people were selfish but that their nature would be changed to become moral and respectful of others as industrialism took hold. Marx focused on economic classes, as did Durkheim in *The Division of Labor*, while Weber examined economic classes as well as status groups, and to some extent, parties. Spencer analyzed shifts in class, political, and gender inequality as societies moved from militant to industrial, and from simple to complex systems. Marx sought the source of inequality in an individual's relationship to the means of production, whereas Weber saw inequality arising from a number of sources, including market situation, lifestyle, and decision-making power. Durkheim argued that although inequality continued to be based on biological and inheritance factors, he assumed that eventually in organic society most social inequality would be founded solely on individual differences in abilities. Spencer placed the sources of the earliest and most rigid forms of inequality in militancy, conquest, and annexation of territory, while later, more fluid forms in industrial societies were based on one's function and performance in the economy. Weber, Durkheim, and Spencer did not see inequality as disappearing in the future, but Marx was more optimistic on this point.

Marx and Weber agreed that classes, class struggle, or both are significant elements in societies. Weber and Marx both felt that capitalism has dehumanizing effects and is class structured and that class is a predominant factor in modern society. Their conceptions of the effects of class anticipated many of the specific effects discussed in later chapters on life chances, crime, and protest. Similar conditions for class consciousness and protest were outlined by Marx and Weber. In contrast to Marx and Weber, Durkheim and Spencer argued that, because of its nature, industrial society contains less alienating and structured forms of inequality.

Table 8.1 highlights the central features of the main theorists covered in this chapter. The theories of Marx, Weber, Durkheim, and Spencer were presented here because their perspectives have helped to shape modern social science. Their impact has not always been obvious, but it has been pervasive.

TABLE 8.1   Summary of Basic Ideas on Inequality from Classical Theorists

| THEORIST | MAJOR CONCERN | THEORIST'S VIEWS ON INEQUALITY | | | |
		Forms	Causes	Inevitability	Future
Marx	Classes in capitalist society	Historical class structures	Private property	No	Revolution and classless society
Weber	Dimensions of inequality and shifts in their prominence	Class, status, party	Market situation; granting of status honor; political power	Yes	Rationalization of society and growing salience of class
Durkheim	Abnormal forms of division of labor	Masters and workers	Anomic and forced divisions of labor	Mixed	Decline of class conflict in industrial society
Spencer	Evolutionary changes in bases and degree of inequality	Classes and gender relations	Form and evolutionary stage of society	Yes	Greater egalitarian ethos and inequality based on achievement

CRITICAL THINKING

1. How important is one's economic position compared to other criteria (e.g., race, gender, lifestyle) in determining ranking in a community?

2. Is a classless society possible or even approachable? If so, what problems, if any, would arise from the classlessness? If no, why not?

3. Capitalism or at least modern industry plays an important role in classical theories of inequality. Do you agree? Why? What features appear to be most closely linked to the creation of inequality? How could capitalism be altered to change the class/status system of the United States?

4. Do you believe that the "survival of the fittest" explains most of the inequality in the United States? Explain and defend your answer.

WEB CONNECTIONS

Marx, Weber, and Durkheim were among the giants of sociology during its classical period. To find out more about them, and to read interviews that Marx and Engels had with various media representatives, go to the Marxist Archive, which also contains information on writers who followed in their footsteps. Comparisons of Marx with Weber and Durkheim can also be carried out by browsing and reading in these two websites: www.marxists.org/ and www2.pfeiffer.edu/~Iridener/DSS/INDEX.HTML.

CHAPTER

9

Contemporary Explanations of Inequality

Social inequality is thus an unconsciously evolved device by which societies insure that the most important positions are conscientiously filled by the most qualified persons.

—Kingsley Davis and Wilbert E. Moore

[The poor] are also separated from the non-poor in the positive sense that they have economic value where they are and hence that there are groups interested, not only in resisting the elimination of poverty, but in actively seeking its perpetuation.

—Michael J. Piori

This chapter consists of a discussion of some of the more recent explanations of social inequality. Generally, theories of inequality tend to stress either the *structural* or *individual* causes of inequality (Gould 2002). Sometimes given explanations incorporate both elements, and try to explain both the *structure of inequality* as well as *individuals' positions within it*. *Structural* explanations focus on the effects of the market's organization, occupational structure, institutional discrimination, and/or the social network of positions on social stratification in a society. Over time, as positions disappear and new ones appear, individuals' class positions also change. Position in the structure affects access, opportunities, and outcomes for individuals. The controversial functionalist theory of Davis and Moore and the dual-labor market theory in this chapter stress the importance of structure and position within it for

understanding inequality in rewards. In the last chapter, Marx and Durkheim's theories are especially representative of this approach. *Individualist* explanations, on the other hand, emphasize the role of individual differences in qualities (traits, talents, education, etc.) in explaining the inequality among people. It is because of differences in effort, ability, training, experience, and the like that inequality in rewards emerges. Neoclassical economic theories that focus on differences in human capital best exemplify this form of theory in this chapter, while Herbert Spencer's explanation from the last chapter is also representative of the individualist type. Some explanations to be encountered shortly incorporate both structural and individualist, macro and micro, elements in them. Included in these are certain forms of social constructionist and reproduction explanations. It can be inferred from some of these theories that even though it is helpful to make the analytical distinction between structural and individualist explanations, it is the case that structure and individual affect each other reciprocally in complex ways.

This chapter is not an exhaustive treatment of all contemporary theories of inequality. The work of Erik Wright, for example, a prominent American Marxist scholar, is not discussed in this chapter. Wright's principal publications have been concerned with the Marxian conceptualization and measurement of class and their application to understanding the shape of class structure in capitalist societies. As a result, his view of the class concept and class structure was reviewed in Chapter 2, along with other perspectives on class structure.

FUNCTIONALIST THEORY OF STRATIFICATION

The arguments of Durkheim that inequality will be based primarily on differences in internal talents and the division of labor are echoed in the 1945 theory of Kingsley Davis and Wilbert Moore. Few theories of stratification have called forth the attention and criticism that the Davis–Moore theory has received.

Like Durkheim's theory, Davis and Moore's theory is based on a functionalist framework. The functional perspective views societies as social systems that have certain basic problems to solve or functions that have to be performed if the society is to survive. One of these problems concerns the motivation of society's members; if that motivation is absent, a society will not survive (Aberle et al. 1950, p. 103). If a society is to continue, important tasks must be specifically delineated and some means for their assignment and accomplishment created; for a society, "activities necessary to its survival must be worked out in predictable, determinate ways, or else apathy or the war of each against all must prevail" (p. 105). And since certain goods of value are scarce (property, wealth, etc.),

"some system of differential allocation of the scarce values of a society is essential" (p. 106). The result of this differential allocation (stratification) must be viewed as being legitimate and "accepted by most of the members—at least by the important ones—of a society if stability is to be attained" (ibid.). Many functional prerequisites are assumed to be necessary for the survival of a society, but it is the assumption of the necessity of stratification that concerns us here.

The most celebrated and damned theory of stratification using the functionalist perspective was formulated by Davis and Moore in 1945. Their ideas are quite simple to grasp and, on the surface, may appear to be common-sensical and even self-evident. One should keep in mind that the kind of thinking that is represented in their theory dominated sociology throughout the 1950s and much of the 1960s in the United States. Let us take a closer look at their reasoning.

Davis and Moore indicated at the outset of their argument what they were trying to do:

1. "To explain in functional terms, the universal necessity which calls forth stratification in any social system."
2. To explain why positions, not persons, are differentially ranked in the system of rewards in any society (Davis and Moore 1945, p. 242).

Assuming that structure is at least minimally divided into different statuses and roles (i.e., a division of labor), Davis and Moore began by arguing that every society has to have some means to place its members in the social structure. A critical issue is the problem of motivating individuals to occupy certain statuses (full-time occupations) and to make sure that they are motivated to adequately perform the roles once they occupy those positions. Since some tasks are more onerous, more important for the society, and more difficult to perform, a system of rewards (inducements) is needed to make certain that these tasks are performed by the most capable individuals. "The rewards and their distribution become a part of the social order, and thus give rise to stratification" (ibid., p. 243). Like Durkheim's view of the ideal industrial society, Davis and Moore assumed that the society will run smoothly because the distribution of rewards to individuals will reflect the "internal inequalities" of their skills and capabilities.

Every society has a variety of rewards that it can use: (1) those "that contribute to sustenance and comfort" (money, goods of different kinds), (2) those related to "humor and diversion" (vacations, leisure plans), and (3) those that enhance "self-respect and ego expansion" (psychological rewards, promotion). Consequently, Davis and Moore are not simply talking about the distribution and system of economic rewards but all kinds of inducements that can promote motivation to perform tasks in the society. Not all positions have equal rewards attached to them, of course, and since that is the case, "the society must be stratified because that is precisely what stratification means. Social inequality is thus an unconsciously evolved device by which societies ensure that the most important positions are conscientiously filled by the most qualified persons" (ibid.). According to this approach, since every society has tasks that are differentially important to its survival, every society is stratified.

Davis and Moore specified two criteria that determine the amount of rewards that accrue to given positions: (1) functional importance of the task and (2) the "scarcity of personnel" capable of performing the task, or the amount of training required (ibid., pp. 243–244). Together these determine the rank of a given position in the system of rewards—that is, in the stratification system. Consequently, "a position does not bring power and privilege because it draws a high income. Rather it draws a high income because it is functionally important and the available personnel is for one reason or another scarce" (pp. 246–247). The exact contribution of each of these criteria, singly and in combination, to the level of rewards is not spelled out, so one can only guess as to how

rewards would be affected if one of these criteria ranked high but the other low on a given position (Abrahamson 1973).

Davis and Moore implied that a third and more radical factor also is involved in determining an *individual's* (as opposed to a position's) rank and reward: economic power or control over resources. They recognized that having a great deal of money can give an individual an advantage in seeking a higher position. Power and prestige can be based on ownership, and "one kind of ownership of production goods consists in rights over the labor of others. . . . Naturally this kind of ownership has the greatest significance for stratification because it necessarily entails an unequal relationship" (1945, p. 247). These comments are repeated in Davis's revised version of the theory. Kemper (1976) stated that it is remarkable that, given all the critics of the theory, none seems to have noticed that economic power also is considered a cause of distribution in the reward system by Davis and Moore. Clearly, however, it takes a secondary place alongside functional importance and training or talent, especially since it is more clearly a determinant of why *individuals*, and not *positions*, are distributed as they are in a reward system.

Societies differ in their stratification systems because they contain different conditions that affect either one or both of the principal determinants of ranking—that is, either functional importance or scarcity. The stage of cultural development and their situation with respect to other societies vary between societies, causing different tasks to be more important in one society than in another, and in personnel being more scarce for certain tasks than for others.

Figure 9.1 outlines the essential argument of the Davis–Moore thesis. Davis and Moore concluded their presentation by noting several dimensions along which stratification systems in different countries can vary. Among others, these include how fine the gradations are between ranks (specialization), the degree of social distance from the top to the bottom, the

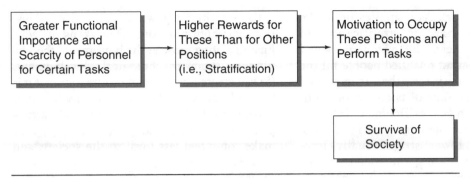

FIGURE 9.1   The Davis–Moore Theory of Stratification

extent of mobility in the system, and the extent to which classes are clearly delineated in the society. What could be more logical? Certain tasks are more important than others, and some are more difficult to carry out. In order to make sure they are performed, more rewards are attached to them. Thus, people are motivated to perform them, and the society continues to function.

Critique of the Functionalist Theory of Stratification

The functionalist theory and the Davis–Moore article, in particular, have precipitated a storm of criticism and counterattacks. The vehemence with which some of the arguments are made and the tenacity with which this debate has held on for almost five decades suggest that a number of fundamental issues are involved. Of the host of criticisms that have been made of the theory, I will focus on three: (1) the issue of the differential functional importance of positions, (2) the question of whether the functionalists are addressing themselves to real societies, and (3) the neglect of the dysfunctions of stratification.

Differential Functional Importance.   A central problem of the Davis–Moore theory is how to establish the *functional necessity* of a task for a society. Davis and Moore acknowledged that it is difficult to define functional necessity, but they suggested two indicators of importance:

(1) "the degree to which a position is functionally *unique*"—that is, there are no functional alternatives to the position, and (2) "the degree to which other positions are *dependent* on the one in question" (Davis and Moore 1945, p. 244, emphasis added).

It is not clear whether Davis and Moore are speaking of the evaluation of positions as being differentially important or of positions being differentially important by some more objective standard. In the 1945 version, the indicators for measuring functional importance suggested that they are speaking of functional importance in an objective sense. But in a later statement, Davis (1948–1949) suggested that it is the *subjective evaluation* of a role's importance that is the significant determinant of its functional importance. And, of course, if this is the case, about whose evaluation is he speaking—all of society or a select few? Moore (1970) also took a more subjective position later when he noted the importance of evaluating performance, qualities, and achievement in determining rewards. The bottom line is that their criteria for defining *functional importance* are not clear nor are their attempts to measure it adequate (Huaco 1963).

The Issue of Dealing with Real Societies.   Another of the principal criticisms of the functional perspective is that it deals with highly abstract social systems (utopias) yet ignores the operation of real societies

(Dahrendorf 1958a). As it applies here, the criticism means that if stratification of rewards is the means by which a society ensures that the most qualified people fill the most important positions, then it is crucial that there be free flow of talent throughout the society. But, in fact, as Tumin (1953) made it plain, this is not the case in real societies. People in the lower strata usually have restricted opportunities, the society is not freely competitive, and people probably are not taking full advantage of the talent they may have. The roles of conflict and lack of opportunity must be considered when trying to understand the socioeconomic arrangement of real societies (Dahrendorf 1958a), and although Davis and Moore did mention the roles of power and wealth in determining and maintaining positions, they did not stress these as major determinants.

One way by which Davis and Moore tried to handle the criticism that some are hindered from attaining a high position was by reiterating that the theory is about *positions*, not the mobility of *people*. However, even given this insistence on their part, people do, in fact, become important in the theory because of Davis and Moore's belief that "it does make a great deal of difference who gets into which positions, not only because some positions are inherently more agreeable than others but also because some require special talents or training and some have more importance than others" (1945, p. 367). Concerns over motivation and scarcity of talent necessarily implicate people in the theory.

Neglect of the Dysfunctions of Stratification. Tumin (1953) was the first major critic to point out that stratification can have numerous dysfunctions for society and the individual, a point ignored in the original Davis–Moore argument. Among the dysfunctions he noted are that stratification (1) inhibits the discovery of talent, (2) limits the extent to which productive resources can be expanded, (3) provides those at the top with the power to rationalize and justify their high position, (4) weakens the self-images among those at the bottom and thereby hinders their psychological development, (5) can create hostility and disintegration if it is not fully accepted by all in society, (6) may make some feel that they are not full participants in the society and, therefore, (7) may make some feel less loyal to the society, and (8) may also make some less motivated to participate in the society.

It is somewhat surprising that the original argument by Davis and Moore would neglect the question of dysfunctions, given their comments about power and wealth affecting the reward system. But, on the other hand, Tumin does not indicate that a condition of full equality may generate problems of its own, such as lack of motivation and feelings of inequity. Wrong (1959), in fact, has indicated that many critics of the Davis–Moore theory point to the dysfunctions of stratification and the role of power and so forth in determining rank, but they neglect the dysfunctional effects of equality of opportunity. In a society where individuals can freely move up on the basis of their talent, would not the failures then suffer even more acutely, knowing that they and not the system are to blame for their low position in the system of rewards?

THEORIES OF SOCIAL CONSTRUCTION AND REPRODUCTION

During the mid- and late 1950s, the functionalist perspective came under a barrage of criticism in sociology. Both symbolic interactionist and conflict models of society proposed alternative ways of interpreting structures of inequality. The functionalist theory focuses on the relative importance of occupations and the difficulty of filling them as the fundamental explanations for differences in rewards among individuals. As such, its emphasis is on the larger economic structure and one's position in it. In sharp contrast, using symbolic interactionist and/or conflict orientations, social construction and reproduction theories examine how, in our everyday behavior and situations, inequality is created and then reproduced over and over again.

Social constructionist theories focus on everyday interactions and often emphasize the importance of words, social categories, and classifications to demonstrate how different categories of people are created and then ranked. These categories are socially invented, not fixed in nature. A good illustration of this is how the U.S. Bureau of the Census has changed its racial classifications over the last several decades. Different races are invented every time such changes are made.

Accepted definitions and classifications for individuals and behaviors are generally invented by those who have economic, political, or social power (Rigney 2001). Consequently, the categories/classifications often reflect their interests and result in dividing up the social world in a manner that privileges them. For example, *intelligence* is generally defined by psychological experts or persons in authority using one's "intelligence quotient" or "IQ," even though in recent decades this definition has come under attack from different, often less privileged groups. Using this definition, only certain persons are defined as "intelligent." Through classifications like this, we create "others" (intellectual, racial, status, etc.) who simply do not measure up to the standards we have created. This process of "othering" creates and helps reproduce inequality (Schwalbe et al. 2000).

The concept of "homosexuality," as discussed in Chapter 6, provides another example of how classifications are created. The classification of heterosexual/homosexual is historically recent, as is the privileging of heterosexuality over homosexuality, for example, in the interpretation of homosexuality as a form of deviance. It was not until 1966 that the American Psychiatric Association introduced homosexuality as a form of sexual disorder. Battles with gay groups over this definition and interpretation later led to changes (Spector and Kitsuse 1977).

Since their interests are at stake, groups will often compete for acceptance of their definition or classification. At different times, different groups may win, and some groups may win almost all of the time. Consequently, classifications may change or they may not. "When one group wins, its vocabulary may be adopted and institutionalized while the concepts of the opposing groups fall into obscurity. . . . The categories and meanings that they have created have direct consequences for the ways such phenomena are conceived, evaluated, and treated" (ibid., pp. 8, 15).

When one puts together all the accepted terms, definitions, classifications, and so forth that proliferate in society, it is easy to see why social constructionists view society as being made up of symbols and words, since it is these that constitute reality for us on a day-to-day basis. Different definitions and classifications suggest different realities. A large number of interpretive and postmodern theories emphasize the importance of language in the construction of society. When sociologists, as "professional experts," create measures of social class, and using data on income, education, and so on, define given individuals as "working class" or "middle class" or "upper class," they are, in effect, inventing these classes or "doing class."

Individuals are "doing race" or "doing gender" when they engage in conversations or behaviors that create or reinforce differences between groups. In this engaging recollection about growing up in a poor minority neighborhood in New York, the White sociologist Dalton Conley discussed how he had to learn what it means to be White or Black: "Learning race is like learning a language. First we try mouthing all sounds. Then we learn which are not words and which have meaning to the people around us" (Conley 2000, p. 37). It did not take long for Conley and his sister to learn the meanings and symbols associated with different groups. In their daily school and neighborhood experiences, they learned what it meant to be rich or poor and Black or White.

Similarly, we learn what gender means by how it is done, that is, by how different individuals are defined and treated. It is in this defining and treatment that different genders are created, beginning early in life when boys and girls are treated differently. In this way, gender is socially constructed and is maintained through the recurrence of distinctions made in school, on the job, in the home, and in other institutions. We then define gender differences as inherent in each individual or as natural, and by treating individuals differently, we reproduce gender inequality (Lorber 2001). It is in our daily interaction with others that gender is invented. Women and men are viewed as being *meant* for different roles and positions. Once constructed, inequalities are then reproduced.

Social reproduction theories are generally built on a conflict model of society and are often aligned with Marxian views on inequality. But rather than focusing on the explanation of the *original appearance* of inequality, these theories focus on outlining the process by which the social class structure is *maintained*. Specifically, they are concerned with the question of how the class structure reproduces itself generation after generation. As MacLeod (1987) stated, "Social reproduction theory explains how societal institutions perpetuate (or reproduce) the social relationships and attitudes needed to sustain the existing relations of production in a capitalist society" (p. 9).

Thus, even though they are concerned with the reproduction of inequality over time, these theories are in sharp contrast to those that emphasize a culture-of-poverty approach—that is, blaming the perpetuation of inequality on the values and other characteristics of poor individuals and their families. Case studies of such individuals make this point unequivocally. "The view that the problem resides almost exclusively with the children and their families, and that some sort of cultural injection is needed to compensate for what they are missing, is not only intellectually bankrupt but also has contributed to the widespread popular notion that the plight of poor whites and minorities is entirely their own fault" (ibid., p. 99). Of the families she studied, Rubin (1976) wrote:

> *These families reproduce themselves not because they are somehow deficient or their culture aberrant, but because there are no alternatives for most of their children. Indeed, it may be the singular triumph of this industrial society . . . that not only do we socialize people to their appropriate roles and stations, but that the process by which this occurs is so subtle that it is internalized and passed from parents to children by adults who honestly believe they are acting out of choices they have made in their own lifetime. (p. 211)*

Needless to say, there are a number of specific theories of reproduction, but only a couple will be summarized here to leave you with the basic outlines of this approach to understanding inequality. Reproduction theories variously focus on the role(s) of (1) institutions, (2) culture, and/or (3) the individual in the perpetuation of social inequality. Following is a summary of these foci and the central catalysts for each in the inequality-reproduction process:

Levels of analysis	Catalysts of reproduction
Macro- and microstructure	Opportunities and barriers
Societal and group culture	Hegemonic values
Individual	Action and reaction

Institutions as social structures create avenues of and barriers to achievement. Societal and subcultural values encourage or discourage attitudes and behaviors that affect achievement. Finally, even though individuals may share values, they may enact them in different ways.

Moreover, since each individual's situation is at least a little different, his or her immediate values that are grounded in this situation may also differ, and thus so may the individual's actions/reactions. Examples of arguments that stress each of these follow.

The role of institutions is stressed by Oliver and Shapiro (1995) in their historical analysis of racial wealth inequality across generations. As reviewed in Chapter 7, governmental agencies and programs have often created opportunities for wealth accumulation for some but not for others. Since degree of access to opportunities allows or prevents the growth of wealth for current and future generations, institutional conditions encourage the cementing and, in some cases, the increasing of economic gaps between racial groups.

Education is another institution prominently displayed in some reproduction theories. Drawing upon Marx's work, Bowles and Gintis's theory addresses how the educational system helps to reproduce class relationships in capitalist society. The educational institution has been studied and considered as an avenue to upward mobility and a means for developing the human personality, but, according to Bowles and Gintis, education has not been seen as an institution to perpetuate the capitalist or class system in U.S. society. However, even early in its development, education was a means "to help preserve and extend the capitalist order. The function of the school system was to accommodate workers to its most rapid possible development. . . . Since its inception in the United States, the public-school system has been seen as a method of disciplining children in the interest of producing a properly subordinate adult population" (Bowles and Gintis 1976, pp. 29 and 37). A higher level of education for most people has not reduced economic inequality, nor has it developed their full creativity. Its structure rewards those who conform to its rules and obey authority.

As in the workplace, obedience to authority and rules is expected. There is a correspon-

dence, Bowles and Gintis argued, between the structure of educational institutions and the workplace. Specifically, there is a similarity between the two spheres in (1) the nature of their authority structures, (2) the student's lack of control over his or her classes and the workers' lack of control over the work process, (3) the role of grades and other rewards (e.g., colored stars on papers in grade schools) and the role of wages as extrinsic motivators in the workplace, (4) ostensibly free competition among students and similar competition among workers, and (5) the specialization and tracking of courses in school and the narrow functional specialization and career paths in the workplace (Bowles and Gintis 1976; MacLeod 1987). These correspondences between the school and workplace reflect a parallelism between them.

In going through the educational process, consequently, individuals are prepared for their respective roles in the economy. In performing this function, "schools are constrained to justify and reproduce inequality rather than correct it" (Bowles and Gintis 1976, p. 102). By providing a setting in which success appears to depend solely on the individual and his or her talent and effort, schools give the appearance of rewarding those who are most meritorious. The school rewards certain attitudes and behaviors, and penalizes others. It rewards those who act and think in a manner that will serve them in the jobs they will perform in the division of labor. Not all who go to school will move on to higher white-collar professional jobs; many will perform the tasks of blue-collar work. As I noted in an earlier discussion of prep schools, education prepares each class differently, depending on the roles they will play when they collectively leave school. This means not only teaching the appropriate skills but also inculcating the appropriate values and demeanor for each class. Schools in different class neighborhoods differ in their organization and value structure.

Parents from different classes and school administrators expect different characteristics from schools. For example, parents from the middle class expect a more open school structure in which autonomy and creativity are valued. This reflects their image of what is needed in middle-class jobs. In contrast, working-class parents know from their job experiences that obedience and discipline are important. This is reflected in the organization and value structure of schools that are made up primarily of working-class students (ibid., pp. 131–134). As Rubin (1976) found in her study of the working and middle classes, "for the working-class parent, school is a place where teachers are expected to be tough disciplinarians; where children are expected to behave respectfully and to be punished if they do not; and where one mark of that respect is that they are sent to school neatly dressed in their 'good' clothes and expected to stay that way through the day" (p. 126).

In contrast, the professional middle-class parent expects school "to be relatively loose, free, and fun; to encourage initiative, innovativeness, creativity, and spontaneity; and to provide a place where children . . . will learn social and interpersonal skills" (ibid., p. 126). In this view, students are perceived as empty vessels that must be filled up with appropriate knowledge and attitudes. To use Freire's (1986) colorful phrase, this is the "banking concept of education" in which teachers and students are seen as being on opposite sides. The teacher is the actor and the student is the object that is acted upon.

This one-way form of education serves the interests of those in the dominant group. It is not liberating to those who receive it. Instead, it serves "to minimize or annul the students' creative power and to stimulate their credulity [which in turn] serves the interests of the oppressors, who care neither to have the world revealed nor to see it transformed" (ibid., p. 60). It launches a "cultural invasion" in which "those who are invaded come to see their reality with the outlook of the invaders rather than their own; for the more they mimic the invaders, the more stable the position of the latter becomes" (ibid., p. 151). The educational experience, then, reproduces different workers for the economy and the social relationships upon which the economy is based.

In sum, schools not only are interested in producing appropriate laborers for the economy but they also serve the long-term goal of perpetuating the institutions and social relationships that will ensure the continued profitability of capitalism. An educational system accomplishes these goals in four ways:

1. It provides some of the skills needed to perform jobs for each class adequately. Curriculum tracking channels individuals from different classes into appropriate courses.

2. Through its structure and curriculum, the educational system helps to justify and legitimate the economic and occupational inequality present in society. It fosters a belief that individuals wind up in different positions solely because of differences in merit.

3. It encourages the development and internalization of attitudes and self-concepts appropriate to the economic roles individuals will perform. Those who conform to prized values (e.g., those of the upper or middle class) are rewarded, while those who do not are negatively labeled.

4. Through the creation of justified status distinctions within the school, education helps to reinforce a taken-for-granted acceptance of social stratification in the wider society (Bowles and Gintis 1976).

MacLeod (1987) has criticized the Bowles–Gintis theory as being too crude and mechanistic because it views individuals as simply outputs of capitalism and the educational system. It does not give adequate attention to the possible individual differences in reactions to structures that constrain the person. Nor does it take into account cultural or subcultural variations in values and lifestyles that may shape unique adaptations to structural barriers. Giroux has similarly criticized Bowles and Gintis for ignoring the active element in the individual within the structural framework of the school and economy. People *experience* the authority structure of the school and its teachers and they react to them, sometimes through acceptance and sometimes through resistance. In Bowles and Gintis's theory, "the subject gets dissolved under the weight of structural constraints that appear to form both the personality and the workplace" (Giroux 1983, p. 85). The complexity of school life, the varied ways and levels in which structural constraints operate and curricula are taught in varied school sites, is reduced, in Bowles and Gintis's approach, to "a homogeneous image of working-class life fashioned solely by the logic of domination" (ibid.).

A more culturally oriented theory of class reproduction is suggested by the work of Pierre Bourdieu. In this perspective, culture is a mediating element between class structure/interests and everyday life and behavior. By appearing to be objective and a source of knowledge, schools that produce both successful and failing students can justify the inequality that follows. Since schools represent the interests of the dominant culture, Bourdieu argued, they value the cultural capital of the dominant class more than that of the lower classes. *Cultural capital* refers to all the sets of beliefs, practices, ways of thinking, knowledge, and skills passed on from one class's generation to the next. Schools, especially those in higher education, espouse the cultural capital that is most characteristic of the privileged classes, thereby denigrating that which is characteristic of the working and lower classes (Bourdieu 1977a,b). Since this occurs in the objective setting of the school, those in the latter classes who do not do well in classes develop an attitude in which they blame themselves and "actively participate in their own subjugation" (Giroux 1983, p. 89).

Generally, Bourdieu suggested that individuals compete within different "fields" in a struggle for economic, cultural, and social capital. These fields constitute networks of relationships among positions (Bourdieu and Wacquant 1992). As a result of these struggles, individuals come to occupy different classes that vary in the amounts and forms of their economic, social, and cultural capital. Research does indeed indicate that variations in capital are reflected in positional arrangements within fields (Anheier, Gerhards, and Romo 1995). Respectively, some possess great amounts of wealth, extensive social networks, and fancy tastes and lifestyles, whereas others do not, and they can use these resources to justify their possession of capital. The presence or absence of these resources forms a large part of the social context in which individuals live, and these objective conditions give rise to particular tastes, lifestyles, and ways of looking at the world. The upper class possesses a "taste of liberty and luxury," whereas the lower has "popular taste." "Distance from necessity" permeates the taste of the upper class, meaning that it is less directly functional and practical compared to that of the lower class.

An individual's *habitus*, or system of stable dispositions to view the world in a particular way, is a direct product of the person's structural situation; in fact, it is the psychological embodiment of the objective conditions in which one lives. Thus, different life conditions give rise to different forms of habitus and those exposed to the same conditions will develop the same habitus (Bourdieu 1990). The habitus, in turn, has a direct, constraining effect on the social action of individuals, which, coming full circle, contributes to reproducing the social structure. Figure 9.2 gives a rough outline of Bourdieu's model. For example, an adolescent who lives within a structure with poor job opportunities as evidenced by the experiences of his or her parents will develop a view that the chances of success are slight and that school makes no

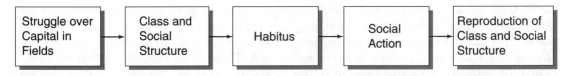

FIGURE 9.2   A General Model of Bourdieu's Explanation of Social Reproduction

difference. This leads to behavior that accommodates him or her to a menial job, which in turn reinforces the existing job opportunity structure. Nothing changes.

Such an image of reproduction of social structure does not lend itself to reconstructing the social order, nor does it acknowledge the possibility of resistance or rebellion on the part of dominated groups (Giroux 1983). In Bourdieu's theory, the prospect of radically altering the educational institution or the system, in general, seems dim, indeed (MacLeod 1987). MacLeod believes that while Bourdieu has incorporated an important cultural element into his theory of reproduction, a necessary corrective to the structural-correspondence theory of Bowles and Gintis, his theory is still too deterministic. To have an adequate theory, "we must appreciate both the importance and the relative autonomy of the cultural level at which individuals, alone or in concert with others, wrest meaning out of the flux of their lives" (ibid., p. 139). Too often, as well, class reproduction theories have ignored the separately lived experiences of women and minority groups, an omission that can seriously limit the theories' ability to understand the habitus of these individuals.

MacLeod's (1987) case study of the conditions and behavior among two groups of adolescent males in a public housing development reveals much about the process by which social positions are reproduced. The "Brothers" are a Black group and the "Hallway Hangers" are White. Over time, the adolescents in these groups develop lower aspirations about their futures. MacLeod's research vividly demonstrates the specific and sometimes different fac-

tors that produce these leveled aspirations. Among the Brothers, for example, there is some evidence that success is possible when they look at the occupations of their siblings. Their parents also believe that conditions have gotten better for Blacks, and thus they encourage their children in their schoolwork. They have been exposed to tenement living for a shorter time, on average, than the Hallway Hangers, and they are antagonistic to the views of the latter group that regards the Blacks with disdain. These conditions lead the Brothers to accept the dominant achievement ideology that opportunity exists and success is possible with the proper effort. What ultimately leads the members of this group to lower their aspirations is a combination of the devaluing of their cultural capital by school officials, lower teacher expectations, tracking, discrimination, and their own self-blame. The school's treatment of them leads to relatively poor performance, and since they subscribe to the achievement ideology which says that it is the individual's own characteristics and efforts that determine how far he or she can get, poor performance leads to self-blame. The combination of self-blame and poor performance results in a lowering of expectations and aspirations. Figure 9.3 outlines the basic processes present in the development of leveled aspirations among the Brothers.

In contrast to the Brothers, the Hallway Hangers do not subscribe to the achievement ideology even though they are White. The conditions of their lives are such that they see little evidence for its validity. Their parents and siblings have not done well even though they are White; their parents believe things are

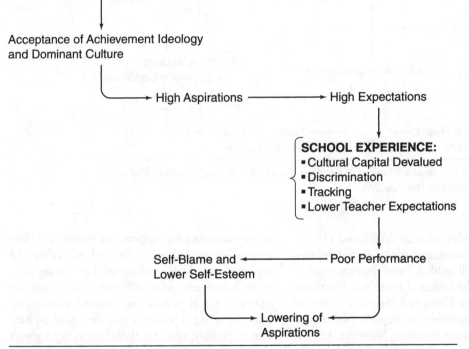

**BACKGROUND
SOCIAL CONDITIONS:**
- Some Evidence of Occupational Success for Siblings
- Significant Others' Support for School and Education
- Some Experience Working
- Shorter Time on Welfare and Less Time in Tenement Living
- Conviction That Discrimination Is Less Than Parents Experienced

Acceptance of Achievement Ideology and Dominant Culture

High Aspirations ──────── High Expectations

SCHOOL EXPERIENCE:
- Cultural Capital Devalued
- Discrimination
- Tracking
- Lower Teacher Expectations

Self-Blame and ◄──── Poor Performance
Lower Self-Esteem

Lowering of ◄──── Aspirations

FIGURE 9.3 Basic Dynamics Involved in Lowering of Aspirations among Brothers
Source: Based on MacLeod 1987, pp. 42ff.

stacked against them; they have lived (or been trapped) in the tenements longer than the Brothers and have a longer history of welfare. They have not seen that education produces many successes in their immediate surroundings. These conditions have bred a feeling of cynicism about the achievement ideology. Their own subculture exerts peer pressure that encourages the rejection of raised aspirations. These experiences and feelings lead to leveled

aspirations and a negative attitude toward school. The latter, in turn, results in poorly rated performance and tracking, which reinforce the leveled aspirations and result in a negative evaluation of them from others. The lowered self-esteem that derives from this negative evaluation leads these adolescents to turn to their own subculture with its own values. But it provides only an imperfect haven from the shame of failure in school, an area highly

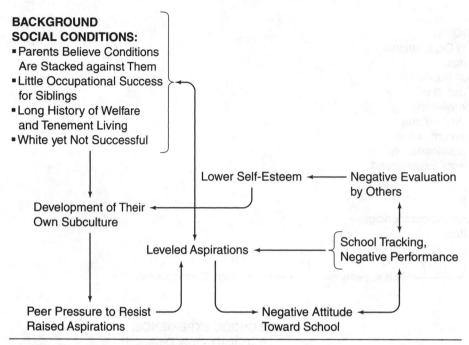

FIGURE 9.4   Basic Dynamics Involved in Leveled Aspirations among Hallway Hangers
Source: Based on MacLeod 1987, pp. 23ff.

valued in the wider society. MacLeod (1987) stated that "the mechanisms of social reproduction" are "well hidden," and thus these adolescents partially blame themselves for their predicament. The Hallway Hangers also resort to racism as a convenient scapegoat. Neither of these interpretations by them, however, results in a full and accurate understanding of their situation or to a radical consciousness on the part of the Hangers. In the last analysis, the conditions that perpetuate their lower class position are repeated. The basic process leading to leveled aspirations among the Hallway Hangers is laid out in Figure 9.4.

LABOR-MARKET THEORIES OF INCOME AND EARNINGS DISTRIBUTION

In contrast to the theories already discussed, labor-market theories of inequality are derived principally from economics and focus narrowly on explanations for income and earnings differences. Some of these are based on rather old explanations of the working of the marketplace, while others are quite different. The treatment that follows is general and aimed at drawing out the core elements of the approaches. Consequently, specific theorists using a given approach may differ on specific elements in the approach. What is immediately appealing about these theories is that they put some meat and teeth into explanations by making the detailed process of inequality more testable. Whereas it might be extremely difficult to satisfactorily test a theory of inequality based on the distribution of sentiments or the functional necessity of inequality, it is possible, for example, to see what the effects of various kinds of human capital investment, such as education and training, are on an individual's earnings.

Most of the theories presented here are principally concerned with explaining poverty and unemployment, but they can easily be used as explanations of the extent of inequality. Each of them focuses on one or another aspect of the labor market in generating inequality.

Neoclassical Labor-Market Theory

This theory is based on several important assumptions: (1) A relatively free and open market exists in which individuals compete for position. (2) Position in that market depends heavily on the individual's efforts, abilities, experience, training, or "human capital." (3) There are automatic mechanisms that operate in the marketplace to ensure that imbalances between one's input (human capital) and one's rewards (wages) are corrected in a way to restore balance.

The ideology of individualism argues that a person should be rewarded to the extent that he or she contributes to the society. In a society in which free competition exists, persons who contribute equal resources in the society receive a wage commensurate with their contributions. The more resources one offers and the greater one's value to any potential employer, the greater the demand for one's services and the higher the wages (Thurow 1969; Leftwich 1977). Thus, factors such as one's education, training, skills, and intelligence are productivity components that are crucial in explaining an individual's wages. These are the elements that must be changed if one's wages are to change (Thurow 1969, p. 26). An extreme version of this argument would assume that individuals are free to choose the amounts of their human capital investments such as education, training, and so on, as well as their occupations. Thus, African Americans and women might be considered to have lower and relatively nonchanging levels of income because they have invested less in education and have less or interrupted work experience (Gordon 1972; Mincer and Polachek 1974). The ultimate result is "that you take out what you put in" (Okun 1975, p. 41). Of course, as we have seen, it often does not work that way.

In addition to one's resources, the demand for one's skills is also important and that demand depends on conditions in the marketplace. Demand for individuals, and therefore their wages, depends on the type of skills they possess and how talented they are at using them. In sum, it is the combination of supply and demand in the market and one's resources (human capital investments) that determines one's wages in the open marketplace (Cain 1976).

If an imbalance develops between what the individuals contribute and the wages they receive, then supply and demand forces are set in motion to restore equilibrium in the market. If the wage is less than is due, the supply becomes smaller, and in the long run the demand for the smaller supply becomes greater. For example, if the perceived crisis in the quality of education in the United States results in the public's raising its view of teachers' contribution to the society, we might expect an upward pressure on their salaries. If greater demand for quality teachers occurs, there should be an increase in the wages employers are willing to pay these workers. In this way, equilibrium is restored. If the opposite occurs—that is, individuals are paid too much for the resource(s) they offer—a large supply of potential workers will appear, too large for the demand for them in the market. In order to ensure getting jobs, they will lower the wages for which they are willing to work. With the lower wages, employment expands, thus leading to a clearing of the labor market and a balancing between supply and demand. Again, equilibrium is restored (Leftwich 1977, p. 76). So, in addition to assuming a competitive market, this approach assumes that automatic mechanisms operate in the market to regulate it toward equilibrium. This tendency toward equilibrium, according to some critics, implies that there is a basic harmony between employers and employees (Gordon 1972, p. 33). Figure 9.5 summarizes the basic elements in the neoclassical explanation of earnings inequality.

Open competitive market

+

Differential free investment in personal human capital

+

Differential supply of and demand for positions

↓

Earnings inequality

FIGURE 9.5   Basic Elements in the Generation of Earnings Inequality according to Neoclassical Theory

If one accepts this argument, then what must be done to reduce earnings inequities is to attack the problems of human capital investment and the choices and returns associated with such investment. Thus, solutions might stress more education and training opportunities as well as accurate and appropriate assessment of individuals' skills and economic payoffs for those skills.

The pure neoclassical model has some distinct limitations, two of which are noted here. First, it is more concerned with wage differentials than with occupational differences and thus is less equipped to deal with sex segregation, for example (Blau and Jusenius 1976). Second, it presents an image of a U.S. economy that is freely competitive and tending toward equilibrium. Like the scarcity and functional-importance factors of the Davis–Moore theory of inequality, this model argues that the level of one's human capital (i.e., how scarce one's talents are) and the demand for them in the market (i.e., their functional necessity) largely determine differences in earnings. Like the kind of society conjured up in the functional approach, Dahrendorf would consider the open, largely conflict-free society of neoclassical theory to be a utopia. It should be mentioned that most economists are aware that the real marketplace does not operate without flaws and imperfections, and that discrimination does limit the opportunities of some in the market.

Dual-Labor Market Thesis

It has become increasingly obvious to some in recent years that explanations of income and earnings distribution that rely on images of the free market and investments in human capital as the primary or sole factors in understanding economic inequalities are inadequate. Critics of the orthodox view say that the market simply does not work the way that pure traditionalists say it does. Rather, the major reasons for inequality lie deep within the workings and cleavages of the capitalist economy.

A number of observations about continuing difficulties in the market have made many analysts skeptical about the orthodox approach and its potential effectiveness in reducing inequality. Among those observations are (1) the continuation of poverty, (2) continued income inequality, (3) the ineffectiveness of educational and training programs in reducing inequality, (4) the use of education as a screening device by employers to procure only culturally acceptable rather than qualified individuals, (5) discrimination against minorities in the labor market, (6) the power of labor unions, employer monopolies, and government intervention to weaken the competitive market, (7) bad attitudes toward work that result from the market itself and not outside the market, and (8) extensive alienation among workers, suggesting that the competitive, equilibrating economy is not working as smoothly as the orthodox model suggests (Cain 1976).

In the face of these alleged anomalies in the economy, some have tried to devise alternate explanations for continued poverty and income inequality. One of the more prominent of these is the dual-labor market approach. Briefly, this thesis consists of four basic elements or assumptions: (1) the private economy is split into two major sectors, (2) the labor market is similarly divided into two parts, (3) mobility, earnings, and other outcomes for workers are contingent on place in the labor market, and (4) a systematic relationship exists between race/ethnicity, gender, and position in the labor market (Hodson and Kaufman 1982).

On observing labor-market processes in the ghetto, a number of economists have come to the conclusion that two markets operating by different rules exist. The poor are members of a separate market that is largely outside the central economy and as such do not participate in the effects of increases in demand, since those demands usually refer only to certain types of occupations. Researchers have found that the kinds of characteristics usually considered as qualifications (such as education) often seem to have little connection with the type of job the person occupies. In effect, some jobs are "race typed" (Reich, Gordon, and Edwards 1977, p. 109). The range of jobs available to minority members, in spite of their qualifications, seems to be quite narrow, and consequently many prefer not to work. In other words, they turn down jobs that are not consistent with their qualifications.

As a result of these observations, more attention has been focused on the kinds of jobs these individuals are actually offered and perform. The tasks seem to be menial, not intellectually demanding, with poor working conditions and low wages. They are isolated and have no internal structures or career system. In other words, they appear to be qualitatively distinct from other kinds of jobs in the market.

Because of the poor nature of the work, workers in this secondary market often quit their jobs, which only encourages the belief that these jobs are unstable, and that performing these types of jobs to the exclusion of others encourages instability in the habits of the workers themselves. This *secondary labor market*, as it has come to be known, is set off from the *primary labor market* in which jobs are characterized by stability, high wages, good working conditions, greater degree of internal job structure, and unionization (Gordon 1972, pp. 43–48).

Within firms in the primary sector, there is an *internal labor market* in which individuals from the outside may enter only at selected points. For example, an outsider may get a job at the bottom of a career ladder in an industrial firm because all other jobs higher up the ladder are being filled from within the firm through promotion. These later jobs are, in effect, protected from outside competition, resulting in a segmentation of the market into competitive and noncompetitive jobs (Doeringer and Piori 1971). Since the skills taught to employees are frequently important, necessary for higher status jobs, and specific to the firm, there will be an attempt by the firm to keep these employees, since training new ones would be costly to the firm. In this protected environment, employees can then work up from the bottom toward the top. In this setting, employees can more easily find security and a lifetime career. Unions also favor the resulting stability for employees, and the employers similarly benefit from retaining trained employees. Given the career system, workers and employers dealing in the primary labor market are less concerned with the perfect balance between earnings and productivity *at a given time* than they are with equity over the long run (ibid.).

By and large, the primary labor market—with its stability, unionization, career systems, and high wages—is limited to a certain sector of the private economy, sometimes called the *core* or *monopoly sector*, whereas the secondary market exists primarily within the *peripheral* or *competitive sector* of the private economy. In the monopoly sector, firms tend to be large, capital intensive, with high productivity per worker, and to possess large, often national and international markets. Examples of firms in this sector would be those in the automobile, railroad, steel, electric, and airlines industries. On the other hand, firms within the competitive sector are much smaller, more labor intensive, with low productivity per worker, more local in their markets, and not in control of any stable product market (O'Connor 1973, pp. 13–16). Examples of firms in this sector would be local restaurants, gas stations, grocery stores, garages, and clothing stores.

Despite the fact that conditions are generally worse for the workers in the secondary market and competitive sector, the tasks performed, though often irregular, are needed in the economy. Consequently, an effort was made historically to stabilize this market and sector; employers worked toward creating a separate market for these workers and these kinds of jobs. Some kinds of workers are in that sector even though they may have the characteristics that would qualify them for work in the primary market. Blacks and women, for example, are usually disproportionately found in the secondary market because of statistical discrimination and other reasons (Gordon 1972, pp. 46–47). Secondary workers were then left with little alternative but to work as part of the secondary labor market in the competitive sector.

The movement toward separate markets has been strengthened by (1) the desirability of retaining individuals who have been carefully trained in large established firms, (2) the presence of unions in some and not other industries, and (3) federal legislation. The trends toward greater job specificity, more on-the-job training in the primary job sector, and the power of custom within given firms have tended to increase the structuring of the internal labor markets within the primary job sector, setting it off more from the unstructured, noncareer patterned secondary job sector (Doeringer and Piori 1971).

Dual-Labor Market and Income Inequality

The existence of segmentation in the U.S. economy, especially in the form of a dual-labor market, helps to perpetuate income inequality and poverty. Generally, there is little intermarket mobility. The market in which individuals are presently working is generally the one in which they began (Gordon 1972, p. 50). Blacks and women are disproportionately found in the lower wage, secondary market and generally do not move up much over their careers. Wolf

(1976) found that women have relatively flat career occupational statuses. She observed that occupations are sex segregated and "we speculate that, at least for most women, these 'women's jobs' are not stepping stones to other more prestigious occupations" (p. 20). Sell and Johnson (1977) also found a great deal of stability in occupational distribution among women across age groups, suggesting that when women leave the labor force, they often reenter the same types of jobs. They also found that changes in the occupational distribution were slight at best during the period from 1960 to 1970 (pp. 10–12). Wolf's research further indicates that contrary to what might be expected, it is not the interruptions in employment ("career contingencies") that primarily account for the occupational attainment of women. Rather, as we observed in an earlier chapter, women simply do not get the same kinds of jobs as men, even when their qualifications are similar.

Figure 9.6 brings together several of the core elements of the dual-labor market argument on the factors that produce earnings inequality. Notice that in sharp contrast with the neoclassical explanation that stresses the characteristics of *persons*, the dual-labor market theory focuses on the importance of *impersonal* labor markets and economic sectors in producing inequality.

Being in either the secondary or primary labor market has an initial impact on an individual's wages. As already mentioned, jobs in the secondary market generally have lower wages than those associated with the primary market. But once in either the secondary or primary market, the determinants of earnings vary. In the primary market, earnings are affected by seniority and whether a person is in a career job hierarchy. O'Connor (1973) stressed that in the monopoly sector, wages and prices are not primarily determined by market forces; prices are largely administered since the corporations in this sector usually have considerable market power. With respect to wages,

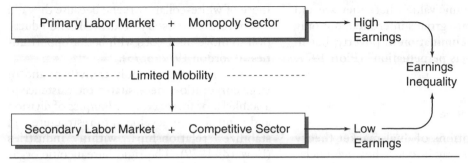

FIGURE 9.6   The Effect of the Dual Private Economy on Earnings

when the demand for labor is low and the supply is large, monopoly industries, because of their attractiveness to workers, can choose from the oversupply at the going rate. In this way, they have an advantage over competitive industries. When labor is in demand, union power, pattern bargaining, and productivity have major impacts on wages and wage movements. But many of the wage increases in the monopoly sector do not trickle down to workers in the competitive sector, which results in a further bifurcation of the working class (ibid., pp. 19–22).

In the competitive sector—that is, for most of those in the secondary labor market—wages are largely determined by market forces. Since the workers in this market are generally considered homogeneous in nature and have little, if any, union power, their wages are primarily the product of supply and demand forces. If the supply of labor is particularly small and the demand consequently high, their earnings are likely to go up because they will work more. Thus, the differences in earnings among those in the secondary labor market are probably due more to differences in the hours worked than to other factors. But because of the homogeneous nature of the work force in this market, wage differences are not likely to be great (Gordon 1972, pp. 50–51). Moreover, in the competitive sector, the raging competition among firms and the poorer and more unstable economic environment in which they operate often mean that they are less able to raise wages

compared with the large firms in the monopoly sector that are relatively free from the extremes of competition (Bluestone 1977).

Osterman's (1975) analysis of a national sample of male workers bears out the hypothesis that the determinants of earnings vary with the labor market in question. His results indeed show that earnings in the secondary market are tied significantly to the numbers of hours worked, with neither experience, race, nor education being important. This supports the view that workers in this market are seen as being interchangeable. In the higher-ranking jobs in the primary market, education, age, and hours worked are important, whereas in the lower tier in the primary market, education is important although less so than in the higher jobs. Age and hours worked are also significant for the lower-ranking jobs in the primary market, as is race. In sum, the human capital argument seems much more viable in the primary than in the secondary market. Osterman's conclusion is that "an individual's income is greatly affected by the segment of the labor market in which the individual works" (ibid., p. 21).

In applying the dual-market theory to poverty, the central conclusion is that many individuals are poor not because they are unemployed or do not participate in the economy but because of the way in which they participate in the economy. Not only are they *excluded* from certain kinds of activities and organizations, they are *included* in the economic structure at particular places because "they have economic value where they are and hence . . . there are groups interested, not only in resisting the elimination of poverty, but in actively seeking its perpetuation" (Piori 1977, pp. 95–96).

Radical Perspective

Many of the notions of dual-market theory have found their way into a radical denunciation of orthodox theory. Basically, the radical argument is that capitalists have found it beneficial to segment the labor market and to stratify the working class so as to prevent its unification and to stabilize the labor market. In this view, if we are to understand the creation of poverty and a particular income distribution, we must understand the historical development and conditions that underlay such distributions.

During the late nineteenth century, the U.S. labor force was becoming increasingly homogeneous and proletarianized; having been herded into factories, the separate craft talents became merged into a mass of semiskilled jobs. The potential threat of a unified working class, especially given the increasing evidence of their militancy, had to be met by employers. To deal with this problem, argued Reich and associates (1977), employers actively promoted labor-market segmentation in order to effectively split up what might otherwise have been a unified work force.

If employers could successfully stratify the working class, it would not only splinter its unity but also, if it could be legitimized, ensure that less desirable (secondary) jobs could be filled. As the clusters of workers were separated from each other, each would develop his or her own habits and lifestyles consistent with the kinds of jobs performed. The result would be stability in the labor market for the capitalist class. "To the extent that employers could accomplish this stratification, it became more likely that blue-collar workers would accept their poorer working conditions (relative to

those of white-collar workers) because they did not have the necessary credentials and education to move on to jobs with better opportunities" (Gordon 1972, p. 73).

The rise of monopoly capitalism and of large corporations necessitated the existence of a stable labor force. New techniques of division and control were developed to restructure and stabilize relationships within industries (Edwards 1979). The rigid bureaucratic organization of firms served this purpose admirably. The clear and minute division of labor and hierarchy of authority associated with this form of organization encouraged the development of an internal labor structure of the kind discussed earlier. Education increasingly became a means of justifying division of the workers, since it became a regularized credential for obtaining certain jobs (Reich, Gordon, and Edwards 1977, p. 111). Those most readily looked down on by unions and the public—namely, women, Blacks, and youth—could more easily be used to fill less-desirable jobs. Stereotypes and dislikes of these groups were used to further segment the labor market (ibid.).

Alongside the conscious efforts of employers to segment the labor market were systemic forces that furthered the segmentation. Racism was and is used to strengthen the hold of employers by weakening the bargaining power of the working class. The result is lower incomes for both Blacks and the White working class and higher profits for the capitalists (ibid., p. 185). Evidence does suggest that White workers do not gain from racism against Blacks but lose while capitalists gain; even income inequality between White capitalists and workers is increased when racism is present (Reich, Gordon, and Edwards 1977). Racism also benefits capitalists by preventing or at least forestalling the unification of Black and White workers into strong and more broadly based unions. Research on the period between World War I and the New Deal indicates that employers fought White worker gains by using available

Blacks as strikebreakers and in place of White workers. This served to help split the working class along racial lines (Bonacich 1976).

As different industrial organizations grew, historically, they advanced at different rates, and a fundamental division developed between them. In one sector were the large, monopoly, capital-intensive, technologically advanced, high-profit, and growth industries, whereas in the other were the more competitive, smaller, lower profit, more labor-intensive organizations. The large organizations required a stable labor force, given their continuous and ongoing production. This sector could not handle, to its benefit, those areas where the work was seasonal or otherwise erratic. Production of those goods and services in which the demand was unstable demanded a certain kind of labor and was subcontracted or exported to the smaller, more competitive firms. Thus, each sector demanded and evolved specific kinds of labor forces—namely, the primary and secondary labor markets—just as the dual-labor market thesis suggested (Reich, Gordon, and Edwards 1977, p. 111). The overall result of this segmentation process has been the segmentation of the economy into monopoly and competitive sectors, segmentation of primary and secondary markets, segmentation within the primary sector into routine and creative jobs, and segmentation by race and sex (ibid., pp. 108–109).

The existence of segmentation of various types in the labor force has been widely accepted, although the dimensions along which that segmentation takes place have not always been agreed on (Osterman 1975). Results reported in Chapters 5 and 7 show Black/White and male/female differences in occupational allocation. Blacks are still underrepresented in the high-reward occupations that involve the exercise of authority, domination by Whites, and/or equal-status contact with customers. But they are overrepresented in lower-status occupations even though some improvement has apparently occurred in recent years.

Gordon (1972, p. 78) suggested that employers will continue to find it beneficial to fill secondary-market jobs with members of minority groups since (1) they are easily distinguishable physically and have been discriminated against before; (2) more than other groups, they have become more resigned to such jobs; and (3) they are least likely to identify with nonminority groups and unite with them against the capitalists. Such segmentation certainly appears to perform certain functions for capitalists. Reich and associates (1977) outlined three of these:

1. It divides the workers and thus prevents unified movements against employers.
2. It establishes qualitative breaks across job hierarchies through the creation of different sets of criteria for access, thereby discouraging mobility aspirations among workers.
3. The division of workers legitimizes the differences in authority between superior and subordinate position holders (p. 112).

Assessment of Labor-Market Theories

In assessing these labor-market theories, it is clear that there are inadequacies in the orthodox explanations, but given the lack of a fully embellished theoretical system by radical theorists, it is not clear how powerful their explanations of occupational and income inequality really are. In fact, perhaps the most valuable contribution of the dual-labor market approach to understanding economic inequality is its emphasis on a textured economy and labor market—that is, on its insistence that these are not homogeneous in nature and that this texture affects rewards for workers (Hodson and Kaufman 1982). The orthodox approach is most likely to be acceptable when it incorporates some of the elements of dual-labor market theory and information about imperfections in the market. Some evidence appears to support radical arguments, as was indicated in our discussion, whereas other critics (e.g., Cain 1976) do not see it as being able to replace orthodox theory. The support for the viability of the radical perspective is clearly split.

Dual-market theory has its evident weaknesses. Within broad sectors, there is a large variety of firms. How are differences among them to be explained? For example, the dual-market theory does not explain differences and sex segregation within each market and differentiation within the female sector (Blau and Jusenius 1976, p. 197). Moreover, within each sector of the economy, there are firms that cater to both the primary and secondary labor markets. Evidence suggests that the tight link assumed by the approach between the primary labor market and core sector on the one hand, and the secondary labor market and peripheral sector on the other, is much looser than suggested by the model. Moreover, the assumption that African Americans and women are concentrated in the peripheral sector is also questionable (Kaufman and Daymont 1981; Wallace and Kalleberg 1981; Hodson and Kaufman 1982). The theory has also been said to be largely of a descriptive rather than explanatory nature, and its concepts to have been improperly measured (Hodson and Kaufman 1982). Finally, splitting the private economy into two parts results in too coarse an image of the real economy within which there are continuous variations among organizations along a variety of dimensions (Baron and Bielby 1984; Hodson 1984).

Splitting the economy and labor market into dichotomous sections ignores changes occurring *within* the national and *between* international economies. As U.S. corporations increasingly enter a world market involving highly competitive adversaries who may also enter the U.S. market, they have reacted by downsizing and streamlining, which has meant lower job stability for many employees. In a sense, what may have been a monopoly sector becomes more competitive, and those employed in those organizations become more vulnerable to fluctuations in economies. In essence, the primary job market takes on some of the characteristics traditionally associated with the secondary market: lower wages, lower job stability, and less unionization. This blurs the distinctions between monopoly/competitive sectors and primary/secondary markets. Further blurring the distinctions in dual markets and sectors is the fact that given firms can contain core *and* peripheral, primary *and* secondary characteristics (Parcel and Sickmeier 1988). In addition, the recent influx of small, entrepreneurial firms into the economy also makes a dual-market perspective appear to be too crude to capture the richer and changing texture of the U.S. economy. Despite weaknesses, however, the dual-market and radical perspectives have properly forced us to address the role of market and economy variations in generating inequality.

THE RECENT FOCUS ON PROCESS IDENTIFICATION

Traditionally, most dominant sociological theories have placed social structure, culture, and similar "social facts" at the center of their arguments. That is, they have tended to focus on the larger, macroworld around us as the principal source for our individual fates and behaviors. There has also been an inclination by theorists to look at inequality on a broad social level rather than to focus on a more fine-grained analysis of the changes occurring *within* occupational groups or classes. But as Myles succinctly puts it: "The aim of the exercise is still to explain who gets what and why" (Myles 2003, p. 556).

In the last several years, there has been a renewed effort to reintroduce the importance of the individual and everyday experience for understanding the mechanisms through which inequalities are created and maintained. Broad theories, part of the argument goes, do not help us understand the everyday inequalities between different individuals who live in unique situations. In traditional theories, "[w]e see an abstract scaffolding of hierarchy manifested in a shell of objective-looking quantitative data. Does this image of fixed, objective hierarchy come to grips with the realities of lived experience?" (Collins 2000, p. 17). Collins contends that these broad, macro theories have to be grounded in more immediate, interpersonal analyses of specific situations and relationships. Social status and deference, for example, operate in a variety of settings (work, church, informal situations, etc.) and may vary in these settings. Situations also change. We need to know more about how inequality operates at the level of the individual life. A renewed focus on the microlevel of the individual is important because historical changes have made the personal, private, and situational aspects of life more prominent today (Collins 2000).

Part of the interest in examining the dynamics of inequality in everyday life is related to a larger concern for understanding the active, real processes by which inequality is generated. How, specifically, are social and economic inequality created? The explanations surveyed in the last and this chapter provide possible general answers to that question. A few more recent attempts have tried to tease out more of the "nitty-gritty" processes involved in the development and maintenance of structures of inequality. They resonate with earlier and previously mentioned undertakings to *ground* theory, such as Omi and Winant's (2005) analysis of how racial categories are actually formed in historical context, for example, and West and Zimmerman's (1987) discussion of how individuals "do gender" in their everyday lives. Among these recent discussions are those by Charles Tilly (1998, 2003) and Roger Gould (2002).

In his model of status hierarchies, Gould argues that hierarchies are produced and reproduced through decentralized, emergent processes. The judgments that individuals make about the qualities possessed by others are "socially influenced." This social influence, in turn, magnifies the differences in perceived qualities between individuals, with higher-status persons being "overvalued" and those of lower status "undervalued." The magnification of differences allows others to follow through with their own judgments of themselves and others. "The status of public figures, then, is the respect accorded to them by each observer *just because* they are accorded respect by everyone else" (Gould 2002, p. 1147, emphasis in original). This legitimizes and helps to stabilize the different status evaluations individuals receive. At the same time, however, individuals will moderate the status they attribute to others depending on the extent to which they themselves receive attention or status from those others. If the demand for reciprocity in attention is pervasive, status inequality can be minimal. In this way, Gould's theory of status hierarchies demonstrates the importance of the social context in which such inequality is created.

One of the most detailed, grounded, and recent explanations of inequality comes from Charles Tilly. Like Gould and others, Tilly is interested in identifying the exact mechanisms that generate and maintain structures of inequality. He cites two mechanisms that produce "durable" inequality, *exploitation* and *opportunity hoarding* (1998, 2003). Inequality becomes established when individuals use their resources to extract something of value (e.g., resources, labor) from others (i.e., exploitation), or when they deprive the access of other groups or categories of people to valued resources (i.e., opportunity hoarding). Among other things, "valued resources" include weapons, labor, land, machines, capital, knowledge, and media control, that is, those items that provide their owner with power over others.

In opportunity hoarding, which categories are selected for exclusion may be determined in part by social categories already existing in the wider society, for example, those involving gender or race. These categories may be borrowed for use in specific situations or organizations, as in the instance when socially defined gender roles are extended to work positions in a corporation. Means that are effective in maintaining dominance over women at home, for example, may be used in the workplace as well. Or racial categories and meanings associated with them may be used to keep Blacks or other minorities out of certain establishments (e.g., Jim Crow laws). This process of borrowing categories from other spheres of life is what Tilly refers to as *emulation*.

Use of such preexisting categories can serve to clarify, justify, and maintain unequal arrangements in the work setting. As with other classifications, social categories of groups simplify relationships among individuals at the same time that they often function to rank them. "Categories matter. . . . categories facilitate unequal treatment by both members and outsiders. . . . The [c]ategories that matter most for durable inequality, however, involve both mutual awareness and connectedness; we know who they are, they know who we are, on each side of that line people interact with each other, and across the line we interact with them—but differently" (Tilly 2003, p. 33). Categories and the meanings attached to them come and go, as we saw with historical shifts in racial classifications. How they come about and change depends heavily on the nature of the contact and interactions between the groups involved.

Adaptation also aids in the maintenance of inequality (Tilly 2003). For example, in his study of total institutions, Goffman (1961) noted that one way inmates or residents adjusted to their controlled position was by becoming "model" inmates or residents, that is, by adjusting to and even accepting the role expected of them. Like emulation, such adaptation helps to sustain hierarchical arrangements. The four mechanisms of exploitation, opportunity hoarding, emulation, and adaptation along with the systematic use of social categories aid in the explanation of inequality structures and their durable nature. As a group, the ventures into identifying processes and mechanisms that create and maintain social inequality are all attempts to clarify the specific and concrete forces that underlie systems of inequality. In her 2002 Presidential Address to the American Sociological Association, Barbara Reskin urged theorists of inequality to focus on *how* rather than *why* inequality is produced by identifying the individual, interpersonal, organizational, and societal mechanisms that shape the structure of inequality (Reskin 2002). The theories just discussed are part of that project.

SUMMARY

The focus in this and the previous chapter has been on general explanations of inequality. Each of the theories covered views the concept of inequality in a different way and is suggestive of different measures of it. Nevertheless, all of them are concerned with the distribution of scarce resources in society, principally political power, economic power, or both. One of the primary values in looking at the classic theorists is that each of them suggests different ways of viewing inequality and makes us sensitive to different aspects of it.

Several of the theories covered in this and the previous chapter have basic elements in common. Most generally, one can see the influence of Marxian thought in social reproduction theory and radical labor-market theory. On the more conservative side, Durkheim's functionalist tradition has been carried through most fully in neoclassical economic theory and the Davis–Moore theory.

All of these theories organize the phenomenon in diverse ways and evoke different images of how the society is to be seen. Some of these, such as the functionalist and labor-market theories, assume a society that is largely free, competitive, and lacking in organized constraints and conflict, while others, most notably social reproduction and dual-labor market theories, view society as consisting of constraining structures and systemic conflict between groups. Because this is so, each of the theories provides us with alternative tools and concepts with which to approach the study of inequality; together, they anticipate the kinds of questions and issues that significantly can be raised about inequality. Each of the theories covered has been primarily concerned with answering the question: How do we explain the existence of inequality, the shape that it takes, and its perpetuation? Indirectly, several devote some attention to a second question of how given individuals become placed in positions in the system of inequality.

Newer developments have emphasized identifying specific mechanisms that account for the development and maintenance of social and economic inequality. These are part of a broader movement to strengthen and fine-tune explanations of inequality that closely consider the specific historical situations of groups and lived experiences of individuals.

CRITICAL THINKING

1. What is wrong with an argument that simply says that rewards, in fact, reflect one's skills and credentials as well as the importance of one's job?

2. If our actions and behaviors serve largely to reproduce the conditions in which we live, how can change in inequality ever occur?

3. How do we know how to rank people in positions? From where or whom do our ideas come?

4. If we "socially construct" gender, race, and class, does this mean that they are not "real"? Are there any hard, concrete realities underlying their construction?

WEB CONNECTIONS

As suggested in this chapter, Pierre Bourdieu is one of the most influential social-reproduction theorists. A summary of his ideas can be found at: http://wikipedia.org/wiki/Pierre_Bourdieu.

10 The Impact of Inequality on Personal Life Chances

There is something about poverty that smells like death. Dead dreams dropping off the heart like leaves in a dry season and rotting around the feet; impulses smothered too long in the fetid air of underground caves. The soul lives in a sickly air.

—Zora Neale Hurston

To go from the bottom 20 percent to the top 20 percent is to enter a magical world where needs are met, problems are solved, almost without any intermediate effort.

—Barbara Ehrenreich

There would not be much point in studying inequality if it had few implications for people. Inequality is an important subject because, ultimately, its existence affects the day-to-day lives of people. The social positions that individuals occupy help to determine who they are, what they think and do, and where they are going. Close your eyes for a moment and imagine yourself as a very poor or extremely wealthy person. What do you see? As a person in either position, how do you feel about life in general and yourself in particular? How do you view the future and your prospects? How do you account for the position you are in?

Most basically, social inequality affects the life chances of individuals. But as Figure 10.1 suggests, its effects are far-reaching, reverberating outward from individuals themselves to their immediate families and the wider society. Chapter 11 will address some aspects of the *social* effects of inequality, beginning with a discussion of its relationship to abuse within families and

proceeding to examination of the broader issues of crime, protests, and environmental justice. The present chapter will focus on the relationship of inequality to *individuals'* chances for physical and mental health, adequate food, and shelter. More specifically, we will see how socioeconomic status, gender, and/or minority status affect personal lives at their most basic level.

BASIC LIFE CHANCES: PHYSICAL HEALTH

There is nothing more basic to life than physical health, and it is evident that individuals rate their own health status differently, depending on their race and income. Generally, Blacks, and Hispanics are more likely than Whites to rate their own health as only fair or poor, and individuals who are poor are more than 3 times as likely as nonpoor persons to consider their health this way. Finally, a slightly greater percentage of women than men classify their health as below average (see Figure 10.2).

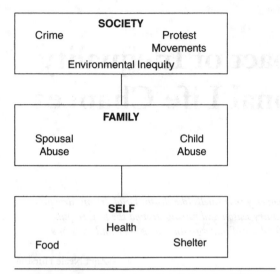

FIGURE 10.1 A Sampling of the Range of Effects of Social Inequality

Interestingly, this self-assessment is a good predictor of a person's actual health, and, indeed, individuals in lower-status categories are worse off on virtually all fundamental health measures (National Center for Health Statistics 2004).

The life expectancies at birth of Blacks and Whites, males and females, have varied historically, and these differences are expected to continue in the twenty-first century. In 2002, average life expectancy for all Americans was over 77 years, which is comparable to that found in the United Kingdom and France, but slightly lower than the life expectancies in Italy, Canada, and the Netherlands. The life expectancy of Whites at birth was more than 5 years longer than that of Blacks, and within each racial group, those with lower incomes lived a shorter time. In 1996, a middle-aged, White man with an income of at least $25,000, for example, could expect to live 6 to 7 years longer than a similar man with an income of under $10,000. Generally, women live longer than men, but the life expectancy of Black women is closer to that of White men than to White women (ibid.).

Differences in mortality rates parallel the discrepancies in life expectancies, and the differences between socioeconomic groups are especially strong among *urban* residents (Hayward, Pienta, and McLaughlin 1997). Moreover, it is not only differences in income that affect mortality, but the kind and variety in sources of income that have an impact. Individuals with assets and income from a variety of sources have lower mortality risks. This may be due in large part to the greater sense of

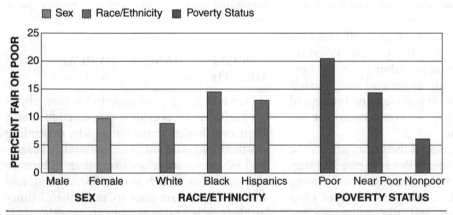

FIGURE 10.2 Percent of Respondents Assessing Health Status as Fair or Poor, by Sex, Race/Ethnicity, and Poverty Status: 2002

Source: U.S. Department of Health and Human Services, *Health, United States, 2004* (Hyattsville, MD: National Center for Health Statistics, 2004), Table 57, p. 217.

stability that is gained from having a secure economic base (Krueger et al. 2003). It identifies another advantage held by those who are wealthy over those who are not.

Mortality rates from different causes also vary by status. Although heart diseases and cancer are the leading causes of death among all groups, the rates are significantly higher for Blacks than for Whites, and the years of life lost to these chronic diseases are also greater for Blacks. Death rates from all causes for those with less than a high school education are much higher than those found among higher educated individuals. This holds for both men and women, although men in general tend to have higher mortality rates regardless of the cause (National Center for Health Statistics 2004).

Status differences in mortality rates extend to children as well. The infant mortality rate among children of Black mothers, for example, is more than twice that of White children. The rate for Hispanic children is lower than it is for either of these groups. For all groups, children of mothers with lower education have higher infant mortality rates. In 2001, the greatest discrepancy in rates existed between White children whose mothers had more than a high school education and Black children whose mothers did not have a high school education (4.3 vs. 14.5) (ibid.).

Health Conditions

The higher mortality rates of lower-status individuals in the United States are related to the generally higher morbidity rates, greater exposure to victimization, and lower rates of preventive care they experience during their lifetimes. "Racial and ethnic disparities for many diseases, health conditions, and outcomes persist in the United States despite economic progress and reduced disparities in health insurance coverage" (Headen, Jr., Manton, and Woodbury 2004). For example, in 2003, the rate of AIDS among Black men was 8 times that of White men; the racial differences were even greater among women. Rates of hypertension and diabetes are higher among minorities, but differences in cancer rates depend on the cancer type. Obesity rates are also generally higher among minorities, especially women. Overall and compared to Whites or the nonpoor, greater proportions of Blacks, Hispanics, and poor persons are limited in their daily activities because of chronic health problems. They also tend to have longer stays when in the hospital. Victimization also plays a role in racial differences in mortality rates. Black men are 9 times and Hispanic men are almost 4 times as likely as White men to be victims of homocide.

The findings of a recent study of almost 7,000 adults over a 15-year period show that the health of Blacks deteriorates more rapidly than that of Whites over time, and that Blacks more often than Whites increasingly view their health as poorer as they get older (Ferraro and Farmer 1996). By both objective and subjective standards, the health of Blacks declines more dramatically with age. A recent study of 8,231 Black and White respondents found that middle-aged Blacks have significantly higher rates than their White counterparts of both fatal chronic (e.g., hypertension, diabetes, stroke) and nonfatal (e.g., asthma, foot/leg, kidney, ulcers, vision, depression) diseases. The poor health disproportionately experienced by Blacks is a continuation of racial differences in health that exist all along the life cycle. Moreover, it appears that it is mostly these racial groups' differing socioeconomic positions (which are heavily linked to their race) that account for their differences in health (Hayward et al. 2000). Proportionately, Blacks lose about twice as many years of life before age 65 as Whites because of chronic conditions. Of those born in 1940, only about 61 percent of Black males were still alive in 1990, compared to 81 percent of White males. Similar discrepancies existed among females.

All these findings make it clear that health is related to *individual* socioeconomic status. But what is also interesting is that the health of individuals also appears to be related to the socioeconomic status of the *community* as a whole and to the degree of income inequality in a *society*, independent of the effects of one's *individual* status. Communities with lower average incomes and higher unemployment rates report higher rates of chronic conditions (Robert 1998). The physical deterioration and social disorder found in poorer neighborhoods, along with the fear that they create, play significant roles in the poorer self-assessments of health and higher rates of chronic disease conditions found among their residents (Ross and Mirowsky 2001). Frustration as a factor in health may be manifested in the finding that greater income and occupational inequality in a metropolitan area is related to higher suicide rates among Blacks in the United States (Burr, Hartman, and Matteson 1999). Keep in mind that the effects of inequality just discussed are independent of those found for differences in socioeconomic status among individuals.

In sum, there have been and continue to be distinct gaps in the health statuses of Blacks and Whites and between those in different socioeconomic groups, and the gap appears to have widened in recent years. This widening reflects not only health gains for those in higher-ranking groups but also simultaneous declines in the health status in lower-status groups. The recent increase in economic inequality, which has already been documented, is a major force behind the growing discrepancies in health status. Economic inequalities appear to be causally related to differences in mortality rates *among* countries and to discrepancies in health statuses among groups *within* countries (Williams and Collins 1995).

Gender is also related to differences in health, but we know less about the factors related to women's health because most medical research has focused on men (Andersen 1997). Although men have higher mortality rates, women have higher rates of disability, of acute conditions such as respiratory, infective, and digestive problems, and of most chronic conditions. Women over the age of 70 are more likely than older men to report difficulty in their daily activities. Their rates of acute conditions are typically 20 to 30 percent higher than those of men. Among chronic conditions, the rates for *nonfatal* varieties are especially higher for women. These include various digestive problems, anemias, arthritis, migraine headaches, urinary infections, and varicose veins. The rates for fatal chronic conditions are higher for men. In 2003, the AIDS rate, for example, was about three times higher among males than among females over 12 years of age (National Center for Health Statistics 2004).

Verbrugge (1999) suggested that important reasons for these gender discrepancies are differences in risks associated with work and leisure, consistent health care, lifestyles and role behaviors of men and women, and the fact that women are more likely to report symptoms and pursue medical help. Women tend to engage in healthier lifestyles and seek more preventive care than men. Women are also more attentive to their bodies and therefore more sensitive to symptoms. They take more continuous care of their health problems than men do. Finally, women are better at reporting minor health problems and this might help minimize the seriousness of those problems later in life and help account for their higher life expectancy. Traditionally in U.S. society, men are supposed to be "strong and silent." But this may work against them. Biological differences are also involved, but are probably less important than other factors. It is expected that gender differences in health will diminish in the twenty-first century as gender differences in exposure to risk factors also diminish (ibid.).

Employment conditions also appear to affect the differential health statuses of men and women. Even when their initial health is the same, women become healthier and have fewer physical limitations the longer and more continuously they are employed than women who are either intermittently employed or not in the labor force. Those who are recently non-employed are the least healthy (Anson and Anson 1987; Pavalko and Smith 1999). In addition to employment itself, the number of work hours also affects health among men. Working more than 40 hours per week has a positive impact on their health, but when their wives work longer than 40 hours per week, the husbands' health suffers. In contrast, long work hours by their husbands do not harm wives' health, nor does the number of their own work hours affect their health (Stolzenberg 2001).

Finally, increases in earnings are positively related to health, but the effects of increases in *spousal* earnings appear to be different for men and women. A national longitudinal study suggests that, among married couples, an increase in wives' earnings raises the chances of husbands dying, whereas the reverse was found for wives when husbands' earnings increase (McDonough et al. 1999). These results on the effects of work hours and earnings on health suggest that men are most likely to suffer when their wives become more involved and success-ful in the world of work, a sphere which, tradi-tionally, has been more of a man's province.

Use of Health Services

Given the differences in health conditions between groups, one would expect to find par-allel differences in the preventive use of physi-cians and other health care providers. There is little disagreement that there are significant differences in the quality of care received by nonpoor Whites on the one hand, and the poor and minorities on the other (Institute of Medicine 2002; Good et al. 2003; Schnittker, Pescosolido, and Croghan 2005). Indeed, Black and Hispanic mothers are less likely to have had a pap smear in the last year, and less likely to have had prenatal care when pregnant, but

more likely to die during pregnancy or while giving birth. Minorities and the poor are less likely to have a family physician that they see on a regular basis, and are less likely to have visited a physician's office in the last year. Poor children are also less likely to have received a full set of vaccinations. Unmet dental needs are more likely among the poor and minorities (National Center for Health Statistics 2004). Among the consequences of lower rates of pre-ventive care among the poor and minorities are greater numbers of emergency-room visits and higher rates of hospitalizations that might have been avoided had preventive care been taken.

There is no widespread agreement on a single reason as to why the poor and minorities receive less than adequate health care. Perhaps it is simply that those in lower socioeconomic positions choose not to seek care for their health problems. This does not appear to be the case, however. A national study found that, regardless of income or education, Blacks are no less likely to seek care than Whites, and may be even more inclined to do so. Nor do they expect less benefit from modern medicine. Disparities in care may result from a confluence of patient and physician expectations, beliefs, and behaviors (Schnittker, Pescosolido, and Croghan 2005). In their 2002 review of more than 100 studies, researchers at the Institute of Medicine also concluded that while patient atti-tudes do not appear to be a major factor, "research suggests that healthcare providers' diagnostic and treatment decisions, as well as their feelings about patients, are influenced by patients' race or ethnicity" (Institute of Medicine 2002, p. 4). A 2004 Gallup poll rein-forced this position, finding that 38 percent of Blacks felt that they were treated unfairly by physicians and health care facilities. Twenty-eight percent of Hispanics but only 17 percent of Whites agreed (McMurray 2004).

The argument that differences in care may be linked to beliefs and expectations held by health care professionals suggests a need for more research on the "culture of medicine."

Most of the attention has been on patient attitudes rather than on professionals' culture. For example, it has been suggested that the interpretation of symptoms by patients varies by race, and that this may affect whether or not health care is sought (Cockerham et al. 1986). But service involves both patient and physician. Stereotypes and general beliefs about racial and ethnic minorities and the poor held by physicians can affect diagnosis and treatment of patients. These orientations, in turn, have their source in racist ideologies that are widely dispersed in the larger society (Institute of Medicine 2002; Good et al. 2003). Despite the potential importance of cultural factors, however, it is most likely that a full explanation of disparities in health care service involves multiple causes.

Other explanations offered for disparities in health care treatment include lack of access and affordability. Kirby and Kaneda found that access to health care was negatively affected by

living in a neighborhood where a disproportionate number of residents were poor, unemployed, and poorly educated. They speculate that such neighborhoods may create fear in residents, receive worse city services than others, and not be attractive to health care providers (2005). Access to effective care may also be compromised by the difficulties that minority physicians have in arranging appropriate care for their patients (Hargraves, Stoddard, and Trude 2001).

High health care costs may also make doctor visits and other services too expensive for many, especially if they do not have health insurance. In 2003, almost 45 million persons were without health insurance coverage of any kind. Almost one-fifth of these were children or youth under 18 years old. Not unexpectedly, minority persons and those lower in socioeconomic status were more likely to be uninsured (see Figure 10.3). In 2002, about one-third of

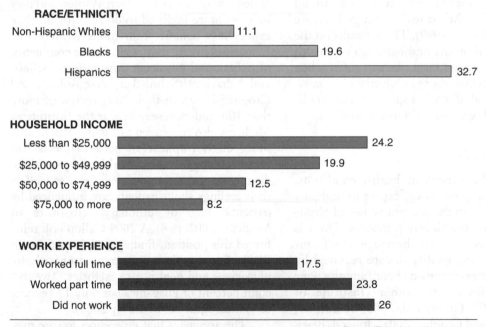

FIGURE 10.3   Percent of Persons Without Health Insurance, by Race/Ethnicity, Income, and Work Experience: 2003

Source: U.S. Census Bureau, *Income, Poverty, and Health Insurance Coverage in the United States: 2003*, Current Population Reports, Series P-60, No. 226, August 2004, Table 5, p. 15.

people in families with incomes below $10,000 compared to only 8 percent in families with incomes over $50,000 were without health insurance ("Providing Health Insurance" 2003–2004). Lack of insurance means that a greater proportion of health care costs have to be borne by private individuals. In the late 1990s, for example, it was estimated that low-income elderly Medicare beneficiaries spent about half of their own incomes on health care (Gross et al. 1999). The controversy about U.S. citizens getting their drugs from Canada because of their lower price indicates the financial strain that health care costs place on persons who have chronic problems.

In addition to racial and socioeconomic disparities, differential treatment is also affected by sex and gender. "When a woman seeks medical care from a physician, there are seventy-eight chances out of one hundred that the person she sees will be a man" (Andersen 1997, p. 216). Doctors tend to bring in their expectations about gender roles and behaviors into their beliefs about health and illness. Male doctors often see illness and complaints among women as having a psychological rather than physiological origin. This suggests that women are not taken as seriously as men who come in with health problems (Andersen 1993).

The negative image of women's bodies and sexist beliefs about women's nature have a long history. In the nineteenth and early twentieth centuries, the female body was considered abnormal compared to the male body. Pregnancies, menstruation, menopause, and similar natural biological events were considered conditions to be "treated" and physicians generally thought that it was in women's nature to be sick (Ehrenreich and English 1981; Rothman 1984). The ovaries and uterus were thought by male physicians to be the absolute core of the female body. Thus, the womb often was viewed as the source for many ailments suffered by women (Ehrenreich and English 1981). At the same time, women were encouraged to develop their "maternal

instincts" and were not believed to have a sex drive as strong as men.

Because of their greater economic and organizational resources, male obstetricians successfully competed against midwives in the delivery of children, enabling them to gain control of a whole area of women's lives (Wertz and Wertz 1981). A captive group of female patients not only provided fees at a time when the number of clientele was dwindling but also their bodies provided "teaching material" for budding male physicians (Rothman 1984, pp. 72–73). Many of these attitudes still survive. An analysis of 27 general gynecology textbooks published since 1943 in the United States revealed that at least 50 percent of them emphasize that women are "destined to reproduce, nurture, and keep their husbands happy" (Scully and Bart 1981, p. 350). Many of these same texts also stress that women's primary interest in sex is for "procreation" rather than "recreation" and that most females are "frigid." The authors of this study concluded: "Gynecologists, our society's official experts on women, think of themselves as the woman's friend. With friends like that, who needs enemies?" (ibid., p. 354).

Class differences also have surfaced in the images of women's health and bodies. Historically, women of the upper class were thought to be more "civilized" and refined than those in the working and lower classes. As a result, they were thought of as more fragile and vulnerable, more susceptible to various maladies. Ehrenreich and English suggested that much of their sickness may have been due to the "sexuo-economic" relationship in their marriages (1981). Essentially, these women were viewed as providing sexual and reproductive services in exchange for economic support from their working husbands. The ill-fitting, heavy clothes expected to be worn by "ladies" of the upper class were responsible, in fact, for many of the illness symptoms experience by these women. But as a consequence of these "health" problems, middle- and upper-class women became a "client caste" to physicians, while poor women received virtually no medical attention. African American, American Indian, and working-class women were seen as being hearty of constitution in contrast to their upper-class counterparts and, therefore, in need of less attention. This stereotype provided a convenient rationale for giving medical care to those who had the financial resources to pay for it (Ehrenreich and English 1981; Wertz and Wertz 1981).

BASIC LIFE CHANCES: PSYCHOLOGICAL HEALTH

Consider for a moment how important physical health is in anyone's life. If affects one's chances in employment, social activities, travel, and relationships with others. Psychological health is also a basic element in contributing to a meaningful life, but are the chances for such health evenly distributed among groups in U.S. society? In 2002, 139,000 men and 207,000 women with "serious mental illnesses" were discharged from non-federal, short-stay hospitals (National Center for Health Statistics 2004). Recent estimates are that about 8.2 million, or about 5 percent of the adult population, suffer mental and emotional problems that "seriously interfered with the ability to work or attend school or to manage day-to-day activities" (Willis et al. 1998). Women, unmarried, unemployed, and poor individuals are overrepresented in this population. A 2001–2002 national survey of adults confirmed higher rates of "serious psychological distress" among minorities, women, and the poor (National Center for Health Statistics 2004). Historically, the vast majority of admittants to inpatient mental health facilities have been White and disproportionately poor. Men and members of minorities, especially Blacks, have been more likely than White women to be placed in state and county psychiatric facilities than in private or general hospitals. Blacks and men were more likely than Whites or women to be *involuntarily* admitted to these hospitals (Manderscheid and Barrett 1987).

Class, Race, Gender, and Distress

"Many studies have found a relationship between lower socioeconomic status and poor physical and mental health" (Latkin and Curry 2003, p. 34). But the nature of the relationship is complex and the direction of causality is a source of controversy. One argument is that individuals who become mentally ill lose their jobs, incomes, and are socially selected or "drift" into a lower class as a result. The alternative view is that the characteristics of a class position create conditions that foster mental health or illness. This is the "social causation" position. Both positions may apply in different circumstances and the nature of the relationship may vary depending upon the specific illness in question (Miech et al. 1999).

But there appears to be little question that economic conditions affect the amount of psychological distress and whether or not individuals receive treatment for it. As poverty rates increase, so does the rate of hospitalization for mental illness. Unemployment increases the amount of distress experienced by individuals, but reduces the rate of hospitalization, perhaps because of inability to meet the costs of treatment (Bye and Partridge 2003).

Besides its economic impact on probability of treatment, how does living in conditions of poverty contribute to mental distress? We know that lower socioeconomic status contributes to an accumulation of physical health problems in later life, which is linked to depression (Miech and Shanahan 2000). At the individual level, family poverty has a long-term impact on children's later feelings of well-being as adults, because it places a strain on relationships within the family, and depresses children's later educational and economic attainment (Sobolewski and Amato 2005). Living in a poor neighborhood also takes its toll on health. Latkin and Curry's study of over 800 respondents in disadvantaged neighborhoods in Baltimore uncovered a strong correlation between perceptions that a neighborhood had serious trash, theft, and vacancy problems and the degree of depression felt by respondents. They link this effect to the high levels of stress and powerlessness along with weak networks of social support produced by living in such neighborhoods (Latkin and Curry 2003). The greater stress and lower support in some family types may also account for the higher rates of depression found among young adults who live in single-parent rather than mother-father families. A smaller percentage of poor individuals live in two-parent families, and such intact families appear to have salutary effects for both the parents and the children. This may also help account for the higher rate of psychological distress among the poor (Simon 2002; Barrett and Turner 2005).

Race and socioeconomic status appear to have their own effects on feelings of distress (Hughes and Thomas 1998). Higher rates of distress and mental illness are found among Blacks. There are disagreements about explanations for the different rates between Blacks and Whites. Blacks, for example, are less likely than Whites to accept "genetic" factors or poor "family upbringing" as reasons. Perhaps this is because these explanations resemble past attacks that have been made on Black intelligence and family structure. Rather, Blacks are more likely to accept "chemical imbalances" or "life stresses" as causes of mental illness (Schnittker, Freese, and Powell 2000).

Evidence does indicate that life stresses are implicated in the psychological distress experienced by minorities. Hispanic and Black youth are less likely than Asian Americans or Whites to attend four-year colleges and to participate fully in school activities. This situation together with their more troubled relationships with parents and/or peers symbolizes the greater difficulty of the route to adulthood that some minorities face. In turn, these conditions contribute to stronger feelings of depression among Hispanics and Blacks (Gore and Aseltine, Jr. 2003). Indeed, lack of social support has been related to increased psychological distress, especially among Blacks (Lincoln,

Chatters, and Taylor 2003). Moving into a middle-class occupation does not necessarily alleviate distress either, since their placement in racially segmented positions creates another source of stress because these individuals compare themselves to others around them who are primarily Whites. Having an occupation that has been labeled as a "Black job" decreases life satisfaction and increases feelings of sadness, hopelessness, and worthlessness (Forman 2003). As Black adults get older and age, they also experience more traumatic losses than Whites, which further enhances the probability of depression (George and Lynch 2003). Data suggest that the relationship between race and feelings of well-being have not changed significantly in recent years (Hughes and Thomas 1998). One of the factors that appears to serve as a buffer against psychological distress for young Black adults is the extent to which they identify with their race. Strong racial identity appears to reduce the distress effects that arise from any racial discrimination young Black adults might experience (Sellers et al. 2003).

Like minorities and the poor, women also experience greater psychological distress when compared to men (Kessler and McRae 1983; Mirowsky and Ross 1995). Clinically defined major depression has been found to be 2–3 times as likely among women than among men, although the gap between them may be narrowing because of the recent increase in depression among young men. These trends have been found not only for the United States but for Sweden, Germany, Canada, and New Zealand as well, but not for Korea or Puerto Rico or among Mexican Americans (Klerman and Weissman 1989).

It also has been discovered in analyses of data from five general population surveys that psychological distress among women is more likely to be affected by some undesirable incidents affecting someone close to them than is the case among men. But women are not *generally* more vulnerable than men to all types of undesirable events. Among the possible contributors to these trends in depression are changes in women's roles and alterations in occupational patterns for men and women (Kessler and McLeod 1984).

It appears that a greater breadth of roles for women may have healthy results. There is evidence that individuals with multiple roles display a greater sense of psychological well-being, and that loss of roles is related to increased feelings of distress. People with multiple roles—for example, employed, married, and parents—tend to have better health than those with none of these roles (Verbrugge 1983). Sociologically, this makes sense since roles provide people with their identities. "The greater the number of identities held, the stronger one's sense of meaningful, guided existence. The more identities, the more 'existential security,' so to speak. A sense of meaningful existence and purposeful, ordered behavior are crucial to psychological health" (Thoits 1983, p. 175).

On the other hand, involvement and responsibility in *too many* areas can increase a person's feeling of loss of personal control and thereby increase stress and depression symptoms (Cleary and Mechanic 1983; Rosenfield 1989). Another factor probably contributing to the greater distress felt by housewives is their little power in the home compared to their employed husbands (Steil 1984). Employment brings power in the family, and distress may be a function of both lack of power and lack of multiple roles outside the family.

Obviously, some conditions and life events may help prepare and strengthen individuals for stressful conditions. Middle-class women who were in or approaching young adulthood during the Great Depression and who suffered serious economic loss because of it are today less likely to feel helpless and are more assertive and in control of their lives than middle-class women who did not experience such losses. Working-class women, on the other hand, who entered the Depression with fewer resources to begin with and experienced serious reductions in economic resources, feel less assertive and have a greater sense of being victimized (Elder and Liker 1982). What this suggests is that life's obstacles are more easily overcome and can even have long-term beneficial effects when those experiencing them have had ample resources on which to build a strong life originally.

Labeling, Diagnosis, and Inequality

General cultural images and expectations pertaining to different categories of people appear to be important for how mental illness symptoms are interpreted. Blacks are diagnosed most frequently with schizophrenia and at a much higher rate than Whites, whereas Whites are more likely to be labeled as having a bipolar disorder (Good et al. 2003; Neighbors et al. 2003). Some research suggests that cultural differences in language and symptom interpretation as well as physician biases enter into diagnoses of illness, although results about the exact effect of the clinician's race have been mixed (Institute of Medicine 2002). Clearly, interpretations of mental illness interact with racial, gender, and class characteristics of patients. The same symptoms in a White patient have been found to be interpreted more negatively when found in a Black patient. Part of the stereotype of Black men is that they are dangerous and potentially violent; this is related to the diagnosis of schizophrenia often given to them (Institute of Medicine 2002; Good et al. 2003).

A study by Loring and Powell (1988) aimed at finding out whether the psychiatrist's or client's race or sex influenced the diagnosis given to the client, even though the symptoms presented in each case vignette did not vary. The authors presented a stratified random sample of 290 psychiatrists with two case studies each, in which the sex and race were either disclosed or not. The point was to see whether these doctors would evaluate the client simply on the basis of symptoms classified in a standard manner by the *Diagnostic and Statistical Manual (DSM-III)* used by clinicians. Some interesting patterns emerged in the research. The authors found the following:

1. White male psychiatrists were more likely to classify a given case in the general schizophrenia category if it involved a White male than if the client were Black or female.
2. Black male and female psychiatrists followed a similar pattern; that is, they were more likely to present the general schizophrenic diagnosis to clients who were of the *same* sex and race as the psychiatrist.
3. Black psychiatrists tended to give the least serious diagnoses to White male patients, and male psychiatrists did not label any White males as having paranoid schizophrenia. In contrast, this was the most frequently given diagnosis for Black male clients by every type of psychiatrist.
4. Male psychiatrists tended to diagnose female clients as having depression disorders, but female psychiatrists shied away from this label.

What these and other results show is that when psychiatrists are not given either the sex or race of the case they are examining, there is widespread agreement among them on the diagnosis. But when such information is provided, if the sex and race are the same as the psychiatrist who is doing the diagnosing, then the diagnosis is basically the same as that which would have been given had no information on sex and race been provided. In other words, the diagnoses appear to be more "objective." In contrast, in those cases where sex and/or gender of client and psychiatrist differ, diagnoses appear more subjective. For example, male psychiatrists, on the whole, are inclined to perceive females as having depressive disorders and to assign White females to the histrionic category, even when the case study itself gives little evidence of such a disorder. It seems that the stereotype of women being emotional is carried over into these diagnoses. Similarly, the diagnoses of Black males also appear to be affected by stereotypical views.

Black males are more likely to be considered as being violent, suspicious, or dangerous, even when their clinical characteristics are the same as those of Whites. Psychiatrists of *both* races tend to give such diagnoses, suggesting internalization of these stereotypes to some extent by both types of psychiatrists. If these biases enter into diagnoses, then official rates of such illnesses for different groups may not accurately reflect the incidence of these disorders among the different sex and racial groups (ibid.).

Stereotypes and gender role expectations may also affect how mental illness in men and women in general is handled. "[I]t is possible that our American culture addresses mental illness differently for women than men, with women seeking treatment when distressed whereas men may be more predisposed to break laws when distressed. There are significantly more men than women incarcerated in the United States . . . many of whom have a mental illness" (Bye and Partridge 2003, p. 44).

Stereotyping and labeling the mentally ill according to traditional gender and racial roles is nothing new, however. In the seventeenth and early eighteenth centuries, the artistic and scientific images of the mad were decidedly male in nature, depicting someone who was "aggressive," "muscular," "seminude," and "raving," with "uncivilized animality." By the first half of the nineteenth century, the image of madness had changed to a feminine one: "antisocial, violent, unruly, and oversexed. . . . The figure of the sexually aggressive madwoman effectively displaced the previously more common figure of the raving male lunatic" (Kromm 1994, pp. 507–508, 530–531). In part, this shift reflected concerns about the increasing political involvement of women in Europe after the French Revolution. This imagery served to control women's power (Kromm 1994).

Other research has found that whether an individual is admitted voluntarily or involuntarily into a state hospital is also related in part to his or her socioeconomic status as well as to the severity of the disorder. Briefly put, individuals from lower socioeconomic levels are more likely to be involuntarily admitted when the disorder is not obvious or severe—that is, when there is room for various interpretations of symptoms (Rushing 1978). Schizophrenia, which is more frequently diagnosed among African Americans, is also a disorder in which individual interpretation by the caregiver plays a large role. It has been labeled as on "open concept" and "fuzzy natural category" (quoted in Gottesman, McGuffin, and Farmer 1987, p. 41).

Similarly, diagnoses of "personality disorders"—which display ambiguous symptoms, are more difficult to identify objectively, and are therefore open to interpretation—show sex biases associated with traditional female roles (Dixon, Gordon, and Khomusi 1995).

Sense of Control, Choice, and Inequality

Mental illness and distress indicate the presence of serious psychological difficulties. But there are other psychological feelings that, while not requiring institutionalization, are indicators of one's general sense of well-being and life satisfaction. Central among these are feelings of control over one's life and that one's actions make a difference. In fact, feelings of control and mastery have been linked to better health (Lachman and Weaver 1998). Those in high-ranking or professional occupational positions are more likely to have such feelings, because those who have spent much of their lives in occupations where they have had autonomy and made the decisions in their work are also likely to feel that they are responsible for and can take control of their lives. Moreover, this effect of work on feelings of self-direction is long lasting (Schooler, Mulatu, and Oates 2004).

In contrast, the greater feelings of distress found in the lower socioeconomic groups have been linked to greater feelings of vulnerability, powerlessness, and alienation, while those in higher positions have a greater feeling of

PL VII.

Early in the nineteenth century, the image of the insane person as female and feminine became established, reflecting concerns about the rising political force of women after the French Revolution.

Source: From Etienne Esquirol's *Des Maladies Mentales*, 1838, courtesy of the National Library of Medicine.

mastery and control (Wheaton 1980; Mirowsky and Ross 1983). This was seen earlier in the relationship between SES and personal control over health. Women, those in lower status jobs, and those who are unemployed have less of a sense of control over their lives (Wheaton 1980; Pearlin et al. 1981; Kohn and Schooler 1982; Mirowsky and Ross 1983). Individuals with a sense of powerlessness have feelings of little control over their lives, believing that they cannot master or determine the paths that life will take. Rather, the belief is that factors outside the individual—fate or "society," for example—determine what happens to them and that there is little they can do to change that. The different conditions of control and choice of those in different occupations is suggested by Barbara Ehrenreich's experience related in Nutshell 10.1.

In sum, feelings of self-mastery and control over one's life appear to be an important set of mediating influences on mental health. Those in low socioeconomic positions generally have a

greater sense than those in higher statuses that their lives are controlled by factors beyond their immediate control. These feelings, in turn, are related to greater depression and less overall satisfaction with life (Lachman and Weaver 1998). The importance of mastery over one's life for mental health is further implied by findings that show that job restructuring and increased job demands, over which individuals have little control, increase depressive feelings and lower a sense of life satisfaction (Tausig and Fenwick 1999). Of course, those with few resources are lacking in the choices available to

---

NUTSHELL 10.1_____

Life as a Low-Wage Worker

In 1998, at the behest of an acquaintance, Barbara Ehrenreich, who has written extensively about the personal impact of social class, decided to find out for herself what life was like for individuals whose earnings hover around the minimum-wage level. In traveling to several states, she worked as a hotel maid, housecleaner, restaurant waitress, dishwasher, and discount-store clerk. She records her experiences and reactions in *Nickel and Dimed* (2001). The following is an excerpt of reflections from her book, which suggests some ways in which the intimate day-to-day lives of the poor and upper-middle class are different:

> It is common, among the nonpoor, to think of poverty as a sustainable condition—austere, perhaps, but they get by somehow, don't they? They are "always with us." What is harder for the nonpoor to see is poverty as acute distress: The lunch that consists of Doritos or hot dog rolls, leading to faintness before the end of the shift. The "home" that is also a car or a van. The illness or injury that must be "worked through," with gritted teeth, because there's no sick pay or health insurance and the loss of one day's pay will mean no groceries for the next. These experiences are not part of a sustainable lifestyle, even a lifestyle

of chronic deprivation and relentless low-level punishment. They are, by almost any standard of subsistence, emergency situations. And that is how we should see the poverty of so many millions of low-wage Americans—as a state of emergency.

> In the summer of 2000 I returned—permanently, I have every reason to hope—to my customary place in the socioeconomic spectrum. I go to restaurants, often far finer ones than the places where I worked, and sit down at a table. I sleep in hotel rooms that someone else has cleaned and shop in stores that others will tidy when I leave. To go from the bottom 20 percent to the top 20 percent is to enter a magical world where needs are met, problems are solved, almost without any intermediate effort. If you want to get somewhere fast, you hail a cab. If your aged parents have grown tiresome or incontinent, you put them away where others will deal with their dirty diapers and dementia. If you are part of the upper-middle-class majority that employs a maid or maid service, you return from work to find the house miraculously restored to order—the toilet bowls shit-free and gleaming, the socks that you left on the floor levitated back to their normal dwelling place. Here, sweat is a metaphor for hard work, but seldom its consequence. Hundreds of little things get done, reliably and routinely every day, without anyone's seeming to do them.

Source: Ehrenreich 2001, pp. 214–215.

others. In a critical sense, lacking a sense of power and control is about lacking choices. The luxury of considering choices is not available for one who is scrambling merely to stay alive or to have a little bit of comfort.

While members of the upper class are likely to feel that one's life can be shaped and directed by the individual, "the essence of lower class position is the belief that one is at the mercy of forces and people beyond one's control, often beyond one's understanding" (Kohn 1969, pp. 189, 192). A young electrician apprentice summarized this feeling well: "See, I feel like I'm being held back, like I'm not on top of things. . . . I don't know what you would call it, maybe sort of powerless, but it's a feeling not about any one thing that's gone wrong" (Sennett and Cobb 1973, p. 34). Falling from their comfortable upper-middle-class life, Kerry Russo reflected on the predicament of her newly unemployed husband: "I look at a successful businessman going through this absolute torture. I can hold him. I can tell him it's going to be okay. But it's out of my hands. And that's the frightening part, how little control we have over our lives. . . . It used to be that if you followed the rules, you'd be fine. That doesn't apply anymore. They've changed the rules" (Safran 1992, p. 115).

It should not be surprising that the self-image of individuals with this perspective would differ from those who feel they can and do control their lives. Consistent with this view are the findings of a recent Gallup survey that revealed that groups with more resources were more likely than others to have excellent self-images. Table 10.1 shows that higher proportions of men, generally those who earned higher incomes and felt their health was excellent, classified their self-images as "excellent." The fact that a higher percentage of non-Whites than Whites consider their self-image this way appears to be inconsistent with this argument. However, recent research suggests that strong racial

TABLE 10.1   Percentage Rating Personal Self-Image* as Excellent, by Income, Employment Status, Race, and Sex: 2003

INCOME	% EXCELLENT
earn less than $20,000 per year	25
earn $20,000–$29,999 per year	26
earn $30,000–$49,999 per year	36
earn $50,000–$74,999 per year	46
earn $75,000 per year or more	44
EMPLOYMENT STATUS	
adults who are not employed	29
adults employed full or part time	40
RACE	
Non-Hispanic Whites	34
Non-Whites	43
SEX	
Women	33
Men	38

*Survey question asked was: "How would you describe your self-image; that is, how you generally feel about yourself—excellent, good, just fair, or poor?"

Source: Joseph Carrol, "Health, Age, and Income Factor into Americans' Self-Image." *Gallup Poll Tuesday Briefing*, August 12, 2003.

identities and unusual adversity may toughen individuals psychologically, helping to create stronger feelings of mastery and purpose in their lives. This is especially the case for Blacks with more education (Ryff, Keyes, and Hughes 2003). Whites, in contrast, are not as likely to think of their whiteness as a race and are in a weaker position to justify their difficulties using external adversities such as discrimination.

Despite the belief that one has little control, Americans have traditionally been brought up to believe in individualism (i.e., the belief that individuals are responsible for their own fates). Imagine how you would feel if you, on the one hand, believed in individualism and, on the other hand, had little opportunity to improve your situation. The personal consequences of being caught in this vise are, in part, psychological. This combination of different amounts of opportunities for classes and an ingrained belief in individual responsibility creates the conditions for self-damaging feelings and doubts among those who are not economically successful on the one hand, and feelings of self-confidence and entitlement among those living in successful families on the other. Sennett and Cobb's (1973) moving study of Boston working-class men and their families who sense a lack of control revealed the corrosive psychological effects that the combination of individualism and varying success has on individuals.

Individualism encourages the desire to excel, and some do excel while others do not. Those who *do* attain positions develop feelings of competence and freedom, while those who *do not* develop feelings of guilt and suspicions of their own inadequacy. For those at the top, individualism reinforces their belief in the deservedness of their position and abilities and reaffirms their high self-worth, while for those at the bottom, especially Whites, individualism has the doubly damaging effect of confirming the deservedness of their lowly position

and reinforcing in their minds that they do not have what it takes. Figure 10.4 summarizes this process.

The lack of control experienced by those below the middle has been linked to their occupational experiences. Those who do repetitive work of little complexity and are closely supervised are more likely to sense a lack of power over their own lives (Blauner 1964). Most jobs of those in the working and lower classes are characterized by a lack of self-direction, which further leads to a feeling of powerlessness (Kohn 1976b). William Thompson worked on the assembly line in a large beef-processing plant and also found the monotony and lack of control difficult. "The assembly line worker became a part of the assembly line. The assembly line is not a tool used by the worker, but a machine which controls him/her" (Thompson 1991, p. 230). To cope with these conditions, workers daydreamed, fooled around, and occasionally engaged in sabotage.

Education is often seen as a way to gain control over one's life, to gain autonomy and

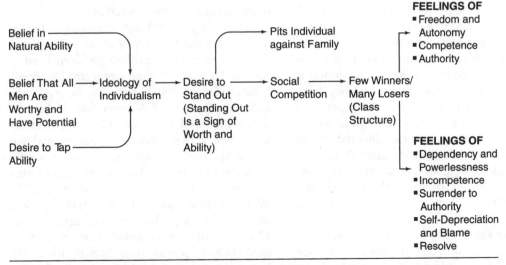

FIGURE 10.4   Ideology, Class Inequality, and Their Effects on Self-Perceptions among Men of Different Classes
Source: Based on Sennett and Cobb 1973.

choices. Indeed, those with lower educations are more likely to feel more vulnerable and less in control of their lives (Umberson 1993). The working-class respondents in Sennett and Cobb's (1973) study realize the potential of education to give their children independence in their lives, but they also suspect that educated people can get away with things that the average person cannot, and that education drives a wedge between less-educated parents and their children. Thus, education becomes a double-edged sword, serving to grant independence but also creating a seemingly permanent breach in understanding between generations. Richard Rodriguez, who went from knowing little English to earning a Ph.D. and becoming a successful writer and professor, described how he and his family drifted further apart: "Years passed. Silence grew thicker, less penetrable" (1982, p. 190).

To summarize, the conditions and resources with which people live affect their beliefs and outlook. The feelings of lack of control, vulnerability, and powerlessness held by many in lower socioeconomic groups generate higher levels of distress and weaken their ability to cope effectively (Wheaton 1980, 1983). In their research review on the relationship between socioeconomic status, beliefs, and distress, Mirowsky and Ross (1986) concluded that "people in lower socioeconomic positions have a triple burden: They have more problems to deal with; their personal histories are likely to have left them with a deep sense of powerlessness; and that sense of powerlessness discourages them from marshalling whatever energy and resources they do have in order to solve their problems. The result for many is a multiplication of despair" (p. 30).

Their sense of powerlessness stems in part from their inability to leave their poor neighborhoods. This immobility leads to greater feelings of distress. Individuals who live in poor neighborhoods where most people have not moved are more likely than residents of stable nonpoor neighborhoods to experience depression and anxiety. This is due in part to perceptions that their neighborhood is physically broken down and dangerous: "The stress of living in a place where the streets are dirty, noisy, and dangerous takes its toll in feelings of depression and anxiety" (Ross, Reynolds, and Geis 2000, p. 594).

BASIC LIFE CHANCES: FOOD AND SHELTER

The research on physical and psychological health clearly shows that economic, racial, and gender inequality are deeply implicated in the chances of individuals for a healthy life. It does not warrant belaboring that food and shelter, like health, are basic to a decent life, and it is the poor who are disproportionately found among the hungry and homeless.

Because of controversies over the definition of *hunger* and the lack of a *consistent national* attempt to assess the magnitude of the problem, there is little agreement on the extent of the problem in the United States.

According to 2001 estimates, almost 34 million persons were hungry or at risk of hunger. In 2003, more than 13 million children lived in households in which food was scarce (America's Second Harvest 2005). A 25-city survey by the U.S. Conference of Mayors found that the demand for food assistance in 2002 increased by an average of 19 percent in those cities, and that almost half of those making such requests were members of families. Thirty-eight percent were employed (U.S. Conference of Mayors 2002). While less prominent than in central-city areas, hunger is also a problem in rural areas. About 12 percent of rural households lack security in food (U.S. Department of Agriculture 2003). Low incomes, poor health, and lack of access are three of the reasons for rural hunger.

Naomi, a 67-year-old woman who lives in a rural area in Louisiana explains:

> *"Even when there's no water, it's 30 miles to the closest big grocery store, and I'm not physically able to drive that far from home anymore. The grocery stores that are closer to us . . . you can't afford to buy a loaf of bread. . . . They have to charge more to cover their costs. The delivery trucks have to come out so far, and they can buy in bulk. It's just a rural store"* (America's Second Harvest 2005).

The problem of hunger, of course, is linked to the issue of good health. The Physician Task Force has argued that inadequate diet has an impact on the health of pregnant women and on the children to whom they give birth. Higher infant mortality rates, low birth weight, slower or deficient brain growth, poorer resistance to infection, and general stunting and anemia are among the conditions related to poor nutrition among children. Other negative effects are found among older persons who are chronically hungry. Many of the health problems among older people—for example, hypertension and weakening of the bone structure (osteoporosis)—require careful attention to quality and quantity of diet, and hunger worsens these maladies (Physician Task Force 1985).

The homeless are among the groups most likely to be hungry. A 1996 governmental survey of homeless assistance centers found that 20 percent eat at most only one meal a day, and 40 percent of the homeless said that they went at least one day in the last month without food (Hombs 2001). Studies of homelessness, which are most often done at the state rather than national level, vary in how they measure homelessness and encounter difficulties in simply counting how many are homeless. "Counting the homeless is a social scientist's nightmare." It is difficult because of the relative "invisibility" of the homeless, hostility among them, the mixing of poverty and homelessness, the frequent movement of the homeless from place to place, and the existence of multiple causes that make it difficult to find them (Redburn and Buss 1986, p. 16).

Consequently, national surveys yield wildly different appraisals on the extent of homelessness in the United States, with estimates ranging from several hundred thousand to several million. The Urban Institute estimated in 2000 that about 3.5 million people were homeless at some point during the year (Urban Institute 2000). Indications are that homelessness has increased over the last two decades. Estimates based on single counts at a given time ("point-in-time counts") tend to be lower than estimates based on counts of those who are homeless sometime during a period of time ("period prevalence counts") (National Coalition for the Homeless, February 1999).

The homeless population has become much more heterogeneous since the 1980s. Families with children are among the fastest growing portion of the homeless population. In 2002, such families made up 41 percent of the homeless in *cities*, up from 33 percent in 1987. Single men constituted another large part (41% vs. 49% in 1987). Of the remainder, 13 percent of the urban homeless population consisted of single women, and 5 percent of unattached youth (U.S. Conference of Mayors 2002). Single men make up a smaller percentage of the *rural* homeless population, which is dominated by "families, single mothers, and children" (National Coalition for the Homeless, June 2001, p. 1). Children and adults who are homeless are also more likely than others to have significant physical and mental health problems. Between 20 and 25 percent have some form of serious, chronic mental illness, and about one-third have some kind of persistent drug abuse problem (National Coalition for the Homeless, April 1999; U.S. Conference of Mayors 2002).

Hunger has become an increasingly serious problem worldwide and in the United States. In 2002, demands for emergency food assistance in the United States went up at least 19 percent over the previous year. In New York, for example, soup kitchens and similar facilities fed 45 percent more individuals in 2002 than in 2000. Similar increases in demand were found in Chicago, Boston, Los Angeles, and other cities.
Photo by David C. Barnett.

What is it like to be homeless? Here are glimpses into the lives of three individuals:

In New York, Frank, a thirty-four-year-old former warehouseman with an "anxiety and nervousness problem," is fearful of being attacked during the night. He sleeps on his side because otherwise, he says, "I be a flat target." . . .

In Houston, Rosa, a forty-two-year-old homeless woman, considers her options. To arrive early to get in line for the free 10:30 meal at the soup kitchen means only an hour or so wait. On the other hand, arriving close to noon will result in no wait at all, but it means going without food for an additional hour and a half . . .

In Detroit, Arch has always been single and a working man for most of his thirty-three adult years "I don't have no friends. I really haven't in a long time," he says while his eyes scan the remnants of neighborhood tenement buildings that are ninety years old. "I sometimes hear them

saying that I've got the v's, y'know, the lines on the back of your neck. It's supposed to mean that you don't have much time. . . ." (Sweeney 1993, pp. 1–3)

These vignettes suggest the unique set of stresses faced by the homeless. Homeless persons suffer greater emotional pressures than those encountered by the housed poor. They have higher levels of depression and are more likely to avoid active confrontation of problems than other members of the poor population (Banyard and Graham-Bermann 1998). Again, the relationship between health and socioeconomic status appears reciprocal. Mental disorder may precipitate homelessness, and homelessness generally intensifies psychological distress. Adding to this distress is the distinct stigma placed on the homeless by the public. National research indicates that the homelessness stigma is over and above the stigma placed on being poor. One supported explanation for the stigma is that the homeless "are viewed as dirty, smelly, lice-ridden, or diseased," resulting in a desire on the part of the public to keep from being contaminated by them (Phelan et al. 1997, p. 333). A recent national telephone survey found that almost two-thirds of respondents felt that "the presence of homeless people threatens the quality of life in America's cities, hurts local businesses, spoils parks for families and children, and makes neighborhoods worse" (Link et al. 1996, p. 145). In the same study, a majority also believed that the homeless were either dangerous, potentially violent, or threatening. Although the public does not fully blame

homeless individuals for their plight, these perceptions of the homeless mark them as a negatively evaluated status group, as defined in Chapter 3.

A number of other factors have been linked to the rise in homelessness. Primary among these is the lack of affordable housing. The higher cost of housing is due in large part to declines in the building of affordable private homes and in public housing. This has left a larger poor population competing for smaller numbers of affordable residences. This increased demand has pushed rents up (Koegel, Burnam, and Baumohl 1996).

The homelessness problem is thus exacerbated by the high cost of what is available. There is evidence that the poor are paying more for their housing. Almost two-thirds of

There has been a significant rise in the amount of homelessness in recent years.
Photo by David C. Barnett.

the poor pay more than half of their income for shelter. In sharp contrast, only 8 percent of the nonpoor pay that high a proportion of their incomes for housing. Federal data indicate that whereas in the late 1970s, there were many more low-cost housing units available than there were the poor needing them, by 1985, that situation was reversed. Immediate causes for this situation include an increase in the number of poor households, a decline in their average incomes, and an increase in the level of rents (Dionne 1989). The destruction or conversion of housing units for other purposes, along with gentrification, has worsened the problem.

Health difficulties and the associated lack of services available to the homeless have also helped maintain homelessness. In addition, the decline in value of the minimum wage has made decent housing difficult to obtain for low-wage workers, most of whom are adults. About one-quarter of the homeless are employed (U.S. Conference of Mayors 2002).

Other factors, then, beyond the characteristics of the homeless themselves, also have contributed to the homeless problem. Deinstitutionalization of those with mental problems, the recession of the early 1980s, the declining value of public assistance benefits, no-fault divorces and increasing numbers of no-children rental rules, the net migration to metropolitan areas, and tighter governmental rules about disabilities have all had an effect on this problem (Hope and Young 1986; Carliner 1987; Hoch 1987; Wright and Lam 1987). Thus, many of the elements that affect the extent of homelessness are "macroprocesses" related to the government and market economy (Rossi and Wright 1989). And it is the poor who are especially vulnerable to shifts in these processes. "As long as the distribution of shelter security remains tied to income and social class the poor will bear the burden of going homeless" (Hoch 1987, p. 29).

SUMMARY

This chapter has focused on a variety of areas concerning personal life chances in different racial, gender, and SES groups. It appears clear that the latter factors are related to physical and mental health in several ways. Moreover, these groups also tend to use health services in different ways, to contact doctors and dentists at different rates, and to differ in the likelihood of possessing health insurance and taking preventive health measures. Inequality also is related to the problems of hunger and homelessness.

Two points should be made about the research conducted on these relationships. First, frequently different measures of SES have been used in studies on the same issue, and, for the sake of convenience, the term *social class* has been used in this chapter as if it were synonymous with SES measures. Second, although significant relationships have been found between race, gender, and SES, on the one hand, and health, on the other hand, I do not want to suggest that these are the only variables or always the most important variables in explaining variations. Rather, the question of interest has been whether inequality in its various forms plays any role in producing various personal life chances. It seems apparent that it does. Indirectly, the organization of a competitive capitalist society and, more directly, the system of inequality that it creates, results in individuals and families being placed in different positions regarding access to and possibilities of gaining the "good things" in life. At the same time, the lack of economic power of some individuals affects relationships at home. Unemployed housewives are more likely to experience various symptoms of distress. In many ways, then, the effects of inequality reach inside the intimate lives of individuals. In Chapter 11, we turn from these personal effects of inequality to more societywide effects—abuse, crime, collective unrest, and environmental justice.

CRITICAL THINKING

1. How do you think your gender, race, and socioeconomic position have affected your path through life thus far?

2. To what extent should individuals be held responsible for their health and actions if these are shaped by their opportunities and circumstances?

3. What can be done to alleviate the negative effects of inequality on people's lives?

4. It is impossible to know everyone personally. Consequently, we often use beliefs about categories of people to orient our feelings and behavior toward them. Does this mean that prejudice or bias is inevitable?

WEB CONNECTIONS

The University of Michigan's Documents Center is a wonderful source of information, and includes data on basic life chances. For example, it provides information on the number of people with mental illness, life expectancy, top hospitals by locale, effects of welfare reform on loss of health insurance, and health insurance ownership by resident's state and socioeconomic characteristics. How does your state compare with others? Visit www.lib.umich.edu/govdocs/sthealth.html/.

11 Deviance, Protest, and Inequality

Odds are, the street thug will do a lot more prison time than the guy who ripped off millions. Where is the justice in that?

—Terry Pluto

The previous chapter focused on how position in the system of social inequality affects an individual's *personal* life, that is, its impact on physical and mental health, access to food, and chances of homelessness. In contrast, the present chapter addresses some of the *social* consequences of inequality—its relationship to family violence, crime, collective protests, and environmental justice.

VIOLENCE IN THE FAMILY

Domestic violence is nothing new. There are records of spousal abuse as far back as the Roman Empire. In the late nineteenth century, it was still legal for "a husband to physically chastise his wife as long as 'the stick was no bigger than his thumb'" (U.S. Department of Justice 2003, p. 339). Domestic abuse includes violence against an intimate partner as well as child abuse and neglect.

In 2003, of the almost 3 million cases referred to child-protective agencies for investigation in the United States, 906,000 children were determined to have been victims of either abuse or neglect. About two-thirds of these cases involved neglect and over one-fourth included physical or sexual abuse. In the same

year, 1,500 children died because of abuse or neglect (U.S. Department of Health and Human Services 2005). For those who live, the effects of such abuse can be longlasting. A greater proportion of women who were abused as children experience depression, low self-esteem, and a higher chance for alcoholism (Langeland and Hartgers 1998; Banyard 1999).

Those most likely to be victims of child abuse were girls under 3 years of age who have some type of disability. Race and ethnicity is also a factor. While about half of all victims were White, a disproportionate 26 percent were Black. The probability of being a victim was greater if the child was Black, American Indian, or an Alaskan Native. The victimization rates for White and Hispanic children were about half that of Blacks, American Indians, or Alaskan Natives. There are racial/ethnic differences in the kinds of abuse most often found, however. A slightly greater percentage of abuse against Black, American Indian, or Alaskan Native children involves *neglect* only (51–67%) than is the case with White children (48%). This might suggest the importance of the lack of adequate resources for understanding abuse. The role of race or ethnicity *in itself* is questionable because of its correlation with other precipitating factors such as poverty, isolation, unemployment, and lack of social support.

Research has repeatedly found an association between lower socioeconomic status and child abuse. Government data indicate that the children who are most at risk are those whose young parents are experiencing heavy stress due to many children, low incomes, drug abuse, isolation, and lack of social support (U.S. Department of Justice 2003). Lower educational and occupational attainment are among the other stressors related to child abuse (Biller and Solomon 1986). Nevertheless, most poor parents do not abuse their children (Faller and Ziefert 1981; Gelles and Cornell 1985). Finally, in 2003, 58 percent of the perpetrators were women and 41 percent were men. However, men are more likely to be the offenders when the abuse is physical or sexual; women are more often involved in child neglect.

In addition to violence against children, domestic violence also involves spousal abuse or abuse between partners. In 2001, almost 700,000 were reported to have been victims of adult abuse; 85 percent of these were women. Considering that these figures do not include mild forms of violence, it is likely that the amount of abuse against women is much higher than these figures suggest (Straus and Gelles 1990). In addition, the total number of victims given is deceiving because many cases of abuse are never reported. Only about half of the victims report their abuse to police; Black women are most likely to file a report. Even confidential reports underestimate the extent of the problem because of the embarrassment and sensitivity of the problem, the belief on the part of some that a certain amount of violence is "normal" and even acceptable, and because many who are abused look for help outside official channels, such as from other couples (Margolin, Sibner, and Glebermen 1988).

One estimate is that about 1 out of 3 adult women will be assaulted by a partner. Women are most likely to be violence victims if they are "black, young, divorced or separated, earning lower incomes, living in rental housing, and living in an urban area" (U.S. Department of Justice 2000, p. 3). These same characteristics apply to men who are victims of violence by a spouse, partner, or girlfriend. Generally, Blacks have been found to be victims at about two and one-half the rate found among other racial and ethnic groups. But again, the relationship between race and violence appears to have less to do with race per se than with the higher rates of poverty, unemployment, and isolation (Sokoloff 2004). Also remember that Black women are more likely than others to report abuse.

Women who live in households with incomes below $7,500 are 7 times as likely to be violence victims than women in households with incomes of at least $75,000 (U.S. Department of Justice 2000). A recent study involving in-depth interviews with over 500 low-income mothers in Texas revealed that "those reporting some violence were significantly more likely to have monthly incomes less than $1,000, to have received cash assistance and food stamps, to have tried to work in the past 3 years, and to have suffered hardships related to the necessities of daily living [e.g., housing, food, utility problems]. They were significantly less likely to be married, to be currently employed, and to have health insurance" (Romero et al. 2003, p. 1235). Young, single women with children seem to be especially vulnerable to violence by a partner (Lauritsen and Schaum 2004).

This research indicates the importance of considering the broader familial and community context in which individuals live when trying to explain abuse rates. It is not only an individual's characteristics but qualities of the social context that are also significant predictors of abuse. For example, communities in which there are a large percentage of female-headed families appear to have higher rates of domestic violence *regardless* of the social status of the individual household (ibid.). Women living in neighborhoods or census tracts with lower levels of education, poorer housing, and higher rates of poverty and unemployment are at greater risk regardless of their *individual* education, employment, or income (Miles-Doan 1998; Pearlman et al. 2003). The broader context in which individuals live and their lack of meaningful ties to the larger society because of segregation or other limited opportunities contribute to stresses that in turn activate abuse. Living in a community with overcrowding, dilapidated housing, inadequate schools, poor public facilities, and lower chances of decent employment creates additional pressures and frustrations for residents.

Unemployment of the husband has been related to greater probability of abuse. Men who work part-time or are unemployed have abuse rates that are about twice as high as those for husbands that are fully employed (Gelles and Cornell 1990). There is also some evidence that the degree of status inconsistency between spouses may be related to wife abuse. Wives whose educational and occupational statuses are higher than those of their husbands may be at greater risk than other wives (Hotaling and Sugarman 1984; Stark and Flitcraft 1988). Moreover, there is some evidence that working wives whose earnings approach or equal those of their working husbands are also at greater risk of abuse by their husbands. This suggests that when the breadwinner role of the husband is jeopardized, the probability of abuse may be greater because his domestic control is at stake. In this context, child abuse as a way of controlling his wife is also more likely (McCloskey 1996). Domestic violence seems to be related to the balance of power within families, with democratic, egalitarian families having the lowest rates of violence (Gelles and Cornell 1990).

If abuse is least likely in societies in which men and women are roughly equal in social status, then we would expect to find that societies that are patriarchal will have higher rates of abuse than more egalitarian societies. Studies involving peasant societies as well as industrial nations indicate that this may indeed be the case. Levinson reports that abuse is more frequent where men are in full authority in the family and control wealth and labor than in societies where women are in control in the household and can acquire wealth and property on their own (Levinson 1988). Yodanis' examination of North American and European countries found that sexual violence against women is greatest in those countries where women's occupational and educational status is low. She suggests that women may be less likely to be seen as a threat to men and be more likely to affect policy in societies where women participate on an equal level with men at work and at institutions of higher education. Consequently, the level of violence against them will be lower (Yodanis 2004). Interestingly, other research indicates that wife abuse may be related to status in a curvilinear manner, with women being most likely to be victims in places where they occupy *either* the lowest *or* highest status (Yllo 1983, 1984).

INEQUALITY AND THE MEASUREMENT OF CRIME

Inequality has been related to the nature and collection of crime statistics, the likelihood of arrest, the social production of crime, and sentencing. In other words, its effect appears to permeate most phases of the criminal justice process. Unfortunately, discussions about the relationship between inequality and crime are mired in disagreements about the definition of *crime* and the varying statistics about it. Controversy about what constitutes crime and how criminals are detected and arrested makes definitive conclusions about this relationship difficult.

Clearly, labels applied to persons and actions have an impact on what behaviors are defined as criminal, how much laws are enforced, and how the behavior of individuals is interpreted. Because of this, the definition of "the crime problem" is a social construction, and the definitions given by some groups may be favored over those of others. Perhaps you consider the crime problem to consist mainly of street crimes such as rape, robbery, murder, and the like, but others may feel that the real crime problem is found in white-collar crime that costs billions of dollars every year and yet receives less attention in the popular press. In the small city in which I live, it is now illegal to "cruise" the downtown in the evenings, a pastime previously engaged in by many youths. What defines *cruising* is rather arbitrary, however. *Loitering* is another rather vaguely defined illegal act. The more one examines various "crimes," the more it becomes evident that they are defined into existence.

Similarly, once laws and crimes are defined, their enforcement is also uneven. This selective enforcement is a means for ensuring that groups are kept in their respective places.

> *Unequal administration of the law is functional because it keeps the status arrangements of society from being disrupted. When, for example, a drunk appears in public, police often react differently in terms of his social status. If he is lower class, he has a good chance of being arrested. If he is upper or middle class, he will more likely be driven home. Middle- and upper-class people, who control the administration of justice, want these laws enforced only against a certain segment of the population. (Reid 1988, p. 36)*

Several scholars have suggested that the police are biased against those in the lower class and, thus, are more likely to arrest them than individuals in higher classes who commit the same offenses (Turk 1969; Quinney 1970). In sum, these and similar observations should make us wary in drawing conclusions about crime because statistics about it have several shortcomings.

Because (1) "crimes" are the result of certain behaviors, and not others, being defined as illegal, and because (2) police actions appear to be affected by the socioeconomic and racial characteristics of citizens, many have questioned the fairness of the criminal justice system. Results of a 2001 national poll revealed that 83 percent of U.S. adults do not believe that all are treated equally in the justice system. Celebrities and the wealthy are thought to get special treatment (Hales 2002). A recent examination of 110 men whose guilty verdicts were later thrown out as a result of DNA tests seems to give credence to these feelings. Most were either working class or poor, and two-thirds were either Hispanic or Black (Cohen and Hastings 2002). The discussion that follows of the relationship between inequality and crime covers "street," "suite" corporate, and hate crimes. Included are discussions of phases of the criminal justice process, starting with arrests and the commission of crime and ending with sentencing.

STREET CRIME AND INEQUALITY

Crime rates are ordinarily determined by using the FBI's Crime Index, which includes both property crimes (burglary, larceny-theft, motor vehicle theft, arson) and violent crimes (murder, forcible rape, robbery, and aggravated assault). One of the problems with this list of "street" crimes is that it does not include any serious, very costly white-collar, corporate, or "suite" crimes, as they are sometimes called. Since the latter are largely crimes perpetrated by middle- or upper-class individuals, it would be a mistake to look only at the Index crimes to reach a conclusion about the relationship between race, sex, socioeconomic status, and crime. To do so would bias the conclusion against individuals in lower social and economic rankings.

Another point to keep in mind is how perceptions about racial groups affect individuals' fears and views of crime rates. Evidence from several cities indicates that respondents' perceptions of the size of the crime rate in a neighborhood is affected by the percentage of residents who are Black. The greater the percentage of Blacks in an area, the more likely is the perception of a high crime rate. In fact, the racial makeup of the neighborhood actually has a stronger impact on perceptions of high crime rates *than the actual crime rate*. This provides ample evidence that racial stereotypes are at work in labeling neighborhoods (Quillian and Pager 2001). Feelings that one might be a victim of crime are also affected by neighborhood racial composition (Chiricos, McEntire, and Gertz 2001).

This stereotyping of neighborhoods as dangerous according to their racial composition appears evident also in research on police interpretations and actions. A recent study in Washington, DC, found that in contrast to Blacks residing in a middle-class neighborhood, Blacks who live in a poor neighborhood are likely to feel they are treated unfairly compared to those who live in White and higher socioeconomic neighborhoods. Blacks in the middle-class neighborhood do not believe that their neighborhood is treated any differently by police than White neighborhoods. This suggests the importance that differences in class have for perceptions among Blacks. But even individuals from middle-class neighborhoods believe police generally treat Blacks and Whites differently. Whites are most likely to use the perceived rate of crime among Blacks as the reason for this disparate treatment (Weitzer 2000).

In general, Blacks are most likely to view the police as biased. Hispanics are significantly less likely to have this perception. Most Whites believe that police treat people impartially. Minorities, however, tend to see law enforcement as another institution that maintains their subordination (Weitzer and Tuch 2005). These views may be shaped by greater negative experiences with police and more exposure to media accounts of police abuse (Weitzer and Tuch 2004). Part of the reason for differences in treatment may also be related to the racial composition of police forces. Evidence suggests that increases in the proportion of minority police lead to more arrests of Whites but not non-Whites, and conversely, increases in the number of White police results in more arrests of non-Whites but not Whites (Donohue and Levitt 2001). The racial characteristics of the victim also seem to make a difference in arrest rates. A South Carolina study showed that when the rate of Black crimes against *Whites* increases, the rate at which Blacks were arrested also increased. When the rate at which Blacks committing crimes against other *Blacks* went up, however, the arrest rate did not increase. This may mean that when Blacks are perceived as a criminal threat against the White majority by authorities, arrest activity intensifies (Eitle, D'Alessio, and Stolzenberg 2002).

Whether or not youth have actual encounters with police or are arrested also appears to be related to the socioeconomic status of the persons involved. Police generally have particular images of delinquents, stereotypes that result in lower-class persons being arrested more often (Sampson 1986). In essence, police have certain expectations of the criminal behavior of youths, and these images lead them to monitor and arrest youths in the lower class more often, regardless of the frequency of their actual criminal behavior (Irwin 1985).

The negative perceptions of lower-class youths by police lead the latter to label whole neighborhoods as being contaminated because they are made up of individuals who are considered undesirable (Irwin 1985; Sampson 1986). The result is that the general socioeconomic status of a neighborhood can influence the attention paid to it and its inhabitants by authorities. A study by Sampson (1986), using data from the Seattle Youth Study, found that the number of contacts and reports by police is strongly and inversely related to the

Minorities who live in poor neighborhoods are more likely than others to view police and other governmental authorities with suspicion and to feel that they are treated unfairly in the justice system. Evidence shows that police label certain neighborhoods as contaminated and that the racial composition of police forces affects the rate of arrests for racial groups. The poster above appeared on a telephone pole in the downtown of a major mid-Atlantic city.

Photo by Brendan R. Hurst.

neighborhood's general SES, independent of the actual extent of criminal and delinquent behavior in the area. He concluded that "for the bulk of offenses typically committed by juveniles (e.g., larceny, fighting, vandalism, burglary, drug violations) official police records and referrals to court are structured not simply by the act itself but by socioeconomic and situational context (e.g., delinquency of friends) as well, a process which may in turn amplify the effect of prior record in later decisions concerning official delinquents" (ibid., p. 884).

All of this research strongly suggests that the ecological area and perceptions of law officials affect the relationship between official rates of crime/delinquency and social class. These additional limitations of official statistics should be kept in mind when viewing the information in Table 11.1, which presents the arrest distributions for Index crimes by race and sex of those arrested. In 2003, there were 1,558,324 arrests made for such crimes, and about three-fourths of all those arrested were men. The highest arrest rate for women was for larceny-theft (37%). In recent years, the arrest rates for women have increased. While most of those arrested in 2003, with the exception of robbery, were Whites, Blacks were disproportionately represented in the arrest rates for all Index crimes, although the percentage of those arrested for various crimes who are Black declined between 2000 and 2003. Forty-nine percent of those arrested for murder in 2000 were Black. In total, 37 percent of all those arrested for violent crimes and 29 percent of those arrested for property crimes were Black. A small percentage of arrests, generally 1 to 3 percent, involved American Indians, Alaskan Natives, Asians, or Pacific Islanders.

Social Class and the Commission of Crime

These statistics suggest strongly that Blacks and males are more likely to commit crimes than their counterparts, and that the differences in arrest rates are too large to believe otherwise (LaFree 1995). However, as you will see in the next section, the differences in rates between Blacks and Whites are not due primarily to cultural differences between these groups, but to differences in the structural contexts in which they live. That is to say that the causes of Black crime are similar to the causes of crime by any group, but Blacks are exposed more forcefully and thoroughly to social contexts that encourage criminal behavior. Much of this context involves elements related to inequality

TABLE 11.1   Arrests by Index Offense Charged, Estimated Distributions by Sex and Race: 2003

| | PERSONS ARRESTED | | | | |
OFFENSE CHARGED	% Male	% Female	% White	% Black	% Other[a]
Murder and nonnegligent manslaughter	90	10	49	49	2
Forcible rape	99	1	64	33	2
Robbery	90	10	44	54	2
Aggravated assault	79	21	65	33	2
Burglary	86	14	71	28	2
Larceny-theft	63	37	69	29	3
Motor-vehicle theft	83	17	61	36	3
Arson	84	16	78	21	2
Violent crime[b]	82	18	61	37	2
Property crime[c]	69	31	68	29	3
Total Index arrests = 1,558,324					

Source: *Crime in the United States 2003: Uniform Crime Reports* (Washington, DC: Federal Bureau of Investigation, 2003).

Note: Totals may not add up to 100 percent because of rounding.

[a]American Indian, Alaskan Native, Asian, or Pacific Islander.

[b]Violent crimes are murder, forcible rape, robbery, and aggravated assault.

[c]Property crimes are burglary, larceny-theft, motor-vehicle theft, and arson.

such as poverty, economic discrepancies, social isolation, poor jobs, and unemployment. For example, one of the arguments used to explain the economic stress faced by minorities has emphasized the role played by the decline of manufacturing and the deindustrialization of cities, leaving only low-wage employment or high rates of unemployment in their wake. Researchers of 683 U.S. metropolitan areas discovered that such "employment volatility" promotes a higher property-crime rate (Bausman and Goe 2004).

In contrast to the apparently clear relationships between race, sex, and crime, the relationship between social class and actual commission of crime/delinquency has been a source of great controversy. Certainly there are arguments that suggest that the definition of crime, the enforcement of laws, and the judicial and sentencing procedures work against the lower classes, which are reflected in higher crime rates and more severe sentencing for those groups.

Overviews of studies done on the relationship between social class/socioeconomic status and crime/delinquency have yielded inconsistent conclusions. Tittle and his colleagues (1978) concluded after their review of 35 studies that the relationship between social status and official crime rates is only weak and that the relationship of status to self-reported crime is nonexistent. They argue that "class and criminality are not now, and probably never were related, at least not during the recent past" (p. 652). However, another review of over 100 studies by Braithwaite (1981) reached the opposite conclusion—that is, that there is quite a bit of support for the inverse relationship between class and crime.

A large part of the explanation for discrepancies in findings on this relationship appears to relate to the measures used for social class and crime (Kleck 1981). Virtually all of the studies in recent years have used occupational prestige, income, or educational hierarchies as measures of class, rather than Marxian measures (e.g., ownership, control over labor, etc.). Hagan and his colleagues (1985, 1987) suggested that differences in power ought to be more fully incorporated into studies of class and crime. This is especially relevant for studies purporting to understand the relationship between gender and crime. When one considers that power differences frequently separate men and women in families and may be directly linked to the probability of white-collar crime, the request for other measures of class seems more than reasonable.

To test their ideas about the importance of power differences in producing common delinquency, Hagan and his associates (1985, 1987) collected data from students in Toronto and used a measure of authority and ownership to determine the position of men and women in the households. The common delinquent acts included less serious behaviors such as minor theft, fighting, minor vandalism, and the like. The authors hypothesized that in families in which wives and daughters have little power, there is less freedom and risk taking on the part of women. Hence, they will be significantly less likely than the sons to commit delinquent acts. It is in these types of families that gender differences in delinquency will be most pronounced. On the other hand, in those in which females have some freedom and can take risks, there will be little difference between the sexes in their delinquency rates. Analyses by Hagan and his colleagues supported these hypotheses and also revealed that the gender differences in delinquency declined as one went down the class hierarchy. Gender differences were largest in the employer class. A large part of the reason for this gender difference seems to be that sons in this class have greater power relative to their mothers and are not taking as great a risk in being punished as are daughters. In other words, the authors pointed out again that gender differences in delinquency are linked to power differences in the family, which in turn are a reflection of power differences in the workplace.

The Structure of Inequality and the Social Production of Crime

When it comes to the commission of crime, an analysis of its relationship to inequality involves more than just examining the connection between the statuses of individuals and the commission of crime. At the social-structural level, or macrolevel, the system of inequality itself may be related to the generation of crime rates. This section examines this possibility as it appears in theory and research.

The generation of crime and varying crime rates appears to be intimately connected to the organization and culture of U.S. society. Homicide and incarceration rates in the United States are higher than those of any other industrialized nation. "In short, at all social levels, America is organized for crime" (Messner and Rosenfeld 1994, p. 6). Our capitalistic emphases on individual competition and economic success at almost any cost in the context of a system in which rewards are unequally divided encourage ventures outside the law, especially because economic success is so frequently used as a measure of a person's worth (Gordon 1973; Messner and Rosenfeld 1994). Gordon theorized that crime in this institutional context becomes a rational response to the manner in which society is organized.

Pratt and Godsey's (2003) study of 47 countries revealed that income inequality in a country was positively related to its homicide rate. Its effect was especially noticeable when the amount of social support provided for the population by the government was low. The percentage of the gross domestic product used in public spending on health care was how the authors measured the degree of "social support." This suggests that the civic and political framework within which citizens live has an impact on the role that inequality plays in generating violent crime. If not paid by the government, health care costs can place an economic strain on individuals, a strain that may, together with other economic needs, instigate property crime. Indeed, economic difficulties accelerate robbery rates by Blacks in racially heterogeneous cities, which, in turn, increase interracial homicides by them (Wadsworth and Kubrin 2004). In sum, societies with high degrees of income inequality create pressures that generate both property and violent crime.

A great deal of research indicates that structural features related to economic inequality are significantly linked to the creation of street crime, and of course it is generally members of minorities and the lower classes that are most likely to experience life on the lower rungs of the economic ladder. At the social level, poverty rates, economic deprivation, income inequality, unemployment, and employment in unstable jobs have all been found to be positively related to crime rates (e.g., Blau and Blau 1982; Williams 1984; Williams and Flewelling 1988; Crutchfield 1995; Kposowa, Breault, and Harrison 1995).

Unemployment rates also have been found to be related to property crime rates. Extensive reviews of studies suggest strongly that unemployment and property crime are positively related (Chiricos 1987; Devine, Sheley, and Smith 1988). These studies rely heavily on official rather than self-reported statistics. In a longitudinal study, Cantor and Land (1985) examined rates for seven Index crimes from 1946 to 1982. Their results are valuable because they indicate that unemployment can have both positive and negative effects on crime, depending on the particular crime in question. Specifically, unemployment can have a dampening effect on the crime rate because it means in part that the opportunity to be a victim of a property or violent crime is lower. When people are unemployed, they are at home, among friends and relatives, "guarding" property more often. This means that they are less likely to be victims of crimes by a stranger. On the other hand, unemployment has a positive effect on criminal motivation, thereby increasing the probability of crime, especially property crime.

At the individual level, employment has been found to be related to a lower probability of committing a crime. An experimental study of over 2,000 ex-offenders in Texas and Georgia revealed that those who were given employment were less likely to commit a crime after being released than those who were not given employment (Berk, Lenihan, and Rossi 1980). Moreover, those who were given some money in the form of transfer payments, which in effect reduced their poverty, were less likely to commit a crime. The latter suggests that there may be a trade-off between unemployment/poverty and crime. Among African American teenagers, employment and criminal behavior do appear to be used as substitutes. Both are viewed as income-producing activities. African American teenagers who are employed engage in fewer criminal behaviors and vice versa. Involvement in criminal activity, in turn, results in less employment (Good and Pirog-Good 1987; Freeman 1989). Not only unemployment itself, but the quality of employment can have an effect on property crime rates. Among young adults, those with poor-paying jobs having bad hours are more likely to be arrested for property crimes (Allan and Steffensmeier 1989).

In addition to property crime, violent crime is also related to inequality of different types. Gender inequality, for example, has been linked to homicide rates in developed countries. Child homicide rates are higher in developed countries in which there is (1) high female labor-force participation but (2) little child support for them and (3) low female status in the society (Fiala and LaFree 1988). This combination creates greater economic stress that heightens the likelihood for child abuse and homicide. Nations that provide more public assistance to mothers in the form of family allowances or social security programs have lower rates of such homicide. It has been argued elsewhere that not alleviating this kind of stress among women in families increases child abuse and is part of the reason why the United States has a higher rate of abuse than many other developed countries (Kamerman 1980; Zigler and Muenchow 1983).

The Blau and Blau (1982) study of inequality and violent crime rates in metropolitan areas used official crime statistics from the largest 125 metropolitan areas in the United States to find out if the crime rates varied with the extent of socioeconomic inequality in the area. Theoretically, they reasoned that in a democracy, inequalities based on skill or other achieved qualities are perceived as justifiable, while those based on ascribed characteristics such as race or sex are not. When a nominal or horizontal trait like race is closely connected to the vertical structure of economic inequality, racial and class differences become consolidated, and conflict between groups results in the society. One result of this situation is higher violent crime rates. Their findings bear out this theory. Economic inequality generally, and racial socioeconomic inequality in particular, is related to the production of violent crimes. Areas with greater inequality have higher crime rates. Inequality, rather than racial composition of an area, is principally related to violent crime rates.

Messner's (1989) cross-national study of homicide rates supports the Blau and Blau theory, as well. Messner predicted that countries with greater ascribed economic inequality in the form of discrimination would have higher homicide rates. While his measures of discrimination are rather crude, the analysis of data from 52 nation-states confirms this hypothesis and, in fact, demonstrates that inequality in the form of economic discrimination is more strongly related to homicide rates than is the extent of overall income inequality. This suggests that the *form* of inequality may be more important than its *extent* in accounting for homicide rates.

A reanalysis of the Blau data by Williams (1984) suggested that poverty may indeed also be related to homicide rates, especially in areas outside the South. This supports the findings of other studies (e.g., Loftin and Hill 1974; Danziger and Wheeler 1975; Messner 1980; Williams and Flewelling 1988). As Williams

and Flewelling stated, "It is reasonable to assume that when people live under conditions of extreme scarcity, the struggle for survival is intensified. Such conditions are often accompanied by a host of agitating psychological manifestations, ranging from a deep sense of powerlessness and brutalization to anger, anxiety, and alienation. Such manifestations can provoke physical aggression in conflict situations" (1988, p. 423).

Given this proposal, let us consider the situation of Blacks living in the interior of a city. Residential segregation of Blacks has been highly intransigent but has declined somewhat since 1980. It continues to be extensive, especially in the East and Midwest. Many of these cities remain "hypersegregated"— "a black core surrounded by a white ring" (Massey and Denton 1993, p. 67). Segregation of Asian and Hispanic immigrants is moderate at worst, although it is increasing as their immigration into the United States has increased. Moving into the suburbs has been marked by the same patterning of racial and ethnic concentration (Charles 2003).

Such residential segregation itself is largely a result of inequality processes. Early in the twentieth century, Blacks moved in large numbers from the South to the North, frequently recruited by employers who were fighting unions and who wished to use Blacks as strikebreakers. This only intensified racist feelings among Whites. Fear by Whites led to "restrictive covenants" in neighborhoods and blockbusting by real estate dealers who hoped to profit from the Black migration. Later, movement of industry out of cities and increasingly poor opportunities for stable employment impoverished these areas. These developments led to the consequent concentration of Blacks into isolated, packed, poor neighborhoods or ghettos.

The current extreme segregation experienced by Blacks is not one of choice; in contrast to Whites, most prefer a decidedly mixed neighborhood. Rather, it has been the actions of government, real estate agencies, banks, and the construction industry that have shaped and maintained segregation through their loan and mortgage policies, gatekeeping of neighborhoods, and construction requirements. Sometimes the stereotypes are evident but the style of discrimination is soft and nuanced as found in these comments by real estate agents who guide Whites away from certain areas:

> "*'Black people do live around here, but it has not gotten bad yet'; [or] 'That area is full of Hispanics and blacks that don't know how to keep clean'; or '(This area) is very mixed. You probably wouldn't like it because of the income you and your husband make. I don't want to sound prejudiced'*" (Farley and Squires 2005, p. 36; see also Charles 2003).

What is important about such segregation is that it "is not a neutral fact; . . . Because of racial segregation, a significant share of black America is condemned to experience a social environment where poverty and joblessness are the norm, where a majority of children are born out of wedlock, where most families are on welfare, where educational failure prevails, and where social and physical deterioration abound. Through prolonged exposure to such an environment, black chances for social and economic success are drastically reduced." The tools and avenues needed to succeed are largely out of reach; access to decent education, health care, and employment is severely limited. The possibility of investing in a desirable home that would increase in value over time, laying a foundation for future wealth, is also almost nonexistent. The conditions perpetuate the low socioeconomic position of residents and freeze the positions of those middle-class persons who live there. As a structural fact, these conditions are beyond the power of any person to change them (Massey and Denton 1993; Farley and Squires 2005). Figure 11.1 captures much of

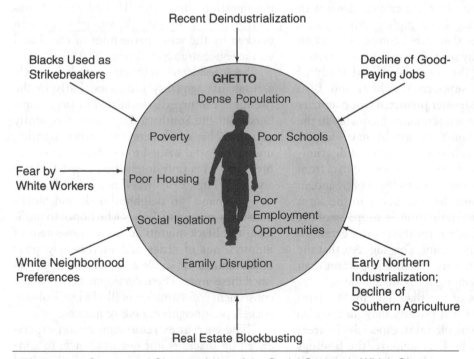

FIGURE 11.1   Causes and Characteristics of the Social Context in Which Ghetto Residents Live

Source: Based on Massey and Denton 1993.

the context in which ghetto residents live and the factors that have created it.

The concentration of poverty and unemployment in these isolated and highly dense areas of cities has led to a stable underclass, the collapse of effective institutions (family disorganization, poor housing, poor employment opportunities), and the development of cultural adaptations that undermine mainstream values. There is little to bind individuals to the community. Consequently, social controls to minimize crime are not in place; neither institutions nor cultural values are effective in controlling crime in this context. Segregation and Black isolation from Whites are highly and directly related to higher rates of violence (Olzak, Shanahan, and McEneaney 1996; Shihadeh and Flynn 1996). This setting results in fewer opportunities and less attachment of Blacks to the wider society and its values. Higher crime rates follow, as do victimization rates, and since it is Blacks who are concentrated in these areas, it is their rates that spiral upward. In 2003, for example, 48 percent of murder victims were Blacks, even though they compose only about 11 percent of the population. The victimization rates of Blacks and low-income individuals for other kinds of violent crimes are also disproportionately higher than those of Whites and higher-income persons. They are also higher for urban dwellers and renters. While somewhat less clearly, the pattern for property-crime victimization follows the same path (see Table 11.2).

What is clear in the research done is that the causes of crime and victimization among Blacks are not unique. Any individual exposed to this environment over time is vulnerable to criminal behavior and victimization (Sampson and Wilson 1995; Kposowa, Breault, and Harrison 1995). Thus, to understand differences in crime and victimization rates between rich and poor, Blacks and Whites, we need to appreciate the social context that generates such differences. And, as you have seen, this is a context largely created by and resulting in multidimensional inequality.

All of these results suggest that changes in the structures of capitalism and inequality would result in changes in crime rates. Danziger and Wheeler's (1975) research suggested that income distribution affects crime rates and that reduced inequality is related to reduced crime rates. They contend, as others have, that inequality generates crime both of the street and suite variety. They concluded from their analysis of 57 large metropolitan areas that "levels of criminal activity are responsive to changes in the distribution of income . . . a one percent reduction in . . . inequality was shown to reduce crime to a larger extent than a one percent increase in deterrence" (ibid., pp. 126–127).

Inequality and Criminal Sentencing

Criminal justice is a process with several stages, beginning with the definition of crime, labeling of individuals as potential criminals, arrest procedures, court procedures, and sentencing. "At all stages of the system—beginning with arrest and proceeding through imprisonment and parole—substantial racial and ethnic disparities are found in virtually all jurisdictions in the United States" (The Sentencing Project 2003, p. 1). Data from the most heavily populated counties in the United States, for example, reveal that even before trial, men, Blacks, and Hispanics are less likely to receive pretrial releases, a major reason being their inability to pay bail. Another factor may be that "judges and other court actors develop 'patterned responses' that express both gender and race-ethnicity assessments relative to blameworthiness, dangerousness, risk of recidivism or flight" (Demuth and Steffensmeier 2004).

If convicted, sentencing is the next stage. Sentencing goes to the heart of questions about the fairness of the criminal justice system. As is the case with likelihood of arrest and conviction, those who are lower in status do worse than others when it comes to sentencing. Even when the type of offense and previous criminal

TABLE 11.2   Estimated Rates of Victimization in Violent and Property Crimes, by Race, Ethnicity, Sex, Income, and Residence: 2002

VICTIM/HOUSEHOLD CHARACTERISTICS	VIOLENT CRIME RATE*	PROPERTY CRIME RATE*
Race		
White	23	165
Black	28	180
Other	15	171.3
Ethnicity		
Hispanic	24	—
Non-Hispanic	23	—
Sex		
Male	26	—
Female	21	—
Household Income		
Under $7,500	46	189
$7,500 to $14,999	32	167
$15,000 to $24,999	30	172
$25,000 to $34,999	27	162
$35,000 to $49,999	26	175
$50,000 to $74,999	19	158
$75,000 and over	19	170
Residence		
Urban	33	215
Suburban	20	145
Rural	18	118
Home Ownership		
Owned	—	136
Rented	—	207

Source: Kathleen Maguire and Ann L. Pastore (Eds.), *Sourcebook of Criminal Justice Statistics—2002*, U.S. Department of Justice, Bureau of Justice Statistics (Washington, DC: U.S. Government Printing Office, 2002), pp. 191, 203, 206.

*Rates for violent crime are per 1,000 persons age 12 and older and do not include murder or manslaughter; rates for property crime are per 1,000 households. All rates rounded.

record are taken into account, lower-income individuals have been found to receive longer sentences. Some studies, however, find that this relationship occurs for some crimes but not for others (D'Alessio and Stolzenberg 1993). In their study of burglary and larceny crimes, Clarke and Koch (1976) argued that lower-income persons have less of a chance for pretrial release on bail and for a private rather than a court-appointed attorney. This may explain why they found that low-income defendants received harsher punishment. After

examining results from many studies, Jeffrey Reiman concluded that, generally, *"for the same crime*, the system is more likely to investigate and detect, arrest and charge, convict and sentence, sentence to prison and for a longer time, a lower-class individual than a middle- or upper-class individual" (Reiman 2004, p. 146).

A review of studies conducted over the last two decades indicates that young, unemployed Black or Hispanic men are especially likely to receive lengthy sentences compared to their White counterparts. Often, although not always, this relationship is found even when other relevant factors such as previous record are taken into account. Harsher penalties are also meted out if the victim of the crime is White and the perpetrator is Black. In cases of murder, the death penalty is more likely to be given to Blacks who have been convicted of killing Whites (The Sentencing Project 2005). Between 1995 and 2000, 72 percent of the 159 cases recommended for prosecution of the death penalty in the federal judicial system included minority defendants. Plea agreements waiving the death penalty were twice as likely to occur if the defendant was White, and prosecuting attorneys were about twice as likely to seek the death penalty in cases with a Black defendant and a non-Black victim. A survey of 28 studies involving cases in state judicial systems revealed the same relationship between defendant/victim characteristics and receipt of the death penalty (ibid.). In January 2003, 43 percent of the 3,692 prisoners under a death sentence were Black, 45 percent were White, and 9 percent were Hispanic. In 2001, over half of death-row prisoners possessed less than a high school education; only about 10 percent had any college education at all. Virtually all (99%) were male (Maguire and Pastore 2002).

In some cases, Blacks may receive more lenient sentences than Whites for the same crimes if (a) the victim involved was Black, (b) White paternalism toward or guilt about Blacks is present, and/or (c) Blacks are perceived as being less responsible because they are exposed to more stressful living conditions than Whites (Kleck 1981).

What accounts for the connection between race and sentencing? Research on the judicial systems in seven states found that Blacks and males are more likely to be sentenced for longer terms than Whites or females if the jurisdiction involved is conservative and subscribes to a "law-and-order" perspective (Helms and Jacobs 2002). So we would expect that the relationship between race and length of sentence would vary across

districts, helping to account for the differences in findings in earlier studies (e.g., Bedau 1964; Thornberry 1973; Burke and Turk 1975; Chiricos and Waldo 1975). Longer sentences are given also, in part, because crime in general is considered "a black phenomenon" (Chiricos, Welch, and Gertz 2004, p. 380). Some crimes in particular, for example, drug offenses, are considered minority crimes, and consequently result in stiffer punishment for Blacks and Hispanics (Steffensmeier and Demuth 2000). A national survey in 2002 suggested that there is a "conflation of race and crime" in the minds of many Americans, part of a broad brush that paints Blacks as bad in general and as a "social threat" in particular (Chirieos, Welch, and Gertz 2004, p. 380). This is consistent with the earlier discussion regarding the image and classification of young, mentally ill Black men as dangerous, paranoid, and schizophrenic.

The concern for crime and punishment in the United States is reflected in its rapidly growing jail and prison populations. In roughly the last 30 years, the rate of *prison* incarceration in the United States has increased 600 percent to reach almost 1.4 million persons in 2002, giving this nation the largest rate of incarceration in the world (Pager 2003). *Jail* inmates totaled over 665,000 in 2002. In that same year, the rate at which Black men were incarcerated was over 6 times the rate for White men (Chiricos et al. 2004). The rate of incarceration in both jails and prisons has continued to grow since 2002. Table 11.3 profiles the populations for jails and state prisons. Compared to the outside population, inmates have lower levels of education. Minorities in general, and Blacks in particular, compose the majority of those populations. In fact, almost 13 percent of Black men aged 25–29 were in jail or prison in 2004 ("Nation's Inmate," April 25, 2005).

The impact of such high rates of minority incarceration reaches beyond prison walls to affect their future employment and present

TABLE 11.3   Percent Distribution of Jail Inmates (2002) and State Prison Inmates (2000)

	JAIL INMATES (2000)	PRISON INMATES (2000)
Sex		
Male	88	94
Female	12	6
Race, Hispanic Origin		
White, non-Hispanic	42	36
Black, non-Hispanic	41	46
Hispanic	15	14
Other	2	2
Education	(1996)	(1997)
8th grade or less	13	14
Some high school	33	26
GED	14	29
High school graduate	26	20
Some college	10	9
College graduate or more	3	2

Source: Kathleen Maguire and Ann L. Pastore (Eds.), *Sourcebook of Criminal Justice Statistics—2000*, U.S. Department of Justice, Bureau of Justice Statistics (Washington, DC: U.S. Government Printing Office, 2000), pp. 503, 519.

political power. Recent research in Milwaukee found that even with identical resumes, not only were job applicants with criminal records less likely than noncriminals to be called back for interviews, but Black *noncriminals* even got fewer callbacks than Whites with *criminal* records. Whether Black or White, having a criminal record decreases the chances for employment. This is especially true for Blacks (Pager 2003). It should not be surprising, therefore, to find that criminal conviction also reduces one's future income, especially if conviction happens when one is young (Kerley, Benson, and Lee 2004). These effects further reduce the chances of building up wealth for the next generation. Prison incarceration also reduces a person's political power since 48 out of 50 states in the United States do not allow prison inmates to vote. Many states also severely limit the chances of individuals voting even after they have served their sentences. About 4.7 million citizens, including 1.4 million Black men, do not have voting rights as a result (The Sentencing Project, April 2005). A recent telephone survey of

adults indicated that a large majority of citizens favor restoring voting rights to ex-felons, but only about one-third believe that felons currently in prison should be allowed to vote (Manza, Brooks, and Uggen 2002). Many of the disenfranchisement rules were passed after the Civil War during Reconstruction, when Blacks were a potential political force. States in which non-Whites make up a large percentage of the prison population are those most likely to have the most restrictive disenfranchisement laws (Behrens, Uggen, and Manza 2003). Such laws can and do affect who gets elected to the U.S. Congress and the Presidency (Uggen and Manza 2002). Whether intentional or not, both imprisonment and disenfranchisement serve as means of controlling and disempowering Black men.

With respect to gender bias, recent studies are more mixed in their results than earlier ones that suggested a paternalistic or chivalric reaction to female offenders. Nagel and Weitzman's (1971) often-cited study of national data concerning over 11,000 criminal cases revealed that while the poor and

Blacks received less favorable treatment than well-off Whites, women were treated more leniently. They were less likely to be held in jail before the trial and to be sentenced to prison. The analysis focused on the crimes of grand larceny and assault. A study by Curran (1983) in Florida supported the leniency argument. She found that at the sentencing stage of the criminal process women received lighter sentences even when relevant legal (e.g., prior arrests, etc.) and other nonlegal factors (race, age, occupational status) were taken into account. Other studies, however, have suggested that the courts have become less chivalrous in their behavior toward women, and that if the criminal act for which a woman is arrested is considered a "manly" crime, she may receive a longer sentence than a man (Simon and Sharma 1979; Kruttschnitt and Green 1984).

Whether a judge is male or female also affects the probability of incarceration and length of sentence. In contrast to the image of women as more lenient, female judges tend to be harsher in their sentencing. They are more likely than male judges to incarcerate an offender and for a longer period of time. Judges of both genders are less likely to incarcerate White, older, and female offenders, but this is especially the case for female judges. Female judges are significantly more likely than their male counterparts to give longer sentences to Black repeat offenders. In other words, offender characteristics affect the decisions of women on the bench more so than those of male judges (Steffensmeier and Hebert 1999).

Regardless of their sentence, women who are sent to prison are sometimes convicted of crimes that were motivated by past abuse. Examining the histories of incarcerated women often reveals that they have been the victims of domestic or other violence that was related to their commission of crimes. In this event, some have suggested that imprisonment constitutes a form of "revictimization" (Dirks 2004; Moe 2004).

WHITE-COLLAR CRIME, CORPORATE CRIME, AND PUNISHMENT

All the adult crimes discussed thus far involve those listed on the FBI's Crime Index. White-collar or "suite" crimes are not part of the FBI's Crime Index, which raises further questions about equity in the treatment of types of crime generally associated with different segments of the population. Generally, though not always, white-collar crime refers to crimes committed by white-collar persons in the course of their occupations. It is the latter part of the definition that is critical; thus, blue-collar workers who steal or defraud in the course of their jobs might be considered guilty of similar crimes, but ordinarily the focus has been on those in the higher status occupations. The classic definition and usual usage of the term are given by Edwin Sutherland: "A crime committed by a person of respectability and high social status in the course of his occupation" (1949, p. 2).

Since the crime occurs in the context of a job, white-collar crime usually involves violation of trust. Thus, such acts as misadvertising, price fixing, identity theft, computer scams, insurance fraud, and other kinds of duplicities and misrepresentations are a part of white-collar crime. More recently, larger-scale corporate scandals have involved alleged insider trading, and accounting irregularities and misrepresentation of company assets that have bilked stockholders and drained the retirement packages of thousands of average employees. Investigations of possible criminality have included large corporations integral to the U.S. economy: Enron, WorldCom, Xerox, Tyco International, Adelphia, Global Crossing, Kmart, Columbia/HCA, and Sunbeam, for example. These acts constitute "corporate crimes," which are crimes committed by businesses or by high-level officials acting in their capacity as representatives of given corporations. Billions of dollars are involved in these cases alone. The savings-and-loans scandals of the 1980s could ultimately cost taxpayers several hundred billion dollars. Government estimates are that corporate crime costs the United States at least $200 billion annually, which is "fifty times the cost of street crime" (Chambliss 1999, p. 152). In addition to its economic costs, corporate crime also has human costs. Estimates suggest that roughly 100,000 individuals die every year because of accidents caused by conditions in industries. Despite their often higher costs to society, however, corporate criminals do not receive anywhere near the attention given to ordinary, street criminals (Chambliss 1999).

Corporate crime appears to be extensive. A survey of 1,043 large corporations searched for evidence of bribery, fraud, illegal political contributions, tax evasion, and antitrust violations (Ross 1980). The examination revealed that 11 percent of them were guilty of at least one violation. In terms of domestic violations, there were 98 cases of antitrust violations and smaller numbers of the other crimes.

Generally, individual white-collar crimes involve many more than one victim. When safety-code violations or price fixing occur, for example, many are harmed or seriously injured. In fact, although one ordinarily does not think of white-collar crime as violent, "there is considerable evidence that so-called 'nonviolent' white-collar criminals kill and maim more people each year in the United States than do violent street criminals" (Messner and Rosenfeld 1994, p. 32). This includes 100,000 who die from job-related illnesses and 30,000 who are killed by unsafe products every year (ibid.). An additional heavy cost of white-collar crime is the erosion of faith in social institutions that occurs when such crime takes place. Trust is a basis of solidarity and when it is damaged, society as a whole suffers. Thus, the damage resulting from white-collar crime radiates from the immediate victims to include many more.

But white-collar crime is not a new phenomenon. A study of white-collar crime during World War II by Marshall Clinard (1946), a sociologist who held an important position in the Office of Price Administration (OPA) at the time, uncovered well over 300,000 violations of the price and rationing rules of the OPA in 1944 alone. In the vast majority of cases, only warnings, dismissals, or minor reprimands were used as punishments. In 1961, a major antitrust violation was taken to court involving General Electric and Westinghouse. Behind closed doors, using hidden codes and meetings, the conspirators negotiated with each other, deciding how the market should be divided among themselves. "A low price would be established, and the remainder of the companies would bid at approximately equivalent, though higher levels" (Geis 1967, p. 122). A newspaper account recorded by Geis described the high-status defendants as they appeared in court as "middle-class men in Ivy League suits—typical businessmen in appearance, men who would never be taken for lawbreakers" (p. 117). One defendant's lawyer called the government's recommendation of a jail sentence "cold blooded" and said that the government did not realize what would happen to "this fine man" if he were put in jail in which there were "common criminals who had been convicted of embezzlement and other serious crimes" (pp. 117–118). One of the witnesses referred to his actions as "illegal . . . but not criminal." Michael Milken's conviction of securities fraud was described by his lawyer as "deviations from an otherwise admirable life" and asked for a sentence of community service instead of prison (Fatsis 1990, p. 113).

At the beginning of this chapter, I noted how crime is often "defined" into existence. The terms used to describe street crime—robbery, theft, murder, and so on,—leave little doubt of the nature of the behavior involved. In contrast, white-collar crimes are often described in more ambiguous and softer terms like financial "malfeasance," book-keeping "irregularities," and "misconduct." "Misconduct" does not seem quite as criminal as "theft," even though *stealing* may be what is involved in both cases. This terminology and the complicated nature of these cases, along with the physical appearance and self-definition of white-collar defendants as upstanding citizens, encourages a different treatment of white-collar defendants. Some argue that the terminology has to become more straightforward: "you've got to boil it down to lying, cheating, and stealing," says a Securities Board commissioner (Leaf 2002, p. 76).

Corporate officials who commit corporate crimes are also usually subject to civil rather than to criminal law, and such violations are handled by agencies rather than by the criminal courts. This is because "corporations" have not, traditionally, been considered "persons" who commit criminal acts with "intent" (Reid 1988). The manner in which white-collar crime is treated—namely, the special kind of legislation, the special kind of enforcement groups used, and the usual minimal types of punishment meted out—indicate that white-collar crime is treated differently than street crime in the U.S. justice system, even though its cost to victims is much greater. Geis (1974) stated the point bluntly: "Upperworld crime portrays the manner in which power is exercised in our society. A review of upperworld violations and the manner in which they are prosecuted and punished tells who is able to control what in American society and the extent to which such control is effective" (p. 114).

Some systematic studies have been done of the relationship between individuals' characteristics and their punishment for white-collar crimes. Wheeler and associates' (1982) study of several white-collar crimes over a three-year period in seven federal districts suggests that socioeconomic status is positively related to being incarcerated and to the length of sentence given those convicted of these crimes. The crimes included in the study were eight federal crimes: "antitrust offenses, securities and exchange fraud, postal and wire fraud, false claims and statements, credit and lending institution fraud, bank embezzlement, IRS fraud, and bribery" (Wheeler, Weisburd, and Bode

1982, p. 642). Paradoxically, the authors found that not only were those with occupations of higher prestige more likely to be imprisoned and given longer sentences but the same was also true for those with less impeccable past lives. They suggested that a "paradox of leniency and severity" runs through a judge's decisions on these matters, impeccability and SES pulling in opposite directions. Other factors, of course, also were found to be related to imprisonment, such as the severity and scope of the crime and the sex of the offender. Men were much more likely to be sent to prison than women, but it is not the role of motherhood that accounts for the differences in treatment. Rather, the authors suggested, "the answer lies deep in the history of sex-role relationships in American society. . . . There is something about the specter of women behind the bars and walls of the prison that leads many judges to a kind of protective paternalism" (p. 656). In making their decisions, judges consider (1) the seriousness of the crime, (2) the "blameworthiness" of the criminal, (3) the category of the offense and the district in which it is committed, and (4) the offender's sex.

Following up on Wheeler and colleagues' model of sentencing, Benson and Walker (1988) studied sentencing for a sample of white-collar criminals in one federal court over a 10-year period. Basically, the crimes examined were the same as those in the previous study, with the addition of embezzlement by a public employee. In contrast to the Wheeler study, Benson and Walker found that SES and impeccability had little to do with the decision to send an offender to prison. They also found that non-Whites were more likely than Whites to be imprisoned even after SES was taken into account. With respect to length of sentence, the researchers found that SES was not related to it, but that being non-White and scoring high in impeccability were related to longer sentences. In essence, most of their results contradict those of Wheeler and associates. They attribute much of this variation to differences in the distribution of crimes among the sample, the differences in the districts studied, and perhaps different values among judges in large urban settings, and those in smaller rural areas. They suggested, in sum, that contextual factors may affect the findings in different studies. The districts studied in the Wheeler and associates research "have larger caseloads, are more urbanized, and are more racially mixed than most federal districts" (Benson and Walker 1988, p. 301). They included the Atlanta, Los Angeles, Dallas, Manhattan and the Bronx, Chicago, and Seattle areas. In contrast, the Benson and Walker study was based on one district in a midwestern state.

As illuminating as these studies may be, they do not address the issues of what percentage of alleged white-collar crimes are actually brought to court, or the length of sentences perpetrators receive. In these areas, there appears to be a greater discrepancy between white-collar and street crime. This is especially the case for high-level crimes: "The U.S. regulatory and judiciary systems . . . do little if anything to deter the most damaging Wall Street crimes" (Leaf 2002, p. 64). White-collar criminals convicted of massive fraud in the 1980s savings-and-loan crisis served an average of just over 3 years in prison, while common burglars (usually stealing $300 or less) received sentences of 4.5 years, and first-time drug criminals got about 5.4 years (ibid.).

In 2000, 8,766 were charged with white-collar crimes and 6,876 (78%) were convicted. Of these, almost 4,000 were sent to prison (Leaf 2002). On closer examination, however, we find that all kinds of crimes, including welfare frauds, are included in the "white-collar" category, and that only 226 of these cases are for securities or commodities fraud. The high-level, "*starched*-collar criminals" are generally not in this group (ibid., p. 68). These starched-collar criminals are often guilty of corporate crimes since they were committing crimes to benefit their companies and as acting officials of their companies. In contrast, white-collar crime like embezzlement,

for example, is a crime committed by an employee for his or her own gain.

Of the 156,238 people in federal prisons in late 2001, only 1,021 were white-collar criminals, and less than 10 percent of these 1,021 were starched-collar criminals. Moreover, over half of the white-collar inmates are in minimal, rather than "medium" or "maximum" security prisons (Leaf 2002).

Since 2002, there have been several high-profile convictions of corporate executives since 2001 for fraud, grand larceny, conspiracy, obstruction of justice, and/or money laundering. These include CEOs at WorldCom, Tyco International, and Adelphia Communications. The lower probability that white-collar or corporate crimes will result in convictions and incarceration reflects deficiencies in the system of justice: case overloads, ambiguous and vague regulatory laws, powerful law teams at the disposal of some but not others, and the complexity of the cases themselves. These deficiencies help to account for the commission of these types of crime.

The Roots of White-Collar and Corporate Crime

What are the main causes of white-collar and corporate crime? One argument focuses on the greed and immorality of individual perpetrators. In this view, white-collar crime is the result of a few "bad apples" with character flaws. A second view emphasizes the role that U.S. and corporate cultures play in encouraging this type of crime. The U.S. culture encourages free enterprise and open competition, honors economic winners and not losers, and winks at those clever people who are able to "pull the wool" over others' eyes. Similarly, and sometimes over other values, corporate culture sometimes encourages success and profit-making and taking full advantage of opportunities to maximize the bottom line. This may even involve intentionally protecting valuable executives from accusations of criminality (Lyons 2002).

The Enron scandal was just the beginning of an increasing number of recent scandals in major corporations. One of the reasons it incensed many was because of the manner in which executives protected their own wealth while demonstrating little concern for average workers in the corporation. Workers were kept in the dark about the real financial situation of the company and were prevented from selling their company stocks while executives cashed in their stock options to make fortunes.

A third, and potentially more perceptive, view involves the political structure and economic context within which corporations operate. This is especially relevant for "corporate" rather than simple "white-collar" crime. A significant part of the structure that affects corporations is the federal regulation to which they are subject. In this case, regulations are often vague and ambiguous, leaving room for multiple interpretations. They are also complex: "[J]uries have a hard time grasping abstract financial concepts, and well-counseled executives have plenty of tricks for distancing themselves from responsibility" (France and Carney 2002, p. 35). The broadness of the regulations means that while a given activity might be considered immoral, it is not necessarily illegal. Sometimes changes in rules create opportunities for crime. Banking deregulation in the 1980s, for example, made it possible for savings and loans associations to engage in fraudulent actions because deregulation removed many of the controls that held these institutions in check. Deregulation created an economic climate in which greed, risk-taking, and corporate crime were encouraged. In addition to regulations, resource inadequacies and case overloads in enforcement agencies encourage illicit and unethical activity by lessening the chances of getting caught or being indicted. Large, complicated cases are costly, and indictment rates are low (Tillman, Calavita, and Pontell 1997). Finally, corporate lobbying for favorable legislation facilitates regulations that are pro-business. The result is that, while the average person may consider certain legal behaviors to be unethical and even "criminal," they may be allowable under law. For example, the "business-judgment rule" permits business executives to carry out almost any transaction as long as it could be interpreted as economically sound and is not clearly illegal. The broadness of this rule has resulted in executives being protected from many legal actions against them. Rules allowing corporations to export earnings to avoid taxation, allowing stock options to be left undefined as company costs, and allowing executives but not other employees to sell company stock during certain times reveal the corporate bias in many regulatory laws. In Charles Derber's opinion, "[T]he business-judgment rule and the growing set of constitutional rights vested in the corporation have created an unaccountable entity with sovereign powers far greater than natural entity theorists of the Gilded Age could ever have imagined" (Derber 2000, p. 148). Favorable rules and laws, when combined with the lobbying power of corporations, optimize the opportunity to *define* what is legal and what is not. As noted at the beginning of the chapter, to a large extent, crimes are defined into existence.

In addition to the political context, economic shifts are another structural element creating a fertile environment for corporate and white-collar crime. For example, downsizing and the economic difficulties encountered by employees and smaller employers made provision of health insurance very costly. Changes in regulations added to the problem when they allowed companies to provide health insurance as part of their employee benefit packages, but exempted these packages from coverage under state insurance laws. The result was an economic and political vacuum in which insurance-fraud criminals could operate (Tillman and Indergaard 1999).

With respect to corporate crime, a capitalist society in which corporations must successfully compete to survive creates pressures to violate the law. The uncertainties in the social, political, and economic environments in which corporate profits must be obtained make success problematic (Box 1983). Corporations, like other large organizations, try to control their environments in order to create a level of certainty in their operations, and they have become powerful actors in their own right (Thompson 1967; Coleman 1982). One of the means to create predictability in the resource and consumer markets is to behave in an illegal manner. When legitimate means to obtaining organizational goals are either difficult to use or unavailable, pressure exists to obtain legitimate goals such as profit by illegitimate means (Sherman 1987). This suggests that capitalism itself helps to generate corporate and white-collar crimes.

HATE CRIMES AND INEQUALITY

Social conditions also affect the extent of crimes committed against members of demeaned status groups. *Hate crimes* are violent or property crimes "committed against a person, property, or society which is motivated, in whole or in part, by the offender's bias against a race, religion, disability [mental or physical], sexual orientation, or ethnicity/national origin" (U.S. Department of Justice 1998, p. 59). One characteristic that distinguishes them from other crimes is the nature of the motivation. Hate crimes have a symbolic function in that they are directed as a *warning* against groups of low status. Consequently, who the specific victims are may be irrelevant to the perpetrator(s) since they serve only as a representative of the group. As warnings, hate crimes are aimed at reaffirming the existing social hierarchies and keeping groups in their place. Thus, their effects of intimidation and fear reach into the entire group, not just the individual victim. Expectations are that hate crimes will not only continue but also increase in the future as the United States becomes more diversified and as pressures mount for dominant groups to share scarce economic, political, and other resources (Perry 2001; Craig 2002).

Knowledge about the extent, causes, and consequences of hate crimes is incomplete for several reasons. First, there has been little systematic research on hate crimes. "The empirical investigation of the causes of hate crime remains a science in its infancy" (Green, McFalls, and Smith 2001, p. 490). Second, states vary in the groups that they include as potential victims, making rate comparisons difficult and conclusions about total numbers suspect. Moreover, some states do not provide any information. Third, statistics collected by the FBI on hate crimes are flawed because of the limited number of groups (e.g., sex is not included) and crimes covered in its definition (i.e., only Index crimes), and because of under-reporting of hate crimes (Perry 2001).

Despite its deficiencies, the FBI data are generally used to reach conclusions about hate crime in the United States as a whole. The gathering of these data began as a result of passage of the Hate Crimes Statistics Act in 1990. In 2003, according to FBI statistics, there were 7,489 hate crime incidents reported, involving 8,715 distinct offenses, and 9,100 victims. Almost two-thirds were crimes against persons, and one-third crimes against property. Just over half were racially motivated, followed by biases based on religion, sexual orientation, ethnicity/nationality, and disability, respectively (see Table 11.4). About two-thirds of the perpetrators were White; two-thirds of the victims were objects of anti-Black feelings.

Extreme concerns about racial and ethnic purity, continued immigration, job competition, residential infiltration, and the sanctity of

TABLE 11.4 Number of Incidents and Victims of Hate Crimes by Bias Motivation: 2003

MOTIVATION	NO. OF INCIDENTS	NO. OF VICTIMS
Race	3,844	4,754
Anti-White	830	1,006
Anti-Black	2,548	3,150
Other	466	598
Religion	1,343	1,489
Anti-Jewish	927	1,025
Other	416	464
Sexual Orientation	1,239	1,479
Anti-male homosexual	783	910
Anti-female homosexual	187	230
Anti-homosexual	247	314
Ethnicity/National Origin	1,026	1,326
Anti-Hispanic	426	595
Other	600	731
Disability	33	43
Anti-physical	24	32
Anti-mental	9	11
Multiple-Bias Incidents	4	9
Total	7,489	9,100

Source: Federal Bureau of Investigation, *Hate Crime Statistics 2003*, November 2004. Washington, DC: U.S. Department of Justice.

marriage and Christianity most often lie behind these biases. Target groups are viewed as threats to the living standards of these hate groups, which see their own way of life as under siege from contaminating elements.

Biases against particular groups are long-standing. As we saw in Chapter 7, abusive acts against Blacks were permitted during slavery, and the creation of the Ku Klux Klan (KKK) after the Civil War helped keep racist fires burning. Current White separatist groups in the United States include the various segments of the KKK, neo-Nazi and Skinhead groups, and some extreme Christian groups such as Christian Identity and the Christian Defense League. Estimates in the mid-1990s put the number of members and supporters of these groups at 200,000 (Dobratz and Shanks-Meile 1997).

One of the more recent publicized instances of a racial hate crime was committed on June 7, 1998, against 49-year-old James Byrd, Jr., a Black man, in Jasper, Texas. Byrd was picked up, beaten, chained to the bumper of a pickup truck, and dragged three miles until his head, shoulder, and other body parts were severed from each other. Showing no remorse and only contempt for his victim and his family, John William King, a White supremacist and one of three White men arrested for the murder, was sentenced to death (Lyman 1999).

A second publicized case, involving a gay man, occurred the fall of 1998. Matthew Shepard, a 21-year-old gay college student, was kidnapped, robbed, beaten, and tied to a fence in Laramie, Wyoming. Shepard died from his ordeal less than a week later (Brooke 1998). Like racism, prejudice against homosexuals has deep historical roots, principally highlighted by laws against sodomy, which were in place as early as the 1600s in the United States, and which required the death penalty or severe mutilation as punishment. In 1997, 21 states still had sodomy laws, and, until recently, human rights laws did not specifically protect gays and lesbians, which allowed continued discrimination against homosexuals in jobs,

housing, and public facilities (Herek and Berrill 1992; American Civil Liberties Union 1997; Button, Rienzo, and Wald 1997). Among other elements, feelings of superiority and concerns about competition over resources demonstrate the role of status inequality in the production of hate crimes.

STRUCTURED INEQUALITY AND COLLECTIVE PROTESTS

It is perhaps inevitable that inequality would be a significant spur for social protest. Perceived competition over positions in social and economic hierarchies, coupled with beliefs about different ethnic, racial, and religious groups, often appear to be instigators of collective protests and violence. And as in understanding the generation of crime, the more concrete structural aspects of inequality and the social context that affects the probability of protest also have to be considered.

Research on strikes has clearly indicated the importance of structural characteristics in the economy and society for the frequency and shape of strikes. Deprivation and/or position in a deprived group are not enough to produce collective action, nor may they even be the most significant predictors of such disorders. Even when frustrations do exist, as they usually and consistently do for deprived groups, one must still explain how individual frustrations develop into collective protests (Snyder and Tilly 1974).

Collective protest depends in large part on conditions that affect the mobilization possibilities of a group and on political conditions in the wider society. "The occasions when protest is possible among the poor, the forms that it must take, and the impact it can have are all delimited by the social structure in ways which usually diminish its extent and diminish its force" (Piven and Cloward 1977, p. 3).

The immediate characteristics and requirements for collective protest are clear: (1) the system being attacked has lost legitimacy in the eyes of the protestors, (2) individuals begin to feel more acutely that they have rights, and (3) they begin to think that their desperate, deprived situation is no longer inevitable but can be changed. Groups of people then collectively defy laws and arrangements that undergird established institutions (ibid., pp. 3–5). It is clear, for example, that from the point of view of the several minority groups that participated in the 1992 Los Angeles riot, the political system had lost its legitimacy. A lack of faith in the police and local political regimes was articulated by different minorities. Korean Americans, whose stores were looted, felt that neither the police nor the National Guard would protect them, and some felt that the media had systematically ignored African American prejudice against Asians, and only recognized White prejudice against African Americans (Awanohara and Hoon 1992; Iyer 1992). Political corruption also poisoned the feeling that government represented the people at large (Davis 1992b). Finally, the Rodney King verdict, in which some police were acquitted for the alleged beating of an African American motorist, only helped to cement belief in the illegitimacy of the entire legal system, and served as a reminder of the violation of minority rights. The lack of educational and occupational opportunities, which are supposed to be available to all Americans, intensified the sense of violation.

These political, educational, and occupational deficiencies in the structure of the community nurtured feelings of extreme frustration and illegitimacy, which, in turn, led to violence. The deficiencies were the "severe maladjustment" of which violence was the symptom (Coser 1967). The lack of opportunities may be related to segregation and the isolation of Blacks from Whites, both of which are related to urban violence. Violence serves as a final means for calling attention to the severe inequities that exist in a community. The critical issue is what and how conditions

in the wider society, especially those relating to the system of political and economic inequality, affect these characteristics in such a way as to enhance the probability of collective disorder.

At least eight elements pertaining to structural conditions have been related to the frequency and form of protest. The *first* of these is the existence of severe concentrated inequality. Severe inequalities in the form of social isolation from Whites, and, paradoxically, increases in desegregation, have both been found to be predictors of the 154 race riots during the 1960–1993 period, which included primarily Black participants.

Lee's interviews with minority merchants and customers in New York and Philadelphia in the late 1990s revealed that although relationships between them were cordial most of the time, the presence of severe inequalities in their immediate context meant that any minor incident could explode into collective protests. Poverty, differing beliefs about a group's legitimate social position, increased immigration, varying rates of social mobility, and perceived special treatment by government for some groups but not others all form part of the potentially explosive context in which relationships between merchants and customers are carried out (Lee 2002).

In their study of Black protests in the period 1948–1997, Jenkins, Jacobs, and Agnone found that "collective grievances stemming from racial income inequality, low-to-high Vietnam War deaths, and low-to-medium unemployment stimulate protest" (2003, p. 293). *High* unemployment, perhaps because it put Blacks in too weak an economic position, dampens protest.

Wrenching changes in society or the local community constitute a *second* structural element underlying collective protests. The transformation of institutions in a society leads to a clash between old and newly developing rules and frameworks for everyday behavior.

Under these conditions, political leaders are more vulnerable, and new opportunities to protest can easily surface, especially if the dislocations are severe and last long enough. Dislocations, then, can create both deprivation and opportunities to protest. Among the basic transformations that would most readily have implications for protest would be drastic fluctuations in the business cycle; shifts in the nature of technology, such as the continued trend toward automation and sophisticated technology; and basic changes in the content of the labor market, such as an increase of immigrants into the market.

Certainly basic and major economic and social changes have taken place in the Los Angeles area in recent decades. Among the *economic* changes are (1) an influx of 400,000 immigrants who work for low wages in southeast Los Angeles County; (2) a decline of at least 40,000 good-paying manufacturing jobs in the area, and a total of 75,000 jobs in general during the 1975–1985 period; (3) an unemployment rate that runs as high as 50 percent in parts of south central Los Angeles; (4) an erosion of the city's tax base as employers and middle-class and White workers move to the suburbs; and (5) a growing gulf between the rich and the poor. These economic downturns have exacerbated social problems arising from the changing composition of the local population. The *social* issues include (1) an interracial and interethnic hostility involving Korean Americans, Hispanics, Whites, African Americans, and other recent immigrants, each of whom is not always similarly situated economically; (2) poor, crowded housing but high rents; and (3) poor-quality education. It appears that while those involved in the 1992 Los Angeles riot were from several ethnic groups, the separation and hostility between them has not been diminished by their common involvement. While they all have economic problems, race remains a divisive force (Davis 1992a, 1992b; "Economic Crisis" 1992; Meyerson 1992).

The Chicano organization NEWS From America blames Central American immigrants for joining the riot; certain black leaders, jealous of the economic success of the Asian community and the coming political success of the Latinos (by sheer weight of numbers), lash out at both; many Koreans conceal a raging anti-black animus behind a wafer-thin veneer of peace rhetoric. Neither multiracial rioting nor multiracial riot defense seems to have loosened the stranglehold that separatism exerts within L.A.'s communities of color. (Meyerson 1992, p. 24)

This description suggests that the animosity is at least partially rooted in the economic and political inequality that is perceived to exist between these groups. Both racism and classism divide the population there, "and it may be futile to try to pinpoint where racism ends and classism begins" (Segal 1992, p. 47).

A *third* societal condition for protest is related to the first. The ideology of the state and its agents can and usually tries to symbolically lighten the burden of deprivation or encourages the belief that the individual is responsible for his or her own fate, not the system against which reaction might otherwise take place (ibid., pp. 6–7). A maintaining ideology is essential: "The willingness of mass publics to follow, to sacrifice, to accept their roles is the basic necessity for every political regime. Without a following there are no leaders." Such sacrifice and willingness to be loyal are legitimized by policy rationales, such as those that appeal to national security and similar symbols (Edelman 1977, p. 5). Severe dislocations can shake adherence to ideologies, and the latter are necessary to maintain peace in the system as it stands. The role of ideology in maintaining inequality is discussed further in Chapter 14.

The *fourth* condition relates directly to the power of the state and political inequality in the society and concerns the power and likely use of repression in dampening unrest. Repression is most likely to be used when the central institutions of the society are being attacked and when concessions have been made, but some continue to protest. Repression raises the cost of protest for those with grievances and thus lowers the odds for successful protest. Snyder and Tilly's (1972) analysis of collective violence in France from 1830 to 1960 found evidence that some measures of the government's repressive action were negatively related to the extent of collective violence.

The *fifth* structural factor is the power of the government to create opportunities and grant concessions. Government can create opportunities by developing acceptable and responsible programs to deal with grievances, and thereby, in effect, reshape the stated demands of the group. In this way, the government can weaken public support of the continued protest and present itself as "a benevolent and responsive government that answers grievances and solves problems" (Piven and Cloward 1977, p. 34). Then when protest dies down, concessions can be safely diluted or taken away; concessions that are not withdrawn can often be made to serve powerful groups as historically has often been the case with unions (p. 35). "Protestors win . . . what historical circumstances have already made ready to be conceded" (p. 36).

The structure of opportunities also affects the tactics protestors must use and the duration of protest. When protestors devise tactics to attain their goals that are then counteracted by successful tactics by the other side, protest is neutralized unless protestors create new tactics and approaches to continue the protest. The life of a movement depends on the ability of its members to constantly develop innovative tactics against those in power. Analysis of the Civil Rights movement during the years 1955 to 1970 demonstrates this process (McAdam 1983). In other words, the maintenance of protest depends on the power structure and opportunities in the social setting.

The *sixth* condition is connected to the fourth and concerns the political position of government vis-à-vis the aggrieved group. If the government is suspected of being supportive or actually does actively support potential protestors, protest is more likely. Jenkins and Perrow (1977) found in their historical study of farmworker movements that some were successful while others failed because of changes in political circumstances in the society. Their success in the late 1960s and early 1970s was heavily due to the fact that government was not solidly against them, and liberals united with workers in publicly denouncing agribusiness. Success requires tolerance or support from those in power or a lack of unity among those who would discourage protest.

The costs of protest are likely to be lower and the possibilities of success higher when political conditions are more favorable to the aggrieved group. Thus, Black protest increased when more liberal and Democratic power in government was strong or Republican presidents were constrained by circumstances to take positions favoring civil rights. As more Black members enter Congress, however, the chances of protest decrease since increased political access provides Blacks with a less costly alternative to protest (Jenkins, Jacobs, and Agnone 2003).

The resources of the group gleaned from inside and outside constitute a *seventh* way in which outside social and economic circumstances affect protest. In discussing strikes, Korpi (1974) suggested that their probability and likelihood of success increase with the strength of resources a group possesses. Relative deprivation may intensify the wish for change, but strikes are more likely if a group has ample power resources from which to draw. These resources can come from individuals or be collective in nature. Coalition formation, for example, can serve as a type of collective resource that can strengthen the position of a discontented group. Since deprivation is usually constantly present for many groups, it is external resources that are needed to organize them and create viable protest. "Disorders do not arise from disorganized anomic masses, but from groups organizationally able to defend and advance their interests" (Jenkins and Perrow 1977, p. 250).

Eighth and finally, the shape of protest is influenced by the structure, function, and ideology of the institutions in which protesting groups are immediately located. They determine the composition of groups that will protest, the avenues of protest, and the terms in which demands are phrased. Students protested war in Vietnam while in college and did so by symbolically attacking the system through their assaults on college administration offices and company interviewers. Factory workers protest through strikes; the unemployed cannot go on strike because they are outside the institution. It is the institutions in which the people are immediately involved that help shape protest. "People cannot defy institutions to which they have no access, and to which they make no contribution" (Piven and Cloward 1977, p. 23).

To sum up, in a number of ways the probability and form of protest are determined by political and economic factors other than feelings of deprivation and powerlessness. Several of those previously listed clearly implicate the system of inequality in the likelihood of protest. For example, the factors of resource availability and likelihood of repression reflect to a large degree the extent of economic and political inequality in society.

SOCIAL INEQUALITY AND ENVIRONMENTAL EQUITY

Criminal justice and collective protests both are issues closely linked to conditions of social inequality, and both affect the community at large. Environmental equity is another social problem that has been linked to social, especially racial, inequality. This problem principally concerns the unequal access to land resources and uneven proximity to dangerous environmental hazards. Generally, environmental equity has not been considered a part of the area of social inequality, and

consequently, few social-inequality researchers have addressed this issue. Indeed, the first serious studies of environmental equity go back only to the early 1980s.

Since it is reasonable to hypothesize that in the competition for a decent and healthy life, those with fewer resources and power will lose out to those with more, and since the accessibility of attractive land and geographic location of potentially dangerous wastes likely affect the chances citizens face for a healthy life, the study of environmental equity legitimately belongs in the field of social inequality. Whatever the effects of accessibility and location are, "those impacts will fall unevenly, along existing divisions of wealth/poverty, power/powerlessness; the transformations of nature will tend to occur in a way that reproduces and exacerbates existing social inequalities. In effect, environmental inequality is one facet or moment of social inequality. . . . [It is] a necessary and inevitable facet of social inequalities, embedded in the very fabric of modern societies" (Szasz and Meuser 1997, pp. 116–117).

The last several decades have witnessed increased competition over land as developers have sought to purchase prime settings, gentrify poor urban neighborhoods, construct gated communities, and gain access to publicly owned areas. The more economically and politically powerful are better positioned to win this competition. As scenic shore land is bought up by those who can afford it, for example, access to some of the country's most beautiful sites becomes restricted. Even access to national parks is limited to those who can afford it because of the need to pay fees.

In addition to battles over owning or controlling access to desirable tracts of land, another component of the conflicts over land is what has been called "environmental racism." This conflict involves the claim that the poor and/or minorities are disproportionately exposed to various kinds of dangerous waste sites and to hazardous chemical contamination. It is this debate that will now be briefly discussed.

Two major events helped give impetus to the "environmental justice movement" in the 1980s. One was a protest. Poor citizens had organized and successfully fought off the building of an industrial-waste landfill in their North Carolina county. A second event involved the publication of three studies which provided evidence that hazardous waste facilities tended to be located in areas with heavy Black populations (Bullard 1983; U.S. General Accounting Office 1983; United Church of Christ 1987). Since the study of environmental racism is relatively new, it should not be surprising that much of the research has suffered from a variety of methodological and substantive deficiencies. Consequently, there is not full agreement that environmental racism even exists. Among the weaknesses of the research have been (1) the use of case studies, which focus on only one geographic area and make generalizations speculative; (2) the varying use of different units of analysis—for example, zip code, county, state, regional, national—which has made comparisons between studies difficult; (3) the inclusion of limited numbers of potential causal variables and types of environmental hazards; and (4) the use of cross-sectional rather than longitudinal data, which makes the direction of causality in the relationship between minority presence and environmental hazards hard to disentangle.

Most of the environmental-racism research examines either (1) the differential location of commercial treatment, storage, and disposal of hazardous waste facilities (TSDFs) or (2) the degree of exposure to toxic chemical releases as measured by the Toxic Release Inventory (TRI). We will discuss examples of each of these types of studies in turn to arrive at a conclusion about the existence of environmental inequity. Anderton and colleagues examined census-tract government data to analyze the relationship between the location of minority populations and the presence of commercial TSDFs (1994). They also sought to find out if either poverty levels and/or the presence of manufacturing/industry were significant

predictors of the location of TSDFs. The authors found no relationship between the percentage of Blacks living in an area and the presence of TSDFs—that is, no significant evidence for environmental racism. They did, however, find a relationship between the percentage of Hispanics and the existence of TSDFs, but this connection was weak. Rather than race or ethnicity, they found that the most consistent predictors of TSDF location were a lower percentage of males employed and a higher percentage of employment in precision manufacturing. That is, TSDFs tend to be found in industrial areas.

The authors cautioned that their results do not mean that environmental racism does not exist, but only that, with their measures and sampling method, they did not find a relationship. In fact, even though their results yielded no evidence of environmental racism, they concluded that "Racism is a continuing, pervasive problem in our society; it would be surprising to find that environmental matters were somehow immune to this problem" (Anderton et al. 1994, p. 244). One significant limitation of this and other studies using commercial TSDFs as a measure is that the latter compose less than 10 percent of all hazardous waste facilities and handle less than 5 percent of all U.S. hazardous waste material (Ringquist 2000). Estimates suggest that there are several hundred thousand unregistered waste sites in the United States that may contain toxic chemicals (Szasz and Meuser 1997). In addition to these facilities, there are nonhazardous waste landfills for which there is no national database as well as other unregulated dumping sites. Moreover, "commercial" TSDFs only *take in* material produced elsewhere; they do not produce their own hazardous waste.

Another investigation of environmental racism using TSDFs as a dependent variable examined the location of all 82 TSDFs in Los Angeles County (Boer et al. 1997). Because it is a case study involving only the Los Angeles area, generalizations from the above study should be made with great caution. Nevertheless, the results support the thesis of environmental racism; TSDFs are more likely to be located in areas with high minority populations. Interestingly, like Anderton and colleagues, researchers found that Hispanics were more likely than Blacks to be residing near a TSDF. The authors suggested that the relationship may, in part, be related to the fact that the Anderton and colleagues' sample was drawn from the Southwest, a region where Hispanics are prominent.

In addition to race and ethnicity, like Anderton and colleagues, this study found that TSDFs were more likely to be sited in areas of industrial use and high employment in manufacturing. Finally, income also was found to be related to TSDF location, but not in a linear manner. Both poor and wealthy areas were less likely than working-class sections to contain TSDFs. The authors suggested that this may be because, on the one hand, poor areas have little employment of any kind (even in TSDFs), and on the other, wealthier neighborhoods can more easily fight off those who would want to build a TSDF in their area. The basic conclusion is that TSDFs are most likely to locate in industrial areas that have a high percentage of minority working-class residents.

General reviews of past TSDF studies concluded that race is a significant predictor of TSDF location, even though these studies have methodological limitations (Ringquist 2000; Lester, Allen, and Hill 2001). Research utilizing exposure to pollutants rather than TSDFs as a measure also tended to find a relationship between minority populations and toxic pollution. Daniels and Friedman (1999) examined aerial release of more than 300 toxic chemicals over all U.S. counties, as recorded by the U.S. Environmental Protection Agency's TRI. Despite its deficiencies, "the TRI is currently—and will likely continue to be—the most consistent and comprehensive source of information on environmental contaminant

releases" (ibid., p. 252). The results showed a positive relationship between the proportion of the population that was Black and the emission of toxic chemicals, even when controls such as urbanization and presence of manufacturing were considered. As in the Boer and colleagues study, researchers found that income was curvilinearly related to the amount of chemical releases. Poor and wealthy areas had lower emissions than moderate-income or working-class counties.

Similar findings were uncovered by Ringquist (1997) in his study of the location of TRI facilities across the country. Briefly, he found that zip codes that had disproportionate numbers of Blacks and Hispanics were also more likely to have TRI facilities. This was also the case for working-class, older, urban, industrial areas. However, somewhat paradoxically, Ringquist also found that even though wealthy areas are less likely to contain any TRI facility at all, when they do they are more likely to have multiple facilities. That is, income is positively related to the *density* of TRI facilities.

The fairly consistent research finding that minority populations are more likely to live near TSDFs or be exposed to toxic chemical releases from manufacturing plants raises the question of causality. How do minority populations come to be at higher environmental risk? Is it pure racism? What were these areas like when plants first decided to move into them? Were they disproportionately composed of minorities? Do such plants intentionally locate in these areas because of the high minority population or for other reasons? Or do minority populations move into these areas because of the greater affordability of homes and availability of industrial jobs? And if they do move into these areas, is it by choice or because they are constrained to do so? The process by which the relationship between minority residence and concentration of environmental risks comes about needs to be identified to reach a fully satisfactory conclusion about the existence and nature of environmental racism.

Some of the described research does suggest that racism may be involved because housing segregation may indirectly contribute to the disproportionate exposure that Blacks receive. That is, because Blacks are more limited than Whites in where they can live, they are more often funneled into living in urban industrial areas in which manufacturers emit toxic chemicals (Boer et al. 1997; Daniels and Friedman 1999). Another potential reason for the relationship is that some areas may have been zoned or targeted for industrial development by local officials, and TSDF plants, for example, may locate in a particular area because of these regulations (Boone and Modarres 1999). On this level, if racism is present, it may have resulted from the actual zoning or local planning process rather than from policies of company plants.

The research on environmental racism is growing and the issue of environmental equity in general will become more salient as competition for land use and population diversity increase across the United States. At the present time, while the bulk of the research suggests that minorities and members of the working class are more exposed to potential toxic chemicals, the research methodologies need to be improved. More information on the location of *all* toxic hazards, more agreement on which is the best unit of analysis to use in studies, and more historical examinations to identify the causal processes involved in explaining exposure levels are required.

SUMMARY

Inequality can affect behavior and social events in several ways. At the outset it was stated that not only individual position in the system of inequality but the system as a whole can have such effects, and in this chapter concern was expressed for both aspects. After discussing how inequality affects the probability of violence in the family, we looked at the relationship between class, race, sex, and crime rates, as well as the relationship between capitalism/inequality and crime rates in general, and found that in each case inequality is implicated in the generation of crime. Official statistics reveal a relationship between being Black and of low income and the probability of being arrested. The bulk of the studies on sentencing suggests a bias against groups of lower socioeconomic standing. A variety of data, then, raise questions about the fairness of the criminal justice system. The definition of the crime problem in terms of FBI Index crimes, which do not include white-collar or corporate crimes, and the special treatment given to white-collar crime, the frequent discovery that SES is related to likelihood of arrests, official reporting of crimes, and type of punishment strongly suggest that justice is not evenly meted out in U.S. society. Moreover, the findings of a relationship between income inequality and property crime rates further suggest that inequality helps produce crime and that reductions in inequality may produce reductions in property crime. Hate crimes, motivated by biases against particular demeaned status groups, also reflect the social inequalities perceived by different clusters of people.

Structures of inequality also help to foment collective protests. Studies of the riots and strikes during the 1960s suggest that the structure of inequality affects the social factors that generate collective protest. The power to mobilize resources, to avoid repression from official sources, to gain concessions, to successfully counter the tactics of those in power, and to discredit official ideology all depend heavily on power arrangements in the society at large.

Finally, recent evidence has raised the possibility of environmental racism. There appears to be a relationship between the presence of minority and working-class populations and the location of hazardous waste facilities and chemical pollution. The social consequence of this inequity is that these populations are disproportionately exposed to potential health hazards. Issues of environmental equity and competition over land will become only more prominent as the U.S. population grows and diversifies.

CRITICAL THINKING

1. What must be done to change the living conditions in ghettos that help generate crime?

2. This chapter emphasized the importance of the social context and conditions for crime and protest. What newly appearing characteristics of current society are likely to have effects on the extent and nature of social inequality? What characteristics are likely to alter the negative effects of inequality on individuals and society?

3. Do you believe the argument that Blacks are more likely to be in prison because of racial stereotypes that suggest that crime is a "Black phenomenon"? Are they in prison because they are believed to be a social threat to White society?

4. What do you think will principally determine how land use is decided as racial/ethnic diversity increases and immigration continues?

WEB CONNECTIONS

The Sentencing Project regularly collects and reviews information on prison populations, state laws, sentencing issues, and criminal justice in general. It is a good place to find summarized data on a variety of law enforcement topics. Go to www.sentencingproject.org.

CHAPTER

12 Social Inequality and Social Movements

Thru this dread shape humanity betrayed, plundered, profaned and disinherited, cries protest to the judges of the world, a protest that is also a prophecy.

—Edwin Markham

In societies where extensive social inequality not only exists but is also perceived as being unjust, it is not unusual for people to demonstrate their feelings against it. A variety of potential devices exist for redressing or reducing such inequality. Systems of inequality instigate social movements aimed at altering them, and conversely, the degree of ultimate success of social movements is measured in terms of their impacts on those systems. The extent to which either of these relationships is actualized, as you will see, depends on structural, cultural, and historical conditions in the society at the time. Economic shifts, prevalent ideologies, political policies, and unique historical events all impress themselves on the shapes of inequality and social movements.

Consistent with the multidimensional focus of treatment, this chapter will explore three social movements related to class, race, and gender that were explicitly aimed at reducing inequality and improving the life chances of the groups in question. The early labor movement of the latter part of the nineteenth century and the first decades of the twentieth century in the United States, the Civil Rights movement of the 1960s, and the women's movement of recent decades are examples of concerted efforts to change social and economic conditions for their constituencies. The purpose here is not to provide an exhaustive history of these movements, but rather to demonstrate systematically how each of them grew out of conditions relating to the structure of social inequality at the time, and how that structure affected the ebb and flow, goals, and tactics of those movements.

THE LABOR MOVEMENT

One of the first things to understand when examining any social movement is that the wider social, historical, and cultural context in which it takes place has an impact on the development, shape, and ultimate fate of the movement. Obviously, the poor conditions and deprivations experienced by industrial workers in the latter part of the nineteenth and early part of the twentieth centuries created dissatisfaction and feelings of hostility. Even though there was some improvement in wages after 1880, hours were long, wages were still low, and work conditions were dangerous. There were few, if any, protections against the hazards of chemicals, machinery, and inhalants from work in the mines and mills. Laborers on the railroads and in construction and logging industries also were exposed to extreme dangers. There was little concern for safety, and many of the wildcat strikes of this time were related to safety issues.

Writing of the period between 1865 and 1917, Asher (1986) observed that "industrial workers have been victimized by low wages, company stores, blacklisting, arbitrary dismissals, forced overtime, sexual exploitation, company spies, police brutality, and a host of other ills" (p. 115). Some of the dangers were inherent in the nature of the work and the technology used, and the fear of competition and concern for profit kept employers preoccupied with matters other than safety (Asher 1986). The early scientific-management movement among employers sought to organize, systematize, and thoroughly gain control of the workplace for management. In order to keep production and efficiency up in the early twentieth century, the pace of work in many plants was accelerated, stopwatches were used, and work was constantly checked by inspectors. This created further alienation among workers.

Living conditions in most instances also left much to be desired. Dubofsky (1975) described a typical immigrant residential area in Pittsburgh: "Situated in what is known as the Dump of Schoenville runs a narrow dirt road. Frequently strewn with tin cans and debris, it is bereft of trees and the glaring sun shines pitilessly down on hundreds of ragged, unkempt, and poorly fed children" (p. 23). The company towns and cramped urban ghettos made for dreary living conditions. In his study of "How the Other Half Lives," Riis (1890) described the conditions in which New York City workers lived. He found "an urban jungle of exploitation, family disintegration, crime, and human degradation" (quoted in Green 1980, p. 20). Even as late as the 1920s, living conditions for most workers were still poor. During these years, although some improvements had been made, work was hard, hours were long, and the level of wages left little money for leisure and recreational activities. In 1929, 42 percent of families had incomes below $1,500, which was barely enough to keep a four-person family going (Zieger 1986).

Despite the awful circumstances of the lives of most industrial workers, however, more is needed to explain the development and continuation of the labor movement over time. Certainly, workers responded to negative changes in their workplaces and in the wider political economy. But it takes more than deprivation to explain the development of collective action on the part of an aggrieved group. While exploitation and deprivation may have induced solidarity among workers, the strength of organized labor depends on other conditions, as well.

The growth of the labor movement was affected by a combination of external and internal factors. Externally, the strength of workers tended to be greater when there was a tight labor market; this gave them greater bargaining power. Strength also grew when economic opportunities were plentiful. The chances of a labor movement being successful also were enhanced when society allowed a variety of political and legal expressions and permitted greater access to resources (Jenkins 1983). For example, this occurred during the 1930s after Franklin Roosevelt's election and passage of the Wagner Act, which legalized the right to unionize. These events created alternate sources of power, and when the potential for political and economic power of labor was high, so was the solidarity of workers. The belief by workers that they would be spending a large part of their lives in their jobs and that they could make a political difference in society also increased their solidarity and the probability of a labor movement.

Sources of Control over Workers

The internal forces affecting the labor movement's shape and direction related heavily to disagreements among workers over membership, goals, and policy, as well as attempts used to break down cohesiveness among workers and thereby control them. Cohesiveness is a source of strength. Greater solidarity means greater organizational or collective power, and the relative strength of organization among opposing groups implicated in the situation affects the probability that a movement will develop (McAdam 1982). Employers who were more often better organized and had broader political resources on their side fought workers in many bloody battles in the latter part of the nineteenth and well into the twentieth century. Around the turn of the twentieth century, as now, it was in the economic interest of employers to minimize the solidarity among workers, thereby hindering the development of a labor movement. A variety of techniques were used to do this (Griffin, Wallace, and Rubin 1986). One of these was the use of largely unskilled immigrant laborers, many of whom, as machine tenders, replaced natives. Blacks and foreign labor also were used as strikebreakers. These moves on the part of employers created animosity against foreign laborers and weakened the cohesiveness of labor in general.

A second technique that created divisions within the ranks of labor involved the redesigning of the division of labor. For much of the nineteenth century, craftsworkers had held control over their work and occupied indispensable positions in the iron, steel, and machinery industries (Dubofsky 1975). Nevertheless, employers and their foremen controlled the workers through direct personal control, "intervening in the labor process often to exhort workers, bully and threaten them, reward good performance, hire and fire on the spot, favor loyal workers, and generally act as despots, benevolent or otherwise" (Edwards 1979, p. 19). The scientific-management movement further strengthened the power of supervisors over workers. It prescribed the dividing of tasks into their smallest, elemental components in order to increase efficiency and output. But in so doing, it also introduced extreme specialization and monotonous work

on the shop floor. Tasks were divided into such small parts that even completely unskilled individuals could perform them.

While not universally implemented in industry, scientific management reflected an important perennial source of labor/management conflict—that is, the issue of who controls the work process. Numerous early confrontations were over the question of who should direct the pace of work tasks (Dubofsky 1975; Piven and Cloward 1977; Edwards 1979; Stephenson and Asher 1986). Through the use of scientific management, management was able to wrest control of production and the labor process from craftsworkers, who, until this point, had been the experts on how to accomplish given work tasks. All of this expropriation of control was done under the guise of being a "scientific" method for organizing work. Scientific management removed the planning and control aspects of the work process from the worker and placed it in the hands of the manager. Workers generally fought the use of scientific management.

The techniques for controlling the work process changed as capitalism perfected its technology. Improved manufacturing techniques such as the assembly line created technical controls. "*Technical control* involves designing machinery and planning the flow of work to minimize the problem of transforming labor power into labor as well as to maximize the purely physically based possibilities for achieving efficiencies" (Edwards 1979, p. 112). Later, control was achieved through the widespread implementation of bureaucratic structure, which builds control into formal sets of rules, positions, and authority hierarchies. Both technical and bureaucratic methods build control into the very fiber of the organization, replacing the personal control of the manager or foreman, which was often perceived as being arbitrary. The evolution of different forms of control can be legitimately viewed as attempts by industrialists to increase efficiency, production, and profit.

But the use of foreign and African American labor along with changes in the mechanisms of control were only two of the techniques used to weaken labor. Industrial management also used welfare capitalism to minimize solidarity among workers. Briefly, welfare capitalism included special savings plans and bonuses, homeownership aid programs, stock-purchasing options, and group insurance plans. Most significant among the programs offered were employee representation plans or work councils and company unions. The latter plans presumably gave workers a meaningful voice in the operation of the organization. Around World War I, the concept of "industrial democracy" had become quite popular. Clearly, these employee representation plans, while suggesting a democratic and more equal relationship between employer and employee, were aimed at reducing worker allegiance to outside unions and slowing their attempts to organize themselves (Brody 1980; Griffin, Wallace, and Rubin 1986).

There is some question as to whether the programs involved in this approach were primarily a conscious attempt by employers to reduce identification with other workers by making workers dependent on and loyal to industry, or rather an honest attempt to deal with the problems that attended changes in industrialization and to treat employees more humanely. The motivation was very likely a combination of paternalistic concern for workers, the belief that a more satisfied work force would increase productivity and efficiency, and a desire on the part of employers to control labor. The latter function, however, appears to have been the most important (ibid.).

A variety of conditions contributed to the demise of welfare capitalism after the late 1920s. Many of the basic concerns of workers were still not being addressed, such as full control over the work process, protection against unemployment, higher wages, and a shorter work week. On top of these factors was the fact that welfare capitalism was expensive and

only some large firms could afford the programs. Hence, it was not widespread among all industries. Finally, the Depression made it virtually impossible for firms to meet the idealized goals of welfare capitalism (Edwards 1979; Brody 1980).

Employers also fought the organized labor movement by fighting against closed or union shops, advocating open shops in their place. In the latter, employees need not be members of unions to remain employed. This push for open shops under the "American Plan" label was especially dominant during the first decade of this century. The National Association of Manufacturers launched a campaign for open shops across industries, while other business-oriented groups (e.g., National Civic Foundation) argued that if unions were to exist and be acceptable, they had to be "responsible" in nature. In response to business attacks on union shops, some trade unions began to take in more unskilled workers as members (Green 1980). The conservative trade unionism of the American Federation of Labor (AFL) was preferable to the more militant and revolutionary approach of the International Workers of the World (IWW) (Griffin, Wallace, and Rubin 1986). The espousal of welfare capitalism and a conservative brand of labor organization helped create an appearance of employers as being reasonable and fair. But neither of these enhanced the ability of labor to organize effectively in its own interests.

Employers had, of course, other resources by which to resist encroachment by labor. Spies were employed to monitor labor activities; legal actions were encouraged against militant workers and organizations; and the power of police, state militia, and federal troops also were used to quell labor unrest. Some states had laws specifically outlawing unions that were considered to be revolutionary or that openly advocated the taking over of industries by workers (syndicalism). Leaders of such unions could be and were put in prison or deported (Perlman and Taft 1935; Griffin,

Wallace, and Rubin 1986). The informal political alliance between business and government was reflected in the frequent use of police or military might in putting down worker protests.

In the late nineteenth century, workers often had the support of local officials, so industries had to get help from state and federal sources (Dubofsky 1975; Green 1980). In numerous strike actions between 1890 and 1920, state militia and federal troops were used against workers. The 1892 steel plant conflict at Homestead, Pennsylvania, and the Pullman railroad boycott of 1894 are only two instances in which soldiers were used against strikers. In Lawrence, Massachusetts, in 1912, the American Woolen mill employed roughly 40,000, about half the city's population. About half of the employees were young women and most were foreign born. But when a group of young Polish women were given reduced wages for no explicit reason, a strike was organized and spread to other mills. In this case, too, police and militia were used against strikers, but after a couple of months, the workers in the "Bread and Roses" strike, as it was called, won wage gains (Green 1980). In 1914, militia in Colorado waged a violent attack on coal miners, shooting strikers and burning their families out of homes. Their violence across the southern part of the state reminded some of the tactics that had been used in the earlier Indian Wars (Zieger 1986). Many other labor–employer confrontations occurred during this period. Throughout World War I and up to 1920, large strikes by rail, meatpacking, and steel workers occurred. In 1919 alone, there were 3,600 strikes (ibid.). But in most cases, employers emerged as the victors (Piven and Cloward 1977; Brody 1980).

In the last years of the nineteenth century and the early years of the twentieth century, workers simply did not have the political or organizational power to be consistently successful against industrial owners. "Whatever force workers mounted against their bosses, whatever their determination and their unity, they could not withstand the legal and military power of the state, and that power was regularly used against them" (Piven and Cloward 1977, p. 102). The only effective legal control on the contract imposed by the employer at the turn of the century was the condition of the labor market. As long as employers had government, the press, and the market behind them and a large number of immigrant workers available, there was little that could get employers to voluntarily improve their contracts with workers (Ginzberg and Berman 1963). All of the preceding discussion demonstrates that changing technological conditions, population composition, and the differential availability of political and economic resources to labor and management decisively affected the development of the labor movement. Access to resources had an especially significant impact on the effectiveness of countermovements and countertactics by each side in the conflict (Griffin, Wallace, and Rubin 1986).

Internal Divisions in the Labor Movement

The particular directions taken by the labor movement have been explained in a variety of ways, but not altogether successfully (cf. Laslett 1987). The varying images of the roles of unions, industrial changes, and social and cultural heterogeneity within the working class and disagreements on the goals of unions all helped to shape the differentiation within the movement. An early approach of the 1880s emphasized the educational function of unions. These organizations were seen as educators of immigrants, proponents of public schools, and often supporters of the socialization of private industry. Thus, in this approach, unions were not seen as being preoccupied with wages and job conditions alone, but with broader issues. The actions and goals of several early unions (Knights of Labor, IWW, Congress of Industrial Organizations [CIO]) make that clear. Another approach to understanding unions saw them as organizations created to buffer the effect of the ill fit between humans who desired to be free and the controls inherent in modern mechanization. The Marxian approach viewed unions as being rooted in class struggle over control of the means of production.

A final and most influential view of labor unions in early America was to view them as tools for increasing the economic benefits of workers. Perlman (1928) argued that in surveying all the changes that have taken place in the economy and technology, workers came to the conclusion that they cannot operate independently as separate entrepreneurs. Rather, Perlman argued, they became reconciled to their positions as employees in businesses owned by others and realized there was not a great deal they could do to change the way things were. Given this situation, workers could hardly be expected to be revolutionary; they were only willing to fight for better wages and job conditions. It should be remembered that Perlman presented his theory before the Great Depression had occurred and before development of the CIO. He also does not appear to give much credit to the imagination and ambition of workers (Laslett 1987).

There is no question that some of these emphases were reflected in the internal structure of the organized labor movement of the early twentieth century. The forms the labor movement took in the United States were also conditioned by industrial changes. In the waning decades of the nineteenth century, the social organization of the economy was undergoing rapid change, and these changes had implications for both employer and employee. For example, the period beginning with the late 1880s was one in which economic enterprises dramatically increased in size and frequently merged with each other. In other words, it was a period in which economic power became more consolidated and concentrated (Edwards 1979). Even though in most of the nineteenth-century

factories authority was decentralized among foremen and various craftsworkers, industrialization brought in its wake a more simplified, detailed division of labor, increasing the need for less-skilled laborers.

Machines often fomented dissatisfaction among skilled craftsworkers and encouraged antagonism between the unskilled industrial workers who could do simple work and operate basic machines, and those who were skilled craftsworkers before machines became dominant (Stephenson and Asher 1986). Machines rapidly took the place of workers, and control over the workplace more frequently fell into the hands of owners and their foremen. "For more and more wage earners, the power over their working lives receded far off into distant central offices and into the hands of men probably unknown to them" (Brody 1980, p. 8). These shifts in technology helped to drive wedges between unskilled and skilled workers, thereby stimulating the different directions in which the organized labor movement would go.

Along with technological changes, productivity rose rapidly, but so did the demand for labor. Immigrants flooded into the United States from a variety of countries. Consequently, the late nineteenth century was also a period in which the size of company work forces increased. The industrial working class grew significantly, but it was composed of individuals from sharply contrasting social and cultural backgrounds. The industrial working class for much of the latter half of the nineteenth century was a conglomeration of native-born craftsworkers, some farmers who had left the land to come to the cities of New York and New England, skilled immigrants from Britain and western Europe, Irish who came to the United States after the potato famine in their native land, and Chinese who became employed primarily in the railroad industry.

After 1880, immigrants from eastern and southern Europe joined the ranks of the less skilled in industry and became an increasingly large part of the industrial working class (Aronowitz 1973). As the demand for labor grew and these immigrants flooded into the country to take lower positions in the mines, mills, and factories, the labor force in the North was almost as segregated by nationality in 1900 as the southern market was by race (Green 1980). Moreover, as the century came to an end, the proportion of women and African Americans involved in industry also increased. In 1900, almost a quarter of all women were in the labor force. The point of all this is that the heterogeneous nature of the working class at this time created divisions that often hindered the solidarity of workers when conflict arose with their employers.

This heterogeneity was used by employers to minimize worker cohesion. Businesses consciously recruited large numbers of unskilled immigrants who served as an available labor supply; this was used to regulate employment and possibly even wages. The employment of ethnically diverse workers stirred antiforeign sentiments among natives, which discouraged the organization of all workers. Blacks, Mexicans, and ethnic Whites also were used as strikebreakers, again discouraging unification among workers.

The racial and ethnic differences within the working class meant language, skill, and religious differences as well, making control of working-class militancy easier. So these internal divisions had direct implications for both the working class and its employers. Some labor leaders had no wish at all to bring non-Whites into the organized labor movement, but rather were primarily interested in advancing the interests of White, skilled craftsworkers. Exclusionary practices, including explicit policies prohibiting admission of non-Whites, were not uncommon among many AFL unions (ibid.). This was to be a bitter source of antagonism within the labor movement. Samuel Gompers, who founded the American Federation of Labor in 1881, was against the inclusion of non-White, nonskilled workers.

In 1905, Gompers proclaimed to a group of union members in Minneapolis that "caucasians" were "not going to let their standard of living be destroyed by Negroes, Chinamen, Japs, or any others" (quoted in ibid., p. 46). The miscellaneous category of "others" referred to people from what were considered at that time the less desirable regions of Europe, such as the Slavic countries and Italy. Keep in mind that ideas about the biological inferiority of different groups were still circulating at this time (see Chapter 7).

In contrast to the American Federation of Labor, which sought to unionize skilled White craftsworkers, other organizers felt that it was crucial to organize all industrial workers. Among those groups that supported the organization of all workers, some had socialist or communist leanings. The Knights of Labor, briefly popular in the 1880s, was among those groups that argued that all workers should be included in the organized labor movement. Rather than advocating the homogeneous composition found in the trade and crafts unions of the AFL, the Knights preferred mixed groupings of workers. The Socialist Party of America, founded in 1901 and under the leadership of the charismatic Eugene Debs, also favored an organizational umbrella that would cover the mass of workers in industry. A few years later, the Industrial Workers of the World, and several decades later, the CIO also actively sought the membership of Blacks and all industrial workers.

As their views about the compositions of labor organizations varied, so did labor leaders' views on the appropriate goals for the labor movement. The goals of the Knights of Labor were broad and involved the reorganization of the industrial order to create a more just society. These utopian goals were eschewed by the newer AFL trade unions that sought more immediate narrow rewards for their members, such as higher wages and better working conditions. This "pure-and-simple" or "business" unionism was more consistent with native

American values according to some interpreters. A large part of the reason for this orientation, argued Lipset (1971), is related to the openness of the class structure, and the values of materialism, egalitarianism, and individual opportunity. Individuals in this context see themselves more as individuals than as members of a class, and see social change as resulting more from individual efforts than from mass organization or social structure. The American values of work, social and geographic mobility, comfort, and common sense also lie behind the belief that individuals do and should determine their own economic fates (Dunlop 1987).

The AFL's trade unionism has aimed at working within the present economic system rather than trying to change it. The emphasis on increasing labor's power has been for the purpose of more effective collective bargaining than for political reasons. Early AFL leaders felt that government should not interfere in labor matters. It should be up to labor to chart its own course and make its own gains (Brody 1971). Gompers's "voluntarism" perspective underscored the brief that labor should not solicit aid from the government for those goals it can accomplish by itself (Green 1980). Paradoxically, this stance helped to create a bond between the AFL and establishment forces, fostering increased cooperation between the union, management, and the government (Rogin 1971; Brody 1980).

In this interpretation, because of cultural and other differences, U.S. workers are not as interested as their European counterparts in a basic change *of* the economic system as much as they are in changing their individual positions *within* the system. "Most men and women live in a real world," wrote Dubofsky (1975), "a world of simple, everyday happenings, small pleasures and recurrent sufferings, which shape their attitudes as much as abstract principles" (p. 48). The trade unions, with their narrow orientation, help to sustain the job consciousness of U.S. workers. Similarly, Brody (1980)

also concluded that in the waning years of the nineteenth century, the labor movement was (1) practical rather than utopian or theoretical, (2) nonrevolutionary with narrow material interests, and (3) impatient with intellectuals and academicians who had theories about the direction the labor movement should pursue.

Despite the narrow orientation of many workers, however, one should not conclude that there has been no revolutionary fervor or concerns within labor. "Such an approach has always been unfair, especially during the heyday of the IWW between 1905 and 1917, and in the early years of the history of the CIO. It was especially untrue during the period of the Knights of Labor . . . which . . . upheld producer's and consumer's cooperation, equal pay for women, and a 'proper share of the wealth that they (the workers) create' " (quoted in Laslett 1987, p. 362). Organized labor has not been a uniform homogeneous mass.

As suggested earlier, differences in races, cultures, goals, and organizing principles have created fissures in the house of labor. There has been a consistent thread of concern among many workers since the nineteenth century over who controls and directs their work. Part of the battle that has been waged between labor and management has involved such issues. "In fact, American workers have waged a running battle over the ways in which their daily work and the human relations at work were organized over the nineteenth century, and in the process they have raised issues which go far beyond the confines of 'wage and job consciousness' or 'bread and butter' unionism, into which historians have long tried to compress the experiences and aspirations of American workers" (Montgomery 1983, p. 389).

Just prior to World War I, then, organized labor contained several different types of organizations and orientations. The trade-union wing, exemplified by the AFL, was solidly on its way but did not incorporate most unskilled and semiskilled industrial workers. The Socialists had political influence on many workers even though the latter's trade-union orientation remained intact. The IWW organized those left out by the more conservative AFL affiliates, was active and militant, and was led by the imposing Big Bill Haywood (Brody 1980).

The Russian Revolution, America's involvement in World War I, and the accompanying patriotic fervor that swept the nation legitimated political and coercive attacks on Socialist organizations and the IWW. As a result, the power of the Left in organized labor declined. "The labor hopes of the American left, hitherto bright, died in World War I and its aftermath" (ibid., p. 41). In the patriotic context of the postwar period, organized labor, in general, was a victim of attacks from industry. The "American Plan" of business proclaimed the consistency of the open shop with U.S. values. In this hostile atmosphere, the AFL became more cooperative with industry and government. With the restrictive immigration laws of the 1920s reducing the inflow of unskilled labor from culturally undesirable countries, industry's source of fresh workers was weakened. By the late 1920s, labor unrest had calmed down even though the benefits of welfare capitalism did not include all industrial workers. Moreover, the cost of living was increasing, erasing many of the gains that had been made by some workers (Zieger 1986).

From the Depression to the Present

On the whole, the 1920s and the early 1930s were not kind to U.S. workers. "The symbol of the twenties is gold . . . the twenties were, indeed, golden, but only for a privileged segment of the American population. For the great mass of people . . . —workers and their families—the appropriate symbol may be nickel or copper or perhaps even tin, but certainly not gold" (Bernstein 1960, p. 47). Bernstein labeled the 1920 to 1933 period as "the lean years" for the worker (ibid.). A litany

of the problems for workers would include the stagnation of the union movement during the period (union membership fell from 5 million in 1920 to 3.5 million in 1929) and the absence of any effective industrywide collective-bargaining tools. Employers could hire who they wanted and workers had little recourse in the matter. Immigration slowed during the 1920s, which meant that it was no longer as easy for native workers to move up occupationally. Older workers found it more and more difficult to hold on to their jobs, as farm migrants and women increasingly entered the urban labor force. Mechanization displaced workers. Between 1920 and 1929, it is estimated that about one-third of those displaced by machines in the manufacturing, coal mining, and railways industries remained unemployed (Bernstein 1960). Moreover, the shift to more mechanized professional positions did not help many workers, who did not have the qualifications for such positions. Income inequality was also extensive in the society. The combined incomes of the top 0.1 percent of families were as great as those of the bottom 42 percent of the population. Within the working class there were also divisions in wages based on regional, ethnic, racial, skill, union membership, sex, and residential differences. Irish, Italian, Jewish, African American, and Mexican workers were generally worse off than native White workers (ibid.).

The effects of the Great Depression on employment were disastrous. In the middle of 1930, almost 4.5 million were without jobs. Shanty areas cropped up in and around cities, places of makeshift residences sometimes called "Hoovervilles." Hunger also rose dramatically. By early 1931, there were an estimated 8.3 million unemployed, but the number was to rise even further to 13.6 million by the end of that year, and to 15 million by early 1933. At that time, about one-third of all wage/salary workers were completely out of work. Many others were only working on a part-time basis (ibid.).

Needless to say, the Depression in the early 1930s changed political dynamics inside and outside the labor movement. The AFL had successfully cultivated close relationships with industrial management and government forces. It stressed union–management harmony and fought against leftist elements in the labor movement. The Depression made many workers and unions realize the need for state help and intervention. It spurred questions among the unemployed about the ability of the present economic and political systems to deal with catastrophic problems, especially as it became clear over the bitter years of the 1930s that it was not the lack of individual efforts but rather broader social forces that were behind much of the misery being experienced (Piven and Cloward 1977). At the same time, however, the vast majority of citizens still had faith in the U.S. system and did not see socialism or communism as a viable alternative. Nor did they think of themselves as a full-fledged working class fighting capitalism (Aronowitz 1973; Zieger 1986).

In the early part of the twentieth century, labor had received little help from the federal government, especially during the Republican administrations of the 1920s. Several critical events strengthened labor's hand during the 1930s, in addition to the political-administration changes that had occurred. One was the rising prospect of war in Europe. U.S. companies that had armament contracts with European countries could not afford major labor unrest to disrupt production. A second event was the passage of the Wagner Act in 1935, which legalized the right of workers to organize and bargain collectively under the protection of the National Labor Relations Board, which could monitor business compliance with the law. This law, bitterly fought by business, resulted in a rapid upsurge in union membership. In the mid- and late 1930s, union membership tripled, reaching about 9 million in 1939 (Zieger 1986). A third event that increased the power of labor was the creation of the CIO in 1935. The CIO unionized many of the previously unorganized mass-production industrial workers. Unlike the AFL, it aimed at being a union for all workers. Its leader, John L. Lewis, also realized that the CIO had to recruit skeptical Blacks to prevent their being used as strikebreakers. In 1937, the CIO had about 4 million members. The New Deal and events during the 1930s left in their wake a triumvirate of power: big government, big business, and big labor. During and after World War II, union membership was still high and growing, and unions were an effective force for improving working conditions for their members.

Despite this growth in union power, the ideological tide had already begun to shift against organized labor by the end of the 1930s. The recession of 1938–1939, which led to a weakening of federal recovery programs, factionalism within the CIO (which many suspected had communist leanings), the growing patriotism during the early years of World War II, and the impatience of many with the increased militancy of workers immediately after the war strengthened conservative forces against unions (ibid.). The increased bureaucratization and job consciousness of unions over the years and the routinization of formal contracts and the "rule of law" in industry also helped to institutionalize labor–industry conflict. Employers were more willing to buy off workers with higher wages than to relinquish control of the production process (Brody 1980; Zieger 1986). The Taft–Hartley Act of 1947 renewed many of the powers that had been lost to business in the Wagner Act. It also curbed the power of unions to strike, required an anti-Communist pledge from workers, and redefined labor's rights in much narrower terms (Piven and Cloward 1977; Zieger 1986).

The increased conservatism and narrowness of unions meant that workers often fought against the wishes of union leadership. The interests of workers and those of the union leadership did not always coincide. This internal division within the labor movement

Historically, union membership has been related to better working conditions and higher earnings. Since their heyday during and after World War II, however, union membership has declined significantly. Recent governmental and corporate actions, along with allegations of corruption, have only served to weaken them further.
Photo by author.

has continued. Although union membership generally grew during the 1950s and 1960s, and more public employees initiated unionization drives, differences of opinion within the labor community surfaced over Vietnam and the Civil Rights and women's movements of the 1960s. In the conservative 1980s and early 1990s, unions were again under attack, membership declined, and union leadership appeared weaker than in the earlier heyday of organized labor. More specifically, the breaking of traditional understandings between unions and management, coupled with vigorous business attacks on unions since the 1970s, helped to beat down the strength of unions. In addition, globalization, and the rapid employment growth in new areas coupled with higher unemployment in traditional occupations, the lack of national unity among unions, and a hostile political climate have certainly contributed to the decline of union power (Western 1993; Clawson and Clawson 1999). But elements internal to labor unions themselves have also contributed to their decline. Publicized corruption, ethnic and gender bias within unions, and a lack of union democracy for rank-and-file workers have weakened their moral authority (Kallick 1994). Unions have yet to fully accommodate the large number of immigrants and the growth in the numbers of women and ethnic groups (especially Hispanics) within the house of labor (DeFreitas 1993; Gooding and Reeve 1993). The face of labor has changed; to maximize their power, unions must successfully handle their heterogeneity. "[I]ssues of race, class, and gender are inextricably woven together. . . . [O]rganizations which successfully combine all these elements and deal with all the intersecting issues hold the promise of merging disciplined action, which members collectively plan and control, and a place where individuals can develop their full potential as critical thinkers and well-rounded human beings" (Leary 2005, p. 35).

The current splintering and weakness of unions is reminiscent of the labor movement of the 1920s, and they come in a three-decade period when wages for many in the middle and working classes have been relatively stagnant and economic strains have been high. The value of the minimum wage in 2003 was 23 percent *less* than it was in 1967. Working at the minimum wage of $5.15 resulted in earnings that were still well below the poverty line. Workers who are not union members have pensions and insurance benefits valued at less than half those of union workers. Retirement and health-insurance benefits have been significantly curtailed in many corporations; in 2003, 45 million were without health insurance.

Historically, union membership has meant significantly higher wages and better benefits, but currently only 13 percent of employees are members of unions. Minority men and women have been the groups who have most benefited economically from union membership (Mishel, Bernstein, and Allegretto 2005). Consequently, they are also the groups most negatively affected by the decline of union power and membership.

Importantly but not surprisingly, the decline of unions is occurring at a time of conservativism, increasing globalization, and open markets, when transnational corporations have gained more economic and political leverage (Faux 2003). The weakness of labor against business does not bode well for a decline in economic inequality. Confrontation by labor against management when support for employees is less than adequate and factory–floor relationships are less than cordial is unlikely when there is no strong union presence (Roscigno and Hodson 2004). Perhaps the labor movement has come full circle and will again mobilize its constituencies to restore labor's power, but to do this in an international

marketplace it may have to embrace not only differences in class, race, and gender, but those of nationality as well. The recent split of the Teamsters and Service Employees International Union from the AFL-CIO also raises questions about labor's cohesiveness, but perhaps raises new possibilities as well.

THE CIVIL RIGHTS MOVEMENT

Although it often discriminated against both Blacks and women, the labor movement was driven by concerns over inequities in political and economic power, and historical, cultural, and social conditions shaped its development and form. In general terms, the same can be said of the Civil Rights movement of the mid-1950s and 1960s. Although an indisputable specific date for its beginning cannot be given, there is general agreement that it began in the period between 1953 and 1955 during which the historic *Brown* v. *Board of Education* Supreme Court decision was made, and systematic bus boycotts had occurred in Baton Rouge, Louisiana, and Montgomery, Alabama. The nonviolent movement extended into the mid-1960s up to the point when other more radical, Black-power elements were becoming increasingly important.

As is the case of the labor movement, there had been many instances of protest by African Americans against Whites before the Civil Rights movement. Revolts by slaves against their masters, the underground railroad, the massive growth of the National Association for the Advancement of Colored People (NAACP) membership to almost half a million during World War II, the demands that led Roosevelt to establish a Fair Employment Practices Committee, and A. Philip Randolph's political activity in Washington and before Congress in the 1940s all provide evidence of racial protest and a push for racial equality before the Civil Rights movement (Morris 1984). Thus, the movements of the 1950s and 1960s did not just suddenly appear out of nowhere. Public activism in movements waxes and wanes as social, economic, and political circumstances in the surrounding environment change. Consequently, what may appear to be the beginning of a social movement may only be a resurgence of activism that had been kept in abeyance because of lack of opportunity structures in the social context (Taylor 1989a). As was found in the labor movement's history, particular historical, political, economic, and social conditions created a context in which effective mass protest could be initiated, and the Civil Rights movement could be nurtured. The actual battle for racial justice predates, then, the so-called modern Civil Rights movement.

In the late nineteenth and early twentieth centuries, African Americans had few resources with which to launch a massive Civil Rights campaign. First of all, racist ideologies discouraged support from Whites. Second, most African Americans were fully but exploitively integrated into the southern economic and political structure. There were few economic opportunities open to them and Jim Crow laws kept them in their assigned place. In other words, the social context offered few political and economic opportunities or alternatives. Third, the federal government did little to alleviate the oppressive conditions under which Blacks lived. Earlier, national leaders had written into the Constitution that Black men, who were unfree, were to be considered only three-fifths persons. Now Congress stood by as Blacks were disenfranchised and violently treated in the South.

The North and the federal government did little while Black subjugation and White supremacy were being systematically institutionalized in the South. This structured inequality was especially evident in the political realm. Blacks were effectively prevented from voting through the use of various devices, including poll taxes, tests of literacy and "good character," grandfather requirements, and primaries limited to Whites. Laws in the South prohibited the integration of Blacks and Whites in schools, hospitals, motels, places of recreation, and even funeral homes and cemeteries. These Jim Crow laws made it legal to spend less public money on Black than on White institutions (Sitkoff 1981).

The Changing Context of Racial Inequality

After World War I, it was clear that changing economic and political conditions would strengthen the power position of African Americans in the United States. Among these economic changes was a decline in the centrality of agriculture in the southern economy coupled with increasing industrialization of the urban South. This agrarian decline was fostered, in part, by declines in immigration and agricultural exports during the war. Accompanying the decline in immigration was an increase in the demand by northern industry for laborers from the South. Both "King Cotton" and industry needed workers, but changing circumstances created a shift in demand from agriculture to industry. Before and after World War I, there was massive African American migration to the North and to cities to seek employment in industries (Piven and Cloward 1977; Sitkoff 1981; McAdam 1982). Southern agriculture suffered again during the Great Depression of the early 1930s. An overproduction of cotton due to decreased demand led to a drastic decline in its price, which spelled disaster for many southern farmers. In Mississippi, at that time perhaps the greatest stronghold of White supremacy, farmers lost their land at about twice the national rate (Bloom 1987). Later, during the 1940s, as mechanization also became more and more essential in agriculture, some farmers left agriculture behind, and the average size of landholdings increased. This meant that more Black as well as White farm workers were economically displaced and needed to seek employment in the industries of northern and southern cities (Piven and Cloward 1977).

Southern agriculture also had to diversify its products to feed the soldiers in military camps during World War II (Bloom 1987). All of these circumstances served to shake up the foundations of the traditional economy in the South.

The changed geographic and economic base of Blacks helped to develop their voting power and the indigenous institutional bases needed for the Civil Rights movement (McAdam 1982). The city provided greater opportunities for Blacks to get organized, to receive more education, and to lay the basis for an expanded Black middle class. The growth of these basic strengths within the Black community was important in the genesis of the Civil Rights movement. There is good evidence that, despite the importance of external resources to the movement, its origins and development can be traced to reliance on institutions indigenous to the Black community (Oberschall 1973; McAdam 1982; Morris 1984; Jenkins and Eckert 1986).

However, some have suggested that professional organizations gave impetus to the Civil Rights movements (McCarthy and Zald 1973). These organizations, in contrast to "mass-based" organizations, have outside leaders, have a full-time staff on salary, have significant outside benefactors, and play the role of "speaking for" aggrieved groups. Despite the argument that the origins of the movement can be traced to these organizations, evidence suggests otherwise. Jenkins and Eckert (1986) traced the involvement and support of indigenous and professional organizations over an approximately 30-year period (the late 1940s to 1980). Their conclusions were clear enough: "Professional SMOs [social movement organizations] were not the model actors at any point in the civil rights movement. Nor did they initiate the challenge, their efforts coming on the heels of indigenous actions. . . . The challenge was initiated by the grassroots groups, especially the churches and student groups" (1986, p. 819).

African American colleges, churches, and civic and fraternal institutions provided not only economic resources but also the communication network and most of the leaders needed to organize the movement. Martin Luther King, Jr., for example, was influential as a movement leader not only because of his charisma but also, crucially, because of the personal and organizational backing he received. The influence of the Southern Christian Leadership Conference during most of the movement's career suggests the relevance of religious institutions. Local colleges also provided most of the students who, early in the 1960s, were involved in the civil disobedience actions that helped bring about legislative changes.

External support of protests generally comes after the protests themselves. These additional resources are a *product* rather than a *cause* of protest (McAdam 1982). The patronage that did come later from outsiders appears to have been given less out of feelings of conscience and injustice than out of concern to keep the movement moderate and weaken the radical element—that is, to exercise some control over the direction of the movement (Jenkins and Eckert 1986). The nonviolent sit-ins of college students and others in the South in the early 1960s, for example, brought much financial and other support from outside, northern groups. The violent protests later in the 1960s in northern and western cities, on the other hand, produced a White backlash, partly because of the violence, but also because of the switch in focus of problems from the rural South to the urban ghettos of the North.

The economic and attending geographic shifts that were occurring in the South, then, provided African Americans with the opportunity to "construct the occupational and institutional foundation from which to mount resistance to White oppression" (Piven and Cloward 1977, p. 205). It has been argued that the southern agricultural power structure benefited most from the traditional racist structure in the South. In this view, the southern agricultural elite (i.e., large plantation owners) had the most to lose from desegregation and equality for African Americans, for they relied on the cheap, accessible African American labor source. On the other hand, cities and businesses stood to suffer from the racial unrest caused by segregationist laws (Bloom 1987). Business growth and investment in Little Rock, Arkansas, were seriously damaged, for example, after the school desegregation confrontations in the late 1950s. With the growth of industries, cities gradually became more influential politically than agrarian areas (ibid.). Consequently, changing economic and social conditions created a split in the "Solid South" between the interests of business and agriculture.

In addition to the shrinking role of agriculture and the expanding presence of industry, the increased stridence and militancy of the reaction against African American protests for equality also helped to isolate the South, especially the Deep South, from the rest of the nation. Thus, changes and reactions to them not only created deeper divisions within the South itself but also served to increasingly alienate the South from the remainder of the country. In other words, Bloom argued, the traditional social and political structure was grounded in a particular kind of economy. A weakening in the basis of that agricultural economy threatened the survival of sociopolitical arrangements that primarily benefited the rich landowner and discriminated against African Americans. "Racial patterns and racial consciousness have as their foundation particular class structures, and they develop and change as these structures themselves change." At the same time, however, "class structure may set the parameters of racial action, but it cannot reduce race to class" (ibid., p. 3).

This last point is very important. Class and economic factors were implicated in the shifting allegiances to racial inequality. However, *racist ideology* was still an underlying element in accounting for not only social and economic inequality in the South but also reactions to Black attempts to eliminate it. Recall that in the latter part of the nineteenth and well into the twentieth centuries, there were a variety of established racial ideologies justifying unequal treatment of Blacks. Beliefs about the inferiority of Blacks go back even further than that to the early founding of the United States (see Chapter 7). The continued significance of racism itself was manifested in the support given by lower-class as well as upper-class White Southerners to the discriminatory treatment of Blacks. Upper-class White Southerners who had vested local economic interests fought the hardest against voting rights for Blacks because to afford this right would have been tantamount to surrendering power to them.

Although the voting regulations effectively eliminated many lower-class Whites as well as Blacks from voting, the former went along with their upper-class brethren in supporting the laws. The southern aristocracy played on racist images of Blacks and used the image of competition between Blacks and Whites as a means to obtain the support of lower-class Whites (Piven and Cloward 1977). In addition, not only southern agricultural aristocrats but also local town and city business people fought against those who pushed for integration into local restaurants, motels, and so on. In essence, both economic factors and racism played roles in the dynamics of racial inequality and reactions to it.

Other social and cultural events gave strength to the Black effort to confront racial inequality. During the 1920s, the Harlem Renaissance encouraged Blacks to take pride in themselves and their cultural and literary heritage. In addition, the Civil Rights activists of the late 1920s and 1930s often fought alongside White radical unionists who were pushing the New Deal policies (Sitkoff 1981). Radical union leaders, it will be recalled, wanted to include not only Whites and skilled workers but also

Blacks and unskilled industrial workers, as well. Both radical unions and Black organizations, however, were often labeled as being infiltrated by Communists. This would become a familiar theme again after World War II, especially with the rise of McCarthyism.

In addition to the changes in the U.S. economy and social-cultural factors that strengthened Black unity, other historical events and conditions also helped to lay the groundwork for the Civil Rights movement that was to come in the 1950s. Political circumstances were weakening the South's grip on Blacks and providing the latter with resources that could be used in their battle against racism. Migration to the North not only meant a greater probability of voting but also led to Blacks holding political office in several major cities (Sitkoff 1981; Bloom 1987). "Estimates of voting strength in 1948 saw Blacks holding the balance of power in sixteen states with a total of 278 electoral votes, compared to 127 electoral votes controlled by the South" (Bloom 1987, p. 76). Politicians with presidential aspirations became increasingly concerned about potential Black political defections and, as a result, often courted the Black vote.

Despite this courtship, governmental policies continued to underrepresent the interests of Blacks. But they also, perhaps inadvertently, strengthened the position of Blacks. As you saw in the history of the early labor movement, the New Deal's policies had an impact on the fate of the labor movement. Similarly, the public works programs of the New Deal provided Blacks with an alternate source of income outside the relatively narrow range of private positions open to them. Having another source of income, which meant less dependence, created a source of power with which to fight oppression (Piven and Cloward 1971, 1982; Bloom 1987). This federal source of work and the increased demand for labor in industry helped to drive wages up— wages that dominant agricultural groups were

increasingly hesitant to pay (Bloom 1987). Federal loans also became available as a substitute for local ones, again making Blacks less dependent on local White funding institutions.

World War II brought further changes to the situation of Blacks. Unionization of Blacks was less difficult than had been the case only a decade earlier. Employment conditions had improved, especially with the wartime economy. But national unity was the preferred emphasis and most Blacks did not favor protest in these circumstances (Sitkoff 1981). Despite continued demands by Black groups, any serious attempts to deal with racial problems took a back seat to dealing with the Axis powers. Although the war brought some positive changes, Blacks were still much worse off than Whites politically and economically, and discrimination was still prevalent.

After the war, several political events occurred that affected efforts for racial equality. The international situation was such that the United States became more involved with a larger number of countries, including some with non-White populations. This change, coupled with the racist overtones of Nazism, against which we had fought, meant that continued racial inequality at home could prove to be an embarrassment. Harry Truman, in running for the presidency in 1948, had to present a platform that showed a strong desire for civil rights if he was to defeat opponents who also were courting the vote of those Blacks who had migrated to the cities of the North. In doing so, however, he alienated democrats from the Deep South who went on to present their own State's Rights Party candidate. He also ordered the desegregation of the military. The economic and political context had shifted to the extent that Truman was advised to court Blacks even at the risk of turning away southern democrats (Piven and Cloward 1977).

A final political element in the late 1940s that affected Civil Rights efforts came out of the developing "Cold War" with the former

Soviet Union. "Red-baiting" was fashionable, and Civil Rights groups and leaders were not immune to accusations of being Communist. White supremacists argued that Communists were behind the movement for Black equality. It will be recalled that similar accusations had been made about unions and their leadership when they also pushed for greater economic and political power. McCarthyism frightened Blacks, and the majority of Black leaders took a gradual and calm approach. "The NAACP became less a protest organization and more an agency of litigation and lobbying after World War II" (Sitkoff 1981, p. 18).

All of the conditions discussed thus far composed the context in which the Supreme Court made its momentous *Brown* v. *Board of Education* decision in 1954. To summarize, several changes had occurred since World War I that changed the social context and the political and economic position of Blacks:

1. The basis of the South's economy had shifted from agriculture to industry, weakening the economic status of the traditional southern upper class. This change led to economic and political splits within the southern upper class. The interests of industrial leaders in the maintenance of Jim Crow laws were simply not as strong nor as necessary as they were for the agricultural elite. The South's social and political structure was becoming increasingly out of step with other macrochanges occurring in the region and the nation.

2. The decline in agriculture and the growth of industry in the nation as a whole opened up new economic opportunities for African Americans, and, for those who moved to cities and to the North, new political/power bases as well. This served to build up institutions within the African American community. In addition, it created a "cognitive liberation" for African Americans, a new understanding of their situation and the potentiality for change (McAdam 1982). The combination of increased internal solidarity within the African American community and being tied to the White economic power structure in an exploitative relationship created a situation favorable to the mobilization of African Americans (Oberschall 1973).

3. Racism continued to provide a backdrop against which economic changes and battles for equality were fought.

4. Political policies brought on by the Depression, the Nazism of World War II, and the growing Black voting bloc were moving in the direction of being helpful for Blacks. Moreover, in the 1950s, growing awareness of independence movements by oppressed non-White groups against colonial powers gave encouragement to Civil Rights forces in the United States. For example, in the late 1940s, India had achieved independence from England, and several African nations had achieved independence from their colonial masters in the late 1950s and early 1960s. These events suggested to the U.S. government that it might make geopolitical sense for the state not to appear racist. The liberation struggles abroad also heartened many Black leaders who became convinced that change was possible (Rollins 1986).

As stated at the beginning of this section, the date on which the Civil Rights movement formally began is debatable. Some tie its start to the 1953 bus boycott in Baton Rouge, Louisiana. Others associate it with Rosa Parks's refusal to give her bus seat to a White man and the Montgomery bus boycott that followed in 1955. In any case, the mid-1950s is generally agreed to mark the start of the movement, and no single event was any more consequential than the Supreme Court's decision of 1954. To suggest the specific dynamics involved in the process, following is a sketchy history of the movement from that point to the mid-1960s when it began to disintegrate into various factions.

A Brief History

The *Brown* v. *Board of Education* decision was a true watershed in the effort for civil rights. It declared segregation in education to be unconstitutional. In concluding his argument, Chief Justice Earl Warren stated simply, "We conclude that in the field of public education the doctrine of 'separate but equal' has no place. Separate educational facilities are inherently unequal" (quoted in Sitkoff 1981, p. 22). This decision had a powerful effect on both Blacks and southern Whites. The Black movement for equality was given a boost, but at the same time a White countermovement was established to fight these advances. While Blacks were jubilant about the decision, the South's White elite were not about to accept it without a fight. Many said unequivocally that they would not comply with the law in this case. "The prospect of desegregating public schools was fundamentally appalling to the average White Southerner. The thought of young 'niggers' mixing in school with little White children jarred the sensibilities of Southern Whites, whether poor farmers or highly placed government officials" (Morris 1984, p. 27). Even though the decision by the Court to segregate had been unanimous, it had not come to this decision easily. In order to get the unanimous ruling, Warren had to agree on a policy of gradual implementation of the desegregation policy. The qualification of gradualism left room for southern dissenters to fight enforcement, and it led to frustration on the part of Blacks who wished speedy implementation of the law.

President Eisenhower demonstrated no strong endorsement of the decision, nor did he actively move to have it enforced. He did not really believe that one could effectively legislate on such moral-laden matters (Sitkoff 1981). Before the decision had been made, he had tried to soften Warren's position by alluding to the basic goodness of the South's people: "These are not bad people. All they are concerned about is to see that their sweet little girls are not required to sit in school alongside some big overgrown Negroes" (quoted in Bloom 1987, p. 106). Eisenhower, then, was not an active supporter of civil rights, but later Black protests and militant White reactions to those actions would force him to intervene.

As mentioned, reaction from the southern White power structure to the Court's decision was immediate and strong. There was no strong push on the part of the government for swift implementation of the law; the dominance by conservative elements of the major political parties in Congress meant no rapid enforcement would be forthcoming. The FBI's J. Edgar Hoover still saw racial unrest as being Communist inspired (Bloom 1987). In the South, White churches and the press generally opposed the ruling, and local White Citizens' Councils were set up to fight desegregation (Sitkoff 1981). In 1956, the membership in these Councils approached 250,000 (Piven and Cloward 1977).

In the mid-1950s, notable bus boycotts by Blacks occurred in Baton Rouge, Montgomery, and Tallahassee. Perhaps the most famous of these was initiated by Rosa Parks in Montgomery in December of 1955. Mrs. Parks, who was an active NAACP participant and had been put off the bus previously for refusing to move to the back, had gotten on a crowded bus and refused to surrender her seat to a White male adult. At the next bus stop, Mrs. Parks was taken off the bus and arrested for violating the local bus ordinance (Sitkoff 1981). News of her arrest spread, and a bus boycott was organized by a group of local Black leaders. Assuming that it would be best to appoint an outsider as its leader, they appointed a hesitant, young, middle-class, nonviolent, and intellectually sophisticated Black minister to lead the boycott.

The Reverend Martin Luther King, Jr. was well educated, a newcomer to the area, and had attended theological school in the North. He was stunned by the blatant racism that seemed to be so out of place in a period when Blacks had become more educated and urbanized (ibid.). Given his background and training, King assumed initially that Whites would respect logic and listen to reason, but he was wrong. "He now realized that the matter was one of power, not reason, that 'no one gives up his privileges without strong resistance' " (ibid., p. 51). Under his new organization, dubbed the Montgomery Improvement Association, King led a nonviolent boycott of the bus system. Local Black churches provided sites for meetings and arranged for alternative modes of transportation. The boycott went on for over a year, and during that time, White resistance had tried a range of tactics to bring it to an end. Legal tactics such as arrests and jailings for minor or fictitious infractions of local laws were used. Economic sanctions also were tried; some deeply involved in the boycott lost their jobs. Finally, violent tactics were used: Many beatings occurred, and four Black churches and the homes of King, his associate Ralph Abernathy, and another supporter were bombed. In the last analysis, however, the nonviolent boycott prevailed and the U.S. Supreme Court declared Alabama's bus segregation laws unconstitutional.

The nonviolent, long-suffering, patient approach of the boycott contrasted in the national media with the harsh White reaction. Many outside the South were appalled at the tactics used by the White resistance. In contrast, King's "neo-Gandhian persuasion" seemed reasonable and acceptable as a means for obtaining equal rights. Above all, it was nonviolent and embraced the Christian beliefs of turning the other cheek and not condemning individual racists. It blamed the system of segregation rather than the individuals who enforced it (King 1958; Sitkoff 1981). As a result of the boycott, King and his approach to injustice

gained world-wide attention. Out of the boycott, other Civil Rights groups were organized, most notably the Southern Christian Leadership Conference (SCLC) under King's leadership.

A familiar pattern of Black/White confrontation began to develop as a result of the early boycotts. Basically, the sequence would begin with nonviolent Black protests, followed by a militant White response, which in turn often led to federal intervention. It did not take long for Black leaders to figure out how to get the attention of federal officials who had been unreliable and largely unresponsive in the past in enforcing rights that were theirs under the Constitution.

Another prominent illustration of Black/White confrontation occurred a couple of years after Mrs. Parks's historic bus ride. In late 1957, Governor Orval Faubus of Arkansas called in National Guard troops to prevent Black students from entering the all-White Central High School in Little Rock. Ignoring another federal court order, troops would still not let these students in the next day. After threats of White mob violence, Eisenhower was forced to act by federalizing National Guard troops and bringing in paratroopers to guarantee safe admission for the students. The troops remained for the rest of the year.

The violent repressive tactics of Whites against nonviolent protestors angered many in the Black community and made them not altogether happy with King's patient, nonmilitant approach. This was especially the case as hostile White resistance intensified during the late 1950s and early 1960s. However, many young college-educated Blacks had had their resolve stiffened by the growing number of successes from King's approach. Beside boycotts and marches, additional nonviolent tactics were used. Among these was the sit-in, which also had been used effectively in the past in union strikes.

In the early 1960s, sit-ins were held throughout the South as a way of protesting segregation of public facilities. Similar protests were held in northern cities to demonstrate sympathetic support of the Civil Rights protestors. These protests involved thousands of individuals, many of them college students. One of the most famous of the sit-ins occurred in early February 1960 in Greensboro, North Carolina. Four Black students sat down at a Woolworth's lunch counter and asked for coffee and donuts. When refused, they kept their seats until the store closed. The next day, more students did the same thing, but White officials remained implacable, and it was only after repeated sit-ins that Greensboro allowed such service six months later. This sit-in inspired similar protests throughout the South and afforded a means by which college students could become meaningfully involved in the Civil Rights movement. Adults also joined in these protests. Within one and one-half years of the Greensboro sit-in, demonstrations had been carried out in over 100 cities and towns in all the southern states (Blumberg 1984). Not only sit-ins at lunch counters, but sleep-ins in the lobbies of motels, swim-ins at pools, play-ins at recreational areas, kneel-ins at churches, and read-ins at libraries followed. Boycotts also were carried out against merchants who refused desegregation (Sitkoff 1981). Local White reactions were often swift and violent. Floggings, kickings, pistol whippings, dog attacks, jailings, and even acid throwings were among the repressive means used against the protestors. But still the sit-ins continued.

One of the results of these demonstrations was that they showed southerners the depth of Black feelings about these matters. They were also powerful in bringing to the attention of the nation the injustice of widespread legal segregation practices. Largely as a result of the active concern of Black college youths, their impatience with years of waiting, and the seemingly futile legal maneuverings of the more conservative approaches in the Civil Rights movement as typified by the NAACP, other, more militant types of organizations (such as the Student Nonviolent Coordinating Committee [SNCC]) began appearing in the early 1960s (Sitkoff 1981; Blumberg 1984).

In 1961, the Congress of Racial Equality (CORE), which had been founded in 1942 and had advocated direct nonviolent means of protest, organized a "freedom ride" from Washington, DC, to New Orleans to see if states and municipalities were complying with the federal law against discrimination in interstate bus terminals. These rides went into the Deep South where White resistance was strongest. As in other peaceful protests, these too evoked violent White resistance. Beatings and deaths of protestors, for example, took place in several Alabama cities, including Birmingham and Montgomery. Again, much of the violence was broadcast through the media.

It was only when waves of public sympathy came that the federal government acted to protect the protestors and enforce the law. When there was no publicity, little was done; violations of the law were left unpunished. It became clear to protestors that they apparently had to elicit a violent response to receive public attention and sympathy, and to trigger the government to act. When the White resistance reacted with legal nonviolent measures, such publicity and sympathy was not as likely, nor as a result, was governmental intervention. Barkan (1984) suggested that had Whites used these means more often, the results may have been different. Examining the confrontations in Montgomery, Selma, Birmingham, Albany (Georgia), and Danville (Virginia), he concluded that in those cities where legal means such as arrests, high bails, court proceedings, and injunctions had been used, protestors were less successful (see also Sitkoff 1981).

Federal officials were always reluctant to intervene in Civil Rights protests. Many of the reasons were political in nature. Both major political parties were still concerned with alienating the power structure and White voters of the Deep South. As in the 1930s, when the federal administration was trying to balance allegiances between labor and business, the government in the 1950s and early 1960s did not want to antagonize either Blacks or Whites. The result was a lot of fence-sitting, and many acts of violence against legitimate protests evoked no response from Washington (Piven and Cloward 1977; Sitkoff 1981).

One of the most brutal reactions to the nonviolent demonstrations of King and the SCLC occurred in Birmingham in the spring of 1963. Sit-ins, marches, and similar techniques had been used to protest local segregation. After these had been going on for a time, the local police commissioner, Eugene "Bull" Connor, came down violently on the protestors. His violent response was seen by millions on television. Officials used dogs, high-pressure hoses, cattle prods, clubs, and even a police tank to beat down the protestors. President Kennedy and his brother, Robert, who had wanted "cooling-down" periods by Blacks and a more gradual approach to desegregation, sent federal representatives to help reach a compromise between King and local officials. But the protestors would not back down. Finally, the SCLC obtained desegregation of some public facilities, a promise of nondiscriminatory hiring, and the formation of a biracial committee in Birmingham (Sitkoff 1981). The local reaction to the agreement was not completely positive. Bombings resulted, causing some Blacks to again question King's nonviolent approach.

As successful protests became more frequent, more working-class Blacks were drawn into the movement. Greater competition among the major Black organizations (SCLC, SNCC, CORE, NAACP) occurred with each group vying for the dominant position. They sponsored massive demonstrations throughout the country. A national March on Washington was made in August 1963, sponsored by numerous Civil Rights, union, and church organizations and involving well over 200,000 individuals. During the summer of 1964, hundreds of individuals worked in Mississippi to increase voter registration, and three workers were brutally murdered. The government asked workers to

remain calm, but this request only deepened their distrust of administration policies and motives. Riots broke out in several cities. President Kennedy began to press for a Civil Rights law in 1963, and shortly thereafter the Civil Rights and Voting Rights Acts were passed under President Johnson. This national legislative response to the basic problems of Blacks, particularly in the South, helped to delegitimize the need for protest, especially in the eyes of northern Whites.

But despite the passage of these laws, as has already been suggested, several other changes had occurred that helped alter the nature of the Black movement from the nonviolent protest tactics of King to cries for "Black Power" and Black "liberation." First, the slow, compromising approach of the federal government to the problems experienced by Blacks on a day-to-day basis, coupled with the patient nonviolent method of King, convinced some in the Civil Rights movement of the need for more drastic action on their own behalf. The consistently violent reactions by Whites to the nonviolent protests of Blacks over the year widened the gap between factions within the Civil Rights movement in the early 1960s.

Second, the focus of the Civil Rights movement had been on the South, but the migration of many Blacks into the cities of the North and West led to a shift in goal emphasis within the movement. The problems of Black city dwellers became the focus: poverty, employment, housing, poor schools, and so on. The Civil Rights movement has been interpreted by some as largely a movement by and for middle-class individuals, while the focus of the Black movement on problems of city residents appeared to demonstrate a greater concern for the Black working and lower classes (Oberschall 1973; Blumberg 1984; Bloom 1987). In total, the shift in the movement was from an emphasis on integration, political and social rights, and nonviolence to one on Black separatism, economic needs, and more militant tactics (Blumberg 1984; Bloom 1987). Different segments stressed the importance of cultural and Black nationalism, while others spoke of Black power. Despite their dissimilarities, all of these more militant perspectives betrayed a basic distrust of White institutions, the need for Blacks to develop their own institutions or identities, and the need for stronger reactions to discrimination against Blacks. Stokely Carmichael's statement about the need for Black power suggests the feelings that some were having: "Power is the only thing respected in this world, and we must get it at any cost" (in Sitkoff 1981, p. 214).

Violent riots occurred during these "long hot summers" in many major cities, including Chicago, Cleveland, Milwaukee, Dayton, San Francisco, Detroit, Newark, New Haven, Boston, Buffalo, and others. During 1967 alone, there were 150 such outbreaks (Sitkoff 1981). Certainly with this turn of events, it was clear that by the mid-1960s, while the Black push for equality was continuing, the nonviolent Civil Rights movement phase had passed.

Since the late 1960s, changes have occurred that have altered the speed and vibrancy of the movement to reduce racial inequality. Over the last couple of decades, shifts in the economy, greater political conservatism and complacency, the rise of Hispanics and concerns about new immigrants, and growing economic inequality outside and inside the Black community have softened the national focus on Blacks' living conditions and created divisions among Blacks themselves. There have even been attempts to eliminate policies originally aimed at equalizing opportunities for all groups. The ongoing assault on

August 8, 1968: Miami policemen drag away a Black youth during a clash between police and rioters in that city's predominantly Black Liberty City district. In 1967 and 1968, race riots occurred across the country in many large cities.
Photo © Bettmann/Corbis.

affirmative action is, in large part, a reflection of fears about competition for jobs and beliefs that changes have largely rectified abuses against Blacks, thus rendering affirmative action unnecessary. Despite the fact that affirmative action appears to have benefited women more than Blacks and that Blacks continue to be worse off than Whites on many socioeconomic and life-chance measures, the broad-based, national sense of urgency to the plight of Blacks appears to have been muted in recent years. Again, this demonstrates how much the health of movements is dependent on changes in the wider society.

THE WOMEN'S MOVEMENT

In both the Civil Rights and earlier labor movements, women had been victims of discrimination. Women needed their own movement to advance their interests. Like the Civil Rights movement, the women's movement has had an uneven history. Its unevenness is reflected in the fact that some scholars suggest that there were two or three separate such movements in history, yet others suggest that a single women's movement went through several phases. Freeman (1975b), for example, stated that "sometime during the 1920s, feminism died in the United States" (p. 448). But as is the case in the other movements, the push for political, economic, and other rights for women never completely "died." Rather, during the natural history of the women's movement, there were times when the movement was widely and publicly active, while in other times, those in the movement were retrenching and the movement was, so to speak, being held in suspension or in abeyance (Taylor 1989a). The point is that what may appear to be separate women's movements can be viewed as distinct phases of one movement. As was the case with the other movements we have surveyed, internal conditions interacted with external circumstances to determine the nature of the movement. Many of those

conditions were related to structures of economic, racial, and sexual inequality in the society, as you will see.

The women's movement in the United States began in the late 1700s and early 1800s and has continued, although not always actively and publicly, to this day (Hole and Levine 1975; Chafe 1977; Snyder 1979). Throughout its history, feminism has incorporated two seemingly paradoxical general goals. One is the belief that since women are, in most respects, the *same* as men in their potential and abilities, they are deserving of the *same* rights as men. The other is the belief that since women are *different* from men, they deserve special protections. At different times and by different groups, each of these positions has been emphasized. Women's rights, then, are defined according to which of these two sets of beliefs and goals is stressed (Cott 1986). For example, in the nineteenth and early twentieth centuries, women argued that they were entitled to the same options and opportunities as men, and that such equal opportunity would allow society to benefit from the unique contributions of both sexes. Harriet Burton Laidlaw, an early suffragist, distilled both these beliefs in her statement that to the extent that women were like men, they ought to have the same rights, but to the extent that they were unlike men, they alone should represent themselves. This bifurcation of beliefs and goals was reflected in the specific goals set by various women's organizations throughout the movement's history. It will be recalled that interpretations of justice and fairness are often based on beliefs about the fundamental differences and similarities between individuals (see Chapter 14).

The earliest organized efforts by women involved attempts to increase their educational rights and to fight for the abolition of slavery, and it was during involvement in the abolitionist movement of the 1830s that some women became acutely aware of their own low political status. As proved to be the case with their involvement in other historical movements, women were not given significant status or voice in the abolitionist movement. Indeed, while this movement was fighting for an end to slavery, women were being prevented from joining some abolitionist organizations and were being muzzled in their attempt to speak in public on the issues. Women had to create their own antislavery organizations because they were being excluded from many of the men's organizations (Hole and Levine 1975). It will be recalled that women had a similar experience in the early labor union movement. While demanding rights and social justice for workers, many unions were at the same time barring women from membership. In those cases where women were members, few held leadership positions.

In 1840, a world antislavery metting was held in London. Men at the meeting, including so-called radicals, were shocked to see women present, and so had them put in galleries where they could not participate effectively in the meeting. Later in 1867, Sojourner Truth, a crusader for both women's and African Americans' rights, wrote of the neglect of women's rights among those who advocated such fights for African Americans: "There is a great stir about colored men getting their rights, but not a word about colored women; and if colored men get their rights and not colored women theirs, you see the colored men will be masters over the women, and it will be just as bad as it was before" (quoted in Ferree and Hess 1985, p. 32). Time and again, it became clear to many women that they would have to have their own organizations and movement if their rights were ever to be granted (Hole and Levine 1975; Snyder 1979).

Two of the women who had attended the antislavery convention in London were Elizabeth Cady Stanton and Lucretia Mott. Convinced of the need for an organization exclusively for women's rights, these women organized a meeting that was held in Seneca Falls, New York, in July of 1848. About 300 men and women attended, including Frederick Douglass and Susan B. Anthony. The attendees approved a "Declaration of Sentiments" based loosely on the wording of the Declaration of Independence. Among other things, this document argued for the basic equality of men and women and stressed that historically men had dominated over women in religious institutions, employment opportunities, and family and political life. Included among the declarations made was a demand for the right to vote. Although this latter demand has been said to signal the beginning of the suffrage movement, most of the women at the Seneca Falls meeting were more concerned with issues in their immediate experience: control of property and earnings, rights over children, rights to divorce, and so forth. From 1848 to the Civil War, women's conventions were held almost every year in different cities of the East and Midwest (Hole and Levine 1975).

The Early Social Context and Directions

The social environment within which women were advocating greater freedoms and rights was not hospitable. Not only was this reflected in women's imposed marginal status in male abolitionist and labor organizations but also in the reactions within other dominant institutions. Religious institutions and the media railed against the embryonic women's movement. It was as if a natural and supernatural order were being violated by the attempts to gain women rights equal to those of men. In order to spread the word, women had to rely on some abolitionist papers and their own journals. Late in the nineteenth century, Stanton and others produced *The Woman's Bible*, a systematic critique to demonstrate that the traditional Bible was a major source of the subjugation of women.

The early formation of the movement also was affected by the forces of early industrialization. Not being allowed to learn skills, women who needed to work were relegated to either household or low-paying work (Huber 1982). Women who were from the middle or upper class, on the other hand, were not expected to work but rather to appear and act as "ladies." "The nineteenth-century concept of a lady was that of a fragile, idle, pure creature, submissive and subservient to her husband and to domestic needs. Her worth was based on her decorative value, a quality that embraced her beauty, her character, and her temperament. She was certainly not a paid employee" (Fox and Hesse-Biber 1984, p. 19). Not only working-class women but also Black women especially were not in a social and economic position to live up to the ideals of this image. They had to work, and in places and ways that did not foster an image of them as "ladies." If a woman was lacking in the qualities expected of a "lady," it "meant a woman was unnatural, unfeminine, and thus a species of a different—if not lower—female order. . . . Women who worked outside the home, or whose race had a history of sexual exploitation, were outside the realm of 'womanhood' and its prerogatives" (Giddings 1984, pp. 48–49). Thus, race as well as class circumstances divided women.

This class division among women had an impact on the membership and goals of the early women's organizations. It was largely middle- and upper-class women who initiated the early movement and who fashioned its goals to fit their problems and desires, such as the desire for education in the professions and civil service and property and voting rights. At the same time, they pushed for lower numbers of hours for female factory workers (Huber 1982). Although the latter appeared as a form of protection for women, it also was seen by many men as a way to minimize work competition from women. This suggests, as discussed earlier, the varying emphases on women as being different as well as the same as men. A desire for protection implies that women are different and more vulnerable than men, whereas the desire on the part of some women for equal employment opportunities implies that they are the equals of men. In sum, the religious and cultural milieu, along with the conditions of industrialization and slavery, helped to shape the form of the early women's movement as well as reactions to it. As you will see later, the 1980s did not afford the movement a hospitable environment either and for some of the same basic reasons.

After the Civil War, when the Fourteenth and Fifteenth Amendments on Black rights were being debated, women were told that attempts to include women in these amendments would only diffuse the focus that was being placed on rights for Blacks alone. The incorporation of women as well as men into the amendments, they were told, would only hinder their passage (Hole and Levine 1975; Snyder 1979). The thrust for a separate women's movement accelerated, and basically two strands developed. One, under Elizabeth Cady Stanton and Susan B. Anthony, formed the National Woman Suffrage Association. It emphasized a variety of rights for women and viewed the vote as a means to obtaining them. The other, exemplified by the American Woman Suffrage Association under Lucy Stone and others, focused only on the vote. Eventually, the emphasis on the vote won out in the movement and the two organizations merged into the National American Woman Suffrage Association (Hole and Levine 1975). "By the decade beginning in 1910 the demand for woman suffrage was a capacious umbrella under which a large diversity of beliefs and organizations could shelter, or . . . an expansive platform on which they could all comfortably, if temporarily, stand" (Cott 1986, p. 52). It is during this period that the term *feminism* came on to the public scene. It would have been unthinkable to use such a term during the "woman movement" of the nineteenth century. Feminism suggested a radical change in all relations with men and also attracted smaller numbers of followers than the earlier "woman movement" (Cott 1987).

Two of the most militantly active groups pushing for the enfranchisement of women were the Congressional Union and the group derived from it, the National Woman's Party (NWP). Both were at the forefront of the movement between 1910 and 1920. Their intellectual leaders, Alice Paul and Lucy Burns, were both highly educated, militant, and single minded in their pursuit of enfranchisement. By all accounts, Paul was a highly charismatic and enthusiastic individual who was an ardent advocate of single-issue politics (ibid.). Apparently, she also practiced a dictatorial style of leadership in the National Woman's Party, which drove some women from the group (Taylor 1989a). The militance of the Party was evident in mass protests, picketing and marches on Wilson's White House, hunger strikes, and even jailings (Hole and Levine 1975; Cott 1987).

The NWP was viewed as having a single objective and any diversion from its pursuit was considered harmful. The rigid adherence to this philosophy resulted in insensitivity to the unique goals and problems of subgroups within the female population. "Only women holding culturally hegemonic values and positions—that is, in the United States, women who are White, heterosexual, middle class, politically midstream—have the privilege (or deception) of seeing their condition as that of 'woman,' glossing over their other characteristics," observed Cott perceptively (1986, p. 58). For example, some Blacks felt that the NWP was basically racist and did not care about the rights of Blacks. Most suffragist groups of the time were imbued with the racism of the broader culture and did little to combat it. Black women's concerns were considered by Paul to be racial rather than feminist problems (Cott 1987).

In 1919, shortly before the passage of the Nineteenth Amendment enfranchising women, Walter White, leader of the NAACP, remarked about the NWP and its leadership: "If they could get the Suffrage Amendment through without enfranchising colored women, they would do it in a moment" (quoted in ibid., p. 69). Just as women had been marginalized in the abolitionist movement by those fighting for Black rights, the specific problems of Blacks were now being put aside to focus on those of women only. In the same vein, some educated women were fighting for the same right to vote that "drunken male immigrant layabouts" possessed. This implied a kind of elitism among some segments of the suffrage movement (Ferree and Hess 1985). But it also reflected a class and race elitism present in the wider society in the early 1900s, a division whose implications for the suffrage movement were not fully understood by its leaders. Those in the movement "profoundly misread the degree to which ethnic, class, and family allegiances undermined the prospect of sex-based political behavior" (Chafe 1977, p. 118).

In April of 1917, the United States entered World War I, but not all groups championed this. The Socialist Party condemned it, while the moderate suffragists in the National American Woman Suffrage Association (NAWSA) took a patriotic stance and endorsed it. The militant National Woman's Party, on the other hand, took no official stand on the war, or on socialism for that matter. The two women's organizations just mentioned were substantially different from each other. The NAWSA was as moderate and nonmilitant in its tactics as the NWP was radical. It was disgusted by the militant and unseemly activities of the NWP (Cott 1987). In a period when anti-Russian and antisocialist feelings were running strong in much of the nation, the alignment of militant feminists with socialists and pacifists alienated the nonaligned NWP from the rest of the country. Antisuffrage groups cropped up attempting to link the "dangers" of socialism, communism, and feminism.

After the enfranchisement of women was accomplished in 1920, the movement for women's rights changed drastically. One interpretation is that "the woman's movement virtually died in 1920 and, with the exception of a few organizations, feminism was to lie dormant for forty years" (Hole and Levine 1975, p. 446). Rather than completely dying, the movement became fractured internally, in large part because the attainment of the franchise had meant different things to different organizations and individuals. In essence, some women saw enfranchisement as an end in itself, while others viewed it as a means to reach more important goals, such as an equal rights amendment (ERA) for women.

The latter was now the goal of the National Woman's Party, while the more conservative National American Woman Suffrage Association fought against the ERA, formed the League of Women Voters, and worked for the active citizenship of women. The idea of universalistic legislation covering women's rights also was opposed by the Women's Bureau of the Department of Labor and a number of voluntary women's organizations. They feared that the legalization of equality with men would remove the shelters women received under the protectionist legislation of the 1920s, which limited women's involvement in the labor force. Some of the motivation on the part of the government for passing protective legislation was concern over the declining fertility rate early in the twentieth century. Officials feared that too drastic a decline would have harmful effects on the size of the defense forces and on the growth of the economy. It was believed that encouraging women to remain at home might stem the tide toward a lower birth rate.

At the bottom of everything, what divided women was the question of the priority of women's maternal roles compared to their employment opportunities. Protectionist legislation was interpreted by its adherents as conserving the maternal role of women (Huber 1982). Those pressing for an ERA, on the other hand, expressed an interest in the full potentiality of women, not merely their roles in the family. In a real sense, this difference of opinion on ERA resurrected the old question about the natures of men and women. Those who were in favor of the ERA were saying that women and men were basically the same, whereas those opposed to it and in support of protective legislation were saying that the two groups were basically different. Although both groups believed that sex inequality existed, the first group saw it as unnecessary and undesirable, yet the second saw it as a given and, therefore, women needed protection. This division in position was duplicated in England (Cott 1986).

The movement also was splintered by the multiple ties of many women to other social movements. Once the Nineteenth Amendment had passed, many women moved on to other causes, such as temperance, birth control, union organizing, and poverty (Ferree and Hess 1985). Black women and working women had concerns other than those held by middle- or upper-class, educated women, and some eventually formed their own organizations. Black women, for example, did not put the passage of the ERA and goals of the birth control movement anywhere near the top of their agenda: "For them, racial concerns overwhelmed those of sex" (Giddings 1984, p. 183). Lynching was a problem that hit much closer to home for them.

Given the class, cultural, employment, racial, and other differences among women, it should be expected that there would be significant fissures within the women's movement. Another source of division among women in the 1920s was a cultural phenomenon of the time. Some women became caught up in the flapper movement of the 1920s and sought to improve their positions through the statuses attained by dress and lifestyle (Snyder 1979). With the defection of many women in different directions, some of the more militant organizations such as the National Woman's Party became increasingly isolated. In sum, whatever mass base existed in the women's movement in 1920 dwindled because of (1) internal divisions, (2) the accomplishment of suffrage, and (3) the growing diversity in the lives of women (Taylor 1989a).

Whether or not significant divisions in a movement can be minimized or made to appear invisible or unimportant depends on the style and message of leadership in the movement, the definition of feminism at the time, and the presence of widespread cultural and social unrest in the society. When the style of leadership is liberal and the interpretation of feminism is broad, the presence of multifaceted rebellion can forge effective though often only temporary alliances among factions. Groups can then fight for the same thing even though it is for different reasons (Cott 1986).

From Limbo to Resurgence

From 1945 to the 1960s, the women's movement was in limbo. In the years immediately after World War II, the social and cultural environment was not hospitable to protest from any minority group. This chapter has mentioned the "anti-Red" climate and the narrow and frightening jingoism of McCarthyism in another context. At the same time, the "feminine mystique" perception of the perfect woman was dominant. This woman was expected to be married, have children, be a helpmate to her husband and his career, and to be happy in her domestic life. In other words, it was a conservative cultural period—one that sanctified the traditional male/female lifestyles. Women who protested or sought "masculine" roles were considered not only unstable and possibly neurotic but also deviant (Rupp 1985; Taylor 1989a). Thus, even if some women wanted to protest, there were few effective avenues through which to do so, and their protests would not have had the support of the federal government. The media ridiculed feminism and reinforced traditional husband/wife roles (Taylor 1989a). It will be recalled that during this postwar expansion period, social inequality, in general, was an issue that was minimized.

Adding to the inhospitality of the social and cultural context, support for feminism also dwindled and extant women's groups had little mass power. The Women's Bureau of the Department of Labor had little influence and was anti-ERA anyway, and the National Woman's Party had been reduced to a relatively small number of faithful followers. None of these groups made much progress during this period, although they kept the movement for women's right alive.

The National Woman's Party's role in this respect has been examined in detail. Most of the women still present in this organization after World War II were White, middle or upper class, employed, well educated, unmarried, and over 50 years of age (Rupp 1985; Taylor 1989a). In other words, it was a very homogeneous group composed of women who had the time, resources, and interest to keep feminist issues alive. A variety of factors held this group together as a cohesive unit:

1. Considering their age, most of the women had gone through similar experiences in the fight for suffrage, and this common participation was a source of identification.
2. All had identified with the "feminist" label despite hostile opposition from the traditional and dominant culture. That is, they had survived some difficult times together.
3. Most were highly, sometimes fanatically, committed to feminist activities and to the cause of the organization.
4. The members had developed deep and enduring friendship networks. They were personally committed to each other.
5. The many shared activities, living accommodations, and meetings at the Alva Belmont House, their national headquarters in Washington, DC, helped fuse them into a unified group (Rupp 1985).

With respect to the last factor, it should be pointed out that social arrangements in the Alva Belmont House, with its own set of hired cooks and servants, suggested the privileges of class. Moreover, the high and almost exclusive commitment demanded of members and their need to travel to meetings in various cities made it difficult for working-class women or those with major family obligations to become involved (ibid.).

In light of its persistence through the difficult climate of the postwar period, the National Woman's Party served as an abeyance organization for the women's movement. It provided tactics, social networks, and an identity to spur the resurgence of the activist phase of the second wave of feminism in the 1960s. The National Organization for Women (NOW), which was founded in 1966, used many of the tactics of the NWP, such as political pressure and lobbying. The NWP activists kept pressure on the government, helping to bring about President Kennedy's decision to form a Presidential Commission on the Status of Women, and to include "sex" in Title VII of the 1964 Civil Rights Act. Some NWP members also were instrumental in the founding of NOW and became openly active in the 1960s. Finally, the NWP became a source of identification for 1960s feminists who could define it as part of the history of their struggle for equal rights. As such, it helped to give the later movement a "collective identity" (Taylor 1989a). The NWP, then, served as a link between the past and the present in the women's movement, and its internal solidarity allowed it to serve as a source for the upsurge in feminist activity in the 1960s.

Although the 1945–1960 period was not marked by significant advances in the women's movement, several other social, cultural, and economic changes were occurring that created the opportunity structure necessary for a later resurgence in the 1960s. External conditions provide the social context in which a movement can either prosper or wither. "Feminism does not have a story discrete from the rest of historical process" (Cott 1986, p. 60). In the period after World War II,

the number of educational degrees given to women was increasing, as was women's participation in the labor force. Opportunities to work, coupled with a trend toward smaller families and a desire for more consumer goods on the part of families who could go on the installment plan, encouraged more women to enter the market. More children were moving on to attend college, which further increased the need in most families for added income. The contours of the female labor force changed from one that had been primarily composed of single women in 1940 to one that consisted mainly of married women and mothers in 1950. But women also experienced significant job segregation following their removal from jobs after the war and the return of more men to the labor force (Freeman 1975a; Huber 1982). Nevertheless, successful participation in traditionally male positions during the war convinced many women that they could do the same jobs as men in most cases. Moreover, their increasing participation in the labor market was at odds with the vision of the perfect family in which the wife/mother stays at home to perform domestic and wifely chores.

In other words, by the time the 1960s arrived, women were more educated, had more earnings, and many had had significant labor-force experience. Women's labor-force experiences brought them face to face with their limited occupational opportunities. This is important because continuous labor-force experience appears to have a positive impact on feminist attitudes (Plutzer 1988). Added to this was the fact that the Civil Rights movement was peaking in the early 1960s and ideas about equality and personal intimacy were becoming more popular. The "sexual revolution" of the mid-1960s, which encouraged control of one's own body and tolerance of different sexual practices, also was consistent with feminist goals (Chafe 1977). All these events and conditions made the context ripe for a resurgence of the women's movement.

It should be kept in mind that this resurgence took place at a time and at the partial expense of the Civil Rights movement. Despite the occurrence of all the racial incidents in the South during this time, sudden concern was deflected from racial issues and focused on the problems of women, especially, it appeared, those of White middle-class women. The concerns that Betty Friedan expressed in *The Feminine Mystique*, those of the bored suburban housewife, seemed far removed from the real everyday problems of Black women. The issues posed clearly described a kind of woman unfamiliar to the average Black woman. Many Black women considered White women to be just another part of the White enemy, and considered their own problems to be both more serious and qualitatively different from those of White women. Further souring feelings between Black and White women was the fact that the women's movement was seen as having benefited from the earlier and heavily paid for efforts of the Civil Rights movement (Giddings 1984).

In 1961, after pleas from Esther Petersen of the Labor Department's Women's Bureau, President Kennedy created the President's Commission on the Status of Women, which, although of short duration, was able to thoroughly document the poor status of women relative to men in the United States. The Commission saw no reason, however, to endorse an equal rights amendment because it thought that such protection was already afforded by the Fourteenth Amendment. One of the most significant outcomes of the Commission's work was the proliferation of state-level commissions on the status of women. One consequence of these commissions was the sharing of information and the generation of a network of activists who were cognizant of the problems faced by women and were convinced of the urgency of change (Freeman 1975a; Ferree and Hess 1985).

It was at a June 1966 meeting of such state commissions in Washington, DC, that the National Organization for Women was created, largely because of the belief that the Equal Employment Opportunity Commission, which had developed out of the Civil Rights Act of 1964 and was supposed to deal with sex discrimination, was doing little about the problems of women in the labor market. Race and sex again appeared to be working at cross purposes. NOW's early emphasis on equal rights, which was attractive to many middle- and upper-class women, turned off Black women and those who were members of unions (Giddings 1984). Conversely, when NOW leaders desired membership in the Leadership Conference on Civil Rights, they were denied with the argument that women's problems did not constitute a Civil Rights issue (Ferree and Hess 1985).

The Civil Rights movement and the newly resurgent women's movement of the 1960s intertwined race and sex issues in other ways as well. Experience in Civil Rights activities provided many women with knowledge about tactics and organizing problems and gave them a sense of their own capabilities. At the same time, however, their participation made it clear, as it had been made clear to women involved in the abolitionist movement, that they needed to develop their own organizations and movement. Women, Black and White, were not accorded high status in the Civil Rights movement, especially in the later Black Power stage. This is despite the fact that, though largely unrecognized, Black women had performed many varied leadership roles in the Civil Rights movement (Barnett 1993). As in society at large, women were treated largely as tools or sex objects. Stokely Carmichael's notorious statement captures one of the dominant feelings about the role of women: "The only position for women in SNCC is prone" (quoted in Freeman 1975b, p. 450).

Black men in the movement often thought of White women as conquests. "Women were sexual conquests, supportive workers behind the scenes, effective organizers on a local level; only in these secondary roles were they welcome in the cause. When women questioned their limited power within the movement, and ultimately in the society, they were ridiculed, abused, and excluded" (Ferree and Hess 1985, p. 47). The perception by many young Black leaders and most Whites who identified with them was that it was the Black male who suffered most from discrimination and poverty because his self-esteem, his "manhood" was being attacked (Ferree and Hess 1985).

Young women's experiences in the student New Left movement also left much to be desired. While the movement preached fewer restrictions on sexuality, the men generally treated the movement women as objects available for the taking. Women did not have positions of power in the New Left. This male arrogance was in sharp contrast to the conditions in the Old Left earlier in this century. In that movement, women were accorded a more important place and the movement supported women who needed child care. It was also ideologically committed to the equality of women, something missing in the New Left (Flacks 1971; Ferree and Hess 1985).

The experiences of many younger women in both the Black Power and New Left movements helped motivate them to create a network of feminists committed to their own unique cause. Thus, another less formal branch of the women's network developed alongside the more centralized and national-level organizations of the women's movement. This strand consisted of more locally based informal groupings composed primarily of younger women. These groups arose all over, in Chicago, Toronto, Detroit, Seattle, Gainesville, and other places. They were not well organized, nor were they intended to be, and they had no central leadership. While the formal national organizations stressed legislation and lobbying as routes to women's rights, the younger, less formal, and more radical strand emphasized the importance of education, consciousness raising, and "rapping" as means to personal power and women's liberation.

The diversity hinted at should suggest the level of richness and depth of the current women's movement. But its complexity, broadness of constituency, and decentralized organization is only one of the ways in which it differs from earlier active abolitionist and suffrage phases of the women's movement. A second difference lies in the fact that its development during the 1960s was more in tune with broader changes in the society at large, as well as more in touch with the real experiences of many women. The cultural contexts during the suffrage and abolitionist movements, it will be recalled, were much more hostile to a woman's movement for equal rights or liberation. Third, in contrast to the earlier active phases of the movement, the goals became much more diverse. The suffrage movement concentrated on a single issue—the vote (Chafe 1977). Similarly, the abolitionist movement concentrated on a single problem—slavery. As you have seen, feminist organizations are attacking a variety of separate problems. Finally, there appears to be more of a concern for the actual transcendence of sex roles rather than a simple concern for equal treatment of men and women under the law.

Its diversity, depth, structural flexibility, relatively broad base of adherents, and institutionalized organization make it likely that the present movement will remain active far longer than the earlier suffrage movement. It has "a momentum of its own, almost independent of the generating conditions that gave rise to it" (Taylor 1989b, p. 484). Some argue that the women's movement's status at the turn of the twenty-first century has been characterized by a decline in vibrancy (Acker 2001; Epstein 2001). This decline has been abetted by the weakening of the labor and Civil Rights movements. The attack on unions has made working-class men more antagonistic toward the women's movement. Others contend that the women's movement remains alive and effective even though it has become heavily institutionalized (Andersen 1997; Disney and Gelb 2000). Rather than deradicalizing the movement, the promotion of some feminists into influential academic and other positions and the solidification of its lobbying abilities have helped expand women's issues and redefine feminist goals as legitimate (Disney and Gelb 2000).

Despite its successes, the women's movement faces an array of fearsome obstacles. The political, economic, and social conditions of the 1980s generated a strong antifeminist countermovement. By the end of the 1970s, many average citizens had been told by the media that women had reached their goals. Added to this message was another which portrayed "feminists as antimale, lesbian, humorless, and politically correct ideologues" (Andersen 1997, p. 313). In 1980, Republicans dropped advocacy of the ERA from their platform after 40 years of supporting it. The New Right began to flower in the late 1970s and has consistently attacked the feminist agenda. This movement is composed of professionals, ministers, and politicians who subscribe to a combination of fundamentalist religious dogma and conservative politics antagonistic to feminism. It has appealed to traditional American labels as a way of discrediting the women's movement. *Family*, *pro-life*, and *Moral Majority* are only some of the buzzwords used to strengthen the countermovement (Taylor 1989b).

At this time, the vast majority of Americans appear to support many of the specific ideas associated with the equality of men and women, even though for most, women's rights is an issue of only moderate importance. A review of surveys from the 1980s and 1990s reveals significant splits in the support for the movement (Huddy, Neely,

and Lafay 2000). While at least two-thirds of Americans are sympathetic with the "women's movement," there is significantly less support for "feminism." Most do not identify themselves as "feminists" probably in part because of the media's negative image discussed earlier. Nor are most women meaningfully involved in the movement. About one-third of U.S. adults view the women's movement as either unnecessary, too powerful, or irrelevant to the lives of some women. They see it as having helped middle-class professional women, but as having yielded few benefits for working-class women, homemakers, or poor women (ibid.). There is also some ambivalence in general support for women, reflecting deeper debates about the underlying basic similarity and differences between the sexes. For example, a large majority of Americans think that it is fine for women, like men, to work full-time outside the home after they marry, but a similar majority is against this once there is a young child in the home (Davis and Smith 1994).

Race and class divisions reveal further differences in opinions about feminism. Black males tend to be more traditional than White males in their ideas about sex roles, especially when it comes to believing that women's place is in the home and the belief that women are not emotionally equipped for active political life. On the other hand, there appear to be few differences among Black and White women in their support of feminism. Finally, among Black males and females, the middle class is more traditional than the working class (Ransford and Miller 1983).

Although Blacks and working-class women have been recruited and attempts have been made to integrate issues of concern to them, the women's movement has traditionally been a White middle-class one and complete integration of these groups has not yet occurred (Ferree and Hess 1985; Taylor 1989b). The diversity within the movement with respect to race, class specific goals, and assumptions about the nature of men and women has provided a source of strength. But under the pressures of a countermovement against feminism, these divisions could widen and splinter the movement. What can be a source of strength can also be a source of damaging division. At this point, the future is still open ended.

INEQUALITY, CONTEXT, AND SOCIAL MOVEMENTS: A SYNTHESIS

In this brief section, and instead of a summary, I will use the preceding discussions on the labor, Civil Rights, and women's movements to distill some more general observations about the implications of social inequality for social movements. The focus here will be on the effects of external economic, political, cultural, and social environmental factors on the development and internal structure of social movements. Because the principal concern of this book is social inequality, particular attention will be paid to the interactions among race, class, and sex outside and inside these social movements.

It is a given that in each case, the social movements centered on deep and systematic grievances on the part of labor, women, or Blacks. It would seem that there would be little reason for a movement to spring up, or for one to develop, were it not for the presence of some perceived injustice or serious problem. Movements do seem to develop when there is a widespread sensitivity to or awareness of injustice (Chafe 1977; Taylor 1989b). Each of the movements, but especially those in the 1960s, can be viewed as movements aimed at inequality. But as has been noted before, such grievance is not sufficient for either the development or continuance of a social movement.

Both the surrounding *structure of opportunities* and *cultural context* affect the probability of a movement developing and flowering over time. Both affect the amount of power

that aggrieved groups can develop. With respect to the structure of opportunities, it is not enough to say that social unrest or upheaval generates social movements. World wars, for example, certainly periods of drastic change in society, often have had a muffling effect on movements. It is the potential economic and political opportunities created by such events, however, rather than the events themselves, that are related to the appearance of social movements. The same can be said of industrialization, which created new opportunities for many individuals. For example, in the early labor movement, it is clear that a tighter labor market created more favorable opportunities for labor, providing it with more bargaining power than it might have had otherwise. Economic expansion and the increased movement of women into the labor force provided them with new opportunities, gave them greater awareness of occupational discrimination, and helped to restructure their images of what was possible for them. It also gave them a greater potential for economic independence. Each of these was important in generating the women's movement. In the case of the Civil Rights movement, massive industrialization created new occupational opportunities for freed Blacks, allowing them to build up a more independent and resource-laden set of social institutions that could serve as a basis for a social movement.

Political opportunities also play a role in creating an environment conducive to social movements. Certainly, at the most fundamental level, a formally democratic political structure is supposed to tolerate dissent, freedom to organize, and peaceful protest. In addition, any political situation favorable to the aggrieved creates another political opportunity. Within the women's movement, the drive to get states to pass the Equal Rights Amendment was strengthened by the support of powerful political allies (Soule and Olzak 2004). In the labor movement, the perception by many that President Roosevelt was sympathetic with their cause provided them with a resource that strengthened their cause. The Wagner Act, the Nineteenth Amendment, and the Civil Rights Act of 1964 all provided political avenues that could be used by aggrieved groups to organize and protest.

Moreover, the political vulnerability of those in power also provided those who perceived themselves as victims (i.e., workers, Blacks, women) with a political trump card to use in organizing. It has been pointed out in the case of each movement, for example, that presidents often acted in support of a minority's cause despite occasional personal feelings to the contrary because of fear of alienating a potentially powerful voting bloc. Roosevelt had to weigh the relative benefits of supporting business against unions and workers. Truman and Eisenhower had to worry about supporting southern politicians against a growing Black voting bloc. Kennedy had to deal with pressure from women's groups and, consequently, created a Presidential Commission to examine discrimination against women.

Finally, social movements themselves often offer opportunities to be used in the genesis of new movements. Many of the younger women active in the current women's movement got much of their tactical and organizational training by working in the Civil Rights movement, and women active in the suffrage movement were also frequently active in the union movement. In sum, the existence of both economic and political structural opportunities creates a social context in which social movements can grow.

The cultural context also affects the life and structure of a social movement. You have seen how a variety of societal values and ideologies have been reflected in the character of labor, women's, and Civil Rights movements. Individualism and antisocialism undergirded several of the goals of the mainstream strand of the early labor movement. The AFL's business unionism, with its emphasis on the accomplishment of narrow, material, economic goals for union members as opposed to goals emphasizing the restructuring of capitalism, is an example of these values at work. A fundamental belief in capitalism on the part of most workers affected what they believed the labor movement should be all about. At the same time, however, the important strain of socialist and communist thinking among a minority of workers helped to diversify the internal structure of the labor movement. The cultural heterogeneity of immigrants who entered the labor force and the anti-Communist feelings following World War I and the Russian Revolution also were factors determining the future direction of the labor movement. These values, along with racism, also affected the composition of the women's suffrage movement, as did the "flapper" values of the 1920s.

Racist, sexist, and class values and their intersection deeply influenced membership in each movement, creating internal divisions and pressures toward homogeneous organizations. In the early labor movement, both Blacks and women were frequently not wanted by unions. When women were permitted into unions, they seldom were permitted to occupy positions of power. Unskilled immigrants also were not invited to join the craft unions of more skilled workers. Women often were seen as potential competitors in the labor force by men. Blacks were used as strikebreakers by employers in factories made up of White workers. In the Civil Rights movement, middle-class Blacks dominated, leaving many immediate working-class concerns for the later development of Black Power in the cities. Women often were used as tools in Civil Rights and Black Power organizations. Earlier, they had been shunned by male abolitionist organizations. Whites as well were discouraged from being part of the Black Power movement of the mid-1960s. With respect to the women's movement, early suffrage organizations often had little use for immigrant or working-class women. Their composition and goals also reflected the racism of the time. Many Black women found themselves in an uncomfortable position in the 1960s feminist movement primarily made up of college-educated, White, middle-class women. Working-class women also did not make up a large part of that movement.

What all this indicates is that prevailing social norms with respect to race, sex, and class impress themselves on the internal dynamics and structure of social movements at the same time that they are related to the structural opportunities afforded each of these groups. The diversity of a movement's membership affects not only its stability but also the diversity and depth of the goals it seeks and the tactics it uses. As we have seen in the histories of each of the three movements covered, there often has been a tendency to develop homogeneous organizations within the movement by barring individuals with undesirable racial, sexual, or class characteristics.

In some cases, the structure of opportunities and the prevailing cultural context are both supportive of minority protests. Such was the case in the 1960s with the women's movements. But in other cases, the structure may provide an amenable setting, but the trend in cultural values is against the minority and its protest. Many of the feelings and dominant ideologies after each war, for example, worked against a movement opening up and expanding. In these instances, a movement is often held in abeyance, squelched, or denied birth. Clearly, the interaction of the structure and culture in a society affect the favorableness of the environment for given social movements. In a culturally hostile setting, countermovements are especially important. In the conservative 1980s and early 1990s, for example, countermovements influenced by fundamentalist religious beliefs and political conservatism offered a serious threat to liberating movements such as feminism. The survival of a movement depends on both its structural strength relative to opposing groups and the cultural values dominant at the time.

In addition to structural opportunities and cultural milieu, the resources available to a group affect the development of a movement. One of the most influential recent theories of social movements, resource mobilization, proposes that access to resources is the most critical factor in the development of movements (Jenkins and Perrow 1977; Jenkins 1983). Resources are of all types and include leadership, organization, money, skills, communication networks, space, and time. Of course, whether an aggrieved group can obtain such resources also depends on the structure of opportunities and the cultural milieu just mentioned. The early Civil Rights movements could rely largely on an indigenous set of religious and educational institutions for many of the resources it needed to develop. Later, as the movement gained strength, the nonviolent nature of the protests, which was consistent with prevailing values, also attracted resources from outside groups. The early suffragists depended on resources from more wealthy donors and supporters among the middle and upper classes of women. In the case of the labor, women's, and Civil Rights movements, effective leadership was also a valuable resource that helped organize and strengthen each movement.

Finally, the presence of opportunities, resources, and a favorable cultural milieu fosters the development of power and a sense of a *cognitive liberation* in which groups of aggrieved individuals redefine their situation and their potential for successful solutions (McAdam 1982). On the other hand, when groups have few opportunities, no resources, and the culture is adverse, the chances of a new revolutionary consciousness and a successful social movement are slim, indeed.

CRITICAL THINKING

1. In addition to those covered in the chapter, what other movements have developed that are fundamentally about issues of inequality? How are they different from and similar to the movements already discussed?

2. What kinds of new inequalities are developing over which movements might develop? What conditions might maximize or minimize the chances for these movements?

3. What conditions would need to be present for a movement to eliminate all socioeconomic inequalities between groups (i.e., a movement that cuts across all class, ethnic, racial, and gender lines)? Is such a movement even possible? Why or why not?

4. Why has it been difficult for those in the labor, Civil Rights, and women's movements to join forces?

WEB CONNECTIONS

Recently, there has been divisiveness in the house of labor. Visit the AFL-CIO's website www.aflcio.org/home.htm. For information on women's involvement in strikes and unions, and important women in the labor movement, visit http://womenshistory.about.com/od/worklaborunions/.

13 Social Mobility and Status Attainment

Openness in U.S. Society

I have put forward the case for calling this occupational stratification or occupational dominance, but whatever one calls it, the empirical fact remains that the apple lands as near the tree as it ever did, if not a little closer.

—Steven Rytina

Children in U.S. society often are told that if they work hard enough and want something badly enough, they will obtain it. The achievement of desired goals depends on the effort individuals are willing to expend. The opportunities are there to be grasped if a person has the aspirations and perseverance required to take advantage of them. The United States as a storied land of opportunity and freedom is chronicled in many myths and fables about how the individual, no matter how humble and lowly, can succeed. The traditional belief has been that ours is a very fluid society in which individuals frequently rise and fall on hierarchies of inequality.

Mobility is seen as resulting from a "contest" with others rather than from "sponsorship" by the powerful. The importance that has been placed on education not only by the public but also by social scientists in their theories of achievement suggests the significance that is attributed to individual effort in the attainment of socioeconomic rewards.

In light of these values concerning the individual and achievement, it is not surprising that a central question raised in the study of inequality has concerned the extent to which the United States has been and continues to be an open society. One important aspect to examine in any system of inequality is its characteristic patterns of mobility.

QUESTIONS CONCERNING OPENNESS

Any conclusions about the openness of a society depend on how the question is posed. Openness has meant different things to different researchers, and the concern for openness has been expressed and studied in a variety of ways. Consequently, it is possible to approach the issue of openness with several different and specific questions:

1. In terms of sheer amount, how much mobility has there been and is there now in the United States? How does the United States compare with other countries on mobility?

2. What is the nature of the mobility that has occurred? Is it more often long-distance or short-range mobility?

3. What have been the trends in intergenerational inheritance? Are individuals more or less likely to have the same occupations as their parents?

4. What has been the pattern of mobility as it pertains to the recruitment and dispersion of individuals into particular occupational strata? When individuals in a given strata do move, into which strata are they most and least likely to move?

5. What role does socioeconomic background play in determining an individual's present status, and has this role changed significantly over time?

6. What conditions in the economic, social, and cultural structures affect the chances for and levels of attainment by individuals?

Each of these questions poses a separate issue, but all of them are relevant to the general question of how open U.S. society is, and each of them has been addressed in research. The first four questions have been the concern of traditional mobility studies, whereas the last two have been a main focus of status-attainment research. We will review both of these areas in later sections, but first we need to clarify some basic methods in the study of mobility.

U.S. MOBILITY OVER TIME

The extent and future of mobility in the United States have been the subject of many debates extending back decades. Serious mobility research began in the 1940s, and even then there was concern about what the future held. Changes in mobility studies since the 1940s have been driven by changes in the databases used and increases in the sophistication of techniques for analyzing them.

Estimate of Mobility Trends from World War II to the 1980s

One of the first attempts to arrive at some conclusions regarding post–World War II mobility trends using national sample data was carried out by Jackson and Crockett (1964). The authors compared data for intergenerational mobility between father and son collected in 1957 by the Survey Research Center at the University of Michigan with national data collected in 1945, 1947, and 1952 to determine trends in mobility from 1945 to 1957. The results suggested that greater mobility occurred in 1952 and 1957 than in 1947. Some mobility would have occurred simply because of changes in the occupational structure between generations. The amount and type of social mobility that occurs in a society is in part affected by the opportunities that are created, changed, or eliminated by the structure within which individuals operate. For example, World War II veterans often received occupational training while in the military; they were also able to take advantage of the educational opportunities afforded by the GI Bill. Taking advantage of these opportunities allowed veterans to strengthen their human capital and later attain higher wages and more prestigious occupations (Teachman and Tedrow 2004). The structure of opportunities had broadened because of the creation of new avenues through which one could be socially mobile. Indeed, many veterans were able to go to college using the GI Bill. The character and composition of the occupational structure at any given point in time also make up part—a very important part—of the *opportunity structure* within which individuals may be able to be mobile. The structure places limits on the possibility and degree of occupational mobility in a society. Increases in the white-collar governmental sector after World War II, for example, even encouraged working-class and middle-class youths to leave high school or college to get jobs in the expanding economy (Shanahan, Miech, and Elder 1998).

In other words, between any two periods of time, some mobility is bound to occur if the occupational distributions in the two generations in question are different. The difference between that minimum amount of *expected* mobility and what *actually* occurs is often referred to as the amount of *circulation mobility*. Most consider this to be a better measure of the openness of a system of inequality than the total amount of mobility because it allegedly already has taken into account changes that have occurred because of alterations in the occupational structure. A greater proportion of the total mobility in 1947 appears to have been due to circulation than to structural conditions, whereas in 1952 and 1957, the reverse is the case.

Blau and Duncan (1967) added 1962 data to those used by Jackson and Crockett. Their data suggested that circulation increased between 1957 and 1962 and that the son's occupation was less dependent on that of the father. In other words, the system of inequality as measured by the amount of circulation appears to have been more open in 1962 than in the earlier years.

Some of the principal findings from the national study on intergenerational mobility by Blau and Duncan (1967) revealed some clear patterns:

1. Despite a good deal of mobility, especially of the short-range variety, occupational inheritance was higher than would be expected if no relationship existed between the father's status and the son's 1962 occupational status.
2. Upward mobility was much more prevalent than downward mobility, most of it being structurally induced.
3. The highest rates of *inflow* into an occupational category from other categories occurred among the lower white-collar and lower blue-collar occupations. That is, they recruited individuals from a wide variety of occupational backgrounds.

4. The highest rates of *outflow* from an occupational category occurred among the two lowest white-collar, blue-collar, and farm groupings. That is, a greater proportion of these sons went to other occupations, suggesting that they had greater chances for mobility. In the salaried professions, on the other hand, just the opposite situation occurred. The sons were much less likely to outflow to other occupations, suggesting a high degree of inheritance.
5. An increasing proportion of men with non-farm/manual origins moved up into the white-collar occupations. But men who started their own careers in a blue-collar occupation were less likely to be mobile than those who began their careers as white-collar workers or farmers (pp. 28–41).

In the 1970s, Featherman and Hauser replicated Blau and Duncan's study and found some similar results. There was a great deal of intra- and intergenerational mobility, most of it short-distance, and there was more upward than downward mobility. More mobility took place than would be expected by only changes in the occupational structure. Most of the mobility took place in the middle of the occupational hierarchy, for example, in upper blue-collar positions. The top and bottom were fairly closed, suggesting "barriers to movement across class boundaries" (Featherman and Hauser 1978, p. 180). Still there was a decline in the relationship between occupational origins and destinations and between fathers' and sons' occupations. Featherman and Hauser concluded that "among American men a reduction of obstacles to occupational change appears to be a long-term and continuing tendency" (ibid., p. 136). At least for men, background seems to have become less important in determining occupational position. This has been substantiated for the period from 1972 to 1985 as well. "Socioeconomic status has become less important for men's and women's occupational mobility since 1972" (Hout 1988,

p. 1389). The decline in the association between an individual's social background and where he or she ends up occupationally appears to be linked to the rise in the proportion of workers who have higher education. This is the case for both men and women (Hout 1988).

Race, farm background, and paternal occupation were still important predictors of occupational status and mobility, but recent changes moderated their impact. On the one hand, the educational level of Blacks increased. Black fathers were more able to pass on their status to sons, and the growing "rationality" of the economy created pressures to reduce discrimination. On the other hand, discrimination did not appear to be any less significant than in the 1960s, racial differences in returns to human-capital investments still remained, and the likelihood of young Blacks being in the labor force was smaller in the 1970s than in the 1960s. Stratification within the Black community became more visible and clear. Blacks became more differentiated with respect to socioeconomic status, creating more distinct classes and greater inequalities among them.

With respect to the last point, results from the analysis of several national surveys conducted between 1972 and 1985 indicated that the openness of the U.S. occupational structure may have increased, whereas changes in the composition of the occupational structure may have slowed. This means that, overall, the extent of observed mobility remains unchanged because the increase in openness has been offset by a reduction in mobility resulting from changes in the occupational structure. In the 1980s, women were more likely to have had parental heads with similar occupational status than was the case even as recently as 1970. The same was true for men. For example, the share of men and women whose origins are upper middle class has grown, whereas those with farm backgrounds have declined in proportion. For most of the twentieth century, the extent of mobility in the United States was due primarily to changes in the occupational structure

between generations. More recently, however, mobility shifts may be due especially to increases in openness and related factors.

Current U.S. Mobility Patterns

In contrast to the Blau and Duncan and Featherman and Hauser studies, which projected a society with increased openness and decreasing inheritance of occupation, recent evidence suggests that occupational mobility had slowed and perhaps even declined in the last decade of the twentieth century. Mobility at the top and bottom of the economic hierarchy remains fairly restricted. For example, it is estimated that a son born into the top 10 percent of the income hierarchy has at least a 1-in-5 chance of attaining the same position, but that one born into the bottom 10 percent has only a 1-in-100 chance in moving up into the top income decile. The chances are much greater that the latter will remain at the bottom (Bowles and Gintis 2002). Nam's study of sons from low-income and high-income backgrounds confirmed this conclusion, finding that intergenerational transmission for those in the high-income group increased over time, but that the chances of low-income persons moving up from their poorer position did not change significantly. "These findings imply that America is not becoming more equal for its children, . . . America is becoming more unequal in that we are not providing children with less equal opportunities to attain high-income status as adults" (Nam 2004, p. 202).

Tracking trends from 1968 to 1986 within a national sample of almost 5,000 families suggests that income mobility has declined while the extent of income inequality has increased since 1980. Thus, individuals have less chance to improve their income positions than they did in the late 1960s (Veum 1992). Rytina's recent longitudinal study of occupational mobility revealed that the relationship between father's and son's specific occupations may be strengthening: "I have put forward the case for calling this occupational stratification or occupational dominance, but whatever one calls it, the empirical fact remains that the apple lands as near the tree as it ever did, if not a little closer" (2000, p. 1270). This raises the issue of the extent to which attainment at the top is due to meritocratic rather than ascribed factors. Both quantitative and qualitative studies of mobility in the higher ranks of organization suggest the importance of subjective criteria in promotion (e.g., Jackall 1988; Bowles and Gintis 2002).

Historically, upward mobility has been heavily attributed to shifts in the occupational structure. The influx of new jobs and restructuring of old jobs due to advances in information technologies such as the Internet have profound implications for mobility patterns now and in the future. This is also true for the further establishment and stability of women in the employed labor force, as mothers' occupations have independent effects on the positions of their children, especially those of their daughters (Khazzoom 1997). Changes in the extent of racial/ethnic discrimination also affect mobility patterns. For instance, between 1940 and 1990, the occupational disadvantages of being Japanese or Chinese American appears to have declined, especially in the white-collar sector (Sakamoto, Liu, and Tzeng 1998).

Mobility toward and at the Bottom

Evidence of growing numbers of poor people, rising income/earnings inequality, and speculation about a declining middle class have spurred questions about whether downward mobility has increased in the United States in recent years. Research suggests that in some respects it has, but that conclusions depend on whether such mobility is measured in absolute or relative terms. *Absolute downward mobility* refers to a downward shift in economic resources without a simultaneous change in an individual's position relative to others. For example, one's income may decline, but because the income of others is also declining or because those below are much poorer, one may still remain in the same place on the income ladder. *Relative downward mobility*, on the other hand, refers to an actual shift in position on the ladder, a switching of position with others. So, for example, one may start out in the third quintile in the income distribution, but then fall into the fourth because of declines in income. Evidence from large nationally representative samples suggests that absolute downward mobility increased during the mid-1980s, but that relative downward mobility did not. Moreover, larger amounts of downward mobility came from the middle and lower quintiles than from the upper quintiles. The chances of falling into poverty are much greater for Blacks and those who are near poor (Rodgers 1995). They are also greater for women than for men. Together with evidence cited earlier about growing economic inequality, these trends fit the saying that the "rich are getting richer and poor getting poorer." While its degree varied, the actual risk of downward mobility increased for most demographic groups during the 1980s (Smith 1994).

Mobility at the bottom of the economic ladder has also become a growing concern as questions about the underclass and possible intergenerational transmission of poverty have arisen. To what extent do those born on the bottom move up and to what extent is poverty passed on to subsequent generations? Several recent studies have used data from the Panel Study of Income Dynamics (PSID), which has followed the economic fortunes of 5,000 families and their children since 1968. These data suggest that the chances of upward mobility of both White and Black children are reduced when raised in a poor family. Being from a Black family increases the negative effects of poverty. Generally, about 25 percent of Blacks who were raised in poor families stay poor in early adulthood, compared to about 10 percent of Whites who were raised poor. In other words, most will move out of poverty, but a minority will be poor like their parents, and the chances of being poor increase significantly for those raised in families where the parents were poor most of the time (Corcoran 1995).

Children who are raised poor are significantly more likely to be poor when they are adults than children brought up in nonpoor families. Even if they move out of poverty, having come from a poor family negatively and significantly affects children's future education, working hours, earnings, and incomes. "Children's futures are clearly constrained by a lack of economic resources. . . . Being poor matters a lot" (ibid., pp. 249, 261). *Why* these effects occur has been a subject of debate. The mechanisms linking background to future poverty are multiple. Lack of economic resources may affect the economic futures of poor children through their negative effects on intellectual development, stress, job networking, and lifestyle choices (Wilson 1987). Children raised in lower-income families are less likely to complete their schooling and more likely to have children out of wedlock (Duncan et al. 1998)—two conditions that would seem to increase the chances of poverty. Not having a high school education, having fewer parental resources, being raised in a troubled family, and not feeling connected to school increase the chances for unemployment among young adults (Caspi et al. 1998). Unemployment, in turn, increases risks for poverty. Evidence also strongly suggests that employment opportunities and neighborhood conditions are important. The number and nature of economic opportunities in an area also affect poverty risks (Haynie and Gorman 1999). Poor neighborhoods then become socially isolated from nonpoor areas as economic and employment flight from them occurs (Wilson 1987).

COMPARATIVE STUDIES OF MOBILITY

During the late 1950s, concerted attempts were made to compare social mobility rates among Western industrialized countries. Most notable among the analyses was one made by Lipset and Zetterberg (1959). A total of nine countries were analyzed, including the United States. On the basis of their research, Lipset and Zetterberg concluded that (1) the rates of observed mobility in industrialized societies were quite similar, (2) the United States is not higher in upward mobility from manual occupations than all other industrialized nations, and (3) mobility into the elite from manual categories was higher in the United States than in the other nations studied.

This study gave rise to increased interest in the apparent relationship between industrialization/development and mobility rates. Essentially, Lipset and Zetterberg (1959) suggested that general social mobility will become increasingly similar in industrial countries because of shifts in the occupational structure. "The overall pattern of social mobility appears to be much the same in industrial societies of various Western countries" (p. 13). Rises in the proportion of urban occupations coupled with the decline of agricultural work, and the growth of service industries, white-collar occupations, and bureaucracy all provide impetus for greater social mobility. Specifically, the *industrialism thesis* contends that "industrialization, directly or indirectly, demolishes old barriers, opens new avenues for ascendance, and shifts the basis of status attainment from ascription to achievement. It, therefore, loosens the dependence of destinations on origins and generates a gradual openness in the mobility structure, in addition to transforming the occupational structure and promoting structural mobility" (Wong 1994, p. 122). According to this argument, industrialism has an "inner logic" that, when introduced into countries, overshadows the distinctive cultural and social characteristics of industrial nations. The expectation is also that specific cultural elements will accompany industrialism, such as the greater significance of relevant qualifications over social background in obtaining occupational positions.

The argument that industrialization inevitably increases upward social mobility in a similar manner in all industrial countries has come under severe attack, however. In the

United States, for instance, income inequality has increased as well as the proportion who are poor or near poor. Concerns about increased *downward* mobility have also intensified in this highly advanced nation. Moreover, as education becomes more important, lack of it gives those on the bottom a smaller chance of moving up.

In addition to the implications from U.S. trends, many recent studies also do not support the industrialism thesis. Simply put, industrial countries vary in their *rates* and *patterns* of mobility. Comparative studies suggest that *overall* observed mobility rates in Western industrial nations are not that similar (e.g., Miller 1975; Grusky and Hauser 1984; Kurz and Muller 1987). Roughly, the same can be said for upward social mobility rates in industrialized nations; in fact, social mobility does not seem to have changed in many of such nations since World War II (Wong 1994). Mobility does not continuously increase with economic development (e.g., Hazelrigg and Garnier 1976; Erikson, Goldthorpe, and Portocarero 1983).

What this suggests is that the industrialism thesis is flawed because it ignores the central role of the often unique historical, cultural, and institutional context of countries in which mobility does or does not occur. The patterns of mobility vary between countries because of differences in their contexts. First of all, the process of industrialization does not follow the same route in all countries. Historical and political conditions help shape the occupational structure and mobility within the country (Hauser and Grusky 1988). Second, varying characteristics of educational institutions affect access to quality education and the connection between education and employment. Thus, the pathways to mobility vary between countries (Kerckhoff 1995). Think about this: Every society provides institutional pathways through which a citizen needs to move if he or she is to be mobile. These pathways differ not only in their structure but, because of the culture, also in terms of who is eligible to use them and when they can use them. Between one's origin

and one's destination lies a patterned structure through which one must pass to be socially mobile. What did your parents have to go through to get where they are? How about your grandparents? The pathways to mobility for different generations vary to the extent that economic, social, political, and cultural structures also change between generations, creating new opportunities while eliminating or altering old ones.

Research generally supports the conclusion that openness or "circulation" mobility has been quite consistent and constant in most industrial countries. For example, not much difference in openness or mobility has been found between Canada and the United States. There appears to be no major discernible trend in mobility at all in these countries (McRoberts and Selbee 1981). Research on Great Britain and the United States has not revealed any significant differences in openness or downward mobility between the countries, even given the suggested differences in values of the two societies (Kerckhoff, Campbell, and Winfield-Laird 1985).

A number of studies also have found support for the conclusion that occupational-structure changes/composition are largely responsible for variations in mobility between countries (e.g., Erikson, Goldthorpe, and Portocarero 1983; Grusky and Hauser 1984; Kerckhoff, Campbell, and Winfield-Laird 1985). Kerckhoff and colleagues (1985), for example, found that the differences in mobility between Great Britain and the United States are due to historical differences in the occupational structures and career paths taken by people in each society. Specifically, the decline in farming and the rise in professional occupations have been more accentuated in the United States than in Britain, and the routes taken by Britons and Americans while pursuing their careers are different. Americans are more likely to begin their careers in professional occupations, whereas Britons, in part because of the availability of apprenticeships, are more likely to have crafts positions as their first jobs.

STATUS ATTAINMENT: WHAT DETERMINES HOW FAR ONE GOES?

Most mobility studies have not provided us with a systematic picture of the *process* through which mobility occurs. That is, they do not lay out the mechanisms and pathways that explain the connection between the positions of parents and their adult children. Status-attainment studies attempt to identify the factors that are primarily responsible for this connection by focusing on *how* individual parental status affects the status of offspring. These studies provide us with another way to measure a society's openness. A society is considered open to the extent that the economic statuses of children are not dependent on those of their parents. It is the extent of this dependence and how it is maintained that has been the focus of status-attainment research.

The first large-scale set of national data specifically collected for the study of intergenerational mobility in the United States became available with the study of Occupational Changes in a Generation (OCG), later published by Blau and Duncan under the title *The American Occupational Structure*. The data were obtained as part of the Current Population Survey (CPS) of the Bureau of the Census in

March 1962. Over 20,000 men formed the basic sample for the OCG study by Blau and Duncan. This sample represents about 45 million men between 20 and 64 years of age who were in the civilian, noninstitutionalized population in March 1962 (Blau and Duncan 1967, pp. 10–19). Thus, this study said nothing about changing economic conditions among women, youths, or the elderly. Nevertheless, the data were considered to be of unusual reliability and completeness because they were collected by trained individuals using established techniques and working for an institution that had been carrying out such surveys for decades.

Blau and Duncan's basic attainment model is presented in Figure 13.1. They are concerned with the relative role of socioeconomic origins in the determination of the son's occupational status. From the diagram, it can be observed that the greatest direct effects on the occupational status of the son in 1962 come from education and status of his first job. A father's education has an indirect effect on 1962 status through its effect on education, whereas a father's occupation has a direct as well as an indirect effect through its connections with the son's first job and education.

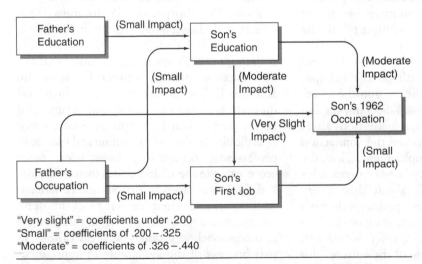

"Very slight" = coefficients under .200
"Small" = coefficients of .200 – .325
"Moderate" = coefficients of .326 – .440

FIGURE 13.1   Effects of Father's Status on Occupational Status of Son
Source: Based on Blau and Duncan 1967.

In summarizing the findings of Blau and Duncan, social origin, education, and first job account for less than 50 percent of the variation that occurs in 1962 occupational attainments. The main factor that affects the chances of individuals moving up are the socioeconomic levels from which they begin. The lower the position from which a person begins, argued Blau and Duncan, the greater the probability that he or she will be upwardly mobile, if only because there are more occupational categories above the individual than below. But as men get older and move through their careers, their social origins appear to have less effect on their attainment than past experience and career accomplishments.

The Blau–Duncan findings also suggest that having a stable family life, having fewer siblings, and being the youngest or oldest male are positively related to occupational success. But those who come from large families *and* overcome obstacles are also likely to move up occupationally more readily than others who have not had such challenges. Moreover, evidence suggested that the role of education, which Blau and Duncan viewed as an achievement variable, had become increasingly important to occupational attainment. They suggested that this indicated an increase in the importance of universalistic factors in attainment.

Blau and Duncan pointed out that the United States does not do as well compared with some other countries when it comes to the dependence of the son's occupational attainment on the father's. They also perceptively observed that *a high degree of mobility can be consistent with extensive inequality and can even help to perpetuate that inequality*. The possibility for mobility may make individuals more complacent about the inequality they observe. Mobility also means changes between generations. Thus, "although high rates of vertical mobility may preserve the status differences observable between *some* individuals, they undermine the status differences between the *same* families that are inherited from one generation to another" (ibid., p. 441, emphases in original).

The American Occupational Structure opened the door to a whole new way of examining the problem of the openness of the system of inequality, gave impetus to scores of studies, and made some valuable contributions to our understanding of movement in the occupational hierarchy, but it has its limitations. Since most of the basic ones relate to limitations in the status-attainment approach generally, comments on this matter will be deferred until after the discussion of more recent status-attainment research.

Explanations of Status Attainment

The first OCG study by Blau and Duncan gave rise, as we saw, to a simple model of status attainment based on characteristics of the individual at different stages of the life cycle. Basically, the Blau–Duncan model relies on *structural* factors as explanatory variables. It is clear that this model does not consider social-psychological factors, such as aspirations and the influences of parents and peers, that may have a significant effect on attainment. That is, it does not lay out "the finer mechanisms through which status attainment takes place" (Haller and Portes 1973, p. 58).

To deal with the issue of the effect of varied social-psychological factors on educational and occupational attainment, Sewell and others developed what is known as the *Wisconsin model* of socioeconomic attainment (e.g., Sewell and Shah 1967; Sewell, Haller, and Ohlendorf 1970). The large volume of studies produced on this model grew out of an initial survey in 1957 of over 10,000 high school seniors in Wisconsin. Most of the early research was devoted to studying the influence of socioeconomic background and social-psychological factors on aspirations. The follow-up surveys were done in 1964 and later decades, with a response rate among the original sample of about 90 percent.

Wisconsin Model. A basic version of the Wisconsin model of early occupational achievement is presented in Figure 13.2. Essentially, it shows that socioeconomic

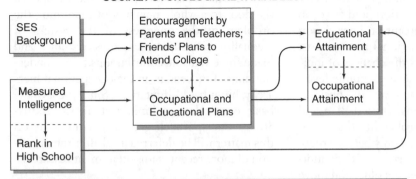

FIGURE 13.2   A Simplified Version of the Wisconsin Model Showing the Mediating Role of Social-Psychological Factors in Individual Attainment

Source: Adapted from Sewell, Haller, and Ohlendorf 1970, p. 1023.

background (father's and mother's education, father's occupational status, and parental income) does not affect grades and is independent of academic ability. However, it does have a sizable ultimate effect on educational and occupational attainments through its influence on the mediating variables of significant others' influences and educational and occupational aspirations. Overall, the model explains about 57 percent of the variation in educational and about 40 percent of the variation in early occupational attainment for the men in the sample. The percentages are somewhat smaller for women (Sewell and Hauser 1976). The model has been applied to individuals with both rural and urban backgrounds, although it was first applied to a sample of farm residents and then later applied to groups from a variety of residential backgrounds.

The Wisconsin model is more effective in explaining the variation in educational and occupational attainment than the basic Blau–Duncan model. The earlier structural model accounts for 26 percent and 33 percent in educational and occupational attainment, respectively. It seems clear from the Wisconsin model that a variety of social-psychological factors play mediating roles linking socioeconomic background and ability to attainment (Haller and Portes 1973, p. 68).

Studies conducted after the development of the Wisconsin model and using national longitudinal samples tended to support the general arguments of the model. Of the factors included in the model, education appears to be the most important factor in predicting occupational attainment, although it explains only a small percentage (9–11%) of the variation in occupational attainment (Alexander, Eckland, and Griffin 1975). And, in contrast to the model, it appears that social-psychological variables play less of a role in accounting for educational attainment than do more objective factors such as "socioeconomic background, recorded ability, and school performance" (Wilson and Portes 1975, p. 354).

What is revealing in the other findings is that none of these models explains very much of the variations that exist among individuals in earnings and income, and what small proportion they do explain (under 20%) is due primarily to the effect of objective factors, such as SES, rather than to social-psychological variables.

The Role of Education in Attainment

The discovery that neither the Blau–Duncan nor the Wisconsin model of attainment accounts for very much of the variation in earnings and income has given rise to a variety of speculations about what the really significant factors might be. The connection between education and economic achievement, while not always strong, has been among the most important predictors included in past achievement models. In considering the role that education plays in future occupational and earnings attainment, it must be kept in mind that the timing of education during one's life cycle has an impact on future earnings. Generally, those who go smoothly through high school, college, and professional training early in their careers do better than those who stop going to school and then either resume their educations later in life or do not return at all. Needless to say, those who come from higher-status backgrounds, especially White males, are more equipped with advantages that allow them to attain their highest level of education early, creating an advantage over others that increases with time. "The enduring effects of social origins and ascribed statuses on educational transitions into adulthood are starkly evident. Childhood socioeconomic status has long-term effects that are not completely reduced by adult strategies to improve human capital" (Elman and O'Rand 2004, p. 154).

The cumulative advantages or disadvantages that accrue to different individuals over time are matched by the inequalities found within different educational systems attended by individuals. Moving from the state level to the classroom level, inequalities abound. Within the public-school system, states vary in their economic support of education and students, and within states, school districts vary in quality. Schools within districts are often unequal, as are classes within schools, and students within classes. This set of telescoping, "nested inequalities" creates different levels of opportunities and cumulative advantages or disadvantages for students in different educational systems (Hochschild 2003). Being a student in a low-level track, in a poor school, in a weak school district, and in a state with minimal support for education has long-term effects for that student.

Most of those concerned with the extent of upward mobility have assumed the importance of education. But the level of its significance has been called into question. The importance of education for men's and women's occupational attainment appears to decline with movement through the life cycle, and its direct effect almost disappears. When it comes to earnings, the impact of education declines more for men than for women. Men start off in occupations that pay significantly more than the positions women initially occupy, and gender differences in earnings continue during careers (Warren, Hauser, and Sheridan 2002).

Even though education is a predictor of first occupation, the explanation for its importance has been a source of controversy. The traditional argument has been that advances in technology and upgrading of the occupational structure have created a need for greater skills and training that education is supposed to supply. Others have argued that the importance of education for attainment does not lie primarily in the cognitive skills it imparts to students. In their survey of findings from other studies, for example, Bowles and Gintis (2002) found that other skills—such as communication ability, attitude, work habits, and other personal characteristics that may be affected by the education experience—affect occupational success independently of any cognitive skills the person may possess.

Collins (1971) also challenged the skill argument, saying there is evidence that what is important about education is not the training it provides but the fact that it represents an introduction into a particular "status culture." Many individuals, argued Collins, are overeducated for their jobs, and those who are better educated do not necessarily perform better on their jobs than the less educated. In fact, Collins stated, U.S. schools generally are not very good at providing students with the vocational skills they need to be successful in the performance of their jobs. What is important about schools for early occupational achievement is that they teach the person a particular set of values and ways of acting and defining things. Employers then select those who would fit into the status culture of the elite and those who might be willing to serve under them because of their adherence to the prescriptions of a particular status culture. In this manner, schools can be used to control membership in economic institutions. It is not known at this point whether the training effect of education on mobility is more important than its role in maintaining class positions across generations (Bielby 1981).

If the variables we have discussed, including education, do not fully explain earnings and income, what else does? Sex, race, labor market, industry, and economic sector of employment are involved. For example, sex segregation in occupation affects the chances for earning increases and joblessness. Working in a male-dominated occupation increases the likelihood for wage promotion for men, but also increases the odds that women will be pushed out of that job. Since male-typed occupations generally have higher earnings than female-typed jobs, access to such positions would seem to be necessary for women to increase their earnings significantly, but the pressures they encounter from resentful men only increase the probability that they will not last in these positions (Maume 1999). Mothers, then, disproportionately enter female-dominated occupations, which, in turn, raise the chances that their daughters will follow a similar path (Khazzoom 1997). Another suggestion is that factors associated with an individual's current experiences may be better predictors of earnings. These might include

on-the-job training, job performance and satisfaction, and the nature of the job and labor markets (Sewell and Hauser 1976). The amount of time spent in the labor force also affects an individual's earnings (Spaeth 1976a). But as already noted, the length of time spent in a high-paying position depends in part on the pressures to which one is subjected.

In addition to these, networking and connections may play important roles in the explanation of earnings and income. Research suggests that individuals who get jobs through personal contacts are more likely to get wage increases and promotion opportunities than those who secure jobs without such contacts. By providing positive information and optimizing the chances of good matches between individuals and jobs, contacts can help create work environments for their acquaintances that are favorable for promotions and pay raises (Coverdill 1998).

Finally, some people just happen to be in the right spot at the appropriate time. For example, you happen to be in a community that has a greater range of jobs than others, or the weather may destroy your jobs in construction, or you happen to be in a city where a new plant locates (Jencks et al. 1973, p. 227). Some of these kinds of events may be appropriately labeled as luck, but others are factors that are systematically related to earnings but have not yet been incorporated into attainment models. The real job of the analyst, as Featherman stated, "is to reduce the size of the residual component toward the limits of 'luck's' imprint on the various occupational accomplishments of workers" (1977, p. 16).

Structures in the Process of Attainment

The notion that luck or being in the right place at the right time may play a role in attainment suggests that one's position in a broader social structure is significant for mobility. Most of the early research on the process of occupational and income attainment focused on characteristics of the individuals involved (i.e., their educations, parents, attitudes, etc.). In asking the question, What determines how far a person gets? especially when compared to their parents, U.S. sociology trained its eye almost solely on human capital factors and the peculiarities of people's backgrounds. This was one of the primary deficiencies of that early research.

Especially since the mid-1980s, however, there has been an emphasis on structural factors in attainment. When one looks outside the individual for reasons for success or failure, one finds that structures in society and in organizations play a significant role in the chances for upward or downward movement. Moreover, while earlier research was concerned primarily with accounting for socioeconomic attainment *in general*, many post-1990 investigations examine the attainment process as it is played out within the structural context of a given economic sector or organization. Attainment always takes place within a concrete organizational or economic context, and variations in the structural networks, hierarchies, and career pathways between organizations can help account for differences in attainment processes and outcomes. This latter realization has led to a focus on intragenerational career job mobility rather than on differences between parents and children.

How, specifically, is structure involved in the attainment process? At a broad level, shifts in the national occupational structure obviously create openings and closures in positions. They create new occupations and eliminate others. For example, there has been a lot of discussion of the United States moving rapidly from a manufacturing to a service-based economy, causing layoffs in one area and creating new openings in the rising service sector. Over the long run, occupations rise and fall in their dominance of a nation's employment structure. These national economic changes are in turn rooted in technology changes, international competition, and the movement of capital between and within

nations. Attendant streamlining, downsizing, and simple shutdowns also affect the alternatives available for attainment.

So-called vacancy-driven models stress the fact "that mobility depends on the availability of empty positions and that the filling of jobs is interdependent. One person's move to a new job or out of a job system creates an opening to be filled" (Rosenfeld 1992). For example, historically, many immigrants have dominated certain types of lower status positions as natives have moved on to the greener pastures of more prestigious jobs. At the national level, attainment is also affected by legislative changes. Affirmative action and equal employment opportunity policies are aimed at broadening the opportunity structures of women and racial/ethnic minorities (ibid.).

Below the national level, attainment is also tied to the structure of opportunities within different economic sectors and organizations. Within large formal organizations of the core economic sector, as was noted earlier, jobs are more likely than in the peripheral sector to be part of a career ladder (i.e., an internal occupational hierarchy along which an individual can move). Frequently, the ladder may be multifaceted or have multiple branches, or an organization may have several job ladders of varying heights, widths, and connections. The relative location of a person in that structure affects the criteria needed and the chances for advancement. Upward mobility is generally slower if one is in a job that is close to the top of a ladder. The pathways to advancement can vary within the same structure (DiPrete and Krecker 1991; Rosenfeld 1992). The presence of this tree-like structure creates opportunities for differential attainment that are independent of the characteristics of individuals.

Some mobility is not vacancy driven, however. For example, in some unionized plants, one's time-in-grade or seniority affects economic advancement, and in colleges and universities, time-in-rank affects promotion up the professorial hierarchy (Rosenfeld 1992). Knowledge about and access to information about the various avenues to advancement within an organization also is important, and this may vary with one's position in it and the internal network of which one is a part. Being an insider, having connections, and being "in the know" affect one's chances for attainment, especially within an organization whose opportunity ladder is open solely or primarily only to current employees (DiPrete and Krecker 1991).

Robert Jackall's intensive study of corporations reveals how critical social skills and personality characteristics are and how they can become more important and eventually displace hard work, education, and other achievement-based factors in moving up the corporate ladder. He found that "managers rarely speak of objective criteria for achieving success because once certain crucial points in one's career are passed, success and failure seem to have little to do with one's accomplishments" (Jackall 1988, p. 41). One manager observed that once a high administrative level is reached, "all have similar levels of ability, drive, competence, and so on. What happens is that people perceive in others *what they like*—operating styles, personalities, ability to get along. Now these are all very subjective judgments" (p. 45, emphasis in original). Having the appropriate mentor and sponsor helps one's chances for upward mobility. Being in a structural location where one knows who is thinking and doing what enhances the probability that one can tailor oneself accordingly.

MOBILITY AND ATTAINMENT PROCESS AMONG AFRICAN AMERICANS

In their landmark study of U.S. men in the early 1960s, Blau and Duncan (1967) argued that Blacks generally start out from a lower position, but instead of moving up in a manner commensurate with their education and other human capital, they become involved in a vicious circle in which they are hindered at each step along the way in the attainment process. That is, their disadvantages are *cumulative*. They have a hard time getting a higher education, and when they do, the occupational returns for that education are less than those received by Whites. Knowledge of this fact may lower the incentive of Blacks to obtain such education, and thereby reinforce the negative stereotype of Blacks as unwilling to be educated. Although southerners and immigrants are disadvantaged, their problems are not of this cumulative nature.

The replication of this national study in the 1970s found that both Blacks and Whites gained in educational attainment, but the gains in recent years were greatest for Blacks and the economic returns to their educations increased. Moreover, Blacks gained in occupational status relative to Whites. Recent changes have moderated the effects of racial barriers, according to Featherman and Hauser, and Black fathers who were in white-collar positions were able to a greater degree to pass on their occupational statuses to their sons.

Despite improvements in educational and occupational status, economic returns from education are not as great for Blacks as for Whites, and significant occupational inequities continue to exist. Moreover, the greater inheritance of occupational status among upper white-collar Black fathers and sons has helped to create greater economic inequality and more "visible" classes within the Black community (Featherman and Hauser 1978; Hout 1984). Blacks who moved up have been disproportionately drawn from more favored socioeconomic backgrounds, and those who had a privileged occupational position, especially in the public sector, were more likely to be able to hold onto it than individuals in manual positions. In other words, "class" factors became more important for Blacks' occupational attainment during the 1960s and 1970s (Hout 1984), even though class divisions have been present and noticed within the Black community since slavery (Cole and Omari 2003).

Research on eminent Black Americans listed in *Who's Who Among Black Americans* also has found that they are more likely to come from privileged backgrounds. Specifically, they are more likely than the average Black to have had parents who are professionals and are highly educated. Further back in their lineage, their ancestors were more likely to have been "free" Blacks with lighter skin (Mullins and Sites 1984). However, the paths to eminence and the occupations that characterize eminent Black Americans have differed historically from those that distinguish eminent White Americans (Lieberson and Carter 1979). Of course, an increase in the impact of class origins among Blacks does not necessarily mean that race has become *less* significant in their lives. Although this research may *suggest* that class is becoming more important than race in determining occupational attainment, Blacks do not perceive it this way. Data from national surveys conducted from the mid-1970s to the mid-1980s show no significant decline in the effects of race on feelings of despair. Blacks are significantly more likely than Whites to feel that things are getting worse rather than better for the average person. In fact, the strength of the relationship between race and such feelings increased between 1980 and 1984 (Austin and Stack 1988).

While middle-class Blacks may be more able to retain the positions, Blacks who were in low-paid jobs were less likely than comparable Whites to be upwardly mobile (Pomer 1986). Movement from the peripheral to the core sector of the economy is especially difficult for Blacks. Mobility into the higher-paying core sector or into a higher status occupation may be hindered by residential segregation which limits access and opportunities to move up, especially in the private sector (Hirschman and Wong 1984; Hout 1986). If Blacks do move up, it is most likely to an adjacent category rather than to an upper nonmanual position. Blacks seldom advance to managerial positions, and in contrast to Whites, most of the movement into the "mainstream" is in the public rather than private sector.

The Black middle class has grown in recent decades. "In a period of slightly more than one hundred years (1865–1970), the Black middle class increased from a small group of 'free Negroes' to a sizable stratum of the Black population" (Durant and Louden 1986, p. 254). A variety of factors have been linked to this growth, including industrialization, urbanization, increased education and collective action, and occupational differentiation. However, much of the growth of the Black middle class can be attributed to the appreciable number who have assumed public or governmental white-collar jobs, rather than managerial or upper-level technical positions in the private sector (Collins 1983; Hout 1984). This makes the Black middle class more potentially vulnerable to shifts within government and its budget.

The instability in the position of Blacks who are in white-collar positions is further indicated by analyses of mobility in earnings using census data from 1967 to 1991 (Gittleman and Joyce 1995). Blacks, especially Black women, who are in the upper quintile of earnings are much less likely than Whites to maintain that position for at least one year. Part of the reason for this earnings instability is related to the fact that White men are more likely to occupy professional and managerial occupations, and Black men are more likely to be found in sales and clerical jobs, positions associated with greater fluctuations in earnings. In general, Blacks are less likely than Whites to be found in the upper-earnings quintile and more likely to be in the bottom quintile. When in the bottom, they are also more likely than Whites to stay there.

Race and the Status-Attainment Process

Research has been done to determine if the models that have been developed to explain educational and occupational attainment apply to Blacks as well as they do to Whites. Since race has an effect on a variety of areas in U.S. life, it may be suspected that what applies to Whites does not apply to Blacks. Since race is an ascribed characteristic, a model based on achievement norms may not fit Blacks as well as Whites. Also, race affects mobility, and the relationship between many of the variables that are included in these standard models differ from one race to another. Finally, the nature of the socialization process in the two races may be different (Porter 1974).

A study by Portes and Wilson (1976) suggested that the process of educational attainment does differ among Blacks. Analyzing a nationwide sample of boys who had been surveyed over a period of several years, and using a variant of the Wisconsin model of status attainment (described earlier), they found several differences between Blacks and Whites:

1. The variables in the model are better at explaining attainment among Whites than among Blacks, which suggests that factors not traditionally considered are more important for Blacks.
2. The more objective factors of socioeconomic background, mental ability, and academic performance are more important for White attainment, whereas among Blacks, the later and more subjective variables of self-esteem and educational aspirations are the significant ones for Blacks.
   a. There is a much stronger connection between mental ability and academic performance and between the latter and educational attainment among Whites than among Blacks. Among Blacks, there is no significant direct connection between academic performance and attainment.
   b. Conversely, the ties of mental ability to self-esteem and the ties of self-esteem to attainment are much stronger among Blacks than Whites.

In summarizing their findings, Portes and Wilson suggested that the results imply a distinction among Whites and Blacks as insiders and outsiders in the U.S. achievement system.

In an open society, one would expect that performance and ability would be quite important, and they are for Whites. But for Blacks, educational attainment is more dependent on self-reliance and ambition. In a manner of speaking, then, while Blacks have had to rely on these qualities, Whites "have at their disposal an additional set of institutional 'machinery' which can, in effect, carry them along to higher levels of attainment" (ibid., p. 430).

Porter (1974) examined early occupational as well as educational achievement among Blacks and Whites and also found significant racial differences in the processes involved. His study of a large sample of males suggests that among Blacks, grades are largely a function of personality factors, such as conformity and ambition, whereas among Whites, both personality and intelligence play roles. As in the Portes and Wilson (1976) findings, subjective rather than objective conditions appear to play a greater part in the attainment process for Blacks. "It would appear that the official sanctions of the school system operate primarily with reference to the visible being of the pupil, and only secondarily, and on the condition that he is White, with reference to academic ability" (Porter 1974, p. 311). Another interesting finding of this study is that in contrast to the results among Whites, grades have no direct effect on either educational or occupational attainment.

Confirming the significance of nonrational, subjective factors in the attainment process of Blacks is the fact that "color" also has an impact on the socioeconomic attainment of African Americans. Simply put, Blacks whose physical appearance more closely approximates the European/U.S. ideal of beauty do better socioeconomically than others (Hill 2000). The importance of "colorism" has been found in other national studies as well (e.g., Hughes and Hertel 1990; Keith and Herring 1991).

Blacks themselves feel that their path to occupational attainment is made more difficult by the lack of decent available jobs for which they are qualified, the concentrated poverty of their neighborhoods, and their lack of social contacts in the inner city. They believe that luck, connections, education, help from those who have made it, and being from the right neighborhood make all the difference:

> "It's not where you go, it's the people; you got to know somebody to get you in."
>
> "Oh, white people got the best chance. . . . They got the top jobs, and in this city, man, you know, it's all who you know."
>
> "If you're from a nice neighborhood I believe it's easier for you to get a job and stuff. . . . The people from the Projects . . . we tend to think of them as being the lowest of the low in society."
>
> "You notice: your own people don't like to help you. Among blacks, I'll put it that way. Because, I got some people in my family . . . they say they'll help you but they won't." (Venkatesh 1994, pp. 171, 173)

These comments suggest the importance of the context in which people live as an explanation for why some get ahead while others remain stuck. In her longitudinal study of women's changing economic fortunes over a 30-year period, Andrea Willson (2003) found that Black women were much more likely than White women to be at financial risk in their old age. White women who were married benefited financially from their marriages; this was not the case for Black women. Poor health, especially that on the part of the husband, significantly reduced household income among married couples. Continuous employment benefited both Black and White women, although Black unmarried women did not get the same income returns from their employment as White women in part because of their generally lower levels of education and lower-status occupations. The higher economic benefit of marriage and continuous employment for White women meant that they lost more than Black women in old age due to widowhood and loss of employment. On the whole, Black women had flatter and lower earnings trajectories over their lifetimes than White women. Consequently, they did not have as far to fall, experiencing smaller declines. This study

demonstrated not only the relevance of marital status for some women, but also the significance of the availability and quality of jobs, and indirectly the importance of education for women's long-term income. The job labor market and education are parts of the varying contexts within which women of different races must navigate their careers.

PATTERNS OF MOBILITY AND ATTAINMENT AMONG WOMEN

The major national studies done on intergenerational mobility during the 1960s and 1970s concentrated on the occupational statuses of *men*. Part of the reason for the omission of women in these studies is that they are based on the assumption that women's positions are dependent on those of their husbands or fathers, and that to know the mobility patterns of men is, therefore, to know the patterns for the entire society. Thus, intergenerational mobility studies involving women most often will compare a woman's position with that of her father rather than her mother, or with her husband or brother(s). If the husband's position is higher than that of the wife's brother, then upward mobility through marriage is said to have occurred. This is the same bias that exists when one argues that a woman's class position can be measured by her father's or husband's position, which is an assumption that pervades much traditional stratification literature (Acker 1973).

The central problem with all this is that women are not considered as independent persons, even though many are unmarried, with their own occupational, educational, and income resources. From discussions earlier in this book, you know that sex and gender inequality exists along a variety of dimensions, and yet people's concepts (like class position) reflect a concern primarily for the attributes of males. The fact of sex inequality needs to be taken into fuller account in measures and studies of mobility (ibid.).

When it comes to believing in their prospects for upward social mobility, most U.S. citizens subscribe to the idea that ambition, hard work, and education will enable them to move up in society. Even many on the bottom endorse this view. While they were divided in the *general* belief that college opportunities were equally available to all, most of the low-income women participating in a vocational program in Bullock and Limbert's (2003) study believed that *they*, personally, would move up in society. They expected to be socially mobile as a result of their training and hard work, and expected to have the opportunities to become successful.

How well do beliefs in the openness of U.S. society mesh with reality? Certainly, along the road to their adult positions, whether people get encouragement, receive help, and get access to opportunities or not plays a role in individuals' attainments. For those at the top, the appropriate resources, values, credentials, and connections are not as problematic as they are for those below them. In her study of "unequal childhoods," for example, Annette Lareau (2003) found that middle-class parents provided their children with more of the social capital and nurtured linguistic and negotiating skills necessary to compete successfully and attain their goals when reaching adulthood. In contrast to working- and lower-class parents who did not intentionally groom their children to be successful professionals, middle-class parents consciously structured the lives of their children to prepare them for their futures. Lareau pointed out that while every childrearing approach has weaknesses and costs, that of the middle class smoothes the pathway to occupational success.

The importance of encouragement and help is perhaps most critical for those at the bottom of the socioeconomic hierarchy. Monthly interviews with low-income minority women in 2000 and 2001 demonstrated the role of social capital in discouraging or promoting upward mobility for these women (Dominguez and Watkins 2003). Strong kin groups can either aid or hinder mobility through their expectations and demands. Sometimes "[s]upport networks can exert a pull away from social mobility ties that is difficult to resist. They enforce kin-scripts that levy time-consuming and professionally limiting expectations on women" (ibid., p. 131). On the other hand, an employment situation can create access to social networks of different people who may have resources or information that open up new possibilities for mobility. "Heterogeneous networks may encourage low-income women to look beyond their present circumstances and learn from those who are more upwardly mobile" (ibid.).

Men and women may come from the same status origins, but they tend to go to different destinations. Although there is a relationship between class of origin and class of destination among both men and women, in general women tend to move into clerical, low-status professional, and service occupations, whereas men go into professional and production occupations. This is the case not only in the United States but in many other industrial countries as well (Roos 1985). The limitations for women in occupational mobility are echoed in their earnings experiences, as well. Among those with salaries or wages, women are *more* likely than men to be and remain at the bottom of the earnings ladder, but are *less* likely than men to be or remain at the top (Gittleman and Joyce 1995).

The likelihood of working in a professional occupation is greatest for daughters from professional or managerial backgrounds, and lowest for those who have fathers who are in farm or production work. This suggests that most of the mobility is short range in nature. At the same time, however, women who have parents with service occupations are more likely to move into white-collar than blue-collar jobs. While parental occupations affect the attainment of their children, it is the mothers' occupations that appear to have more impact on the destination of their daughters (Khazzoom 1997).

The occupational attainment of women who are employed is affected by a pattern of factors that is different from the pattern that affects the attainment path of men. Thus, the attainment process of employed women is quite different from that of married, nonemployed women, whose attainment path is directly tied to that of their husbands. The differences are largely due to the features of the opportunity structure that women encounter when they move into the labor force—features that frequently involve curves, bumps, and walls not often experienced by men. Think of the road to attainment as akin to a maze, and some mazes are more complex and difficult than others. How successful one is in getting through it may depend partially on individual attributes, but it also depends heavily on the structure of the maze itself.

Obstacles and Pathways in Status Attainment for Women

To fully understand the process of status attainment, it is important to remember that such mobility always takes place within a given social and cultural context. This context helps define the ease with which attainment can occur. Some pathways make attainment much easier than others. The shape, smoothness, and contours of the opportunity structure for men make attainment a less troublesome process than is the case for women. The opportunity structure for women is replete with narrow passageways, dead-ends, obstacles, steep hills, shaky bridges, and guarded gates that make the process more problematic (Tolbert 1982; DiPrete and Soule 1988).

By and large, status attainment in the United States for both men and women occurs within a culture in which there are different beliefs about and expectations for men and women that affect their role prospects. It should not be surprising, then, that women are more affected by household-related variables than are men. The presence of a child, for example, has a dampening effect on the upward mobility of women, but it has no similar effect for men (Waddoups and Assane 1993).

Attainment also takes place within a private economic structure in which firms are differentiated in terms of formalization, complexity, size, market, and other characteristics. This structure contains both stable, powerful and unstable, less-powerful sectors. It also contains a wide variety of occupations and positions, some more autonomous and specialized than others. Within the economy, each organization or industry has an internal labor market that constitutes a pathway for mobility.

Some kinds of movements within the economic structure are more difficult than others. In a study of 20,000 men in the civilian labor force, Snipp (1985) found that the most difficult barriers to cross in the path to mobility are those that divide manual from nonmanual labor, professional from nonprofessional, and skilled crafts from semi- or unskilled labor, respectively. Similarly, for women there are also broad occupational divides that are difficult to cross. For example, it is harder for women than for men to move from the secondary labor market or lower rungs of the primary market into the well-paying, stable professional, managerial, and craft positions at the top of the primary labor market (Waddoups and Assane 1993).

The patterns of mobility and immobility being described are shaped in part by the expectations people have about categories of individuals, and, in the absence of knowledge about a person, external characteristics such as sex and/or race are used to provide clues to what might be expected (Berger, Cohen, and Zelditch 1972; Berger et al. 1977). Sex segregation and the level of earnings associated with it are affected by what Petersen and Saporta called "the opportunity structure for discrimination" (2004, p. 852). This refers to the variety of opportunities available to employers to discriminate against given categories of individuals. Using data collected over a 9-year period, Petersen and Saporta's (2004) research on a large service-producing organization revealed that employers were most likely to discriminate against women at the point of hiring, rather than during their job tenure because discrimination is less detectable and costly at this juncture. When hired, women were more often placed in lower-level jobs and received lower wages than men even though their educational levels were roughly similar. Thus, women went through a gatekeeping or filtering process that resulted in their being relegated into specific kinds of positions. This was a feature of the opportunity structure within which women had to operate. Interestingly, the authors found that women were more likely to be promoted and received higher salary raises than men. Possible reasons for this included the company's desire to change its sexist image and concerns for lawsuits alleging discrimination, which is more detectable and measurable at this point of employment. But while women were more likely to be promoted once in a job, women were not likely to occupy the highest positions because (a) they were unlikely to be placed in these positions when hired and (b) there was only a small pool of women with seniority who were eligible to be promoted into the top echelons of the organization.

Traditional U.S. culture contains beliefs about the usual behavior and personality characteristics of each sex. These expectations help to generate and maintain sex segregation in occupations, which, in turn, reinforce expectations. Women, for example, are much less likely than men to be corporate executives, meaning that when someone below or outside the organization is being considered for a top executive position, most of those involved in making the decision will be men who have been socialized into having particular expectations about male and female candidates.

In her study of an industrial corporation, Kanter (1977a) found that at the top is an inner circle of individuals who have to be counted on to share a similar view of the organization and to behave in a manner consistent with that view. There are distinct pressures for homogeneity and conformity at the managerial level. A large part of the reason for this pressure to conform arises from the open nature of organizations and the managerial positions within them. Since position tasks are not well defined at that level and the organization operates in a "turbulent" environment with other organizations, the conclusion is that executives have to be able to trust each other and see each other's behavior as predictable. "Women were decidedly placed in the category of the incomprehensible and unpredictable" (ibid., p. 58).

Consistent with this conclusion, additional research has found that middle-level managers *believe* that upwardly mobile men are more likely to be promoted because of greater support and sponsorship within the organization, and that men's future power and mobility would be greater because of this support and sponsorship. The managers also thought that promoted men would be considered to be more successful than women who had been promoted, even if their performances were not any better (Wiley and Eskilson 1983). What all this research suggests is that the external characteristic of sex is used as a criterion to conclude that it may be too much of a risk to have women and other "unpredictable" individuals within management. By continually recruiting men into those positions, the inequality in occupational positions between the sexes is perpetuated.

One of the difficult dilemmas for women's mobility concerns the fact that the hiring and promoting of women at given managerial levels may depend on the proportion of women already present in an organization at or below those levels. A recent study of managerial positions in 333 savings-and-loan associations suggests that the chances for hiring and promotion into a managerial position are increased as the proportion of women in or below that position goes up. They are also optimized when a solid proportion, though not a majority, of those in higher decision-making positions are also women. Thus, women appear to have to be present in relatively high percentages before women are hired or promoted in good numbers. But the question remains: "Although having women present in managerial positions is crucial to bringing more women into management, it remains unclear how women initially attain managerial positions" (Cohen, Broschak, and Haveman 1998, p. 723).

Women, of course, have traditionally been socialized into the same general beliefs about the sexes as men, and their beliefs can have an impact on the probability of their being upwardly mobile. For example, the willingness to move is an important factor in career mobility, but generally women are less willing to move than men. Research among white-collar employees in a federal agency, for example, found that regardless of their education and other factors, women express less desire to move (Markham et al. 1983). Part of the reason may be that women see more family conflict arising as a result of moving. Perhaps this sensitivity is due to the socialization among women to have the family as a central focus of their lives. A significant factor in the reluctance to move is that most men consider themselves to be the "primary providers," and most women do not. Women who *do* see themselves in these terms are just as willing to move as men in similar circumstances (ibid.).

These self-definitions and expectations combine with occupational segregation and the internal market structure of organizations to limit mobility by women. When women are in a position that is part of an internal labor market, they benefit less from that position than men do, in large part because a majority of them do not make job changes within a firm but move to other employers.

Thus, women do not participate as fully as men in the career ladders available in many organizations, and this contributes heavily to the wage differences between the sexes (Felmlee 1982). In any case, "women's" positions are less likely to be linked to apprenticeships and career ladders and more likely to be surrounded by "dead space"—that is, not connected to a distinct career-promotion ladder (Seidman 1978). Moreover, when women are in "female" white-collar positions, such as that of secretary, and perform admirably because of their accumulated but very specific job expertise, they may have less chance to be occupationally mobile within an organization (Kanter 1977a). Being promoted or not promoted is not always based on merit at the level of the concrete organization (Hartmann 1987). These obstacles in the attainment process for women may provide some of the reasons past research has shown that the career trajectories of women are relatively flat when compared to those of men.

In other words, the entry-level jobs and job families are structured, often even in large firms, to maintain sex segregation. Moreover, if a position is a dead end, it will have consequences on the behavior and demeanor of the individual in that position.

> *Opportunity structures shape behavior in such a way that they confirm their own prophecies. Those people set on high-mobility tracks tend to develop attitudes and values that impel them further along the track: work commitment, high aspirations, and upward orientations. Those set on low-mobility tracks tend to become indifferent, to give up, and thus to "prove" that their initial placement was correct. . . . It is graphically clear how cycles of advantage and cycles of disadvantage are perpetuated in organizations and in society. (Kanter 1977a, p. 158)*

Once in a low-status, "female" job, it is difficult to move out. This result only reconfirms the position as a "female" one and, therefore, one with certain characteristics. "It may be because the jobs are done by women that they are viewed as unskilled and are lower paid, not just that low-wage (low-skills) jobs are created and women are channeled into them" (Hartmann 1987, p. 63).

While improvements have been made, status-attainment studies have traditionally suffered from gender-related inadequacies. For example, as a factor in explaining attainment, the emphasis has generally been on the father's rather than mother's occupation and education. In addition, housework as a type of occupation has usually been omitted from these studies. Finally, the focus on individual background characteristics as predictors of attainment has often led to neglect of the role of discrimination and other biases in explaining attainment.

SUMMARY

This chapter has surveyed some of the research that has dealt with the trends in the openness of industrial societies, especially the United States. Summaries of various studies of mobility were presented which, up until 1962, relied either on local data or research that had not been specifically designed for the study of mobility. Generally, the findings of mobility studies suggest that the trend in mobility has not been altogether uniform in U.S. society. Most of the mobility that occurred in the twentieth century appears to have been brought about by changes in the occupational structure over time rather than through greater democracy and freedom in the society. The United States has more upward than downward mobility, but most of the upward mobility is of short distance. There does not appear to have been much significant change through most of the twentieth century in the extent to which the occupational status of the son is dependent on that of the father, and in general, the last couple of

decades have witnessed at least a stabilization, if not a decline, in overall occupational mobility in the United States. Some broad socioeconomic advances have occurred for Blacks and women in recent years, but they still lag significantly behind White males.

The second major part of the chapter concerned status-attainment research, which has dominated much of the stratification research over the last 40 years and has reshaped the study of mobility. Two basic models of status attainment surfaced early: the Blau–Duncan model, which emphasizes the importance of structural factors for attainment, and the Wisconsin model, which incorporates social-psychological elements into its explanation. Both models explain occupational and educational attainment better than they account for differences in earnings and income. The effect of education is conditioned by the level of one's occupation and the society involved. Other factors of importance include economic and organizational opportunity structures and one's place in them. The process of attainment among African Americans and females varies from that found among White males. Both experience nonrational barriers not faced by White males. Traditional status attainment studies often neglected discrimination as a significant factor in mobility, instead focusing on individuals' personal characteristics and backgrounds as predictors. This made attainment models less effective in explaining the attainment processes of minorities and women. Discrimination, along with the varying opportunity structures available to different groups, can help us understand why some are rich and others poor, or why some occupy positions of high status or power while others are stuck farther down the social ladder. The continued presence of these inequalities raises the possibility that many may consider them unjust. Chapter 14 explores the issue of legitimacy and perceived fairness in greater detail.

CRITICAL THINKING

1. The United States is often thought of as a land of opportunity, one in which there are few obstacles in the path of anyone who wants to move up. What do you think most accounts for this image?

2. Trace your own social mobility or that of your parents. What best explains the degree of attainment and its route?

3. Is the United States becoming a more open or closed society? Explain your answer.

4. Which do you think is more important for one's level of attainment as an adult—*childhood* experiences and background OR experiences and conditions encountered as an *adult*? How would you defend your position?

WEB CONNECTIONS

Change in the occupational structure was the primary factor behind social mobility for most of the twentieth century. What occupations are growing the fastest? Which are declining in employment? What trends exist in wages for specific occupations? How do these vary by state? Search your state for trends in occupations and wages: www.acinet.org/acinet/.

CHAPTER

14 Justice and Legitimacy

Assessments of the Structure of Inequality

The study of injustice is at the heart of the sociological imagination. The classic queries of the discipline concern the distribution of power and resources; who gets what and why remain the fundamental questions we must ask.

—Kelly Hoffman and Miguel Angel Centeno

Unquestionably, social justice appears as a recurring concern around the globe. For that reason alone, we sociologists must vigorously engage issues of social justice or become largely irrelevant to the present and future course of human history.

—Joe R. Feagin

Think about situations where you were rewarded differently from someone else. If the situations were important to you, undoubtedly you had feelings about whether such treatment was or was not justified. These feelings become issues and problems when you feel that your treatment was unjustified. What made the difference in whether you felt you were treated fairly or unfairly, and why are some unequal distributions of rewards considered just while others are thought of as unjust?

Virtually every chapter in this book so far has provided evidence of extensive economic, political, gender, and racial inequality in U.S. society. There is no denying that this inequality is present, but is it unfair? It is difficult, if not impossible, to avoid the question of fairness in the presence of such pervasive inequality. The issue of fairness and justice, and how it is defined by individuals, is a legitimate topic of inquiry because of its strong connection with inequality: "The issues of social inequality and distributive justice are joined when individuals come to believe that they deserve what they get and get what they deserve" (Shepelak and Alwin 1986). The study of distributive justice is also important because "the sense of justice is thought to be implicated in outcomes ranging from personal distress and divorce to revolution and international conflict" (Jasso 1999, p. 133).

Is it fair that, in 2003, the average chief executive officer (CEO) at a major corporation received more pay for working one day than an average worker got for working 52 weeks? Or that on average CEOs' pay was 185 times that of the average worker? (Mishel, Bernstein, and Allegretto 2005). Or that the richest 1 percent in the United States holds one-third of all wealth while the bottom 40 percent own well under 1 percent? What is fair? Who considers it fair? What determines whether individuals think the present distribution of resources is just? What criteria do people use before reaching a conclusion about the fairness of inequality? These are the empirical questions to be addressed in this chapter.

How people evaluate the inequality around them depends, in part, on what they think is primarily responsible for it, on the criteria they use when making their evaluative assessment about the extent of inequality, and on the effectiveness of national ideologies and institutions in justifying extensive inequality. When individuals come to the conclusion that a given distribution of rewards is fair, then they also tend to believe that it is legitimate. Beliefs in the fairness and legitimacy of the structure of inequality in a society are two elements that contribute to its stability and continuity over time. Thus, when trying to account for its perpetuation, it is important to know how people feel about inequality and what factors underlie its legitimacy. Believing that a given distribution is unfair and therefore illegitimate, however, does not necessarily mean that individuals will rise up against it by initiating riots or social movements. We will explore the conditions behind these reactions fully in the next chapter. Here, we are concerned only with individuals' attitudes toward the structure of inequality and the conditions that foster legitimation.

We begin with a discussion of how people feel about inequality, proceed to a survey of ideas on what constitutes a just distribution of resources, and finish with an examination of factors that contribute to the legitimation of inequality. In essence, we are concerned with the principles used to define justice and then the evaluation of our present system of inequality using those principles. The next chapter will focus on "justice consequences," the reaction to injustice in the form of social movements (Jasso 1994).

U.S. ATTITUDES ABOUT THE DISTRIBUTION OF INCOME AND WEALTH

Americans often have ambivalent attitudes about social and economic inequality. Their ambivalence is manifested in their sporadic anger, confusion, and inconsistent attitudes about these matters (Sennett and Cobb 1973; Hochschild 1981). Lengthy telephone interviews with over 2,200 Americans confirm the operation of an "underdog" principle in reactions to equality and inequality (Kluegel and Smith 1986). As a group, Blacks are more likely than Whites to consider economic inequality as unjust, to desire more equality, and to feel that income should be based more on need than on skills. Women also are more likely than men to see occupational inequality and their own personal income as being unfair. Conversely, Whites with higher incomes are more likely than others to endorse the present unequal distribution of income, to believe that income should be based more on skills than on needs, and to be skeptical about the positive outcomes from a more equal distribution.

Despite these differences in opinion, there is still widespread support, even among underdogs, for a system of inequality. A majority of adults believe that "people should be allowed to accumulate as much wealth as they can even if some make millions while others live in poverty," and that inequalities in earnings are required to motivate workers to take on extra responsibilities (Davis and Smith 1996). A recent analysis of large national samples in nine industrial countries, including the United States, revealed that the United States was among those favoring a higher degree of income inequality between top and bottom occupations (Kelley and Evans 1993).

How people feel about existing inequalities depends on what they think brought them about. Inequalities are viewed as justified or not, depending on their perceived sources. Being given an equal chance and personal effort are perceived as important for a just distribution.

Almost 9 out of 10 adults believe that equality of opportunity should be promoted rather than equality of economic outcomes, but almost half are not satisfied with the opportunities for a poor person to move up or with the mobility chances for the next generation. Even a majority of Blacks believe that inequality can be just in principle, especially if it is based more on skills than on need. Only among the poor does there appear to be clear support for need as a dominant criterion in determining income distribution (Kluegel and Smith 1986).

The international survey of nine countries alluded to earlier confirmed that citizens feel that those in the highest-ranking occupations should be paid, on average, three to five times the salary of those in the lowest-ranking positions (Kelley and Evans 1993). More so than their citizen counterparts, older persons with higher education, incomes, and self-identified social classes favor greater pay for individuals in high-ranking occupations. For example, a conservative, high-income 60-year-old man with a college education who identifies with the upper class, and who is also a supervising manager of

---

NUTSHELL 14.1

Our Values and Fairness in Policy

Sharon Hays spent three years talking to welfare recipients and visiting two welfare offices in different-sized cities. Her study, *Flat Broke with Children*, examined the cultural values underlying welfare reform and the effects of reform policy on the poor. Oftentimes, controversies involving fairness or justice are based in allegiances to different and seemingly contradictory values. Current welfare policies reflect these contradictions that are then visited upon the poor who must adhere to these policies. In the excerpt below, Hays argues that we need to make some wage changes and changes in caregiving policy to be more just. Do her ideas seem fair or just to you?

> The welfare program established in 1935 with the New Deal called on the state to support those women who were without an "independent" breadwinner to care for them, and they called on the market to offer men wages that were adequate to support a family of "dependent" wives and children. Under current conditions, both the state and the market operate as if children did not exist and as if there is no caregiving work left to be done. If we are to be true to our principles, it is now time to call on the state and the market to provide all people with the means to do both. . . . More specifically, we

could, first, offer genuine public support for the work of caregiving, not just a kiss on the cheek and the imaginary pedestal, but substantial tax credits to caregivers, universal supplements to cover the costs of children, and national standards to assure the quality and compensation of paid caregivers. We could provide workplace family leave policies that positively value the work of care, and we could offer adequate flexibility on the job to allow all workers to respond to family responsibilities. . . . At the same time, we need to make it possible for all adults to achieve financial independence. The fact that the nation has moved farther away from this goal is a central reason for the rise of single parenting and the rise of the welfare rolls that occurred from 1970 to 1995. . . . By 1997, the 57 million Americans in the bottom fifth were earning just 7 cents on every dollar earned by the 57 million at the top. To address this tremendous income disparity requires raising the minimum wage to the level of a "living wage" that is sufficient to support children. It means reassessing tax burdens and tax breaks and government subsidies that disproportionately favor the wealthy. Further, to make the vision of independent productive citizenship a reality, the creation of widely available, fully subsidized job-training programs and public works employment are not altogether unfathomable ideas.

Source: Sharon Hays, *Flat Broke with Children* (New York: Oxford, 2003), pp. 235–236.

his own company, feels that those in high-prestige positions should be paid seven times the minimum wage. In contrast, an individual with the opposite characteristics believes that a person in that kind of occupation should receive a salary of only three times the minimum wage. When it comes to the lowest-status jobs, however, the results are distinctly different. There is general consensus across groups about the appropriate wages for unskilled workers. Surprisingly, the single difference shows those with higher incomes favoring higher pay for those at the bottom. In essence, then, the only major disagreement among individuals revolved around the size and legitimacy of the salaries accorded high-prestige occupations. At the same time, however, virtually no one in these countries was in favor of a completely egalitarian distribution of income.

While a recent survey showed that a majority of U.S. adults believe that individuals should be free to legally accumulate as much wealth as they are able, the same survey also shows that almost two-thirds of adults feel that income inequality has gotten too large in the United States and that inequality continues because it helps the rich and powerful (Davis and Smith 1996). Keep in mind that the United States has a higher degree of income inequality than virtually any other industrial country in the world. When combined with this fact, perhaps the cynical attitude expressed by a majority of adults about why inequality continues is related to their belief in a link between wealth and corruption. Jong-sung and Khagram's study of the relationship between inequality and beliefs in corruption in 129 countries revealed that higher degrees of inequality are associated with stronger beliefs in the presence of corruption. "Inequality increases corruption, especially in democracies, and corruption produces policy outcomes closer to those preferred by the rich than those favored by the median voter" (Jong-sung and Khagram 2005, p. 154).

When combined, all these results suggest that U.S. adults believe in a ceiling and floor, outside of which the degree of income inequality is unjust. A majority of Americans appear to support the *principle* of income inequality as being fair, but they do not see the present system as necessarily equitable. As the same time, they are decidedly split on whether or not the government should do something about income inequality. In sum, Americans' attitudes about inequality are complex and often contradictory.

WHAT IS A JUST DISTRIBUTION?

The question of what constitutes a just distribution of scarce and desired goods is an issue that has been wrestled with for centuries. There seem to be two broad principles used in such definitions, but each of these is more complex that at first appears. One basically argues that a just distribution exists when equal people are treated equally and unequal people are treated unequally. It assumes that people (1) start out with different abilities and traits, (2) are free to realize those potentials, and (3) are therefore entitled to make different claims on scarce resources and rewards. This is what Hochschild (1981) called the "principle of differentiation" and it approximates what Ryan (1981) called the principle of "fair play." Given that individuals vary in their talents, abilities, and interests, it is predictable that they also will and should vary in their socioeconomic success, and that those with high levels of appropriate talents will assume higher positions in the hierarchy of inequality (ibid.). If persons of *unequal* talent and ability are given *equal* rewards, then this must be justified (Hochschild 1981). While this position is consistent with a belief in meritocracy, one complication is that one's competencies and motivations may be due to luck related to biology or environment, factors over which one may have little control. So if people are not fully responsible for their competencies or motivations, a question can be raised as to whether they really *merit* what they get (Marshall, Swift, and Roberts 1997). Generally speaking, this position is consistent with conservative theories such as functionalism and human-capital theory, both of which imply that one should get out of a system what one puts into it. Findings from the international study just cited are broadly consistent with this view.

A second broad principle, the "principle of equality," argues that people are of "equal value and can make equal claims on society. Differences in treatment must be justified" (Hochschild 1981, p. 51). This conception approximates Ryan's (1981) notion of "fair shares" as a basis for a just distribution. People ought to have equal rights and equal access to society's resources in order to live decent lives. This principle is consistent with more radical, Marxian views of inequality and its roots, such as those that consider private property to be a major source of explanation. Although there are a number of variations on these two principles, none of which are agreed upon by all, we cannot pursue them here. While these two conceptions appear to be incompatible, there is some evidence that people's perceptions of the fairness of inequality are affected by both of these criteria (i.e., on their personal assessment of both the distributive *outcome* of rewards as well as the *process* that led to it). Moreover, how they feel about the process is related to their feelings about the outcome, and vice versa (Törnblom and Vermunt 1999).

Causal Attributions for Inequality

How do Americans define a just distribution of economic rewards in society? This partly depends on their characteristics and history, the criteria suggested by the society's dominant ideology, and their beliefs about the causes of economic inequality (Shepelak and Alwin 1986; Stolte 1987). With respect to the latter, Americans appear to give mixed messages when asked what they believe determines an individual's economic position.

Generally, most people attribute poverty and wealth to either *individualistic* or *structural* factors. "Individual" arguments include beliefs that poverty or wealth is due to personal qualities such as effort, ability, and ambition, while those who take a "structural" position argue that one's economic status is due to factors beyond the individual's control, such as inheritance, government policy, wage rates, discrimination, and availability of work. Historically, Americans have more often aligned themselves with the individualistic position, believing that hard work, ambition, personal investment in education, and natural ability are critical for economic success (Ritzman and Tomaskovic-Devey 1992). The widespread endorsement of this position is consistent with the belief that the United States is a free and open society in which anyone can succeed. Most Americans subscribe to the dominant ideology that (1) opportunity for economic mobility is prevalent; (2) each individual is personally responsible for the extent of his or her own economic success; and (3) in general, therefore, the system of inequality is fair (Kluegel and Smith 1986). "In . . . the United States, principles of justice are based on the assumption that the playing field is level and that opportunities to succeed are the same for everyone" (Flanagan et al. 2003, p. 717).

Not everyone, of course, is equally likely to subscribe to the belief that individuals are primarily responsible for where they wind up. Social class affects one's perceptions. In Bullock and Limbert's study, for example, when low-income women were asked what they believed were the principal causes of poverty, structural explanations were favored over individualistic ones (2003; see also Hunt 2004). Inheritance and being able to go the best schools, that is, being privileged were the most frequently given explanations for why some people are wealthy (Bullock and Limbert 2003). These results were consistent with earlier findings (Kluegel and Smith 1986). In another study comparing teens from "security" societies (e.g., Russia, Bulgaria) with those from "opportunity" countries (Australia, United States), Flanagan and associates found that working-class teens in the United States were more likely than middle-class youth (especially girls) to endorse the individualistic argument, that is, to believe that this nation is a meritocracy (Flanagan et al. 2003). Males in general were more likely than females to believe in individualistic causes. Women are more likely than men to take a structural position and to believe that the government should help care for the poor (see also Kluegal and Smith 1986). The two studies just described appear to indicate that the poor and working class may differ in their views on the causes of wealth and poverty. Flanagan and associates suggest that working-class adolescents may endorse the meritocratic perspective because "self reliance and hard work for the working class is indispensable. There is no other way for people 'like them' to make it." They do not have the resources and opportunities that middle- and upper-class youth have at their disposal (2003, p. 727).

In addition to class position and gender, beliefs about the sources of poverty and wealth are also related to race and ethnicity. Interviews in 2000 with over 1,000 White and minority individuals in Los Angeles revealed that, as a group, respondents were more likely to attribute wealth to individualistic causes such as ambition, effort, and talent, but attribute poverty to structural causes such as inheritance, connections, dishonesty or the economy. In other words, most believe that the "sky is the limit" for most people, but that those at the bottom are held down by factors beyond their control (Hunt 2004). Hunt found that Whites, Blacks, and Latinos were equally likely to attribute wealth to individualistic causes, but Blacks and Latinos were more likely than Whites to also attribute wealth to structuralist sources. Interestingly, Blacks and Latinos are more structuralist but *also* more individualist than Whites in their beliefs about what causes

poverty. This "dual consciousness" is more prevalent among minorities (ibid., p. 845).

What Americans believe the determinants of income *are*, of course, may be different from what they believe *should* be the determinants. When asked to judge what incomes certain kinds of hypothetical households received, respondents in an Indianapolis study, perhaps not unexpectedly, associated higher occupational status, higher education, being White, and being male in a single-person household with higher incomes, whereas those with larger families were believed to receive lower incomes (Shepelak and Alwin 1986). Another study presented hypothetical vignettes to a sample of 200 White adults (Jasso and Rossi 1977). The individuals in these vignettes varied in sex, marital status, number of children, educational attainment, occupation, and earnings. Respondents were asked if the fictitious person in each of a limited number of vignettes presented to them was (1) overpaid, (2) fairly paid, or (3) underpaid. There was a nine-point rating scale ranging from "extremely underpaid" to "fairly paid" to "extremely overpaid." The results revealed some interesting patterns. Single females were more likely than married females to be seen as being overpaid. Those with higher education and occupational status (especially males) and those with a greater number of children who are married and male were more likely than opposite groups to be viewed as underpaid.

These findings indicate that people use a mixture of achievement-related and unrelated criteria to make decisions about what is fair. While occupation and education are used to make judgments, so are sex and marital status. Most Americans, including African Americans and women, also apparently feel that income should be based more on skills than on level of need (Kluegel and Smith 1986). A direct implication of all these findings is that an equal distribution of income among the individuals in these vignettes would be considered unfair, although respondents were not in favor of the range of incomes that presently exists. When respondents were asked in the Jasso and Rossi study to attribute a fair income to each of the fictitious individuals, the responses ranged from just over $7,000 for a single female with seven years of education and a low-status job, to about $34,500 for a college-educated married couple with high-status professional jobs. This suggested fair range in earnings is much smaller than the range that actually exists in the labor market. The conclusion that most Americans believe that the range of incomes from bottom to top is too great is supported by other research as well (Rainwater 1974; Alves and Rossi 1978; Kluegel and Smith 1986; Davis and Smith 1989). Thus, Americans not only have identifiable opinions about the factors on which individuals' incomes should be based but also about the overall fairness of the current extent of economic inequality.

BASES FOR THE LEGITIMATION OF STRUCTURED INEQUALITY

The preceding studies indicate that most people in the United States believe that it is the individual more than anything else that determines upward mobility in the socioeconomic hierarchy. Most Americans subscribe to the dominant ideology mentioned earlier. Fitting this in with the theories of a just distribution, most people use the "principle of differentiation" in defining a just distribution. It is the *process* that must be seen as being just. The evidence also suggests that criteria over which the individual presumably has great control, such as education and skills, *should be* used more than other kinds of factors to determine income. These beliefs obviously fit into the dominant American ideology that if people invest in themselves, they can improve their economic fate in life. Yet, as mentioned earlier, the evidence suggests that there are obstacles to equal opportunity for certain categories of individuals, and that not everyone with the same kind of job and education earns the same amount of income.

The question, then, is how do individuals come to accept a belief system even though there is evidence that contradicts it? How is an ideology internalized so that Americans come to believe that inequality is legitimate and justified?

In this section, various mechanisms through which the system of inequality in the United States is legitimated will be explored. These mechanisms exist on the microlevel of the *individual* in her or his everyday experiences as well as on the *institutional* macrolevel, working through the family, the education system, and other institutions. Let us begin at the level of the individual to see how people internalize the belief that inequality is fair.

Legitimation at the Level of the Individual

How do ideologies become internalized by people? This is a question addressed by Della Fave (1980), who tried to describe how individuals develop self-evaluations and judgments about the fairness of inequality. Interaction seems to be critical. To begin with, individuals are social beings—that is, they develop only in relationship with each other. As individuals grow and develop, they come into contact with greater numbers of people who react to them in a variety of ways. Individuals learn the expectations others have of them by noticing how others behave toward them. This combination of the expectations and reactions of others toward us makes up what Mead called the "generalized other" (ibid.). It is through the relationship with the generalized other that individuals develop a definition and image of themselves. Seeing how others react to us leads to the development of a particular self-image. We can see ourselves as others see us; we can view ourselves as an object, from the outside, as it were. By viewing ourselves as others see us, we come to a conclusion about our own worth and our contributions to society. A consistent self-image over time requires the social support of others. "A person who maintains a self-definition with no social support is mad; with minimum support, a pioneer; and with broad support, a lemming. Most of us are lemmings" (Huber 1988, p. 92).

The generalized other, rooted in social relationships, helps us understand why we evaluate *ourselves* as we do. How we evaluate the quality of *others* also depends on interaction. When individuals with different *amounts* of money or other resources *and* different *kinds* of noticeable nominal characteristics (e.g., race, sex, age) interact recurrently, each person draws associations between those characteristics, competence, and the differential amount of resources. Eventually, there develops a belief in the greater competence of those with more resources. One result is that better-off individuals can and are expected to present their opinions more forcefully and effectively, resulting in higher esteem for them and lower esteem for the less well-off. To the extent that the better-off tend to be male or White, beliefs in the greater quality of these types of people develop and are accepted by both parties in these interactions. "In effect, double dissimilar encounters [i.e., those in which individuals differ in resources and nominal characteristics] become beacons that continually broadcast support for status beliefs about the nominal distinction, encouraging and underpinning their diffusion and eventually their consensuality as well" (Ridgeway et al. 1998, p. 334).

Further strengthening of beliefs in the legitimacy of "who has how much" occurs because, as we have seen, people believe that hard work and ambition are critical and justifiable reasons for wealth. Thus, the wealthy are viewed as deserving of their high positions. This positive assessment of the wealthy influences not only individual images of them but people's own self-images.

But how does the individual reach the conclusion that those who are wealthy work harder, contribute more to society, and therefore deserve more than others? Briefly, Della Fave (1980) argued that individuals reach con-

clusions about the reasonableness of their beliefs from what they consider to be an "objective outside observer." In other words, it is from this observer that individuals develop ideas about what reality is and how it operates, and it is this observer whose judgments are internalized. It is the generalized other who fulfills the role of this observer, and it is the reactions of the generalized other to others that individuals internalize. Since a wide variety of people subscribe to the dominant ideology mentioned earlier, they react to the wealthy as being deserving. This appears to be an objective evaluation, and so they come to interpret them, others, and themselves accordingly. Those who are reacted to favorably or treated as if they were important by almost everyone, including other important people, develop a very positive self-image, whereas others develop self-evaluations that are not quite as positive. "It is from the generalized other that individuals form an evaluation of self and, thus, of the worth of their 'contributions.' It is upon these evaluations, in turn, that judgements of equity are made in accordance with the principle of distributive justice" (ibid., p. 961).

Those who are successful also develop feelings of self-efficacy; that is, they believe that their own actions can bring about successful rewards. This is largely because of positive reactions to their success by others, which then encourages them to do more and reinforces their high self-efficacy. Viewing their own success as being a result of their own actions, they come to define it as legitimate and deserving (Stolte 1983).

Those who possess very positive self-evaluations, in turn, come to view their own high level of rewards as being deserved relative to others, whereas those with more negative self-images see themselves as being worthy of fewer rewards. In a large complex society, individuals generally have to piece together broad images of what others are like and what their contributions are on the basis of the limited information to which they have access. Thus, individuals make conclusions about the contributions of others based on the information that shows on the surface—namely, their wealth and income. Those with high incomes, in turn, can use their resources to manage the impressions that others have of them—that is, manipulate the interpretations of others in such a way that the latter develop a positive image of them (Goffman 1959). As was noted in Chapter 3, the demeanor of upper-class people can be tailored in such a way as to elicit deference and respect. Moreover, their ability to maintain high positions in educational, work, and other institutions reinforces the image of their greater contributions and worthiness for higher rewards. Those with greater amounts are viewed as making greater contributions, as deserving of their economic resources, given the widespread belief that rewards should be commensurate with contributions. Essentially, the process of legitimation in this case is circular: Those with greater rewards elicit greater respect and the feeling

from others that they deserve what they have, which in turn reinforces the inequality found in the hierarchy of rewards (Della Fave 1980). A skeletal interpretation of this process is presented in Figure 14.1.

According to Della Fave (1980), the entire internalization and social process just described bears directly on the extent to which the system of inequality is legitimated. The greater the degree to which the distribution of self-evaluations in society matches the distribution of rewards, the more legitimate the system of inequality will be considered and the more stable the society's structure of inequality will be. Conversely, if the two sets of distributions are not matched, then the stratification system is less likely to be defined as legitimate. This is consistent with Durkheim's views on the importance of the match between internal differences and rewards.

Several of the relationships suggested have been tested recently. Following Della Fave's theory, Shepelak (1987) tested relationships among income, self-evaluations, and the belief

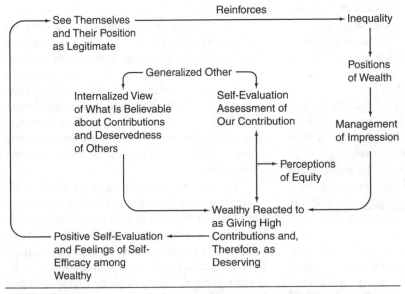

FIGURE 14.1 The Internalized Process of the Legitimation of Inequality
Source: Based on Della Fave 1980, pp. 955–958.

in individual responsibility for a person's position. Her interviews with over 300 Indianapolis residents revealed that those with higher incomes did indeed have more favorable self-evaluations than those with low incomes, and that those with better self-evaluations were more likely than others to attribute their incomes to their own effort. However, the latter explanations were not related either to family income or estimates of equity/fairness. Family income and self-appraisals were both found to be positively related to the feeling that an individual's income was fair. Conversely, those with low incomes were more likely to say that they were being underrewarded. In other words, contrary to Della Fave's self-evaluation theory, those with lower incomes do not feel that they deserve less than those above them. In fact, family income is more strongly linked to beliefs in the fairness of one's family income than are either self-evaluations or explanations of income level. "These findings fail to substantiate the view that disadvantaged persons believe they deserve less" (ibid., p. 501). Rather, they provide support for those who found that income is inversely related to the belief that the system of inequality is legitimate (e.g., Robinson and Bell 1978). On the other hand, support was found for the conclusions that a person's income standing and explanation of present position do affect feelings of self-worth. Figure 14.2 shows the interrelationships found among self-evaluations, income, perceptions of fairness, and perceived causes of income.

In addition to the self-evaluation process just discussed, there are other bases of legitimacy that exist at the level of the everyday lives of individuals. Most people, perhaps especially those who have to scramble to eke out a living, are too wrapped up in their ordinary lives and personal troubles to give much thought to the broad public issues of legitimacy and stability. "What ordinary men are directly aware of and what they try to do are bounded by the private

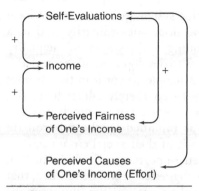

FIGURE 14.2 Relationships between Self-Evaluations, Income, and Fairness

Source: Based on Shepelak 1987, pp. 500–501.

orbits in which they live; their visions and their powers are limited to the close-up scenes of job, family, neighborhood; in other milieux, they move vicariously and remain spectators" (Mills 1959, p. 3). They may not be happy with the way things are, but they are unsure of the structural sources of this vague discontent. The result is that more often than not they go along with the way things are and do not question the culture or social structure of the society, thereby lending legitimacy to social arrangements by default.

Some research studies show that the social activities of those in the working and lower classes are usually limited to those involving friends and relatives; exposure to a wide range of types of people and geographic areas is restricted. The value and belief system that develops out of involvement in this immediate environment is basically accommodative in nature, helping individuals to make sense out of their everyday concrete situation. Thus, it also tends to be parochial— tailored to explain or deal with the specific and immediate context in which these individuals live (Parkin 1971). As it concerns social inequality, part of the accommodation in this value system is to accept inequality but also to try to improve one's position within it.

Thus, the value system generated in the local neighborhood does not ordinarily lead to a basic questioning of the system of inequality and its bases or to development of a radical ideology. Rather, people accept it in the abstract and then try to concretely adjust to it. So, "dominant values are not so much rejected or opposed as modified by the subordinate class as a result of their social circumstances and restricted opportunities" (ibid., p. 92). Marx further suggested, it will be recalled, that close-up involvement in the monotonous routine of everyday life by members of the working class leads them to begin to believe that their situation is normal and natural, and not to believe in or even to imagine an alternative situation.

Legitimation at the Cultural/Institutional Level

Although it is clear that self-evaluation and similar social-psychological processes are involved in legitimating social inequality, a society's culture and its social institutions are also directly implicated in the legitimation process. As in the case of self-evaluation's role, the basic question is, How do institutions and cultural values operate in ways that justify and maintain the hierarchy of social inequality?

It has been noted several times that Americans have ambivalent feelings about inequality. A large part of the reason for this ambivalence lies in the frequently inconsistent values that make up U.S. culture. At the abstract level, a core value in the culture is the belief in equal opportunity or fair play. But, in addition, Americans also tend to believe in competition, achievement, success, work or activity, efficiency, individual personality, freedom, nationalism, racism, humanitarianism, and morality (Williams 1970). Although these values are not all consistent with each other—for example, the belief in the sacredness of the individual versus the value of racism—most of these values help justify social and economic inequality in U.S. society. We have seen that differential rewards are more often believed to be the result of differential effort or work by individual personalities striving to achieve success in a context of free, open competition with others. To attack capitalism or the structure of inequality that has existed for generations would be, for many, not only unfair but also unpatriotic. So these values, by and large, push people in the direction of supporting the existing system, while other, though apparently fewer, values such as humanitarianism and moralism imply that inequality is inequitable.

The impact of values is often reflected in stereotypes that are held about different groups, and these stereotypes, in turn, often help to justify and sustain social inequalities. For example, images of what are appropriate attitudes and behavior for women have discouraged their movement into high corporate executive positions. As recently as 1989, male management students still believed that the qualities necessary to be a successful manager are more likely to be found in men than women. Consequently, these students were less likely to view women as being qualified for such positions. This is essentially the same belief as was held by male managers in the 1970s (Schein, Mueller, and Jacobson 1989). Part of the reason for this mistaken belief is probably the conviction that women are not as serious about their jobs and do not really work as hard as men at them.

Even when out in the labor force, as an increasing number of women are, traditional domestic stereotypes hold sway. Employed mothers are seen as being more masculine, less feminine, and less desirable than other kinds of mothers (Riedle 1991). Women who are physically attractive are also thought to be less qualified than unattractive ones for managerial positions, and, when they are in such positions, their performance is unjustifiably rated as being of less quality. Interestingly, attractiveness is considered a disadvantage for females in high positions, but it is considered an asset for them in clerical positions, a traditionally "female" occupation (Spencer and Taylor 1988). When in high positions that have been dominated by males historically, women are often pressured to adopt traditional feminine attitudes and behaviors, and if they don't, they suffer the consequences. "Women who do not wish to be classified . . . as deviant . . . must persist in playing the 'proper' role by following the interpersonal behavior pattern prescribed for them. Followed repeatedly, these patterns function as a means of control" (Henley and Freeman 1984, p. 475). In sum, images and stereotypes function to justify and maintain occupational inequality between men and women. Obviously, negative stereotypes of racial or ethnic minority groups perform a similar function. Perceiving Blacks, for example, as being less intelligent, less interested in education, and having less work incentive than Whites also serves to legitimize the economic and political inequalities that exist between the races. The power of these beliefs persists even when the evidence in each of these cases does not warrant such beliefs.

The beliefs and values that individuals endorse derive, in large part, from the broader institutional and cultural framework in which they are embedded. The task now is to describe how the system of inequality and the supporting values infiltrate the social institutions so that institutions foster activities and reinforce beliefs that legitimate inequality. How do institutions help to maintain the hierarchy of social inequality?

Before examining the roles of specific institutions, let us look at several ways in which dominant institutions influence behavior and attitudes, in general. Institutions consist of rules and structures that circumscribe what can and cannot be done. Moreover, these features of institutions help to define what is permissible and what is not, what is a legitimate issue or problem and what is not. Smith (1987) related how her research on mothering and education, which might help parents organize their collective interests in the schools, was controlled by

the local school system. All research in the schools has to be cleared by the school board, and because of this, it has to be organized, proposed, and conducted in a manner that is consistent with the perspective of professional educators, not parents. *Professionalism* defines what is allowable and professionalism is defined by those most esteemed and dominant in the profession (generally White, higher status males). This creates limits on what information can be collected and what can be done with it.

The preceding example suggests that one of the tools used by institutions to legitimate social structure, including the system of inequality, is to frame the image of that structure and the processes associated with it in a particular way with the use of certain kinds of concepts and terms. Language can greatly influence the interpretations placed on issues such as poverty, welfare, and political participation. The terms used to describe what is defined as a social problem also can influence how people react to them. "Quiescent public acceptance of poverty as a fact of social life depends upon how it is defined, far more than upon its severity" (Edelman 1977, p. 7). Governments can affect the extent to which citizens interpret "poverty" as legitimate by using particular symbols to describe it. To indicate that some people are "on welfare" to most Americans suggests something about the character of these individuals and their responsibility for their fate. Someone who is seen as a "welfare case" by an outsider is usually thought to be a person who does not work and probably does not want to work, one who is "living off" the rest of society. The term itself evokes an image quite different from the term *poor.*

When poverty is attributed glibly to "human nature" or to "economic laws," it allows people to justify denying help to the poor yet at the same time permits them to feel sorry for the poor. The result is that inequality is accepted and policies do not change (Edelman 1977). When arguments explaining the existence of inequality are couched in terms that cannot be tested empirically yet are emotionally powerful, it is difficult to argue against such reward differences. Referring to income as "rewards" or "earnings" plants the belief that the money is earned and thus deserved. Attributing the high rewards of a position to its "functional importance" to society helps to legitimize differential rewards. People have been socialized to react positively to the needs of society, the national interest, and earnings. Terms such as these encourage the acceptance and legitimation of "material sacrifices, constricted roles, political weakness, existing power hierarchies, and unfulfilled lives" (ibid., pp. 153–154).

Institutions of all types use language and symbols to create an imagery that legitimates the existing social reality. The use of certain terms to evoke images and thus to encourage the acceptance of inequalities between individuals applies not only to economic differences between rich and poor but also between men and women and Blacks and Whites. Because of the symbolic power of the concepts used by institutions and because of the intrusion of major institutions into most corners of their lives, people develop certain interpretations about society and other people, including those who are meritorious and deserving and those who are not. The images of the poor will be discussed more fully in Chapter 15.

The family, education, and religion all contain elements that encourage acceptance of inquality. Let us explore some of the ways in which each of these institutions fosters legitimation of social inequality.

Family.   The family is a principal instrument of socialization. It is within the domestic sphere that men and women learn much about how they should define themselves, their proper roles, and what they can expect from each other and society. Women are associated traditionally with an *expressive* role in the family; their primary responsibility is for nurturing and addressing the emotional needs of family members. In the urban setting of modern society, "the woman's fundamental status is that of her husband's wife, the mother of his children, and traditionally the person responsible for a complex of activities in connection with the management of the household, care of children, etc." (Parsons 1964b, p. 95). Woman can, of course, choose to pursue a career instead, but if this occurred on a large scale, it would be necessary to bring about "profound alterations in the structure of the family" (ibid., p. 96).

Men, on the other hand, have been expected to perform an *instrumental* role, which means that while the women's focus is on the internal life of the family, men's concerns are with adapting to the outside world, primarily in making a living to support the family. Functionalists such as Parsons have viewed this role differentiation as a source of complementarity and efficiency. Women have a central role in reproduction and, since this occurs in the domestic sphere, it is more efficient and more natural to have them be responsible for the expressive role in the family. The whole trend in social evolution, in this view, has been toward increased specialization and differentiation of function, which further legitimizes the role specialization of the two sexes.

Over generations, the continual socialization of men and women into these roles leads them eventually to be thought of as natural. The fact that this role differentiation has generally been thought of in the past as ideal by many Americans, and that most women have been content with the role indicates how powerful this ideology has been (Bem and Bem 1970). The balance that comes from the complementarity of these roles in the traditional functionalist view has integrative consequences for the society; it keeps society functioning smoothly. Of course, the behavior of others outside the family—such as nurses at the hospital when the child is born, babysitters, teachers, and relatives—further reinforces the gender-role distinctions considered appropriate for the sexes (Bernard 1981). The personality stereotypes of the sexes are consistent with their traditional roles. Men are still thought of favorably as being basically competitive, ambitious, independent, and logical, and women are well thought of for having good manners and being gentle, warm, soft-hearted, and affectionate (Werner and LaRussa 1985).

Although it may appear to be reasonable to view these personality traits and roles as merely complementary, as different but equal, the status and the power connected with each of them are quite different. As was pointed out earlier, capitalism and its values have shaped major institutions in modern society. This means that the social statuses attributed to families by individuals outside the family are based on what the occupational statuses of breadwinners are and how much income they bring home. As was noted in Chapter 5, the differences in status and power between the sexes are linked to the division of labor between them.

Education.   Schools perpetuate and legitimize inequality between the sexes, races, and classes through a variety of mechanisms. In general, it has been argued that one of the principal integrative functions of education is to have individuals perceive the educational system as a microcosm of the wider society in which their attainment is dependent on hard work and appropriate skills. The view is that, in education, individuals with varying abilities and levels of effort are channeled into appropriate levels of the occupational structure. The school appears as a forum in which students openly compete with each other and then are objectively evaluated by the experts. "The educational system fosters and reinforces the belief that economic success depends essentially on the possession of technical and cognitive skills—skills which it is organized to provide in an efficient, equitable, and unbiased manner on the basis of meritocratic principle" (Bowles and Gintis 1976, p. 103). But, Bowles and Gintis argued, the skills learned in school and IQ and test scores do not have a strong effect on an individual's economic success. Rather, according to this argument, schools are in the business of preparing students to be funneled into work roles at appropriate status levels.

At another level, various aspects of teacher–student relations encourage acceptance of an individual's traditional place in the structure of inequality. By teaching students about the nature of social reality, such as the values of the free market, intellectuals help to support the status quo. In Gramsci's (1971) phrase, intellectuals often have been "managers of legitimation." This includes members of the helping professions, such as social workers, psychiatrists, and teachers. Although educators often have encouraged happiness through adjustment to the status quo, those involved in these professions "have reinforced inequality by equating adjustment to existing social, economic, and political institutions with psychological health" (Edelman 1977, p. 152). People who deviate from their expected roles or who criticize the social structure are defined as "deviant" and are dealt with accordingly (Mills 1959).

Some of the teacher behaviors that encourage adjustment also reinforce traditional gender roles in U.S. society. Teachers in elementary schools pay more attention to males when they fight, suggesting that boys are more prone to aggression. At the same time, they pay more attention to the needs of girls by giving them more assistance than boys, thereby inadvertently encouraging their dependence on authority figures (Serbin et al. 1973; Fagot 1977). Since men are more likely to be in positions of authority (e.g., as principals in schools), children learn that it is normal for men rather than women to have power. Exposure to opposite situations appears to reduce the chances of children developing stereotypical views of gender roles (Paradiso and Wall 1986). What children read and how men and women are portrayed pictorially in textbooks also have an impact. When children act in a way that violates traditional sex-role expectations, they are usually ridiculed by their peers (Lamb, Easterbrooks, and Holden 1980).

Thorne's (1989) study in a California working-class elementary school further reveals the variety of ways in which traditional sex roles and inequalities are legitimated. Through participant observation research, she found that boys and girls frequently engage in "border-work." This refers to "forms of cross-sex inter-action which are based upon and reaffirm boundaries and asymmetries between girls' and boys' groups" (p. 76). Types of borderwork include various contests inside and outside the classroom in which the sexes are pitted against each other. Another form is chasing, in which boys and girls tease and try to elude each other on the playground. Invasions also occur in which members of one sex will "invade" the game being played by the other sex. These activities and what is said while each is going on reinforce and legitimize traditional ideas about what is appropriate for each sex. The dominance of boys in this informal world is demonstrated by (1) the greater playground space that they control, (2) the greater probability of invasion by boys in girls' games, and (3) the association of greater pollution (e.g., "cooties") with girls.

Class content is another avenue through which political and economic inequalities are legitimated. By and large, the information presented in classrooms and textbooks serves to reinforce a favorable interpretation of the United States and its history. Children have seldom been told in detail about unethical acts by national leaders or of the brutalization of such groups as American Indians. "None of this is very surprising. . . . Throughout history all children have been socialized to accept the dominant values and institutions of their society" (Kerbo 1983, p. 388).

Teacher expectations of Blacks and Whites and students from higher and lower classes also have been shown to be different. The images teachers have of lower status groups influence their expectations of them. Less is expected from them, which ultimately affects how well they do in school. Their lower performance only reinforces the initial negative image held by teachers, resulting in a self-fulfilling prophecy. Their lower performance also appears to justify their lower attainment, further strengthening the belief that attainment is linked to merit. The lower expectations by teachers of lower status individuals influence the teachers to place these students in lower non-college-oriented tracks. Their placement in these tracks helps to ensure their lower educational attainment (Farley 1988).

Not only the curricula but also the social organization of schools at the secondary and university levels are different for those that primarily serve students who will enter relatively low-status positions after graduation, and those that have students who will enter elite positions. In the lesser junior colleges and lower tracks of high school, "students will be given more frequent assignments, have less choice in how to carry out those assignments, and will be subject to more detailed supervision by the teaching staff" (Hurn 1987, p. 331). This is in sharp contrast to the greater autonomy and flexibility permitted at more elite schools. The organization, rules, and curricula of each level of education are organized to prepare students for the tasks they will confront in the occupations they will likely enter. In this sense, education helps to keep the system of inequality intact by accommodating its students to the demands of the economy. Social reproduction explains more fully how the educational process works to maintain inequality from generation to generation (see Chapter 9).

What is important about all these mechanisms is that their effects are largely unrecognized, while most perceive that attainment is the result of individual effort and abilities. Schools are for learning, teachers are the objective experts, and students study and take valid tests, are judged on the basis of their performance, and are placed accordingly in the hierarchy of attainment. Where students end up appears to be solely up to them. This reinforces the individualist ideology accounting for social inequality in the wider society.

Religion.   French sociologist Emile Durkheim argued that the religious institution was functional for both the individual and society. For individuals, it helps them to deal with difficult problems, provides some answers to difficult questions, and makes their lives meaningful. For society, religion is integrative because its beliefs and rituals take individuals out of their secular lives and bring them together to form a community. Religion, for Durkheim, was primarily a *social institution* rather than a *personal psychological experience*. It is out of the social gathering of individuals that feelings of a superior force or power outside individuals first arise. Thus, Durkheim argued that the worship of supernatural forces in religious rituals is really an adoration of the powers in society. "In the divine, men realize to themselves the moral authority of society, the discipline beyond themselves to which they submit, which constrains their behavior even in spite of themselves, contradicts their impulses, rewards their compliance, and so renders them dependent and grateful for it" (Sahlins 1968, pp. 96–97).

Given this description, it should come as no surprise that images of the supernatural world often mirror the social structure of society. Swanson (1974) showed concretely in his study of non-Western societies that a social hierarchy on earth is reflected in a social hierarchy among the supernatural. In societies in which older people occupied positions of importance, ancestors were a subject of worship, and in societies in which there was a great deal of social inequality, religion helped to legitimate the differences between the top and the bottom. A good example of this legitimation occurs in Hinduism in which the concepts of karma, dharma, and samsara combine to explain and justify the continuous inequality generation after generation. *Karma* indicates the belief that a person's present situation is the result of his or her actions in a previous life, and *dharma* refers to the duties and norms attached to each caste. Finally, *samsara* refers to the continual birth and rebirth of life. In other words, central beliefs in Hinduism absolve society or others from responsibility for social inequality. It is the result of individual actions (Turner, B. 1986).

Particular branches of Christianity also, of course, have legitimated people's beliefs about inequality. Protestantism, in general, which focuses on the individual relationship between each individual and God, stresses the importance of hard work and equality of opportunity in attaining success. Success is expected to be the result of self-denial and continuous effort, not the result of easy inheritance. This kind of spirit is what is embodied in Weber's concept of the "Protestant Ethic" and is especially associated with specific forms of Protestantism. Hard work and religious beliefs were intermingled by many famous preachers early in U.S. history. Cotton Mather, a charismatic Puritan preacher of the late seventeenth century, lectured that business and people's occupations were "callings" and not to be ignored. If individuals do not engage in their occupations, but rather remain idle (slothful), poverty will befall them. Riches are the result of industry, and poverty is the result of individual laziness. Those who are poor should expect no help from others since it is their own behavior that has resulted in their dismal situation. By engaging in business, people are doing what God intended: "Yea a *calling* is not only our *Duty*, but also our *Safety*. Men will ordinarily fall into horrible *Snares*, and infinite *Sins*, if they have not a *Calling*, to be their preservative. . . . If the Lord Jesus Christ might find thee, in thy *Store House*, in thy *Shop*, or in thy *Ship*, or in thy *Field*, or where thy *Business* lies, who knows, what *Blessings* He might bestow upon thee?" (cited in Rischin 1965, pp. 24, 26,). It is only a short jump from this statement to the belief that those who are successful are so because of their own efforts and are among the favored of God, while those on the bottom do not work and are sinful.

Advocates of Dutch Calvinism justified slavery by viewing Blacks as sinners and slavery as a just condition for their sins and inferiority in the eyes of God. The legacy of these beliefs can be found in the contemporary dilemmas of inequality in South Africa (Turner, B. 1986; also see Chapters 6 and 8). In the United States, a slave catechism was used in many churches during the period of slavery to justify domination by masters, to encourage work, and to attribute lack of work to personal laziness. White pastors told Blacks that God created the masters over them and that the Bible tells them that they must obey their White masters (Fishel and Quarles 1967). There are also elements in Christianity that have been used to support continual subordination of women to men, including the biblical argument about the origins of woman out of man and the injunctions to obey one's husband in marriage.

Civil religion also uses religion to justify the "American way of life." It is a mixture of religious and political ideology in which the U.S. social structure and culture are seen as favored by God. God and Americanism go hand in hand in this ideology. This is a nation "under God" and its institutions are sanctified by the Almighty. At civil ceremonies and during certain public occasions, such as the opening of Congress, presidential inaugurations, and the pledge of allegiance, God is mentioned and the United States is his (her) benefactor. A recent study indicated that most elementary school children believe that the United States "has been placed on this earth for a special purpose," that it has a "chosen" status with God, and that it is successful because it is morally good (Smidt 1980). The "American way" that is so blessed incorporates the values of individualism, freedom, capitalism, and equality of opportunity, which make up a core part of the ideology supporting inequality. Preachers such as Pat Robertson and Jerry Falwell conjoin Christianity and Americanism in a manner that makes them not only mutually supportive but almost indistinguishable. In this ideology, to attack Americanism becomes tantamount to committing a serious sin. Americanism is supposed to be accepted, not criticized or undermined.

Karl Marx viewed religion under capitalism as having many of the effects on inequality just discussed. People are expected to put up with inequality; religion lulls them into a false sense of complacency. That is, it makes them *falsely conscious* of their real situation. It blinds them to the real causes of their predicament (i.e., class exploitation, not personal sin). In this way, socioeconomic inequality is seen as legitimate by those who blame only themselves or look forward to another life when conditions will be better for them.

Of course, Marx realized that historically, before capitalism, religion had been used to support the oppressed; even in our own time, religions have not always supported the status quo. Martin Luther King, Jr., and the Southern Leadership Christian Conference used religious ideas to try to improve conditions of Blacks in the United States, and Catholic bishops have fought on the side of the poor against many Latin American dictatorships (Hehir 1981; Light, Keller, and Calhoun 1989). Catholicism also has been a force for change in communist Eastern Europe (Parkin 1971). Despite these instances where religion has opposed inequality, historically it has been more closely associated with its legitimation and maintenance. This has been the case with each of the social institutions we have discussed. By and large, each has served to support the dominant value system as it pertains to inequality, and it is through each of them that individuals come to believe that the social inequality around them is legitimate.

SUMMARY

The principal focus of this chapter has been on examining the reactions to the fairness of social and economic inequality, the criteria that define such fairness, and to explore the factors that contribute to the legitimation and, therefore, the stability of inequality in the United States. Americans are clearly torn on the fairness issue. On the one hand, they believe that hard work, education, and similar personal investments are important for economic achievement and believe that they should be important. On the other hand, most feel that the extent of inequality is too great, but they do not think that full equality of income or wealth would be fair either. Moreover, when asked what they think determines success, they tend to overestimate the significance of some factors and underestimate the impact of others, most notably race and sex. Attributing poverty and wealth to individualistic and/or structuralist causes varies with one's class, gender, and minority status. In their assessments of criteria to be used in determining a fair income, Americans tend to use a mixture of achievement and other factors (e.g., education, martial status, sex, occupational status).

The system of inequality itself is legitimated at the individual and institutional levels. Individuals develop interpretations of their own and others' rewards and contributions from the reactions of others to inequality. Their position in the rewards hierarchy affects their own self-evaluations and their appraisal of the fairness of their own incomes. At the same time, those with positive self-evaluations interpret their own incomes as being the result of their own efforts.

Through its culture and institutions, society helps to encourage traditional beliefs about the causes of inequality, thereby maintaining the structure of inequality. Generally, the values impressed on members and clients of those institutions are those of individualism and capitalism. Through the language and symbols used and their rules of knowledge, institutions define what is real and proper. In the case of the family and education, institutions shape beliefs and roles for those in different positions of the system of inequality and encourage a belief in the legitimacy of their positions. Religion also has used its resources on many occasions to legitimate the socioeconomic inequality that surrounds individuals.

At one point in the chapter, we noted conditions under which such inequality might be perceived as illegitimate. Illegitimacy is one of the factors motivating attempts to change the structure of inequality. The next chapter deals more fully with concerted attempts to bring about such change by examining formal government policies aimed at dealing with issues of economic inequality and poverty.

CRITICAL THINKING

1. What role, if any, should compassion play in determining the distribution of scarce resources? Should this issue even be a subject of debate? Why or why not?

2. Is it possible to develop a formula for the fair distribution of resources that is objective and generally agreed upon by most in society? Explain your answer. If you agree that such a formula could be developed, what might go into such a formula?

3. How does the actual distribution of resources affect attitudes about the distribution of them?

4. Why would Blacks and Latinos be more likely than Whites to *simultaneously* subscribe to structuralist *and* individualist arguments about the causes of poverty?

WEB CONNECTIONS

The term "justice" can be interpreted in a variety of ways. To help you think about the meaning of justice, visit the website of the Center for Economic and Social Justice, www.cesj.org/thirdway/economicjustice-defined.htm.

Addressing Inequality and Poverty

Programs and Reforms

The ongoing similarities between welfare reform at the closure of the twentieth century and the previous half a millennium are striking. Both the "menace" of welfare and its "cures" have not really changed. Welfare policy . . . still lies in the shadow of the sturdy beggar.

—Joel F. Handler

One of the greatest pains to human nature is the pain of a new idea.

—Walter Bagehot

The discussion in the last chapter showed that Americans consider equality of opportunity to be an important part of a just system, and most of the nonpoor also believe that the primary reasons for poverty lie within the individual. At the same time, a majority believes that the current system of inequality is too unequal, and many believe that forces beyond the control of the individual are an important cause of poverty. These paradoxical views are manifested in the contradictions found within U.S. governmental programs aimed at addressing inequality and poverty. This closing chapter (1) analyzes and assesses recent major governmental programs aimed at alleviating poverty and inequality, (2) describes proposed welfare reform alternatives, and (3) reviews current state welfare policies and their success.

Traditionally and significantly, governmental programs have focused their attention on *poverty* rather than the broader and more difficult issue of *inequality*. By focusing on the poor alone, attention has been deflected away from the systemic nature of the poverty problem and toward the conclusion that poverty is an isolated problem generated within a specific segment of the population. The notion that poverty is fostered by a system of social inequality has not been enthusiastically embraced in policy circles. It has been more consistent with the belief in individualism to conclude that the problems of those on the bottom—be they the poor, minority groups, or women—are peculiar to them. Consequently, the programs suggested to alleviate their troubles have focused on them rather than on the broader society. The belief has been that it is not society but rather particular groups within it that have a problem. In sum, *U.S. policy has been more concerned with addressing the poverty of individuals than the social inequality of society.*

ADDRESSING INEQUALITY

Although little attention has been given by policymakers to programs that directly address the reduction of social inequality, the federal income tax system, government transfers, and affirmative action purportedly address the issue of distribution of economic resources among groups in the United States. The tax system is supposed to be "progressive"—that is, to lessen income differences between income strata by taxing higher-income groups at higher rates. To what extent does it accomplish this goal? Looking at Table 15.1, we find that in the distribution of *pretax private* income, 1.1 percent of all income goes to the bottom 20 percent of the population, while 55.1 percent is received by the top 20 percent. This is income only from private sources and before taxes; no government cash transfers (e.g., social security, welfare money) are included. These two percentages give an idea of what the distribution of income would be without the effect of governmental tax or benefit programs. Income is most highly concentrated in this definition (Index = 0.506). The poverty rate is also highest under this definition (18.5).

When pretax income from governmental sources is added to the definition as is done in the first line of Table 15.1, both the index of income concentration and poverty rates fall to 11.8 and 0.447, respectively. This suggests that government transfers help to reduce income inequality. When the effect of taxes is combined with the effect of government transfers, the index of income concentration and poverty rates decline significantly (0.411 and 8.8, respectively). However, the effect of taxes is only minor. The main reason for this decline is social security payments (Zandvakili and Mills 2001). The decline in poverty in Canada and its rise in the United States during the 1980s appears to have been due to the expansion of transfer programs in Canada and the contraction of transfer programs in the United States, further suggesting the impact of such programs on poverty (Hanratty and Blank 1992).

Recent data indicate that the wealthy provide most of the individual tax payments received by the Internal Revenue Service. In 2004, the top 20 percent in income paid 81 percent of all personal federal income taxes. This may suggest to some that the government is taking away from the rich

TABLE 15.1   Poverty Rates and Income Inequality under Four Definitions of Income: 1999 and 2000

INCOME MEASURE	1999 POVERTY RATE	INDEX OF INCOME CONCENTRATION	PERCENT OF INCOME RECEIVED BY	
			Lowest Quintile	*Highest Quintile*
Pretax income	11.8	0.447	3.6	49.7
Pretax private income	18.5	0.506	1.1	55.1
Posttax private income	18.3	0.486	1.4	51.2
Posttax income + all transfers	8.8	0.411	4.6	46.7

Source: U.S. Bureau of the Census, *Money Income in the United States: 2000*. Current Pop. Reports, Series P60, No. 213, September 2001, Table G; and U.S. Bureau of the Census, *Poverty in the United States: 1999*. Current Pop. Reports, Series P60, No. 210, September 2000, Table 5.

Note: "Pretax income" is before-tax income from all sources but excluding capital gains; "pretax private income" is before-tax income from only private sources plus capital gains and health insurance supplements to salary or wages; "posttax private income" is after-tax income from private sources only; "posttax income + all transfers" is after-tax income plus the value of means-tested government cash and noncash transfers.

more than from the poor, and indeed, the official tax rates are higher for those in higher income brackets. Two points should be kept in mind, however, before reaching this conclusion. First, tax rates have declined most precipitously for the higher-income groups in the past 20 years. While those in the highest income quintile paid most of the taxes, those payments reduced their adjusted gross incomes only by 25 percent (Andrews 2004). Part of the reason for this is that a much higher percentage of the incomes of the wealthy comes from capital gains, which are taxed at a lower rate than earnings from employment. The latter is the principal source of income for those in the middle and working classes. This suggests the second point, namely, that the higher amount paid by the wealthy is testament to the large size of their incomes. Conversely, the much smaller amounts of taxes contributed by those on the bottom give evidence to the meagerness of their incomes.

When considering the mild effect of *individual* federal income tax on income inequality, it should be noted that *corporate* taxes are not included, nor is the value of nonincome wealth. The proportion of total federal government revenue that comes from corporate taxes steadily declined throughout the twentieth century. In 2003, only 9.9 percent of internal revenue collections came from corporate taxes compared to 50.5 percent from individual income taxes (U.S. Bureau of the Census, *Statistical Abstract* 2004–2005). Increasingly, corporations have sought to incorporate parts of their businesses outside the United States in order to avoid payment of corporate taxes. As of 2002, such "inversions" as they are called, were legal under U.S. law. Locating elsewhere allows companies to benefit from advantageous tax and banking laws in the chosen countries (Barry 2002). The Internal Revenue Service recently estimated that about $70 billion in taxes were lost in 2001 because of offshore accounts. At the same time, the agency has made it more difficult for lower-income individuals to qualify for earned-income tax credits, credits they receive because of their low incomes

(Walsh 2003). A recent federal bankruptcy law has also made it more difficult for average citizens to evade payment of their debts, debts that are in large part due to costs derived from medical bills, divorce, and loss of jobs. These are not costs that are the result of a lavish lifestyle.

Just as corporations benefit from current law, so too do the wealthy who benefit from recent changes in estate tax laws. The latter changes allow individuals to pass on more of their wealth (eventually up to $1 million) without being taxed on it. This encourages the sedimentation of wealth discussed in an earlier chapter. Consequently, the inequality of economic resources is not reduced by either corporate or estate taxes, both of which allow the well-to-do to keep more of their wealth. Maintenance of wealth is also optimized by the fact that those with incomes above $100,000 are three times *less* likely than the working poor to be audited by the IRS (Johnston 2002). As a whole, the current tax system has not done much to make the income distribution more equal.

Affirmative Action Programs

Like taxes, affirmative action is also aimed at reducing inequality between groups. Overall, affirmative action programs can be viewed "as a conscious effort to increase the representation of women and other designated groups in particular organizations, occupations, programs, and a wide range of activities" (Orlans and O'Neill 1992, p. 7). Most notably, affirmative action attempts have been associated with improving the socioeconomic chances and conditions of racial and ethnic minorities, especially African Americans. In this sense, in contrast to taxes, affirmative action aims at redressing racial and gender inequities.

The general argument for such programs is rooted in the unique historical experiences of African Americans in this country. In contrast to other ethnic groups and women, African Americans came as the property of others rather than as free individuals. While others

The tax system has become less progressive in recent decades and has not served as a major source of income redistribution. Although many organizations are listed as major influences on government policy, they are also often tax-exempt and do not have to pay taxes.
Cartoon by Joe Heller.

were free to engage in the pursuit of property, "Blacks had to cease being property before they could begin to acquire it" (Hamilton 1992, p. 14). Because of their distinctive skin color, African Americans could not as easily disavow or hide their ethnic background and melt into the landscape. Finally, in contrast to the discrimination experiences of many White ethnic immigrants, the discrimination faced by African Americans was virtually comprehensive and widespread until the mid-1960s (Jencks 1992).

These unique conditions and history implied that a special set of programs was needed to address the problem of racial inequality. There have been two general approaches and meanings to affirmative action. The first, dominant until the late 1960s, stresses the prejudice and lack of opportunity that some minorities have expe-

rienced, and therefore aims at implementing "equality of opportunity" to improve the status of minorities vis-à-vis the majority. This approach is consistent with the American belief in individualism and the definition of fairness as equal opportunity. A good example of this approach is found in the policy of the Equal Employment Opportunity Commission (EEOC) created in 1965 to foster nondiscrimination in employment.

The second approach, more significant since the Nixon presidency, stresses the importance of continuing and ingrained institutional racism as the principal source of racial inequality, and therefore aims at implementing equal group representation or "equality of results" to improve minority status. This approach is more reflective of the idea that fairness means equality of result or conditions and, in the view of some, minority preference (Graham 1992). The Office of Federal Contract Compliance, which monitors the active hiring of minorities, is an example of a program built on this approach.

Affirmative action programs have been a focus of controversy, especially since the 1970s. Those who support them argue that past wrongs and continued discrimination against minorities warrant such policies, even though they may be temporary. As Supreme Court Judge Harry Blackmun argued, "In order to get beyond racism, we must first take account of race" (Orlans and O'Neill 1992, p. 8). Proponents have also argued that such programs have been effective in reducing racial discrepancies. Increased compliance by employers and increased enrollments in colleges by minorities during the 1970s are cited as illustrations of the success of such programs, but other results are more mixed (Jencks 1992; Taylor and Liss 1992).

The arguments against affirmative action have centered on beliefs and some evidence that such programs may reduce work and training incentives, and reinforce stereotypes that Whites have of minorities (Loury 1992). Policies that appear to give special preference to particular groups (race-specific programs) rather than the same preference to all individuals (universalistic programs) are especially distasteful to many Americans. They feel like Frederick Douglass did after the Civil War—that "promoting an image of blacks as privileged wards of the state" will only help to sustain stereotypical beliefs that Blacks do not have what it takes to make it on their own (Lipset 1992, p. 73). The psychological fallout for Blacks from these programs is also damaging, because they encourage the conclusion among those who benefit that they did not *earn* their success (Jencks 1992). There is also the issue of whether Civil Rights laws have become so broadly defined that *every* kind of group and type of person is encouraged to think of themselves as a victim of rights violation and is entitled to pursue legal action. In a word, the critics say these broad interpretations create a sense of unwarranted victimization.

The problem with many of these criticisms of affirmative action programs is that they are built on existing prejudicial views about minorities that are left unquestioned. For example, the concern that these programs reinforce stereotypes of minorities would not be necessary if such stereotypes were addressed as problems and attacked. Moreover, the worry that Blacks, women, and other beneficiaries of affirmative action might not be seen as having *earned* their success is due in large part to a lack of understanding of barriers to success over which these groups have little if any control. These complaints may say more about those who have these perceptions than it does about the individuals against whom discrimination has been directed.

Plous (1996) has recently listed and countered many of the myths about affirmative action; several of her observations are as follows:

Myth #1: We need color-blind policies, not those aimed at only particular groups. Plous has argued that such policies would leave advantages long held by dominant groups unchanged. Some groups would continue to have an initial advantage in economic competition.

Myth #2: Affirmative action has not been successful. Evidence from governmental studies on employment and contract gains for women and minorities suggests otherwise.

Myth #3: Average citizens want to eliminate all affirmative action. Most citizens continue to support some forms of affirmative action, want to keep many of the programs, and want to see only some of them changed.

Myth #4: Affirmative action programs harm many White workers. Given the differences in the sizes of Black and White populations, even if every unemployed Black replaced a White employee, less than 2 percent of White workers would be displaced. The principal causes of job displacement are factory closings, downsizing, and technological changes.

Myth #5: Affirmative action damages the self-esteem of its beneficiaries because they suspect they obtained their positions under false pretenses. In fact, most employed Blacks and women do not question their own abilities, and the employment may actually raise their self-esteem.

Myth #6: Affirmative action results in the hiring of unqualified candidates. Most supporters of these programs do not endorse the hiring of unqualified applicants. Indeed, the most accepted form of affirmative action is that which allows the hiring of a minority person from among a pool of at least roughly comparable candidates. The hiring of unqualified persons is illegal under federal affirmative action regulations.

Additional myths about affirmative action exist, and many continue because they give solace or support to privileged groups and the status quo. Programs like affirmative action that have attempted to reduce social and economic inequality have generally been controversial because they dredge up old arguments about helping individuals versus groups, providing equal opportunity versus equal results, and showing color blindness rather than color preference. In periods of general economic recession, we can expect this controversy to intensify. Given this controversy and the dominance of U.S. values like individualism and equal opportunity, it should not be surprising that U.S. policies have aimed at helping the poor rather than reducing inequality. To many, inequality is both necessary and inevitable; it is poverty that is the problem that needs to be addressed.

THE CONUNDRUM OF DEFINING POVERTY

The statistics on poverty, its definition, and the characteristics of income-maintenance programs are riddled with hidden assumptions and social values that have affected approaches to understanding and grappling with poverty.

We begin with the thorny issue of defining *poverty*, then proceed with an analysis of the social values and orientations and myths that have affected the approach to poverty in the United States. From there, we review the statistics on the extent of poverty among various groups and survey some of the major programs that have been at the heart of the U.S. income-maintenance system.

Defining *poverty* is basically a political act because how it is defined depends largely on one's values and the relative power of interest groups to get their preferred definition accepted. The battle over definition is important because it affects our perceptions of the magnitude of poverty rates and, consequently, what we think needs to be spent to alleviate the problem. The result is a variety of suggestions for how poverty should be defined.

In *broad* definitions, poverty is considered multidimensional. What it *means* to be poor includes not only income but also access to basic services, health, self-respect, housing, educational opportunities, and political participation. This contrasts with a *narrow* definition that defines poverty only in terms of income. In addition to the broad/narrow issue, some define the income–poverty line using only income from private sources, such as wages, pensions, gifts, alimony, and child support. Government transfers are not included in determining income in this *pretransfer* measure. A *posttransfer* measure would include the impact on income of cash and/or noncash government benefits. Needless to say, the use of the latter measure results in a picture of lower poverty in the country. Finally, there is debate about whether poverty should be defined *absolutely* or *relatively*. In an absolute definition, a poverty line or threshold is set and anyone falling below that line is defined as poor. One of the problems with determining the absolute minimum necessary to live above the poverty level is that what is defined as a "necessity" varies from time to time and group to group. Moreover, setting an absolute poverty line does not address the issue of the *distribution* of income throughout the income hierarchy. In contrast, relative measures of poverty are tied to how others in society are doing in terms of income. The assumption is that poverty is relative to the social and economic context in which people live. That is, the poverty–income line would fluctuate with the fortunes of the rest of society. For example, one proposal is to set the poverty line at 50 percent of the median household income in the United States. This would set the income much higher than the absolute poverty threshold currently used by the government. The latter has not kept pace with rises in median income. Relative measures such as the one suggested here usually result in the poverty rate being defined as higher than under the official government measure. One can see from this how easily the defining of poverty would become a political issue.

The Official Measure of Poverty

The official government definition of poverty is based on a formulation developed by the Social Security Administration (SSA) in 1965, which was then formally adopted by the government in 1969. In this definition, total family income refers to posttransfer *cash income before taxes*. It does not include capital gains or losses. The poverty threshold was determined by using the Department of Agriculture's 1961 economy food plan, which reflects the different consumption needs of families of different sizes and composition, with heads of different sex and age, and place of residence. This food plan, in turn, had been developed using the Department of Agriculture's 1955 survey of food consumption, which revealed that families of three or more persons spent about one-third of their incomes on food. A family was then defined as poor if it spent more than one-third of its income while following the economy food plan. The poverty level, consequently, was set as being equal to three times the cost of the

food plan. In the early 1960s, for example, it was estimated that the minimal diet would cost $1,000. Thus, the poverty level was set at $3,000 in 1964. In 2003, the average poverty threshold for a family with two parents and two children under age 18 was $18,660. Every year, the level is adjusted according to changes in the Consumer Price Index. Adjustments are also made for differences in the size and composition of families. In the table that appears later in the chapter, this conception of poverty is referred to as the "official definition" of poverty.

Problems with the Official Measure.   One of the major sources of debate about the official poverty measure is that it does not include the noncash transfers to the poor such as food stamps, Medicaid, subsidized housing, and school lunches. There are also problems with the measure of income used. First, there appears to be little question that individuals' net or disposable incomes are a better measure of the economic resources available to them than their incomes before taxes (Sawhill 1988). Yet the Bureau of the Census continues to use pretax income in its official measure of poverty.

In addition, its use of *current* instead of permanent income creates difficulties in assessing the "true levels of well-being" of families at the proposed poverty level (Plotnick and Skidmore 1975, p. 35). Assessing a family's economic status by using its income at one point does not allow us to distinguish those who have consistent levels of income from those whose incomes have fluctuated from year to year. Moreover, by using the one-year snapshot as the unit for determining how many are and who is poor, the official measure does not permit distinctions to be made between those who are poor only for a short time from those who are more "persistently poor." This distinction is important because these groups have different characteristics, which means that the programs that may prove effective in reducing their poverty would probably differ.

Finally, the use of the 33 percent formula to arrive at the poverty threshold assumes that the Department of Agriculture's costing method and food plan apply to all families of a given type. This may not be the case at all. Given the differences in sizes and age distributions of families, and therefore varying demands or needs among them, it is unrealistic to assume that one-third of the budgets of all these families is spent on food. Perhaps most importantly, the official formula was based on an emergency, temporary budget, not on food budgets actually observed among families under ordinary circumstances (Duncan 1984; Haveman 1987).

LEVELS OF AND TRENDS IN POVERTY

Even though the concern for the poor was increasing during the latter half of the nineteenth century, there was little information about the actual extent of poverty at the time. Jacob Riis estimated that between 20 and 30 percent of the population of New York lived in poverty near the end of the nineteenth century; Spahr also suggested that the number of poor was quite large (Bremner 1956). Using a minimum decency standard, Hartley (1969) estimated that the proportion of the population

in poverty was about 45 percent in 1870 and 35 percent in 1910, indicating a general decrease in the intervening decades. Using another minimum-decency standard, Ornati (1966) put the proportion of the population in poverty in the mid-1930s at around 45 percent. With the exception of 1944, poverty in the 1940s appears to have been near the 30 percent mark, and in the early 1950s, it was between 22 and 29 percent of the population (Ornati 1966; Hartley 1969; Weinstein and Smolensky 1978).

Poverty from 1959 to the Present

Poverty data based on the official government definition were first collected for 1959. Using that measure, the poverty rate fell significantly from 22 to 12 percent between 1960 and 1969 (see Figure 15.1). During that decade, the number of children and adults who were poor dropped from 39.8 million to 24.1 million. Between 1970 and 1979, the number of poor people vacillated between 23 and 26 million. The poverty rate for those years varied between 11.1 and 12.6 percent. However, from 1980 to 1983, the poverty population increased by 44 percent, going from 26 million in 1979 to 35.3 million in 1983. After 1983, the poverty rate fell but rose

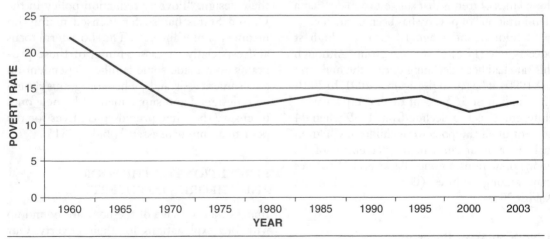

FIGURE 15.1 U.S. Official Poverty Rate, 1960–2003

Source: U.S. Census Bureau, *Income, Poverty, and Health Insurance Coverage in the United States: 2003*, Current Population Reports, Series P-60, No. 226, August 2004, Table B-1, p. 40.

again in 1990 and continued to rise through 1993. After that, it fell so that in 2000 the poverty rate was 11.3 percent, meaning that over 31 million were poor. This rate is about what it was in the mid-1970s and about half the poverty rate of 1959 (U.S. Bureau of the Census 2001). But after 2000, the poverty rate rose each year, reaching 12.5 percent (35.9 million) in 2003.

Among racial/ethnic groups, Blacks have experienced the greatest decline in poverty rates since the early 1970s, but the 2003 poverty rates for Blacks and Hispanics were still about three times (24.4% and 22.5%) that of non-Hispanic Whites (8.2%). Nevertheless, non-Hispanic Whites made up 43 percent of the poor population that year.

Among families, the poverty rate of those with female householders has also decreased. In 1959, about 43 percent of such families were poor, compared to 30 percent in 2003. However, the percentage of poor who live in families with female householders has increased dramatically since 1959. In 1959, about 18 percent of all poor lived in families headed by female householders, compared to about 35 percent in 2003. This trend is especially visible among Blacks. In 2003, about 58 percent of all poor Blacks lived in families headed by females. It is these kinds of trends that suggest to many that a "feminization" of poverty has been occurring.

Children under age 18 have the highest poverty rate (17.6) of any age group. Although this rate had been declining during the mid- and late 1990s, it began to rise again in 2001. In 2003, 12.9 million or 36 percent of all the poor were children. This is a decline from 1959 when 44 percent of all the poor were children. Children make up a significantly higher percentage of the poor populations among Blacks and Hispanics than among Whites (U.S. Census Bureau, August 2004).

A Note on Asset Poverty

The discussion on poverty just completed focused on poverty as measured by individual or household *income*. Recently, however, the concept of "asset poverty" has been proposed as a more complete measure of the economic stability of a household. This mirrors our earlier discussion on the benefits of looking at *wealth* rather than income as a fuller indicator of a household's economic position. Caner and Wolff defined an "asset poor" household as one in which "access to 'wealth-type resources' is insufficient to enable the household to meet its 'basic needs' for some limited 'period of time'" (Caner and Wolff 2004, p. 496). For the purposes of their study, they defined that *period of time* to be three months. Examining data from a national longitudinal study for the period 1984–1999, Caner and Wolff found that at least 26 percent of the households were asset-poor, regardless of the asset measure used. The college-educated and married were among the groups that experienced a decline in asset poverty between 1984 and 1999. In contrast, among those with less than a high school education, asset poverty as measured by net worth increased between 1989 and 1999, as it did for non-Whites. Whites' asset poverty rate declined during the study period. In their conclusion, Caner and Wolff urged that "poverty" programs be revised to incorporate assets in their design: "Poverty reduction policy in the United States has so far focused mainly on income maintenance. . . . The short-term focus and especially the asset limits of these programs even made some families dependent on government assistance. These programs should be redesigned and supplemented by new ones to ensure that they provide incentives for the poor to accumulate assets" (ibid., p. 515).

PERCEPTIONS OF THE POOR AND THEORIES OF POVERTY

Images that we have of the poor are bound up with our explanations for their poverty. Our deeper cultural values affect the theories of poverty that we find acceptable and they color our perceptions of the poor. Rather than treating them separately, the following discussion combines comments about popular images of the poor with theories about why they are poor. Recall that the broad theories of inequality covered earlier differ in what they include as the main source of inequality between individuals and groups. Some stress individual differences (e.g., Spencer, human capital), while others stress broader social, economic, or cultural causes (e.g., Marx, Durkheim, social reproduction, dual labor market). Correspondingly, each explanation of poverty tends to stress one of four different factors: (1) individual flaws, (2) value and lifestyle deficiencies of the poor, (3) stresses in the living situation of the poor, or (4) societal economic and political conditions that create poverty rates of different levels. While the first two place the blame for poverty on the poor themselves, the second two emphasize forces outside the poor over which they have little control. As we will see, all of these have been implicated in arguments about how to deal with the problem of poverty, but U.S. policies and programs have historically been based more upon (1) and (2) than on (3) and (4). This should not be surprising given the central position that individualism occupies in the United States' pantheon of values. Consequently, the discussion that follows traces the roots of individualistic theories and the myths about the poor associated with these explanations. Evidence suggests that the poor have most of the same basic values as the nonpoor and values are not the major cause of poverty. Rather, labor market conditions, technological shifts, legislation, and related social conditions directly affect changes in poverty rates.

Most of the images of the poor and the causes of poverty that have dominated U.S. history have focused in one way or another on alleged weaknesses among the poor themselves. This focus on the individual's characteristics as the basic cause of poverty emerged in fourteenth-century Europe with the rise of industrialism, the new freed wage-laborer, and the growth of international commerce. The massive economic changes occurring on the continent during this period—in addition to famines, widespread diseases, and war—generated a large number of paupers and beggars. Something had to be done to deal with these individuals. At the same time, the process of industrialization required the ready availability of workers.

As the dominant source of relief and welfare moved progressively out of the hands of the church and private charity and into the hands of public institutions and officials, a clear distinction between the "deserving" and "undeserving" poor developed in the late fifteenth century. Women who were pregnant, individuals who were seriously ill, and the elderly were among those who were considered worthy of help. Individuals who could but did not work were considered undeserving of assistance. The principle of "less eligibility" was used—that is, the idea that any relief given not be great enough to discourage work. The amount of relief was not expected to be higher than the wages of the lowest worker in the community (Dolgoff and Feldstein 1984).

The Elizabethan Poor Law of 1601 distinguished among the "able-bodied poor," the "impotent poor," and "dependent children." The former were required to work; refusal to do so would mean punishment, and nonpoor citizens were forbidden to aid them. Those classified as being "impotent"—such as the disabled, deaf, blind, elderly, and mothers with small children—were given either "in-door relief" (placed in an institution or almshouse) or given "outdoor relief" (allowed to stay in their own homes but given relief such as food, clothing, or other needed goods). "Dependent children" who could not be supported by their families were farmed out as apprentices, taught trades, and expected to serve in this capacity until early adulthood (Zastrow 1982). To be eligible for aid, the poor person was expected to have been a stable member of the community and without family support.

The distinction between the deserving and undeserving poor found in the Elizabethan Poor Law became deeply ingrained in the approaches taken to the poor and welfare in Britain and the United States and have remained so to this day. In early America, poverty was becoming a serious problem. Before the Civil War, upheavals in the economy, sickness, immigration, and demographic changes generated large numbers of poor individuals. Specifically, the decline of home manufacture of goods, unemployment, the rise of low-wage labor, the seasonality of much work, and crop failures were among the economic changes responsible for poverty. Growing population pressure on the land, the changing age structure of the population, and increasing immigration also led to increased poverty levels (Katz 1986).

Reaction to the poverty problem was heavily influenced by the English reaction. Relief was considered a public responsibility. It was to be locally administered and controlled; it was not to be given to those who had families who could support them, and those who could work were expected to do so (ibid.). Even then, however, many believed that any relief would discourage the motivation to work and weaken character. Efforts were placed then, as now, on seeking out and eliminating the "able-bodied" from the relief rolls. The Quincy Report, a 1821 Massachusetts study of poverty and welfare, made the by-now familiar distinction between the impotent poor and the able poor. The "poorhouse," an early attempt to take care of the poor, aimed at (1) eliminating the undeserving from help by requiring work and banning alcohol for residents and (2) encouraging children and the deserving able poor by stressing work education and discipline in the hopes that such treatment would set them on the path out of poverty. The goal was to transform the character and behavior of its residents (ibid.).

The poorhouses did not work out very well. The conflict in goals that plagues many current welfare programs was already present in the early poorhouse program. A concern for order, cost, routine, and custody overcame the initial goal of reforming the individuals in them. Many became rundown and the care given became less than adequate. Officers of the poorhouses were often found to be guilty of graft. Inmates had greater and greater control over their behavior in the poorhouse; discipline was not enforced nor was useful work found for most inmates (ibid.).

Cultural Values and the Poor

Historically, perceptions of the poor have been conditioned by the cultural context. A number of U.S. values have had a significant impact on our views of the poor. Among the most central of these are (1) individualism/autonomy and (2) the belief in work, intertwined with its moral character. The roots of these values go back several centuries and originated in intellectual and religious events in Europe.

Individualism/Autonomy.   The image of the quintessential pioneer as someone who was an island unto himself or herself, a singular and stalwart rock against the rigors of frontier life, has captivated the idea of what true Americans should be like. Despite the fact that most early Americans traveled and lived in groups, the idea of the rugged individual has had great appeal (Boorstin 1967). Basic to this ideal image of the heroic American are several components:

1. This person is physically and psychologically independent; he or she needs no help from others.
2. Individual achievement is sought despite difficult obstacles.
3. Achievement under even difficult circumstances means that anyone can succeed if he or she tries hard enough.
4. Those who do not make it either lack the ability or are lazy and therefore immoral.

In any case, they do not have what it takes to succeed.

5. The possibility of material gain is needed to motivate people (Dolgoff and Feldstein 1984).

These components suggest the scenario that being poor or rich is largely a result of "contest mobility" in which the best win and the worst fail. Clearly in this view, individuals who are poor either do not have the personal qualities necessary to succeed or do not put forth enough effort. Moreover, being poor and on welfare indicates dependency, and therefore flies in the face of the ideal autonomous person.

The Enlightenment of the eighteenth century and Adam Smith's economic theories also provided intellectual support to the centrality of the autonomous individual. It was believed that intelligent individuals, equipped with modern knowledge, could do almost anything for themselves as well as society. Smith's economic theories stressed a laissez-faire approach to economic affairs. Free individuals, unencumbered by governmental and other regulations, seeking their own goals would create the most efficient and productive society. Governmental interference in the form of any aid was believed to violate the intricate processes of freely working, "natural systems." "The 'inefficient poor' like inefficient businesses, were to die off through natural selection" (Tropman 1989, p. 137).

The beliefs that individuals should be self-reliant, exercise self-restraint, and take responsibility for their own lives are still reflected today in polls that show a large majority of Americans favoring policies that require work, impose time limitations on welfare benefits, and allow no increases in benefits when women on welfare have more children (Shaw and Shapiro 2002).

The Moral Character of Work. "God helps those who help themselves" goes the old saying. The belief that individuals are responsible for their own destinies can be traced back to religious doctrines that meshed with a society having a large frontier to be explored, conquered, and populated by a motley collection of individuals who had emigrated from Europe largely in the nineteenth century. One of these religious strands was Calvinism, which Miller (1977) has called "the most individualistic development out of the most individualistic wing of the most individualistic part of the Judeo-Christian heritage" (p. 3). Calvinism is a puritanical, grim religion that stresses the importance of the individual and his or her own work as an indication of whether he or she is among the "elected." Under this doctrine, work is considered crucial to a meaningful life. Idleness is not only a sin but a social evil as well. People who become poor do so because they lack character. Since they are not successful, it is a sign that they are not among God's elect. Calvin was against even free almsgiving to those he considered idle and lazy (Dolgoff and Feldstein 1984).

The American Puritan minister Cotton Mather (1663–1728) confirmed the religious importance of work in his exhortations about the importance of having "a calling." Every man should have an occupation through which he contributes to society, argued Mather, otherwise he cannot expect anything from society. "How can a man Reasonably look for the *Help of other men*, if he be not in some *Calling* Helpful to *other men*?" wrote the minister. When men do not put forth their efforts, what happens? "By *Slothfulness* men bring upon themselves . . . Poverty . . . Misery . . . all sorts of Confusion . . . On the other Side . . . a *Diligent* man is very rarely an *Indigent* man" (Rischin 1965, pp. 24–28, emphases in original). It would be easy to see why those in positions of wealth and power might subscribe to these views, since they not only justify the wealth of those at the top but also locate the source of poverty in a lack of effort by the poor individual.

Although the explicitly religious character of many of these pronouncements has become less evident, the hold of the essential ideas is still strong. To place the reason for economic success or failure on the individual is (1) to exonerate society and others from playing a role in the creation of poverty, and, just as important, (2) to isolate the poor from the rest of society and to foster a "them versus us" imagery of the population. The further perception, though inaccurate, of most of the poor as Black intensifies the belief that the poor are qualitatively different in character from the rest of the population. A recent poll suggested that U.S. adults are more likely to view Blacks as more lazy than either Hispanics or Asian Americans (Shaw and Shapiro 2002).

The work ethic is at the heart of the rationale in current welfare policies. The thrust is on getting able-bodied people to work outside the home so that they will not take advantage of welfare benefits. Only the deserving poor should receive help. The notion that those without jobs, especially during times of relative prosperity, are to blame for their own economic troubles goes back deep in our history. As Bremner (1956) noted in his analysis of reactions to poverty during the nineteenth century, "In normal times Americans were accustomed to think of unemployment as exclusively the problem of the inefficient and indolent. Conservatives stuck to this view even in depression years." It was also believed that the presence and fear of poverty served as incentives to work and to use one's abilities to the fullest (ibid., pp. 16–17).

The beliefs in individualism, work, and its moral character influence present-day images of the poor and welfare. This is not to say that other values are not also implicated in current images. A sense of community and compassion (humanitarianism), the beliefs in achievement and success as upward mobility, and the belief that the family is supposed to play a crucial role in maintaining its members are all additional values that have helped to shape our perceptions

of the poor and what is to be done with them. The focus here has been on individualism and the work ethic because, more often than not, these values have been most salient in those perceptions and have informed those responsible for crafting welfare policies.

Myths About the Poor

Consistent with the above values, a review of recent surveys finds that almost half of all adults feel that the poor have it easy and could get along without governmental support. About 40 percent believe that lack of effort is the main reason for poverty, and three-quarters think that the poor have become too dependent on government for help. People on welfare are viewed much more negatively than are the poor in general (Shaw and Shapiro 2002).

Values and beliefs often distort social reality by suggesting that most of the poor have characteristics that they, in fact, do not possess. This is why individualistic explanations of poverty are so weak; too much evidence contradicts them. Blacks are often believed to make up the bulk of those who are poor and on welfare, but, in fact non-Hispanic Whites comprised just under half of the poor in 2000. Given their beliefs about work and their images about those on welfare, some people assume that the majority of those receiving aid are able-bodied, middle-aged men who are too lazy to work. In fact, almost half of the poor are either below 18 or over 65 years old. Of the remainder, there are also those nonaged who are disabled in some way and families in which no husband is present. Thus, the majority are not able-bodied, middle-aged men. But women who receive aid are now considered part of the "able-bodied poor." They are viewed as the new paupers of poverty. That is, they are considered a danger to society if they do not work and are also considered to be perfectly capable of working.

There are other misconceptions about the poor that reinforce the belief that they are

NUTSHELL 15.1_____

Remembrance of Ridicule as a Poor Child

Vivyan C. Adair has written poignantly about the images and treatment of the poor and those on welfare, and how they demean and punish their victims. Currently in the Department of Women's Studies at Hamilton College, Adair gives a partial reflection of her experiences and feelings growing up in a poor family:

> What I recall most vividly about being a child in a profoundly poor family was that we were constantly hurt and ill, and, because we could not afford medical care, small illnesses and accidents spiraled into more dangerous illnesses and complications that became both a part of who we were and written proof that we were of no value in the world.
>
> In spite of my mother's heroic efforts, at an early age my brothers and sister and I were stooped, bore scars that never healed properly, and limped with feet mangled by ill-fitting, used Salvation Army shoes. When my sister's forehead was split open by a door slammed in frustration, my mother "pasted" the angry wound together on her own, leaving a mark of our inability to afford medical attention, of our lack, on her very forehead. When I suffered from a concussion, my mother simply put borrowed ice on my head and tried to keep me awake for a night. And when throughout

elementary school we were sent to the office for mandatory and very public yearly checkups, the school nurse sucked air through her teeth as she donned surgical gloves to check only the hair of poor children for lice.

> We were read as unworthy, laughable, and often dangerous. Our schoolmates laughed at our "ugly shoes," our crooked and ill-serviced teeth, and the way we "stank," as teachers excoriated us for our inability to concentrate in school, our "refusal" to come to class prepared with proper school supplies, and our unethical behavior when we tried to take more than our allocated share of "free lunch." Whenever backpacks or library books came up missing, we were publicly interrogated and sent home to "think about" our offenses, often accompanied by notes that reminded my mother that as a poor single parent she should be working twice as hard to make up for the discipline that allegedly walked out the door with my father. When we sat glued to our seats, afraid to stand in front of the class in ragged and ill-fitting hand-me-downs, we were held up as examples of unprepared and uncooperative children. And when our grades reflected our otherness, they were used to justify even more elaborate punishment that exacerbated the effects of our growing anomie.

Source: Vivyan C. Adair, "Branded with Infamy: Inscriptions of Poverty and Class in the United States." *Signs* 27: 456–457.

---

undeserving. One is that they have a significantly greater number of children than the nonpoor. This is plainly not the case. There is only a slight difference in the average size of poor and nonpoor families. In 1991, the average size of U.S. families in general was 3.17, whereas that of poor families was 3.52, about a third of a person larger. A 1998 survey by the Department of Labor found that food-stamp households containing minors had an average of 4.1 persons in the household with 2.4 children under 18 years of age. Non-food-stamp households with minors present averaged a similar 4.0 persons in total, with 1.8 of them under 18 years of age (U.S. Department of

Labor, August 2000). Thus, the differences in household composition between those on and those not on "welfare" are not nearly as great as welfare stereotypes would suggest.

Nor is there any good evidence that poor mothers have children, including illegitimate ones, to increase their benefits. Yet a majority of Americans apparently believe that the presence of welfare encourages young women to have children and discourages those who get pregnant from marrying the fathers (Davis and Smith 1989). The assumption that people have children to get more support from the government simply does not hold up when the evidence is examined (Morris and Williamson 1986).

First, the vast majority of unmarried mothers on welfare have only one child and illegitimacy rates tend to be lower in states with higher welfare benefits (Ellwood and Bane 1984; Bell 1987). Second, welfare benefits are quite low, making it uneconomical to have more children to receive more benefits. In 2003, the average monthly food stamp benefit, for example, was $83.90, and the average child support payment was $4,274 per year (U.S. Census Bureau 2005).

When one considers that in 1999 even families with incomes under $36,000 spent well over $100,000 to raise a child to age 18, receiving under $100 per month for each child hardly makes it economically worthwhile to have large numbers of children (Zastrow 1982; Children's Defense Fund 1999). In European countries, in fact, which generally have much higher benefits for children than the United States, there have been concerns over the *declining* birth rates in recent years (Bell 1987). This again suggests that benefit levels are not a major cause of birth rates.

Another reason why many balk at giving the poor too many cash benefits is that they are perceived as wasting their money on frivolous purchases. However, evidence from the 1999 Consumer Expenditure Survey conducted by the U.S. Department of Labor suggests that the poor spend most of their incomes on basic needs. Table 15.2 compares the percentages and amounts of income spent on different items by the 10 percent who spent the least in 1999 with the percentages and amounts spent by all other expenditure groups. Total expenditures for those in the lowest expenditure group are about one-fifth those of other groups ($8,391 vs. $40,937). In terms of how income is spent, about 70 percent of the $8,391 in outlays is spent on housing and food by the lowest-level households, transportation and health account for another 14 percent, while only 3 percent is spent on clothing. Significant for future quality of life, only 4 percent of the expenditures of the lowest-expenditure group is put aside for insurance and pensions. In contrast, while they spend more in each category, a smaller percentage is spent by other households on housing, food, and health care, but a greater proportion is spent on transportation, especially vehicles, and on insurance and pensions. These households spend 13 times as much money on insurance and pensions than the lowest-expenditure group, providing for a more stable future.

A final image of those on welfare is that they are usually guilty of fraud and cheating.

TABLE 15.2 Average Annual Expenditures and Expenditure Percentages of Outlays for Consumer Units in Lowest Decile Group and Consumer Units in All Other Decile Groups: 1999

	LOWEST DECILE		ALL OTHER DECILES	
MAJOR OUTLAY CATEGORY	*Amount*	*% of Outlays*	*Amount*	*% of Outlays*
Housing	$3,766	45%	$16,154	39%
Food	$2,127	25%	$5,620	14%
Transportation	$654	8%	$6,984	17%
Health Care	$470	6%	$1,713	4%
Clothing	$279	3%	$1,611	4%
Personal Insurance and Pensions	$333	4%	$4,398	11%
Other Outlays	$762	9%	$4,457	11%
Average Total Outlays	$8,391	100%	$40,937	100%

Source: U.S. Department of Labor, *Characteristics and Spending Patterns of Consumer Units in the Lowest 10 Percent of the Expenditure Distribution.* Issues in Labor Statistics. Summary 01–02 May 2001.

But in fact, only an extremely small percentage cheat and then, in almost all cases, only a small amount of money is involved. More prevalent and more serious than cheating by recipients are the honest mistakes and errors made by public officials when determining eligibility for and level of public aid (Zastrow 1982; Bell 1987). In addition, recent exposures of pervasive fraud by building contractors and others who profit from the government's housing program, extensive overcharging by contractors charged with cleaning up polluted areas, and overcharging and similar behaviors by health-care providers strongly suggest that if fraud is a problem in poverty programs, the poor are not its primary source.

When considering the deservedness of those who receive welfare and who they are, one should remember that many nonpoor also receive governmental welfare, although one usually does not think of middle-class or wealthy persons or corporations as receiving such aid. For this reason, it has been called *phantom welfare* (Huff and Johnson 1993). Direct cash and credit subsidies, tax exemptions and deductions, subsidized or reduced-cost services, and various trade restrictions are among the assistance programs provided to businesses. In total, the estimated cost of these benefits has been put at $150 to 200 billion per year (ibid.). Not only businesses but also nonpoor persons receive heavy amounts of aid. Among the benefits to the middle class in the "fiscal welfare system" are tax deductions for mortgages and exemptions for parents of college students (Abramovitz 2001, p. 298). Despite the many governmental benefits that flow to the nonpoor, it is generally only the poor who are perceived as receiving "welfare" and often seen as undeserving of that aid. Yet, if the degree to which it is deserved is a measure of whether governmental benefits should go to a group, then the phantom welfare that is given to nonpoor individuals and organizations needs to be given more attention than it has received.

The Poor and Incentive to Work.   Perhaps the most consequential perception of the poor involves their attachment to work and the work ethic. As mentioned earlier, the value of work is deeply ingrained in U.S. culture, as is the belief that most people can succeed if they try hard enough. These beliefs force us to raise some important questions about the poor. First, are people poor primarily because they do not work? Second, do the poor believe in the work ethic or do they prefer not to work? With respect to the first question, census data indicate that a significant proportion of the poor work, many of them full-time. In 1999, 43 percent of poor individuals over 16 years of age worked during the year, and over one-quarter of these did so full-time, year-round. Fully 64 percent of the incomes of poor two-parent families come from earnings, while 23 percent is derived from welfare programs. In 1999, 2.5 million poor adults worked full-time year-round, and 6.6 million more worked part-time, year-round. Yet they are still poor, and low wages are an important part of the reason. The 1996 legislation to raise the minimum wage to $5.15 per hour still gave a family of three only 87 percent of the income they needed to reach the poverty threshold. Among poor female-headed families with children, the patterns are different. While over half obtain income from earnings, only 29 percent of their income comes from earnings. Welfare is the source for over half their income (Schiller 1998). The low level of the minimum wage, the elimination of many high-paying, unionized jobs, and the lack of adequate childcare programs for poor women who want to work suggest the central roles that situational and structural factors play in perpetuating poverty.

On the question of a work ethic among the poor, most poor adults who do not work cite, in order of frequency, family reasons, school, illness, and inability to find work as reasons for not working (U.S. Bureau of the Census,

September 1998c). "It's an interesting phenomenon," stated Patrick McGrath, director of a county Department of Human Services in Ohio, "A lot of our people do work and are still eligible for assistance. It's a myth that our people are lazy and don't work" (Brett 1989). Of those poor who did not work at all in the United States in 1991, over half were either ill, disabled, retired, or going to school. Roughly another third were not working because they were keeping house. When one considers that a majority of the poor are old, children, or disabled, the image that these figures conjure up for the poor as a whole is not one of laziness.

What these data indicate is that many poor individuals work, but despite their efforts, they remain poor. Because of the importance of earnings as a source of income for most families, it is important that programs be designed with work incentives in mind. Both the poor and the nonpoor respond to such incentives (Danziger, Haveman, and Plotnick 1986). Most Americans want to work. When asked if they would continue to work even if they had enough money to live on comfortably for the rest of their lives, a vast majority of Americans say they would continue to work (Davis and Smith 1989). Given that work is a hub around which many Americans' most cherished values revolve, these findings should not be surprising. Work is a major source of self-esteem and identity. "In America, this hold on the psyche is true even for those only marginally employable and thus barely sharing in the economic, social, and psychic rewards of work. . . . [And] paid, employed work is a central identifier of the self. The characteristic used as a person's overall social identification and evaluation is his or her general occupational status" (Gamst 1995, pp. 5 and 13). A large number of studies have found that there is virtually no difference between the poor and nonpoor in their desire to work (Kaplan and Tausky 1972, 1974; Davidson and Gaitz 1974; Smith 1974; Goodwin 1983; Moris and Williamson 1986).

POVERTY PROGRAMS

Historically, there have been different kinds of attempts to address the problem of poverty. Some of the earliest were private and local in nature, whereas many of the contemporary programs involve different levels of governmental participation. The extent to which government should be directly involved in solving this problem has been a source of controversy.

The most stringent view—the *residual*, or conservative view—holds that social welfare aid should only be given to the poor when their families and their involvement in the private economy have not been able to lift them out of poverty. In this sense, welfare is only to provide a "residual" function, coming in only after other more traditional, nongovernmental sources of help have been exhausted. As this function implies, social welfare expenditures and programs are expected to be kept to a minimum and only those who demonstrate indisputably that they are in need are considered eligible for welfare help. Even then, benefits will be low and short term so as to provide a work incentive. Poverty is viewed as being caused primarily by individual defects and character flaws, rather than by wider social or cultural conditions. The result is that there is a social stigma for those seeking welfare under these circumstances. This also helps keep aid to the desired minimum. Up until the New Deal, this approach to welfare dominated the U.S. welfare system (Zastrow 1982; Bell 1987), and it still maintains a strong grip.

The second view of social welfare—the *institutional*, or liberal perspective—has basically the opposite characteristics from the residual approach. Specifically, it assumes that social welfare programs are an integral part of the institutional structure of modern society, and that like other institutions, they play a vital role in dealing with many of the problems generated by society's social structure and events, such as aging, which are largely inevitable. The institutional approach is consistent with the situational and structural theories of poverty. Since poverty is largely beyond the control of most poor, people should be able to expect help without stigmas being attached to such aid. Beginning with the New Deal in the 1930s, an institutional element was formally introduced on a broad scale into the general income-maintenance system of the United States. The result is that the present system is largely a mixture of both approaches.

A third view of social welfare programs interprets them differently than either conservatives or liberals. Instead of being considered either an unnecessary burden on government or as an integral and humane part of it, this more radical perspective views social welfare programs as a means of controlling the working class and the poor. Social welfare programs expand when there is rising unrest among these groups and contract when these groups are calm (Piven and Cloward 1971). This pacifying function of welfare is closely related to the uneven operation of the capitalist economy. Oversupplies of labor lead to increases in government-sponsored programs. At the same time, however, the work requirements and benefit levels of welfare programs are stringent enough to ensure the availability of a cheap labor force to employers.

A Profile of Some Major Programs

Current U.S. income-maintenance programs can be divided into two general parts: social insurance and public assistance. Both parts include cash and in-kind benefits. *Social insurance* is aimed at replacing income lost because of death, unemployment, disability, or retirement. Most of the social insurance programs were developed under the Social Security Act of 1935; they include old-age insurance, survivors' insurance, disability insurance, unemployment insurance, and, in many cases, worker's compensation. Medicare is also a social insurance program. These programs are financed by the insured through payroll taxes, by the employer, and by the government. Eligibility for participation depends on the extent of a person's prior work history. As long as individuals satisfy certain basic requirements, they are automatically eligible for these programs. There is little stigma attached to participation in these programs because individuals are thought of as deserving of such benefits. These programs are most illustrative of the "institutional" perspective on welfare.

Public-assistance programs, which have been more "residual" in the assumptions built into them, are "means-tested" programs that aim at temporarily assisting poor individuals and families. These make up what most people think of as "welfare." The major programs included in the public-assistance category are Temporary Assistance to Needy Families (TANF replaced Aid to Families with Dependent Children (AFDC)), Supplemental Security Income (SSI), food stamps, and Medicaid. In addition, local general assistance and housing also are included under this category. Public-assistance programs are financed by general revenues, and instead of individuals being automatic participants upon the satisfaction of basic requirements, persons wishing to receive welfare (i.e., public assistance) must prove that their income is low enough to justify their receiving aid (Lynn 1977; Sawhill 1988). Thus, there tends to be more of a stigma attached to applying for and receiving welfare than is the case, for example, when one receives social security income in the mail. However, the stigma appears to be largely attached to recipients by others rather than one held by the recipients themselves (Morris and Williamson 1986).

Table 15.3 indicates number of recipients and federal amounts for the major social insurance and public-assistance programs in 2002. Social security is by far the most expensive of the income maintenance programs. In 2002, mandatory outlays exceeded $453 billion and the program served over 46 million beneficiaries.

TABLE 15.3   Number of Recipients and Federal Expenditures for Major Social Insurance and Public-Assistance Programs: 2002

PROGRAM	NO. OF RECIPIENTS (IN MILLIONS)	EXPENDITURES (IN BILLIONS)
Social Insurance		
Social Security (total)	46.5	$453.6
Social Security (retirement)	32.4	$304.0
Social Security (survivors)	6.9	$84.0
Social Security (disability)	7.2	$65.6
Medicare	39.6[a]	$267.1
Public Assistance		
Supplementary Security Income	6.9[b]	$38.5
Food Stamps	20.2[b]	$24.1
Temporary Assistance for Needy Families	5.1[b]	$13.0
Medicaid	50.9[b]	$258.2

Source: U.S. Census Bureau, *Statistical Abstract of the United States 2004–2005*, pp. 347, 350.

Note: [a]number of *enrollees* in program.   [b]average number of *monthly* recipients.

Social security provides monthly benefits to eligible retired and disabled workers, as well as to their spouses, children, and survivors. Retirement benefits make up most of these expenses. In 2002, the average monthly retirement benefit was $895.

Although most of the benefits from the social security retirement program go to non-poor recipients, millions are protected from falling into poverty because of the program. Despite this benefit, social security has become a source of contention between younger and older generations. As its costs have gone up due to an aging population and a comparatively smaller base of workers to support it, younger workers resent the program's immediate cost to them and worry whether it will be able to support them when they retire.

In addition to the retirement program of social security, *survivors' and disability insurance* are also a part of social security. Under the first, a worker's surviving dependents receive cash benefits. These survivors can include children under age 18, spouses who have a child in their care who is under 16 years of age, dependent parents of the deceased, and disabled unmarried children of any age. Disability insurance

provides protection against the loss of family income resulting from a "breadwinner" being disabled. In 2002, almost $66 billion was spent on disability costs (see Table 15.3).

In 1965, *Medicare* was added to the social security package. Its purpose is to provide hospital and medical insurance to people age 65 or older and those who are disabled but covered by social security. Payment under Medicare is made directly to the care provider. At the present time, Medicare does not pay for all medical services. For example, it does not cover custodial or routine dental care, nor does it pay for long-term nursing home care. The latter has been an issue of increasing concern, especially as the number of elderly increases. Medicare expenditures totaled almost $231 billion in 2002, more than doubling the amount spent in 1990.

Public-Assistance Programs.   The programs that we have been discussing are largely based on the assumption that their beneficiaries have contributed both to the financial support of those programs and to the society through their years of employment. Thus, the benefits are interpreted more as a right than as a handout; that is, they are viewed as deserved. In contrast, public-assistance programs are controversial in large part because they are not always seen as serving the truly deserving. It is with these programs that questions about fraud, laziness, and deservedness arise most often. Groups that traditionally have been the most vulnerable to poverty conditions are most likely to receive welfare. These include women, children, Blacks, Hispanics, and the elderly.

Under the public-assistance umbrella have been AFDC (now TANF), food stamps, Medicaid, and SSI programs (see Table 15.3). All of them are *means tested*; that is, individuals are required to prove that their level of need is such that they require help. Most of them involve at least two levels of government in their administration or funding. The federal government has given states wide latitude in determining eligibility criteria. The form of benefit also varies. The benefits from the TANF and SSI programs come in the form of cash assistance, while those from food stamps and Medicaid come in the form of in-kind benefits (e.g., checks are not sent to the beneficiaries; rather it is goods or services that are provided). Let us look briefly at each of these major programs.

Largely because of its cost and the controversy surrounding it, Aid to Families with Dependent Children was replaced in 1996 with block grants to states (TANF), which could then exercise greater control over the manner in which funds are spent. The professed purpose of AFDC was to provide financial support for poor families with children who did not have parental support and for families with children who needed emergency support. The program was a combined federal/state effort, with each state determining what constitutes "needy" and a "suitable home," as well as the level of payment. Consequently, a great deal of variation existed between states. In every state, however, recipients were required to register for employment and training and

pass income and asset tests to prove their eligibility. Federal expenditures for TANF were $13 billion in 2002.

One reason for the controversy over AFDC concerned the profile of the typical recipient. Compared to their non-AFDC counterparts, AFDC mothers were younger, more likely to be Black or Hispanic, less educated, more likely to be unemployed, and had a much lower income. The changing racial and marital-status composition of the beneficiary group tended to increase dissatisfaction with the program on the part of taxpayers (Morris and Williamson 1986; U.S. Bureau of the Census, March 1995). Also speeding the program's demise were convictions that it encouraged the breakup of families and discouraged individuals from working. The new TANF program places a heavy emphasis on the need to work and the amount of time over which a person can receive benefits. The stated aim is to move abled-bodied individuals off welfare as soon as possible.

Supplemental Security Income (SSI) is another cash-benefit welfare program aimed at people who are in financial need, and who are either 65 years of age or older, blind, or disabled. Implemented in 1974, it replaced federally reimbursed programs being run by the state to help the elderly, blind, and disabled. In 2002, almost 7 million persons received SSI payments per month. Monthly payments ranged from $330 for the elderly to $425 for disabled persons and $445 for blind individuals.

The *food stamp program* is much larger, consequently, it is one of the major in-kind public-assistance programs offered by the federal government. Although such a program operated during the period from 1939 to 1943, it was not reinstituted again until the early 1960s. Although some experts would have preferred increases in cash benefits to a food stamp program, the program has grown significantly since its reintroduction in the 1960s. In 2002, about $24 billion in food stamps were allotted and during any given month there were 20 million recipients. This is a decline since March 1994, when 28 million received stamps, but an increase since 2000. Still, only about 60 percent of those eligible sign up to receive stamps. Just over half of the participants in the program were children, and about one-fourth of these households contained a disabled person. In 2002, the average monthly allotment in coupons for each recipient was about $80. The majority of households that received food stamps did not receive TANF, SSI, or Social Security cash benefits. Although almost one-quarter of these households had someone who worked, almost 90 percent were living below the poverty line (U.S. Department of Agriculture, July 2003). A full profile of the food-stamp population is provided in Table 15.4.

Medicaid is another in-kind program aimed at providing financial assistance to states to pay for the medical care of those on public assistance, children, pregnant women, and the elderly who meet basic economic requirements. It is different from Medicare in a number of ways. First, it is a selective program, whereas

TABLE 15.4   Profile of Food-Stamp Participants: 2002

Female	59%
Male	41%
Under 18 years old	51%
18–59 years old	40%
60 or older	9%
Non-Hispanic White	42%
Non-Hispanic Black	35%
Hispanic	18%
Other	5%
Households with children	54%
Households with elderly	19%
Households with disabled	27%
Households with earned income	28%
Households with unearned income	75%
Households with no income	11%

Source: U.S. Census Bureau, *Statistical Abstract of the United States 2004–2005*, Table 553, p. 361.

Medicare is a universal program. This means that applicants have to satisfy certain economic requirements before they can receive the service; that is, the program is means tested. In contrast, everyone in a particular age category is qualified to receive basic Medicare benefits, regardless of income. Second, Medicaid is a federal- and state-administered program, whereas Medicare is nationally administered. Finally, at least on paper, Medicaid covers all kinds of services, whereas Medicare is more restrictive in coverage (Dolgoff and Feldstein 1984).

To participate in the Medicaid program, states are required to cover several groups of eligible people, including some low-income elderly, women, and children, and disabled individuals. They must also provide hospital care, nursing-home care, and physician services. Medicaid covers about one-fourth of all children and two-thirds of nursing-home residents. The elderly and disabled compose less than one-third of beneficiaries, but they account for almost two-thirds of its costs. Finally, Medicaid serves at least half the adults with AIDS, and about 90 percent of children with AIDS. In 2002, federal expenditures for the roughly 51 million recipients per month who received Medicaid benefits totaled over $258 billion.

There seems to be fairly widespread agreement that programs such as Medicare and Medicaid have made it possible for more people to get needed medical care. More people have used more health services than before the inception of these programs. Despite these salutary trends, however, problems still remain. Variations between states in their coverage rules and the optional facilities/services available create inequalities among individuals who are equally in need of medical care. Also, the availability of Medicaid has not erased the differences in the care of the poor and nonpoor discussed earlier in the text. Many physicians still hesitate to take Medicaid patients (Morris and Williamson 1986).

FLAWS IN PRE-1996 ASSISTANCE PROGRAMS

Problems with assistance plans as they existed before 1996 eventually led to the overhaul of some of the main programs. Among these were controversies over (1) equity, (2) adequacy, (3) goal conflicts, (4) family incentives, and (5) work disincentives.

Not all individuals in equal need were given the same assistance because of differences in regulations and assistance levels between demographic groups and states. Individuals over age 65, for example, were more likely to be lifted out of poverty by governmental programs, especially social security. Traditionally, male heads were less likely to get assistance than female heads. However, female heads of families face some unique problems as a result of divorce, labor-market discrimination, and lack of adequate child care for their children. There are also geographical inequities, with some states having higher benefits or greater flexibility in their programs than others.

Lack of adequate support was a second deficiency of past programs. None of the public-assistance programs had—or has—a standard benefit level that will enable a recipient to live comfortably. In 1998, for example, households that contained children and were on food stamps received an average total of $4,806 from public assistance programs and Supplemental Security Income, with food stamps making up 47 percent of that amount. When one considers that these households contained an average of 4.1 persons, it is easy to see how meager the amount of assistance is (U.S. Department of Labor, August 2000). Since the 1970s, the value of public assistance benefits in real terms has not even kept pace with inflation. Cutbacks to programs in the 1980s exacerbated this problem. Finally, the inadequacy of existing programs was suggested by comparative research which demonstrated that out of 15 affluent industrialized nations, U.S. assistance programs were the least effective in lifting individuals out of poverty, largely because of the low level of benefits (Kenworthy 1999).

Conflict in the goals of programs created additional problems. Satisfying the goal of adequacy, for example, might mean raising the cost of a program, or raising the level of benefits might endanger work incentives by making recipients feel complacent about seeking employment. This problem is complicated by the fact that the poor population is heterogeneous, and changes in one goal may be more important for one group than another. For example, how important is it that the work-incentive goal be maximized for those who are elderly, disabled, or under age? Perhaps adequacy is more important for them.

A great deal of controversy exists over whether public assistance fosters the disintegration of marriages and encourages illegitimacy (Murray 1984). Most studies have found no relationship between benefit levels, family dissolution, and illegitimacy (e.g., Winegarden 1974; Ellwood and Bane 1984; Danziger, Haveman, and Plotnick 1986; Ellwood and Summers 1986; Wilson 1987). Nor have higher state benefit levels been linked to increases in the number of female-headed households (Greenstein 1985). Welfare is not the most significant cause of the increase in female-headed households (Sawhill 1988). In fact, the number of female-headed households grew even when benefit levels declined (O'Hare 1987). Rather, changes in family composition are more closely tied to shifts in attitudes about families and divorce as well as to broader events in the economy. Family dissolution and reluctance to marry are related, for example, to the greater employment opportunities for women and the employability problems encountered by Black men (Ellwood and Summers 1986; Sawhill 1988).

Finally, many believe that public-assistance programs have built-in work disincentives (Murray 1984). Behind this belief is the conviction that "generous" benefit levels discourage recipients from seeking employment. However, this relationship is not as straightforward as it may appear. In the mid-1970s, low-income individuals were given an incentive to work in the form of the Earned Income Tax Credit (EITC). This allowed low-income workers to claim a tax credit of 10 percent of their earned income up to $5,000, giving them a maximum benefit of $500 (Levitan 1985). If low benefit levels encourage one to seek work, one would think that due to the combined effect of the EITC and the decreased value of benefits in the 1970s, unemployment would be down as individuals elected to go into the labor force. Instead, unemployment rose during the 1970s. While high benefit levels and benefit penalties if one works may have some disincentive effects, it appears that broader economic conditions are more closely related to employment rates than are welfare benefits (Danziger, Haveman, and Plotnick 1986; Sawhill 1988).

Moreover, the fact that most who had been on welfare were not on for very long further suggests that most do not become dependent for long periods of time (Bane and Ellwood 1994). Once on welfare, teenage women with children and with less than a high school education, who had never been married, had no significant work experience, and who were members of a minority were more likely than other groups to be on it for a long period. But even for this group, only one-third, at most, would have been welfare recipients for 10 years. Only about 15 percent are constantly on welfare (Handler 1995). "Welfare does not typically become a permanent way of life in which recipients make few efforts to escape and remain on welfare for generations" (Bane and Ellwood 1994, p. 42). Despite the lack of strong evidence of permanent dependency and the minor work disincentive effects of traditional public assistance programs, the images projected in these arguments combined with the lack of equity, adequacy, and consistency in goals led to welfare reform in 1996.

WELFARE REFORM

Despite the daunting task of reforming the welfare system, the Congress passed a welfare-reform package in 1996. At first glance, changes brought about by the Personal Responsibility and Work Opportunity Reconciliation Act of 1996, as its title suggests, are based on many of the same assumptions of past programs: individual characteristics are responsible for poverty, policymakers have to get tough with those on welfare to save them, people need to be pushed off welfare into work, welfare creates dependency, and single mothers form the core of those on public assistance. The 1996 Act was designed to reform the welfare system through an emphasis on making welfare recipients less dependent on public aid by pressuring them to find and accept work in the marketplace. Consistent with past policy and welfare recipients, the provisions of the law assume that those on welfare need to be pushed into work, that, if given the chance, they would prefer to remain dependent on welfare. But in contrast to past legislation, it does not guarantee public aid to a poor person. Among the Act's provisions are the following:

1. Able-bodied adults are required to work after two years of aid or lose benefits.
2. Aid is limited to five years over a person's lifetime.
3. Block grants are given to states that can devise their own programs (Aid to Families with Dependent Children [AFDC] is eliminated).
4. Future legal immigrants are ineligible for benefits in their first five years.
5. Spending on food stamps is lowered by about $24 billion over a six-year period, and guarantees of cash assistance for children are eliminated.
6. Medicaid coverage is continued for people on welfare and for one year after leaving it if they are working.
7. Encouragement is given for teenage mothers to identify fathers of their children, stay in school, and live at home with parents.

Proponents hailed the new package as a reflection of American values of work and independence and as a way of forcing those on welfare to be "responsible." Critics claimed that it created few, if any, jobs in which welfare recipients could work and would push more than a million more children into poverty. In many ways, the new legislation appeared to have many of the same flaws that plagued past policies.

President Clinton also signed into law a raise in the minimum wage to $5.15. Although many believe that good wages and earned income tax credits are a better way to remove people from poverty than welfare programs, this wage increase alone will not raise most poor families out of poverty. If one worked full time, 40 hours a week, 52 weeks a year, minimum wage earnings would still total $10,712, well below what is needed to raise an average poor family above the poverty line. Inadequacy has been a traditional weakness of American welfare programs, and, as suggested, some critics feared that more children would be thrown into poverty by the 1996 changes.

The block grants resulting from the welfare reforms of 1996 were aimed at giving states more leeway in shaping their own programs and encouraging individuals to reduce their assumed dependency on welfare by becoming employed as soon as possible. Consequently, by July 1997, every state had devised its own mixture of programs and requirements that fall within federal guidelines (National Governors' Association Center for Best Practices 1999). Some states impose lifetime limits of 60 months on assistance, while others have shorter limits. Some require individuals to be working before two years of aid are over, while others hold to the two-year limit. States also vary on how they treat interstate immigrants, assistance to drug felons, available transitional child care, and the existence of caps on total assistance amounts.

A central feature of these reforms is the Temporary Assistance for Needy Families (TANF) program, which replaced AFDC. Thus, it is likely to be one of the more controversial dimensions of welfare reform. In Wisconsin, one of the first states to experiment with extensive welfare reform, the W-2 (Wisconsin Works) program replaced AFDC. Individuals participating in W-2 are "guided to the best available immediate job opportunity." In the event individuals do not find jobs, they are given subsidized or community employment, or are required to enter a work training program. The aim is to remove individuals from welfare rolls as soon as possible. After two years, they are on their own, and can only be in the program for a total of five years over their lifetimes. To provide transitional support while in employment or training, Wisconsin has provided job centers, some child support, emergency loans to keep them working, transportation assistance, and health care (Medicaid) (Department of Workforce Development 1999). The programs of all the states emphasize self-sufficiency as a goal and impose time limitations beyond which individuals are no longer eligible for benefits.

An Assessment of the Reform Act of 1996

Given the controversial nature of the Personal Responsibility and Work Opportunity Reconciliation Act of 1996, it should not be surprising that there is similar disagreement about its effects on welfare recipients. Most of the popular press has emphasized criteria of success that show the Act to have had positive effects, and have downplayed criteria and evidence that suggest the Act's negative impacts (Schram and Soss 2001). Indeed, whether or not welfare reform is viewed as having been a success depends on how "success" is measured.

By some measures—number on welfare, employment, child poverty—there has been success. First, between 1996 and the middle of 2000, the number of welfare recipients fell by 53 percent (6.5 million). The number of people on welfare is lower than it has been since 1969, and the percentage on cash assistance is the lowest it has ever been (Lichter and Jayakody 2002). Second, women who had been on welfare have been pressed to end their dependency and enter the labor force in large numbers. Between 1996, the year of the reform legislation, and mid-1998, an additional 741,000 mothers who had never been married moved into the labor force (Lerman and Ratcliffe 2001). Third, the child poverty rate fell from 20.5 percent in 1996 to 16.2 percent in 2000, although it increased to 17.6 percent in 2003 (U.S. Census Bureau, August 2004). There has also been a decline since 1996 in the rate of pregnancy among unwed teenagers (Lichter and Jayakody 2002).

Even for the above positive effects, however, there is debate about the role of welfare reform in creating them. A strong economy at the time of legislation is also thought to have contributed heavily to reductions in welfare rolls and increased employment, resulting in reductions in child poverty (Corcoran et al. 2000; Kaushal and Kaestner 2001; Lens 2002). The question is whether reform will have the same effect when the economy is not so robust. Greenberg and Bernstein provide an answer to the question, noting that between 2001 and 2004, the number of people on welfare fell at the same time that the poverty rate increased. It appears that welfare reform "generally performed well during the tightest labor market in 30 years [mid-to-late 1990s] but has been far less effective amid the slack labor market that has prevailed since the 2001 recession" (2004, p. B2).

Other evidence on reform's work effects is also less positive about the impact of welfare reform. While many mothers who have left welfare are employed, most are not working 40 hours per week consistently, many are in low-wage positions that do not offer many health or other benefits, and most are unlikely to move up into more stable positions with significantly higher pay. Tracking the employment transitions of young women from unemployment through work in bad jobs to work in good jobs, Pavetti and Acs estimated that by their late 20s most of the women on welfare

will either still be working in bad jobs or will not be working regularly. Only a minority will be in good jobs (Pavetti and Acs 2001). Consequently, many of these new workers have simply joined the ranks of the working poor for incomes that are often lower that those they had before leaving welfare (Abelda 2001; Bavier 2001; Cancian 2001; Lens 2002).

In her three-year ethnographic study conducted among welfare families and at welfare offices, Sharon Hays found that 40 percent of the women and children who had gotten off welfare had *no* source of income, and of the remaining 60 percent, about half were still poor. Similarly, Cancian and Meyer's (2004) study of former welfare participants in Wisconsin found that while more than 50 percent have gotten out of poverty, they have not achieved economic independence, and continue to rely on non-cash benefits from the government. There is some evidence that the wages of former welfare recipients will grow, assuming that they can continue to gain experience and maintain a full-time position (Corcoran et al. 2000). But the latter is much less of a certainty and varies with the state of the economy and the place of residence.

Most of the employment is in metropolitan rather than rural areas even though many of the latter have some of the highest poverty rates in the United States. In fact, there is evidence that, because of its urban bias, welfare reform may have actually worsened economic conditions among poor rural mothers. "Rural America . . . is too often forgotten in the welfare policy debates. Most predominately rural states provide low TANF benefits in comparison to generous urban states" (Lichter and Jayakody 2002). Recent interviews with over 400 low-income rural mothers confirmed the desperate conditions that many face ("Study Examines," 2002). About 50 percent work one to three jobs, averaging 32 hours per week and earning just under $800 per month. More hours are simply not available from their employers. As a result, child care is often unaffordable and frequently costs more than the income brought in by the job. The availability of adequate child-care centers and transportation continues to be a significant issue.

At the present time, poor parents are caught in the gears of policies that make contradictory demands upon them. On the one hand, they are encouraged by welfare policies to work at the same time that their schools and their students are being monitored and expected to raise educational standards and performance. The more time poor parents spend working, the less time they have to help their children perform better in school. Parents need to work to support their families, but support for today is not the same as support for tomorrow. It is the degree of investment in their children's education that may very well affect the chances that the next generation will be out of poverty (Newman and Chin 2003).

These problems tend to fall disproportionately on young single mothers who have little education. Those most likely to be helped by welfare reform and to be early leavers are those who are most likely to find employment—that is, the able-bodied, better educated, skilled, and experienced. This leaves a core of less-educated, less-experienced, disabled individuals who are less likely to be able to become self-sufficient and who find it difficult to move off welfare. It may be much more difficult to enforce TANF rules with this group (Bavier 2001; Lichter and Jayakody 2002).

The full consequences of the 1996 legislation will probably not be known for years. For reform to have a chance of being effective, all of the components needed to make recipients self-sufficient have to be in place. This requires solving the problems of child care, transportation, and training/education. It also demands addressing the broader issues of employment supply and sex discrimination in the workplace. The latter is significant because many of those who are and will be seeking employment are younger mothers.

SUGGESTIONS FOR REDUCING INEQUALITY

Historically, the focus of welfare discussions and programs has been on the reduction of poverty rather than inequality. Poverty and inequality have been viewed as separate issues by most people primarily because the former has been interpreted as an *individual* phenomenon while the latter is generally seen as a characteristic of *social* structure. Poverty has widely been considered a problem that must be confronted, while few have called for a full-fledged assault on social and economic inequality. Yet poverty and inequality are interlinked because poverty is basically a problem rooted in economic and inequality processes in U.S. society.

How can we explain the reluctance to view poverty in terms of economic inequality? Why inequality is defined as a major problem by most of the public?

Since social services and programs that arise from policies do not originate with the poor, they rarely call for fundamental changes in the economic and/or political conditions in the society. Rather, the emphasis is on working within present economic and political arrangements, thereby maintaining the status quo.

The continued persistence of poverty has suggested to some that the poor may serve basic functions for the society, and particular nonpoor groups within it. Indeed, having an "undeserving" poor population serves many functions for the rest of us:

1. It justifies their poor treatment, makes us feel superior, and provides us with a convenient scapegoat for societal problems.
2. Conceiving the poor as a separate group creates a whole battery of jobs for those who are not poor, including a wide variety of "helping" professional positions.
3. The undeserving label justifies pushing the poor out of the legitimate labor market and provides an easily available group of

laborers to do work in the informal and illegal economy, and to serve as a surplus army to hire when nonpoor workers balk at working under poor conditions.

4. Our labeling and hostile treatment of the poor serves to reinforce and legitimate our own lives and institutions.

5. Their violation of mainstream values helps to remind us of those values, thereby constantly reaffirming them.

6. Blaming the poor for their own problems relieves others and social institutions of any blame for their situation.

7. The poor's lowly position and their label as undeserving weakens their political power and strengthens that of higher classes.

8. Labeling the poor as undeserving permits the agencies that deal with them to treat them in a way that reinforces and reproduces the stigma associated with poverty (Gans 1995).

By indicating these and other basic functions performed by the poor in U.S. society, Gans implied that poor people are not an *isolated* group who are poor because of their lack of integration into the mainstream of society, but rather are an *integral* part of the society. Alternative poverty programs that have been suggested vary in the extent to which their recommendations focus on the uniqueness and isolated nature of the poor, or on the nature of their integration into society. Those that stress the former tend to believe that the root causes of poverty lie in the flawed characters and characteristics of the poor themselves, whereas those in the latter camp are more likely to see social structures and processes as forces that create a poor population.

Those who see the operation of wider social forces in the generation of poverty and inequality also tend to argue that broader-based policies and programs must be implemented to address these problems. For more than a decade, William Julius Wilson has stressed that for any program to be fully accepted by the public it must be seen as benefiting everyone, not just particular groups. "I am convinced," wrote Wilson in 1987, "that, in the last few years of the twentieth century, the problems of the truly disadvantaged in the United States will have to be attacked primarily through universal programs that enjoy the support and commitment of a broad constituency" (1987, p. 120).

Most recently, Wilson has again stressed the crucial importance of a universally agreed-upon approach and a broad-based coalition to reduce the gap dividing the privileged and underprivileged (1999). Part of the problem with programs like affirmative action is that they are seen as preferential, privileging some groups over others. Consequently, they are viewed as unfair and unacceptable by many. Some of this is due to the language used in labeling the program and inferred by those who interpret it. Affirmative action, for example, is linked, in the minds of many, with "quotas" and "preferential treatment." Instead of focusing on numbers, Wilson proposes, we ought to relabel our efforts as "affirmative opportunity" since "it echoes the phrase *equal opportunity*, which connotes a principle that most Americans still support, while avoiding connotations now associated (fairly or not) with the idea of affirmative action—connotations such as quotas, lowering standards, and reverse discrimination, which most Americans detest" (Wilson 1999, p. 111,). Perhaps most fundamentally, Wilson believes that racial, ethnic, and other groups need to deemphasize how they are *different* from one another, and emphasize and act on the values, goals, and destinies that they have in *common*. Organized coalitions of different groups that focus on problems that they all share are more likely to be effective: "In the final analysis, unless groups of ordinary citizens embrace the need for mutual political cooperation, they stand little chance of generating the political muscle needed to ease their economic and social burdens" (ibid., p. 123).

Since we are all part of one society, economic events and inequality have implications for all of our lives.

Perhaps the most controversial and recent proposal to address broad-based inequality in the United States has been put forward by Ackerman and Alstott (1999). Their argument recalls Oliver and Shapiro's demonstration that inequality develops over generations as the structure of opportunities allows some groups to prosper and pass on their prosperity to future generations, while others are left to languish and struggle, leaving little to their children (1995). In this way, inequality becomes fixed and individuals from different groups but in the same generation start out their lives with unequal amounts of advantages.

Briefly, Ackerman and Alstott suggest that the most direct way to address economic inequality between individuals is to grant every young adult a "stake" so they can begin their adult lives on a more equal level. Specifically, they suggest a one-time stake of $80,000 for young adults to use as they wish to develop their futures. Individuals take responsibility for the success or failure of their choices, and in old age they would have an obligation to repay the stake if they are able to do so. To fund the $80,000 stakes for beginning adults, a tax of 2 percent on all wealth would need to be levied. Ackerman and Alstott believe this is fair, since "every American has an obligation to contribute to a fair starting point for all" (1999, p. 5). Like Wilson, they imply the importance of stressing that all citizens are in the American enterprise together, and thus we have to work together to reach a more just society. Existing programs of the welfare state have been too divisive, and we need a plan that will invigorate common values. A "stakeholder society" will do that, say Ackerman and Alstott. They believe that beneficiaries of their proposed policy "will locate themselves in a much larger national project devoted to the proposition that all men are created equal. By invoking this American ideal in their own case, they link themselves not only to all others in the past who have taken steps to realize this fundamental principle but also to all those who will do so in the future" (ibid., p. 7).

Attempts at reform have frequently gotten hung up because of the difficulty of trying to balance conservative and liberal approaches, trying to be tough but compassionate at the same time. Suggestions aim at helping those who need help but also at encouraging individual responsibility. American values encourage us to be generous but to encourage others to realize that there is no "free lunch." Both society and the individual have obligations. "Any successful social policy must strike a balance between collective compassion and individual responsibility," wrote Christopher Jencks (1992, p. 87). Historically, the reform pendulum has swung between these two kinds of themes.

Recent federal suggestions have mirrored some of the preceding state efforts, but have also incorporated elements of compassion. The Family and Medical Leave Act of 1993 requires those who employ at least 50 workers to provide three months of unpaid leave per year for child care or medical reasons. But only about half of the private labor force is covered, along with government workers (Landers 1993). Suggestions have also been made to increase the Earned Income Tax Credit (EITC) to low-income families. Last, the 1996 Kennedy-Kassebaum health plan allows currently insured individuals to take their insurance with them if they change employers, and minimizes the chances of anyone being denied health insurance because of a preexisting condition. All of these efforts reflect a concern for compassion, but as you have seen, many of the aspects of current policy mirror a harsher, tougher view of those on welfare. Humanity as well as inhumanity have been mixed into our recipes for welfare. As yet, the recipe is not perfected.

SUMMARY

This chapter has discussed approaches and programs aimed at addressing problems associated with inequality and poverty. Affirmative action and taxes aim at reducing income, racial, and gender inequality, but since these are controversial, more federal programs have been focused on the reduction of poverty. There is no question that the measurement of poverty is laden with political implications. Depending on what is included under the category of economic resources, poverty rates may be higher or lower. The controversies surrounding the definition and measurement of poverty alone make the topic a political "hot potato."

Adding to this controversy are people's images of the poor, especially those on public assistance (welfare). The traditional values of individualism, independence, hard work, material success, and others encourage a negative attitude toward those who are not economically successful. At the same time, humanitarian and community values encourage people to take care of those who are less fortunate than themselves. Believing that virtually all people can make it if they try hard, but at the same time knowing from historical events such as the Depression, plant closings, and market declines that not everything about their economic fates is in their hands to control has resulted in a somewhat bifurcated approach to income-maintenance programs for the needy. There are elements of both a residual and institutional approach in this system.

In one category, social insurance programs such as social security retirement, disability, and Medicare insurance provide universal coverage with a minimum of stigma to a wide variety of individuals who fall into a particular demographic category. There is no means-testing or demeaning administrative process suggesting that these recipients are receiving welfare. In the other category of public assistance are those who are poor but not elderly and/or disabled. Individuals with these characteristics—often women who head their own households, children, and members of minorities—must provide proof that they are indigent. They must prove that they are deserving of benefits from food stamps, Medicaid, and similar programs.

Problems of inequity, inadequacy, and goal conflict have permeated public assistance programs for the poor. In addition, questions about how they affect work incentive, family composition, and effectiveness have also generated heated debate. Alternative proposals attempt to grapple with the problems of adequacy, employment, work incentives, and so on. Many have suggested economic growth and full employment as the key to the puzzle of poverty. This would mean greater self-sufficiency for everyone. Indeed, the welfare reform act of 1996 focuses on pushing individuals into the labor force. But this leaves some pessimistic, and the follow-ups on those leaving state welfare are decidedly mixed. In many cases, policies have deepened poverty, at least in the short run. More time is needed, however, to fully assess state reform's full impact.

As difficult as poverty may be to understand, we still have not confronted the even thornier issue of economic inequality. A focus on inequality unavoidably involves all of us, since we all live out our lives within its structure. The suggestions of Wilson, Ackerman, and Alstott, as improbable as they may seem, are based realistically on a recognition that any effective policy to reduce inequality must incorporate groups from every strata, not just the poor. In one way or another, we need to reach across the widening gaps that separate us. If inequality continues to grow as it has in recent years, we may be forced to address this topic. The real question is whether poverty, let alone inequality, can be eliminated within a democratic capitalist society. This brings us back to some of the core questions with which we began this book.

If poverty is generated not merely by differences among individuals, but by conditions that are part of a capitalist economy, such as unemployment and the pressure for profit and lower wages, then a permanent solution, as Morris and Williamson suggested, is very unlikely unless fundamental changes in the political economy occur. Are inequality and poverty inevitable? Given the present social structure, the answer is probably *yes*. Are inequality and poverty desirable? It depends. Although it is a serious problem for those who must suffer with it, poverty appears to be functional for others. It helps maintain the attractiveness of low wages and menial jobs, especially when coupled with low benefits from programs. At the same time, it provides employment for many middle-class professionals. As to the immediate future of inequality and poverty, the fact that income and wealth inequality has increased in recent years, despite the presence of income-maintenance programs, suggests that either (1) we do not really consider inequality to be a major problem, (2) we do not really know what causes it to fluctuate, and/or (3) some find inequality beneficial.

Evidence strongly suggests that what happens in the economy has a major impact on both inequality and poverty. At the dawn of the twenty-first century, many organizations are streamlining and downsizing in an effort to maintain profits in the face of intensified domestic and foreign competition. While executives and shareholders frequently reap the economic benefits of these leaner and more efficient organizational structures, the attendant layoffs have led many in the middle class to fall near or into poverty. These shifts have also exacerbated the poor financial conditions of those already on the bottom and are also likely to cause further tensions among racial/ethnic groups and between the sexes. In sum, the rewards and punishments of recent economic changes are clearly and unequally divided. The combination of the economic trends and their varied effects on different groups, together with our reluctance to address the problem of inequality and to recognize its social roots, are not good omens. The signs do not look good for a systematic reduction of social inequality in the near future.

CRITICAL THINKING

1. Why have policymakers tended to focus on poverty rather than inequality as an economic problem? Why has poverty been so difficult to define and measure?

2. Can the conflicting goals of welfare policy ever be reconciled to produce an effective welfare policy? Explain your answer.

3. What specific data on welfare help to eliminate the negative stereotype of the

"welfare mother"? Is simply having the facts enough to eliminate this stereotype? Explain your answer.

4. Given what has been suggested in this chapter, what do you think should be the cornerstone features of any effective antipoverty plan?

WEB CONNECTIONS

The Finance Project is a nonprofit research and assistance firm that provides information on welfare, income supplements, job training, and asset development. Visit their website at www.financeproject.org/irc/win.asp.

GLOSSARY OF BASIC TERMS

absolute downward mobility a downward shift in economic resources without a simultaneous change in an individual's position relative to others.

anomic division of labor an abnormal condition in which the rules of relationships among those in the production process and limits in the marketplace are unclear.

asset poverty condition in which a household does not have sufficient wealth resources to meet its basic needs for a specified period of time.

assimilationist theory an explanation of race relations that views minority groups as being on a one-way road to blending in with the rest of society.

berdaches in traditional Navajo society, persons who were men anatomically, but were considered to be in a third gender and intersexed.

brown-bag test criterion used to screen individuals from membership in a group or organization if their skin color is darker than a brown grocery bag.

burakumin a minority outcaste group in Japan distinguished and discriminated against on the basis of the impurity of their occupations and place of residence.

capitalism an economic system based on private ownership, competition, and open markets.

caste system a closed social ranking system dividing categories of individuals in which position is ascribed and which is legitimated by cultural and/or religious institutions.

chronic illness health problems that continue over a long period of time.

circulation of elites Pareto's argument that as conditions change, those most competent to rule move into positions of power while the incompetent move into the governed class.

circulation mobility mobility that reflects the cultural and social openness of a society.

class defined variously as individuals or groups who (1) occupy the same position on hierarchies of occupational prestige, income, and education; or (2) are in the same relation to the system of production; or (3) are in the same relation to the system of production and are also class conscious.

class consciousness the full awareness within a group of its class position and relationship with other classes, along with action based on this awareness.

closed society a society in which little social mobility occurs and position is entirely dependent on the position into which one is born.

competitive race relations a set of relationships between races most often found in industrial systems and characterized by competition and aggressive rather than accommodative behavior.

core economic sector the section of the private economy occupied by large, capital-intensive, highly productive firms with large sometimes international markets (also called **monopoly sector**).

crises of overproduction the inability of capitalism to sell all that it produces, largely because of the inconsistency between low, impoverished wages and advanced technology.

cross-gender the situation of one sex regularly performing and acting in a manner socially and culturally expected of a different sex.

cultural capital a group's cultural values, experiences, knowledge, and skills passed on from one generation to the next.

dependency theory the argument that countries are interlinked through economic and political ties that perpetuate development or underdevelopment.

derivations Pareto's term for justifications or reasons people give for their behavior.

drift hypothesis in the study of the relationship between mental illness and social class, the argument that illness causes one's downward mobility through the class system.

dual economy the view of the economy as being split between large, economically powerful, monopolistic firms on the one hand, and small, less stable, local, poorer economic organizations on the other.

economic hardship spending more than 40 percent of one's income on debt payment.

embourgeoisement the taking on by the working class of middle-class cultural and social characteristics.

environmental equity/justice   concerns the extent to which groups have equal access to public land resources and equal exposure to environmental hazards.

estate system   a fairly rigid system of ranking based primarily on land ownership, and usually sanctioned by the state and religion.

ethnic group   a group distinguished on the basis of its native cultural and linguistic characteristics.

Eugenics Movement   an early twentieth-century movement concerned with heredity and mating as means for the perfection of a race.

financial wealth   those forms of wealth that can be easily and quickly converted to cash.

forced division of labor   an abnormal condition in which the distribution of accorded positions and occupations is inconsistent with the distribution of talents and skills among individuals.

functionalist theory of stratification   the argument that stratification is a necessary device for motivating talented people to perform the society's most difficult and important tasks, and that it arises from scarcity of talent and the differential social necessity of tasks.

gender   a set of attitudinal, role, and behavior expectations, which are socially and culturally defined, associated with each sex.

globalization   *economically*, the acceleration of international trade and flow of financial capital; *politically*, the opening of national borders to foreign goods and services; and *socially*, the free flow and exchange of cultural ideas and structural arrangements among nations.

habitus   Bourdieu's term for a system of stable dispositions to view the world in a particular way.

hate crime   a violent or property crime committed against a person that is motivated at least in part by a bias against the person's race, religion, disability, sexual orientation, ethnicity, or national origin.

health maintenance organization (HMO)   a health organization that provides a variety of core services to individuals for a fixed monthly premium.

hermaphrodites   individuals who lack an enzyme at birth that would allow them to develop male genitals and are, consequently, defined as females even though male features later begin to develop.

homosocial reproduction   process by which groups or individuals in specific organizational positions recruit new persons who are similar to them on criteria deemed to be important.

honor killing   an extreme form of discrimination in which the person, usually a minority or female individual, is killed for ostensibly violating a cultural norm or tradition related to that person's behavior.

human capital   the investments one makes in oneself (i.e., education, acquisition of skills, and experience).

hyperghettoization   the extreme concentration of underprivileged groups in the inner city.

hypersegregation   the isolation, clustering, and heavy concentration of Blacks in given geographic areas, especially the center of the city.

income deficit   how far below the poverty level one's income falls.

Index of Income Concentration   a measure of how far the actual distribution of income is from perfect equality (also called Gini coefficient).

individual-level analysis   a focus on individuals or individual actions in the analysis of relationships between variables.

industrialism thesis   the argument that, regardless of the country, industrialization breaks down barriers to social mobility and results in an emphasis on achievement rather than ascription as a basis for vertical mobility.

inflow table   an intergenerational mobility table showing the degree to which those with different occupational backgrounds move into the same occupational category.

in-kind benefits   noncash outlays given to recipients of government programs, such as food stamps, medical assistance, and job training.

inner circle   a network of leaders from large corporations who serve as top officers at more than one firm, who are politically active, and who serve the interests of the capitalist class as a whole.

inner/outer orientation   a view of the environment as hospitable, fruitful, and freely giving (inner) or as one in which the environment is alien and hostile, and must be conquered (outer).

institutional view of social welfare   belief that since poverty is often beyond the control of individuals, and one of government's legitimate roles is to help those in need, welfare should be available to help people out of poverty.

intergenerational mobility   a change in economic or social hierarchical position between generations.

internal colonialism   a situation in which a minority group is culturally, socially, and politically dominated as if it were a colony of the majority group.

intragenerational mobility vertical economic or social movement within one's own lifetime.

jati the complex system of local castes found in Indian villages.

labor power the mental and physical capacities exercised by individuals when they produce something of use.

legitimation process the means and manner by which social inequality is explained and justified.

marital mobility vertical social mobility that occurs because of one's marriage.

mass society a society in which the vast majority of the population is unorganized, largely powerless, and manipulated by those at the distant top.

means of production the material (e.g., machines) and nonmaterial (e.g., lectures) techniques used to produce goods and services in an economy.

microinequities everyday ways in which, because of their social ranking, individuals are ignored, put down, highlighted, or demeaned.

militant societies societies in which there is heavy regulation of individuals and groups; the regulatory system is the dominant institution in the society; contrasted with industrial societies and associated with Spencer.

mobility ratio the percentage of offsprings of employed parents who are in a given occupation, divided by the percentage of the labor force that is in that category.

mode of production the particular type of economic system in a society, including its means of production (e.g., technology) and social/authority relations among workers and between workers and owners. Capitalism and feudalism are two modes of production.

near poor those whose total income falls between 100 percent and 125 percent of the poverty threshold.

necessary labor the labor needed to reproduce workers and their replacements.

nested inequality inequalities existing at various levels within a given institutional sphere that have a cumulative or layered effect.

net worth one's wealth minus one's debts.

opportunity structure characteristics of the cultural, social, political, legal, occupational, economic, and other institutions that affect chances of social mobility either positively or negatively.

origin myths in this context, the view of the world's origin as being due to either masculine or feminine forces.

party an association aimed at or specifically organized for gaining political power in an organization or society (Weber).

paternalistic race relations a system of somewhat stable established relationships most likely to be found in complex agricultural systems in which relationships between races are dictated by a recognized social code and in which members of the dominant race treat members of the subordinated race as if they were children.

path analysis a statistical technique used to uncover the nature and strength of causal connections within a set of variables.

patriarchy a complex of structured interrelationships in which men dominate women.

peripheral economic sector part of the private economy occupied by small, local, labor-intensive, less productive, and less stable economic organizations (also called **competitive sector**).

phantom welfare government cash, tax, and in-kind programs and policies that largely benefit the nonpoor.

pluralism the view stressing that power is distributed throughout society among various groups rather than concentrated.

political action committee (PAC) a group that organizes around a broad or narrow common interest to influence political policy in its favor.

posttransfer poverty having an income below the official poverty level, even when government benefits are taken into account.

power elite a small group or set of groups that dominate the political process and masses in a society.

prestige the social ranking accorded a position or occupation; a synonym for status honor.

pretransfer poverty having an income below the official poverty level, not taking into account any kind of government assistance.

primary labor market the labor market associated with jobs that are stable, good paying, and unionized; have good working conditions; and in which there is an internal job structure through which one can move.

principle of differentiation the belief that it is fair that those with unequal talents should receive unequal rewards.

principle of equality the belief that since all people are ultimately of equal value, they should therefore receive equal consideration or treatment.

proletarianization the conversion of white-collar and middle-class occupations into occupations with traditional working-class characteristics (i.e., boring, routine, etc.).

public assistance cash and in-kind government programs for the poor that are means tested (i.e., require that an individual prove his or her eligibility) and to which there is a social stigma attached.

race-specific programs programs of government aid that target particular racial groups for help.

rationalization the increasing bureaucratic, technological, and impersonal character of the modern world (Weber).

relations of production the nature of relationships among workers, between workers and managers/supervisors, and between owners and nonowners in an economic system.

relative downward mobility a shift in one's position on the economic ladder to a lower position and involving a switch in place with another person or group.

relative income the distance an income is from the middle of the income distribution.

residual view of social welfare the belief that since poverty is caused by personal flaws, welfare programs should be minimal, with low benefits and strict eligibility requirements to discourage use of them.

residues Pareto's term for manifestations of underlying basic human propensities or basic drives.

ruling class the broad Marxian view that the upper class, or an active arm of it generally dominates the political process in society to protect its interests.

scientific management a system of control used by management in which labor tasks are simplified and standardized by being broken down into their smallest elements.

secondary labor market the labor market associated with poor, unstable, low-paying, and often dead-end jobs.

sedimentation the reproduction and perpetuation of lower levels of wealth over generations for given groups.

sex stratification the degree to which access to valued resources is restricted because of sex.

slave system a system of inequality based on ownership of human beings.

social causation thesis in the study of the relationship between mental illness and social class, the argument that social class position is causally related to the probability of mental illness.

social constructionism a perspective that explains how social phenomena are socially created through definitions, classifications, and categorizations used by individuals.

Social Darwinism a social philosophy stressing perfection of society through a natural, unfettered process of survival of the fittest.

social insurance government programs, such as social security, for which individuals who have worked for a certain period of time are automatically eligible and seen as deserving of aid.

social-level analysis a focus on examining relationships between group, aggregate, or societal characteristics rather than those between individuals.

social reproduction the process by which structural conditions reproduce themselves.

social stratification a condition in which the ranking system among groups or categories of individuals is firmly established, resulting in a set of social layers separated by impermeable boundaries.

socioeconomic status a person's position on several continuous social and economic hierarchies, such as education, income, occupation, and wealth.

stages of capitalism capitalism's movement through phases of cooperation, manufacture, and modern industry (Marx).

status the ranking of individuals and groups on the basis of *social* and evaluated characteristics; contrasts with class, which is largely an *economic* ranking.

status attainment the study of the factors and processes that account for the educational, occupational, and economic attainment of individuals.

strategic elites individuals who serve fundamental coordinating functions that have significant relevance for a whole society.

street crime crimes listed by the FBI's Crime Index, including burglary, larceny-theft, motor vehicle theft, arson, murder, forcible rape, robbery, and aggravated assault.

structural mobility mobility that is due to shifts in the occupational distribution or changes in technology.

suite crime a synonym for **white-collar crime**.

surplus labor labor time that is left over after socially necessary labor has been subtracted from the total labor time spent on the job. It produces profit for the employer.

transgendered   referring to individuals who deviate from traditional gender binaries of Western society and who sometimes define themselves as belonging to a third gender.

underclass   a small, urban, largely unemployed, chronically poor, welfare-dependent group of individuals living in impoverished neighborhoods and whose children often wind up in the same position.

vacancy-driven mobility   mobility that depends on the availability and distribution of open positions.

varna   a major ritual caste in India, such as the Brahmins.

welfare capitalism   special benefits used by management to minimize solidarity among workers.

white-collar crime   crimes committed by individuals of high status or corporations using their powerful positions and generally involving violations of trust and extensive victimization.

whitening   the social process by which individuals can change their racial classification because of their education, occupation, or high-class position.

Wisconsin model   a model of status attainment that stresses the impact of social-psychological as well as structural factors on attainment.

world inequality   the total amount of inequality between nations and the average of amount of inequality within nations combined.

REFERENCES

Aaronson, Daniel, and Daniel G. Sullivan. 1998. "The Decline of Job Security in the 1990s: Displacement, Anxiety, and Their Effect on Wage Growth." *Economic Perspectives* 22:17–43.

Abelda, Randy. 2001. "Fallacies of Welfare-to-Work Policies." *Annals of the American Academy of Political and Social Science* 577:66–77.

Aberle, D. F., A. K. Cohen, A. D. Davis, M. J. Levy, and F. X. Sutton. 1950. "The Functional Prerequisites of a Society." *Ethics* 60:100–11.

Abrahamson, Mark. 1973. "Functionalism and the Functional Theory of Stratification: An Empirical Assessment." *American Journal of Sociology* 78:1236–46.

Abramovitz, Mimi. 2001. "Everyone Is Still on Welfare: The Role of Redistribution in Social Policy." *Social Work* 46:297–308.

Acker, Joan. 1973. "Women and Social Stratification: A Case of Intellectual Sexism." *American Journal of Sociology* 78:936–45.

Acker, Joan. 2001. "Different Strategies Are Necessary Now." *Monthly Review* 53(5):46–49.

Ackerman, Bruce, and Ann Alstott. 1999. *The Stakeholder Society*. New Haven: Yale University Press.

Adams, Bert N., and R. A. Sydie. 2002. *Classical Sociological Theory*. Thousand Oaks, CA: Pine Forge Press.

Adams, Charles Francis, ed. 1969. *The Works of John Adams*, vol. IX. Freeport, NY: Books for Libraries Press.

Adler, Patricia A., and Peter Adler. 1998. *Peer Power*. New Brunswick, NJ: Rutgers University Press.

Alderson, Arthur S., and Francois Nielsen. 2002. "Globalization and the Great U-Turn: Income Inequality Trends in 16 OECD Countries." *American Journal of Sociology* 107:1244–99.

Alexander, Herbert E. 1992. "The PAC Phenomenon." Pp. ix–xv in *Almanac of Federal PACs: 1992*, edited by E. Zuckerman. Washington, D.C.: Amward.

Alexander, Karl L., Bruce K. Eckland, and Larry J. Griffin. 1975. "The Wisconsin Model of Socioeconomic Achievement: A Replication." *American Journal of Sociology* 81:324–42.

Allan, Emilie Anderson, and Darrell J. Steffensmeier. 1989. "Youth, Underemployment, and Property Crime: Differential Effects of Job Availability and Job Quality on Juvenile and Young Adult Arrest Rates." *American Sociological Review* 54:107–23.

Allen, Michael Patrick. 1987. *The Founding Fortunes: A New Anatomy of the Super-Rich Families in America*. New York: Truman Talley Books.

Allen, Robert L. 1969. *Black Awakening in Capitalist America*. Garden City, NY: Anchor.

Almond, Gabriel A. September 1991. "Capitalism and Democracy." *PS: Political Science & Politics* 24:467–74.

Almquist, Elizabeth McTaggart. 1984. "Race and Ethnicity in the Lives of Minority Women." Pp. 423–53 in *Women: A Feminist Perspective*, edited by J. Freeman. Palo Alto, CA: Mayfield.

Altman, Dennis. 2005. "The Globalization of Sexual Identities." Pp. 216–26 in *Gender Through the Prism of Difference*, edited by M. B. Zinn, P. Hondagneu-Sotelo, and M. A. Messner. New York: Oxford.

Alves, W. M., and P. H. Rossi. 1978. "Who Should Get What? Fairness Judgments of the Distribution of Earnings." *American Journal of Sociology* 84:541–65.

American Civil Liberties Union. 1997. "Antidiscrimination Laws Protect Equal Rights for Gays and Lesbians." Pp. 143–51 in *Gay Rights*, edited by T. L. Roleff. San Diego: Greenhaven.

America's Second Harvest. 2005. Available at www.secondharvest.org.

Andersen, Margaret L. 1993. *Thinking about Women*. New York: Macmillan.

Andersen, Margaret L. 1997. *Thinking about Women*. Boston: Allyn & Bacon.

Anderson, Elijah. 1999. *Code of the Street*. New York: W. W. Norton.

Anderson, Sarah, John Cavanagh, Chris Hartman, Scott Klinger, and Stacey Chan. 2004. *Executive Excess 2004*. Washington, D.C.: Institute for Policy Studies; and Boston, MA: United for a Fair Economy.

Anderton, Douglas L., Andy B. Anderson, John Michael Oakes, and Michael R. Fraser. 1994. "Environmental Equity: The Demographics of Dumping." *Demography* 31:229–48.

Andrews, Edmund L. October 6, 2004. "Initiative by Bush on the Income Tax Has Innate Conflicts." *New York Times*, pp. C1, C3.

Anheier, Helmut K., Jurgen Gerhards, and Frank P. Romo. 1995. "Forms of Capital and Social Structure in Cultural Fields: Examining Bourdieu's Social Topography." *American Journal of Sociology* 100:859–903.

Anson, Ofra, and Jon Anson. 1987. "Women's Health and Labour Force Status: An Enquiry Using a Multi-Point Measure of Labor Force Participation." *Social Science & Medicine* 25:57–63.

Appalachian Regional Commission. 1985. *Appalachia: Twenty Years of Progress*. Washington, D.C.: Author.

Aristotle. "Justice." Pp. 16–27 in *Justice: Selected Readings*, edited by J. Feinberg and H. Gross. Encino, CA: Dickenson Publishing.

Aronowitz, Stanley. 1973. *False Promises: The Shaping of American Working Class Consciousness*. New York: McGraw-Hill.

Asher, Robert. 1986. "Industrial Safety and Labor Relations in the United States, 1865–1917." Pp. 115–30 in *Life and Labor: Dimensions of American Working-Class History*, edited by C. Stephenson and R. Asher. Albany, NY: State University of New York Press.

Ashley, David, and David Michael Orenstein. 1990. *Sociological Theory: Classical Statements*. Needham Heights, MA: Allyn & Bacon.

Austin, Roy L., and Steven Stack. 1988. "Race, Class, and Opportunity: Changing Realities and Perceptions." *The Sociological Quarterly* 29:357–69.

Avery, Robert B., and Michael S. Rendall. 2002. "Lifetime Inheritance of Three Generations of Whites and Blacks." *American Journal of Sociology* 107:1300–46.

Awanohara, Susumu, and Shim Jae Hoon. May 14, 1992. "Melting Pot Boils Over." *Far Eastern Economic Review*, pp. 10–11.

Bachrach, Peter, and Morton S. Baratz. 1962. "Two Faces of Power." *American Political Science Review* 56:947–52.

Badgett, M. V. Lee. 2001. *Money, Myths, and Change: The Economic Lives of Lesbians and Gay Men*. Chicago: University of Chicago.

Bagehot, Walter. Quote from *The Oxford Dictionary of Quotations*, 3rd ed. Oxford: Oxford University Press, p. 29.

Bailey, J. Michael. 1996. "Gender Identity." Pp. 71–93 in *The Lives of Lesbians, Gays, and Bisexuals*, edited by R. C. Savin-Williams and K. M. Cohen. Fort Worth, TX: Harcourt Brace.

Baker-Sperry, Lori, and Liz Grauerholz. 2003. "The Pervasiveness and Persistence of the Feminine Beauty Ideal in Children's Fairy Tales." *Gender & Society* 15:711–26.

Baltzell, E. Digby. 1958. *Philadelphia Gentleman: The Making of a National Upper Class*. Glencoe, IL: The Free Press.

Bane, Mary Jo, and David T. Ellwood. 1994. *Welfare Realities*. Cambridge, MA: Harvard University Press.

Banyard, Victoria L. 1999. "Childhood Maltreatment and the Mental Health of Low-Income Women." *American Journal of Orthopsychiatry* 69:161–71.

Banyard, Victoria L., and Sandra A. Graham-Bermann. 1998. "Surviving Poverty: Stress and Coping in the Lives of Housed and Homeless Mothers." *American Journal of Orthopsychiatry* 68:479–89.

Baran, Paul, and Paul Sweezy. 1966. *Monopoly Capital*. New York: Monthly Review Press.

Barkan, Steven E. 1984. "Legal Control of the Southern Civil Rights Movement." *American Sociological Review* 49:552–65.

Barnett, Bernice McNair. 1993. "Invisible Southern Black Women Leaders in the Civil Rights Movement." *Gender & Society* 7:162–82.

Baron, James N., and William T. Bielby. 1984. "The Organization of Work in a Segmented Economy." *American Sociological Review* 49:454–73.

Barr, Bob, Steve Largent, Jim Sensenbrenner, Sue Myrick, Ed Bryant, Bill Emerson, Harold Volkmer, and Ike Skelton. 1996. *Defense of Marriage Act. 5/96 H.R. 3396 Summary/Analysis*. Web site: http://www.lectlaw.com/files/leg-23.htm.

Barrera, Mario. 1979. *Race and Class in the Southwest: A Theory of Racial Inequality*. Notre Dame, IN: University of Notre Dame Press.

Barrett, Anne E., and R. Jay Turner. 2005. "Family Structure and Mental Health: The Mediating Effects of Socioeconomic Status, Family Process, and Social Stress." *Journal of Health and Social Behavior* 46:156–69.

Barringer, Felicity. January 11, 1990. "The Dress for Success: A Second Time Around." *New York Times*, p. A18.

Barry, John S. 2002. "Corporate Inversions: An Introduction to the Issue and FAQ." *Fiscal Policy Memo. Tax Bites*, May 30. The Tax Foundation.

Batteau, Allen. 1984. "The Sacrifice of Nature: A Study in the Social Production of Consciousness." Pp. 94–106 in *Cultural Adaptation to Mountain Environments*, edited by P. D. Beaver and B. L. Purrington. Athens, GA: The University of Georgia Press.

Bausman, Kent, and W. Richard Goe. 2004. "An Examination of the Link Between Employment Volatility and the Spatial Distribution of Property Crime Rates." *American Journal of Economics and Sociology* 63:665–95.

Bavier, Richard. July 2001. "Welfare Reform Data from the Survey of Income and Program Participation." *Monthly Labor Review*, pp. 13–24.

Baxter, Janeen, and Erik Olin Wright. 2000. "The Glass Ceiling Hypothesis: A Comparative Study of the United States, Sweden, and Australia." *Gender & Society* 14:275–94.

Beaver, Patricia D. 1984. "Appalachian Cultural Adaptations: An Overview." Pp. 73–93 in *Cultural Adaptation to Mountain Environments*, edited by P. D. Beaver and B. L. Purrington. Athens, GA: The University of Georgia Press.

Beck, E. M., Patrick M. Horan, and Charles M. Tolbert, II. 1980. "Industrial Segmentation and Labor Market Discrimination." *Social Problems* 28:113–30.

Beckfield, Jason. 2003. "Inequality in the World Polity: The Structure of International Organization." *American Sociological Review* 68:401–24.

Bedau, H. A. 1964. "Death Sentences in New Jersey." *Rutgers Law Review* 19:1–55.

Behrens, Angela, Christopher Uggen, and Jeff Manza. 2003. "Ballot Manipulation and the 'Menace of Negro Domination': Racial Threat and Felon Disenfranchisement in the United States, 1850–2002." *American Journal of Sociology* 109:559–605.

Bell, Winifred. 1987. *Contemporary Social Welfare*. New York: Macmillan.

Bellas, Marcia L. 1994. "Comparable Worth in Academia: The Effects of Faculty Salaries of the Sex Composition and Labor-Market Conditions of Academic Disciplines." *American Sociological Review* 59:807–21.

Beller, Andrea H. 1984. "Trends in Occupational Segregation by Sex and Race, 1960–1981." Pp. 11–26 in *Sex Segregation in the Workplace: Trends, Explanations, Remedies*, edited by B. F. Reskin. Washington, D.C.: National Academy Press.

Bem, Sandra L., and Daryl J. Bem. 1970. "Case Study of a Nonconscious Ideology: Training the Woman to Know Her Place." Pp. 89–99 in *Beliefs, Attitudes and Human Affairs*, edited by D. J. Bem. Belmont, CA: Brooks/Cole.

Benokraitis, Nijole V., and Joe R. Feagin. 1986. *Modern Sexism*. Englewood Cliffs, NJ: Prentice Hall.

Bensman, Joseph. 1972. "Status Communities in an Urban Society: The Musical Community." Pp. 113–30 in *Status Communities in Modern Society*, edited by H. R. Stub. Hinsdale, IL: Dryden.

Benson, Michael L., and Esteban Walker. 1988. "Sentencing the White-Collar Offender." *American Sociological Review* 53:294–302.

Benston, Margaret. 1969. "The Political Economy of Women's Liberation." *Monthly Review* 21:15–16.

Berger, J., P. Cohen, and M. Zelditch, Jr. 1972. "Status Characteristics and Social Interaction." *American Sociological Review* 37:241–55.

Berger, J., M. H. Fisek, R. Z. Norman, and M. Zelditch, Jr. 1977. *Status Characteristics and Social Interaction: An Expectation States Approach*. New York: Elsevier.

Bergmann, Barbara R. 1974. "Occupational Segregation, Wages and Profits When Employers Discriminate by Race or Sex." *Eastern Economic Journal* 1:103–10.

Berk, Richard A., Kenneth J. Lenihan, and Peter H. Rossi. 1980. "Crime and Poverty: Some Experimental Evidence from Ex-Offenders." *American Sociological Review* 45:766–86.

Berle, Adolf. 1959. *Power without Property*. New York: Harcourt Brace Jovanovich.

Bernard, Jessie. 1972. *The Sex Game*. New York: Atheneum.

Bernard, Jessie. 1981. *The Female World*. New York: The Free Press.

Bernstein, Aaron. February 26, 1996. "Is America Becoming More of a Class Society?" *BusinessWeek* pp. 86–96.

Bernstein, Irving. 1960. *The Lean Years: A History of the American Worker 1920–1933*. Boston: Houghton Mifflin.

Berreman, Gerald D. 1960. "Caste in India and the United States." *American Journal of Sociology* 66:120–27.

Berreman, Gerald D. 1972. "Race, Caste, and Other Invidious Distinctions in Social Stratification." *Race* 13:385–414. Reprinted on pp. 21–39 in *Majority & Minority: The Dynamics of Race and Ethnicity in American Life*, edited by N. R. Yetman. Boston: Allyn & Bacon, 1985.

Bertrand, Marianne, and Kevin F. Hallock. 2001. "The Gender Gap in Top Corporate Jobs." *Industrial and Labor Relations Review* 55:3–21.

Beteille, Andre. 1996. *Caste, Class, and Power: Changing Patterns of Stratification in a Tanjore Village*, 2nd ed. New Delhi: Oxford University Press.

Bibb, Robert, and William H. Form. 1977. "The Effects of Industrial, Occupational, and Sex Stratification on Wages in Blue-Collar Markets." *Social Forces* 55:974–96.

Bielby, Denise D., and William T. Bielby. 1988. "She Works Hard for the Money: Household Responsibilities and the Allocation of Work Effort." *American Journal of Sociology* 93:1031–59.

Bielby, William T. 1981. "Models of Status Attainment." Pp. 3–26 in *Research in Social Stratification and Mobility*, edited by D. J. Treiman and R. V. Robinson. Greenwich, CT: JAI Press.

"Bigotry in the Military." August 30, 1999. *New York Times*, p. A22.

Biller, Henry B., and Richard S. Solomon. 1986. *Child Maltreatment and Paternal Deprivation*. Lexington, MA: Lexington Books.

Billings, Dwight. 1974. "Culture and Poverty in Appalachia: A Theoretical Discussion and Empirical Analysis." *Social Forces* 53:315–24.

Bittman, Michael, Paula England, Nancy Folbre, Liana Sayer, and George Matheson. 2003. "When Does Gender Trump Money? Bargaining and Time in Household Work." *American Journal of Sociology* 109:186–214.

Black, Dan, Gary Gates, Seth Sanders, and Lowell Taylor. 2000. "Demographics of the Gay and Lesbian Population in the United States: Evidence from Available Systematic Data Sources." *Demography* 37:139–54.

Black, Sandra E., and Elizabeth Brainerd. 2004. "Importing Equality? The Impact of Globalization on Gender Discrimination." *Industrial and Labor Relations Review* 57:540–59.

Blackwell, James E. 1985. *The Black Community: Diversity and Unity.* New York: Harper & Row.

Blair-Loy, Mary, and Jerry A. Jacobs. 2003. "Globalization, Work Hours, and the Care Deficit Among Stockbrokers." *Gender & Society* 17:230–49.

Blau, Francine D. 1978. "The Data on Women Workers, Past, Present, and Future." Pp. 29–62 in *Women Working,* edited by A. H. Stromberg and S. Harkess. Palo Alto, CA: Mayfield.

Blau, Francine D. 1984. "Occupational Segregation and Labor Market Discrimination." Pp. 117–43 in *Sex Segregation in the Workplace,* edited by B. F. Reskin. Washington, D.C.: National Academy Press.

Blau, Francine D., and Marianne A. Ferber. 1986. *The Economics of Women, Men, and Work.* Englewood Cliffs, NJ: Prentice Hall.

Blau, Francine D., and Carol L. Jusenius. 1976. "Economists' Approaches to Sex Segregation in the Labor Market: An Appraisal." *Signs: Journal of Women in Culture and Society* 1:181–99.

Blau, Judith R., and Peter M. Blau. 1982. "The Cost of Inequality: Metropolitan Structure and Violent Crime." *American Sociological Review* 47:114–29.

Blau, Peter M., and Otis Dudley Duncan. 1967. *The American Occupational Structure.* New York: John Wiley & Sons.

Blauner, Robert. 1964. *Alienation and Freedom: The Factory Worker and His Industry.* Chicago: University of Chicago Press.

Blauner, Robert. 1972. *Racial Oppression in America.* New York: Harper & Row.

Block, Fred. 1977. "The Ruling Class Does Not Rule: Notes on the Marxist Theory of the State." *Socialist Revolution* 7:6–28.

Bloom, Jack M. 1987. *Class, Race & the Civil Rights Movement.* Bloomington, IN: Indiana University Press.

Bluestone, Barry. 1977. "The Characteristics of Marginal Industries." Pp. 97–102 in *Problems in Political Economy: An Urban Perspective,* edited by D. M. Gordon. Lexington, MA: D.C. Heath.

Blumberg, Rae Lesser. 1978. *Stratification: Socioeconomic and Sexual Inequality.* Dubuque, IA: William C. Brown.

Blumberg, Rae Lesser. 1984. "A General Theory of Gender Stratification." Pp. 23–101 in *Sociological Theory,* edited by R. Collins. San Francisco, CA: Jossey-Bass.

Blumberg, Rhoda Lois. 1984. *Civil Rights: The 1960s Freedom Struggle.* Boston: Twayne.

Boer, J. Tom, Manuel Pastor, Jr., James L. Sadd, and Lori D. Snyder. 1997. "Is There Environmental Racism? The Demographics of Hazardous Waste in Los Angeles County." *Social Science Quarterly* 78:793–810.

Bonacich, Edna. 1976. "Advanced Capitalism and Black/White Relations in the United States: A Split Labor Market Interpretation." *American Sociological Review* 41:34–51.

Bonacich, Edna. 1980. "Class Approaches to Ethnicity and Race." *Insurgent Sociologist* 10(2).

Bonacich, Edna. 1985. "Class Approaches to Ethnicity and Race." Pp. 62–77 in *Majority and Minority: The Dynamics of Race and Ethnicity in American Life,* edited by N. R. Yetman. Boston: Allyn & Bacon.

Bonilla-Silva, Eduardo. 2004. "From Bi-Racial to Tri-Racial: The Emergence of A New Racial Stratification System in the United States." Pp. 224–39 in *Skin Deep: How Race and Complexion Matter in the "Color-Blind" Era,* edited by C. Herring, V. Keith, and H. D. Horton. Chicago: University of Illinois.

Boone, Christopher G., and Ali Modarres. 1999. "Creating a Toxic Neighborhood in Los Angeles County." *Urban Affairs Review* 35:163–87.

Boorstin, Daniel J. 1967. *The Americans.* New York: Vintage.

Bottomore, Tom B. 1964. *Elites and Society.* Baltimore: Penguin.

Bottomore, Tom B. 1966. *Classes in Modern Society.* New York: Pantheon.

Bottomore, Tom B., and Maximilien Rubel, eds. 1956. *Karl Marx: Selected Writings in Sociology and Social Philosophy.* New York: McGraw-Hill.

Bourdieu, Pierre. 1977a. "Cultural Reproduction and Social Reproduction." Pp. 487–510 in *Power and Ideology in Education,* edited by J. Karabel and A. H. Halsey. New York: Oxford University Press.

Bourdieu, Pierre. 1977b. *Outline of a Theory of Practice.* Cambridge: Cambridge University Press.

Bourdieu, Pierre. 1990. *The Logic of Practice.* Stanford, CA: Stanford University Press.

Bourdieu, Pierre, and Loic J. C. Wacquant. 1992. *An Invitation to Reflexive Sociology*. Cambridge, MA: Polity Press.

Bowles, Samuel, and Herbert Gintis. 1976. *Schooling in Capitalist America*. New York: Basic Books.

Bowles, Samuel, and Herbert Gintis. 2002. "*Schooling in Capitalist America* Revisited." *Sociology of Education* 75:1–18.

Bowman, Phillip J., Ray Muhammad, and Mosi Ifatunji. 2004. "Skin Tone, Class, and Racial Attitudes Among African Americans." Pp. 128–58 in *Skin Deep: How Race and Complexion Matter in the "Color-Blind" Era*, edited by C. Herring, V. Keith, and H. D. Horton. Chicago: University of Illinois.

Box, Steven. 1983. *Power, Crime, and Mystification*. London: Tavistock.

Braithwaite, John. 1981. "The Myth of Social Class and Criminality Reconsidered." *American Sociological Review* 46:36–57.

Bremner, Robert H. 1956. *From the Depths: The Discovery of Poverty in the United States*. New York: New York University Press.

Brett, Regina. February 5, 1989. "Myths Disguise Extent, Severity of problem." *Akron Beacon Journal*, p. A7.

Brody, David, ed. 1971. *The American Labor Movement*. New York: Harper & Row.

Brody, David. 1980. *Workers in Industrial America: Essays on the Twentieth Century Struggle*. New York: Oxford University Press.

Brooke, James. October 13, 1998. "Gay Man Dies from Attack, Fanning Outrage and Debate." *New York Times*, pp. A1, A17.

Brooks, John. 1979. *Showing Off in America*. Boston: Little, Brown.

Brown, B. Bradford, and Mary Jane Lohr. 1987. "Peer-Group Affiliation and Adolescent Self-Esteem: An Integration of Ego-Identity and Symbolic-Interaction Theories." *Journal of Personality and Social Psychology* 52:47–55.

Browne, Irene, and Joya Misra. 2003. "The Intersection of Gender and Race in the Labor Market." Pp. 487–513 in *Annual Review of Sociology*, edited by K. S. Cook and J. Hagan. Palo Alto, CA: Annual Reviews.

Bruchac, Joseph. 2004. "Indian Renaissance." *National Geographic* 206:77–93.

Bruins, Jan. 1999. "Social Power and Influence Tactics: A Theoretical Introduction." *Journal of Social Issues* 55:7–14.

Brunsma, David L., and Kerry Ann Rockquemore. 2002. "What Does 'Black' Mean? Exploring the Epistemological Stranglehold of Racial Categorization." *Critical Sociology* 28:101–21.

Bullard, Robert D. 1983. "Solid Waste Sites and the Black Houston Community." *Sociological Inquiry* 53:273–88.

Bullock, Heather E., and Wendy M. Limbert. 2003. "Scaling the Socioeconomic Ladder: Low-Income Women's Perceptions of Class Status and Opportunity." *Journal of Social Issues* 59:693–709.

Burke, Peter, and Austin Turk. 1975. "Factors Affecting Postarrest Dispositions: A Model for Analysis." *Social Problems* 22:313–32.

Burr, Jeffrey A., John T. Hartman, and Donald W. Matteson. 1999. "Black Suicide in the U.S. Metropolitan Areas: An Examination of the Racial Inequality and Social Integration-Regulation Hypotheses." *Social Forces* 77:1049–81.

Button, James W., Barbara A. Rienzo, and Kenneth D. Wald. 1997. *Private Lives, Public Conflicts*. Washington, D.C.: Congressional Quarterly Press.

Bye, Lynn, and Jamie Partridge. 2003. "Factors Affecting Mental Illness Hospitalization Rates: Analysis of State-Level Panel Data." *The Social Science Journal* 40:33–47.

Cain, Glen G. December 1976. "The Challenge of Segmented Labor Market Theories to Orthodox Theory." *Journal of Economic Literature* 14: 1215–57.

Cairns, Robert B., and Beverley D. Cairns. 1994. *Lifelines and Risks: Pathways of Youth in Our Time*. Cambridge: Cambridge University Press.

Campaign Financing Monitoring Project, Common Cause. 1974. *1972 Federal Campaign Finances Interest Groups and Political Parties*. Washington, D.C.: Common Cause.

Campo-Flores, and Howard Fineman. 2005. "A Latin Power Surge." *Newsweek*, May 30:25–31.

Cancian, Maria. 2001. "Rhetoric and Reality of Work-Based Welfare Reform." *Social Work* 46:309–14.

Cancian, Maria, and Daniel R. Meyer. 2004. "Alternative Measures of Economic Success among TANF Participants: Avoiding Poverty, Hardship, and Dependence on Public Assistance." *Journal of Policy Analysis and Management* 23:531–48.

Caner, Asena, and Edward N. Wolff. 2004. "Asset Poverty in the United States, 1984–99: Evidence from the Panel Study of Income Dynamics." *Review of Income and Wealth*, Series 50:493–518.

Cantor, David, and Kenneth C. Land. 1985. "Unemployment and Crime Rates in the Post-World War II United States: A Theoretical and Empirical Analysis." *American Sociological Review* 50:317–32.

Cantor, Muriel G. 1987. "Popular Culture and the Portrayal of Women: Content and Control." Pp. 190–214 in *Analyzing Gender*, edited by Beth B. Hess and Myra Marx Ferree. Newbury Park, CA: Sage.

Caplan, Pat, ed. 1987. *The Cultural Construction of Sexuality*. London: Tavistock.

Carawan, Guy, and Candie Carawan. 1975. *Voices from the Mountains*. New York: Knopf.

Carli, Linda L. 1999. "Gender, Interpersonal Power, and Social Influence." *Journal of Social Issues* 55:81–99.

Carliner, Michael S. 1987. "Homelessness: A Housing Problem?" Pp. 119–28 in *The Homeless in Contemporary Society*, edited by R. D. Bingham, R. E. Green, and S. B. White. Newbury Park, CA: Sage.

Carlson, Lewis H., and George A. Colburn. 1972. *In Their Place: White America Defines Her Minorities 1850–1950*. New York: John Wiley & Sons.

Carmichael, Stokely, and Charles V. Hamilton. 1967. *Black Power*. New York: Vintage.

Carr, Debovah. 2005. "Political Polls." *Contexts* 4:32.

Carter, Prudence L. 2003. "'Black' Cultural Capital, Status Positioning, and Schooling Conflicts for Low-Income African American Youth." *Social Problems* 50:136–55.

Case, Mary Anne C. 1995. "Disaggregating Gender from Sex and Sexual Orientation: The Effeminate Man in the Law and Feminist Jurisprudence." *Yale Law Journal* 105:2–3.

Cash, Thomas F., and Patricia E. Henry. 1995. "Women's Body Images: The Results of a National Survey in the U.S.A." *Sex Roles* 33:19–28.

Casper, Lynne M., and Loretta E. Bass. 1998. *Voting and Registration in the Election of November 1996*. Current Population Reports, Series P20, No. 504. Washington, D.C.: U.S. Government Printing Office.

Caspi, Avshalom, Terrie E. Moffitt, Bradley E. Entner Wright, and Phil A. Silva. 1998. "Early Failure in the Labor Market: Childhood and Adolescent Predictors of Unemployment in the Transition to Adulthood." *American Sociological Review* 63:424–51.

Catanzarite, Lisa. 2003. "Race-Gender Composition and Occupational Pay Degradation." *Social Problems* 50:14–37.

Caudill, Harry M. 1962. *Night Comes to the Cumberlands: A Biography of a Depressed Area*. Boston: Little, Brown.

Cauthen, Kenneth. 1987. *The Passion for Equality*. Totowa, NJ: Rowman & Littlefield.

Center for Mental Health Services and National Institution of Mental Health. 1992. *Mental Health, United States, 1992*. Ronald W. Manderscheid and Mary Anne Sonnenschein, eds. DHHS Pub. No. (SMA) 92–1942. Washington, D.C.: U.S. Government Printing Office.

Chafe, William H. 1977. *Women and Equality: Changing Patterns in American Culture*. New York: Oxford University Press.

Chafetz, Janet Saltzman. 1984. *Sex and Advantage: A Comparative, Macro-Structural Theory of Sex Stratification*. Totowa, NJ: Rowman & Allanheld.

Chafetz, Janet Saltzman. 1988. *Feminist Sociology: An Overview of Contemporary Theories*. Itasca, IL: F. E. Peacock.

Chakravarti, Anand. 1983. "Some Aspects of Inequality in Rural India: A Sociological Perspective." Pp. 129–81 in *Equality and Inequality: Theory and Practice*, edited by A. Beteille. Delhi: Oxford University Press.

Chambliss, William J. 1999. *Power, Politics, and Crime*. Boulder, CO: Westview.

Charles, Camille Zubrinsky. 2003. "The Dynamics of Racial Residential Segregation." Pp. 167–207 in *Annual Review of Sociology*, edited by K. S. Cook and J. Hagan. Palo Alto, CA: Annual Reviews.

Children's Defense Fund. 1999. *Extreme Child Poverty Rises by More than 400,000 in One Year, New Analysis Shows*. Washington, D.C.: Author.

Chinn, Menzie D., and Robert W. Fairlie. 2005. "Assessing the Global Digital Divide." *La Follette Policy Report* 15:1–2, 10–14.

Chira, Susan. February 12, 1992. "Bias against Girls Is Found Rife in Schools, with Lasting Damage." *The New York Times*, pp. A1, B6.

Chiricos, T. G. 1987. "Rates of Crime and Unemployment: An Analysis of Aggregate Research Evidence." *Social Problems* 34:187–212.

Chiricos, T. G., and G. P. Waldo. 1975. "Socioeconomic Status and Criminal Sentencing: An Empirical Assessment of a Conflict Proposition." *American Sociological Review* 40:753–72.

Chiricos, Ted, Ranee McEntire, and Marc Gertz. 2001. "Perceived Racial and Ethnic Composition of Neighborhood and Perceived Risk of Crime." *Social Problems* 48:322–40.

Chiricos, Ted, Kelly Welch, and Marc Gertz. 2004. "Racial Typification of Crime and Support for Punitive Measures." *Criminology* 42:359–89.

Chow, Esther Ngan-ling. 2003. "Gender Matters: Studying Globalization and Social Change in the 21st Century." *International Sociology* 18:443–60.

Cigler, Allan J., and Burdett A. Loomis, eds. 1995. *Interest Group Politics*. Washington, D.C.: Congressional Quarterly.

Clarke, Stevens H., and Gary G. Koch. 1976. "The Influence of Income and Other Factors on Whether Criminal Defendants Go to Prison." *Law and Society Review* 11:57–92.

Clawson, Dan, and Mary Ann Clawson. 1999. "What Has Happened to the U.S. Labor Movement? Union Decline and Renewal." Pp. 95–119 in *Annual Review of Sociology*, edited by K. S. Cook and J. Hagan. Palo Alto, CA: Annual Reviews.

Cleary, Paul D., and David Mechanic. 1983. "Sex Differences in Psychological Distress among Married People." *Journal of Health and Social Behavior* 24:111–21.

Clinard, Marshall B. 1946. "Criminological Theories of Violations of Wartime Regulations." *American Sociological Review* 11:258–70.

Cockerham, William C., Gerhard Kunz, Guenther Leuschen, and Joe L. Spaeth. 1986. "Symptoms, Social Stratification and Self-Responsibility for Health in the United States and West Germany." *Social Science & Medicine* 22:1263–71.

Cockerham, William C., Guenther Leuschen, Gerhard Kunz, and Joe L. Spaeth. 1986. "Social Stratification and Self-Management of Health." *Journal of Health and Social Behavior* 27:1–14.

Cohen, Lisa E., Joseph P. Broschak, and Heather A. Haveman. 1998. "And Then There Were More? The Effect of Organizational Sex Composition on the Hiring and Promotion of Managers." *American Sociological Review* 63:711–27.

Cohen, Philip N., and Matt L. Huffman. 2003. "Occupational Segregation and the Devaluation of Women's Work Across U.S. Labor Markets." *Social Forces* 81:881–908.

Cohen, Sharon, and Deborah Hastings. June 2, 2002. "Exonerated, 110 Inmates Unprepared." *Akron Beacon Journal*, pp. A1, A10.

Cole, Elizabeth R., and Safiya R. Omari. 2003. "Race, Class and the Dilemmas of Upward Mobility for African Americans." *Journal of Social Issues* 59:785–802.

Coleman, James S. 1982. *The Asymmetric Society.* Syracuse, NY: Syracuse University Press.

Collins, Chuck, Betsy Leondar-Wright, and Holly Sklar. 1999. *Shifting Fortunes.* Boston: United for a Fair Economy.

Collins, Patricia Hill. 1990. *Black Feminist Theory.* Boston, MA: Unwin Hyman.

Collins, Randall. 1971. "Functional and Conflict Theories of Educational Stratification." *American Sociological Review* 36:1002–19.

Collins, Randall. 1975. *Conflict Sociology: Toward an Explanatory Science.* New York: Academic Press.

Collins, Randall, ed. 1984. *Sociological Theory 1984.* San Francisco: Jossey-Bass.

Collins, Randall. 1986. *Weberian Sociological Theory.* Cambridge and New York: Cambridge University Press.

Collins, Randall. 1988. *Theoretical Sociology.* New York: Harcourt Brace Jovanovich.

Collins, Randall. 2000. "Situational Stratification: A Micro-Macro Theory of Inequality." *Sociological Theory* 18:17–43.

Collins, Sharon. 1983. "The Making of the Black Middle Class." *Social Problems* 30:369–81.

Collins, Sharon. 1993. "Blacks on the Bubble." *The Sociological Quarterly* 34:429–47.

Conley, Dalton. 2000. *Honky.* Berkeley: University of California.

Connell, R. W. 2005. "Masculinities and Globalization." Pp. 36–48 in *Gender Through the Prism of Difference,* edited by M. B. Zinn, P. Hondagneu-Sotelo, and M. A. Messner. New York: Oxford.

Connolly, William E. 1969. *The Bias of Pluralism.* New York: Lieber-Atherton.

Cookson, Peter W., Jr., and Caroline Hodges Persell. 1985. *Preparing for Power: America's Elite Boarding Schools.* New York: Basic Books.

Coontz, Stephanie, and Peta Henderson, eds. 1986. *Women's Work, Men's Property: The Origins of Gender and Class.* London: Verso.

Corcoran, M. 1995. "Rags to Rags: Poverty and Mobility in the United States." Pp. 237–67 in *Annual Review of Sociology,* edited by J. Hagan and K. S. Cook. Palo Alto, CA: Annual Reviews.

Corcoran, Mary, Sandra K. Danziger, Ariel Kalil, and Kristin S. Seefeldt. 2000. "How Welfare Reform Is Affecting Women's Work." Pp. 241–69 in *Annual Review of Sociology,* edited by K. S. Cook and J. Hagan. Palo Alto, CA: Annual Reviews.

Coreil, Jeannine, and Patricia A. Marshall. 1982. "Locus of Illness Control: A Cross Cultural Study." *Human Organizations* 41:131–38.

Coser, Lewis A. 1967. *Continuities in the Study of Social Conflict.* New York: The Free Press.

Coser, Lewis A. 1971. *Masters of Sociological Thought.* New York: Harcourt Brace Jovanovich.

Cott, Nancy F. 1986. "Feminist Theory and Feminist Movements: The Past Before Us." Pp. 49–62 in *What Is Feminism?* edited by J. Mitchell and A. Oakley. New York: Pantheon.

Cott, Nancy F. 1987. *The Grounding of Modern Feminism.* New Haven, CT: Yale University Press.

Cotter, David A., Joan M. Hermsen, and Reeve Vanneman. 2003. "The Effects of Occupational Gender Segregation Across Race." *Sociological Quarterly* 44:17–36.

Counts, George S. 1925. "The Social Status of Occupations: A Problem in Vocational Guidance." *School Review* 33:16–27.

Coverdill, James E. 1988. "The Dual Economy and Size Differences in Earnings." *Social Forces* 66:970–93.

Coverdill, James E. 1998. "Personal Contacts and Post-Hire Job Outcomes: Theoretical and Empirical Notes on the Significance of Matching Methods." *Research in Social Stratification and Mobility* 16:247–69.

Cox, Oliver C. 1942. "The Modern Caste School of Race Relations." *Social Forces* 21:218–26.

Cox, Oliver C. 1945. "Race and Caste: A Distinction." *American Journal of Sociology* 50:360–68.

Cox, Oliver C. 1948. *Caste, Class and Race.* New York: Monthly Review Press.

Cox, Oliver C. 1959. *The Foundations of Capitalism.* New York: Philosophical Library.

Cox, Oliver C. 1964. *Capitalism as a System.* New York: Monthly Review Press.

Cox, Oliver C. 1976. *Race Relations: Elements and Social Dynamics.* Detroit: Wayne State University Press.

Craig, Kellina M. 2002. "Examining Hate-Motivated Aggression: A Review of the Social Psychological Literature on Hate Crimes as a Distinct Form of Aggression." *Aggression and Violent Behavior* 7:85–101.

Crandell, N. Fredric, and Marc J. Wallace, Jr. 1998. *Work & Rewards in the Virtual Workplace.* New York: American Management Association.

Crane, Diane. 2000. *Fashion and Its Social Agendas.* Chicago: University of Chicago.

Crompton, Rosemary, and Gareth Jones. 1984. *White Collar Proletariat: Deskilling and Gender in Clerical Work.* Philadelphia: Temple University Press.

Crutchfield, Robert D. 1995. "Ethnicity, Labor Markets, and Crime." Pp. 194–211 in *Ethnicity, Race, and Crime,* edited by D. F. Hawkins. Albany: State University of New York Press.

Cunningham, Frank. 1975–1976. "Pluralism and Class Struggle." *Science and Society* 39:385–416.

Curran, Debra A. 1983. "Judicial Discretion and Defendant's Sex." *Criminology* 21:41–58.

Currie, Elliott, and Jerome H. Skolnick. 1988. *America's Problems: Social Issues and Public Policy.* Glenview, IL: Scott, Foresman.

Dahrendorf, Ralf. 1958a. "Out of Utopia: Toward a Reorientation of Sociological Analysis." *American Journal of Sociology* 64:115–27.

Dahrendorf, Ralf. 1958b. "Toward a Theory of Social Conflict." *Journal of Conflict Resolution* 2:170–83.

Dahrendorf, Ralf. 1959. *Class and Class Conflict in Industrial Society.* Stanford, CA: Stanford University Press.

Dahrendorf, Ralf. 1970. "On the Origin of Inequality Among Men." Pp. 3–30 in *The Logic of Social Hierarchies,* edited by E. O. Laumann, P. M. Siegel, and R. W. Hodge. Chicago: Markham.

D'Alessio, Stewart J., and Lisa Stolzenberg. 1993. "Socioeconomic Status and the Sentencing of the Traditional Offender." *Journal of Criminal Justice* 21:71–74.

Dale, Maryclaire. May 13, 2005. "Pension Cuts Hit Many Retirees." *Akron Beacon Journal,* pp. D1–D2.

Dalton, Harlan. 2002. "Failing to See." Pp. 15–18 in *White Privilege,* edited by P. S. Rothenberg. New York: Worth Publishers.

Damiano, Christin M. 1998/1999. "Lesbian Baiting in the Military: Institutionalized Sexual Harassment Under 'Don't Ask, Don't Tell, Don't Pursue.' " *American University Journal of Gender, Social Policy & the Law* 7:499–522.

Daniels, Glynis, and Samantha Friedman. 1999. "Spatial Inequality and the Distribution of Industrial Toxic Releases: Evidence from the 1990 TRI." *Social Science Quarterly* 80:244–62.

Danziger, Sheldon, and David Wheeler. 1975. "The Economics of Crime: Punishment or Income Distribution." *Review of Social Economy* 33:113–31.

Danziger, Sheldon H., Robert H. Haveman, and Robert D. Plotnick. 1986. "Antipoverty Policy: Effects on the Poor and the Nonpoor." Pp. 50–77 in *Fighting Poverty: What Works and What Doesn't,* edited by S. H. Danziger and D. H. Weinberg. Cambridge, MA: Harvard University Press.

Darling, Sharon. 1984. "Illiteracy: An Everyday Problem for Millions." *Appalachia* 18:22–23.

Das, Man Singh, and F. Gene Acuff. 1970. "The Caste Controversy in Comparative Perspective: India and the United States." *International Journal of Comparative Sociology* 11:48–54.

D'Augelli, Anthony R. 1998. "Developmental Implications of Victimization of Lesbian, Gay, and Bisexual Youths." Pp. 187–210 in *Stigma and Sexual Orientation,* edited by G. M. Herek. Thousand Oaks, CA: Sage.

D'Augelli, A. R., and A. H. Grossman. 2001. "Disclosure of Sexual Orientation, Victimization, and Mental Health among Lesbian, Gay, and Bisexual Older Adults." *Journal of Interpersonal Violence* 16:1008–27.

Davidson, Chandler, and Charles M. Gaitz. 1974. "Are the Poor Different? A Comparison of Work Behavior and Attitude among the Urban Poor and Nonpoor." *Social Problems* 22:229–45.

Davies, James C. 1969. "The J-Curve of Rising and Declining Satisfactions as a Cause of Some Great Revolutions and a Contained Rebellion." In *Violence in America: Historical and Comparative Perspectives,* edited by H. D. Graham and T. R. Gurr. Washington, D.C.: National Commission on the Causes and Prevention of Violence.

Davies, James C. 1971. "Introduction." Pp. 3–9 in *When Men Revolt and Why,* editing by J. C. Davies. New York: The Free Press.

Davis, Angela. 1981. *Women, Race and Class.* New York: Random House.

Davis, James Allan, and Tom W. Smith. 1989. *General Social Surveys, 1972–1989.* Principal Investigator, James A. Davis; Director and Co-Principal Investigator, Tom W. Smith. NORC ed. Chicago: National Opinion Research Center, producer;

Storrs, CT: The Roper Center for Public Opinion Research, University of Connecticut, distributor.

Davis, James Allan, and Tom W. Smith. 1994. *General Social Surveys, 1972–1994*. Principal Investigator, James A. Davis; Director and Co-Principal Investigator, Tom W. Smith. NORC ed. Chicago: National Opinion Research Center, producer; Storrs, CT: The Roper Center for Public Opinion Research, University of Connecticut, distributor.

Davis, James Allan, and Tom W. Smith. 1996. *General Social Surveys, 1972–1996*. Principal Investigator, James A. Davis; Co-Principal Investigator, Tom W. Smith. NORC ed. Chicago: National Opinion Research Center, producer; Storrs, CT: The Roper Center for Public Opinion Research, University of Connecticut, distributor.

Davis, John A. 1974. "Justification for No Obligation: View of Black Males Toward Crime and the Criminal Law." *Issues in Criminology* 9:69–87.

Davis, Kingsley. 1948–1949. *Human Society*. New York: Macmillan.

Davis, Kingsley, and Wilbert E. Moore. 1945. "Some Principles of Stratification." *American Sociological Review* 10:242–49.

Davis, Mike. 1992a. *City of Quartz*. New York: Vintage.

Davis, Mike. June 1, 1992b. "In L. A., Burning All Illusions." *The Nation*, pp. 743–46.

Davis, Mike. Summer 1992c. "The L. A. Inferno." *Socialist Review*, pp. 57–80.

de Tocqueville, Alexis. 1969. Quoted in *Democracy in America*, edited by J. P. Mayer. New York: Doubleday.

DeFreitas, Gregory. 1993. "Unionization among Racial and Ethnic Minorities." *Industrial and Labor Relations Review* 46:284–301.

Della Fave, Richard. 1980. "The Meek Shall Not Inherit the Earth: Self-Evaluation and the Legitimacy of Stratification." *American Sociological Review* 45:955–71.

Demuth, Stephen, and Darrell Steffensmeier. 2004. "The Impact of Gender and Race-Ethnicity in the Pretrial Release Process." *Social Problems* 51:222–42.

Department of Workforce Development. June 22, 1999. *Wisconsin Works Overview*. Madison, WI: Author.

Derber, Charles. 2000. *Corporation Nation*. New York: St. Martin's Griffin.

Devine, Joel A., Joseph F. Sheley, and M. Dwayne Smith. 1988. "Macroeconomic and Social-Control Policy Influences on Crime Rate Changes. 1948–1985". *American Sociological Review* 53:407–20.

DeVos, George A., and Hiroshi Wagatsuma, eds. 1966. *Japan's Invisible Race: Caste in Culture and Personality*. Berkeley: University of California Press.

DeVos, George A., and William O. Wetherall. 1983. *Japan's Minorities: Burakumin, Koreans, Ainu and Okinawans*. London: Minority Rights Group.

"Did Milken Get Off Too Lightly?" May 7, 1990. *U.S. News and World Report*, pp. 22–24.

Dionne, E. J., Jr. April 18, 1989. "Poor Paying More for Their Shelter." *New York Times*, p. A18.

Dionne, E. J. June 13, 2004. " 'E Pluribus Unum'?" *Akron Beacon Journal*, p. B2.

DiPlacido, Joanne. 1998. "Minority Stress among Lesbians, Gay Men, and Bisexuals." Pp. 138–59 in *Stigma and Sexual Orientation*, edited by G. M. Herek. Thousand Oaks, CA: Sage.

DiPrete, Thomas, and Margaret L. Krecker. 1991. "Occupational Linkages and Job Mobility within and across Organizations." Pp. 91–131 in *Research in Social Stratification and Mobility*, vol. 10, edited by R. Althauser and M. Wallace. Greenwich, CT: JAI Press.

DiPrete, Thomas A., and Whitman T. Soule. 1988. "Gender and Promotion in Segmented Job Ladder Systems." *American Sociological Review* 53:26–40.

Dirks, Danielle. 2004. "Sexual Revictimization and Retraumatization of Women in Prison." *Women's Studies Quarterly* 32:102–15.

Disney, Jennifer Leigh, and Joyce Gelb. 2000. "Feminist Organizational 'Success' The State of U.S. Women's Movement Organizations in the 1990s." *Women & Politics* 21:39–76.

DiversityBusiness. 2005. Top 500 Women Owned Businesses Announced. Available at http://div2000.com/Resources/DivLists/2003/Women/2003.

Dixon, Jo, Cynthia Gordon, and Tasnim Khomusi. 1995. "Sexual Symmetry in Psychiatric Diagnosis." *Social Problems* 42:429–46.

Dobratz, Betty A., and Stephanie L. Shanks-Meile. 1997. *White Power, White Pride*. New York: Twayne.

Doeringer, Peter B., and Michael J. Piori. 1971. *Internal Labor Markets and Manpower Analysis*. Lexington, MA: D.C. Heath.

Dolgoff, Ralph, and Donald Feldstein. 1984. *Understanding Social Welfare*. New York: Longman.

Dollar, David, and Aart Kraay. 2004. "Trade, Growth, and Poverty." *The Economic Journal* 114: F22–F49.

Dollard, John. 1957. *Caste and Class in a Southern Town*. Garden City, NY: Doubleday.

Domhoff, G. William. 1971. *The Higher Circles*. New York: Vintage.

Domhoff, G. William. 1998. *Who Rules America?* Mountain View, CA: Mayfield.

Dominguez, Silvia, and Celeste Watkins. 2003. "Creating Networks for Survival and Mobility: Social Capital among African-American and

Latin-American Low-Income Mothers." *Social Problems* 50:111–35.

Donohue, John J. III, and Steven D. Levitt. 2001. "The Impact of Race on Policing and Arrest." *Journal of Law and Economics* 44:367–94.

Dowd, Mavreen. May 5, 2005. "Ugly Duckling Has No Chance." *Akron Beacon Journal.* p. B2.

Dublin, Thomas. 1979. *Women at Work.* New York: Columbia University Press.

Dubofsky, Melvyn. 1975. *Industrialism and the American Workers, 1865–1920.* Arlington Heights, IL: AHM Publishing.

DuBois, W. E. B. 1973. *The Philadelphia Negro.* Millwood, NY: Kraus-Thompson.

Duke, James T. 1976. *Conflict and Power in Social Life.* Provo, UT: Brigham Young University Press.

Duncan, Cynthia M., ed. 1992. *Rural Poverty in America.* New York: Auburn House.

Duncan, Cynthia M. 1999. *Worlds Apart.* New Haven, CT: Yale.

Duncan, Greg J. 1984. *Years of Poverty, Years of Plenty: The Changing Economic Fortunes of American Workers and Families.* Ann Arbor, MI: Institute for Social Research, University of Michigan.

Duncan, Greg J., Jeanne Brooks-Gunn, W. Jean Yeung, and Judith R. Smith. 1998. "How Much Does Childhood Poverty Affect the Life Chances of Children?" *American Sociological Review* 63:406–23.

Duncan, Otis Dudley. 1961. "A Socioeconomic Index for All Occupations." Chapter 6 in *Occupations and Social Status,* edited by Albert J. Reiss, Jr. New York: The Free Press.

Dunlop, John T. 1987. "The Development of Labor Organization: A Theoretical Framework." Pp. 12–22 in *Theories of the Labor Movement,* edited by S. Larson and B. Nissen. Detroit: Wayne State University Press.

Durant, Thomas J., Jr., and Joyce S. Louden. 1986. "The Black Middle Class in America: Historical and Contemporary Perspectives." *Phylon* 47:253–63.

Durkheim, Emile. 1933. *The Division of Labor in Society.* New York: The Free Press.

Dye, Thomas R. 2002. *Who's Running America? The Bush Restoration.* Upper Saddle River, NJ: Prentice Hall.

Eakins, Barbara W., and R. Gene Eakins. 1978. *Sex Differences in Human Communication.* Boston: Houghton Mifflin.

Eckert, Penelope. 1989. *Jocks & Burnouts.* New York: Teachers College Press.

"The Economic Crisis of Urban America." May 18, 1992. *BusinessWeek,* pp. 38–43.

Edelman, Murray, 1977. *Political Language: Words That Succeed and Policies That Fail.* New York: Academic Press.

Eder, Donna. 1995. *School Talk: Gender and Adolescent School Culture.* New Brunswick, NJ: Rutgers University Press.

Edwards, Alba M. 1943. *Comparative Occupations Statistics for the United States.* Washington, D.C.: U.S. Government Printing Office.

Edwards, Richard. 1979. *Contested Terrain: The Transformation of the Workplace in the Twentieth Century.* New York: Basic Books.

Ehrenreich, Barbara. September 7, 1986. "Heading for a Two-Tier Society." *Akron Beacon Journal,* p. F1.

Ehrenreich, Barbara. 2001. *Nickel and Dimed.* New York: Metropolitan Books.

Ehrenreich, Barbara, and Deirdre English. 1981. "The Sexual Politics of Sickness." Pp. 327–50 in *The Sociology of Health and Illness: Critical Perspectives.* New York: St. Martin's Press.

Ehrenreich, Barbara, and Arlie Russell Hochschild. 2005. "Global Woman." Pp. 49–55 in *Gender Through the Prism of Difference,* edited by M. B. Zinn, P. Hondagneu-Sotelo, and M. A. Messner. New York: Oxford.

Eisenstein, Hester. 2001. "The Broader Picture." *Monthly Review* 53(5):49–52.

Eisenstein, Zillah. 1977/1990. "Constructing a Theory of Capitalist Patriarchy and Socialist Feminism." *Insurgent Sociologist* 7(1977):3–17. Reprinted on pp. 114–45 in *Women, Class, and the Feminist Imagination: A Socialist-Feminist Reader,* edited by K. V. Hansen and I. J. Philipson. Philadelphia: Temple University Press.

Eisenstein, Zillah. 1981. *The Radical Future of Liberal Feminism.* New York: Longman.

Eisler, Benita, ed. 1977. *The Lowell Offering.* Philadelphia: J. B. Lippincott.

Eitle, David, Steward J. D'Alessio, and Lisa Stolzenberg. 2002. "Racial Threat and Social Control: A Test of the Political, Economic, and Threat of Black Crime Hypotheses." *Social Forces* 81:557–76.

Elder, Glen H., and Jeffrey K. Liker. 1982. "Hard Times in Women's Lives: Historical Influences across Forty Years." *American Journal of Sociology* 88:241–69.

Elkins, Stanley. 1959. *Slavery: A Problem in American Institutional and Intellectual Life.* Chicago: University of Chicago Press.

Eller, Ronald D. 1982. *Miners, Millhands, and Mountaineers: Industrialization of the Appalachian South, 1880–1930.* Knoxville, TN: University of Tennessee Press.

Elliott, James R., and Ryan Smith. 2004. "Race, Gender, and Workplace Power." *American Sociological Review* 69:365–86.

Ellwood, David T., and Mary Jo Bane. 1984. "The Impact of AFDC on Family Structure and Living

Arrangements." Working paper prepared for the U.S. Department of Health and Human Services under grant no. 92A-82.

Ellwood, David T., and Lawrence H. Summers. 1986. "Poverty in America: Is Welfare the Answer or the Problem?" Pp. 78–105 in *Fighting Poverty: What Works and What Doesn't*, edited by S. H. Danziger and D. H. Weinberg. Cambridge, MA: Harvard University Press.

Elman, Cheryl, and Angela M. O'Rand. 2004. "The Race Is to the Swift: Socioeconomic Origins, Adult Education, and Wage Attainment." *American Journal of Sociology* 110:123–60.

Engels, Frederick. 1973. "The Origin of the Family, Private Property and the State." Pp. 204–334 in *Karl Marx and Frederick Engels: Selected Works*. Moscow: Progress Publishers.

England, Paula. 1984. "Socioeconomic Explanations of Job Segregation." Pp. 28–46 in *Comparable Worth and Wage Discrimination*, edited by H. Remick. Philadelphia: Temple University Press.

England, Paula, and Dana Dunn. 1985. "Why Men Dominate." *The Women's Review of Books* 2:14–15.

England, Paula, and George Farkas. 1986. *Households, Employment, and Gender: A Social, Economic and Demographic View*. New York: Aldine.

England, Paula, George Farkas, Barbara Kilbourne, and Thomas Dou. 1988. "Explaining Occupational Sex Segregation and Wages: Findings from a Model with Fixed Effects." *American Sociological Review* 53:544–58.

Epstein, Barbara. 2001. "What Happened to the Women's Movement?" *Monthly Review* 53:1–13.

Erikson, Kai T. 1976. *Everything in Its Path*. New York: Simon & Schuster.

Erikson, Robert, John H. Goldthorpe, and Lucienne Portocarero. 1983. "Intergenerational Class Mobility and the Convergence Thesis: England, France, and Sweden." *British Journal of Sociology* 34:303–43.

Eskridge, Jr., William N., and Philip P. Frickey. 1995. *Cases and Materials on Legislation: Statutes and the Creation of Public Policy*. St. Paul, MN: West Publishing.

Evans, Lorraine, and Kimberly Davies. 2000. "No Sissy Boys Here: A Content Analysis of the Representation of Masculinity in Elementary School Reading Textbooks." *Sex Roles* 42:255–70.

Evertsson, Marie, and Magnus Nermo. 2004. "Dependence within Families and the Division of Labor: Comparing Sweden and the United States." *Journal of Marriage and Family* 66:1272–86.

Fackler, Martin. April 14, 2002. "Chinese Farm Women Commit Suicide to Escape Oppression." *Columbus Dispatch*.

Fagot, Beverly I. 1977. "Consequences of Moderate Cross-Gender Behavior in Preschool Children." *Child Development* 48:902–07.

Faller, Kathleen Coulborn, and Marjorie Ziefert. 1981. "Causes of Child Abuse and Neglect." Pp. 32–51 in *Social Work with Abused and Neglected Children*, edited by K. C. Faller. New York: The Free Press.

Fanon, Frantz. 1963. *The Wretched of the Earth*. New York: Grove Press.

Farley, John E. 1988. *Majority-Minority Relations*. Englewood Cliffs, NJ: Prentice Hall.

Farley, John E., and Gregory D. Squires. 2005. "Fences and Neighbors: Segregation in 21st Century America." *Contexts* 4:33–39.

Farough, Steven D. 2004. "The Social Geographies of White Masculinities." *Critical Sociology* 30:241–64.

Farrell, Ronald A. 1971. "Class Linkages of Legal Treatment of Homosexuals." *Criminology* 9:49–68.

Fatsis, Stefan. November 22, 1990. "Milken Gets 10 Years in Wall Street Scandal." *Akron Beacon Journal*, pp. A1, A13.

Faux, Jeff. January 2003. "Corporate Control of North America." *The American Prospect*, pp. 24–28.

Feagin, Joe R. 2001. "Social Justice and Sociology: Agendas for the Twenty-First Century." *American Sociological Review* 66:1–20.

Featherman, David L. 1977. "Has Opportunity Declined in America?" Institute for Research on Poverty Discussion Paper No. 437–77. Madison, WI: University of Wisconsin.

Featherman David L., and Robert M. Hauser. 1978. *Opportunity and Change*. New York: Academic Press.

Feldstein, Stanley, ed. 1972. *The Poisoned Tongue: A Documentary History of American Racism and Prejudice*. New York: William Morrow.

Felmlee, Diane H. 1982. "Women's Job Mobility Processes within and between Employers." *American Sociological Review* 43:142–51.

Fenton, Steve. 1984. *Durkheim and Modern Sociology*. Cambridge: Cambridge University Press.

Ferraro, Kenneth F., and Melissa M. Farmer. 1996. "Double Jeopardy to Health Hypothesis for African Americans: Analysis and Critique." *Journal of Health and Social Behavior* 37:27–43.

Ferree, Myra Marx, and Beth B. Hess. 1985. *Controversy and Coalition: The New Feminist Movement*. Boston: Twayne.

Fiala, Robert, and Gary LaFree. 1988. "Cross-National Determinants of Child Homicide." *American Sociological Review* 53:432–45.

Firebaugh, Glenn. 1999. "Empirics of World Income Inequality." *American Journal of Sociology* 104:1597–1630.

Firebaugh, Glenn. 2000. "The Trend in Between-Nation Income Inequality." Pp. 323–39 in *Annual*

Review of Sociology, edited by K. S. Cook and J. Hagan. Palo Alto, CA: Annual Reviews.

Firebaugh, Glenn, and Brian Goesling. 2004. "Accounting for the Recent Decline in Global Income Inequality." *American Journal of Sociology* 110:283–312.

Firestone, Shulamith. 1970. *The Dialectic of Sex: The Case for Feminist Revolution*. New York: William Morrow.

Fishel, Leslie, Jr., and Benjamin Quarles. 1967. *The Negro American: A Documentary History*. Glenview, IL: Scott, Foresman.

Flacks, Richard. 1971. *Youth and Social Change*. Chicago: Markham.

Flanagan, Constance A., Bernadette Campbell, Luba Botcheva, Jennifer Bowes, Beno Csapo, Petr Macek, and Elena Sheblanova. 2003. "Social Class and Adolescents' Beliefs about Justice in Different Social Orders." *Journal of Social Issues* 59:711–32.

Flowers, Paul, and Katie Buston. 2001. " 'I Was Terrified of Being Different': Exploring Gay Men's Accounts of Growing-Up in a Heterosexist Society." *Journal of Adolescence* 24:51–65.

Foerstel, Karen. 2002a. "Campaign Finance Bill Finds New Energy in Enron Ruins." *Congressional Quarterly Weekly* January 19:168–71.

Foerstel, Karen. 2002b. "Campaign Finance Passage Ends a Political Odyssey." *Congressional Quarterly Weekly* March 23:799–804.

Foner, Philip S. 1979. *Women and the American Labor Movement*, vol. 1. New York: The Free Press.

Forbes 400 Index. 2004. Available at http://www.forbes.com/lists.

Form, M. H., and G. P. Stone. 1957. "Urbanism, Anonymity, and Status Symbolism." *American Journal of Sociology* 62:504–14.

Forman, Tyrone A. 2003. "The Social Psychological Costs of Racial Segmentation in the Workplace: A Study of African Americans' Well-Being." *Journal of Health and Social Behavior* 44:332–52.

Fox, Mary Frank, and Sharlone Hesse-Biber. 1984. *Women at Work*. Palo Atto, CA: Mayfield.

France, Mike, and Dan Carney. July 2002. "Why Corporate Crooks Are Tough to Nail." *BusinessWeek* 1:35–38.

Frank, Robert. May 20, 2005. "In Palm Beach, The Old Money Isn't Having a Ball." *New York Times*, pp. A1, A11.

Franklin, John Hope. 1980. *From Slavery to Freedom: A History of Negro Americans*. New York: Knopf.

Frazier, E. Franklin. 1937. "Negro Harlem: An Ecological Study." *American Journal of Sociology* 43:72–88.

Frazier, E. Franklin. 1957. *Race and Culture Contacts in the Modern World*. Westport, CT: Greenwood Press.

Fredrickson, George M. 1981. *White Supremacy: A Comparative Study in American and South African History*. New York: Oxford University Press.

Freeman, Jo, ed. 1975a. *Women: A Feminist Perspective*. Palo Alto, CA: Mayfield.

Freeman, Jo. 1975b. "The Women's Liberation Movement: Its Origins, Structures, Impact, and Ideas." Pp. 448–60 in *Women: A Feminist Perspective*, edited by J. Freeman. Palo Alto, CA: Mayfield.

Freeman, Richard B. 1989. "The Relation of Criminal Activity to Black Youth Employment." *Review of Black Political Economy* 16:99–107.

Freire, Paulo. 1986. *Pedagogy of the Oppressed*. New York: Continuum.

Freitag, Peter J. 1975. "The Cabinet and Big Business: A Study of Interlocks." *Social Problems* 23:137–52.

French, Jr., John R., and Bertram H. Raven. 1959. "The Bases of Social Power." Pp. 150–67 in *Studies in Social Power*, edited by D. Cartwright. Ann Arbor, MI: Institute for Social Research.

Fuwa, Makiko. 2004. "Gender and Housework in 22 Countries." *American Sociological Review* 69:751–67.

Gagne, Patricia, and Richard Tewksbury. 1998. "Conformity Pressures and Gender Resistance among Transgendered Individuals." *Social Problems* 45:81–101.

Galbraith, John Kenneth. 1952. *American Capitalism: The Concept of Countervailing Power*. Boston: Houghton Mifflin.

Galinsky, Ellen, and James T. Bond. 1996. "Work and Family: The Experiences of Mothers and Fathers in the U.S. Labor Force." Pp. 79–103 in *The American Woman 1996–97*, edited by C. Costello and B. K. Krimgold. New York: W. W. Norton.

Gallup, George, Jr. 1989. *The Gallup Poll: Public Opinion 1988*. Wilmington, DE: Scholarly Resources.

Gallup, George, Jr. 1997. *The Gallup Poll: Public Opinion 1997*. Wilmington, DE: Scholarly Resources.

The Gallup Report, January/February 1987. Report No. 256–57, p. 14.

Gamson, Joshua, and Dawne Moon. 2004. "The Sociology of Sexualities: Queer and Beyond." Pp. 47–64 in *Annual Review of Sociology*, edited by K. S. Cook and J. Hagan. Palo Alto, CA: Annual Reviews.

Gamst, Frederick, ed. 1995. *Meanings of Work*. Albany: State University of New York Press.

Gans, Herbert J. 1968. *More Equality*. New York: Vintage.

Gans, Herbert J. 1972. "Positive Functions of Poverty." *American Journal of Sociology* 78:275–89.

Gans, Herbert J., ed. 1974. "The Equality Revolution." Pp. 7–35 in *More Equality*, edited by H. J. Gans. New York: Vintage.

Gans, Herbert J. 1995. *The War against the Poor.* New York: Basic Books.

Garbarino, Merwyn S. 1976. *American Indian Heritage.* Boston: Little, Brown.

Gaventa, John. 1980. *Power and Powerlessness: Quiescence and Rebellion in an Appalachian Valley.* Urbana: University of Illinois Press.

Gaventa, John. 1984. "Land Ownership, Power, and Powerlessness in the Appalachian Highlands." Pp. 142–55 in *Cultural Adaptation to Mountain Environments*, edited by P. D. Beaver and B. L. Purington. Athens: University of Georgia Press.

Geis, Gilbert. 1967. "The Heavy Electrical Equipment Antitrust Cases of 1961." Pp. 139–50 in *Criminal Behavior Systems*, edited by M. Clinard and R. Quinney. New York: Holt, Rinehart and Winston.

Geis, Gilbert. 1974. "Upperworld Crime." Pp. 114–37 in *Crime Perspectives on Criminal Behavior*, edited by A. S. Blumberg. New York: Knopf.

Gelles, Richard J., and Claire Pedrick Cornell. 1985 and 1990. *Intimate Violence in Families.* Beverly Hills, CA: Sage.

George, Linda K., and Scott M. Lynch. 2003. "Race Differences in Depressive Symptoms: A Dynamic Perspective on Stress Exposure and Vulnerability." *Journal of Health and Social Behavior* 44:353–69.

Gerson, Kathleen. 1998. "Gender and the Future of the Family." Pp. 11–12 in *Challenges for Work and Family in the Twenty-First Century*, edited by D. Vannoy and P. J. Dubeck. New York: Aldine de Gruyter.

Gerth, Hans H., and C. Wright Mills, eds. 1962. *From Max Weber: Essays in Sociology.* New York: Oxford University Press.

Giddens, Anthony. 1973. *The Class Structure of the Advanced Societies.* New York: Harper & Row.

Giddens, Anthony. 1978. *Emile Durkheim.* New York: Penguin.

Giddens, Anthony. 1982. *Sociology: A Brief but Critical Introduction.* New York: Harcourt Brace Jovanovich.

Giddings, Paula. 1984. *When and Where I Enter: The Impact of Black Women on Race and Sex in America.* New York: Bantam.

Gilbert, Dennis. 2003. *The American Class Structure.* Belmont, CA: Wadsworth.

Gilliam, Franklin D., Jr. 1986. "Black America: Divided by Class." *Public Opinion* 9:53–60.

Gillison, Gilliam. 1980. "Images of Nature in Gimi Thought." Pp. 143–73 in *Nature, Culture and Gender*, edited by C. MacCormack and M. Strathem. Cambridge: Cambridge University Press.

Ginzberg, Eli, and Hyman Berman. 1963. *The American Worker in the Twentieth Century.* New York: The Free Press.

"Girl Watching." November 2, 1992. *Fortune*, p. 146.

Giroux, Henry A. 1983. *Theory & Resistance in Education: A Pedagogy for the Opposition.* South Hadley, MA: Bergin & Garvey.

Gittleman, Maury, and Mary Joyce. September 1995. "Earnings Mobility in the United States, 1967–91." *Monthly Labor Review*, pp. 3–11.

Gladstone, Rick. May 9, 1988. "Despite Crash Executive Salaries Keep Rising." *Wooster Daily Record*, p. 34.

Glasgow, Douglas G. 1987. "The Black Underclass in Perspective." Pp. 129–44 in *The State of Black America 1987.* New York: National Urban League.

Goesling, Brian. 2001. "Changing Income Inequalities within and between Nations: New Evidence." *American Sociological Review* 66:745–61.

Goffman, Erving. 1959. *The Presentation of Self in Everyday Life.* Garden City, NY: Doubleday.

Goffman, Erving. 1961. *Asylums.* Garden City, NY: Doubleday Anchor Books.

Goffman, Erving. 1967. *Interaction Ritual.* Garden City, NY: Anchor Books, Doubleday.

Goldberg, Steven. 1973. *The Inevitability of Patriarchy.* New York: Morrow.

Goldthorpe, John H. 2002. "Globalisation and Social Class." *West European Politics* 25:1–28.

Gonsiorek, John C. 1996. "Mental Health and Sexual Orientation." Pp. 462–78 in *The Lives of Lesbians, Gays, and Bisexuals*, edited by R. C. Savin-Williams and K. M. Cohen. Fort Worth, TX: Harcourt Brace.

Good, David H., and Maureen A. Pirog-Good. 1987. "A Simultaneous Probit Model of Crime and Employment for Black and White Teenage Males." *Review of Black Political Economy* 16:109–27.

Good, Mary-Jo DelVecchio, Cara James, Byron J. Good, and Anne E. Becker. 2003. "The Culture of Medicine and Racial, Ethnic, and Class Disparities in Healthcare." Pp. 594–625 in *Unequal Treatment: Confronting Racial and Ethnic Disparities in Health Care*, edited by B. D. Smedley, A. Y. Stith, and A. R. Nelson. Washington, D.C.: National Academies Press.

Gooding, Cheryl, and Pat Reeve. 1993. "The Fruits of Our Labor. Women in the Labor Movement." *Social Policy* 23:56–64.

Goodman, William C., and Timothy D. Consedine. 1999. "Job Growth Slows during Crises' Overseas." *Monthly Labor Review* 122:3–23.

Goodwin, Leonard. 1983. *Causes and Cures of Welfare: New Evidence on the Social Psychology of the Poor.* Lexington, MA: Lexington Books.

Gordon, David M. 1972. *Theories of Poverty and Underemployment.* Lexington, MA: D.C. Heath.

Gordon, David M. 1973. "Class and the Economics of Crime." Warner Modular Publication Reprint No. 350. Andover, MA: Warner Modular Publications.

Gordon, Milton M. 1949. "Social Class in American Sociology." *American Journal of Sociology* 55:262–68.

Gore, Susan, and Robert H. Aseltine, Jr. 2003. "Race and Ethnic Differences in Depressed Mood Following the Transition from High School." *Journal of Health and Social Behavior* 44:370–89.

Gossett, Thomas F. 1963. *Race: The History of an Idea in America.* Dallas, TX: Southern Methodist University Press.

Gottesman, Irving L., Peter McGuffin, and Anne E. Farmer. 1987. "Clinical Genetics as Clues to the 'Real' Genetics of Schizophrenia." Pp. 39–63 in *Special Report: Schizophrenia 1987*, edited by D. Shore. Rockville, MD: U.S. Department of Health and Human Services.

Gottfried, Heidi. 2004. "Gendering Globalization Discourses." *Critical Sociology* 30:9–15.

Gould, Roger V. 2002. "The Origins of Status Hierarchies: A Formal Theory and Empirical Test." *American Journal of Sociology* 107:1143–78.

Grabb, Edward G. 1984. *Social Inequality: Classical and Contemporary Theorists.* Toronto: Holt, Rinehart and Winston of Canada.

Graham, Hugh Davis. 1992. "The Origins of Affirmative Action: Civil Rights and the Regulatory State." *The Annals of the American Academy of Political and Social Science* 523:50–62.

Gramsci, Antonio. 1971. *Selections from the Prison Notebooks.* London: Lawrence and Wishart.

Green, Charles. April 11, 1992. "Bush Endorses Drastic Wisconsin Welfare Reforms." *Akron Beacon Journal*, p. A4.

Green, Donald P., Laurence H. McFalls, and Jennifer K. Smith. 2001. "Hate Crime: An Emergent Research Agenda." Pp. 479–504 in *Annual Review of Sociology*, edited by K. S. Cook and J. Hagan. Palo Alto, CA: Annual Reviews.

Green, Gordon, John Coder, and Paul Ryscavage. March 1992. "International Comparisons of Earnings Inequality for Men in the 1980s." *The Review of Income and Wealth* 38:1–15.

Green, James R. 1980. *The World of the Worker: Labor in Twentieth-Century America.* New York: Hill and Wang.

Green, John C. 2000. "Anti-Gay: Varieties of Opposition to Gay Rights." Pp. 121–38 in *The Politics of Gay Rights*, edited by C. A. Rimmerman, K. D. Wald, and C. Wilcox. Chicago: University of Chicago.

Greenberg, Mark, and Jared Bernstein. December 6, 2004. "Holes Starting to Open in Welfare Reform." *Akron Beacon Journal*, p. B2.

Greenstein, Robert. March 1985. "Losing Faith in 'Losing Ground.' " *The New Republic* 25:12–17.

Grenzke, Janet M. 1989. "PACs and the Congressional Supermarket: The Currency Is Complex." *American Journal of Political Science* 33:1–24.

Griffin, Larry J., Michael E. Wallace, and Beth A. Rubin. 1986. "Capitalist Resistance to the Organization of Labor before the New Deal: Why? How? Success?" *American Sociological Review* 51:147–67.

Grodsky, Eric, and Devah Pager. 2001. "The Structure of Disadvantage: Individual and Occupational Determinants of the Black-White Wage Gap." *American Sociological Review* 66:542–67.

Gross, David, Lisa Alecxih, Mary Jo Gibson, John Corea, Craig Caplan, and Normandy Brangan. 1999. "Out-of-Pocket Health Spending by Poor and Near-Poor Elderly Medicare Beneficiaries." *Health Services Research* 34:241–54.

Grubb, W. Norton, and Robert H. Wilson. June 1992. "Trends in Wage and Salary Inequality, 1967–88." *Monthly Labor Review* 115:23–39.

Grusky, David B., and Robert M. Hauser. 1984. "Comparative Social Mobility Revisited; Models of Convergence and Divergence in 16 Countries." *American Sociological Review* 49:19–38.

Guillen, Mauro F. 2001. "Is Globalization Civilizing, Destructive, or Feeble? A Critique of Five Key Debates in the Social Science Literature." Pp. 235–60 in *Annual Review of Sociology*, edited by K. S. Cook and J. Hagan. Palo Alto, CA: Annual Reviews.

Gusfield, Joseph R. 1962. "Mass Society and Extremist Politics." *American Sociological Review* 27:19–30.

Hacker, Helen. 1951. "Women as a Minority Group." *Social Forces* 30:60–69.

Haddock, Geoffrey, and Mark P. Zanna. 1998. "Authoritarianism, Values, and the Favorability and Structure of Antigay Attitudes." Pp. 82–107 in *Stigma and Sexual Orientation*, edited by G. M. Herek. Thousand Oaks, CA: Sage.

Hagan, John, A. R. Gillis, and John Simpson. 1985. "The Class Structure of Gender and Delinquency: Toward a Power-Control Theory of Common Delinquent Behavior." *American Journal of Sociology* 90:1151–78.

Hagan, John, John Simpson, and A. R. Gillis. 1987. "Class in the Household; A Power-Control Theory of Gender and Delinquency." *American Journal of Sociology* 92:788–816.

Haider-Markel, Donald P. 2000. "Lesbian and Gay Politics in the States: Interest Groups, Electoral Politics, and Policy." Pp. 290–346 in *The Politics of Gay Rights*, edited by C. A. Rimmerman, K. D. Wald, and C. Wilcox. Chicago: University of Chicago.

Hales, Dianne. February 10, 2002. "What Americans Say about Our Justice System." *Parade Magazine*, pp. 10, 12–13.

Haller, Archibald O., and Alejandro Portes. 1973. "Status Attainment Processes." *Sociology of Education* 46:51–91.

Hamilton, Charles V. 1992. "Affirmative Action and the Clash of Experiential Realities." *The Annals of the American Academy of Political and Social Science* 523:10–18.

Hamilton, Richard F. 1966. "The Marginal Middle Class: A Reconsideration." *American Sociological Review* 31:192–93.

Hanagan, Michael. 2000. "States and Capital: Globalizations Past and Present." Pp. 67–86 in *The Ends of Globalization*, edited by D. Kalb, M. van derLand, R. Staring, B. van Steenbergen, and N. Wilterdink. Lanham, MD: Rowman & Littlefield.

Handler, Joel F. 1995. *The Poverty of Welfare Reform*. New Haven, CT: Yale University Press.

Hanratty, Maria J., and Rebecca M. Blank. 1992. "Down and Out in North America: Recent Trends in Poverty Rates in the United States and Canada." *Quarterly Journal of Economics* 107:233–54.

Hao, Lingxin. 2003. *Immigration and Wealth Inequality in the U.S.* Russell Sage Foundation Working Paper #202.

Hargraves, J. L., J. J. Stoddard, and S. Trude. 2001. "Minority Physicians' Experiences Obtaining Referrals to Specialists and Hospital Admissions." *Medscape General Medicine*. Available at www.medscape.com/Medscape/GeneralMedicine/journal/2001.

Harris, Kathleen Mullan. 1996. "Life after Welfare: Women, Work and Repeat Dependency." *American Sociological Review* 61:407–26.

Harris, Olivia. 1980. "The Power of Signs: Gender, Culture and the Wild in the Bolivian Andes." Pp. 70–94 in *Nature, Culture and Gender*, edited by C. MacCormack and M. Strathem. Cambridge: Cambridge University Press.

Harris, Richard J., Juanita M. Firestone, and William A. Vega. 2005. "The Interaction of Country of Origin, Acculturation, and Gender Role Ideology on Wife Abuse." *Social Science Quarterly* 86:463–83.

Hartley, W. B. 1969. *Estimation of the Incidence of Poverty in the United States, 1870–1974*. Ph.D. dissertation, University of Wisconsin, Madison.

Hartmann, Heidi. 1976/1990. "Capitalism, Patriarchy, and Job Segregation by Sex." *Signs: A Journal of Women in Culture and Society* 1:137–69. Reprinted in *Women, Class, and the Feminist Imagination: A Socialist-Feminist Reader*, edited by K. V. Hansen and I. J. Philipson. Philadelphia: Temple University Press.

Hartmann, Heidi. 1981. "The Unhappy Marriage of Marxism and Feminism." Pp. 15–29 in *Women and Revolution*, edited by L. Sargent. Boston: South End Press.

Hartmann, Heidi. 1987. "Internal Labor Markets and Gender: A Case Study of Promotion." Pp. 59–92 in *Gender in the Workplace*, edited by C. Brown and J. A. Pechman. Washington, D.C.: Brookings Institution.

Harvey, David. 1989. The *Condition of Postmodernity*. Oxford: Blackwell.

Hauser, Robert M., and David B. Grusky. 1988. "Cross-National Variation in Occupational Distribution, Relative Mobility Chances, and Intergenerational Shifts in Occupational Distributions." *American Sociological Review* 53:723–41.

Haveman, Robert H. 1977. "Poverty Income Distribution and Social Policy: The Last Decade and the Next." *Public Policy* 25:3–24.

Haveman, Robert H. 1987. *Poverty Policy and Poverty Research: The Great Society and the Social Sciences*. Madison, WI: University of Wisconsin Press.

Hawley, Amos. 1963. "Community Power and Urban Renewal Success." *American Journal of Sociology* 68:422–31.

Haynes, Norris. 1995. "How Skewed Is the Bell Curve?" *Journal of Black Psychology* 21:275–92.

Haynie, Dana L., and Bridget K. Gorman. 1999. "A Gendered Context of Opportunity: Determinants of Poverty across Urban and Rural Labor Markets." *Sociological Quarterly* 40:177–97.

Hays, Sharon. October 17, 2003. "Studying the Quagmire of Welfare Reform." *Chronicle of Higher Education*, pp. B7–B9.

Hayward, Mark D., Eileen M. Crimmins, Toni P. Miles, and Yu Yang. 2000. "The Significance of Socioeconomic Status in Explaining the Racial Gap in Chronic Health Conditions." *American Sociological Review* 65:910–30.

Hayward, Mark D., Amy M. Pienta, and Diane K. McLaughlin. 1997. "Inequality in Men's Mortality: The Socioeconomic Status Gradient and Geographic Context." *Journal of Health and Social Behavior* 38:313–30.

Hazelrigg, Lawrence E. 1972. "Class, Property, and Authority: Dahrendorf's Critique of Marx's Theory of Class." *Social Forces* 50:473–87.

Hazelrigg, Lawrence E., and Maurice A. Garnier. 1976. "Occupational Mobility in Industrial Societies: A Comparative Analysis of Differential Access to Occupational Ranks in Seventeen Countries." *American Sociological Review* 41:498–511.

Headen, Alvin E., Jr., Kenneth G. Manton, and Max A. Woodbury. 2004. "Co-Morbidity and Black and White Disparities in Health and Functional Status." *Review of Black Political Economy* 31:9–33.

Hebert, L. Camille. 2001. "Sexual Harassment as Discrimination 'Because of . . . Sex': Have We Come Full Circle?" *Ohio Northern University Law Review* 27:439–84.

Hechter, Michael. 2004. "From Class to Culture." *American Journal of Sociology* 110:400–45.

Hehir, J. Bryan. April 10, 1981. "The Bishops Speak on El Salvador." *Commonwealth*, pp. 199, 223.

Helms, Ronald, and David Jacobs. 2002. "The Political Context of Sentencing: An Analysis of Community and Individual Determinants." *Social Forces* 81:577–604.

Henderson, A. M., and Talcott Parsons, trans. 1947. *Max Weber: The Theory of Social and Economic Organization.* New York: The Free Press.

Henley, Nancy, and Jo Freeman. 1984. "The Sexual Politics of Interpersonal Behavior." Pp. 465–77 in *Women: A Feminist Perspective*, edited by J. Freeman. Palo Alto, CA: Mayfield.

Herdt, Gilbert. 1997. *Same Sex, Different Cultures.* Boulder, CO: Westview Press.

Herek. Gregory M. 2002. "Gender Gaps in Public Opinion about Lesbians and Gay Men." *Public Opinion Quarterly* 66:40–66.

Herek, Gregory M., and Kevin T. Berrill, eds. 1992. *Hate Crimes.* Newbury Park, CA: Sage.

Herring, Cedric. 2004. "Skin Deep: Race and Complexion in the 'Color-Blind' Era." Pp. 1–21 in *Skin Deep: How Race and Complexion Matter in the "Color-Blind" Era*, edited by C. Herring, V. Keith, and H. D. Horton. Chicago: University of Illinois.

Herrnstein, Richard J., and Charles Murray. 1994. *The Bell Curve: Intelligence and Class Structure in American Life.* New York: The Free Press.

Hershey, William. June 16, 1993. "Temporary Workers Growing in Numbers." *Akron Beacon Journal*, p. B7.

Herz, Diane E., and Barbara H. Wootten. 1996. "Women in the Workforce: An Overview." Pp. 44–78 in *The American Woman 1996–97*, edited by C. Costello and B. K. Krimgold. New York: W. W. Norton.

Hewitt, Christopher. 1995. "The Socioeconomic Position of Gay Men: A Review of the Evidence." *American Journal of Economics and Sociology* 54:461–79.

Higley, John, and Given Moore. 1981. "Elite Integration in the United States and Australia." *American Political Science Review* 75:581–97.

Higley, Stephen Richard. 1995. *Privilege, Power, and Place.* Lanham, MD: Rowman & Littlefield.

Hill, Mark E. 2000. "Color Differences in the Socioeconomic Status of African American Men: Results of a Longitudinal Study." *Social Forces* 78:1437–60.

Hill, Mark E. 2002. "Race of the Interviewer and Perception of Skin Color: Evidence from the Multi-City Study of Urban Inequality." *American Sociological Review* 67:99–108.

Hirschfeld, Julie R. January 20, 2001. "Congress of Relative Newcomers Poses Challenge to Bush, Leadership." *Congressional Quarterly Weekly*, pp. 178–82.

Hirschman, Charles, and Ellen Kraly. 1988. "Immigrants, Minorities, and Earning in the United States in 1950." *Ethnic and Racial Studies* 11:332–65.

Hirschman, Charles, and Morrison G. Wong. 1984. "Socioeconomic Gains of Asian Americans, Blacks, and Hispanics: 1960–1976." *American Journal of Sociology* 90:584–606.

Hoch, Charles. 1987. "A Brief History of the Homeless Problem in the United States." Pp. 16–32 in *The Homeless in Contemporary Society*, edited by R. D. Bingham, R. E. Green, and S. B. White. Newbury Park, CA: Sage.

Hochschild, Jennifer. 1981. *What's Fair: American Beliefs about Distributive Justice.* Cambridge, MA: Harvard University Press.

Hochschild, Jennifer L. 2003. "Social Class in Public Schools." *Journal of Social Issues* 59:821–40.

Hodge, Robert W., Paul Siegel, and Peter H. Rossi. 1964. "Occupational Prestige in the United States. 1925–1963." *American Journal of Sociology* 70:286–302.

Hodson, Randy. 1984. "Companies, Industries, and the Measurement of Economic Segmentation." *American Sociological Review* 49:335–48.

Hodson, Randy, and Robert L. Kaufman. 1982. "Economic Dualism: A Critical Review" *American Sociological Review* 47:727–39.

Hoffman, Donna L., and Thomas P. Novak. 1998. "Bridging the Racial Divide on the Internet." *Science* 280:390–91.

Hoffman, Kelly, and Miguel Angel Centeno. 2003. "The Lopsided Continent: Inequality in Latin America." Pp. 363–90 in *Annual Review of Sociology*, edited by K. S. Cook and J. Hagan. Palo Alto, CA: Annual Reviews.

Hole, Judith, and Ellen Levine. 1975. "The First Feminists." Pp. 436–47 in *Women: A Feminist*

Perspective, edited by J. Freeman. Palo Alto, CA: Mayfield.

Hollingshead, August B., and Fredrick Redlich. 1958. *Social Class and Mental Illness*. New York: John Wiley & Sons.

Holloway, Steven R., and Elvin K. Wyly. 2001. "'The Color of Money' Expanded: Geographically Contingent Mortgage Lending in Atlanta." *Journal of Housing Research* 12:55–90.

Holmes, Malcolm D., and Judith A. Antell. 2001. "The Social Construction of American Indian Drinking: Perceptions of American Indian and White Officials." *Sociological Quarterly* 42:151–73.

Holt, Douglas B. 1997. "Distinction in America? Recovering Bourdieu's Theory of Tastes from Its Critics." *Poetics* 25:93–121.

Hombs, Mary Ellen. 2001. *American Homelessness*. Santa Barbara, CA: ABC-CLIO.

hooks, bell. 1981. *Ain't I a Woman: Black Women and Feminism*. Boston: South End Press.

Hope, Marjorie, and James Young. 1986. *The Faces of Homelessness*. Lexington, MA: Lexington Books.

Horrigan, M. W., and S. E. Haugen. 1988. "The Declining Middle-Class Thesis: A Sensitivity Analysis." *Monthly Labor Review* 111:3–13.

Hotaling, G. T., and D. B. Sugarman. 1984. "An Identification of Risk Factors." In *Domestic Violence Surveillance System Feasibility Study, Phase I Report*. Rockville, MD: Westat.

Hout, Michael. 1984. "Occupational Mobility of Black Men: 1962 to 1973." *American Sociological Review* 49:308–22.

Hout, Michael. 1986. "Opportunity and the Minority Middle Class: A Comparison of Blacks in the United States and Catholics in Northern Ireland." *American Sociological Review* 51:214–23.

Hout, Michael. 1988. "More Universalism, Less Structural Mobility: The American Occupational Structure in the 1980s." *American Journal of Sociology* 93:1358–400.

Huaco, George A. 1963. "A Logical Analysis of the Davis-Moore Theory of Stratification." *American Sociological Review* 28:801–04.

Huber, Joan. 1982. "Toward a Sociotechnological Theory of the Women's Movement." Pp. 24–38 in *Women and Work: Problems and Perspectives*, edited by R. Kahn-Hut, A. K. Daniels, and R. Colvard. New York: Oxford University Press.

Huber, Joan. 1988. "From Sugar and Spice to Professor." Pp. 92–101 in *Down to Earth Sociology: Introductory Readings*, edited by J. M. Henslin. New York: The Free Press.

Huddy, Leonie, Francis K. Neely, and Marilyn R. Lafay. 2000. "The Polls—Trends: Support for the Women's Movement." *Public Opinion Quarterly* 64:309–50.

Huff, Daniel D., and David A. Johnson. 1993. "Phantom Welfare: Public Relief for Corporate America." *Social Work* 38:311–16.

Huffman, Matt L., and Philip N. Cohen. 2004a. "Racial Wage Inequality: Job Segregation and Devaluation across U.S. Labor Markets." *American Journal of Sociology* 109:902–36.

Huffman, Matt L., and Philip N. Cohen. 2004b. "Occupational Segregation and the Gender Gap in Workplace Authority: National Versus Local Labor Markets." *Sociological Forum* 19:121–47.

Hughes, Michael, and Bradley R. Hertel. 1990. "The Significance of Color Remains: A Study of Life Chances, Mate Selection, and Ethnic Consciousness Among Black Americans." *Social Forces* 68:1105–20.

Hughes, Michael, and Melvin E. Thomas. 1998. "The Continuing Significance of Race Revisited: A Study of Race, Class, and Quality of Life in America, 1972 to 1996." *American Sociological Review* 63:785–95.

Hull, Kathleen E., and Robert L. Nelson. 2000. "Assimilation, Choice, or Constraint? Testing Theories of Gender Differences in the Careers of Lawyers." *Social Forces* 79:229–64.

Human Rights Campaign. 2005a. *Answers to Questions About Marriage Equality*. Washington, D.C.: Human Rights Campaign.

Human Rights Campaign. 2005b. *Marriage/Relationship Laws: State by State*. Available at http://www.hrc.org/Template.cfm?Section=Laws_Legal_Resources.

Hunt, Matthew O. 2004. "Race/Ethnicity and Beliefs about Wealth and Poverty." *Social Science Quarterly* 85:827–53.

Hunter, Herbert M., and Sameer Y. Abraham, eds. 1987. *Race, Class, and the World System: The Sociology of Oliver C. Cox*. New York: Monthly Review Press.

Hurn, Christopher. 1987. "Theories of Schooling and Society: The Functional and Radical Paradigms." Pp. 322–33 in *Introducing Sociology*, edited by R. T. Schaefer and R. P. Lamm. New York: McGraw-Hill.

Ibarra, Peter R., and John I. Kitsuse. 2003. "Claims-Making Discourse and Vernacular Resources." Pp. 17–50 in *Challenges & Choices*, edited by J. A. Hostein and G. Miller. Hawthorne, NY: Aldine de Gruyter.

Institute of Medicine. 2002. *Unequal Treatment*. Washington, D.C.: National Academies Press.

International Bank for Reconstruction and Development/ The World Bank. 1992. *World Development Report 1992*. New York: Oxford University Press.

Irwin, John. 1985. *The Jail: Managing the Underclass in American Society*. Berkeley: University of California Press.

Iyer, Pica. June 1, 1992. "Goneril's Lament." *The New Republic*, p. 12.

Jackall, Robert. 1988. *Moral Mazes: The World of Corporate Managers*. New York: Oxford.

Jackman, Robert W. 1975. *Politics and Social Equality: A Comparative Analysis*. New York: John Wiley & Sons.

Jackson, Elton F., and Harry J. Crockett, Jr. 1964. "Occupational Mobility in the United States: A Point Estimate and Trend Comparison." *American Sociological Review* 29:5–15.

Jacobson, Sharon, and Arnold H. Grossman. 1996. "Older Lesbians and Gay Men: Old Myths, New Images, and Future Directions." Pp. 345–73 in *The Lives of Lesbians, Gays, and Bisexuals*, edited by R. C. Savin-Williams and K. M. Cohen. Fort Worth, TX: Harcourt Brace.

Jamieson, Amie, Hyon B. Shin, and Jennifer Day. February 2002. *Voting and Registration in the Election of November 2000*. Current Population Reports Series P20, No. 542. Washington, D.C.: U.S. Census Bureau.

Jasso, Guillermina. 1994. "Assessing Individual and Group Differences in the Sense of Justice." *Social Science Research* 23:368–406.

Jasso, Guillermina. 1999. "How Much Injustice Is There in the World? Two New Justice Indexes." *American Sociological Review* 64:133–68.

Jasso, Guillermina, and Peter Rossi. 1977. "Distributive Justice and Earned Income." *American Sociological Review* 42:639–51.

Jefferson, Alphine W. 1993. "Contemporary Diaspora and the Future." Pp. 102–18 in *Africana Studies*, edited by M. Azevedo. Durham, NC: Carolina.

Jencks, Christopher. 1992. *Rethinking Social Policy*. New York: HarperCollins.

Jencks, Christopher, Marshall Smith, Henry Acland, Mary Jo Bane, David Cohen, Herbert Gintis, Barbara Heyns, and Stephen Michelson. 1973. *Inequality: A Reassessment of the Effect of Family and Schooling in America*. New York: Colophon Books.

Jenkins, J. Craig. 1983. "Resource Mobilization Theory and the Study of Social Movements." Pp. 527–53 in *Annual Review of Sociology*, edited by R. H. Turner and J. F. Short, Jr. Palo Alto, CA: Annual Reviews.

Jenkins, J. Craig, and Craig M. Eckert. 1986. "Channeling Black Insurgency: Elite Patronage and Professional Social Movement Organizations in the Development of the Black Movement." *American Sociological Review* 51:812–29.

Jenkins, J. Craig, David Jacobs, and Jon Agnone. 2003. "Political Opportunities and African-American Protest, 1948–1997." *American Journal of Sociology* 109:277–303.

Jenkins, J. Craig, and Charles Perrow. 1977. "Insurgency of the Powerless: Farm Worker Movements (1946–1972)." *American Sociological Review* 42:249–68.

Johnson, Cathryn. 1994. "Gender, Legitimate Authority, and Leader-Subordinate Conversations." *American Sociological Review* 59:122–35.

Johnson, Harry A., ed. 1976. *Ethnic American Minorities*. New York: R. R. Bowker.

Johnson, Jennifer. 2002. *Getting By On the Minimum*. New York: Routledge.

Johnston, David Cay. April 7, 2002. "Wealthy More Likely to Escape Tax Audit, IRS Data Show." *The Columbus Dispatch*, p. A7.

Joint Center for Political and Economic Studies. 1990. *Black Elected Officials: A National Roster*. Washington, D.C.: Author.

Joint Center for Political Studies. 1989. *Black Elected Officials: A National Roster*. Washington, D.C.: Author.

Jones, Woodrow, Jr., and K. Robert Keiser. 1987. "Issue Visibility and the Effects of PAC Money." *Social Science Quarterly* 68:170–76.

Jong-sung, You, and Sanjeev Khagram. 2005. "A Comparative Study of Inequality and Corruption." *American Sociological Review* 70:136–57.

Judis, John B. January 21, 1990. "Pulling U.S. Strings: Japanese Money Buys Influence." *Akron Beacon Journal*, pp. E1, E4.

Kabeer, Naila. 2004. "Globalization, Labor Standards, and Women's Rights: Dilemmas of Collective (In)Action in an Interdependent World." *Feminist Economics* 10:3–35.

Kaiser, S. 1985. *The Social Psychology of Clothing and Personal Adornment*. New York: Macmillan.

Kallick, David. 1994. "Toward a New Unionism." *Social Policy* 25:2–6.

Kamerman, Sheila B. 1980. *Parenting in an Unresponsive Society: Managing Work and Family Life*. New York: The Free Press.

Kanter, Rosabeth Moss. 1977a. *Men and Women of the Corporation*. New York: Basic Books.

Kanter, Rosabeth Moss. 1977b. "Some Effects of Proportions on Group Life: Skewed Sex Ratios and Responses to Token Women." *American Journal of Sociology* 82:965–90.

Kaplan, H. Roy, and Curt Tausky. 1972. "Work and the Welfare Cadillac: The Function of and Commitment to Work among the Hardcore Unemployed." *Social Problems* 19:469–83.

Kaplan, H. Roy, and Curt Tausky. 1974. "The Meaning of Work Among the Hardcore Unemployed." *Pacific Sociological Review* 17:185–98.

Kasarda, John D. 1989. "Urban Industrial Transition and the Underclass." *Annals of the American Academy of Political and Social Science* 501:26–47.

Katz, Jonathan Ned. 2004. " 'Homosexual' and 'Heterosexual'." Pp. 44–46 in *Sexualities: Identities, Behaviors, and Society*, edited by M. S. Kimmel and R. F. Plante. New York: Oxford.

Katz, Michael B. 1986. *In the Shadow of the Poorhouse: A Social History of Welfare in America*. New York: Basic Books.

Katz-Gerro, Tally. 2002. "Highbrow Cultural Consumption and Class Distinction in Italy, Israel, West Germany, Sweden, and the United States." *Social Forces* 81:207–29.

Kaufman, Robert L., and Thomas N. Daymont. 1981. "Racial Discrimination and the Social Organization of Industries." *Social Science Research* 10:225–55.

Kaushal, Neeraj, and Robert Kaestner. 2001. "From Welfare to Work: Has Welfare Reform Worked?" *Journal of Policy Analysis and Management* 20:699–719.

Keister, Lisa A., and Stephanie Moller. 2000. "Wealth Inequality in the United States." Pp. 63–81 in *Annual Review of Sociology*, edited by K. S. Cook and J. Hagan. Palo Alto, CA: Annual Reviews.

Keith, Verna M., and Cedric Herring. 1991. "Skin Tone and Stratification in the Black Community." *American Journal of Sociology* 97:760–78.

Keller, Suzanne. 1969. "Beyond the Ruling Class-Strategic Elites." Pp. 520–24 in *Structured Social Inequality*, edited by C. S. Heller. New York: Macmillan.

Keller, Suzanne. 1987. "Social Differentiation and Social Stratification: The Special Case of Gender." Pp. 329–49 in *Structured Social Inequality*, edited by Celia S. Heller. New York: Macmillan.

Kelley, Jonathan, and M. D. R. Evans. 1993. "The Legitimation of Inequality: Occupational Earnings in Nine Nations." *American Journal of Sociology* 99:75–125.

Kemper, Theodore D. 1976. "Marxist and Functionalist Theories in the Study of Stratification: Common Elements That Lead to a Test." *Social Forces* 54:559–78.

Kendall, Diana. 2002. *The Power of Good Deeds*. Lanham, MD: Rowman & Littlefield.

Kennelly, Ivy. 1999. "That Single-Mother Element': How White Employers Typify Black Women." *Gender & Society* 13:168–92.

Kenworthy, Lane. 1999. "Do Social-Welfare Policies Reduce Poverty? A Cross-National Assessment." *Social Forces* 77:1119–39.

Kephart, William M. 1950. "Status after Death." *American Sociological Review* 15:635–43.

Kerbo, Ronald R. 1983. *Social Stratification and Inequality: Class Conflict in the United States*. New York: McGraw-Hill.

Kerckhoff, Alan C. 1995. "Institutional Arrangements and Stratification Processes of Industrial Societies." Pp. 323–47 in *Annual Review of Sociology*, edited by J. Hagan and K. S. Cook. Palo Alto, CA: Annual Reviews.

Kerckhoff, Alan C., Richard T. Campbell, and Idee Winfield-Laird. 1985. "Social Mobility in Great Britain and the United States." *American Journal of Sociology* 91:281–301.

Kerley, Kent R., Michael L. Benson, and Matthew R. Lee. 2004. "Race, Criminal Justice Contact, and Adult Position in the Social Stratification System." *Social Problems* 51:549–68.

Kessler, Ronald C., and James A. McRae, Jr. 1983. "Trends in the Relationship between Sex and Attempted Suicide." *Journal of Health and Social Behaviour* 24:98–110.

Kessler, Ronald C., and Jane D. McLeod. 1984. "Sex Differences in Vulnerability to Undesirable Life Events." *American Sociological Review* 49:620–31.

Khazzoom, Aziza. 1997. "The Impact of Mothers' Occupations on Children's Occupational Destinations." *Research in Stratification and Mobility* 15:57–89.

Kiely, Ray. 2004. "The World Bank and 'Global Poverty Reduction': Good Policies or Bad Data?" *Journal of Contemporary Asia* 34:3–20.

King, Deborah K. 1988. "Multiple Jeopardy, Multiple Consciousness: The Context of a Black Feminist Ideology." *Signs* 14:42–72.

King, Martin Luther. 1958. *Stride toward Freedom*. New York: Harper & Row.

Kinney, David A. 1993. "From Nerds to Normals: The Recovery of Identity among Adolescents from Middle School to High School." *Sociology of Education* 66:21–40.

Kirby, James B., and Toshiko Kaneda. 2005. "Neighborhood Socioeconomic Disadvantage and Access to Health Care." *Journal of Health and Social Behavior* 46:15–31.

Kite, Mary E. and Bernard E. Whitley, Jr. 1996. "Sex Differences in Attitudes toward Homosexual Persons, Behavior, and Civil Rights: A Meta-Analysis." *Personality and Social Psychology Bulletin* 22:336–53.

Kite, Mary E., and Bernard E. Whitley, Jr. 1998. "Do Heterosexual Women and Men Differ in Their Attitudes toward Homosexuality?" Pp. 39–61 in *Stigma and Sexual Orientation*, edited by G. M. Herek. Thousand Oaks, CA: Sage.

Klawitter, Marieka M., and Victor Flatt. 1998. "The Effects of State and Local Antidiscrimination Policies on Earnings for Gays and Lesbians." *Journal of Policy Analysis and Management* 17:658–86.

Kleck, Gary. 1981. "Racial Discrimination in Criminal Sentencing: A Critical Evaluation of the Evidence with Additional Evidence on the Death Penalty." *American Sociological Review* 46:783–805.

Klerman, Gerald L., and Myrna M. Weissman. 1989. "Increasing Rates of Depression." *Journal of the American Medical Association* 261:2229–35.

Kluegel, James R., and Eliot R. Smith. 1986. *Beliefs about Inequality: Americans' Views of What Is and What Ought to Be*. New York: Aldine de Gruyter.

Kmec, Julie A. 2003. "Minority Job Concentration and Wages." *Social Problems* 50:38–59.

Kochhar, Rakesh. 2004. *The Wealth of Hispanic Households: 1996 to 2002*. Washington, D.C.: Pew Hispanic Center.

Koegel, Paul, M. Audrey Burnam, and Jim Baumohl. 1996. "The Causes of Homelessness." Pp. 24–33 in *Homelessness in America*, edited by J. Baumohl. Phoenix, AZ: Oryx Press.

Kohn, Melvin L. 1969. *Class and Conformity*. Homewood, IL: Dorsey.

Kohn, Melvin. 1976a. "The Interaction of Social Class and Other Factors in the Etiology of Schizophrenia." *American Journal of Psychiatry* 133:177–80.

Kohn, Melvin. 1976b. "Occupational Structure and Alienation." *American Journal of Sociology* 82:111–30.

Kohn, Melvin L., and Carmi Schooler. 1982. "Job Conditions and Personality: A Longitudinal Assessment of Their Reciprocal Effects." *American Journal of Sociology* 87:1257–86.

Kolenda, Pauline. 1978. *Caste in Contemporary India*. Prospect Heights, IL: Waveland Press.

Korpi, Walter. 1974. "Conflict, Power, and Relative Deprivation." *American Political Science Review* 68:1569–78.

Kotlowitz, Alex. 1991. *There Are No Children Here*. New York: Doubleday.

Kposowa, Augustine J., Kevin D. Breault, and Beatrice M. Harrison. 1995. "Reassessing the Structural Covariates of Violent and Property Crimes in the USA: A County Level Analysis." *British Journal of Sociology* 46:79–105.

Kriesberg, Louis. 1979. *Social Inequality*. Englewood Cliffs, NJ: Prentice Hall.

Kromm, Jane E. 1994. "The Feminization of Madness in Visual Representation." *Feminist Studies* 20:507–35.

Krotz, Joanna L. July/August 1999. "Getting Even." *Working Woman*, pp. 42–50.

Krueger, Patrick M., Richard G. Rogers, Robert A. Hummer, Felicia B. LeClere, and Stephanie A. Bond Huie. 2003. "Socioeconomic Status and Age: The Effect of Income Sources and Portfolios on U.S. Adult Mortality." *Sociological Forum* 18:465–82.

Krugman, Paul, and Anthony J. Venables. 1995. "Globalization and the Inequality of Nations." *Quarterly Journal of Economics* 110:857–77.

Kruttschnitt, Candace, and Donald E. Green. 1984. "The Sex-Sanctioning Issue: Is It History?" *American Sociological Review* 49:541–51.

Kuriloff, Peter, and Michael C. Reichert. 2003. "Boys of Class, Boys of Color: Negotiating the Academic and Social Geography of an Elite Independent School." *Journal of Social Issues* 59:751–69.

Kurz, Karin, and Walter Muller. 1987. "Class Mobility in the Industrial World." Pp. 417–42 in *Annual Review of Sociology*, vol. 13, edited by W. R. Scott and J. F. Short, Jr. Palo Alto, CA: Annual Reviews.

Labich, Kenneth. March 8, 1993. "The New Unemployed." *Fortune*, pp. 40–49.

Lacey, Marc. December 7, 2004. "From Broken Lives, Kenyan Women Build Place of Unity." *New York Times*.

Lachman, Margie E., and Suzanne L. Weaver. 1998. "The Sense of Control as a Moderator of Social Class Differences in Health and Well-Being." *Journal of Personality and Social Psychology* 74:763–73.

LaFree, Gary. 1995. "Race and Crime Trends in the United States: 1946–1990." Pp. 169–93 in *Ethnicity, Race, and Crime*, edited by D. F. Hawkins. Albany: State University of New York Press.

Lamb, Michael E., M. Ann Easterbrooks, and George W. Holden. 1980. "Reinforcement and Punishment among Preschoolers: Characteristics, Effects, and Correleates." *Child Development* 51:1230–36.

Lamont, Michèle. 2000. *The Dignity of Working Men*. Cambridge, MA: Harvard.

Landers, Susan. March 1993. "Family Leave Ushers in New Era." *NASW News* 38:1, 8.

Langeland, Willie, and Christina Hartgers. 1998. "Child Sexual and Physical Abuse and Alcoholism: A Review." *Journal of Studies on Alcohol* 59:336–48.

Lannoy, Richard. 1975. *The Speaking Tree: A Study of Indian Culture and Society*. New York: Oxford University Press.

Lapham, Lewis H. 1988. *Money and Class in America*. New York: Weidenfeld & Nicolson.

Lareau, Annette. 2003. *Unequal Childhoods*. Berkeley: University of California.

Laslett, John H. M. 1987. "The American Tradition of Labor Theory and Its Relevance to the Contemporary Working Class." Pp. 359–78 in *Theories of the Labor Movement*, edited by S. Larson and B. Nissen. Detroit: Wayne State University Press.

Lasswell, Thomas E. 1965. *Class and Stratum*. Boston: Houghton Mifflin.

Latkin, Carl A., and Aaron D. Curry. 2003. "Stressful Neighborhoods and Depression: A Prospective Study of the Impact of Neighborhood Disorder." *Journal of Health and Social Behavior* 44:34–44.

Laumann, Edward O., John H. Gagnon, Robert T. Michael, and Stuart Michaels. 1994. *The Social Organization of Sexuality*. Chicago: University of Chicago Press.

Lauritsen, Janet L., and Robin J. Schaum. 2004. "The Social Ecology of Violence Against Women." *Criminology* 42:323–57.

Lauzen, Martha M., and David M. Dozier. 2005. "Maintaining the Double Standard: Portrayals of Age and Gender in Popular Films." *Sex Roles* 52:437–46.

Leacock, Eleanor. 1986. "Women, Power and Authority." Pp. 107–35 in *Visibility and Power: Essays on Women in Society and Development*, edited by L. Dube, E. Leacock, and S. Ardener. Delhi: Oxford University Press.

Leaf, Clifton. March 18, 2002. "White-Collar Criminals: They Lie, They Cheat, They Steal, and They've Been Getting Away with It for Too Long." *Fortune*, pp. 61–76.

Leary, Elly. 2005. "Crisis in the U.S. Labor Movement." *Monthly Review* 57:28–37.

Lee, Jennifer. 2002. "From Civil Relations to Racial Conflict: Merchant-Customer Interactions in Urban America." *American Sociological Review* 67:77–98.

Lee, Jennifer, and Frank D. Bean. 2004. "America's Changing Color Lines: Immigration, Race/ Ethnicity, and Multiracial Identification." Pp. 221–42 in *Annual Review of Sociology*, edited by K. S. Cook and J. Hagan. Palo Alto, CA: Annual Reviews.

Leftwich, Richard H. 1977. "Personal Income and Marginal Productivity." Pp. 78–81 in *Problems in Political Economy: An Urban Perspective*, edited by D. M. Gordon. Lexington, MA: D.C. Heath.

Lehmann, Jennifer M. 1995. "The Question of Caste in Modern Society: Durkheim's Contradictory Theories of Race, Class, and Sex." *American Sociological Review* 60:566–85.

Lengermann, Patricia Madoo, and Jill Niebrugge-Brantley. 1988. "Contemporary Feminist Theory." Pp. 282–325 in *Contemporary Sociological Theory*, edited by George Ritzer. New York: Knopf.

Lens, Vicki. 2002. "TANF: What Went Wrong and What to Do Next." *Social Work* 47:279–90.

Lenski, Gerhard. 1988. "Rethinking Macrosociological Theory." *American Sociological Review* 53:163–71.

Lerman, Robert I., and Caroline Ratcliffe. July, 2001. "Are Single Mothers Finding Jobs Without Displacing Other Workers?" *Monthly Labor Review*, pp. 3–12.

Lester, James P., David W. Allen, and Kelly M. Hill. 2001. *Environmental Injustice in the United States: Myths and Realities*. Boulder, CO: Westview.

Levine, Steven B. 1980. "The Rise of American Boarding Schools and the Development of a National Upper Class." *Social Problems* 28:63–94.

Levinson, David. 1988. "Family Violence in Cross-Cultural Perspective." Pp. 435–55 in *Handbook of Family Violence*, edited by V. B. Van Hasselt, R. L. Morrison, A. S. Bellack, and M. Hersen. New York: Plenum.

Levitan, Sar A. 1985. *Programs in Aid of the Poor*. Baltimore: Johns Hopkins University Press.

Levy, Frank, and Richard J. Murnane. 1992. "U.S. Earnings Levels and Earnings Inequality: A Review of Recent Trends and Proposed Explanations." *Journal of Economic Literature* 30:1333–81.

Lewis, Amanda E. 2004. " 'What Group?' Studying Whites and Whiteness in the Era of 'Color Blindness'." *Sociological Theory* 22:623–46.

Lewis, Gregory B. 2003. "Black-White Differences in Attitudes toward Homosexuality and Gay Rights." *Public Opinion Quarterly* 67:59–78.

Lewis, Gregory B., and Jonathan L. Edelson. 2000. "DOMA and ENDA: Congress Votes on Gay Rights." Pp. 193–216 in *The Politics of Gay Rights*, edited by C. A. Rimmerman, K. D. Wald, and C. Wilcox. Chicago: University of Chicago.

Lewis, Helen. 1974. "Fatalism or the Coal Industry." P. 222 in *Appalachia: Its People, Heritage, and Problems*, edited by Frank S. Riddel. Dubuque, IA: Kendall/Hunt.

Lichter, Daniel T. 1988. "Racial Differences in Underemployment in American Cities." *American Journal of Sociology* 93:771–92.

Lichter, Daniel T., and Rukamalie Jayakody. 2002. "Welfare Reform: How Do We Measure Success?" Pp. 117–41 in *Annual Review of Sociology*, edited by K. S. Cook and J. Hagan. Palo Alto, CA: Annual Reviews.

Lieberson, Stanley, and Donna K. Carter. 1979. "Making It in America: Differences between Eminent Blacks and White Ethnic Groups." *American Sociological Review* 44:347–66.

Light, Donald, Susanne Keller, and Craig Calhoun. 1989. *Sociology*. New York: Knopf.

Ligner, Isabelle. December 14, 2001. "Pakistan Women Targeted by 'Crimes of Honour'." *Agence France Presse*, International News Section.

Lincoln, Karen D., Linda M. Chatters, and Robert Joseph Taylor. 2003. "Psychological Distress among Black and White Americans: Differential Effects of Social Support, Negative Interaction and Personal Control." *Journal of Health and Social Behavior* 44:390–407.

Lindert, Peter, and Jeffrey G. Williamson. 1976. "Three Centuries of American Inequality." Institute for Research on Poverty Discussion Paper No. 333–76. Madison: University of Wisconsin, Madison.

Link, Bruce G., Jo C. Phelan, Ann Stueve, Robert E. Moore, Michaeline Bresnahan, and Elmer L. Struening. 1996. "Public Attitudes and Beliefs about Homeless People." Pp. 143–48 in *Homelessness in America*, edited by J. Baumohl. Phoenix, AZ: Oryx Press.

Lipman, Joanne. April 14, 1993. "The Nanny Trap: The Dark Side of Child Care Is How Poorly Workers Are Sometimes Treated." *Wall Street Journal*, pp. A1, A8.

Lipset, Seymour Martin. 1971. "Trade Unionism and the American Social Order." Pp. 7–29 in *The American Labor Movement*, edited by D. Brody. New York: Harper & Row.

Lipset, Seymour Martin. 1992. "Equal Chances versus Equal Results." *The Annals of the American Academy of Political and Social Science* 523:63–74.

Lipset, Seymour Martin, and Hans L. Zetterberg. 1959. "Social Mobility in Industrial Societies." Pp. 11–75 in *Social Mobility in Industrial Society*, edited by S. M. Lipset and R. Bendix. Berkeley: University of California Press.

Lo, Jeannie. 1990. *Office Ladies, Factory Women: Life and Work at a Japanese Company*. Armonk, NY: M. E. Sharpe.

Loftin, Colin, and Robert H. Hill. 1974. "Regional Subculture and Homicide: An Examination of the Gastil-Hackney Thesis." *American Sociological Review* 39:714–24.

Loftus, Jeni. 2001. "America's Liberalization in Attitudes toward Homosexuality, 1973 to 1998." *American Sociological Review* 66:762–82.

Long, J. Scott, and Mary Frank Fox. 1995. "Scientific Careers: Universalism and Particularism." Pp. 45–71 in *Annual Review of Sociology 1995*, edited by J. Hagan and K. S. Cook. Palo Alto, CA: Annual Reviews.

Lopreato, Joseph, and Lawrence E. Hazelrigg. 1972. *Class, Conflict, and Mobility*. Corte Madera, CA: Chandler & Sharp.

Lorber, Judith. 1996. "Beyond the Binaries: Depolarizing the Categories of Sex. Sexuality, and Gender." *Sociological Inquiry* 66:143–59.

Lorber, Judith. 2001. *Gender Inequality*. Los Angeles: Roxbury.

Loring, Marti, and Brian Powell. 1988. "Gender, Race, and DSM-III: A Study of the Objectivity of Psychiatric Behavior." *Journal of Health and Social Behavior* 29:1–22.

Loury, Glenn C. 1992. "Incentive Effects of Affirmative Action." *The Annals of the American Academy of Political and Social Science* 523:19–29.

Low, Jason, and Peter Sherrard. 1999. "Portrayal of Women in Sexuality and Marriage and Family Textbooks: A Content Analysis of Photographs from the 1970s to the 1990s." *Sex Roles* 40:309–18.

Lowe, Marian, and Ruth Hubbard, eds. 1983. *Women's Nature: Rationalizations of Inequality*. New York: Pergamon.

Ludwig, Jack. 2003. "Is America Divided into 'Haves' and 'Have-Nots'?" *Gallup Poll Tuesday Briefing*. May 1:1–4.

Luibheid, Eithne. 1998. " 'Looking Like a Lesbian': The Organization of Sexual Monitoring at the United States-Mexican Border." *Journal of the History of Sexuality* 8:477–506.

Lurie, Alison. 1987. "Fashion and Status." Pp. 124–30 in *The Social World*, 3rd ed., edited by Ian Robertson. New York: Worth Publishers.

Lurie, Nancy Oestreich. 1982. "The American Indian: Historical Background." Pp. 131–44 in *Majority & Minority: The Dynamics of Race and Ethnicity in American Life*, 3rd ed., edited by N. R. Yetman and C. H. Steele. Boston: Allyn & Bacon.

Lyman, Rick. February 24, 1999. "Man Guilty of Murder in Texas Dragging Death." *New York Times*, pp. A1, A12.

Lynn, Laurence E., Jr. 1977. "A Decade of Policy Developments in the Income-Maintenance System." Pp. 55–117 in *A Decade of Federal Antipoverty Programs*, edited by R. H. Haveman. New York: Academic Press.

Lyons, Daniel. July 22, 2002. "Bad Boys." *Forbes*, pp. 99–104.

MacCormack, Carol P. 1980. "Nature, Culture and Gender: A Critique." Pp. 1–24 in *Nature, Culture and Gender*, edited by C. MacCormack and M. Strathern. Cambridge: Cambridge University Press.

MacLeod, Jay. 1987. *Ain't No Makin' It: Leveled Aspirations in a Low-Income Neighborhood*. Boulder, CO: Westview.

Madon, Stephanie. 1997. "What Do People Believe about Gay Males? A Study of Stereotype Content and Strength." *Sex Roles* 37:663–85.

Maguire, Kathleen, and Ann L. Pastore. 2002. *Sourcebook of Criminal Justice Statistics—2002.* Washington, D.C.: U.S. Department of Justice.

Mahler, Vincent A. 2004. "Economic Globalization, Domestic Politics, and Income Inequality in the Developed Countries." *Comparative Political Studies* 37:1025–53.

Makoba, Johnson W. 2002. "Globalization and Marginalization of Labor in the Third World." Paper delivered at Pacific Sociological Association meeting, Vancouver, Canada, April 18–21.

Manderscheid, Ronald W., and Sally A. Barrett, eds. 1987. *Mental Health, United States, 1987.* Washington, D.C.: U.S. Government Printing Office.

Manley, John F. 1983. "Neo-Pluralism: A Class Analysis of Pluralism I and Pluralism II." *American Political Science Review* 77:368–83.

Mantsios, Gregory. 2004. "Class in America-2003." Pp. 193–207 in *Race, Class, and Gender in the United States*, edited by P. S. Rothenberg. New York: Worth.

Manza, Jeff, Clem Brooks, and Christopher Uggen. 2002. "Public Attitudes towards Felon Disenfranchisement in the United States." *Harris Interactive Survey*, July 2002.

Marden, Charles F., and Gladys Meyer. 1973. *Minorities in American Society.* New York: Van Nostrand.

Marger, Martin. 1997. *Race and Ethnic Relations.* Belmont, CA: Wadsworth.

Margolin, Gayla, Linda Gorin Sibner, and Lisa Gleberman. 1988. "Wife Battering." Pp. 89–117 in *Handbook of Family Violence*, edited by V. B. Van Hasselt, R. L. Morrison, A. S. Bellack, and M. Hersen. New York: Plenum.

Markham, Edwin. 1958. "The Man with the Hoe." Reprinted in *One Hundred and One Famous Poems*, compiled by R. J. Cook. Chicago: Reilly & Lee. (poem is out of print).

Markham, William T., Patrick O. Macken, Charles M. Bonjean, and Judy Corder. 1983. "A Note on Sex, Geographic Mobility, and Career Advancement." *Social Forces* 61:1138–46.

Marshall, Gordon, Adam Swift, and Stephen Roberts. 1997. *Against the Odds? Social Class and Social Justice in Industrial Societies.* New York: Oxford University Press.

Marshall, Ray, and Beth Paulin. 1987. "Employment and Earnings of Women: Historical Perspective." Pp. 1–36 in *Working Women: Past, Present, Future*, edited by K. S. Koziara, M. H. Moskow, and L. D. Tanner. Washington, D.C.: Bureau of National Affairs.

Martyna, W. 1978. "What Does 'He' Mean? Use of the Generic Masculine." *Journal of Communication* 28:131–38.

Marx, Karl. 1967. *Capital*, vol. I. New York: International Publishers.

Marx, Karl, and Frederick Engels. 1969 and 1970. *Selected Works*, vols 1, 2, 3. Moscow: Progress Publishers.

"Mass Layoffs in December 2001." Report available at ftp://ftp.bls.gov/pub/news.release/History/mmls. 01292002.news.

Massad, J. 2002. "Re-orienting Desire: The Gay International and the Arab World." *Public Culture* 14:361–85.

Massey, Douglas S. 1995. "Review of the Bell Curve." *American Journal of Sociology* 101:747–53.

Massey, Douglas S., and Nancy A. Denton. 1993. *American Apartheid.* Cambridge, MA: Harvard University Press.

Matthaei, Julie A. 1982. *An Economic History of Women in America.* New York: Schocken Books.

Matthews, Donald R. 1954. "United States Senators and the Class Structure." *Public Opinion Quarterly* 18:5–22. Reprinted on pp. 331–42 in *Social Stratification: A Reader*, edited by J. Lopreato and L. S. Lewis. New York: Harper & Row.

Maume, David J., Jr. 1999. "Occupational Segregation and the Career Mobility of White Men and Women." *Social Forces* 77:1433–59.

Maume, David J., Jr. 2004. "Wage Discrimination over the Life Course: A Comparison of Explanations." *Social Problems* 51:505–27.

Mayer, Kurt B., and Walter Buckley. 1970. *Class & Society.* New York: Random House.

Maynard, Micheline. May 11, 2005. "United Air Wins Right to Default on Its Pensions." *New York Times*, pp. A1, C2.

McAdam, Doug. 1982. *Political Process and the Development of Black Insurgency, 1930–1970.* Chicago: University of Chicago Press.

McAdam, Doug. 1983. "Tactical Innovation and the Pace of Insurgency." *American Sociological Review* 48:735–54.

McCall, Leslie. 2001. "Sources of Racial Wage Inequality in Metropolitan Labor Markets: Racial, Ethnic, and Gender Differences." *American Sociological Review* 66:520–41.

McCarthy, John D., and Mayer N. Zald. 1973. *The Trend of Social Movements in America: Professionalization and Resource Mobilization.* Morristown, NJ: General Learning Press.

McCloskey, Laura Ann. 1996. "Socioeconomic and Coercive Power within the Family." *Gender & Society* 10:449–63.

McDonough, Peggy, David R. Williams, James S. House, and Greg J. Duncan. 1999. "Gender and the Socioeconomic Gradient in Mortality." *Journal of Health and Social Behavior* 40:17–31.

McFate, Katherine. June 1987. "Defining the Underclass." *Focus*, pp. 8–12.

McIntosh, Peggy. 1988. "White Privilege and Male Privilege: A Personal Account of Coming to See Correspondences through Work in Women's Studies." Center for Research on Women Working Paper No. 189. Wellesley, MA: Wellesley College.

McKissack, Fredrick L., Jr. June 1998. "Cyberghetto: Blacks Are Falling through the Net." *The Progressive*, pp. 20–22.

McMurray, Coleen. 2004. "Do Blacks Receive Second-Class Healthcare?" *Gallup Poll Tuesday Briefing*, July 20.

McRoberts, Hugh A., and Kevin Selbee. 1981. "Trends in Occupational Mobility in Canada and the United States: A Comparison." *American Sociological Review* 46:406–21.

Mead, Margaret. 1963. *Sex and Temperament in Three Primitive Societies*. New York: William Morrow.

Meiksins, Peter F. 1988. "A Critique of Wright's Theory of Contradictory Class Locations." *Critical Sociology* 15:73–82.

Melchionno, Rick. Spring 1999. "The Changing Temporary Work Force." *Occupational Outlook Quarterly*, pp. 25–32.

Memmi, Albert. 1965. *The Colonizer and the Colonized*. New York: Orion.

Merten, Don E. 1997. "The Meaning of Meanness: Popularity, Competition, and Conflict among Junior High School Girls." *Sociology of Education* 70:175–91.

Messner, Steven F. 1980. "Income Inequality and Murder Rates: Some Cross-National Findings." *Comparative Social Research* 3:185–98.

Messner, Steven F. 1989. "Economic Discrimination and Societal Homicide Rates: Further Evidence on the Cost of Inequality." *American Sociological Review* 54:597–611.

Messner, Steven F., and Richard Rosenfeld. 1994. *Crime and the American Dream*. Belmont, CA: Wadsworth.

Meyer, Ilan H., and Laura Dean. 1998. "Internalized Homophobia, Intimacy, and Sexual Behavior among Gay and Bisexual Men." Pp. 160–86 in *Stigma and Sexual Orientation*, edited by G. M. Herek. Thousand Oaks, CA: Sage.

Meyer, Lisa B. 2003. "Economic Globalization and Women's Status in the Labor Market." *Sociological Quarterly* 44:351–83.

Meyerson, Harold. May 25, 1992. "Fractured City." *The New Republic*, pp. 23–25.

Miech, Richard Allen, and Michael J. Shanahan. 2000. "Socioeconomic Status and Depression over the Life Course." *Journal of Health and Social Behavior* 41:162–76.

Miech, Richard A., Avshalom Caspi, Terrie E. Moffitt, Bradley R. Entner Wright, and Phil A. Silva. 1999. "Low Socioeconomic Status and Mental Disorders: A Longitudinal Study of Selection and Causation during Young Adulthood." *American Journal of Sociology* 104:1096–1131.

Miles-Doan, Rebecca. 1998. "Violence between Spouses and Intimates: Does Neighborhood Context Matter?" *Social Forces* 77:623–45.

Miliband, Ralph. 1977. *Marxism and Politics*. New York: Oxford University Press.

Miller, Casey, and Kate Swift. 1993. "Women and Names." Pp. 77–84 in *Experiencing Race, Class, and Gender in the United States*, edited by Virginia Cyrus. Mountain View, CA: Mayfield.

Miller, S. M. 1963. *Max Weber: Selections from His Work*. New York: Thomas Y. Crowell.

Miller, S. M. 1975. "Comparative Social Mobility." Reprinted in part on pp. 79–112 in *Social Mobility*, edited by A. P. M. Coxon and C. L. Jones. Baltimore: Penguin.

Miller, William Lee. 1977. *Welfare and Values in America: A Review of Attitudes toward Welfare Policies in Light of American History and Culture*. Durham NC: Welfare Policy Project. Institute of Policy Sciences and Public Affairs of Duke University, The Ford Foundation.

Mills, C. Wright. 1951. *White Collar*. New York: Oxford University Press.

Mills, C. Wright. 1956. *The Power Elite*. New York: Oxford University Press.

Mills, C. Wright. 1959. *The Sociological Imagination*. New York: Oxford University Press.

Mills, C. Wright. 1962. *The Marxists*. New York: Dell.

Mills, Mary Beth. 2003. "Gender and Inequality in the Global Labor Force." Pp. 41–62 in *Annual Review of Anthropology*, edited by W. H. Durham, J. Comaroff, and J. Hill. Palo Alto, CA: Annual Reviews.

Milner, Murray, Jr. 1994. *Status and Sacredness*. New York: Oxford University Press.

Milner, Murray, Jr. 2004. *Freaks, Greeks, and Cool Kids*. New York: Routledge.

Mincer, Jacob, and Solomon Polachek. 1974. "Family Investments in Human Capital: Earnings of Women." *Journal of Political Economy* 82:76–110.

Minnich, Daniel J. 2003. "Corporatism and Income Inequality in the Global Economy: A Panel Study of 17 OECD Countries." *European Journal of Political Research* 42:23–53.

"Minorities in the 109th Congress." 2004. *Congressional Quarterly Weekly*, November 6:2637.

Mintz, Beth. 1975. "The President's Cabinet, 1897–1972: A Contribution to the Power Structure Debate." *Insurgent Sociologist* 5:131–48.

Mirowsky, John, and Catherine E. Ross. 1983. "Paranoia and the Struture of Powerlessness." *American Sociological Review* 48:228–39.

Mirowsky, John, and Catherine E. Ross. 1986. "Social Patterns of Distress." Pp. 23–45 in *Annual Review of Sociology*, vol. 12, edited by R. H. Turner and J. F. Short, Jr. Palo Alto, CA: Annual Reviews.

Mirowsky, John, and Catherine E. Ross. 1995. "Sex Differences in Distress: Real or Artifact?" *American Sociological Review* 60: 449–68.

Mishel, Lawrence, Jared Bernstein, and John Schmitt. 2001. *The State of Working America 2000–2001*. Ithaca, NY: Cornell University.

Mishel, Lawrence, Jared Bernstein, and Sylvia Allegretto. 2005. *The State of Working America 2004/2005*. Ithaca, NY: Cornell University.

Mitzman, Arthur. 1971. *The Iron Cage: An Historical Interpretation of Max Weber*. New York: Grosset & Dunlap.

"Mixed Messages." April 12, 1993. *Newsweek*, pp. 28–29.

Moe, Angela M. 2004. "Blurring the Boundaries: Women's Criminality in the Context of Abuse." *Women's Studies Quarterly* 32:116–38.

Montgomery, David. 1983. "The Past and Future of Workers' Control." Pp. 389–405 in *Workers' Struggles, Past and Present: A "Radical America" Reader*, edited by James Green. Philadelphia: Temple University Press.

Moore, Mark P., and Priya Ranjan. 2005. "Globalisation vs Skill-Biased Technological Change: Implications for Unemployment and Wage Inequality." *The Economic Journal* 115:391–422.

Moore, Wilbert E. 1970. "But Some Are More Equal Than Others." Pp. 143–48 in *The Logic of Social Hierarchies*, edited by E. O. Laumann, P. M. Siegel, and R. W. Hodge. Skokie, IL: Markham.

Morris, Aldon D. 1984. *The Origins of the Civil Rights Movement: Black Communities Organizing for Change*. New York: The Free Press.

Morris, Michael, and John B. Williamson. 1986. *Poverty and Public Policy: An Analysis of Federal Intervention Efforts*. New York: Greenwood Press.

Mouw, Ted. 2000. "Job Relocation and the Racial Gap in Unemployment in Detroit and Chicago, 1980 to 1990." *American Sociological Review* 65:730–53.

Muller, Edward. 1988. "Democracy, Economic Development, and Income Inequality." *American Sociological Review* 53:50–68.

Mullins, Elizabeth I., and Paul Sites. 1984. "The Origins of Contemporary Eminent Black Americans: A Three-Generation Analysis of Social Origins." *American Sociological Review* 49:672–85.

Murray, Charles. 1984. *Losing Ground: American Social Policy 1950–1980*. New York: Basic Books.

Murray, Charles. 1985. "Have the Poor Been 'Losing Ground'?" *Political Science Quarterly* 100:427–45.

Murray, Charles. Summer 1986. "No, Welfare Isn't Really the Problem." *The Public Interest*, pp. 3–11.

Murray, Stephen O. 1996. *American Gay*. Chicago: University of Chicago Press.

Myles, John. 2003. "Where Have All the Sociologists Gone? Explaining Economic Inequality." *Canadian Journal of Sociology* 28:551–59.

Myrdal, Gunnar. 1944. *An American Dilemma: The Negro Problem and Modern Democracy*. New York: Harper and Brothers.

Nagel, S. S., and L. J. Weitzman. 1971. "Women as Litigants." *Hastings Law Journal* 23:171–98.

Nam, Yunju. 2004. "Is America Becoming More Equal for Children? Changes in the Intergenerational Transmission of Low- and High-Income Status." *Social Science Research* 33:187–205.

Nasar, Sylvia. August 16, 1992. "The Rich Get Richer, But Never the Same Way Twice." *New York Times*, p. E3.

Nathans, Stephen J. 2001. "Twelve Years after Price Waterhouse and Still No Success for 'Hopkins in Drag'." *Villanova Law Review* 46:713–43.

National Center for Health Statistics. 2004. *Health, United States, 2004*. Washington, D.C.: U.S. Department of Health and Human Resources.

National Coalition for the Homeless. February 1999. "Who Is Homeless?" *NCH Fact Sheet #5*. Washington, D.C.: Author.

National Coalition for the Homeless. April 1999. "Mental Illness and Homelessness." *NCH Fact Sheet #5*. Washington, D.C.: National Coalition for the Homeless.

National Coalition for the Homeless. June 2001. "Homeless Families with Children." *NCH Fact Sheet #7*. Washington, D.C.: National Coalition for the Homeless.

National Gay and Lesbian Task Force. 2005. *"How Unequal Are Civil Unions?"* Los Angeles: National Gay and Lesbian Task Force.

National Governors' Association Center for Best Practices. 1999. *Round Two Summary of Selected Elements of State Programs for Temporary Assistance for Needy Families*. Washington, D.C.: National Governors' Association.

National Telecommunications and Information Administration. 1999. *Falling through the Net: Defining the Digital Divide*. Washington, D.C.: U.S. Government Printing Office.

"Nation's Inmate Population Increased 2.3 Percent Last Year." April 25, 2005. *New York Times*, p. A14.

Neft, Naomi, and Ann D. Levine. 1997. *Where Women Stand.* New York: Random House.

Neighbors, Harold W., Steven J. Trierweiler, Briggett C. Ford, and Jordana R. Muroff. 2003. "Racial Differences in DSM Diagnosis Using a Semi-Structured Instrument: The Importance of Clinical Judgment in the Diagnosis of African Americans." *Journal of Health and Social Behavior* 43:237–56.

Newman, Katherine S., and Margaret M. Chin. 2003. "High Stakes: Time Poverty, Testing, and the Children of the Working Poor." *Qualitative Sociology* 26:3–34.

Newport, Frank. July 1998. "Americans Remain More Likely to Believe Sexual Orientation Due to Environment, Not Genetics." *The Gallup Poll Monthy*, pp. 14–16.

Newport, Frank. February 2001. "Americans See Women as Emotional and Affectionate, Men as More Aggressive." *The Gallup Poll Monthly*, pp. 34–38.

Nicholson, Linda J. 1984. "Making Our Marx." *The Women's Review of Books* 1:8–9.

Nielsen, Francois. 1994. "Income Inequality and Industrial Development: Dualism Revisited." *American Sociological Review* 59:654–77.

Nielsen, Francois. 1995. Review of the Bell Curve. *Social Forces* 74:337–41.

Nielsen, Francois, and Arthur S. Alderson. 1995. "Income Inequality, Development, and Dualism: Results from an Unbalanced Cross-National Panel." *American Sociological Review* 60:674–701.

Noel, Donald L. 1968. "A Theory of the Origin of Ethnic Stratification." *Social Problems* 16:157–72. Reprinted on pp. 109–20 in *Majority and Minority: The Dynamics of Race and Ethnicity in American Life,* edited by N. R. Yetman, 1985. Boston: Allyn & Bacon.

Oberschall, Anthony. 1973. *Social Conflict and Social Movements.* Englewood Cliffs, NJ: Prentice Hall.

O'Connor, James. 1973. *The Fiscal Crisis of the State.* New York: St. Martin's Press.

Offe, Claus. 1975. "The Theory of the Capitalist State and the Problem of Policy Formation." In *Stress and Contradiction in Modern Capitalism,* edited by L. Lindberg et al. Lexington, MA: D.C. Heath.

O'Hare, William P. 1987. *America's Welfare Population: Who Gets What?* Publication No. 13. Washington, D.C.: Population Reference Bureau.

Okun, Arthur. 1975. *Equality and Efficiency: The Big Tradeoff.* Washington, D.C.: Brookings Institution.

Oliver, Melvin, and Thomas Shapiro. 1995. *Black Wealth and White Wealth: A New Perspective on Racial Inequality.* New York: Routledge.

Ollman, Bertell. 1968. "Marx's Use of Class." *American Journal of Sociology* 73:573–80.

Ollman, Bertell. 1987. "How to Study Class Consciousness and Why We Should." *The Insurgent Sociologist* 14;57–96.

Olzak, Susan, Suzanne Shanahan, and Elizabeth H. McEneaney. 1996. "Poverty, Segregation, and Race Riots: 1960 to 1993." *American Sociological Review* 61:590–613.

Omi, Michael, and Howard Winant. 1986. *Racial Formation in the United States: From the 1960s to the 1980s.* New York: Routledge, Kegan and Paul.

Omi, Michael, and Howard Winant. 2005. "Racial Formation." Pp. 193–99 in *Great Divides,* edited by T. M. Shapiro. Boston: McGraw-Hill.

opensecrets. 2004. *2004 Election Overview.* Available at www.opensecrets.org.

Oppel, Jr., Richard. May 23, 2002. "White House Acknowledges More Contacts with Enron." *New York Times*, pp. A1, C4.

Orlans, Harold, and June O'Neill. 1992. "Preface." *The Annals of the American Academy of Political and Social Science* 523:7–9.

Ornati, Oscar. 1966. *Poverty Amid Affluence.* New York: The Twentieth Century Fund.

Ortner, Sherry B. 1974. "Is Female to Male as Nature Is to Culture?" Pp. 67–87 in *Woman, Culture & Society,* edited by M. Z. Rosaldo and L. Lamphere. Stanford, CA: Stanford University Press.

Ortner, Sherry B., and Harriet Whitehead, eds. 1981. *Sexual Meanings: The Cultural Construction of Gender and Sexuality.* Cambridge: Cambridge University Press.

Ossowski, Stanislaw. 1963. *Class Structure in the Social Consciousness.* New York: The Free Press.

Osterman, Paul. 1975. "An Empirical Study of Labor Market Segmentation." *Industrial and Labor Relations Review* 28:508–23.

Ostrander, Susan. 1984. *Women of the Upper Class.* Philadelphia: Temple University Press.

O'Sullivan, Katherine, and William J. Wilson. 1988. "Race and Ethnicity." Pp. 223–42 in *Handbook of Sociology,* edited by N. J. Smelser. Newbury Park, CA: Sage.

Pager, Devah. 2003. "The Mark of a Criminal Record." *American Journal of Sociology* 108:937–75.

Paradiso, Louis V., and Shauvan M. Wall. 1986. "Children's Perceptions of Male and Female Principals and Teachers." *Sex Roles* 14:1–7.

Parcel, Toby L., and Charles W. Mueller. 1983. *Ascriptions and Labor Markets: Race and Sex Differences in Earnings.* New York: Academic Press.

Parcel, Toby L., and Marie B. Sickmeier. 1988. "One Firm, Two Labor Markets: The Case of

McDonald's in the Fast-Food Industry." *Sociological Quarterly* 29:29–46.

Parenti, Michael. 1970. "Power and Pluralism: A View from the Bottom." *The Journal of Politics* 32:501–30.

Parkin, Frank. 1971. *Class Inequality and Political Order.* New York: Praeger.

Parkin, Frank. 1979. *Marxism and Class Theory: A Bourgeois Critique.* London: Tavistock.

Parlee, Mary Brown. 1979. "Conversational Politics." *Psychology Today* 12:48–91.

Parsons, Talcott. 1964a. "A Revised Analytical Approach to the Theory of Social Stratification." Reprinted on pp. 386–439 in *Essays in Sociological Theory,* rev. ed., by T. Parsons. 1964. New York: The Free Press.

Parsons, Talcott. 1964b. *Essays in Sociological Theory,* rev. ed. New York: The Free Press.

Pattillo-McCoy, Mary. 1999. *Black Picket Fences.* Chicago: University of Chicago.

Pavalko, Eliza K., and Brad Smith. 1999. "The Rhythm of Work: Health Effects of Women's Work Dynamics." *Social Forces* 77:1141–62.

Pavetti, LaDonna, and Gregory Acs. 2001. "Moving Up, Moving Out, or Going Nowhere? A Study of the Employment Patterns of Young Women and the Implications for Welfare Mothers." *Journal of Policy Analysis and Management* 20:721–36.

Pearlin, L. I., E. G. Menaghan, M. A. Lieberman, and J. T. Mullan. 1981. "The Stress Process." *Journal of Health and Social Behavior* 22:337–56.

Pearlman, Deborah N., Sally Zierler, Annie Gjelsvik, and Wendy Verhoekoftedahl. 2003. "Neighborhood Environment, Racial Position, and Risk of Police-Reported Domestic Violence: A Contextual Analysis." *Public Health Reports* 118:44–58.

Perlman, Selig. 1928. *A Theory of the Labor Movement.* New York: Macmillan.

Perlman, Selig, and Philip Taft. 1935. *History of Labor in the United States, 1896–1932. Volume IV: Labor Movements.* New York: Macmillan.

Perry, Barbara. 2001. *In the Name of Hate.* New York: Routledge.

Pessen, Edward. 1973. *Riches, Class and Power before the Civil War.* Lexington, MA: D.C. Heath.

Petersen, Trond, and Ishak Saporta. 2004. "The Opportunity Structure for Discrimination." *American Journal of Sociology* 109:852–901.

Peterson, Richard A., and Albert Simkus. 1992. "How Musical Tastes Mark Occupational Status Groups." Pp. 152–86 in *Cultivating Differences: Symbolic Boundaries and the Making of Inequality,* edited by M. Lamont and M. Fournier. Chicago: University of Chicago Press.

Pew Research Center. 2003. *Republicans Unified, Democrats Spilt on Gay Marriage.* Washington, D.C.: Pew Research Center for the People & the Press.

Phelan, Jo, Bruce G. Link, Robert E. Moore, and Ann Stueve. 1997. "The Stigma of Homelessness: The Impact of the Label 'Homeless' on Attitudes toward Poor Persons." *Social Psychology Quarterly* 60:323–37.

Phelan, Shane. 2001. *Sexual Strangers: Gays, Lesbians, and Dilemmas of Citizenship.* Philadelphia: Temple University Press.

Phelps, Linda. 1981. "Patriarchy and Capitalism." Pp. 161–73 in *Building Feminist Theory: Essays from Quest.* New York: Longman.

Philipson, Ilene J., and Karen V. Hansen. 1990. "Women, Class, and the Feminist Imagination: An Introduction." Pp. 3–40 in *Women, Class, and the Feminist Imagination: A Socialist-Feminist Reader,* edited by K. V. Hansen and I. J. Philipson, Philadelphia: Temple University Press.

Physician Task Force on Hunger in America. 1985. *Hunger in America: The Growing Epidemic.* Middletown, CT: Wesleyan University Press.

Pierce, Jennifer L. 1995. *Gender Trials.* Berkeley: University of California.

Piori, Michael J. 1977. "The Dual Labor Market: Theory and Implications." Pp. 93–97 in *Problems in Political Economy: An Urban Perspective,* edited by D. M. Gordon. Lexington, MA: D.C. Heath.

Piven, Frances Fox, and Richard A. Cloward. 1971. *Regulating the Poor: The Functions of Public Welfare.* New York: Random House.

Piven, Frances Fox, and Richard A. Cloward. 1977. *Poor People's Movements: Why They Succeed, How They Fail.* New York: Pantheon.

Piven, Frances Fox, and Richard A. Cloward. 1982. *The New Class War.* New York: Pantheon.

Piven, Frances Fox, and Richard A. Cloward. 1987. "The Historical Sources of the Contemporary Relief Debate." Pp. 3–43 in *The Mean Season: The Attack on the Welfare State,* edited by F. Block, R. A. Cloward, B. Ehrenreich, and F. F. Piven. New York: Pantheon.

Plotnick, Robert D., and Felicity Skidmore. 1975. *Progress against Poverty: A Review of the 1964–1974 Decade.* New York: Academic Press.

Plous, S. 1996. "The Affirmative Action Debate: What's Fair in Policy and Programs?" *Journal of Social Issues* 52:25–31.

Plutzer, Eric. 1988. "Work Life, Family Life, and Women's Support of Feminism." *American Sociological Review* 53:640–49.

PollingReport. 2005. *Law and Civil Rights.* Available at http://www.pollingreport.com/civil.htm.

Pomer, Marshall I. 1986. "Labor Market Structure, Intergenerational Mobility, and Discrimination: Black Male Advancement Out of Low Paying Occupations 1962–1973." *American Sociological Review* 51:650–59.

Porter, James N. 1974. "Race, Socialization, and Mobility in Educational and Early Occupational Attainment." *American Sociological Review* 39:303–16.

Portes, Alejandro, and Kenneth L. Wilson. 1976. "Black-White Differences in Educational Attainment." *American Sociological Review* 41:414–31.

Portes, Alejandro, and Ruben G. Rumbaut. 2005. "Not Everyone Is Chosen." Pp. 271–283 in *Great Divides*, edited by T. M. Shapiro. Boston: McGraw-Hill.

Poulantzas, Nico. 1973. *Political Power and Social Classes*. London: New left Books.

Powell, G. Bingham, Jr. 1986. "American Voter Turnout in Comparative Perspective." *American Political Science Review* 80:17–43.

Prabhakar, A. C. 2003. "A Critical Reflection on Globalisation and Inequality: A New Approach to the Development of the South." *African and Asian Studies* 2:307–45.

Pratt, Travis C., and Timothy W. Godsey. 2003. "Social Support, Inequality, and Homicide: A Cross-National Test of An Integrated Theoretical Model." *Criminology* 41:611–43.

Presser, Harriet B. 1998. "Toward a 24 Hour Economy: The U.S. Experience and Implications for the Family." Pp. 39–47 in *Challenges for Work and Family in the Twenty-First Century*, edited by D. Vannoy and P. J. Dubeck. New York: Aldine de Gruyter.

Presthus, Robert. 1962. *The Organizational Society*. New York: Vintage Books.

Prewitt, Kenneth, and Alan Stone. 1973. *The Ruling Elites*. New York: Harper & Row.

"Price Waterhouse v. Hopkins." 1989. No. 87–1167. Supreme Court of the United States. 490 U.S. 228: 231–95.

"Providing Health Insurance for the Uninsured." 2003–2004. *La Follette Policy Report*, Winter:2–3.

Public Citizen. 1999. *NAFTA at Five: School of Real Life Results*. http://www.citizen.org/pctrade/nafta/reports/5years.htm.

Pyke, Karen, and Tran Dang. 2003. " 'FOB and 'Whitewashed': Identity and Internalized Racism among Second Generation Asian Americans." *Qualitative Sociology* 26:147–72.

Quillian, Lincoln, and Devah Pager. 2001. "Black Neighbors, Higher Crime? The Role of Racial Stereotypes in Evalutions of Neighborhood Crime." *American Journal of Sociology* 107:717–67.

Quinney, Richard. 1970. *The Social Reality of Crime*. Boston: Little, Brown.

Raabe, Phyllis Hutton. 1998. "Being a Part-Time Manager: One Way to Combine Family and Career." Pp. 81–91 in *Challenges for Work and Family in the Twenty-First Century*, edited by D. Vannoy and P. J. Dubeck. New York: Aldine de Gruyter.

Ragsdale, Lyn. 1998. *Vital Statistics on the Presidency: Washington to Clinton*. Washington, D.C: Congressional Quarterly.

Rainwater, Lee. 1974. *What Money Buys*. New York: Basic Books.

Ramsey, P. G. 1991. "Young Children's Awareness and Understanding of Social Class Differences." *Journal of Genetic Psychology* 152:71–82.

Ransford, H. Edward, and Jon Miller. 1983. "Race, Sex and Feminist Outlooks." *American Sociological Review* 48:46–59.

Ransom, Montrece McNeill. 2001. "The Boy's Club: How 'Don't Ask, Don't Tell' Creates a Double-Bind for Women." *Law and Psychology Review* 25:161–77.

Raven, Bertram H. 1965. "Social Influence and Power." Pp. 399–444 in *Current Studies in Social Psychology*, edited by I. D. Steiner and M. Fishbein. New York: Wiley.

Redburn, F. Stevens, and Terry F. Buss. 1986. *Responding to America's Homeless: Public Policy Alternatives*. New York: Praeger.

Reich, Michael. 1977. "The Economics of Racism." Pp. 183–88 in *Problems in Political Economy: An Urban Perspective*, edited by D. M. Gordon. Lexington, MA: D.C. Heath.

Reich, Michael, David M. Gordon, and Richard C. Edwards. 1977. "A Theory of Labor Market Segmentation." Pp. 108–13 in *Problems in Political Economy: An Urban Perspective*, edited by D. M. Gordon. Lexington, MA: D.C. Heath.

Reid, Pamela Trotman. 1984. "Feminism versus Minority Group Identity: Not for Black Women Only." *Sex Roles* 10:247–55.

Reid, Sue Titus. 1988. *Crime and Criminology*. New York: Holt, Rinehart and Winston.

Reiman, Jeffrey. 2004. *The Rich Get Richer and the Poor Get Prison*. Boston: Allyn & Bacon.

Reiss, Albert J., Jr., ed. 1961. *Occupations and Social Status*. New York: The Free Press.

Reissman, Leonard. 1959. *Class in American Society*. Glencoe, IL: The Free Press.

Reskin, Barbara F. 1984. "Introduction." Pp. 1–7 in *Sex Segregation in the Workplace: Trends, Explanations, Remedies*, edited by B. F. Reskin. Washington, D.C.: National Academy Press.

Reskin, Barbara F. 2003. "Including Mechanisms in Our Models of Ascriptive Inequality." *American Sociological Review* 68:1–21.

Reskin, Barbara F., and Debra Branch McBrier. 2000. "Why Not Ascription? Organizations' Employment of Male and Female Managers." *American Sociological Review* 65:210–33.

Resnick, Stephen, and Richard Wolff. 2003. "The Diversity of Class Analyses: A Critique of Erik Olin Wright and Beyond." *Critical Sociology* 29:7–27.

Reuveny, Rafael, and Quan Li. 2003. "Economic Openness, Democracy, and Income Inequality." *Comparative Political Studies* 36:575–601.

Richardson, Laurel. 1987. *The Dynamics of Sex and Gender: A Sociological Perspective*. New York: Harper & Row.

Ridgeway, Cecilia L., Elizabeth Heger Boyle, Kathy J. Kuipers, and Dawn T. Robinson. 1998. "How Do Status Beliefs Develop? The Role of Resources and Interactional Experience." *American Sociological Review* 63:331–50.

Riedle, Joan E. 1991. "Exploring the Subcategories of Stereotypes: Not All Mothers Are the Same." *Sex Roles* 24:711–22.

Riesman, David, with Reuel Denney and Nathan Glazer. 1950. *The Lonely Crowd*. New Haven, CT: Yale University Press.

Rigney, Daniel. 2001. *The Metaphorical Society*. Lanham, MD: Rowman & Littlefield.

Riis, Jacob. 1890. *How the Other Half Lives*. Williamstown, MA: Corner House.

Ringquist, Evan J. 1997. "Equity and the Distribution of Environmental Risk: The Case of TRI Facilities." *Social Science Quarterly* 78:811–29.

Ringquist, Evan J. 2000. "Environmental Justice: Normative Concerns and Empirical Evidence." Pp. 232–56 in *Environmental Policy*, edited by N. J. Vig and M. E. Kraft. Washington, D.C.: CQ Press.

Rischin, Moses, ed. 1965. *The American Gospel of Success*. New York: Quadrangle/The New York Times Books.

Risman, Barbara J. 2005. "Gender as Structure." Pp. 292–99 in *Great Divides*, edited by T. M. Shapiro. Boston: McGraw-Hill.

Ritzman, Rosemary, and Donald Tomaskovic-Devey. 1992. "Life Chances and Support for Equality and Equity as Normative and Counternormative Distribution Rules." *Social Forces* 70:745–63.

Robbins, Alexandra. 2004. *Pledged: The Secret Life of Sororities*. New York: Hyperion.

Robert, Stephanie A. 1998. "Community-Level Socioeconomic Status Effects on Adult Health." *Journal of Health and Social Behavior* 39:18–37.

Robinson, Robert, and Wendell Bell. 1978. "Equality, Success and Social Justice in England and the United States." *American Sociological Review* 43:125–43.

Robison, Jennifer. 2003. "Social Classes in U.S., Britain, and Canada." *Gallup Poll Tuesday Briefing*, August 6:1–3.

Rodgers, Joan R. 1995. "An Empirical Study of Intergenerational Transmission of Poverty in the United States." *Social Science Quarterly* 76:178–94.

Rodriguez, Richard. 1982. *Hunger of Memory: The Education of Richard Rodriguez*. New York: Bantam Books.

Rogin, Michael. 1971. "Voluntarism: The Political Functions of an Anti-Political Doctrine." Pp. 100–18 in *The American Labor Movement*, edited by D. Brody. New York: Harper & Row.

Rollins, Judith. 1986. "Part of a Whole: The Interdependence of the Civil Rights Movement and Other Social Movements." *Phylon* 47:61–70.

Romero, Diana, Wendy Chavkin, Paul H. Wise, and Lauren A. Smith. 2003. "Low-Income Mothers' Experience with Poor Health, Hardship, Work, and Violence: Implications for Policy." *Violence Against Women* 9:1231–44.

Romero, Mary. 1992. *Maid in the USA*. London: Routledge.

Roos, Patricia A. 1985. *Gender & Work: A Comparative Analysis of Industrial Societies*. Albany: State University of New York Press.

Roos, Patricia A., and Barbara F. Reskin. 1984. "Institutional Factors Contributing to Sex Segregation in the Workplace." Pp. 235–60 in *Sex Segregation in the Workplace: Trends, Explanations, Remedies*. Washington, D.C.: National Academy Press.

Roosevelt, Franklin Delano. 1966. "Second Inaugural Address." In *Poverty in the Affluent Society*, edited by H. H. Meissner. New York: Harper & Row.

Roscigno, Vincent J., and Randy Hodson. 2004. "The Organizational and Social Foundations of Worker Resistance." *American Sociological Review* 69:14–39.

Rose, Arnold M. 1968. *The Power Structure*. New York: Oxford University Press.

Rosencranz, Mary Lou. 1962. "Clothing Symbolism." *Journalism of Home Economics* 54:18–22.

Rosenfeld, Rachel A. 1992. "Job Mobility and Career Processes." Pp. 39–61 in *Annual Review of Sociology*, vol. 18, edited by J. Blake and J. Hagan. Palo Alto, CA: Annual Reviews.

Rosenfield, Sarah. 1989. "The Effects of Women's Employment: Personal Control and Sex Differences in Mental Health." *Journal of Health and Social Behavior* 30:77–91.

Rospenda, Kathleen M., Judith A. Richman, and Stephanie J. Nawyn. 1998. "Doing Power: The Confluence of Gender, Race, and Class in Contrapower Sexual Harassment." *Gender & Society* 12:40–60.

Ross, Catherine E., and John Mirowsky. 2001. "Neighborhood Disadvantage, Disorder, and Health." *Journal of Health and Social Behavior* 42:258–76.

Ross, Catherine E., John R. Reynolds, and Karlyn J. Geis. 2000. "The Contingent Meaning of Neighborhood Stability for Residents' Psychological Well-Being." *American Sociological Review* 65:581–97.

Ross, Irwin. 1980. "How Lawless Are Big Companies?" *Fortune* 102:57.

Rossi, Peter H., and James D. Wright. 1989. "The Urban Homeless: A Portrait of Urban Dislocation." *Annals of the American Academy of Political and Social Sciences* 501:132–42.

Rossides, Daniel W. 1976. *The American Class System: An Introduction to Social Stratification*. Boston: Houghton Mifflin.

Roth, Guenther, and Claus Wittich, eds. 1968. *Max Weber: Economy and Society*. 3 vols. New York: Bedminster Press.

Roth, Louise Marie. 2004a. "Engendering Inequality: Processes of Sex-Segregation on Wall Street." *Sociological Forum* 19:203–28.

Roth, Louise Marie. 2004b. "Bringing Clients Back In: Homophily Preferences and Inequality on Wall Street," *Sociological Quarterly* 45:613–35.

Roth, Wendy. 2005. "The End of the One-Drop Rule? Labeling of Multiracial Children in Black Intermarriages." *Sociological Forum* 20:35–67.

Rothenberg, Paula S. 2002. *White Privilege*. New York: Worth Publishers.

Rothman, Barbara Katz. 1984. "Women, Health, and Medicine." Pp. 70–80 in *Women: A Feminist Perspective*, edited by J. Freeman. Palo Alto, CA: Mayfield.

Rowley, Anthony. 1990. "Unmentioned Underclass." *Far Eastern Economic Review* 150:36–37.

Rubenstein, Ruth P. 2001. *Dress Codes*. Boulder, CO: Westview.

Rubin, Lillian Breslow. 1976. *Worlds of Pain: Life in the Working-Class Family*. New York: Basic Books.

Rudra, Nita. 2004. "Openness, Welfare Spending, and Inequality in the Developing World." *International Studies Quarterly* 48:683–709.

Rupp, Leila J. 1985. "The Women's Community in the National Women's Party, 1945 to the 1960's." *Signs: Journal of Women in Culture and Society* 10:715–40.

Rushing, William A. 1978. "Status Resources, Societal Reactions, and Type of Mental Hospital Admission." *American Sociological Review* 43:521–33.

Ryan, William. 1981. *Equality*. New York: Random House.

Ryff, Carol D., Corey L. M. Keyes, and Diane L. Hughes. 2003. "Status Inequalities, Perceived Discrimination, and Eudaimonic Well-Being: Do the Challenges of Minority Life Hone Purpose and Growth?" *Journal of Health and Social Behavior* 44:275–91.

Rytina, Steven. 2000. "Is Occupational Mobility Declining in the U.S.?" *Social Forces* 78:1227–76.

Sachs, Jeffrey D. 2005. "The End of Poverty." *Time*, March 14:44–54.

Sacks, Karen. 1975. "Engels Revisited: Women, the Organization of Production, and Private Property." Pp. 211–34 in *Toward an Anthropology of Women*, edited by R. R. Reiter. New York: Monthly Review Press.

Safran, Claire. 1992. "The New Faces of Poverty." *Redbook* 179:84–87.

Sahlins, Marshall D. 1968. *Tribesmen*. Englewood Cliffs, NJ: Prentice Hall.

Sakamoto, Arthur, Jeng Liu, and Jessie M. Tzeng. 1998. "The Declining Significance of Race among Chinese and Japanese American Men." *Research in Social Stratification and Mobility* 16:225–46.

Salin, Denise. 2003. "Ways of Explaining Workplace Bullying: A Review of Enabling, Motivating and Precipitating Structures and Processes in the Work Environment." *Human Relations* 56:1213–32.

Sampson, Robert J. 1986. "Effects of Socioeconomic Context on Official Reaction to Juvenile Delinquency." *American Sociological Review* 51:876–85.

Sampson, Robert J., and William Julius Wilson. 1995. "Toward a Theory of Race, Crime, and Urban Inequality." Pp. 37–54 in *Crime and Inequality*, edited by J. Hagan and R. D. Peterson. Stanford: Stanford University Press.

Sanday, Peggy Reeves. 1981. *Female Power and Male Dominance: On the Origins of Sexual Inequality*. Cambridge: Cambridge University Press.

Sandler, Bernice R. 1986. "The Campus Climate Revisited: Chilly for Women Faculty, Administrators, and Graduate Students." Washington, D.C.: Association of American Colleges.

Sassen, Saskia. 2000. "The State and the New Geography of Power." Pp. 49–65 in *The Ends of Globalization*, edited by D. Kalb, M. van der Land, R. Staring, B. van Steenbergen, and N. Wilterdink. Lanham, MD: Rowman & Littlefield.

Save the Children. 2004. *State of the World's Mothers 2004*. Westport, CT: Save the Children.

Savin-Williams, R. C., and R. G. Rodriguez. 1993. "A Developmental, Clinical Perspective on Lesbian, Gay Male, and Bisexual Youths."

Pp. 77–101 in *Adolescent Sexuality*, edited by T. P. Gullotta, G. R. Adams, and R. Montemayor. Newbury Park, CA: Sage.

Savin-Williams, Ritch C. 1996. "Dating and Romantic Relationships among Gay, Lesbian, and Bisexual Youths." Pp. 166–80 in *The Lives of Lesbians, Gays, and Bisexuals*, edited by R. C. Savin-Williams and K. M. Cohen. Fort Worth, TX: Harcourt Brace.

Savin-Williams, Ritch C., and Kenneth M. Cohen. 1996. "Psychosocial Outcomes of Verbal and Physical Abuse among Lesbian, Gay, and Bisexual Youths." Pp. 181–200 in *The Lives of Lesbians, Gays, and Bisexuals*, edited by R. C. Savin-Williams and K. M. Cohen. Fort Worth, TX: Harcourt Brace.

Sawhill, Isable V. 1988. "Poverty in the U.S.: Why Is It So Persistent?" *Journal of Economic Literature* 26:1073–1119.

Schaefer, Richard T. 1987. "Racial Prejudice in a Capitalist State: What Has Happened to the American Creed?" Pp. 162–68 in *Introducing Sociology: A Collection of Readings*, edited by R. T. Schaefer and R. P. Lamm. New York: McGraw-Hill.

Schaefer, Richard T. 2006. *Racial and Ethnic Groups*. Upper Saddle River, NJ: Pearson Education.

Schein, Virginia, Ruediger Mueller, and Carolyn Jacobson. 1989. "The Relationship between Sex Role Stereotypes and Requisite Management Characteristics among College Students." *Sex Roles* 20:103–10.

Schellenberg, E. Glenn, Jessie Hirt, and Alan Sears. 1999. "Attitudes towards Homosexuals among Students at a Canadian University." *Sex Roles* 40:139–52.

Schiller, Bradley R. 1998. *The Economics of Poverty and Discrimination*. Englewood Cliffs, NJ: Prentice Hall.

Schlegel, Alice, ed. 1977. *Sexual Stratification: A Cross-Cultural View*. New York: Columbia University Press.

Schneider, William. July 1992. "The Suburban Century Begins." *The Atlantic Monthly*, pp. 33–44.

Schnittker, Jason, Jeremy Freese, and Brain Powell. 2000. "Nature, Nurture, Neither, Nor: Black-White Differences in Beliefs about the Causes and Appropriate Treatment of Mental Illness." *Social Forces* 78:1101–30.

Schnittker, Jason, Bernice A. Pescosolido, and Thomas W. Croghan. 2005. "Are African Americans Really Less Willing to Use Health Care?" *Social Problems* 52:255–71.

Scholte, Jan Aart. 2000. *Globalization: A Critical Introduction*. New York: St. Martin's Press.

Schooler, Carmi, Mesfin Samuel Mulatu, and Gary Oates. 2004. "Occupational Self-Direction, Intellectual Functioning, and Self-Directed Orientation in Older Workers: Findings and Implications for Individuals and Societies." *American Journal of Sociology* 110:161–97.

Schram, Sanford F., and Joe Soss. 2001. "Success Stories: Welfare Reform, Policy Discourse, and the Politics of Research." *Annals of the American Academy of Political and Social Science* 577:49–65.

Schultz, T. Paul. 1998. "Inequalities in the Distribution of Personal Income in the World: How It Is Changing and Why." *Journal of Population Economics* 11:307–44.

Schwalbe, Michael, Sandra Godwin, Daphne Holden, Douglas Schrock, Shealy Thompson, and Michele Wolkomir. 2000. "Generic Processes in the Reproduction of Inequality: An Interactionist Analysis." *Social Forces* 79:419–52.

Schwartz, Michael, ed. 1987. *The Structure of Power in America*. New York: Holmes & Meier.

Scott, Janny, and David Leonhardt. May 15, 2005. "Class in America: Shadowy Lines That Still Divide." *New York Times*, pp. A1, A16.

Scott, Sarah. November 1, 2000. "The Deepest Cut of All." *Chatelaine*, p. 191.

Scully, Diana, and Pauline Bart. 1981. "A Funny Thing Happened on the Way to the Orifice: Women in Gynecology Textbooks." Pp. 350–55 in *The Sociology of Health and Illness: Critical Perspectives*, edited by P. Conrad and R. Kern. New York: St. Martin's Press.

Secombe, Wally. 1973. "The Housewife and Her Labour Under Capitalism." *New Left Review* 83:19.

Sedgwick, Eve Kosofsky. 1998. "What's Queer?" Pp. 183–87 in *Gender Inequality*, edited by J. Lorber. Los Angeles: Roxbury.

Segal, Troy. May 18, 1992. "The Riots: 'Just as Much about Class as about Race.'" *BusinessWeek*, p. 47.

Seider, Maynard S. 1974. "American Big Business Ideology: A Content Analysis of Executive Speeches." *American Sociological Review* 39:802–15.

Seidman, Ann. 1978. *Working Women: A Study of Women in Paid Jobs*. Boulder, CO: Westview Press.

Select Committee on Hunger. 1992. *Hunger in America: Who Cares?* Series 102–28. Washington, D.C.: U.S. Government Printing Office.

Sell, Ralph R., and Michael P. Johnson. 1977. "Income and Occupational Differences between Men and Women in the United States." *Sociology and Social Research* 62:1–20.

Sellers, Robert M., Cleopatra H. Caldwell, Karen H. Schmeelk-Cone, and Marc A. Zimmerman. 2003. "Racial Identity, Racial Discrimination, Perceived Stress, and Psychological Distress among African American Young Adults." *Journal of Health and Social Behavior* 43:302–17.

Sennett, Richard, and Jonathan Cobb. 1973. *The Hidden Injuries of Class*. New York: Vintage.

Serbin, Lisa A., K. Daniel O'Leary, Ronald N. Kent, and Illene J. Tonick. 1973. "A Comparison of Teacher Response to the Preacademic and Problem Behaviors of Boys and Girls." *Child Development* 44: 796–804.

Seshanna, Shubhasree, and Stephane Decornez. 2003. "Income Polarization and Inequality Across Countries: An Empirical Study." *Journal of Policy Modeling* 25:335–58.

Sewell, William H., Archibald O. Haller, and George W. Ohlendorf. 1970. "The Educational and Early Occupational Status Attainment Process: Replication and Revision." *American Sociological Review* 35:1014–27.

Sewell, William H., and Robert M. Hauser. 1972. "Causes and Consequences of Higher Education: Models of the Status Attainment Access." *American Journal of Agricultural Economics* 54:851–61.

Sewell, William H., and Robert M. Hauser. 1976. "Recent Developments in the Wisconsin Study of Social and Psychological Factors in Socioeconomic Achievement." Center for Demography Working Paper No. 76–11. Madison: University of Wisconsin.

Sewell, William H., and Vimal Shah. 1967. "Socioeconomic Status, Intelligence, and the Attainment of Higher Education." *Sociology of Education* 40:1–23.

Shamir, Ronen. 2005. "Without Borders? Notes on Globalization as a Mobility Regime." *Sociological Theory* 23:197–217.

Shanahan, Michael J., Richard A. Miech, and Glen H. Elder, Jr. 1998. "Changing Pathways to Attainment in Men's Lives: Historical Patterns of School, Work, and Social Class." *Social Forces* 77:231–56.

Shaw, Greg M., and Robert Y. Shapiro. 2002. "The Polls-Trends: Poverty and Public Assistance." *Public Opinion Quarterly* 66:105–28.

Shepelak, Norma J. 1987. "The Role of Self-Explanations and Self-Evaluations in Legitimating Inequality." *American Sociological Review* 52:495–503.

Shepelak, Norma J., and Duane Alwin. 1986. "Beliefs about Inequality and Perceptions of Distributive Justice." *American Sociological Review* 51:30–46.

Sherman, Lawrence W. 1987. "Deviant Organizations." Pp. 52–62 in *Corporate and Governmental Deviance*, edited by M. D. Ermann and R. J. Lundman. New York: Oxford.

Sherrod, Drury, and Peter M. Nardi. 1998. "Homophobia in the Courtroom." Pp. 24–38 in *Stigma and Sexual Orientation*, edited by G. M. Herek. Thousand Oaks, CA: Sage.

Shifman, Pamela. 2003. "Trafficking and Women's Human Rights in a Globalized World." *Gender and Development* 11:125–32.

Shihadeh, Edward S., and Nicole Flynn. 1996. "Segregation and Crime: The Effect of Black Social Isolation on the Rates of Black Urban Violence." *Social Forces* 74:1325–52.

Shils, Edward A. 1970. "Deference." Pp. 420–28 in *The Logic of Social Hierarchies*, edited by Edward O. Laumann, Paul M. Siegel, and Robert W. Hodge. Chicago: Markham.

Shirley, Carla, and Michael Wallace. 2004. "Domestic Work, Family Characteristics, and Earnings: Reexamining Gender and Class Differences." *Sociological Quarterly* 45:663–90.

Simon, Angela. 1998. "The Relationship between Stereotypes of and Attitudes toward Lesbians and Gays." Pp. 62–81 in *Stigma and Sexual Orientation*, edited by G. M. Herek. Thousands Oaks, CA: Sage.

Simon, Lawrence H. 1994. *Karl Marx: Selected Writings*. Indianapolis: Hackett Publishing.

Simon, R. J., and Navin Sharma. 1979. *The Female Defendant in Washington, D.C.: 1974 and 1975*. Washington, D.C.: INSLAW.

Simon, Robin W. 2002. "Revisiting the Relationships among Gender, Marital Status, and Mental Health." *American Journal of Sociology* 107:1065–96.

Simpson, George Eaton, and J. Milton Yinger. 1965. *Racial and Cultural Minorities*. New York: Harper & Row.

Singleton, Judy. 1998. "The Impact of Family Caregiving to the Elderly on the American Workplace: Who Is Affected and What Is Being Done?" Pp. 201–14 in *Challenges for Work and Family in the Twenty-First Century*, edited by D. Vannoy and P. J. Dubeck. New York: Aldine de Gruyter.

Sitkoff, Harvard. 1981. *The Struggle for Black Equality, 1954–1980*. New York: Hill and Wang.

Sivaramayya, B. 1983. "Equality and Inequality: The Legal Framework." Pp. 28–70 in *Equality and Inequality: Theory and Practice*, edited by A. Beteille. Delhi: Oxford University Press.

Skocpol, Theda. 1988. "An 'Uppity Generation' and the Revitalization of Macroscopic Sociology." Pp. 145–59 in *Sociological Lives*, edited by M. W. Riley. Newbury Park, CA: Sage.

Slater, Courtenay M., and Cornelia J. Strawser, eds. 1998. *Business Statistics of the United States*. Washington, D.C.: Bernan Press.

Sloane, David Charles. 1991. *The Last Great Necessity: Cemeteries in American History*. Baltimore: Johns Hopkins University.

Smidt, Corwin. 1980. "Civil Religious Orientations among Elementary School Children." *Sociological Analysis* 41:24–40.

Smith, Dorothy E. 1987. *The Everyday World as Problematic: A Feminist Sociology.* Boston: Northeastern University Press.

Smith, James D. 1987. "Recent Trends in the Distribution of Wealth in the U.S.: Data, Research Problems, and Prospects." Pp. 72–89 in *International Comparisons of the Distribution of Household Wealth*, edited by Edward D. Wolff. Oxford: Clarendon Press.

Smith, James P., and Barry Edmonston, eds. 1997. *The New Americans: Economic, Demographic, and Fiscal Effects of Immigration.* Washington, D.C.: National Academy Press.

Smith, Kevin B., and Robert A. Bylund. 1983. "Cognitive Maps of Class, Racial, and Appalachian Inequalities among Rural Appalachians." *Rural Sociology* 48:253–70.

Smith, Mapheus. 1943. "An Empirical Scale of Prestige Status of Occupations." *American Sociological Review* 8:185–92.

Smith, Patricia K. 1994. "Downward Mobility: Is It a Growing Problem?" *American Journal of Economics and Sociology* 53:57–72.

Smith, Vernon K. 1974. *Welfare Work Incentives: The Earnings Exemption and Its Impact upon AFDC Employment, Earnings, and Program Costs.* Lansing, MI: Michigan Department of Social Services.

Smucker, Philip. February 25, 2001. "Egyptian Women Fight Circumcision: Activists Making Gains against Ancient Rite of Mutilation." *Pittsburgh Post-Gazette*, p. A4.

Snipp, C. Matthew. 1985. "Occupational Mobility and Social Class: Insights from Men's Career Mobility." *American Sociological Review* 50:475–93.

Snipp, C. Matthew. 2003. "Racial Measurement in the American Census: Past Practices and Implications for the Future." Pp. 563–88 in *Annual Review of Sociology*, edited by K. S. Cook and J. Hagan. Palo Alto, CA: Annual Reviews.

Snyder, David, and Charles Tilly. 1972. "Hardship and Collective Violence in France, 1830–1960." *American Sociological Review* 37:520–32.

Snyder, David, and Charles Tilly. 1974. "On Debating and Falsifying Theories of Collective Violence." *American Sociological Review* 39:610–13.

Snyder, Eloise C., ed. 1979. *The Study of Women: Enlarging Perspectives of Social Reality.* New York: Harper & Row.

Sobel, Michael E. 1983a. "Lifestyle Differentiation and Stratification in Contemporary U.S. Society." Pp. 115–44 in *Research in Social Stratification and Mobility*, vol. 2, edited by Donald W. Treiman

and Robert V. Robinson. Greenwich, CT: JAI Press.

Sobel, Michael E. 1983b. "Structural Mobility, Circulation Mobility and the Analysis of Occupational Mobility: A Conceptual Mismatch." *American Sociological Review* 48:721–27.

Sobolewski, Juliana M., and Paul R. Amato. 2005. "Economic Hardship in the Family of Origin and Children's Psychological Well-Being in Adulthood." *Journal of Marriage and Family* 67:141–56.

Sokoloff, Natalie J. 2004. "Domestic Violence at the Crossroads." *Women's Studies Quarterly* 32:139–47.

Soltow, Lee. 1975. *Men and Wealth in the United States.* New Haven, CT: Yale University Press.

Sontag, Susan. 1973. "The Third World of Women." *Partisan Review* 60:201–03.

Sorensen, Aage B. 2000. "Symposium on Class Analysis: Toward a Sounder Basis for Class Analysis." *American Journal of Sociology* 105:1523–58.

Soule, Sarah A., and Susan Olzak. 2004. "When Do Movements Matter? The Politics of Contingency and the Equal Rights Amendment." *American Sociological Review* 69:473–97.

Spaeth, Joe L. 1976a. "Cognitive Complexity: A Dimension Underlying the Socioeconomic Achievement Process." In *Schooling and Achievement in American Society*, edited by W. H. Sewell, R. M. Hauser, and D. L. Featherman. New York: Academic Press.

Spain, Daphne. 1992. *Gendered Spaces.* Chapel Hill: The University of North Carolina Press.

Spain, Daphne. April 21–24, 1993. "Built to Last: Public Housing as an Urban Gendered Space." Paper presented at the Urban Affairs Association, Indianapolis.

Spector, Malcolm, and John I. Kitsuse. 1977. *Constructing Social Problems.* Menlo Park, CA: Cummings Publishing.

Spencer, Barbara, and G. Stephen Taylor. 1988. "Effects of Facial Attractiveness and Gender on Causal Attributions of Managerial Performance." *Sex Roles* 19:273–85.

Spencer, Herbert. 1892/1946. *The Man versus the State.* Caldwell, ID: The Caxton Printers.

Spencer, Herbert. 1897. *The Principles of Ethics.* Vol. II. New York: D. Appleton.

Spencer, Herbert. 1909. *The Principles of Sociology.* Vol. II. New York: D. Appleton.

Spencer, Herbert. 1912. *The Principles of Sociology.* Vol. I. New York: D. Appleton.

Spencer, Herbert. 1961. *The Study of Sociology.* Ann Arbor: University of Michigan.

Spilerman, Seymour. 2000. "Wealth and Stratification Processes." Pp. 497–524 in *Annual Review of*

Sociology, edited by K. S. Cook and J. Hagan. Palo Alto, CA: Annual Reviews.

Stack, Steven, and Delores Zimmerman. 1982. "The Effect of World Economy on Income Inequality: A Reassessment." *The Sociological Quarterly* 23:345–58.

Stanley, Thomas J., and William D. Danko. 1996. *The Millionaire Next Door.* Atlanta, GA: Longstreet Press.

Stark, Evan, and Anne Flitcraft. 1988. "Violence among Intimates: An Epidemiological Review." Pp. 293–317 in *Handbook of Family Violence*, edited by V. B. Van Hasselt, R. L. Morrison, A. S. Bellack, and M. Hersen. New York: Plenum.

Steffensmeier, Darrell, and Chris Hebert. 1999. "Women and Men Policymakers: Does the Judge's Gender Affect the Sentencing of Criminal Defendants?" *Social Forces* 77:1163–96.

Steffensmeier, Darrell, and Stephen Demuth. 2000. "Ethnicity and Sentencing Outcomes in U.S. Federal Courts: Who is Punished More Harshly?" *American Sociological Review* 65:705–29.

Steil, Janice M. 1984. "Martial Relationships and Mental Health: The Psychic Costs of Inequality." Pp. 113–23 in *Women: A Feminist Perspective*, edited by J. Freeman. Palo Alto, CA: Mayfield.

Stephenson, Charles, and Robert Asher, eds. 1986. *Life and Labor: Dimensions of American Working-Class History.* Albany, NY: State University of New York Press.

Stern, Philip M. 1988. *The Best Congress Money Can Buy.* New York: Pantheon.

Stolte, John F. 1983. "The Legitimation of Structural Inequality: Reformulation and Test of the Self-Evaluation Argument." *American Sociological Review* 48:331–42.

Stolte, John F. 1987. "The Formation of Justice Norms." *American Sociological Review* 52:774–84.

Stolzenberg, Ross M. 2001. "It's About Time and Gender: Spousal Employment and Health." *American Journal of Sociology* 107:61–100.

Stone, Gregory P. 1962. "Appearance and the Self." Pp. 86–118 in *Human Behavior and Social Processes*, edited by Arnold M. Rose. Boston: Houghton Mifflin.

Strathern, Marilyn. 1980. "No Nature, No Culture: The Hagen Case." Pp. 174–222 in *Nature, Culture and Gender*, edited by C. MacCormack and M. Strathern. Cambridge: Cambridge University Press.

Straus, Murray A., and Richard J, Gelles. 1990. *Physical Violence in American Families.* New Brunswick, NJ: Transaction.

Strobe, Leigh. August 17, 2004. "The Haves Have More; Have-Nots Have Less." *Wisconsin State Journal*, pp. A1, A8.

"Study Examines Rural Low-Income Families in Light of Welfare Reform." June 6, 2002. *The Wayne Journal*, p. 28.

"Study Shows Shift to Lower-Pay Jobs." September 2, 1988. *Akron Beacon Journal.*

Sturm, James L. 1977. *Investing in the United States, 1798–1893.* New York: Arno Press.

Sutherland, Edwin H. 1949. *White Collar Crime.* New York: Dryden.

Swanson, Guy E. 1974. *The Birth of the Gods.* Ann Arbor, MI: University of Michigan.

Sweeney, Richard. 1993. *Out of Place: Homelessness in America.* New York: HarperCollins.

Szafran, Robert F. 1982. "What Kinds of Firms Hire and Promote Women and Blacks? A Review of the Literature." *The Sociological Quarterly* 23:171–90.

Szasz, Andrew, and Michael Meuser. 1997. "Environmental Inequalities: Literature Review and Proposals for New Directions in Research and Theory." *Current Sociology* 45:99–120.

Szymanski, Albert. 1978. *The Capitalist State and the Politics of Class.* Cambridge, MA: Winthrop.

Tabb, William K. September 4–11, 1970. "Black Americans: Internal Colony or Marginal Working Class." Paper presented at the Seventh World Congress of Sociology of the International Sociological Association, Varna, Bulgaria.

Tausig, Mark, and Rudy Fenwick. 1999. "Recession and Well-Being." *Journal of Health and Social Behavior* 40:1–16.

Taylor, Timothy. 2002. "The Truth about Globalization." *The Public Interest* 147:24–44.

Taylor, Verta. 1989a. "Social Movement Continuity: The Women's Movement in Abeyance." *American Sociological Review* 54:761–75.

Taylor, Verta. 1989b. "The Future of Feminism: A Social Movement Analysis." Pp. 473–90 in *Feminist Frontiers II: Rethinking Sex, Gender, and Society*, edited by L. Richardson and V. Taylor. New York: Random House.

Taylor, William L., and Susan M. Liss. 1992. "Affirmative Action in the 1990s: Staying the Course." *The Annals of the American Academy of Political and Social Science* 523:30–37.

Teachman, Jay, and Lucky M. Tedrow. 2004. "Wages, Earnings, and Occupational Status: Did World War II Veterans Receive a Premium?" *Social Science Research* 33:581–605.

The Sentencing Project. 2003. *Annotated Bibliography: Racial Disparities in the Criminal Justice System.* Washington, D.C.: The Sentencing Project.

The Sentencing Project. 2005. *Racial Disparity in Sentencing: A Review of the Literature.* Washington, D.C.: The Sentencing Project.

The Sentencing Project. 2005. *Felony Disenfranchisement Laws in the United States.* Washington, D.C.: The Sentencing Project.

"The Women of Islam." December 3, 2001. *Time,* p. 50.

Thoits, Peggy A. 1983. "Multiple Identities and Psychological Well-Being: A Reformulation and Test of the Social Isolation Hypothesis." *American Sociological Review* 48:174–87.

Thompson, James D. 1967. *Organizations in Action.* New York: McGraw-Hill.

Thompson, William E. 1991. "Hanging Tongues: A Sociological Encounter with the Assembly Line." Pp. 225–34 in *Down to Earth Sociology,* edited by James M. Henslin. New York: The Free Press.

Thornberry, T. P. 1973. "Race, Socioeconomic Status and Sentencing in the Juvenile Justice System." *Journal of Criminal Law and Criminology* 64:90–98.

Thorne, Barrie. 1989. "Girls and Boys Together . . . But Mostly Apart: Gender Arrangements in Elementary Schools." Pp. 73–84 in *Feminist Frontiers II: Rethinking Sex, Gender, and Society,* edited by L. Richardson and V. Taylor. New York: Random House.

Thurow, Lester C. 1969. *Poverty and Discrimination.* Washington, D.C.: The Brookings Institution.

Thurow, Lester C. June 1999. "Building Wealth." *Atlantic Monthly,* pp. 57–69.

Tienda, Marta, and Ding-Tzann Lii. 1987. "Minority Concentration and Earnings Inequality: Blacks, Hispanics, and Asians Compared." *American Journal of Sociology* 93:141–65.

Tillman, Robert, Kitty Calavita, and Henry Pontell. 1997. "Criminalizing White-Collar Misconduct." *Crime, Law & Social Change* 26:53–76.

Tillman, Robert, and Michael Indergaard. 1999. "Field of Schemes: Health Insurance Fraud in the Small Business Sector." *Social Problems* 46:572–90.

Tilly, Charles. 1998. *Durable Inequality.* Berkeley: University of California Press.

Tilly, Charles. 2003. "Changing Forms of Inequality." *Sociological Theory* 21:31–36.

Tittle, Charles R., Wayne J. Villemez, and Douglas A. Smith. 1978. "The Myth of Social Class and Criminality: An Empirical Assessment of the Empirical Evidence." *American Sociological Review* 43:643–56.

Tolbert, Charles M., II. 1982. Industrial Segmentation and Men's Career Mobility." *American Sociological Review* 47:457–77.

Törnblom, Kjell Y., and Riel Vermunt. 1999. "An Integrative Perspective on Social Justice: Distributive and Procedural Fairness Evaluations of Positive and Negative Outcome Allocations." *Social Justice Research* 12:39–64.

Treiman, Donald J., Heidi I. Hartmann, and Patricia A. Roos. 1984. "Assessing Pay Discrimination Using National Data." Pp. 137–54 in *Comparable Worth and Wage Discrimination,* edited by H. Remick. Philadelphia: Temple University Press.

Tropman, John E. 1989. *American Values & Social Welfare: Cultural Contradictions in the Welfare State.* Englewood Cliffs NJ: Prentice Hall.

Tumin, Melvin M. 1953. "Some Principles of Stratification: A Critical Analysis." *American Sociological Review* 18:387–94.

Turk, Austin T. 1969. *Criminality and Legal Order.* Chicago: Rand McNally.

Turner, Bryan S. 1986. *Equality.* New York: Methuen.

Turner, Jonathan H. 1985. *Herbert Spencer.* Beverly Hills: Sage.

Turner, Jonathan H. 1986. *The Structure of Sociological Theory.* Chicago: Dorsey.

Turner, Jonathan H., Royce Singleton, Jr., and David Musick. 1984. *Oppression: A Socio-History of Black-White Relations in America.* Chicago: Nelson-Hall.

Turner, Jonathan H., and Charles E. Starnes. 1976. *Inequality: Privilege and Poverty in America.* Pacific Palisades, CA: Goodyear.

Turner, Margery Austin, and Felicity Skidmore. 1999. *Mortgage Lending Discrimination: A Review of Existing Evidence.* Washington, D.C: The Urban Institute.

Turner, Richard. May 17, 1999. "The $25 Million Secret." *Newsweek,* p. 35.

Turner, William H. 1986. "The Black Ethnographer 'At Home' in Harlem: A Commentary and Research Response to Stephenson and Greer." *Human Organization* 45:279–92.

U.S. Bureau of the Census. 1979. *The Social and Economic Status of the Black Population in the United States: An Historical View, 1790–1978.* Current Population Reports, Series P-21, No. 80. Washington, D.C.: U.S. Government Printing Office.

U.S. Bureau of the Census. 1987. *Money Income and Poverty Status of Families and Persons in the United States: 1986.* Current Population Reports, Series P-60, No. 157.

U.S. Bureau of the Census. August 1987. *Male-Female Differences in Work Experience, Occupation, and Earnings: 1984.* Current Population Reports, Series P-70, No. 10. Washington, D.C.: U.S. Government Printing Office.

U.S. Bureau of the Census. 1990. *Statistical Abstract of the United States 1990.* Washington, D.C.: U.S. Government Printing Office.

U.S. Bureau of the Census. September 1990. *Money Income and Poverty Status in the United States 1989.* Current Population Reports, Series P-60, No. 168. Washington, D.C.: U.S. Government Printing Office.

U.S. Bureau of the Census. March 1992. *Workers with Low Earnings: 1964 to 1990.* Current Population Reports, Series P-60, No. 178. Washington, D.C.: U.S. Government Printing Office.

U.S. Bureau of the Census. August 1992a. *Money Income of Households, Families, and Persons in the United States: 1991.* Current Population Reports, Series P-60, No. 180. Washington, D.C.: U.S. Government Printing Office.

U.S. Bureau of the Census. August 1992b. *Poverty in the United States: 1991.* Current Population Reports, Series P-60, No. 181. Washington, D.C.: U.S. Government Printing Office.

U.S. Bureau of the Census. August 1992c. *Measuring the Effects of Benefits and Taxes on Income and Poverty: 1979 to 1991.* Current Population Reports, Series P-60, No. 182-RD. Washington, D.C.: U.S. Government Printing Office.

U.S. Bureau of the Census. September 1993. *Poverty in the United States 1992.* Washington, D.C.: U.S. Government Printing Office.

U.S. Bureau of the Census. January 1994. *Household Wealth and Asset Ownership: 1991.* Current Population Reports, Series P-70, No. 34. Washington, D.C.: U.S. Government Printing Office.

U.S. Bureau of the Census. 1995. *Statistical Abstract of the United States 1995.* Washington, D.C.: U.S. Government Printing Office.

U.S. Bureau of the Census. March 1995. *Statistical Brief: Mothers Who Receive AFDC Payments.* Washington, D.C.: U.S. Government Printing Office.

U.S. Bureau of the Census. April 1996. *Income, Poverty, and Valuation of Noncash Benefits: 1994.* Current Population Reports, Series P-60, No. 189. Washington, D.C.: U.S. Government Printing Office.

U.S. Bureau of the Census. September 1996. *Money Income in the United States: 1995.* Current Population Reports, Series P-60, No. 193. Washington, D.C.: U.S. Government Printing Office.

U.S. Bureau of the Census. 1998. *Statistical Abstract of the United States 1998.* Washington, D.C.: U.S. Government Printing Office.

U.S. Bureau of the Census. September 1998a. *Health Insurance Coverage: 1997.* Current Population Reports, Series P-60, No. 202. Washington, D.C.: U.S. Government Printing Office.

U.S. Bureau of the Census. September 1998b. *Money Income in the United States: 1997.* Current Population Reports, Series P-60, No. 200. Washington, D.C.: U.S. Government Printing Office.

U.S. Bureau of the Census. September 1998c. *Poverty in the United States: 1997.* Current Population Reports, Series P-60, No. 201. Washington, D.C.: U.S. Government Printing Office.

U.S. Bureau of the Census. October 1999. *Health Insurance Coverage.* Current Population Reports, Series P-60, No. 208. Washington, D.C.: U.S. Government Printing Office.

U.S. Bureau of the Census. September 2001. *Poverty in the United States: 2000.* Current Population Reports, Series P-60, No. 214. Washington, D.C.: U.S. Government Printing Office.

U.S. Census Bureau. February 2002. *The American Indian and Alaska Native Population: 2000.* Census 2000 Brief, No. 01–15. Washington, D.C.: U.S. Government Printing Office.

U.S. Census Bureau. August 2004. *Income, Poverty, and Health Insurance Coverage in the United States: 2003.* Current Population Reports, Series P-60, No. 226. Washington, D.C.: U.S. Government Printing Office.

U.S. Census Bureau. 2005. *Statistical Abstract of the United States: 2004–2005.* Washington, D.C.: U.S. Government Printing Office.

U.S. Census Office. 1903. *Statistical Atlas of the United States, 1900.* Washington, D.C.: U.S. Government Printing Office.

U.S. Conference of Mayors. 1998. *A Status Report on Hunger and Homelessness in America's Cities: 1998.* Washington, D.C.: Author.

U.S. Conference of Mayors. 2002. *A Status Report on Hunger and Homelessness in America's Cities.* Washington, D.C.: U.S. Conference of Mayors.

U.S. Department of Agriculture. 2003. *Household Food Security in the United States.* Washington, D.C.: U.S. Department of Agriculture.

U.S. Department of Agriculture. July 2003. *Characteristics of Food Stamp Households: Fiscal Year 2002 (Advance Report).* Washington, D.C.: U.S. Government Printing Office.

U.S. Department of Commerce and Labor, Bureau of Statistics. 1911. *Statistical Abstract of the United States, 1911.* Washington, D.C.: U.S. Government Printing Office.

U.S. Department of Education. March 1990. *Faculty in Higher Education Institutions, 1988.* Washington, D.C.: U.S. Government Printing Office.

U.S. Department of Health and Human Services. 2005. *Child Maltreatment 2003.* Washington, D.C.: U.S. Government Printing Office.

U.S. Department of Justice. 1976. *Capital Punishment 1975.* National Prisoner Statistics Bulletin, Law Enforcement Assistance Administration, National Criminal Justice Information and Statistics Service.

U.S. Department of Justice. 1998. *Uniform Crime Reports for the United States 1997.* Washington, D.C.: Federal Bureau of Investigation.

U.S. Department of Justice. 2000. *Special Report: Intimate Partner Violence.* Washington, D.C.: Bureau of Justice Statistics.

U.S. Department of Justice. 2003. "Violence among Family Members and Intimate Partners." Pp. 339–49 in *Crime in the United States 2003.* Washington, D.C.: U.S. Department of Justice.

U.S. Department of Labor. April 1999. *Highlights of Women's Earnings in 1998.* Report 928. Washington, D.C.: U.S. Government Printing Office.

U.S. Department of Labor. August 2000. *A Comparison of the Characteristics and Spending Patterns of Food Stamp Recipients and Nonrecipients.* Summary 00-14. Washington, D.C.: U.S. Government Printing Office.

U.S. Department of Labor. May 2001. *Characteristics and Spending Patterns of Consumer Units in the Lowest 10 Percent of the Expenditure Distribution.* Summary 01-02. Washington, D.C.: U.S. Government Printing Office.

U.S. Department of Labor. February 2004. *Women in the Labor Force: A Databook.* Report 973. Washington, D.C.: U.S. Government Printing Office.

U.S. Department of Labor. September 2004. *Highlights of Women's Earnings in 2003.* Report 978. Washington, D.C.: U.S. Government Printing Office.

U.S. Department of Labor. January 2005. *Employment & Earnings.* Washington, D.C.: U.S. Government Printing Office.

U.S. Department of Labor, Bureau of Labor Statistics. March 1982. *Analysis of Work Stoppages, 1980.* Bulletin 2120. Washington, D.C.: U.S. Government Printing Office.

U.S. Department of Labor, Bureau of Labor Statistics. June 1985. *Handbook of Labor Statistics, Bulletin 2217.* Washington, D.C.: U.S. Government Printing Office.

U.S. Department of Labor, Bureau of Labor Statistics. January 1989. *Employment and Earnings.* Washington, D.C.: U.S. Government Printing Office.

U.S. Department of Labor, Bureau of Labor Statistics. March 1989. *Monthly Labor Review.* Washington, D.C.: U.S. Government Printing Office.

U.S. Department of Labor, Bureau of Labor Statistics. June 1989. *Current Wage Developments.* Washington, D.C.: U.S. Government Printing Office.

U.S. Department of Labor, Bureau of Labor Statistics. Spring 1998. *The 1996–2006 Job Outlook in Brief.* Washington, D.C.: U.S. Government Printing Office.

U.S. Department of Labor, Bureau of Labor Statistics. January 2002. *Employment & Earnings.* Washington, D.C.: U.S. Government Printing Office.

U.S. Department of Labor, Women's Bureau. 1947. *Women's Occupations through Seven Decades.* Washington, D.C.: U.S. Government Printing Office.

U.S. General Accounting Office. 1983. *Siting of Hazardous Waste Landfills and Their Correlations with Racial and Economic Status of Surrounding Communities.* Washington, D.C.: U.S. Government Printing Office.

Uchitelle, Louis, and N. R. Kleinfield. March 3, 1996. "The Downsizing of America: A National Heartache." *New York Times.*

Uggen, Christopher, and Amy Blackstone. 2004. "Sexual Harassment as a Gendered Expression of Power." *American Sociological Review* 69:64–92.

Uggen, Christopher, and Jeff Manza. 2002. "Democratic Contraction? Political Consequences of Felon Disenfranchisement in the United States." *American Sociological Review* 67:777–803.

Umberson, Debra. 1993. "Sociodemographic Position, World Views, and Psychological Distress." *Social Science Quarterly* 74:575–89.

United Church of Christ. 1987. *Toxic Wastes and Race: A National Report on the Racial and Socio-Economic Characteristics of Communities with Hazardous Waste Sites.* New York: United Church of Christ.

United Nations. 1995. *The World's Women 1995: Trends and Statistics.* New York: United Nations.

United Nations. 1998. *Human Development Report 1998.* New York: Oxford University Press.

United Nations. 2001. *Human Development Report 2001.* New York: Oxford University Press.

University of California-Davis. 2005. *Sexual Prejudice: Prevalence.* Available at http://psychology.ucdavis.edu/rainbow/html/prej_prev.html.

Urban Institute. 2000. *A New Look at Homelessness in America.* Washington, D.C.: Urban Institute.

Urgent Relief for the Homeless Act. February 4, 1987. *Hearing before the Subcommittee on Housing and Community Development of the Committee on Banking, Finance and Urban Affairs, House of Representatives.* Serial No. 100–3. Washington, D.C.: U.S. Government Printing Office.

Useem, Michael. 1978. "The Inner Group of the American Capitalist Class." *Social Problems* 25:225–40.

Useem, Michael. 1979. "The Social Organization of the American Business Elite and Participation of Corporation Directors in the Governance of American Institutions." *American Sociological Review* 44:553–72.

Useem, Michael. 1980. "Which Business Leaders Help Govern?" Pp. 199–225 in *Power Structure Research*, edited by G. W. Domhoff. Beverly Hills, CA: Sage.

Useem, Michael. 1984. *The Inner Circle: Large Corporations and the Rise of Business Political Activity in the U.S. and U.K.* New York: Oxford University Press.

Valdes, Francisco. 1995. "Queers, Sissies, Dykes, and Tomboys: Deconstructing the Conflation of 'Sex,' 'Gender,' and 'Sexual Orientation' in Euro-American Law and Society." *California Law Review* 83:129–204.

van den Berghe, Pierre L. 1967. *Race and Racism: A Comparative Perspective.* New York: John Wiley & Sons.

van den Berghe, Pierre L. 1985. "Review of J. S. Chafetz's Sex and Advantage." *American Journal of Sociology* 90:1350.

Vanneman, Reeve, and Fred C. Pampel. 1977. "The American Perception of Class and Status." *American Sociological Review* 42:422–37.

Veblen, Thorstein. 1953. *The Theory of the Leisure Class.* New York: The New American Library.

Venkatesh, Sudhir Alladi. 1994. "Getting Ahead: Social Mobility among the Urban Poor." *Sociological Perspectives* 37:157–82.

Verba, Sidney, Nancy Burns, and Kay Lehman Schlozman. 2003. "Unequal at the Starting Line: Creating Participatory Inequalities across Generations and among Groups." *The American Sociologist*, Spring/Summer:45–69.

Verba, Sidney, and Norman H. Nie. 1972. *Participation in America: Political Democracy and Social Equality.* New York: Harper & Row.

Verba, Sidney, and Gary R. Orren. 1985. *Equality in America: The View from the Top.* Cambridge, MA: Harvard University Press.

Verbrugge, Lois M. 1983. "Multiple Roles and Physical Health of Women and Men." *Journal of Health and Social Behavior* 24:16–30.

Verbrugge, Lois M. 1999. "Pathways of Health and Death." Pp. 377–94 in *Health, Illness, and Healing*, edited by K. Charmaz and D. A. Paterniti. Los Angeles: Roxbury.

Veum, Jonathan R. December 1992. "Accounting for Income Mobility Changes in the United States." *Social Science Quarterly* 73:773–85.

Vogel, David. 1987. "Political Science and the Study of Corporate Power. A Dissent from the New Conventional Wisdom." *British Journal of Political Science* 17:385–405.

Vogel, Lise. 1983. *Marxism and the Oppression of Women.* New Brunswick, NJ: Rutgers University Press.

Vogeler, Ingolf. 1975. "American Peasantry." *Anthropological Quarterly* 48:223–35.

Volgy, Thomas J., John E. Schwarz, and Lawrence E. Imwalle. 1996. "In Search of Economic Well-Being: Worker Power and the Effects of Productivity, Inflation, Unemployment and Global Trade on Wages in Ten Wealthy Countries." *American Journal of Political Science* 40:1233–52.

Wacquant, Lois J. D., and William Julius Wilson. 1989. "The Cost of Racial and Class Exclusion in the Inner City." *Annals of the American Academy of Political and Social Science* 501:8–25.

Waddoups, Jeffrey, and Djeto Assane. 1993. "Mobility and Gender in a Segmented Labor Market: A Closer Look." *American Journal of Economics and Sociology* 52:399–411.

Wade, Robert Hunter. 2004. "Is Globalization Reducing Poverty and Inequality?" *World Development* 32:567–89.

Wadsworth, Tim, and Charis E. Kubrin. 2004. "Structural Factors and Black Interracial Homicide: A New Examination of the Causal Process." *Criminology* 42:647–72.

Wald, Kenneth D. 2000. "The Context of Gay Politics." Pp. 1–28 in *The Politics of Gay Rights*, edited by C. A. Rimmerman, K. D. Wald, and C. Wilcox. Chicago: University of Chicago.

Waldman, Amy. April 29, 2005. "Mystery of India's Poverty: Can the State Break its Grip?" *New York Times*, p. A4.

Wallace, Michael, and Arne L. Kalleberg. 1981. "Economic Organization, Occupations, and Labor Force Consequences: Toward a Specification of Dual Economy Theory." Pp. 77–117 in *Sociological Perspectives on Labor Markets*, edited by I. Berg. New York: Academic Press.

Walsh, Mary Williams. April 25, 2003. "I.R.S. Tightening Rules for Low-Income Tax Credit." *New York Times*, pp. A1, C4.

Walton, Anthony. January 1999. "Technology versus African-Americans." *Atlantic Monthly*, pp. 14–18.

Warren, John Robert, Robert M. Hauser, and Jennifer T. Sheridan. 2002. "Occupational Stratification across the Life Course: Evidence from the Wisconsin Longitudinal Study." *American Sociological Review* 67:432–55.

Weber, Max. 1964. *The Theory of Social and Economic Organization*, edited by Talcott Parsons. New York: The Free Press.

Webster, Murray, Jr., and James E. Driskell, Jr. 1983. "Beauty as Status." *American Journal of Sociology* 89:140–65.

Weeden, Kim A. 2002. "Why Do Some Occupations Pay More Than Others? Social Closure and Earnings Inequality in the United States." *American Journal of Sociology* 108:55–101.

Weinstein, Michael M., and Eugene Smolensky. 1978. "Poverty." *Dictionary of American Economic History*.

Weiss, Micheal J. 1988. *The Clustering of America*. New York: Harper & Row.

Weitzer, Ronald. 2000. "Racialized Policing: Residents' Perceptions in Three Neighborhoods." *Law & Society Review* 34:129–53.

Weitzer, Ronald, and Steven A. Tuch. 2004. "Race and Perceptions of Police Misconduct." *Social Problems* 51:305–25.

Weitzer, Ronald, and Steven A. Tuch. 2005. "Racially Biased Policing: Determinants of Citizen Perceptions." *Social Forces* 83:1009–1030.

Welch, Susan, and Michael W. Combs. 1985. "Intraracial Differences in Attitudes of Blacks: Class Cleavage or Consensus." *Phylon* 46:91–97.

"The Well-Heeled: Pricey Sneakers in Inner City Help Set Nation's Fashion Trend." December 1, 1988. *Wall Street Journal*, pp. A1, A6.

Werner, Paul D., and Georgina Williams LaRussa. 1985. "Persistence and Change in Sex-Role Stereotypes." *Sex Roles* 12:1089–100.

Wertz, Richard W., and Dorothy C. Wertz. 1981. "Notes on the Decline of Midwives and the Rise of Medical Obstetricians." Pp. 165–83 in *The Sociology of Health and Illness: Critical Perspectives*, edited by P. Conrad and R. Kern. New York: St. Martin's Press.

Wessel, David. May 13, 2005. "As Rich-Poor Gap Widens in the U.S., Class Mobility Stalls." *Wall Street Journal*, pp. A1, A7.

West, Candace, and Don Zimmerman. 1987. "Doing Gender." *Gender & Society* 1:125–51.

West, Cornel. 1993. *Race Matters*. Boston: Beacon.

West, Darrell M. 2000. *Checkbook Democracy*. Boston: Northeastern University.

Western, Bruce. 1993. "Postwar Unionization in Eighteen Advanced Capitalist Countries." *American Sociological Review* 58:266–82.

Western, Mark, and Erik Olin Wright. 1994. "The Permeability of Class Boundaries to Intergenerational Mobility among Men in the United States, Canada, Norway and Sweden." *American Sociological Review* 59:606–29.

Wheaton, B. 1980. "The Sociogenesis of Psychological Disorder: An Attributional Theory." *Journal of Health and Social Behavior* 21:100–24.

Wheaton, B. 1983. "Stress, Personal Coping Resources, and Psychiatric Symptoms: An Investigation of Interactive Models." *Journal of Health and Social Behavior* 24:208–29.

Wheeler, Stanton, David Weisburd, and Nancy Bode. 1982. "Sentencing the White-Collar Offender: Rhetoric and Reality." *American Sociological Review* 47:641–59.

White, Jack E. 1997. "I'm Just Who I Am." *Time*, May 5:34.

Wiley, Mary Glenn, and Arlene Eskilson. 1983. "Scaling the Corporate Ladder: Sex Differences in Expectations for Performance, Power and Mobility." *Social Psychology Quarterly* 46:351–59.

Williams, David R., and Chiquita Collins. 1995. "U.S. Socioeconomic and Racial Differences in Health: Patterns and Explanations." Pp. 349–86 in *Annual Review of Sociology 1995*, edited by J. Hagan and K. S. Cook. Palo Alto, CA: Annual Reviews.

Williams, Gregory Howard. 1995. *Life on the Color Line*. New York: Dutton.

Williams, Kirk R. 1984. "Economic Sources of Homicide: Reestimating the Effects of Poverty and Inequality." *American Sociological Review* 49:283–89.

Williams, Kirk R., and Robert L. Flewelling. 1988. "The Social Production of Criminal Homicide: A Comparative Study of Disaggregated Rates in American Cities." *American Sociological Review* 53:421–31.

Williams, Robin M., Jr. 1970. *American Society: A Sociological Interpretation*. New York: Knopf.

Willie, Charles Vert. 1979. *The Caste and Class Controversy*. Bayside, NY: General Hall.

Willis, Angela Gonzalez, Gordon B. Willis, Alisa Male, Marilyn Henderson, and Ronald W. Manderscheid. 1998. "Mental Illness and Disability in the U.S. Adult Household Population." Pp. 113–18 in *Mental Health, United States, 1998*, edited by R. W. Manderscheid and M. J. Henderson. Washington, D.C.: Center for Medical Health Services.

Willson, Andrea E. 2003. "Race and Women's Income Trajectories: Employment, Marriage, and Income Security over the Life Course." *Social Problems* 50:87–110.

Wilson, Kenneth L., and Alejandro Portes. 1975. "The Educational Attainment Process: Results from a National Sample." *American Journal of Sociology* 81:343–63.

Wilson, William J. September 14–19, 1970. "Race Relations Models and Explanations of Ghetto Behavior." Paper presented at the Seventh World Congress of Sociology of the International Sociological Association, Varna, Bulgaria.

Wilson, William Julius. 1982. "The Declining Significance of Race-Revisited But Not Revised." Pp. 399–405 in *Majority & Minority: The Dynamics of Race and Ethnicity in American Life,* edited by N. R. Yetman and C. H. Steele. Boston: Allyn & Bacon.

Wilson, William Julius. 1987. *The Truly Disadvantaged: The Inner City, the Underclass, and Public Policy.* Chicago: University of Chicago Press.

Wilson, William Julius. 1999. *The Bridge over the Racial Divide.* Berkeley: University of California Press.

Winegarden, C. R. 1974. "The Fertility of AFDC Women: An Economic Analysis." *Journal of Economics and Business* 26:159–66.

Wolf, Naomi. 1991. *The Beauty Myth: How Images of Beauty Are Used against Women.* New York: Morrow.

Wolf, Wendy C. 1976. "Occupational Attainments of Married Women: Do Carrer Contingencies Matter?" Madison, WI: Center for Demography and Ecology Working Paper No. 76–3, University of Wisconsin.

Wolff, Edward N. May 1992. "Changing Inequality of Wealth." *American Economics Review* 82:552–58.

Wolff, Edward N. 1995. "How the Pie Is Sliced." *The American Prospect* 22:58–64.

Wolff, Edward N. 1998. "Recent Trends in the Size Distribution of Household Wealth." *Journal of Economic Perspectives* 12:131–50.

Wolff, Edward N. April 2000. *Recent Trends in Wealth Ownership, 1983–1998.* Working Paper No. 300.

"Women-Owned Businesses Employ More People than the Fortune 500." April 20, 1993. *Akron Beacon Journal,* p. D6.

Wong, Raymond Sin-Kwok. 1994. "Postwar Mobility Trends in Advanced Industrial Societies." Pp. 121–44 in *Research in Social Stratification and Mobility,* edited by R. Althauser and M. Wallace. Greenwich, CT: JAI Press.

"Worker Displacement during the Late 1990s." Displaced workers summary report available at http://www.bls.gov/bls/news.release/disp.nr0.htm.

The World Bank. 1999. *World Development Report: Knowledge for Development 1998/99.* Oxford: Oxford University Press.

Wright, Erik Olin. 1976. "Class Boundaries in Advanced Capitalist Societies." *New Left Review* 98:3–41.

Wright, Erik Olin. 1977. "Class Structure and Occupation: A Research Note." Institute for Research on Poverty Discussion Paper No. 415–77. Madison: University of Wisconsin-Madison.

Wright, Erik Olin. 1978. "Race, Class, and Income Inequality." *American Journal of Sociology* 83:1368–97.

Wright, Erik Olin, Janeen Baxter, and Gunn Elisabeth Birkelund. 1995. "The Gender Gap in Workplace Authority in Seven Nations." *American Sociological Review* 60:407–35.

Wright, Erik Olin, and Donmoon Cho. 1992. "The Relative Permeability of Class Boundaries to Cross-Class Friendships: A Comparative Study of the United States, Canada, Sweden, and Norway." *American Sociological Review* 57:85–102.

Wright, Erik Olin, and Bill Martin. 1987. "The Transformation of the American Class Structure 1960–1980." *American Journal of Sociology* 93:1–29.

Wright, Erik Olin, and Luca Perrone. 1977. "Marxist Class Categories and Income Inequality." *American Sociological Review* 42:32–55.

Wright, James D., and Julie A. Lam. 1987. "Homeless and the Low-Income Housing Supply." *Social Policy* 17:48–53.

Wrong, Dennis. 1969. "Social Inequality without Social Stratification." Pp. 513–20 in *Structured Social Inequality,* edited by C. S. Heller. New York: Macmillan.

Wrong, Dennis H. 1959. "The Functional Theory of Stratification: Some Neglected Considerations." *American Sociological Review* 24:722–82.

Yamaguchi, Kazuo, and Yantao Wang. 2002. "Class Identification of Married Employed Women and Men in America." *American Journal of Sociology* 108:440–75.

Yanagisako, Sylvia Junko, and Jane Fishburne Collier. 1987. "Toward a Unified Analysis of Gender and Kinship." Pp. 14–50 in *Gender and Kinship: Essays toward a Unified Analysis,* edited by J. F. Collier and S. J. Yanagisako. Stanford, CA: Stanford University Press.

Yang, Alan S. 1997. "Attitudes toward Homosexuality." *Public Opinion Quarterly* 61:477–507.

Yllo, K. 1983. "Sexual Equality and Violence against Wives in American States." *Journal of Comparative Family Studies* 14:67–86.

Yllo, K. 1984. "The Status of Women, Marital Equality and Violence against Wives." *Journal of Family Issues* 5:307–20.

Yodanis, Carrie L. 2004. "Gender Inequality, Violence against Women, and Fear." *Journal of Interpersonal Violence* 19:655–75.

Youngman, Judith. 2001. "Women in the Military: The Struggle to Lead." Pp. 139–66 in *The American Women 2001–2002,* edited by C. B. Costello and A. J. Stone. New York: Norton.

Zakaria, Fareed. 2005. "Does the Future Belong to China?" *Newsweek,* May 9:28–40.

Zandvakili, Sourushe, and Jeffrey A. Mills. 2001. "The Distributional Implications of Tax and Transfer Programs in the U.S." *Quarterly Review of Economics and Finance* 41:167–81.

Zastrow, Charles. 1982. *Introduction to Social Welfare Institutions: Social Problems, Services and Current Issues*. Homewood, IL: Dorsey.

Zeitlin, Irving. 1968. *Ideology and the Development of Sociological Theory*. Englewood Cliffs, NJ: Prentice Hall.

Zieger, Robert H. 1986. *American Workers, American Unions. 1920–1985*. Baltimore: The Johns Hopkins University Press.

Zigler, Edward, and Susan Muenchow. 1983. "Infant Day Care and Infant-Care Leaves." *American Psychologist* 38:91–94.

Zimmer, Michael J., Charles A. Sullivan, Richard F. Richards, and Deborah A. Calloway. 2000. *Cases and Materials on Employment Discrimination*. New York: Aspen Law & Business.

Zimmerman, Don H., and Candace West. 1975. "Sex Roles, Interruptions and Silences in Conversation." Pp. 105–29 in *Language and Sex: Difference and Dominance*, edited by B. Thorne and N. Henley. Rowley, MA: Newbury House.

Zipp John F. 1994. "Government Employment and Black-White Earnings Inequality, 1980–1990." *Social Problems* 41:363–82.

Zuckerman, Edward, ed. 2005. *The Almanac of Federal PACs: 2004–2005*. Hedgeville, W. Va.: Amward. Publications.

INDEX